LEARN, TEACH...

SUCCEED...

With **REA's TExES™ Core Subjects 4–8 (211)**
test prep, you'll be in a class all your own.

TExES™

TEXAS EXAMINATIONS OF EDUCATOR STANDARDS™

CORE SUBJECTS 4-8 (211)

Ann Cavallo, Ph.D.

Karen Allmond, Ed.D.

Mary D. Curtis, Ph.D.

Marci Smith Deal, M.Ed.

Christina Gawlik, Ph.D.

Melissa Hulings, Ph.D.

Candace Joswick, Ph.D.

Kathleen C. Tice, Ph.D.

Research & Education Association

www.rea.com

Research & Education Association
1325 Franklin Ave., Suite 250
Garden City, NY 11530
Email: info@rea.com

TExES™ Core Subjects 4–8 (211)
with Online Practice Tests, 2nd Edition

Printed in the United States of America

Library of Congress Control Number 2022949007

ISBN-13: 978-0-7386-1282-9
ISBN-10: 0-7386-1282-0

The competencies and associated descriptive statements presented in this book are copyright © 2020 by the Texas Education Agency and were created and implemented by the Texas Education Agency and Pearson Education, Inc., or its affiliate(s). Texas Examinations of Educator Standards and TExES are trademarks of the Texas Education Agency. All other trademarks cited in this publication are the property of their respective owners.

Cover image: © iStockphoto.com/FatCamera

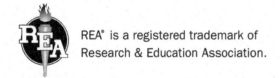

REA® is a registered trademark of Research & Education Association.

Contents

Chapter 5
Subject Test III: Social Studies (808) 237

CONTENTS

Chapter 6
Subject Test IV: Science (809)   379

About Our TExES Exam Experts

Core Subjects 4–8 Lead Author and Science Co-Author

Dr. Ann Cavallo is Assistant Vice Provost and Director of the Center for Research on Teaching and Learning Excellence, Co-director of UTeach Arlington, and Distinguished University Professor of Science Education at The University of Texas at Arlington. Dr. Cavallo has held faculty appointments at the University of Oklahoma, the University of California–Davis, and Wayne State University. She joined the faculty at the University of Texas at Arlington in 2006 as Associate Professor and earned the rank of Professor in 2009 in her field of Science Education. Dr. Cavallo received the 2015 Distinguished Record of Research or Creative Activity Award from UT Arlington. She is Principal Investigator of three National Science Foundation (NSF) grants totaling over $3 million. Dr. Cavallo's research has investigated high school and college students' learning approaches and strategies, scientific reasoning, and self-efficacy, as well as students' acquisition of conceptual understandings of science. Dr. Cavallo has been published in more than 40 internationally and nationally refereed journals and proceedings, and has authored several books and book chapters (including content for REA's top-selling TExES Core Subjects EC–6 (391) Book + Online test prep). She has secured more than $12 million in grants and gifts from various funding agencies to support her work. She serves on the STEM Teacher Preparation Advisory Board for NSF and the American Association for the Advancement of Science. Dr. Cavallo earned her B.S. from Niagara University, and her M.S. in Science Education/Biology, M.S. in Natural Science, and Ph.D. in Science Education from Syracuse University. She holds secondary teacher certification in Biology, Chemistry, Earth Science, and General Science, and taught middle and high school science prior to earning her graduate degrees.

Science Co-Author

Dr. Melissa Hulings is an Assistant Professor of Science Education at The University of Texas at Arlington, based in the Department of Curriculum and Instruction. She was a classroom teacher for eight years, with experience teaching science in Grades 6–12, before becoming a full-time doctoral student. As a doctoral student, she was a graduate research/teaching assistant. Upon completing her doctoral program, she became a clinical assistant professor before being named to her current position in 2020. Dr. Hulings is a recipient of the UTA College of Education 2016–2017 Award for Excellence in Teaching by a Clinical Faculty Member. She earned her B.S. in Secondary Science from Oklahoma State University, her M.Ed. from Northeastern State University, and her Ph.D. in Professional Education Studies from Oklahoma State University. She holds secondary teacher certification in Chemistry, Earth Science, Biological Sciences, and Mid-Level Science, and has taught middle school and high school science.

ELAR Author

Dr. Kathleen Copeland Tice is a Clinical Assistant Professor in the Department of Curriculum and Instruction at The University of Texas at Arlington. Dr. Tice teaches courses in literacy studies at both the undergraduate and graduate level. Her research has focused upon teacher knowledge development and service-learning in teacher preparation. She has served as the annual conference Program Chair for the Service-Learning & Experiential Education–Special Interest Group of the American Educational Research Association. She is a co-editor of the *International Journal of Research on Service-Learning in Teacher Education*. Honored with the University of Texas System Regents' Outstanding Teacher Award, Dr. Tice is also an eight-time recipient of a Literacy Grant from the Honor Society of Phi Kappa Phi, the nation's oldest and most prestigious collegiate honor society for all academic disciplines. Her teaching experience runs the gamut from the Houston Independent School District to migrant high school students in Rural Upward Bound. She holds a B.S. in Elementary Education and M.Ed. in Reading Education from the University of Houston, and earned her Ph.D. in Language Arts Education/Reading Education from the University of Texas at Austin.

ELAR Contributor

Dr. Luis A. Rosado is a Professor of Bilingual Education and the Founding Director of the Center for Bilingual and ESL Education in the College of Education and Health Professions at The University of Texas at Arlington. Dr. Rosado has more than 36 years of teaching experience at the elementary, high school, and college levels. He has taught in Puerto Rico, Massachusetts, and Texas. Dr. Rosado has received more than $5.6 million in state and federal funding to prepare bilingual and ESL teachers as well as school administrators, and to provide services to support high school students. He holds a B.A. in Secondary Social Studies from the University of Puerto Rico–Rio Piedras, an M.Ed. in Bilingual and Multicultural Studies from Boston State College (now the University of Massachusetts), and an Ed.D. in Bilingual Education from Texas A&I University (now Texas A&M–Kingsville). Dr. Rosado is the author of REA's TExES Bilingual Education Supplemental (164) test prep, for which he was named a silver medalist for Best Academic Themed Book in the International Latino Book Awards.

Mathematics Co-Authors

Dr. Karen Allmond is an Adjunct Associate Professor in the Department of Curriculum and Instruction at The University of Texas at Arlington. Formerly she was Program Coordinator for UTA's Accelerated Online program for teachers working toward their Master in Education degree with an emphasis on Mathematics and Science. She has worked with pre-service teachers in the College of Education and UTeach program, a science and mathematics teacher preparation program at UT Arlington. Dr. Allmond's experience in the field of education spans over 25 years. She taught in Texas public schools for 18 years, serving in the Arlington, Mansfield, and North East Independent school districts. Her work with Title I schools met the needs of diverse students and learners, including students in Special Education, General Education, English Learners, and Gifted and Talented students. Her certifications include Special Education, ESL, and Principal. She earned her B.A. in Interdisciplinary Studies and M.Ed. in Educational Leadership from UT Arlington. She earned her Ed.D. in Educational Leadership from the University of Phoenix.

Dr. Christina Gawlik is a former Assistant Professor of Mathematics and Mathematics Education at Texas Woman's University in Denton and Saint Xavier University in Chicago. She earned her B.S.Ed. and M.S.Ed. degrees from the University of Kansas, and her Ph.D. from Kansas State University. Prior to earning her doctorate, she taught high school mathematics and served as adjunct faculty at several two- and four-year institutions across Kansas. Dr. Gawlik is a leader in professional development for teaching mathematics who has presented extensively at national and international conferences. She has facilitated workshops for K–12 mathematics teachers across the United States, Canada, and Dubai. Dr. Gawlik has published student workbooks, learning guides, and videos for K–12 and higher education, and is actively developing resources for developmental mathematics and courses in mathematics for non-math majors.

Dr. Candace Joswick is an Assistant Professor of Mathematics Education in the Department of Curriculum and Instruction at The University of Texas at Arlington, where she is also Program Coordinator of STEM Education. Dr. Joswick began her career in education as a middle grades mathematics teacher. Her research focuses on learning trajectories and progressions, teacher development, technology as a tool for teaching and learning, and classroom interactions and discourse. Dr. Joswick is the Principal Investigator and Co-Principal Investigator on two U.S. Department of Education grants totaling over $15 million. She is the 2022 recipient of The University of Texas at Arlington Department of Curriculum and Instruction Outstanding Teaching Award for Pre-Tenure Faculty, and the UTA College of Education awards for Outstanding Faculty Research Early Career and Pre-Tenured Faculty Teaching. She earned her B.A. in Mathematics from Wittenberg University, and her M.A. and Ph.D. in Mathematics Education from The Ohio State University.

Mathematics Consultant

Stu Schwartz is a 35-year veteran of the mathematics classroom. His experience includes preparing teacher candidates for teacher certification exams in math. He offers mathematics resources for students and teachers alike at his website, *MasterMathMentor.com*. Mr. Schwartz is a recipient of the Presidential Award for Excellence in Mathematics and Science Teaching, the United States' highest honor for teachers of science, technology, engineering, and mathematics.

Social Studies Co-Authors

Dr. Mary D. Curtis is a veteran K–16 educator and researcher. She holds a secondary teacher certification in Social Studies and taught at the high school level for 10 years. Additionally, Dr. Curtis has held significant leadership positions in professional organizations and has been recognized for her impact as an educator. She has worked to further social science education at the district, state, and national levels, through presentations at professional conferences and published research. Dr. Curtis's research investigates teacher learning, instructional strategies, and technological pedagogical content knowledge (TPACK) with particular regard for geospatial technology. Dr. Curtis earned her B.A. from Texas A&M University; her M.S. in Instructional Technology from the University of Houston–Clear Lake; and her Ph.D. in Geography Education from Texas State University.

Marci Smith Deal is the K–12 Social Studies Coordinator for Hurst-Euless-Bedford ISD in Texas. She has been in public education for over 39 years. Ms. Deal has served as the Vice President and then President of the Texas Social Studies Supervisors Association, each for two separate terms. In 2012 she was named the Texas Social Studies Supervisor of the Year. She has also served as the Vice President of the Texas Council for the Social Studies. Since 1988 she has served as a teacher consultant for the National Geographic Society. For 25 years, she served as the Texas State Coordinator for the National Geographic Society's Geography Bee and other Geographic Competitions. She is a member of the Texas Alliance for Geographic Education (TAGE) and the National Council for Geographic Education (NCGE). In 2000 she received the TAGE Distinguished Service Award, and in 2001 was honored with the NCGE Distinguished Teaching Achievement Award. She is a member of the World Affairs Council of Dallas/Fort Worth and serves on the council's Education Advisory Board. In 2022 she was named the council's International Educator of the Year. Ms. Deal holds a B.S. in Economics from The University of Texas at Arlington and a Master of Education degree from the University of North Texas, Denton.

About REA

Founded in 1959, Research & Education Association (REA) is dedicated to publishing the finest and most effective educational materials—including study guides and test preps—for students of all ages. Today, REA's wide-ranging catalog is a leading resource for students, teachers, and other professionals. Visit *www.rea.com* to see our complete catalog.

Acknowledgments

Publisher: Pam Weston

Editorial Director: Larry B. Kling

Digital Content Prep: Heidi Gagnon

Composition and File Prep: Jennifer Calhoun

Copy Editors: John Kupetz and Karen Lamoreux

Proofreader: Fiona Hallowell

Mathematics Accuracy Checker: Ryann Shelton

Indexer: Casey Indexing and Information Service

REA extends special thanks to the Texas teacher candidates who beta-tested this Book + Online product—Mahnoor Agha, Katie Block, Emma Klee, and Malissa Williams—to succeed on the TExES Core Subjects 4–8 test.

Getting Started

Congratulations! By taking the TExES Core Subjects 4–8 (211) test, you're on your way to a rewarding career as a teacher of young students in Texas. Our book, and the online tools that come with it, give you everything you need to succeed on this important exam, bringing you one step closer to being certified to teach in Texas.

This TExES Core Subjects 4–8 test prep package includes:

- A **complete overview** of the TExES Core Subjects 4–8 (211) test

- A **comprehensive review** for all four subject tests in the TExES Core Subjects 4–8 test battery

- An **online diagnostic test** to pinpoint your strengths and weaknesses and focus your study

- **Two full-length practice test batteries:** one in the book and online, plus an additional test online that comes with powerful diagnostic tools to help you personalize your prep

HOW TO USE THIS BOOK + ONLINE PREP

About Our Review

The review chapters in this book are designed to help you sharpen your command of all the skills you'll need to pass the Core Subjects 4–8 test. Each of the skills required for all four subject tests in the 4–8 battery is discussed at length to optimize your understanding of what the exam covers. Keep in mind that your schooling has taught you most of what you need to know to answer the questions on the test. Our content review is designed to reinforce what you have learned and show you how to relate the information you have acquired to the specific competencies on the test. Studying your class notes and textbooks together with our review will give you an excellent foundation for passing the test.

About the REA Study Center

We know your time is valuable and you want an efficient study experience. At the REA Study Center (*www.rea.com/studycenter*), you will get feedback right from the start on what you know and what you don't to help make the most of your study time. Here is what you will find at the REA Study Center:

- **Diagnostic Test**—Before you review with the book, take our online diagnostic test. Your score report will pinpoint topics for which you need the most review, to help focus your study.

- **2 Full-Length Practice Test Batteries**—Our practice tests give you the most complete picture of your strengths and weaknesses. After you've studied with the book, test what you've learned by taking the first of two practice exams (online or in the book) for each of the four subjects. Review your score reports, then go back and study any topics you missed. Take the second practice test online to ensure you've mastered the material.

Our online exams simulate the computer-based format of the actual TExES test and come with these features:

- **Automatic scoring**—Find out how you did on your test, instantly.

- **Diagnostic score reports**—Get a specific score tied to each competency, so you can focus on the areas that challenge you the most.

- **On-screen detailed answer explanations**—See why the correct response option is right, and learn why the other answer choices are incorrect.

- **Timed testing**—Learn to manage your time as you practice, so you'll feel confident on test day.

AN OVERVIEW OF THE TEST

What is assessed on the Core Subjects 4–8 test?

The Core Subjects exam is actually a battery of four subject tests, with four unique test codes:

- English Language Arts and Reading (806)

- Mathematics (807)

- Social Studies (808)

- Science (809)

The TExES Core Subjects 4–8 test is a criterion-referenced examination constructed to measure the knowledge and skills that an entry-level educator in Texas public schools must have. The test, along with the Science of Teaching Reading (293) exam, is a requirement for candidates seeking a Core Subjects 4–8 certificate. Because it's a computer-administered test, the exam is available throughout the year at numerous locations across the state and at select locations nationally. For more information about certification requirements and what you must do to meet them, visit the Texas Education Agency website at *www.tea.texas.gov/str*. To find the test center near you, visit *www.tx.nesinc.com*.

Candidates are limited to five attempts to take any of Texas's teacher certification tests, but in the event you don't pass the Core Subjects 4–8 test, you need to retake only the individual subject test where your score falls short. Below is an overview of the four subject tests that make up the Core Subjects exam. The table covers the percentage and number of questions on each subject test, as well as the time allocated for each subject test. These subject tests and the competencies rooted in them represent the knowledge that teams of teachers, subject area specialists, and district-level educators have determined to be necessary for beginning teachers.

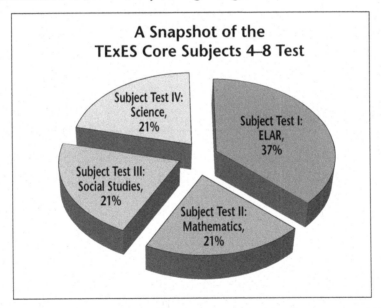

A Snapshot of the TExES Core Subjects 4–8 Test

Subject Test	Competencies	Total Items	Percentage of Total Test	Time
English Language Arts and Reading (ELAR)	9	74	37%	1 hour and 55 minutes
Mathematics	19	42	21%	1 hour and 5 minutes
Social Studies	7	42	21%	50 minutes
Science	23	42	21%	50 minutes
Total	55	200	100%	4 hours and 40 minutes

What is the format of the TExES Core Subjects 4–8 test?

The test includes a total of 200 multiple-choice items. You may encounter non-scorable questions but you won't know which is which, so they surely aren't worth worrying about. Your final scaled score will be based only on the scorable items. The test is organized into four subject tests.

Multiple-Choice Questions

Although all the questions on the test are multiple-choice, they may not all be the type of multiple-choice question with which you're familiar. The majority of questions on the Core Subjects test are standard multiple-choice items. The questions are not intended merely to test your command of facts but also your critical-thinking skills. For example, you may be asked to analyze information and compare it with knowledge you have, or make a judgment about it. To acquaint yourself with all the standards and competencies covered on the test, be sure to download Pearson Education's test framework at *www.tx.nesinc.com*.

Some multiple-choice questions are self-contained while others are clustered, branching off a common stimulus. Each question will generally have four choices: A, B, C, and D. (Some questions may have more.) In most cases, the correct answer will require you to identify the single best response. Some questions, however, will require you to select *all* valid responses. In such instances, you may need to click check boxes instead of ovals. In addition, be aware that this test occasionally presents non-traditional, technology-driven formats for multiple-choice items, both to present the information and to allow you to select the best answer. A rundown of these new formats follows.

Unfamiliar Question Types

There are several unfamiliar question types that may show up on the Core Subjects test. First, let's look at the kind of question that asks test-takers to identify more than one correct response option to a question.

Example

1. Which of the following led to the American Revolution? Select *all* that apply.

    A.   the French and Indian War

    B.   the Intolerable Acts

    C.   the French Revolution

    D.   the Articles of Confederation

Answer and Explanation

Options (A) and (B) are correct. The French and Indian War (A), fought from 1754 to 1763, served as a powerful vehicle by which the British Empire extended its reach in North America. The British sought to impose taxation on the colonists to finance the defense of the newly acquired territory, which aggravated growing discontent with British governance. The Intolerable Acts (B) embraced measures enacted by the British Parliament in 1774 to strike back at the colonists' defiance (e.g., the Boston Tea Party in 1773) of British rule. The move backfired, spawning the First Continental Congress later that year. Simple chronology helps you root out the French Revolution (C) as an incorrect option. The French Revolution, fought from 1787 to 1799, is an anachronistic response that could not have led to the American Revolution, which ended in 1783. Finally, the Articles of Confederation instead of leading to the American Revolution actually *resulted from* it. The Articles were drafted in 1776–77 and adopted by Congress on Nov. 15, 1777, as the first U.S. constitution.

According to the Texas Education Agency, the Core Subjects 4–8 test may use interactive questions that may include audio or video clips instead of, say, a static map or reading passage.

Item formats may ask you to select the correct answer(s) by any of these means:

1. Click on a sentence or sentences, or on parts of a graphic representation, such as a map, chart, or figure—sometimes termed a "hot spot."

2. Drag and drop answer options into "target" areas in a table, piece of text, or graphic.

3. Use a drop-down menu.

More than anything, these innovative item types require that you read the instructions carefully to be sure you are fully responsive to the question.

The TExES Core Subjects test is scored based on the number of questions you answer correctly. With no penalty for guessing, you won't want to leave any item unanswered.

When should the test be taken?

Traditionally, teacher preparation programs determine when their candidates take the required tests for teacher certification. These programs will also clear you to take the examinations and make final recommendations for certification to the Texas State Board for Educator Certification (SBEC).

A candidate seeking 4–8 certification may take the appropriate Core Subjects test at such time as his or her Educator Preparation Program (EPP) determines the candidate's readiness to take the test, or upon successful completion of the EPP, whichever comes first. The EPP will determine readiness through benchmarks and structured assessments of the candidate's progress throughout the preparation program.

The test is generally taken just before graduation. Taking all appropriate TExES examinations is a requirement to teach in Texas, so if you are planning on being an educator, you must take and pass these tests.

How do I register for the test?

To register for the test, you must create an account in the Pearson online registration system. Registration will then be available to you online, 24/7, during the regular, late, and emergency registration periods. Visit Pearson's TExES website at *www.tx.nesinc.com* and follow the instructions.

You must pay a registration fee to take the TExES tests, and you will also incur additional late fees when registering after the scheduled date.

What's the passing score?

Your score on each of the TExES 211's four subject tests (test codes 806 to 809) will be reported on a 100–300 scale. A scaled score of 240 is set as the minimum passing score. To put this in context, you want to be confident you can answer between 70% and 80% of the questions correctly. To achieve the 70% level, you must get 140 questions correct; to reach the 80% level, you need to get 160 questions correct. As you work your way through our practice tests, scores in this range will suggest that you are sufficiently absorbing the test content. On the actual test, however, some (unknown number) of the questions will be field-tested and thus will not be scored. There is no holistic score for the full Core Subjects 4–8 battery; overall results are reported as "Passed" or "Not Passed" because, as the Texas Education Agency puts it, "there is no total scaled score for the overall exam."

If you do not get a passing score on our online diagnostic test or the practice tests, review your online score report and study the detailed explanations for the questions you answered incorrectly. Note which types of questions you answered wrong, and re-examine the corresponding review content. After further review, you may want to retake the practice tests online.

When will I receive my score report?

As part of the registration process to take TExES examinations, test candidates set up an account with Pearson in which they are assigned a username and password. Use this account to access your score report information on Pearson's TExES website. Scores for the TExES 211 exam are reported within 7 days of testing. Score reports will be posted by 10 p.m. CT on the score reporting date and will be available for 90 days.

What if I don't pass each subject test?

You must pass all parts of the Core Subjects 4–8 test in order to meet the examination requirement for Texas's Core Subjects 4–8 certificate. If you don't do well on every part of the Core Subjects test, don't panic. You can retake the entire test or any single subject exam up to four times. Both options require a 30-day waiting period after the first and subsequent attempts. After your first attempt, each testing session counts as another try, regardless of whether the session includes the entire exam battery or an individual subject test.

How should I prepare for the test?

It is never too early to start studying for the TExES. The earlier you begin, the more time you will have to sharpen your skills. Do not procrastinate. Cramming is not an effective way to study, since it does not allow you the time needed to learn the test material. It is important for you to choose the time and place for studying that works best for you. Be consistent and use your time wisely. Work out a study routine and stick to it.

When you take our diagnostic test and practice tests, simulate the conditions of the actual test as closely as possible. Go to a quiet place free from distraction. Read each question carefully, consider all answer choices, and pace yourself.

As you complete each test, review your score reports, study the diagnostic feedback, and thoroughly review the explanations to the questions you answered incorrectly. But don't overdo it. Take one problem area at a time; review it until you are confident that you have mastered the material. Give extra attention to the areas giving you the most difficulty, as this will help build your score. Because the test covers content areas in grades 4–8, you should review the state curricula for these grades (Texas Essential Knowledge and Skills) available at *http://www.tea.state.tx.us*.

TEXES CORE SUBJECTS 4–8 STUDY SCHEDULE

Week	Activity
1	Take the online Diagnostic Test Battery at the REA Study Center. Your detailed score report will identify the topics where you need the most review.
2–3	Study the review chapters. Use your Diagnostic Test score report to focus your study. Useful study techniques include highlighting key terms and information and taking notes as you read the review. Learn all the competencies by making flashcards and targeting questions you missed on the Diagnostic Test.
4	Take Practice Test Battery 1 either in the book or online at the REA Study Center. Review your score report and identify topics where you need more review.
5	Reread all your notes, refresh your understanding of the test's competencies and skills, review your college textbooks, and read class notes you've taken. This is also the time to consider any other supplementary materials that your advisor or the Texas Education Agency suggests. Visit the agency's website at *http://www.tea.state.tx.us/*.
6	Take Practice Test Battery 2 online at the REA Study Center. Review your score report and restudy the appropriate review section(s) until you are confident you understand the material.

Are there any breaks during the test?

Although there is no designated break during the Core Subjects test, you do have a little time to use for the restroom or snacking or stretching outside the testing room. The total time allotted for all the subject tests is 4 hours and 40 minutes. But the grand total for the entire testing period is 5 hours. That leaves you 20 minutes to make your own break.

Bear in mind the following:

- You need to get permission to leave the testing room.

- You cannot take a break during any of the subject tests—only between tests.

- The overall test clock never stops.

- The timer for individual subject tests starts only when you begin a test.

- Consult your test admission materials for further details, including updates from Pearson and the Texas Education Agency.

What else do I need to know about test day?

The day before your test, check for any updates in your Pearson testing account. This is where you'll learn of any changes to your reporting schedule or regarding the test site.

On the day of the test, you should wake up early after a good night's rest. Have a good breakfast and dress in layers that can be removed or added as the conditions in the test center require. Arrive at the test center early. This will allow you to relax and collect your thoughts before the test, and will also spare you the anguish that comes with being late. As an added incentive to make sure that you arrive early, keep in mind that no one will be admitted into the test center after the test has begun.

Before you leave for the testing site, carefully review your registration materials. Make sure you bring your admission ticket and two unexpired forms of identification. Primary forms of ID include:

- Passport

- Government-issued driver's license

- State or Province ID card

- National ID card

- Military ID card

You may need to produce a supplemental ID document if any questions arise with your primary ID or if your primary ID is otherwise valid but lacks your full name, photo, and signature. Without proper identification, you will not be admitted to the test center.

Strict rules limit what you can bring into the test center. We recommend that you consult the Texas Education Agency's complete rundown on what to expect on test day. You may not bring watches of any kind, cellphones, smartphones, or any other electronic communication devices or weapons of any kind. Scrap paper, written notes, books, as well as any printed material are all prohibited.

No smoking, eating, or drinking is allowed in the testing room. Consider bringing a small snack and a bottle of water to partake of beforehand to keep you sharp during the test.

Good luck on the TExES Core Subjects 4–8 (211) test!

Proven Test-Taking Strategies for TExES Core Subjects

All test-taking strategies have the same practical goal: to show you the best way to answer questions so you can improve your score.

The strategies and tips that follow come straight from teacher education students who have passed the TExES Core Subjects tests. We have worked directly with students just like you to see what works best.

Remember: There is no one right way to study. Savvy test-takers sharpen their skills while minimizing obstacles such as poor time management and test anxiety. As you assess these strategies, identify those you already use in your daily life and adapt the approaches that best address your problem areas—that is, the ones for which you'll need to invest more study time.

To make the most of whatever strategies you use, it's best to have an overall plan in mind. Our strategy list can be adjusted according to your needs, which no one knows better than you. Do what best fits your style of learning and method of study.

1. Guess Away

One of the most frequently asked questions about the TExES Core Subjects test is: Can I guess? The answer: Absolutely! There is no penalty for guessing on the test. That means if you refrain from guessing, you may lose points. To guess smartly, use the process of elimination (see Strategy No. 2). Your score is based strictly on the number of correct answers. So answer all questions and take your best guess when you don't know the answer.

2. Process of Elimination

Process of elimination is one of the most important test-taking strategies at your disposal. Process of elimination means looking at the choices and eliminating the ones you know are wrong, including answers that are partially wrong. Your odds of getting the right answer increase from the moment you're able to get rid of a wrong choice.

3. All in

Review all the response options. Just because you believe you've found the correct answer—or, in some cases, all the answers that apply—look at each choice so you don't mistakenly jump to any conclusions. If you are asked to choose the *best* answer, be sure your first answer is really the best one.

4. Choice of the Day

What if you are truly stumped and can't use the process of elimination? It's time to pick a fallback answer. On the day of the test, choose the position of the answer (e.g., the third of the four choices) that you will pick for any question you cannot smartly guess. According to the laws of probability, you have a higher chance of getting an answer right if you stick to one chosen position for the answer choice when you have to guess an answer instead of randomly picking one.

5. Use Choices to Confirm Your Answer

The great thing about multiple-choice questions is that the answer has to be staring back at you. Have an answer in mind and use the choices to *confirm* it. For the Math test, in the cases in which you're given a problem to solve, try to find the match among the choices. Or try the opposite: *backsolving*—that is, working backwards—from the choices given.

6. Watch the Clock

Among the most vital point-saving skills is active time management. The breakdown and time limits of each section are provided as you begin each test. Keep an eye on the timer on your computer screen. Make sure you keep track of how much time you have left for each section and never spend too much time on any one question. Remember: Most multiple-choice questions are worth one raw point. Treat each one as if it's the one that will put you over the top. You never know, it just might. The last thing you want on test day is to lose easy points because you ran out of time and focused too much on difficult questions.

7. Read, Read, Read

It's important to read through all the multiple-choice options. Even if you believe answer choice A is correct, you can misread a question or response option if you're rushing to get through the test. While it is important not to linger on a question, it is also crucial to avoid giving a question short shrift. Slow down, calm down, read all the choices. Verify that your choice is the best one, and click on it.

8. Take Notes

Use the noteboard booklet and erasable pen provided to you by the test proctor to make notes or do calculations.

9. Isolate Limiters

Pay attention to any limiters in a multiple-choice question stem. These are words such as *initial, best, most* (as in *most appropriate* or *most likely*), *not, least, except, required,* or *necessary.* Especially watch for negative words, such as "Choose the answer that is *not* true." When you select your answer, double-check yourself by asking how the response fits the limitations established by the stem. Think of the stem as a puzzle piece that perfectly fits only the response option(s) that contain the correct answer. Let it guide you.

10. It's Not a Race

Ignore other test-takers. Don't compare yourself to anyone else in the room. Focus on the items in front of you and the time you have left. If someone finishes the test 30 minutes early, it does not necessarily mean that person answered more questions correctly than you did. Stay calm and focus on *your* test. It's the only one that matters.

11. Confirm Your Click

In the digital age, many of us are used to rapid-clicking, be it in the course of emailing or gaming. Look at the screen to be sure to see that your mouse-click is acknowledged. If your answer doesn't register, you won't get credit. However, if you want to mark it for review so you can return later, that's your call. Before you click "Submit," use the test's review screen to see whether you inadvertently skipped any questions.

12. Creature of Habit? No Worries.

We are all creatures of habit. It's therefore best to follow a familiar pattern of study. Do what's comfortable for you. Set a time and place each day to study for this test. Whether it is 30 minutes at the library or an hour in a secluded corner of your local coffee shop, commit yourself as best you can to this schedule every day. Find quiet places where it is less crowded, as constant background noise can distract you. Don't study one subject for too long, either. Take an occasional breather and treat yourself to a healthy snack or some quick exercise. After your short break—5 or 10 minutes can do the trick—return to what you were studying or start a new section.

13. Knowledge is Power

Purchasing this book gives you an edge on passing the TExES Core Subjects test. Make the most of this edge. Review the sections on how the test is structured, what the directions look like, what types of questions will be asked, and so on. Take our practice tests to familiarize yourself with what the test looks and feels like. Most test anxiety occurs because people feel unprepared when they are taking the test, and they psych themselves out. You can whittle away at anxiety by learning the format of the test and by knowing what to expect. Fully simulating the test even once will boost your chances of getting the score you need. Meanwhile, the knowledge you've gained will also save you the valuable time that would have been eaten up puzzling through what the directions are asking. As an added benefit, previewing the test will free up your brain's resources so you can focus on racking up as many points as you can.

14. B-r-e-a-t-h-e

Anxiety is neither unusual nor necessarily unwelcome on a test. Just don't let it stifle you. Take a moment to breathe. This won't merely make you feel good. The brain uses roughly three times as much oxygen as muscles in the body do: Give it what it needs. Now consider this: What's the worst that can happen when you take a test? You may have an off day, and despite your best efforts, you may not pass. Well, the good news is that this test can be retaken. Fortunately, the TExES Core Subjects test is something you can study and prepare for, and in some ways to a greater extent than other tests you've taken throughout your academic career. In fact, study after study has validated the value of test preparation. Yes, there will be questions you won't know, but neither your teacher education program nor state licensing board (which sets its own cut scores) expects you to know everything. When unfamiliar vocabulary appears or difficult math problems loom, don't despair: Use context clues, process of elimination, or your response option of the day (i.e., choose either A, B, C, or D routinely when you need to resort to a guess) to make your choice, and then press ahead. If you have time left, you can always come back to the question later. If not, relax. It is only one question on a test filled with many. Take a deep breath and then exhale. You know this information. Now you're going to show it.

Subject Test I: English Language Arts and Reading (806)

CHAPTER 3

OVERVIEW OF SUBJECT TEST I: ELA AND READING (806)

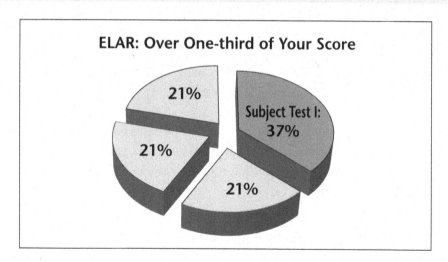

ELAR: Over One-third of Your Score

English Language Arts and Reading, or ELAR, accounts for approximately 37% of the questions you will see on the TExES Core Subjects 4–8 test. That makes this by far the largest subject test in the test battery. This is the section where you are expected to spend most of your time and where you will encounter the most questions. You'll be allotted 1 hour and 55 minutes to answer 74 test items. That gives you just over 1.5 minutes for each question. (Each of the four subject tests that make up the Core Subjects 4–8 test is individually timed.)

The ELAR subject test assesses eight Texas educator standards in connection with the statewide curriculum, known as Texas Essential Knowledge and Skills (TEKS). These

English Language Arts and Reading, or ELAR, accounts for approximately 37% of the questions you will see on the TExES Core Subjects 4–8 test. That makes this by far the largest subject test in the test battery. This is the section where you are expected to spend most of your time and where you will encounter the most questions. You'll be allotted 1 hour and 55 minutes to answer 74 test items. That gives you just over 1.5 minutes for each question. (Each of the four subject tests that make up the Core Subjects 4–8 test is individually timed.)

The ELAR subject test assesses eight Texas educator standards in connection with the statewide curriculum, known as Texas Essential Knowledge and Skills (TEKS). These

15

standards frame what it takes to teach middle school English Language Arts and Reading, including that the teacher:

I. Understands the importance of oral language, knows the developmental processes of oral language and provides a variety of instructional opportunities for students to develop listening and speaking skills.

II. Understands the foundations of reading and early literacy development.

III. Understands the importance of word analysis skills (including decoding, blending, structural analysis, sight word vocabulary) and reading fluency and provides many opportunities for students to practice and improve their word analysis skills and reading fluency.

IV. Understands the importance of reading for understanding, knows the components of comprehension and teaches students strategies for improving their comprehension.

V. Understands that writing is a developmental process and provides instruction that helps students develop competence in written communication.

VI. Understands the importance of study and inquiry skills as tools for learning and promotes students' development in applying study and inquiry skills.

VII. Understands how to interpret, analyze, evaluate, and produce visual images and messages in various media and to provide students with opportunities to develop skills in this area.

VIII. Understands the basic principles of assessment and use a variety of literacy assessment practices to plan and implement instruction.

The subject test embraces nine competencies, which are based on the above standards and broadly define "what an entry-level educator in this field in Texas public schools should know and be able to do," according to the Texas Education Agency. Let's look at each competency in turn.

COMPETENCY 001: ORAL LANGUAGE

The teacher understands the importance of oral language, knows the developmental processes of oral language, and provides a variety of instructional opportunities for students to develop listening and speaking skills.

The beginning teacher:

A. Knows basic linguistic concepts (e.g., phonemes, segmentation) and developmental stages in acquiring oral language, including stages in phonology, semantics, syntax, and pragmatics, and recognizes that individual variations occur.

B. Knows characteristics and uses of informal and formal oral language assessments and uses multiple, ongoing assessments to monitor and evaluate students' oral language skills.

C. Provides language instruction that acknowledges students' current oral language skills and that builds on these skills to increase students' oral language proficiency.

D. Plans, implements, and adapts instruction that is based on informal and formal assessment of students' progress in oral language development and that addresses the needs, strengths, and interests of individual students, including English learners (ELs), in accordance with the English Language Proficiency Standards (ELPS).

E. Recognizes when oral language delays or differences warrant in-depth evaluation and additional help or intervention.

F. Knows how to provide explicit, systematic oral language instruction and supports students' learning and use of oral language through meaningful and purposeful activities implemented one-to-one and in a group.

G. Selects and uses instructional materials and strategies that promote students' oral language development; that respond to students' individual strengths, needs, and interests; that reflect cultural diversity; and that build on students' cultural, linguistic, and home backgrounds to enhance their oral language development.

H. Understands relationships between the development of oral language and the development of reading and provides instruction that interrelates oral and written language to promote students' reading proficiency and learning (e.g., preview-review, discussion, questioning).

I. Knows similarities and differences between oral and written language and how to promote students' awareness of these similarities and differences.

J. Selects and uses instructional strategies, materials, activities, and models to strengthen students' oral vocabulary and narrative skills in spoken language and teaches students to connect spoken and printed language.

K. Selects and uses instructional strategies, materials, activities, and models to teach students skills for speaking to different audiences for various purposes and for adapting spoken language for various audiences, purposes, and occasions.

L. Selects and uses instructional strategies, materials, activities and models to teach students listening skills for various purposes (e.g., critical listening to evaluate a speaker's message, listening to enjoy and appreciate spoken language) and provides students with opportunities to engage in active, purposeful listening in a variety of contexts.

M. Selects and uses instructional strategies, materials, activities, and models to teach students to evaluate the content and effectiveness of their own spoken messages and the messages of others.

N. Knows how to promote students' development of oral communication skills through the use of technology and applications found in smartphones, tablets, and e-readers.

The Centrality of Oral Language

Educators may assume that by the time students reach Grades 4–8, most will know enough about speaking and listening to carry on fluent conversation. In addition, lingering gaps in speaking skills may not be expected. Teachers will also recognize that much at this stage remains to be accomplished in reading and writing. As a result, oral language development may fall by the wayside. Yet theory and research point to the centrality of oral language development in literacy instruction. Proficiency in oral language plays a critical role developing proficiency in reading and writing. At the same time, speaking and listening can be tools for thinking and learning as students engage in reading and writing. Furthermore, there's a strong social element involved: After all, speaking and listening are primary ways for students to establish relationships with others.

Students proficient in reading and writing typically have had certain types of oral language experiences that propel them into successful reading and writing development. But even when they engage in day-to-day speaking and listening, students' vocabulary may still not be strong enough for reading and writing in school. But a strong vocabulary is not all that is required for successful reading and writing. Students must transcend merely knowing word meanings and identifying individual words. Instead, students need to know how to create meaning by knowing how to bring together individual words, sentences, or thoughts to develop a complete mental representation of the message on the page or screen. A thought or sentence mentioned in one part of the text needs to be brought together with others to create meaning.

When students engage in everyday listening, they are not required to understand longer texts. Likewise, in everyday speaking, students do not have to compose longer texts to have a conversation. However, when students gain opportunities to listen to longer texts, such as in hearing books read aloud, they improve the listening comprehension abilities they need for reading. In the course of gaining experiences in extended dialog where they are called upon to sustain a thought and thus engage their intellect and imagination, they also will gain proficiency in writing.

In fact, even in the course of composing an essay, students can represent their thoughts in writing more effectively when they discuss what they want to write about. This can be part of a dialog with a teacher during writing conferences. Similarly, when students talk with each other as part of ongoing subject-matter learning, the collaboration allows them to refine their language skills and expand their learning abilities as they collaborate.

Oral language development is of course valuable in its own right. Talking and listening provide a way for students to build and strengthen connections with class members and the teacher, thereby helping foster a sense of belonging in school and the broader community. Indeed, speaking and listening skills also are essential—later on in the child's development—for effective civic participation and in the workplace. The language opportunities that schooling provides can build upon and expand the oral language at home. As students continue their schooling, their opportunities for growth in speaking and listening should continue. Schooling serves as a springboard to opportunities to use everyday language as well as the academic language that students learn in the subject areas. Teachers should ensure that students engage in a range of speaking and listening situations that enhance social development as well as the learning environment across the subject spectrum.

Oral Language Acquisition and Development

As educators cultivate students' oral language development, they can gain insights from what research tells us about how students acquire language. Long before children begin their schooling, they already have made strides in their language development. In fact, by age 5 they typically are able to speak and listen in at least one language. Because oral language acquisition occurs so regularly and routinely, it is possible for educators to overlook its significance. Remarkably, however, between birth and the start of their schooling, children learn the complex, abstract thinking needed for them to acquire a language.

How does this happen? The child's environment plays a role. Parents, caretakers, and others surround a child with talking and conversation, which contributes to children's language acquisition as well as the honing of a particular dialect. Nonetheless, research shows that children have an innate ability to acquire language, allowing them with ease—and no special effort—to construct their knowledge of language. Children thus do not acquire language with a formal sequence of lessons, but instead discern and apply the underlying principles of language on their own.

As children apply those principles, the adults around them are seen and heard creating messages in the language; in this way, adults model how to reply to messages from others, but they do not consciously address how letters and words are combined to speak and write. Adults know how sounds can be combined to form words and how those words can be combined when they talk and listen, but they cannot specify the principles.

In acquiring language, children do not simply imitate what they hear from people around them. Rather, as studies have shown, they also pick up forms of language they have not heard, such as when they overgeneralize a rule they are learning. For example, a child may say *went* but at a later point misapply the conjugation rule by saying *goed* [sic] as part of learning about adding -ed to form the regular past tense. Or a child may say *feets* [sic] while learning to form plurals. Eventually the child comes to use the conventional forms by figuring out the governing linguistic rules.

Understanding how young children acquire language enables teachers to foster language development in school. Students' oral language development continues throughout schooling, and oral language development can work in tandem with reading and writing development.

Components of Oral Language

As they acquire oral language, children gain mastery of the sounds of the language, known as the **phonemes**, and how those sounds can be combined. Children also learn **semantics**, or the ways meaning is generated in a language, which includes not only the meanings of words but also the way words, phrases, and sentences combine in ways that make sense. The semantic component entails **morphemes**, the smallest units of meaning that can be combined. Some morphemes are free morphemes because they can occur alone as a word, such as *car*. Other morphemes are called bound morphemes because these cannot occur alone as a word, such as when -*s* is used to form a plural. The plural noun cats, for example, consists of two morphemes, *cat* and -*s*. Additionally, children learn how words/morphemes can be placed together. This entails creating grammatical structure, the **syntax** of the language. Children combine two words, such as in "more juice," to convey meaning, but later will learn to create complex statements and questions. Language growth also includes adding prefixes (e.g., *un-*), suffixes (e.g., *-ful*), and inflectional endings added to the root word to change its number or tense (e.g., -*s*, -*ed*, -*ing*).

Language development also includes **pragmatics**, that is, knowing how to use language appropriately, depending on the context. Pragmatics is part of communicative competence, or knowing how to adjust speech to match the particular circumstances in which speakers find themselves. A person may describe the same event in different ways, depending upon whom they are talking with and whether it is an informal or formal situation.

Social Dimensions of Language Use

When children acquire language, they do so as part of communicating for everyday reasons. Children acquire language to connect with others and make sense of experience as they interact with the world around them. These social dimensions of language growth cannot be disentangled from cognitive growth. Teachers can provide opportunities for students to continue to grow in oral language by encouraging students to use language for day-to-day interaction in the classroom and, more broadly, valuing opportunities for letting students talk in a variety of situations for different purposes. Talking also can continue to be a tool for thinking and learning.

Stages of Oral Language Acquisition

By the time children are around 12 to 18 months old, they typically produce one-word utterances. Children entering the telegraphic stage use two or more words together to begin to create sentence-like utterances, such as "more juice" to communicate "I want more juice" to the parent.

By the time a child is 4 to 4½ years old, language skills become more complex in the types of statements, questions, and vocabulary (or lexicon) acquired. By age 5, children are able to talk easily with others who speak the same language or dialect.

Children vary in exactly when they begin to talk. For some, this happens before they are 12 months old. Children also can vary as they continue their oral language development. Some may use more complex sentences at 3½ years old as compared to other children who do not do so until they reach 4½-year mark.

Theories of Language Acquisition

How is language acquisition best explained? Behaviorists say it entails children gradually moving from simple to more complex utterances. Children begin with babbling and then say one- or two-word utterances until they can produce longer messages. Children respond to positive reinforcement, such as when a mother smiles or gives the child a glass of juice when the child says "juice."

Although children do move from babbling to one- and two-word utterances to the more complex sentences, and people do respond, cognitive theorists argue that behaviorist theory does not account for many other aspects of language acquisition. These factors include the fact that *adults* are able to produce and understand language they have never heard before, involving more than imitation and positive reinforcement for their utterances.

According to **Noam Chomsky**, children would not be equipped to produce and understand the infinite number of possibilities to form sentences were they relying solely on input from the environment. So Chomsky proposed the notion of humans uniquely having an innate mechanism that he called a **Language Acquisition Device** (LAD). He held that children are born with **Universal Grammar**, which contains all the information children need to acquire the grammar of a language. As a result, children are able to acquire language structures beyond those heard from the adults around them.

However, some psycholinguists did not totally accept Chomsky's notion of Universal Grammar, maintaining instead that children might use more general cognitive principles. This view holds that children are born with the ability to acquire language, and that the development is gradual. As a result, when a child hears a sufficient number of linguistic constructions, the child will discern the underlying principles that make it possible for the child to understand and create messages.

Oral Language Development in Schooling

As indicated, speaking and listening development is required in curriculum, but reading and writing development is often viewed as meriting particular attention and legitimacy. This can create the mistaken impression that oral language should be a lower priority. Educators may assume that students who are native speakers already know what they need to know about speaking and listening. Students often are expected to work on their own. Yet in our communities and in the workplace, successfully interacting with others (and even getting a job) often hinges on proficiency in speaking and listening.

Research tells us that proficiency in oral language depends upon people using language for a range of purposes, in different situations, with various sizes and types of of audiences. Planning for oral language development does not require teachers to add another area to be taught. Rather, speaking and listening can be integrated into students' experiences during the school day. Schooling can also contribute toward greater oral proficiency in special ways because students engage in speaking and listening situations that expand the types of audience, functions (or purposes), and situations (or registers) that children will face as they grow.

Audience

Teachers can systematically incorporate opportunities for students to engage in a range of situations that vary by the size and type of audience. The demands of using language differ when students are talking to one another one-on-one, versus in a small group, or in a whole-class or large group. Audience in schools also can vary in terms of familiarity, which also provides opportunities for students to become more comfortable expressing ideas to strangers. The age of the participants also can play a role. Speakers may need to adjust their comments depending on the age and familiarity of the listener.

Functions of Language

Halliday (1973) provides a description of various functions of language, which teachers can use to ensure that students experience the full spectrum of functions to suit different contexts and **purposes**. With sufficient scaffolding and support from their teachers, students can gain language proficiency with these language functions:

- **Instrumental:** used to obtain something

- **Regulatory:** used to request or control

- **Personal:** used to express self

- **Interactional:** used to connect with others and maintain social relationships

- **Heuristic:** used to gain information or explore

- **Imaginative:** used to create

- **Representational:** to inform and exchange information

Providing ways for students to engage in the Halliday functions does not require additional lessons. In fact, educational objectives can be enhanced as students interact with their peers for various purposes. For example, rather than completing an assignment on their own, students can work with partners or small groups in math or science. As the students learn in the subject area, they also engage in heuristic, representational, and regulatory functions.

Language Register

In oral and written language development, growth includes knowing how to adjust the level and style of language depending upon the situation. A more formal register is appropriate for some situations, whereas informal registers are most appropriate when communicating with family and friends. By offering students multiple opportunities to use language that range from informal to more formal, students can learn how to be proficient in using registers.

Key Guidelines for Oral Language Development in Classrooms

Here's a look at key guidelines for fostering students' abilities in listening and speaking.

- **Speaking and listening can be developed without sacrificing subject-matter learning.** Teachers should integrate speaking and listening in subject-matter learning. Teachers may believe that they do not have time to add speaking and listening to their classroom schedules. In addition, they know that formal assessments focus on reading and writing. However, by slightly revising learning experiences, many written language experiences can include talking and listening. Learning experiences where each student works solo by writing can be presented so that students discuss the information these experiences illuminate. Students work with the teacher and other students in completing a written learning task, incorporating speaking and listening. In fact, the demonstrations and collaboration provided by speaking and listening can enhance learning. Ultimately, students need to be able to work independently in completing a task, but they can achieve at a faster pace when oral language situations are intertwined supportively alongside reading and writing.

- **Provide students an array of opportunities to engage in authentic speaking and listening activities.** We know that being able to talk easily with family and friends does not necessarily translate into being able to talk easily with someone recently met, such as in a job interview. In other words, different types of language situations make different demands on speakers and listeners. Consider ways to let students use language for **different purposes** and in various **types of situations** that range from informal to more formal situations, such as talking with a classmate or having a panel discussion about a recently read book. Consider also how to provide various **types of audiences**, such as communicating with people who are familiar or less familiar, who are the same age, younger, or older. Audiences also can vary, alternately involving speaking with another individual, or in groups large and small.

- **Provide modeling.** Students can gain when teachers engage in discussions with a group of students as well as talk with individual students. The modeling that the teacher provides can expand the adult models provided in the home and the community. Also, in school, the uses of language can be different, because adult modeling for a particular purpose may not exist at home.

- **Provide helpful growth opportunities in using conventional language rather than focusing on errors.** Students need to learn about conventional ways of speaking. However, it is not helpful to criticize their dialect, which by definition may break with convention. Rather than saying the student is "wrong" or incorrect, the teacher can reply by using the conventional way to express the thought and thereby reinforce the meaning. For example, if the child says, "He goed with me," the teacher could reply, "Oh, it is great that he went with you." In this way, the student gets to hear the conventional form while also feeling safe in talking with the teacher. Keep in mind that the expressions students use could come directly from their parents and other loved ones. Over time, students also can acquire more fully conventional uses of language when given opportunities to demonstrate it in the classroom with the guidance of the teacher, such as when the teacher models.

- **Let students engage talking and listen daily as part of routines.** Research on language development tells us that we grow in language by using it daily, for everyday meaningful reasons. Talking and listening are ways we form connections, and the social dimensions of learning cannot be disentangled from the cognitive.

- **Rather than focusing upon what students cannot do, adults should focus on what they *can*.** Most students are successful in acquiring at least one language by the time they reach age 5. A student may mispronounce a word or not use it exactly in accord with convention. Nevertheless, most students eventually will use the more conventional forms as they engage in talking and listening. Some students are more reticent, and some are more talkative, especially in particular situations. But as certain talking situations become more familiar, many students who are initially reticent begin to talk more. If teachers make it possible for students to engage in a range of talking situations that are authentic, students will grow in using language.

- **Seek advice when needed.** When a student has difficulty hearing or seems to be far behind peers in communicating, the teacher should seek advice; the child may need the help of other professionals who specialize in speech and hearing.

- **Keep in mind that students rely upon knowing a language through speaking and listening to be able to read and write in that language.** Students do not need to wait to achieve proficiency in speaking to begin reading and writing instruction. However, they do draw upon knowing vocabulary and how to combine sounds and words when they read and write. Short-changing oral language development hampers growth in reading and writing.

Conditions for Learning Oral and Written Language

As discussed earlier, in learning how to speak and listen, children do more than imitate the what they hear. They learn the underlying principles for how words can be combined, which makes it possible for language learners to understand sentences they have never heard before and to produce sentences they have never said before. However, parents, caretakers, and others play an invaluable role in children's language acquisition. Children hear language being used, or are provided modeling. Also, others respond to the child's utterances. Moreover, through interactions with others, children are given real reasons to communicate.

Brian Cambourne (1988) delineated eight conditions for learning language based on his study of children's language development. These conditions for learning are present in the environment when children acquire oral language most easily, and these conditions also can guide the acquisition of written language.

1. **Immersion:** Students should be imbued with authentic ways to use oral and written throughout the curriculum. Teachers can do this by, for example, reading aloud to students, letting students work in small groups, and providing students daily opportunities to write.

2. **Demonstrations:** Students need demonstrations of oral and written language use. Modeling on the part of the teacher and other students, as well as the language of books and other sources, makes it possible for students to see the various ways that language can be used.

3. **Engagement:** Regardless of their proficiency levels, students can actively engage and realize that they can read and write when they are provided an environment where they can try out using language in a supportive environment.

4. **Expectation:** Have high but realistic expectations for each student, knowing they will make gains in language development over time.

5. **Responsibility:** With meaningful support, students can be responsible for their learning and make choices about what they read and write.

6. **Approximation:** Students will gradually become more proficient in oral and written language use when their best efforts are valued and when they are guided toward accuracy and self-correction.

7. **Use:** Students need multiple opportunities to use oral and written language in a variety of ways for real reasons.

8. **Response:** Students will gain most when teachers and others listen to them, read their writing, and provide genuine comments.

Ways Oral and Written Language Development Can Work in Tandem

Speaking and listening can contribute to students' growth in reading and writing. By incorporating effective instructional practices on a daily basis, teachers can capitalize on speaking and listening to help their students grow as readers and writers. Such practices are able to make an impact when they become part of the routines in classrooms; growth will take place, but it will happen over time. Gains can be seen immediately, but they will gather steam and widen once students develop familiarity with procedures and experiences. These instructional practices also make it possible for teachers to provide oral language experiences whereby students participate in different types of language situations that vary according to (1) **types of audiences**, (2) **informal to more formal registers**, and (3) **purposes or functions**.

Reading Aloud

We know that being a successful reader entails more than identifying words correctly. Even when students can say words correctly, many still cannot understand what they are reading as they reach the third and fourth grades, where the content of reading is longer and fewer pictures provide support. A major reason why students can face difficulty is because they have not developed the abilities needed for reading longer texts.

Developing students' listening comprehension can make it possible for students to navigate longer texts when they read because they have developed the types of thinking needed as they gained in listening comprehension. When students talk with others outside of school, they encounter brief segments of language. In speaking with friends and family, the exchanges are short, with one person saying something and the other person replying typically in relatively rapid-fire snippets. Through these oral language experiences, students gain much, but they do not gain the listening comprehension that will foster success when reading. With mostly shorter language exchanges under their belt, students' listening comprehension abilities will not be sufficiently advanced to succeed when encountering longer segments of language. Students cannot sustain attention or bring together ideas encountered to create understanding. We also know that students' oral language experiences will not afford them the wide range of vocabulary they encounter in reading. However, students' listening comprehension and vocabulary can be developed in relatively short periods of time by reading quality literature aloud. Quality literature for youth will engage students, which, in turn, leads to vocabulary and comprehension development.

By reading aloud quality literature, teachers can help students gain in sustaining attention and creating understanding as they gradually acquaint themselves with longer passages and different types of books. Students should read independently daily, but they also can gain from read-aloud experiences because their listening comprehension gradually will increase over time if reading aloud occurs daily. Reading aloud also is critical for showing students what books offer. Assigning reading may or may not work with reluctant readers. Conversely, when teachers read aloud quality literature that students enjoy, even reluctant readers can be buoyed to read and want to do it independently.

Writing Conferences

Speaking and listening can support writing development. Writing conferences with students can help them talk about a topic, which provides scaffolding for writing. Similarly, individual and whole-class writing conferences with students can support writing development as class members supply feedback on what they liked or learned and then pose genuine questions that "tell" the writer where clarification or elaboration is needed.

Buddy Reading (Partner Work)

Reading with partners, known as **buddy reading** or **partner work**, provides students opportunities for students to participate in productive reading while also providing oral language development. Rather than completing an activity on their own, students can learn content more efficiently and learn how to learn when they and the teacher work together, or they are shown how to work in small groups.

Grand Conversations

Traditionally, reading assignments to measure understanding have involved writing answers to questions or completing packets for which students complete an array of written assignments as part of reading a book. The same learning objectives can be met by engaging in grand conversations with students on a daily basis. Rather than using question-and-answer recitations, the teacher and students share their thoughts about what took place in a work and big ideas that emerge from the reading selection. This works especially well when the teacher models sharing and participates in the conversation.

Just as readers do generally, students enjoy discussing books they've read when given the opportunity. In addition, the comments of students show that they can think at high levels about what they have read as they make inferences, evaluate their readings, and share connections to their lives and other reading experiences. These discussions can provide the basis for subsequent discussion of literary elements featured in a work. Regular discussion also provides support for students as they learn how to write about what they have read. The students' oral composing development will make it easier for them to be able to compose when writing because of the practice they've gotten.

Retelling

After students have read a section or part of a selection independently, the teacher can ask the group to retell what was read. This should be a casual conversation, allowing students to feel safe to talk. If students leave out a part, the teacher can add the missing portion to provide modeling and accuracy (e.g., "Yes, that happened, but just before that…."). If students stop, the teacher can provide a brief prompt, such as "What happened next?," to encourage the students. If students are reluctant to begin, the teacher can start to model and invite students to share along the way.

Retelling is a way of encouraging students to pay attention to the text as they read. When teachers use this approach each time a story is read independently by students or when students read expository texts, it can lead to gains in proficiency in remembering and retelling. Retelling also can be used to assess whether students have understood what they have read. The retelling of a student may not show higher levels of comprehension, but higher levels of comprehension can be developed through conversations about the book. Moreover, recalling what was read through retelling provides a basis for making inferences, producing evaluations, achieving synthesis, and applying what is learned.

Technology and Audio-Assisted Reading

Students can receive additional experiences in hearing stories read through audiobooks. Quality literature can be shared beyond the read-aloud experiences provided. These experiences provide opportunities to expand vocabulary and listening comprehension.

Cooperative Learning

Students can make greater gains in vocabulary and overall oral language development by participating in small-group work on some assignments and by working in pairs. Such learning experiences also can be used to provide scaffolding for students who need more help to complete a task independently. Cooperative learning is especially useful for English learners (ELs) as well as other students facing similar circumstances.

"Turn and Talk"

Traditionally, teachers will ask an entire group of students a question or set of questions to encourage interaction in the classroom. Many children are reluctant to share because they are not confident in talking in a whole-group setting. Nonetheless, they can gain in confidence and ability when given the opportunity to talk and listen with another classmate first.

"Turn and Talk" is a prime tool for getting students to think more about a topic or experience. Rather than an individual child answering the teacher's question, children turn and talk to a partner to help crystallize their thinking and develop their oral language abilities. After talking with a partner, the children then can share what they talked about with the whole group. For instance, after the children have learned in science class about the function of tree bark, the teacher could ask the children to turn and talk about one thing they learned about the topic that day. Then the children could share and talk as a whole group. The teacher also could write to record a list of ideas that could be reviewed in later lessons of the unit on trees. "Turn and Talk" works best when the teacher makes sure all students have partners who can help them grow in speaking and listening. For example, it may be best to place a reticent child with one who is confident but also supportive. Teachers also should help students learn about how to be polite listeners. Teachers use the "turn and talk" strategy in situations where the children can briefly address the topic at hand (in, say, 30 to 60 seconds). However, letting students talk with a partner or work together could also be a part of classroom learning for longer periods of time.

Assessing Listening and Speaking in K–12

Performance-based activities can be used to provide students opportunities to use language, and they also can provide a context for gathering information about a student's proficiency in listening and speaking. These listening and speaking activities work best when they are an ongoing part of classroom learning. Students' speaking abilities also can be assessed in the classroom with a structured checklist identifying specific features that teachers want to observe. The checklist could be organized to feature social as well as academic situations and/or proficiency levels.

Here's an example of a "Speaking and Listening Checklist":

- ✓ Listens to others during whole-class conversations
- ✓ Listens to others during small-group conversations
- ✓ Contributes to whole-class conversations
- ✓ Contributes to small-group conversations
- ✓ Talks with individual students
- ✓ Speaks clearly
- ✓ Uses courteous language
- ✓ Uses social registers that are appropriate
- ✓ Provides comments that relate to the topic
- ✓ Asks questions related to the topic

Language Assessment of English Learners (ELs)

The Texas Education Agency (TEA) designed the Texas English Language Proficiency Assessment System (TELPAS) to assess the progress that English learners make in learning the English language. English language proficiency assessments in Grades K–12 are required by the federal government to evaluate the progress of English learners (ELs). The TELPAS assesses proficiency in listening, speaking, reading, and writing. For students in Grades K–1 the TELPAS includes ratings based upon classroom observations. Students in Grades 2–12 receive a score on the multiple-choice questions of the TELPAS reading test. Speaking and listening proficiency ratings are based upon classroom observations, and writing scores are based upon a collection of each student's writing. Students receive a composite score based on the four levels of English proficiency identified by the state education agency (SEA)—beginner, intermediate, advanced, and advanced high. These scores are then reported to the U.S. Department of Education to document changes in the English proficiency of the learners.

Beginning—Students at this level have a small vocabulary of common words and little ability to use English in academic settings. Students often communicate by using English words and phrases that they have memorized.

Intermediate—Students at this level can communicate about familiar topics, are able to understand simple conversations, but they may not understand all the details. Students are able to use basic English, and they need language support to understand.

Advanced—Students can understand most of what they hear in social situations, but they may have difficulty with unfamiliar vocabulary and grammar. Students at this level can understand and use grade-appropriate academic English when they have support.

Advanced High—Students at this level can communicate in most situations. These students can use grade-appropriate academic English with minimal support even when encountering new information. A score of advanced high is one of the criteria used when considering reclassifying students as fluent English speakers.

English Proficiency Standards (ELPS)

Chapter 19 TAC §74.4E of the Texas Education code defines English Proficiency Standards (ELPS) as a series of instructional standards that outline the linguistic modifications needed to support ELs in the process of content mastery when instruction is provided in English. The ELPS delineate specific strategies in each of the language skills—listening, speaking, reading, and writing—so teachers can guide ELs in the process of content and language mastery. To comply with the ELPS mandate, which is now also mandated by federal legislation, teachers with at least one EL in their classroom are required to incorporate content and language objectives in lesson planning to facilitate content-area mastery and the development of academic English.

The ELPS addresses expectations for student mastery of (1) learning strategies, (2) listening, (3) speaking, (4) reading, and (5) writing. This means that ELs need to be able to learn in a discipline and make gains in the four language domains listed above. Supporting ELs requires making sure they have many targeted opportunities to use English across the curriculum. Using pictures and gestures can help ELs new to English. Providing scaffolding and support for learning in disciplines is necessary for all students, but especially ELs. Ways to support students include making sure they (1) use language daily, (2) are shown ways to build upon what is known in English and about a topic, (3) experience interesting learning opportunities, and (4) are able to participate with appropriate pacing and level of difficulty. These approaches are effective for all students, allowing ELs and native speakers to participate in the same types of learning experiences, but more scaffolding is needed for ELs, depending on a student's language proficiency.

COMPETENCY 002: EARLY LITERACY DEVELOPMENT

The teacher understands the foundations of early literacy development.

The beginning teacher:

A. Understands the significance of phonological and phonemic awareness for reading and typical patterns in the development of phonological and phonemic awareness and recognizes that individual variations occur.

B. Understands elements of the alphabetic principle (e.g., letter names, graphophonemic knowledge, the relationship of the letters in printed words to spoken language) and typical patterns of students' alphabetic skills development, and recognizes that individual variations occur.

C. Understands that comprehension is an integral part of early literacy.

D. Understands that not all written languages are alphabetic and that many alphabetic languages are more phonetically regular than English and knows the significance of this for students' literacy development in English.

E. Understands that literacy acquisition generally develops in a predictable pattern from prereading (emergent literacy) to conventional literacy and recognizes that individual variations occur.

F. Understands that literacy development occurs in multiple contexts through reading, writing, speaking, and using various media.

G. Knows characteristics of informal and formal literacy assessments (e.g., screening devices, criterion-referenced state tests, curriculum-based reading assessments, informal reading inventories, norm-referenced tests).

H. Knows how to select, administer, and use results from informal and formal assessments of literacy acquisition.

I. Knows how to use ongoing assessment to determine when a student needs additional help or intervention to bring the student's performance to grade level, based on state content and performance standards for reading in the Texas Essential Knowledge and Skills (TEKS).

J. Analyzes students' errors in reading and responds to individual students' needs by providing focused instruction to promote literacy acquisition.

K. Selects and uses instructional materials that build on the current language skills of individual students, including English learners (in accordance with the ELPS), to promote development from emergent literacy to conventional literacy.

L. Knows how to promote students' early literacy development skills through the use of technology and applications found in smartphones, tablets, and e-readers.

Phonological and Phonemic Awareness

Before children learn to read print in an alphabetic language, such as English and Spanish, they need to understand that words are made up of speech sounds, or phonemes. In reading, they will need to account for the sounds of a word as they remember the word. **Phonemes** are the smallest parts of sound in a spoken word that make a difference in the word's meaning. For example, changing the first phoneme in the word *mop* from /m/ to /t/ changes the word from *mop* to *top*, and thus the meaning as well.[1]

As they learn to speak, children discover individual phonemes of their language and the corresponding sounds that can be combined to create words. However, this knowledge is acquired unconsciously. In learning to read and write, children must have a conscious knowledge that words are made up of sounds because they need to account for those sounds as they relate letters and sounds. Children can use letter-sound knowledge for reading once they know that words are made up of individual sounds that blend together and that words can be segmented into their constituent sounds.

Phonological awareness is the ability to identify and manipulate the oral components of sentences and words, and the highest level is identifying and manipulating individual sounds in words, which is **phonemic awareness**.

Phonological awareness abilities exist on a continuum of complexity that moves from larger to smaller units of language. That is, the complexity moves from listening to sentences and detecting words, noticing beginnings and endings of **words, syllables, onset and rime**, and **individual sounds (phonemes) of words**.

The continuum of phonological awareness from the less complex to the more complex is as follows.

- Segmenting **sentences** of speech into **words**.

  Teacher says: Move a token for each word you hear in the sentence. My cat runs.

  Child: (Detects three words.)

- **Detecting rhyme.**

  Teacher says: Do *hat* and *cat* sound the same at the end?

  Child: "Yes." The teacher also could provide pictures for the student to match according to whether the pictures rhyme.

---

[1] A letter between slash marks shows the phoneme, or sound, that the letter represents, and not the name of the letter. For example, the letter *h* in English represents the unvoiced sound /h/ as in *help* or *hand*.

- **Detecting alliteration.**

  Teacher says: Sally sells seashells by the seashore

- **Syllable counting and detection** of words.

  Teacher says: Clap for sounds you hear in this word *baby*.
  Child: Claps twice.

- Blending and segmenting **onset and rime**. The onset is the consonant sound before the vowel of a syllable, and the rime is the vowel and other sounds of the syllable, such as for *sun*: /s/ -onset /un/ -rime

  Teacher says: Say the two parts you hear in a word and blend them back together. *bat*
  Child: /b/ /at/ *"bat"*

- **Phonemic awareness,** or understanding that words are made up of individual sounds. Below we look at the levels of phonemic awareness and the ways each level can be assessed or taught.

Phonemic Awareness is the highest level or subcomponent of phonological awareness. It addresses the ability to identify and manipulate individual phonemes or sounds in spoken words.

The continuum of **phonemic awareness** from the less complex to the more complex follows and includes examples of how to assess and teach a skill:

- **Initial sound identification.**

  Teacher says: Say the sound you hear at the beginning of these words (which are spoken, not shown in print): *see, sun, so*
  Child: (/s/)

- **Final sound identification.**

  Teacher says: Say the sound you hear at the end of these words (which are spoken, not shown in print): *man, sun, in.*
  Child: /n/

- **Blending phonemes,** or combining individual sounds provided to say a word.

  Teacher says: Blend these sounds to make a word: /s/ /u/ /n/
  Child: *"sun"*

- **Segmenting phonemes,** or breaking down a word to identify the individual sounds.

  Teacher says: Say each sound you hear in the word, *sun* (which is spoken, not shown in print)
  Child: /s/ /u/ /n/ The teacher also can ask the child to say the word and move a token into boxes to account for each sound.

- **Phoneme addition**, or adding a speech sound to sounds to the beginning or end to make a word.

Teacher says:	If you added /s/ to the beginning of /it/ (spoken, not shown in print), what word would you make?
Child:	*"sit"*

Teacher says:	If you added /s/ to the end of /bat/ (spoken, not shown in print), what word would you make?
Child:	*"bats"*

- **Phoneme substitution**, or changing a sound in a spoken word to make a different word.

Teacher says:	Say the word *mat*. Now change the /m/ to /s/ (spoken, not shown in print). What is the word now?
Child:	*"sat"*

- **Phoneme deletion**, or removing a sound to make a different word.

Teacher says:	Say the word *mat*. Now say *mat* without the /m/ (spoken, not shown in print).
Child:	*"at"*

Supporting Students' Development in Phonological and Phonemic Awareness

Although students reading and spelling on grade level in Grades 4–8 will have mastered phonological and phonemic awareness, some students experience difficulty in reading and spelling words. The lack of achievement could be the result of the lack of effective instruction in the early grades or special needs not addressed. If students lack phonemic awareness, they can experience difficulty in learning to read and spell, and the early reading failure can lead to subsequent failure in subsequent grades as well as diminished motivation. If teachers in Grades 4–8 are aware of how to address reading difficulties, their students can gain the support they need to succeed in reading and spelling words.

As teachers plan instruction, they can confuse *phonics* and *phonological awareness*. Phonological awareness activities (including phonemic awareness) do not entail using print. Instead, children *listen* to language spoken to become aware of sounds in language. Teachers also may use pictures for the students to say, such as a picture of a cat and a hat for detecting rhyming words or to segment the sounds. Phonics pertains to learning ways sounds are represented by printed letters.

Be careful not to confuse *phonological awareness* with *phonemic awareness*. Keep in mind that phonological awareness is like an overall umbrella. Phonemic awareness is a level of phonological awareness and fits under the umbrella, being the most advanced type of phonological awareness.

Even though phonological awareness experiences entail spoken language, early writing and reading experiences can foster phonemic awareness. Students use **invented spelling**, writing a representation of each sound in a word even though the word is not spelled in a conventional way (e.g., mkrone for *macaroni*). To be able to write and account for each sound, students are engaging in segmenting phonemes as they say the word and then account for each sound. Students surely need to learn conventional spelling, but these early efforts contribute to their spelling development. Reading poems daily for shared reading can foster sensitivity to rhyming words, an early level of phonological awareness. As part of phonics instruction, early instruction in letter-sound correspondences and word families, groups of words that have the same endings (e.g., *bat, cat, hat, sat*), strengthens phonemic awareness. Such awareness highlights the predictability of sound-symbol correspondences to produce written language. As students learn to read a word and account for the letters, the students blend phonemes/sounds.

If students in Grades 4–8 experience difficulty in reading and spelling words, teachers can examine the TEKS (Texas Essential Knowledge and Skills) to determine they types of abilities students need to acquire. The TEKS (Texas Essential Knowledge and Skills) delineates which levels of phonological awareness need to be addressed in kindergarten–Grade 2. Although there is overlap, easier levels of phonological awareness are addressed first, such as identifying and producing rhyming words in kindergarten and producing rhyming words in Grade 1. The most advanced level for kindergarten involves segmenting one-syllable words into individual phonemes, a level of phonemic awareness. By first grade, teachers should offer activities where students are segmenting one-syllable words of three to five phonemes into individual phonemes, including words with initial and/or final consonant blends. Similarly, easier levels of phonological awareness are addressed first within a grade. For example, in kindergarten, after rhyming words are addressed, children are taught to recognize alliteration, identify words in a sentence, and identify syllables in spoken words.

In Grade 2, students encounter the more advanced levels of phonemic awareness where they manipulate phonemes, or recognize a change in a spoken word when a specified phoneme is added, changed, or removed. Thus, while phonemic awareness is necessary for learning to read, more advanced levels of phonemic awareness accompany progress in reading.

In deciding which words to say for phonemic awareness instruction, teachers should use one-syllable words. Students can blend and segment words with two or three sounds before advancing to four sounds. Single consonant sounds (e.g., /s/) and consonant digraphs (e.g., /sh/) that make one sound are easier than blends, such as *bl*, which has two consonant sounds in a row, /b/ and /l/.

Consonant sounds can be classified. Teachers do not need to teach about the classifications to students, but the classifications can provide guidance for instruction.

Continuous sounds (continuants) can be held continuously, such as /f/, /l/, m/, /n/, /r/, /s/, /v/, /w/, /y/, /z/. Continuous sounds are easier to blend, so it is best to start with continuous sounds. **Stop sounds** are more difficult to use because they are not held continuously, rather the airflow is completely stopped: /b/, /d/, /g/, /k/, /p/, /t/.

Consonant sounds also can be classified as voiced or unvoiced. **Voiced sounds** are made with the vocal cords vibrating: /b/, /d/, /g/, /n/, /m/, /v/, /j/, /w/, /y/, /l/, /r/. **Unvoiced sounds** are made with the vocal cords not vibrating: /p/, /t/, /d/, /k/, /f/, /s/, /h/. If a student is having difficulty making a sound, the student might be making an unvoiced phoneme voiced and might find it helpful to feel their throat to feel whether or not it is vibrating.

Guidelines for Assessment and Instruction

Following are guidelines for assessing and teaching phonological and phonemic awareness:

- Oral language abilities are a prerequisite for phonological awareness. Children need to have basic listening skills, and be able to understand what others say, share their ideas, and produce basic sentences.

- When working with young children, teachers often use a puppet or stuffed animal for phonemic awareness activities. For example, the teacher may say, "Mr. Dog speaks slowly. Let's see if we can tell what he says: /s/ /u/ /n/." Children say the word or point to a picture to show the ability to blend individual sounds.

- For an activity, teachers should model first for any assessment and instruction so children understand the task. Children may seem to not have the phonemic awareness ability when they actually did not understand what they are being asked to do.

- Children vary in their abilities, but with instruction many will make progress. A child's lack of progress does not necessarily indicate a disability; rather, it could be because that child has not been provided effective instruction. Teachers should seek the advice of specialists when trying to ascertain whether the child has progressed, or whether progress is being impeded despite effective instruction.

- Phonemic awareness activities can be beneficial but are not a substitute for literacy instruction. Students also need experiences with print in classrooms. Students make gains in phonemic awareness as they encounter print and account for sounds, such as the following: when using "invented" spelling at the writing center; when engaging in shared reading and choral reading where word patterns and rhyming words are seen and heard, and when learning letter-sound correspondences. Students also need to make gains in listening comprehension by hearing books and poetry read aloud.

- Start with continuous sounds, known as continuants, that are easier to blend and can be held continuously, such as /f/, /l/, m/, /n/, /r/, /s/, /v/, /w/, /y/, /z/. Stop sounds are more difficult to use because they are not held continuously; rather, the airflow is completely stopped, viz., /b/, /d/, /g/, /k/, /p/, /t/.

- Use the levels of phonological and phonemic awareness to determine which to focus upon first. Start with easier tasks such as rhyming, and then move to counting syllables.

- Start with larger units of language such as words and onset-rime and then move to individual phonemes.

- Children's "invented" and "phonological" spelling should not be discouraged because accounting for each letter in a word is an effective way to develop phonemic awareness.

- Some teachers assume that spelling the word incorrectly will impede the child's spelling development. However, children who use "invented" or "phonological" spelling make strong progress in spelling. The "errors" are reduced as the children develop conventional spelling as they account for the letters that create the correct spelling.

Alphabetic Principle

In alphabetic languages, like English and Spanish, the letters (and letter patterns) of the alphabet represents the sounds of the language. Along with understanding that words are made up of individual speech sounds, children must understand that speech sounds, also called phonemes, are represented in print by a letter or group of letters, which is thus termed the alphabetic principle. A set of graphs or characters is used to represent the phonemes. Like English, Spanish also relies on the alphabetic principle, and the letters used in both English and Spanish are based on the Latin alphabet. Spanish is highly regular in the way sounds and letters relate. English and French, however, are examples of languages where the sound-and-symbol relations can be irregular. Other alphabet systems of the world include Russian, Hindi, Greek, and all romance languages. The Korean alphabetic syllabary stands apart because, unlike English, where letters are written in sequential order, Korean letters are arranged as syllable blocks.

Arabic and Hebrew are consonant-based systems whose alphabets represent consonants and some vowels, where vowels can be represented by diacritics. A syllabary writing system represents syllables, which typically is a consonant and a single vowel. Pictographs and ideographs are complex systems where symbols represent sounds and meaning, objects of the world and ideas and abstract ideas.

As children make gains in acquiring the alphabetic principle in English, they learn the sounds associated with specific letters or start to learn phonics, which relates sounds to letters. Through phonics instruction, children learn how to apply the alphabetic principle as they learn patterns in the relationships between sounds and letters.

Not all words in English have regular spellings where phonics generalizations apply, so students must identify words in other ways, such as knowing the word automatically or reading parts of the word to decode the entire word (e.g., *disappear*). Additionally, after students learn about sounds and letters or phonics, teachers can emphasize morphemic analysis, where even words in English that seem to be irregular or cannot be "sounded out" can be shown to have common aspects. Students can internalize regularities and patterns in spelling as teachers provide instruction in morphemic analysis, where, for example, *nation*, *national*, and *nationality* are taught to show the commonality in a root word, spelling, and meaning.

To master the alphabetic principle, students must be able to identify letters easily. Before they can make strong gains in their reading vocabulary, children need to learn how to distinguish between **lowercase and uppercase, or capital letters**. Learning to form letters is the most effective way to help children learn to identify them, and knowing how to write letters is needed for spelling. Beginning readers can read words without identifying any of the letters. However, being able to remember a large stock of words requires knowing the letters of the word to aid in its retention. Thus, letter identification is part of early reading instruction.

Stages of Reading Acquisition

Students move though stages of reading development, and within a given classroom, students may be at different stages of development. Students within a stage may vary in what they know, and their development will take place at different paces.

In the initial stages of reading development, students learn to decode words, so instruction in spelling and reading focuses upon making gains in letter identification and word identification skills, viz.: sight vocabulary, phonics, structural analysis (word parts), and the use of context clues. Together with broad learning strategies, students learn to use sources of information or cues to read. The **emergent**, **progressing**, and **transitional stages** are the initial stages characterized by learning how to identify words. At the **fluent stage**, students have mastered word identification.

Even once after reaching the fluent stage, students continue to profit from guided reading or small-group instruction. However, instruction at this stage still focuses more on vocabulary development and more sophisticated reading abilities because students will now know how to decode well. Students should be reading a variety of types of literature, including informational texts. Increased time should be devoted to independent reading, but students still gain from hearing books read aloud so that their listening comprehension increases and so they continue to be reinforced in what books offer. Along with reading for pleasure, students must be shown how to read to learn in various disciplines.

Students in beginning stages speak in a soft voice or read silently after a teacher introduces a text to make sure students can read it. Fluent readers may be able to read the section independently after the text is introduced by the teacher, and the group meets later to discuss the selection. Instruction also focuses on understanding literary terms and techniques authors use as well as how to read informational texts.

Following is a summary of what to expect from children at each stage of reading development. Experts stress the behaviors (rather than age or grade) associated with each stage.

Emergent Stage

Emergent readers:

- Know that written language presents a message

- Have made gains in concepts of print in knowing that print moves left to right, top to bottom, and can make a return sweep

- May know what a letter is as compared to what a word is

- Can make a voice-print match by pointing with a finger

- Can turn pages and "pretend read"

- May be able to "play with" sounds for the beginning and ending of words

- May know some high-frequency words

- Can use picture clues

- Can make connections to the text by using oral language and knowledge of story structure

- Start by reading books with one to two lines of print with predictable sentence patterns and illustrations that provide much support

Progressing Stage

Progressing readers:

- Are developing a knowledge of high-frequency words they know automatically

- May begin in this stage by reading a variety of simple sentences but later a variety of more sentence patterns

- Can read stories with a beginning, middle, and end

- Start to attend to punctuation

- Can search for cues and self-correct

- Start by reading multiple lines of print with some similar sentence patterns and illustration with much or moderate support

Transitional Stage

Transitional readers:

- Know a large number of high-frequency words automatically

- Are more adept at using phonics (letter-sound correspondences) and structural analysis (word parts) for word identification

- Use sources of information as they identify words by using knowledge of visual cues, meaning cues, and language structure (or how words can go together)

- Become more proficient monitoring their reading

- Understand how to use punctuation marks correctly as part of developing reading fluency

- Begin to read longer, complex texts with some support from illustrations

- Read fiction, poetry, and informational texts

Fluent Stage

Fluent readers:

- Use all sources of information to identify words quickly and self-correct

- Consistently monitor for understanding

- Read fluently

- Increasingly can read challenging vocabulary

- Know how to adjust their rate depending upon the purpose for reading

- Read a variety of genres

- Can engage in discussion of the text and use details from the text to support comments

- Understand literary terms and how to apply them in understanding how literature works

- Become more proficient in reading to learn from informational texts

Role of Instruction

Students need effective instruction to reach their potential as readers. Teachers can provide sound learning experiences that meet students' needs while also demonstrating that literacy experiences can be rewarding. Effective instruction takes into account the **ability of the student** and the **demands of the text**, while also **providing support at a pace that helps the student succeed**.

Through **reading aloud**, teachers can help students make gains in understanding how written language works and show students that reading can be rewarding. Through **small-group instruction**, teachers can help students increase their ability to identify words, read independently, and discuss texts. Students can orchestrate skills by **reading independently** daily. Even when students cannot read independently for long stretches of time, students can engage in reading through other experiences, such as **buddy reading** or **audio-assisted reading**.

Importance of Comprehension Development

Comprehension development is essential from the outset. Without a focus on it as part of early literacy instruction, students are at risk of becoming "word callers"; this means they can identify words accurately while being able to comprehend none or very little of the texts they read.

Beginning readers will read simple texts with words repeated because their ability to decode is limited, and repeated words help students gain a sight vocabulary or know a word immediately. Such shorter texts supported by picture clues do not make the demands on comprehension characteristic of the longer texts that students encounter in middle and upper grades.

However, teachers can develop comprehension by reading aloud texts longer than what students can read. Teachers also can encourage students to monitor their understanding as they decode by thinking about what would make sense rather than solely focusing upon print. By asking students to retell what they read and talk about stories, teachers can show students that comprehending is needed for reading to take place and take hold.

Sources of Information in Proficient Reading

Proficient readers use sources of information or cues as they read. Teachers should acquaint themselves with the pertinent cueing systems and sources, and assess students' oral reading accordingly.

- **Visual cues** are the letters or printed words that children use for word identification and to learn or refine a skill. Phonics, structural analysis (or morphemic analysis), and sight words help students make gains with visual cues, allowing them to read successfully.

- **Discerning meaning** entails paying attention to what makes sense in identifying a word. When students rely upon what they know about **semantics** of language, they are using **meaning cues** because they are paying attention to what would make sense.

- **Structure cues** (or language structure cues) entails using knowledge of **syntax**, or how words are put together in English.

When students are learning to speak in English, they can be expected to have more difficulty in using their knowledge of semantics of English or meaning cues. English learners are not generally as adept in using knowledge of syntax or language structure because they are less certain of how words can be put together in a language. However, when teachers read aloud to students and provide effective oral language development experiences, English learners will make progress in using meaning and structure cues.

Analyzing Oral Reading Errors

Teachers can help students use all sources of information or cueing systems if teachers are aware of what to observe when assessing students' oral reading. Students' oral reading errors are miscues because such errors can reveal which cues a student is not using.

Visual cues entail using the print for word identification. As a key part of phonics instruction, students will learn that letter-sound correspondences occur in a specific sequence, in a word's initial, middle, and final position. The student may use structural analysis or word parts to identify certain words. The ability to identify sight words goes a long way toward letting children deal effectively with many of the high-frequency terms they will encounter.

What can go wrong as students try to build their facility with visual cues? In this example of a miscue, the student is not sufficiently attentive to word identification in print.

Student: After school, Fred **wanted** to go to the mall.
Text: After school, Fred **decided** to go to the mall.

The student substitutes the word *wanted* for *decided*. Thus, the student failed to use visual cues to identify this word.

In this example of a miscue, the student pays attention to **some, but not all, visual cues, in identifying a word**.

Student: Next week we will **combine** leaves we find for our science unit.
Text: Next week we will **collect** leaves we find for our science unit.

Notice that in the example above the student substitutes the word *combine* for *collect*. This points a miscue or oral reading error, but the student still **marshals some visual cues** in identifying this word.

Meaning cues require paying attention to what makes sense in a single sentence while also considering the context of the story.

In the following example of a miscue, the student **pays attention to meaning**.

Student: After school, Fred **wanted** to go to the mall.
Text: After school, Fred **decided** to go to the mall.

Notice that the student is not using visual cues but rather using meaning or semantic cues.

In the following example of a miscue, the student **is not paying attention to meaning**.

Student: After school, Fred went to the mall with his **freeze**.
Text: After school, Fred went to the mall with his **friends**.

In the following example, the student is using some visual cues (i.e., the consonant blend, *fr*), but is not using meaning/semantic cues because what student says does not make sense.

- **Structure cues** use grammar to arrange words in accordance with how language is used conventionally.

In the next example of a miscue, the student misses (language) structure cues.

Student: After school, Fred **depended** to go to the mall.
Text: After school, Fred **decided** to go to the mall.

You can see that the student uses some visual cues (i.e., the *de-* and the *-ed*), but no structure cues. In so doing, the student disregards the patterns of conventional English. Notice that the student does not pick up meaning either, as what is said does not cohere. In fact, meaning cues and structure cues often are misconstrued in tandem.

Responding to Students' Oral Reading Miscues (Errors)

Proficient readers use cues or sources of information when they read. Teachers can help students use all cueing systems by being aware of what to look for when assessing students' oral reading. Analyzing students' oral reading errors or miscues can be used to inform instruction. An immediate, important way to provide instruction is to provide a prompt when students make a miscue. The prompt should encourage students to self-correct by using all available cues: visual, meaning, structure. The type of prompt the teacher provides matters because teachers can help students become stronger in reading independently by providing an effective prompt. The teacher can listen to students read individually while other students read silently during guided reading or small-group reading instruction.

Guidelines for Responding to Miscues (Oral Reading Errors)

Following are guidelines and context for dealing effectively with student miscues.

- **Realize that miscues can result from rushing while reading.** Students may think that fast reading is better. Encourage them to read, with expression, at an appropriate pace.

- **Respond by providing a prompt that helps the student gain independence in reading.** Students will confront unknown words as they read, such as the texts of state exams, as well as the texts they read outside of school. The most effective prompts help students use all cueing systems, including visual cues, meaning cues, and structure cues. When students use the first letter sound(s) of a word and the rest of the words in the sentence as context clues, they can decode most unknown words and continue reading the text.

- **Do not ask students to "sound it out," as this is not a reliable approach.** Many words in English do not follow phonics generalizations, so they cannot be "sounded out" when they are unknown words, such as *said* (which does not follow the rule for *ai* as does *wait* and *sail*) or *come*, which does not follow the rule for the long *o* sound (versus *home*, for example). At the same time, we do want students to know phonics/patterns in spelling so they can identify words immediately.

- **Do not tell the student the unknown word right away.** Revealing the unknown word at the outset leads to the student's overreliance on the teacher and generally creates a mistaken sense that someone will always be there to supply the unknown words.

- **Encourage the student to read to the end of the sentence before providing a prompt.** In the course of making a miscue, the student may self-correct the miscue after reading to the end of the sentence. If the student does not know a word, encourage him or her to read to the end of the sentence before providing a prompt so that the student is able to use the full context of the sentence along with the print to identify the word. The context of the phrasing up to the unknown word may not be enough to identify it.

- **If the student's miscue makes sense, the teacher should provide a prompt that acknowledges using meaning while also encouraging the student to use visual cues.** A simple prompt can help students solve the problem of the unknown word while also being able to internalize wording. Respond this way: "That makes sense, but look more carefully at the word."

- **If the student's miscue does not make sense, the teacher can encourage using all cues and comprehension monitoring:** Ask the student, "Does that make sense?"

- **If a student still does not know a word, determine whether the word can be identified by using initial consonant sounds and the context of the sentence.** Then point this out to the student with a response like this: "This word starts with *w*. Think about what word could start with *w* that would make sense in this sentence."

- **Some words need to be identified by also using visual cues at the end of a word or in the middle,** such as in the next scenario:

Text:	Where did he go?
Student:	When did he go?
Teacher Prompt:	"That makes sense, but look more carefully at the end of the first word."

- **When students do not recognize multisyllabic words, the teacher uses aspects of structural analysis to help them break the word into parts.** This includes pointing out the prefix, suffix, and or inflectional endings (such as -*s* to identify the short plural and the third person singular). To identify the meaning of compound words, teachers may guide students to notice the two words, and ask them to read each of them to see if the meaning of the individual words contribute to understanding the unknown word.

- **Teachers may not be able to listen to all students read each day, but should be systematic in listening to students read-aloud during guided reading or small-group instruction.** The teacher's prompts serve as instruction because, over time, students internalize the questions and self-correct. To have time to listen to individual students read aloud while the other students read silently, the teacher can tell students they can read the section again or read ahead to the next chapter of a longer work.

- **Even brief anecdotal notes may be useful when the teacher jots what is observed when hearing a student read aloud.** Teachers can then make sure to provide instruction based on the students' miscues.

Running Records

A running record is an assessment tool in which teachers listen to students read orally to know how to best meet the students' needs. The teacher creates a shorthand record of the students' reading. The notations represent what the students did or said for each word the student reads: whether the student (1) correctly reads a word, (2) makes an oral reading error or miscue, (3) repeats a word or series of words, (4) self-corrects, or (5) is unable to attempt to read a word.

At the beginning of a year, running records can be used to assign students to a guided reading or small instructional group. A group needs to be homogeneous so that students in a group have similar needs. Similarly, running records can be used to find the level of book that is best for students. If students read a text that is too hard, they will be kept from using all sources of information, and they will not comprehend what they are reading. Teachers can use benchmark books or selections that are at varying levels of difficulty and correspond to different reading levels.

Teachers can use running records throughout the year to make sure students are making steady progress in the books they have read once or twice during their guided reading instruction. Teachers can assess when they listen to students read individually while other students read silently during guided reading, or teachers can assess at other times of the day.

Teachers also can analyze running records to understand what type of instruction student needs to make progress in reading. Running records can be used to document progress of a student over a period of time.

Running records provide insights into students' oral reading. Comprehension can be achieved by asking the student to retell what was read or by questioning the student about the text. Once students are proficient in word identification, teachers rely more on assessing students' comprehension in determining the level of text and how to meet students' needs.

Taking a Running Record

- Select the text you will use for assessment. When forming reading groups, various levels could be needed. If the assessment is for reading instruction in guided reading groups, the text will be a section currently being read to recently finished.

- Students do not need to read an entire story or book. Instead, they can read a portion of the text that is 100 to 200 words.

- Have a blank sheet of notebook paper or a running record form. The notations are made on the paper, not on copies of the reading selection or text.

- On the sheet, write the student's name, the title of the selection, and the date.

- Sit next to the student so you can see each word as it's read.

- On the sheet of paper or running record form, use the notation system and place a mark on the sheet for each word in the text to indicate what the student did.

- The marks should be arranged just the same as the words on the page. Move left to right, starting a new line when the text does, and indicate page numbers so you will be able to refer back to what the child said.

- Use a horizontal line to show new page numbers.

- Each correct word read correctly is indicated with a check mark. The example that follows shows the words in the text, what the student read, and what the running record would look like.

> Text: After school, we are going to my friend's house.
> Student: After school, we are going to my friend's house.
> Running Record: ✓　✓　✓　✓　✓　✓✓　✓　✓

Other marks are used to indicate errors. What the student says goes above a line of text, and what the text or teacher says goes below the line. Punctuation is not included.

> Text: After school, we are going to my friend's house.
> Student: After stool, we are going to my friend's house.
> Running Record: ✓　stool　✓ ✓　✓　✓ ✓　✓　✓
> 　　　　　　　　school

Students' Reading, Notation, and Error Count

Accurate Reading—The student reads the word correctly.

✓

Types of Miscues Counted as an Error:

Substitution—The student says a word that does not match what's in the text. Such substitution is counted as an error unless the student self-corrects. Repeating names are counted wrong only once.

> Student   depended
> Text   decided

Omission—The student leaves out the word in the text.

> Student   —
> Text   a

Insertion—The student adds or inserts a word that is not in the text.

Student   <u>the</u>

Text   —

Not Counted as Error: Repetition—Takes place when a student re-reads a word or section of words. A repetition is not counted as an error because the student knows the words, but this behavior is still noted because it can point to the student's inability to automatically recognize a word. A line is drawn over the word or words repeated.

       ↓   R

      ✓ ✓ ✓ ✓ ✓ ✓ ✓

Self-Correction—The student makes a substitution but then the student corrects the error. This is not counted as an error, but it is still noted.

Student   <u>depended</u>| SC

Text   decided

Intervention—One Error: Appeal/Told—Following an appeal for help from the student, each teacher-given, or told, word is counted as an error. During assessment, the teacher strives to tell a student a word or give prompts for word identification so that an accurate assessment of what the student can do is obtained. Teachers should provide prompts during instruction because the dual goal is both teaching and assessment as they listen to students read aloud individually during guided reading or small-group work. However, when a student does not make an attempt, the teacher tells the word only after waiting 5 to 10 seconds, to give the student a chance to figure it out.

Student   _____ A

Text   decided T

Scoring a Running Record

Scoring a running record is based upon the total number words the student reads correctly. The running words (RW) is the number of words the student reads. Errors (E) is the number of miscues counted as an error.

The **accuracy rate** is found by determining the percentage of words read correctly out of the total number of words read:

$RW - E/RW \times 100$

Example:

RW = 100

Errors = 2

100 − 2/100 × 100 = 98%

The accuracy rate can help determine whether a text is at the independent, instructional, or frustration level.

95%—100%	Independent Level (easy)
90%—94%	Instructional Level (can be read with support/instruction)
Below 90%	Frustration Level (too difficult)

Analyzing Miscues

By analyzing the miscues of a running record, the teacher can understand the sources of information a student is using. Students who use **visual cues** are using what is printed in the book to identify words.

Students use their knowledge of (language) **structure cues** when they use what they know about how words go together in the language to figure out an unknown word, such as in the following:

I like to eat _____.

Even though the student may not know the exact term to fill in the blank, she or he would still intuitively know the *types* of words that would fit in the blank (e.g., that the unknown word could not be a verb). Knowing how words can be put together is using **knowledge of syntax**, also called *language structure*.

Students use their knowledge of **meaning** when they think about what would make sense such as in the example above: I like to eat _____. Because the student knows that people can eat, the student knows that the unknown word (i.e., the blank) will be some kind of food (not a car, for example). Using meaning is using **knowledge of semantics**.

Failure to use **visual cues** may indicate a problem in an area of word identification. Instruction in phonics, structural analysis (or morphemic analysis), and sight words help students gain in using visual cues.

Failure to use **structure cues** may point to a need for help in using context clues or more oral language development to gain proficiency in the syntax of English. Similarly, students who do not use meaning cues may need help with context clues or more oral language development to gain syntactical proficiency. Such students may also need to monitor comprehension. The examples that follow show how to analyze a miscue.

Example of Analysis of a Miscue of a Running Record

Student: I have a bag dog.

Text: I have a big dog.

✓ ✓ ✓ <u>bag</u> ✓

big

- **Meaning cues:** No, the miscue neither makes sense nor shows the use of semantic knowledge.

- **Structure cues:** No, the miscue does not show the use of syntactic knowledge.

- **Visual cues:** Yes, the miscue indicates the reader has used visual cues by identifying the initial and final consonant letters.

- **Needed instruction:** The student used short *a*, and did not know short *i*, so short *i* needs to be taught.

Student: This vase is under because it is broken.

Text: This vase is unacceptable because it is broken.

✓   ✓   ✓   <u>under</u>   ✓   ✓✓   ✓

unacceptable

- **Meaning cues:** No, the miscue neither makes sense nor shows the use of semantic knowledge.

- **Structure cues:** No, the miscue does not show the use of syntactic knowledge.

- **Visual cues:** Yes, the reader used *un* when trying to identify the word.

- **Needed instruction:** The student needs to be taught how to identify multisyllabic words by examining the prefix and base word. The student also may not know the base word, *acceptable*.

Informal Assessments

Informal assessments such as running records are beneficial for teachers because they can provide data to inform their instruction daily. Informal assessments also are beneficial because they provide specific feedback about a student. The assessments can be used to revise instruction; determine abilities at designated milestones for the year; monitor progress; and share progress with parents. Common forms of informal assessment follow.

Letter Identification—Students are given a worksheet with capital (uppercase) letters and lowercase letters arranged left-to right. The letters are not presented in alphabetical order. As the teacher points to the letters, the student identifies them. Students also can be assessed to determine whether they can write each letter. The teacher keeps a record sheet for each child.

Sight Words—Students are asked to read leveled lists of high-frequency sight words. Students also can be assessed to determine whether they can spell the words. The teacher keeps a record sheet for each child.

Phonics Generalization Word Lists—Students are asked to read lists of words that feature phonics generalizations. For example, if the student can read the word *tape*, the student indicates the ability to read words with the long *a* sound and the structure C-V-C-E silent E pattern. Being able to read the word chop indicates understanding the sound of consonant digraph *ch*. Students also can be assessed to determine whether they can spell the words. The teacher keeps a record sheet for each child.

Reading Logs—A reading log is a type of journal used by students to record their reading activity. Students list the title, author, and illustrator of each book they read during independent reading. This assessment documents independent reading and the types of literature the student is reading.

Anecdotal Notes—Teachers jot comments or write longer entries to remember what a student did and said. An example would be asking a student to read individually during guided reading or documenting what happened during a writing conference.

Writing Samples and Written Checklists—Teachers maintain a cumulative folder for student checklists that track students' ability to (1) compose and (2) follow the conventions of spelling, punctuation, and usage. Students' writing samples are dated, and they can include rough drafts fastened to the final draft.

COMPETENCY 003: WORD IDENTIFICATION SKILLS AND READING FLUENCY

The teacher understands the importance of word identification skills (including decoding, blending, structural analysis, and sight word vocabulary) and reading fluency and provides many opportunities for students to practice and improve word identification skills and reading fluency.

The beginning teacher:

A. Understands that many students develop word analysis skills and reading fluency in a predictable sequence and recognizes that individual variations occur.

B. Understands differences in students' development of word identification skills and reading fluency and knows instructional practices for meeting students' individual needs in these areas.

C. Understands the connection of word identification skills and reading fluency to reading comprehension.

D.   Knows the continuum of word analysis skills in the statewide curriculum and grade-level expectations for attainment of these skills.

E.   Knows how students develop fluency in oral and silent reading.

F.   Understands that fluency involves rate, accuracy, and intonation and knows the norms for reading fluency that have been established in the Texas Essential Knowledge and Skills (TEKS) for various age and grade levels.

G.   Knows factors affecting students' word identification skills and reading fluency (e.g., home language, vocabulary development, learning disability).

H.   Understands important phonetic elements and conventions of the English language.

I.   Knows a variety of informal and formal procedures for assessing students' word identification skills and reading fluency on an ongoing basis and uses appropriate assessments to monitor students' performance in these areas and to plan instruction for individual students, including English learners (in accordance with the ELPS).

J.   Analyzes students' errors in word analysis and uses the results of this analysis to develop and adjust future instruction.

K.   Applies norms and expectations for word identification skills and reading fluency, as specified in the Texas Essential Knowledge and Skills (TEKS), to evaluate students' reading performance.

L.   Knows how to use ongoing assessment of word identification skills and reading fluency to determine when a student needs additional help or intervention to bring the student's performance to grade level, based on state content and performance standards for reading in the Texas Essential Knowledge and Skills (TEKS).

M.   Knows strategies for decoding increasingly complex words, including using the alphabetic principle, structural cues (e.g., prefixes, suffixes, roots) and syllables, and for using syntax and semantics to support word identification and confirm word meaning.

N.   Selects and uses instructional strategies, materials, activities, and models to teach students to recognize high-frequency irregular words (e.g., by completing analogies, identifying meanings of foreign words commonly used in written English, identifying and explaining idioms and multiple-meaning words) to promote students' ability to decode increasingly complex words and to enhance word identification skills for students reading at different levels.

O.   Selects and uses appropriate instructional strategies, materials, activities, and models to improve reading fluency for students reading at different levels (e.g., having students read independent-level texts, engage in repeated reading activities, use self-correction).

Word Identification

Instruction in word identification provides students the ability to analyze unknown words or recognize words they encounter as they read. Word identification is necessary for reading, but students also need to comprehend what they read. Early literacy instruction must help students decode print, but from the outset, students need to see word identification as a means to understand what they read.

Proficiency and Rationale for Instruction

By the time students have reached fourth grade, many are proficient in correctly pronouncing the words they encounter in reading materials at their grade level. Along with knowing words, these students can figure out words they have not seen before. At the same time, many students are unable to recognize words when reading materials at their grade level. In fact, students in an eighth-grade classroom could be reading on the first- or second-grade level.

Being able to identify words immediately is critical in reading. Siphoning attention to figuring out a word creates a type of "bottleneck" in short-term memory, which can result in losing the thread necessary to create meaning and comprehension. Nonetheless, it's also possible for students to correctly read every word in a passage yet not comprehend it.

Some in literacy education lay down a rough marker that up to third grade, students' literacy development focuses more on *learning to read*, while after third grade, development focuses more on *reading to learn*. However, many students need specific instruction on learning how to identify words even after third grade. A variety of factors cause students to read below—or even far below—grade level. We know these students can make progress, but they often need to rely strongly on a teacher with the expertise to help them.

How Readers Identify Words

Readers use four major ways to identify/recognize words: (1) **sight words**, (2) **phonics**, (3) **structural analysis**, and (4) **context clues** (where surrounding words and/or pictures are used to figure out an unknown word). Capable readers use all four approaches; instruction should thus include assessment of what students know and take students' needs into account.

Sight Words: Assessment and Instruction

Sight words are words students recognize instantly. The first sight words students need to know are high-frequency words, that is, those likeliest to be encountered, and likewise the ones that will be used the most when students write. To avoid struggling with fluency, children need to know how to read and write 20 to 30 sight words before they can engage in guided reading lessons.

Children who are not ready for guided reading can read with the teacher, who can point to the words to make a voice-print match. This is known as choral, or shared reading.

One noted sight-word list is the Dolch list. Dr. Edward W. Dolch developed the list by studying the most common words students encountered when reading. The list includes approximately 300 words. The words are sometimes organized in sets of 100 or by grade level, ranging from Pre-K through Grade 3.

The Fry list, developed by Dr. Edward Fry, is an expanded version of the Dolch list. The Fry list, encompassing 1,000 words, is based on the most common words in reading materials; in fact, these words represent approximately 90% of the words in a typical book, website, or news article. This list can be used with students in Pre-K to high school grades. As previously stated, the Fry words are listed by the frequency with which they occur and are often broken down into groups of 100. The first 100 Fry words are thus the 100 most frequently occurring words in the English language.

Sight words lists are presented by levels. Students can be assessed by reading a list of words, and if a student is able to read the words, a higher-level word list can then be assessed.

Students should be able to spell high-frequency words because they will use these often when they write. A student may be able to read a word but not be able to spell it, even if the student is reading on grade level. Spelling tests can be given to isolate the words students do not know so those words can be learned.

Phonics: Assessment and Instruction

Phonics pertains to the relationship of sounds and letters. Irregular spellings, and the various irregular pronunciations that accompany them, make numerous English words resistant to sounding-out. Still, some patterns or generalizations occur often enough to be helpful in reading and spelling. The phonics generalizations that follow can help students discern such generalizations.

What are proven, complementary methods of phonics assessment? Ask students to write/spell one-syllable words that feature the generalization. Students benefit from learning to spell words that feature the generalization so that they start to see the pattern, as in learning short *a* words, such as *cap, had, bat*. From words that students learn to read and spell, they can also broaden out to learn word families. Once they know how to read/spell *bat*, for example, they can learn *cat, fat, hat, mat, sat*; this is an analogic approach, which lets students learn how to detect patterns. In a synthetic approach, students learn the sounds of each letter and letter combinations, and blend individual sounds to pronounce the word. Effective instruction can include both approaches, and provides for sufficient practice in reading and spelling words so that students master phonics generalizations.

Major Phonics Generalizations

Let's delve into major phonics generalizations. Effective instruction ensures that students apply phonics generalizations as part of word identification. However, such instruction does not ask students to memorize rules. Rather, it entails providing enough practice in reading and spelling words that feature a generalization to the point that students internalize the pattern.

Consonants

In English, the alphabet is composed of vowels and consonants. The vowels are *a, e, i, o, u*—and sometimes *y* (e.g., *play*) or *w* (e.g., *snow*). Consonants are the other letters of the alphabet.

- **Initial consonant sounds:** When a single consonant is at the beginning of a word, it is considered an initial consonant. For example, *y* and *w* are in the initial position of *yellow* and *with*.

- **Final consonant sounds:** Once students know final sounds, they typically do not have difficulty identifying sounds of the letters in a final position; however, such consonants work like vowels when combined with another vowel, such as in *play*, *cow*, and *snow*.

- **Consonant blends:** Consonant blends are when two or three consonant sounds blend in sequence. For fluent adults, such combinations are read with automaticity. Children, however, need to be given ways to distinguish words that start with a blend from those that begin with the first letter in the blend – for instance, to perceive that the initial sound of *brown* sounds different from the initial sound of *boat*. The three major categories of consonant blends are as follows:

  - *l* blends (such as *bl, cl, fl, pl*)
  - *r* blends (such as *br, cr, dr, fr, pr, tr*)
  - *s* blends (such as *st, sp, str, spr*)

- **Consonant digraphs:** In consonant digraphs, the sounds do not blend. Two consonants together create a new sound, such as the following: **ch**urch, **sh**ower, **wh**at, **th**em, and **th**ink

Vowels

Vowel sounds are not as consistent as those of consonants. The sound of a vowel depends upon orthographic patterns: how the letters surrounding the vowel are arranged. Students do not need to be able to say whether the vowel is "long" or "short" to read words with vowels. Instead, they need to be able to discern the pattern by seeing many examples of that pattern. For example, children will discern the pattern of short *a* by seeing instances of **short *a* words** in a spelling list when first learning these words (rather than having short *a* words combined with other short vowel words).

Subsequently they can be shown how the sound changes depending upon what surrounds the *a* (such as *can* vs. *car* or *can* vs. *cane*).

Short vowels: Consonant(s)-Vowel-Consonant(s) or CVC, CVCC, and CCVC patterns

short *a*	cap, man, had
short *e*	bed, pet, test
short *i*	sit, fish, ship
short *o*	dog, hot, mop
short *u*	cut, rug, must

Long vowels: The vowel "says" its name, and this takes place in three major patterns:

1. **Two vowels together**—The first one says its name, and the second one is silent pattern.

long *a*	ai (*wait*)	ay (*play*)
long *e*	ea (*seat*)	ee (*green*)
long *i*	ie (*lie*)	
long *o*	oa (*boat*)	ow (*snow*—but not long in *cow*)
long *u*	ui (*fruit*)	

2. **VCe-Vowel-Consonant-silent *e* pattern**

long *a*	name
long *e*	Pete
long *i*	kite
long *o*	code
long *u*	flute

3. **Single vowel after a consonant**—Words with a single vowel after a consonant (e.g., *me, so*) are learned as sight words. Thus, they usually are taught that way.

R-controlled vowels: When a vowel is followed by an *r*, the vowel appears as part of a CVC pattern but the *r* changes its sound so that it is neither long nor short. Consider the sound of these examples: *car, fern, stir, corn, turn.*

Vowel digraphs: A vowel digraph has two vowels come together to create a new sound that is neither long, short, nor *r*-controlled.

au, aw	haul or saw
oo	look, book; soon, pool

Diphthongs: Diphthongs, a special case of vowel digraphs, involve the slurring of two letters.

oy, oi	boy or boil
ou, ow	house or cow

Structural Analysis or Word Parts Instruction-Assessment and Instruction

Readers use structural analysis or word parts by examining the units of meaning of a word. Students begin to develop this ability in the early grades once they know sight words. Students use structural analysis as they encounter words that have more than one syllable and when they examine word roots as part of vocabulary development.

Forming plurals

-s	cat—cats	rake—rakes
-ies (y-drop)	puppy—puppies	

Adding -es when the word ends in x, s, sh, ch

box—boxes	bus—buses	dish—dishes	church—churches

Special cases of forming plurals

wolf—wolves
foot—feet
deer—deer or sheep—sheep
potato—potatoes
child—children

Other examples of inflectional endings: adding -s, -ed, -ing, er, est

walk—walks (3rd person singular)
walk—walked (regular past tense)
walk—walking (present progressive)
tall—taller (comparative)
large—largest (superlative)

Possession

singular vs. plural
dog's bone vs. *the two dogs' bone*

Compound words: Two words can come together to create a new word, such as *hotdog* or *something*. With the notable exception of words like *nightmare* and *butterfly*, the component words combined to create compound words provide clues to identify the new meaning.

Contractions: In contractions, the apostrophe is used to show where one or more letters (or sounds) have been omitted. Students have an easier time learning to spell contractions when they are shown the logic of the placement of the apostrophe. By presenting the original, longer version and then spelling the contraction below it, students can see that when a letter (or letters) is removed, we must add the apostrophe to replace the omitted letter(s).

The use of contractions represents a particular challenge for ELs, who might not recognize the meaning of contractions like these: *I've* (I have), *it's* (it is), *didn't* (did not), *can't* (cannot), *I'll* (I will), *we're* (we are), *they're* (they are). To introduce contractions to ELs, teacher should use the long forms first and systematically introduce each contraction. Teachers can also present the contracted form with an explanation of the intended meaning. Also, when reading contractions, teacher should present both versions (as shown below) to be sure all students understand the use of contractions in English.

Presenting contractions

it is	did not
↓	↓
it's	didn't

Prefixes and Suffixes

Prefixes and suffixes are morphemes that, when attached to a word stem, create new words. These components have meaning in isolation; thus, they can be used as a foundation for decoding words. Some affixes can also change the syntactic classification of the new word; these are identified as derivational morphemes. These types of morphemes can change the syntactic classification of the word. For example, the word *aware* is an adjective, but when the derivational morpheme *-ness* is added, it creates a noun, *awareness*. Following are examples of prefixes and suffixes paired with their meaning.

Prefixes: Prefixes are affixes attached at the beginning of a word.

Prefixes	Meaning	Sample words
un-	not or opposite of	unhappy, unaware
dis-	not, opposite of	disappear, discover
trans-	across	transportation, transmit
sub-	under, beneath	submarine, subway

Suffixes: Suffixes are affixes attached at the end of a word stem

Suffixes	Meaning	Sample words
-ful	full of	helpful, playful
-less	without	homeless, powerless
-ly	manner of—creating an adverb	sadly, slowly
-able, -ible	can be	capable, audible

Syllables: A syllable is a unit, forming the whole or part of a word, which contains a minimum of one vowel sound. For example, the phrase "a car" contains two monosyllabic words—*a* and *car*. The first word—*a*—contains one vowel, and the second word—*car*—contains one vowel and two consonants. Examples of multisyllabic words follow:

Walk-ing (two syllables)   se-nile (two syllables)   *cheer-ful-ly* (three syllables)

Knowing syllable patterns can help students as they spell and read. Common types of syllables are as follows:

- **Open syllable** ends with a single vowel sound created by a single. One-syllable-examples include *me* and *so*, and multisyllabic examples include *ho-tel* and *me-te-or*. The vowel makes a long sound in an open syllable.

- **Closed syllable** occurs when a vowel is "closed" by a consonant, such as *bag* or *bag-gage*. The vowel makes a short sound in a closed syllable.

- **Vowel-Consonant-Silent *e* (VCe)** syllable has a long vowel sound spelled with a sequence of vowel, consonant, silent *e*, such as in *bike* or *com-plete*.

- **Vowel Teams syllable** occurs when two vowels combine to make one sound. The sound can be the long vowel sound, such as in *play, wait, keep, seat, boat, snow, fruit, pie* or *snowing, playing*. **Vowel digraphs** can be considered vowel teams, such as in *paw* and *aw-ful* or *book* and *book-ing*. Vowel teams also can include **dipthongs**, such as in *joy, joy-ful, cow, pow-er*.

- **Vowel-*r* (or *r*-controlled) syllable)** contains *ar*, *er*, *ir* or *or*, *ur*, such as we see in *turn*, *pur-chase*, *bark*, *bark-ing*.

- **Schwa syllable** contains the schwa vowel sound, which is common but does not have one standard sound. The schwa sound is close to the short *u* sound and is an unaccented syllable, such as we see in *dam-age*, *oc-cur*, *em-pha-size*.

The knowledge students gain in learning phonics and sight words helps them as they learn syllable patterns. By learning to spell words that illustrate various types of syllables, students gain an understanding of how to read and write multisyllabic words.

Morphemic Analysis

Morphemic analysis, which is related to **structural analysis**, takes place when students use prefixes, suffixes, and roots or base words to determine or recall word meanings. This is a facet of vocabulary development.

- A **morpheme** is either a word (a free morpheme) or part of a word that has meaning.

- A **bound morpheme** is not a word on its own, and thus cannot stand on its own. A bound morpheme appears with a root. Bound morphemes include affixes (which are prefixes and suffixes), such as the prefix *dis-* in *disappear* or the suffix *-s* in *dogs*.

- A **free morpheme** can stand on its own (e.g., *appear*).

- A **compound word** (e.g., *football*) is made up of two free morphemes. Through structural or morphemic analysis, students analyze parts of words to arrive at word identification or understanding of words. Structural analysis begins early on in schooling as students learn how to apply plurals, such as in *cat → cats* or adding an inflectional ending such as *-s*, *-ed*, *-ing* to a verb, as in *walks → walked → walking*.

Structural and morphemic analysis becomes more complicated as students learn to read and spell such plurals like *puppies* for *puppy*, which typically require that plurals involving *-y* endings be formed with *-ies* taking the place of the *-y*. Structural and morphemic analysis is further complicated as students learn to identify multisyllabic words and break words into syllables.

Learning affixes of **Latin and Greek roots and derivations** can help students increase their vocabulary and understand new words they encounter more readily, especially as they also use context clues of the text.

Examples of Greek Roots and Derivations

Root	Definition	Example
auto-	self	autobiography
bio-	life	biography
homo-	same	homogenous, homophone
hydr-	water	hydration, dehydrated
logy-	study of	biology, geology

Examples of Latin Roots and Derivations

Root	Definition	Example
cord-, cor-, cardi-	heart	cordial, discord, cardiogram
duc-, duct-	to lead	conduct, reduction
fract-, frag-	Break	fraction, fragment
loc-	Place	location, relocate
port-	to carry	export, transportation

Cognates are words in two languages that share a similar meaning, spelling, and pronunciation. English learners can benefit from being shown these similarities. Examples of cognates in English in Spanish can be found in words that have common Greek and Latin roots:

Cognates

Greek root	Translation	English example	Spanish example
astr-	star	astrology	astrología
bio-	life	biography	biología
phon-	sound	microphone	micrófono
Latin root	**Meaning**	**English example**	**Spanish example**
aud-	to hear	auditorium	auditorio
dict-	to tell, speak	dictate	dictar
mit-, mis-	send	mission	misión

Idioms and Commonly Confused Words

Idioms and commonly confused words also warrant instruction. Idioms are expressions that cannot be interpreted in a literal way, and they cannot create confusion, especially for English learners. Common idioms include the following:

Idioms

beat around the bush	avoiding coming to the point
left out in the cold	not included; ignored
cutting corners	doing a task in a way that weakens quality

Commonly confused words include homophones, homographs, and homonyms.

Homophones are words that sound alike but have different meanings. Homophones can have different spellings, such as *know—no, flour—flower, stair—stare, accept—except*. However, some homophones have the same spelling, such as *rose* (the flower), and *rose* (act of getting or going up).

Homographs are words that have the same spelling but different meanings, such as *right* (correct) and *right* (opposite of left). Homographs are not necessarily pronounced the same, such as *bow* (v. to kneel) and *bow* (n. looped ribbon).

Homonyms are words that are either pronounced or spelled the same. In other words, homonyms can be homophones or homographs. Readers use context to deduce the meaning and intended pronunciation.

Context Clues

To identify an unknown word, readers use surrounding words as context clues. Context clues also can be the illustrations on a page or, more broadly, the text's subject matter or setting.

Knowing how words can be combined requires **knowledge of syntax**. Another term for this is **language structure**. In using context, students use their knowledge of language structure because they know what types of words can be placed together. For example, in the following sentence, which we used earlier, the blank or unknown word would be a thing (noun), not a verb or preposition.

I like to eat _____.

Children who know English also intuitively know this even though they may not know the term *noun*; they do not need to know the parts of speech to figure out the unknown word. Even young children will know this intuitively because they discern principles of language as they acquire it.

In the course of using context clues, students deploy their knowledge of **meaning** because they know what would make sense such as in the example above. Because they know English and know what people can eat, they know that the unknown word (the blank) must be some kind of food (as opposed to, say, a rock).

Students also can use accompanying images to reveal context, and this especially takes place with beginning readers. A child can look at the illustration on the page to decide that in this sentence the unknown word is *cake*, when given a picture of a child eating a piece of cake: I like to eat _____.

To be equipped to use context clues effectively, students need to know sight words. Readers may use the initial consonant sound (which is phonics) with context clues, such as the following:

I will ride to school on the b_____.

The context clues above allow the reader to figure out the missing word, *bus*.

In the following example, the student may break the word *instead* into syllables (which is structural analysis) and use context clues to decide what would make sense:

I want to eat this dessert _____(instead).

Children who know how to speak English can use context more readily. They will pick up knowledge about semantics (meaning) and syntax (language structure) in the course of learning how to speak. Using context clues is the fastest way for students to figure out words, and students can do this even before they know all of the phonics and structural analysis generalizations. Oral language development thus plays a central role in learning how to recognize words in English.

Effective Word Analysis Development

Spelling

One of the best ways for students to learn word analysis or identification skills is through **spelling**. Spelling helps students focus on each letter of a word, and as students learn to spell words, they learn to read words. With a systematic spelling program, students can gain mastery of phonics, sight words, and structural analysis when they learn how to spell words that feature phonics generalizations, get acquainted with sight words, and achieve proficiency in structural/morphemic analysis.

Through systematic instructions, students can learn (1) which individual letters correspond with which sounds, (2) phonics generalizations, (3) high-frequency words, (4) types of syllables, and (5) morphemic information (i.e., prefixes, suffixes, and root words). By focusing on a designated list of words that feature a particular focus, such as consonant-vowel consonant (CVC) for short *a* words, teachers can help students discern patterns and regularities. Similarly, teachers can focus on patterns like adding *-ed* and *-ing* or words in a list sharing the same Latin root.

Word Games

To strengthen students' vocabulary acquisition, teachers can provide small-group learning or learning stations where students play word games, such as bingo. Once students have been shown how to work together in playing the game, they will be able to do so while the teacher works with other students. As students learn new words, the teacher adds those words to the game.

Demonstrations Using Context and Cloze Procedure

Teachers also can **demonstrate** how to use context clues by showing students how to use surrounding words of a sentence to figure out an unknown word. This can be done by listening to students read aloud individually or as part of group instruction, including guided reading groups. Using sentences from the reading section, the teacher can model how to determine an unknown word's meaning by reading up to and after the word in the sentence to decide what would make sense. **Cloze** passages leave blanks at designated points to see if students can read and understand the texts with the missing words. Students are asked to supply the missing words, which gauges their ability to use context clues. Either students need to be able to read the surrounding words to be able to supply the missing word, or teachers need to read the sentences for the student. Cloze activities also can help students review words they are learning by providing a word bank from which to find the best match to fill in the missing word in a sentence.

Independent Reading

With daily reading, students become more proficient in word identification. Gains in reading are associated with the amount of time students invest in texts. Specific instruction in spelling and skills is needed, but students also must hone their skills by engaging in sustained reading. Daily instruction should provide opportunities for students to **read independently** books they themselves select. Even books that are easy allow students to make gains because such books make it possible to gain fluency. Daily read-alouds make students more apt to want to read because these teacher-led activities highlight what books offer; in fact, students will often select a book or the author of a book the teacher has read aloud.

Daily **shared reading**, during which the teacher and students read a text together, makes it possible for students to learn words and then read on their own either that day or after subsequent readings with the teacher. Poems students enjoy are ideal for shared reading, which is also applicable to content areas, which present a steady stream of unknown words that students must decode. Students also can read **with a partner** or read along **with an audio recording** during small group work while the teacher works with a group for guided reading. These learning experiences work especially well for students unable to engage in sustained silent reading.

Guided Reading Groups and Small-Group Instruction

Guided reading is small-group instruction where the teacher works with students reading at approximately the same reading level. Although students can profit from heterogeneous groups for the independent work, guided reading groups work best with homogeneous grouping where students are reading a text at the instructional level for all. Students can be overwhelmed and rendered unable to make gains when they are reading texts that are too hard, owing to too many unknown words. The texts for guided reading are what students can read with some support from the teacher, to allow them to make gains. Through this small-group instruction, the teacher also can provide more individualized attention. The three parts of a guided reading lesson work together: before reading, during reading, and after reading.

Before reading, the teacher builds or activates **background knowledge** helpful for understanding the text. This can include providing a gist statement, or brief synopsis. The teacher also helps students be prepared for reading aspects of the text with which students are unfamiliar, such as **unknown words** or features of the text such as speech bubbles, charts, or bold print.

During reading, students **read silently** (or in a soft voice if the students are young children/ beginning readers) the story or designated segment. Students who finish ahead of others are instructed to read the text again, which helps build fluency. The teacher **listens to individual students read aloud** to assess the students' ability to recognize words and interpret prompts to help them figure out unknown words. The teacher usually cannot listen to everyone read in one day, but can always listen to the rest the next day.

During reading is a critical time because the teacher can determine what needs to be addressed during word study, such as which words students do not know, whether students read fluently, and whether students can use multiple cues for word analysis. Teachers create brief anecdotal notes to log and address the needs of students. The teacher should log and respond to all miscues, as students are evaluated for their ability to thread together all the sources of information and cueing systems. This encompasses accurately reading the print words (**visual** cues such as letter shapes), considering what sounds right (language **structure** cues), and deciding what makes sense (**meaning** cues).

After reading, the teacher and students discuss the story. Teachers can begin by asking students to recall what happened to ensure they comprehend, recall, and are able to say what happened. After **retelling**, students can **discuss** the story to engage in higher levels of comprehension by making inferences, forming connections among texts **(text-to-text connections)** or connections to their lives **(text-to-self connections)**. Student also can discuss big ideas or lessons that emerge from the text. After the teacher and students share their personal responses to the fiction and poetry, subsequent discussion can focus on literary elements as well as strategies writers use to achieve their purpose. Once students are familiar with the story and have made their connections, through talking, the students and teacher can look again at the text to discuss plot, setting, characterization, and/or themes.

When reading informational texts, such discussions can include learning how to take notes with headings to catalog and remember details about a topic. After reading also is devoted to word study, where the teacher can instruct students how to spell a few words and address meanings of words when vocabulary instruction is needed. In addition, teachers reinforce strategies that may need to be elaborated or reinforced, such as how to use context, how to read with expression, or how to read charts.

Round-robin reading was a longstanding method to gauge students' proficiency at decoding words. The teacher calls on students one by one to read aloud. However, reading experts maintain that this method has a number of drawbacks and actually can hamper students' progress in word identification. The intention in round-robin is that while each student reads aloud, the other students follow along silently. But the reality is that students read at different rates, and a student who reads at a slower rate will have trouble following the student who reads aloud faster. As a result, students who read faster are asked to slow down their rate to follow along with the student who reads slower, which works against fluency. Moreover, students can be embarrassed and come to dread reading if they lose their spot or make errors. In addition, students may end up reading less because they're focused on predicting what they will read when their turn is called.

The alternative to round-robin sessions is to show students how to read in soft voices or silently through guided reading/small-group instruction. Teachers can teach students in small groups while the rest of the class engages in independent reading activities. To assess students, teachers can listen to a student read aloud while others in the group are reading silently or softly. Teachers also can provide prompts when students make a miscue. Teachers can assess whether students read words accurately, automatically, and with expression (all of which defines fluency, which we'll take up in the next section).

Guided reading/small-group reading can take place during language arts blocks, but it also can take place during science and social studies when students learn from textbooks whose content is more difficult to read. If students cannot read the textbook on their own, teachers can use shared reading, where students follow along with the teacher. In time, with reinforcement, students will expand their sight vocabulary so that they can read a text independently.

Fluency

Fluency in reading is essential for comprehension. When students read fluently, they can focus on constructing the meaning of the text because they do not have to devote attention to decoding print. Additionally, fluency is important because if students do not read easily and with understanding, they are less apt to enjoy reading. Students who do not enjoy reading tend to read less and thus do not make the gains in reading development that come from reading extensively. Although fluency measures include timed readings, fluency should not be confused with speed reading. Fluency entails **accuracy**, **automaticity**, **rate**, and **prosody**.

Accuracy, automaticity, and rate depend upon having strong word identification skills so that students not only can identify a word but do so automatically. When readers identify or decode words slowly, they cannot devote attention to creating meaning because they must devote attention to decoding. In other words, effective reading includes automaticity – recognizing words automatically. The process of creating meaning also is disrupted when readers fail to identify words accurately. Inaccurate word recognition can impede comprehension. Students with strong word identification abilities can decode the text even when they encounter words they have never seen. Readers who use sight words, phonics, structural/morphemic analysis, and context clues are able to call upon a repertoire of ways to identify words they read: Phonics helps students see patterns in words rather than relying on memorizing every word.

- Knowledge of sight words/high-frequency words enables students to automatically know many of the words they will encounter, including those with irregular spellings that do not adhere to phonics patterns, such as *said* and *come.*

- Structural/morphemic analysis provides expertise in identifying multisyllabic words, including base words with prefixes or suffixes.

- When students are aware of context clues, they can use their knowledge of language structure (or syntax) along with meaning (or semantics) as they decode. In turn, this helps students monitor how they identify visually similar words even as they decide whether what they're reading makes sense or sounds like the way something is said. This is the process by which readers determine, for example, what the correct preposition should be in the following sentence: *We ride to school in our car (not on our car).*

Prosody (or expression) includes appropriate phrasing and paying attention to punctuation. If students are reading with expression/using appropriate intonation and using appropriate phrasing, they are more apt to pay attention to what is being conveyed in the text. This includes, for example, recognizing that a question mark at the end of a sentence signals rising intonation. Students may be able to read words accurately and automatically, yet not comprehend the text. Evaluating prosody gets at whether students are constructing meaning (comprehending) as they read rather than merely word calling.

Key Factors in Assessing Fluency

Following are the prime factors relevant to assessing fluency.

- Screening, diagnosing, and progress monitoring make it possible to support students' growth in fluency by using assessment to inform instruction.

- By listening to students read, teachers can make sure they are reading fluently.

- Assessment of fluency must address accuracy, rate (automaticity), and prosody (expression).

- If only rate is observed and measured, students may suffer in comprehension because attention is not given to prosody or reading with expression, which indicates students are paying attention to meaning as they read. Stressing rate may cause fluency to be conflated with speed reading.

- If only accuracy is observed and measured, students may be only "word calling" and thus reading so slowly they cannot devote attention to constructing meaning as they read.

Procedures for Assessing Fluency

- Use a passage from a grade-level text to know how well a student performs at grade level. The passage can be 100 to 245 words.

- Students read the text aloud individually for 1 minute.

- Count the number of words the student read correctly to obtain words read correctly per minute (WCPM).

- Because the 1-minute testing is short, multiple passages can be used, with the median (or middle) score used.

- Research studies have established norms for **reading rates** (the number of words a student reads per minute). These benchmark rates, reported as WCPM, are established for assessment intervals across the school year to determine whether students are making progress.

- Teachers can compare a student's reading rates to the reported ranges rates. See the reading rates averages recommended in Hasbrouck & Tindal (1992).

- Hasbrouck and Tindal (1992) have provided guidance for Grades 1–8, and the fluency norms are provided for three assessments during a school year:

National Oral Reading Fluency (ORF) Target Rate Norms

Grade	Fall (WCPM)	Winter (WCPM)	Spring (WCPM)
1		10–30	30–60
2	30–60	50–80	70–100
3	50–90	70–100	80–110
4	70–110	80–120	100–140
5	80–120	100–140	110–150
6	100–140	110–150	120–160
7	110–150	120–160	130–170
8	120–160	130–170	140–180

Source: Hasbrouck, J.E., & Tindal, G. (1992). Curriculum-based oral reading fluency norms for students in Grades 2 through 5. *Teaching Exceptional Children*, 24, 41–44.

- To find the **accuracy rate**, count the number of errors the student did not correct to obtain a percentage of words read accurately. For example, if a student makes 10 errors in a 100-word text, the accuracy rate is 90%.

- The **accuracy rate** can help determine whether the grade-level text is at the independent, instructional, or frustration level.

  95%–100%   Independent Level (easy)

  90%–94%   Instructional Level (can be read with support/instruction)

  Below 90%   Frustration Level (too difficult)

- **Prosody** can be assessed by noting the extent to which the student reads with expression. This can include whether the student seems to consistently read in a natural way, note punctuation, and whether they read at a good volume as opposed to very quiet. Prosody assessment can include noting whether students read mostly word by word, two- to three-word phrases or longer, smooth phrasing.

Instructional Support for Fluency

Using Assessment to Inform Teaching

- If a student does not read a text accurately, the student may need more instruction in an area of word identification.

- If the student has difficulty in word identification, the teacher needs to determine what type of word identification is needed. The student may need additional support in phonemic awareness, letter identification, sight vocabulary, phonics, structural analysis, using context clues/oral language development.

- If the student does not read with expression, they may need practice in reading the text smoothly, with expression, and/or paying attention to punctuation.

- If the student can identify words, they may need a teacher to model how to read fluently, such as paying attention to punctuation and reading with expression.

- If the text used for fluency assessment is too difficult for a student to read, a text at a lower reading level should be used for instruction. When students cannot identify at least 90% of the words in a text, they are reading at their frustration level.

- Using an easier text may indicate that the student is able to read fluently and understand the text.

- Students make gains in fluency when they can read at least 95% of the words so that they do not need to devote attention to word analysis, and it is best when the student can read 98%–100% of the words of a text.

Reading Materials

- Providing daily opportunities for students to read independently helps them develop fluency. Students should be able to self-select what they read so they experience reading the way readers do in the real world, and they should have ample materials to select that are at their independent reading level or are easy for them to read.

- Students need the opportunity to read texts where they know most of the words, or text at their independent reading level, which is when they can recognize 95%–100% of words in a text.

- Grade-level books can be too hard for some students to read independently. Because the students have to devote so much attention to identifying words, they are unable to make gains in fluency.

- Grade-level texts used for assessment provide a way to see how a student compares to what is considered grade-level proficiency, but it is easy texts that allow students to make gains in fluency.

Rereading

- Reading again texts for instruction can make it possible for students to reach the independent reading level for the texts, so rereading a text on a subsequent day after a guided reading lesson can be a valuable instructional activity.

- Multiple readings are feasible when students read again shorter texts, and poetry is ideal. Many teachers provide shared reading of a poem daily. If the teacher selects quality poetry for youth, students enjoy the reading experiences.

Choral Reading and Shared Reading

- Choral reading takes place when the teacher and students read a text or part of a text together. Choral reading can take place through an enlarged text a group of students can see, or it can take place when the teacher and students read the same text.

- In shared reading, the teacher reads first to model, and students follow along. In subsequent readings, the student reads with the teacher until they can read on their own. Choral reading and shared reading begin by the teacher reading aloud the selection so that (1) the teacher models fluent reading, and (2) students then can enjoy the story or poem and think about its meaning.

- Many teachers present a poem for daily shared reading. Once students can read the poem, a new poem is introduced, either during the week or the next week. Shared reading provides differentiated instruction because students will gain what they need, whether it is new words or reading with expression.

- The multiple readings of poetry can include pointing out to students how to pay attention to punctuation and expression. Students can be shown to not pause when reading until they see a comma, period, or question mark in the poem even when coming to the end of the line. Students also can be shown how to consider the "voice" of the poem in reading with expression.

Showing Fluent Reading

- Teachers can model how to read fluently. This can take place during reading aloud daily. Teachers also can model as part of teaching at the end of a guided reading lesson or when working with students individually. The teachers can provide a short lesson for the student. The teacher can read a short segment to model, and then let the student read with the teacher. The student then reads.

Audio-Assisted Reading

- Students can read along with the person reading on the audio recording a text.

- If the reading materials is easy for the student, the student can focus on reading smoothly and with expression. Audio-assisted reading can be a learning station or independent activity to teach to students. Students can participate while the teacher works with a small group for guided reading or the small-group work. Students will enjoy the reading if the teacher selects quality poetry, picture books, or short stories that meet the needs of youth.

Readers' Theater

- Readers' theater is a type of drama where the presentation takes place through reading a script. Readers' theater does not involve memorizing lines of a script as in a formal play. The presentation does not involve moving, as would story dramatization. Instead, the presentation comes alive through the readers' voices.

- Readers' theater can be a rewarding way for students to revisit a story or content in textbooks. The subsequent reading can help foster comprehension and vocabulary development as students review content. The rereading also helps with word recognition as students strive to read in a fluent way as they practice the script for a presentation. Fluency also is enhanced as students strive to become the character and say something the way the character would and observe punctuation, using the correct intonation.

- Readers' theater does not involve costumes and memorizing, so it is an easy drama activity to incorporate while also fostering fluency, vocabulary, and comprehension and oral language development. Oral language development takes place as students talk in presenting and others listen.

Readers' theater is an ideal way to develop oral and written language because students are using language for reasons, not dummy runs. Various forms of literature can provide the basis of the script, but the script needs to be at students' independent reading level for fluency development. By reading the script with the teacher or with other students, students can practice a script at their instructional level of 90%–94% word identification. With practice, students can reach 100% of the words they read in the script.

Partner Reading

Students can be shown how to read in pairs to practice reading a poem the students have read during shared reading with the teacher to help students make gains in fluency. Students also can reread a story with which they have engaged previously during their guided reading instruction with the teacher. When students are shown how to read together in productive ways, partner reading can be a beneficial literacy station or independent activity while the teacher meets with small groups for guided reading or other instruction.

COMPETENCY 004: READING COMPREHENSION AND ASSESSMENT

The teacher understands the importance of reading for understanding, knows components and processes of reading comprehension and teaches students strategies for improving their comprehension.

The beginning teacher:

A. Understands reading comprehension as an active process of constructing meaning.

B. Understands the continuum of reading comprehension skills in the statewide curriculum and grade-level expectations for these skills.

C. Understands factors affecting students' reading comprehension (e.g., oral language development, word analysis skills, prior knowledge, language background, previous reading experiences, fluency, vocabulary development, ability to monitor understanding, characteristics of specific texts).

D. Knows characteristics of informal and formal reading comprehension assessments (e.g., criterion-referenced state tests, curriculum-based reading assessments, informal reading inventories, norm-referenced tests).

E. Selects and uses appropriate informal and formal assessments to monitor and evaluate students' reading comprehension.

F. Analyzes student errors and provides focused instruction in reading comprehension based on the strengths and needs of individual students, including English learners (in accordance with the ELPS).

G. Knows how to use ongoing assessment to determine when a student needs additional help or intervention to bring the student's performance to grade level, based on state content and performance standards for reading in the Texas Essential Knowledge and Skills (TEKS).

H. Understands metacognitive skills, including self-evaluation and self-monitoring skills, and teaches students to use these skills to enhance their own reading comprehension.

I. Knows how to determine students' independent, instructional and frustration reading levels and uses this information to select and adapt reading materials for individual students and to guide their selection of independent reading materials.

J. Uses various instructional strategies to enhance students' reading comprehension (e.g., linking text content to students' lives and prior knowledge, connecting related ideas across different texts, engaging students in guided and independent reading, guiding students to generate questions and apply knowledge of text topics).

K. Knows how to provide students with direct, explicit instruction in the use of strategies to improve their reading comprehension (e.g., previewing, self-monitoring, visualizing, retelling, summarizing, paraphrasing, inferring, identifying text structure).

L. Uses various communication modes (e.g., written, oral) to promote students' reading comprehension.

M. Understands levels of reading comprehension and how to model and teach literal, inferential, and evaluative comprehension skills.

N. Knows how to provide instruction to help students increase their reading vocabulary.

O. Understands reading comprehension issues for students with different needs and knows effective reading strategies for those students.

P. Knows the difference between guided and independent practice in reading and provides students with frequent opportunities for both.

Q. Knows how to promote students' development of an extensive reading and writing vocabulary by providing them with many opportunities to read and write.

Reading Comprehension and Assessment

Successful reading entails being able to comprehend what is being read. To be able to comprehend texts, students must be able to decode or recognize words fluently. However, comprehension also depends upon language comprehension. Language comprehension includes being able to understand vocabulary, sentences, and longer texts or discourse. To know how to help all students reach their potential, teachers need to assess to determine whether students have difficulties in (a) decoding and/or (b) dimensions of language comprehension: understanding vocabulary, deciphering various sentence structures, and sustaining understanding of various types of discourse (such as informational texts and stories).

By the time students reach the middle and upper grades, many can pronounce correctly the words they read or decode, but they struggle in understanding what they have read. The difficulties in comprehension can take place if students received effective instruction in word identification, but not effective instruction in comprehension. Instruction in reading comprehension should begin as students learn to read and proceed as students continue in schooling.

Beginning readers need to retell and talk about books they read early on to cultivate their comprehension skills. However, the short texts appropriate for beginning readers do not provide the opportunity for students to build the kind of comprehension eventually needed for tackling longer texts. This is why it's key for teachers to read aloud daily, which allows students to undertake increasingly longer texts, as well as to develop and refine listening comprehension needed as they rise toward the upper grades.

Talking experiences can help students gain in language comprehension. At the same time, however, students need to hear the language of books, which provides vocabulary and sentence structures not found in everyday conversations. To maintain this path, teachers need to read aloud daily to students in upper grades to continue to build the listening comprehension skills needed increasingly complex reading comprehension.

Not all students who have reached Grade 4 can identify or decode words. Some students may have struggled in decoding from the outset of their early literacy instruction, with their needs never met. ELs in particular could thus have gaps in their schooling, and some in the broader student population may lack instruction in word identification in English. Students with dyslexia or other learning difficulties could have adequate or even strong language comprehension, and have no trouble understanding ideas presented orally. Nonetheless, they may experience difficulty in decoding, which leads to difficulty in reading comprehension even when students demonstrate strong language comprehension.

Dimensions of Comprehension

Asking students well-developed questions about a text is an excellent way to assess comprehension. However, comprehension instruction should not be limited to providing passages and how to answer particular types of questions. Rather than solely assessing comprehension, teachers should teach it. Such instruction helps students deal with the specifically challenging aspects of engaging in various types of texts and reading for different purposes.

Reading is an active, constructive process that is a transaction between the reader and the text. As discussed, to be able to construct meaning, readers must be able to decode. In constructing meaning, readers use their (1) **knowledge of language**, (2) **knowledge of the world**, and (3) **print awareness**. Setting the **reader's purpose for reading** while weaving in different texts and **text structures** also helps the reader extract the meaning present in the writing.

The varied backgrounds readers bring to the classroom afford opportunities to make valuable connections with lived experience. Because readers use knowledge of language to comprehend, teachers can help them grow in applying that knowledge to understand texts. This is achieved by activating and building the background knowledge students need as they read a selection of fiction, poetry, or nonfiction. Teachers also can help students learn to navigate various types of texts and how to adjust how they read according to varying purposes. Additionally, students need to be explicitly taught how to monitor their reading, to see whether they are comprehending what they are reading so they can revise their approach accordingly.

Knowledge of Language and Comprehension

Teachers can help students increase their knowledge of language by providing oral language experiences that let students use language in a variety of ways on a daily basis. At the same time, teachers need to help students meet the demands of written language. Even though students may be able to communicate in informal ways by talking and listening, they may not be proficient in written language.

In applying their knowledge of language, students must be able to understand words they encounter in the text, which may include some that are seldom or never used in informal communication. Students also must understand the principles of syntax, or the ways sentences are made. In addition, readers must understand that the format and the language features used in oral communication differ from those used in written communication. In oral communication, speakers construct meaning by relying on the prosodic features of language (i.e., stress, tone, and word juncture), as well as nonverbal clues.

By reading aloud and independently daily, students begin to see how written language works, just as they did when acquiring oral language. Students who write daily also can learn more about how print is used to convey meaning. Reading experiences inform the students' writing, but students also grow as readers as they make choices akin to those other writers make in developing a message.

Knowledge of the World and Comprehension

Before students read a selection, they should be equipped with pre-reading support. One way teachers can provide this is to **build or activate background knowledge** needed to comprehend the text well. Capable readers draw upon their background knowledge without knowing it, and teachers should assume students will, and guide them in doing so. Consequently, teachers can show students this is a part of reading by activating their background knowledge (schemata).

Teachers may want to activate specific background knowledge when students read a text that is similar to one they've read before. For example, while reading a variant of a folktale, the teacher may remind students of a prior version they had read. Or if students are reading another book in a series, the teacher may want to briefly discuss connections between the two texts that help define why they are part of the series. Or teachers can review concepts needed to understand the next section in a textbook.

For students lacking background knowledge, teachers should step in and **build background knowledge**. For example, if students are reading a work of historical fiction that takes place during the Great Depression, teachers can set the scene by providing the historical context. For students who have not mastered concepts they need to know to understand a content-area text, the teacher should teach the applicable concepts.

Preparing students to read a text (pre-reading) includes helping them understand **unfamiliar vocabulary**. Vocabulary development includes understanding concepts as well as how to pronounce unfamiliar words. Asking students to look up the definition of words in a glossary is not an effective way to help students understand unfamiliar concepts. Rather, teachers should (1) present a word, (2) ask the student to repeat the word, (3) explain the concept using student-friendly language and provide examples that close the gap, (4) present the word in the sentence that is in the text, and (5) use photos, objects, gestures, pantomime, and/or morphemic analysis (e.g., relate the word *territorial* to *territory* and the Latin root *terra* along with the Spanish cognate *la tierra*). The amount of instruction needed can vary depending on the demands of the text, the students' experiential background, and the difficulty of the concept. Consider, for example, that in reading a story that takes place at a circus, the teacher may briefly explain content-specific terms such as *big top* or *trapeze*. Similarly, before students read *The Little Red Hen*, defining terms like *mill* or *cottage* would be in order.

On the other hand, some concepts and vocabulary may require more discussion for students to grasp the new information they are encountering in informational (or expository) texts or to understand the plot of a story.

Pre-reading also can include a gist statement for reading fiction, where the teacher provides the names of characters and a sentence or two that provides an overview of the plot without telling what exactly happens. For reading informational text, pre-reading includes surveying the text to scan the title, headings, illustrations, captions, maps, and any text features that helps the students be better prepared for navigating the text as they read.

Navigating Print: Knowledge of Text Structure, Purposes for Reading, and Monitoring

Along with being able to identify words, successful students can read various types of texts that differ because of the **text structure**. Narrative texts encountered when reading stories make different demands on readers than informational or expository texts. Even young children can remember and retell stories they hear by using a schema, or cognitive framework, for organizing and interpreting stories they encounter. Similarly, older students may readily comprehend fiction but struggle with informational texts.

Informational texts make different demands on readers than fictional stories; facing these varied demands can be a major obstacle to reading success. What differs? Critically, the text structures of informational texts are not like those of stories. Whereas readers have a schema for stories, they need to figure out the text structure of informational texts. As a result, informational (or expository) texts often must be read more than once to be able to understand and recall the information.

The text structures of informational texts can vary, depending upon how the information is organized in the discipline or is needed for relating the information. For example, when presenting a chapter about rocks, the authors may use headings—such as *igneous*, *sedimentary*, and *metamorphic*—that signal how the information is organized. Within each section, each type of rock is described. Latching onto these headings to guide their reading gives students a way of organizing individual facts or units of information. Students also can use headings to see how concepts relate to one another, such as how *magma*, once it cools, allows for the formation of igneous rocks, or how *sedimentary* rock forms from weathering and erosion.

As students reach the middle grades, they are increasingly required to read longer informational texts that make greater demands on their memory. Teachers can help students read and remember information by giving them tools to discern how information is organized in the text so they can better learn and retain the concepts they encounter.

Following are **major types of text structures** writers use when producing informational texts:

- **Description**—The writer presents the topic by presenting a list of characteristics.

- **Sequence**—The writer presents a series of events or steps in a process.

- **Compare/contrast**—The writer compares or contrasts concepts and events by showing how they are alike or different.

- **Problem/solution**—The writer presents a problem followed by a solution.

- **Cause/effect**—The writer presents information that explains a relationship between one thing that triggers or is responsible for another.

While different types of text structures can be described individually, students need to be shown that more than one type of text structure can exist within a text. For example, a chapter in a history textbook may use sequence in presenting the chronology of the American Revolution while also showing cause and effect and offering a description.

It is essential for students to be able to apply knowledge of text structure as they read, rather than being able to define text structures per se. Familiarity with text structures should be viewed as a tool for learning or a way to read to learn successfully. As students apply knowledge of text structures as they read in various disciplines, they build flexibility and expertise. Nonetheless, they can become frustrated when asked to use text structure without having been provided enough scaffolding.

Teachers must keep in mind that story maps and retelling of the story pertain to the structure of fiction, but do not work for nonfiction/informational text. These tools aid students in recalling characters, describing the setting and problem of the story, and explaining what took place to resolve the problem. When it comes to reading nonfiction, students surely should talk about what they have read, but they need to focus on reading small chunks to be able to connect individual ideas with the stated or implied topic heading. "How wolves communicate" could be such a subtopic in a text about wolves.

Vocabulary Development

Reading proficiently depends on recognizing and understanding words instantly. Readers who can do this are then equipped to devote attention to creating meaning, or comprehension. Understanding meaning is also key to success in instructional experiences that rely on listening and speaking.

Before children enter school, they have gained in their speaking and listening vocabularies through meaningful interactions with others. Even without being taught directly, children gradually acquire and refine their knowledge of words. Schooling provides opportunities for students to expand their **speaking** and **listening vocabularies** while doing likewise for their **reading** and **writing vocabularies**.

Although students continue to make gains in vocabulary development in less formal ways through their interactions with others, instruction at school plays a decisive role in helping students make the gains they need to succeed academically and in their day-to-day lives. Acquiring vocabulary entails being able to (1) understand a word when it is used, (2) define a term in one's own words, (3) decode and spell a word, and (4) know multiple meanings when it comes time to apply them.

Vocabulary Development and Instruction

Vocabulary development entails **connecting a word** (or label) **with concepts**. When students understand a concept, they are able to remember and use the word associated with it. Learning how to use a dictionary is critical to this endeavor. However, dictionary use alone is not enough to lock in gains in vocabulary development; long-term gains require more than looking up words and memorizing.

Vocabulary development takes place when students expand their understanding of a known concept and learn new words that can be used as a label for a known concept. Other times, students relate new concepts to existing labels or words they know, distinguishing, for example, between the *bark* of a dog versus the *bark* of a tree. In schooling, children may need to learn both a concept and a label, such as when they are learning about a process like photosynthesis.

The type of instruction varies depending upon what students need. A brief example may be sufficient if students understand the concept and are learning a new word in conjunction with it. On the other hand, students need more experiences in instances when they understand a concept but are learning a word in a language other than their native tongue. Students may be especially challenged when they are required to simultaneously understand a concept while learning new words that characterize the concept.

Many concepts students encounter in content areas (e.g., science, social studies) are abstract, so instruction must be devoted to making the abstraction tangible. At the same time, instruction must help students acquire the vocabulary that is needed and used in discussing and learning the concept.

When students understand a concept at a deeper level, they understand how related concepts are linked. Students gain in conceptual development by encountering a concept either firsthand or via oral or written language.

Types of Instruction for Vocabulary Development

Reading Aloud and Independent Reading

A pivotal way teachers help students make gains in vocabulary development is by reading aloud to students each day as well as providing time for students' daily independent reading experiences. As they spread their wings across new reading materials, students encounter words that are likely to transcend their oral language experiences. Students understand and learn new words by using **contextual analysis**, which requires using adjacent words and illustrations to help them figure out meanings. Although teachers are not teaching words directly, students make substantial gains through their engagement with reading. The words that become a part of their reading vocabularies may now become part of their speaking, listening, and writing vocabularies. Exposing students to a variety of types of literature makes students more apt to undergo more extensive gains. Teachers should read aloud not just fiction and poetry but also nonfiction, or informational, books.

Systematic Vocabulary Instruction

Vocabulary development also needs to include systematic instruction that helps students attain strategies for gaining vocabulary. Teacher can provide instruction before, during, and after reading. Deciding when to teach or review vocabulary depends on what is needed to help students succeed in view of both the specific task they need to engage in and their overall oral and written language development.

As discussed, vocabulary development can take place **before reading** to help students encounter new concepts and words so that students can comprehend the text. Teachers need to consider students' background knowledge and ways they can relate new concepts to students' previous learning or background knowledge. Rather than just asking students to look up a word in a glossary of the textbook, teachers should provide student-friendly definitions, examples, gestures, features, pictures, or diagrams. Teachers also need to show students how illustrations or diagrams establish a context to thread together vocabulary and associated concepts. Pre-reading also should include reading the word in a sentence, and that sentence should be one that appears in the text.

Systematic, direct instruction includes helping students learn how to use **word structure** to understand and recall new words. **Morphemes** are the smallest units of meaning in language. They may have meaning in themselves (e.g., *happy*). However, they also can be word parts that have no meaning on their own (bound morphemes) but instead change or expand the meaning of words to which they are added; in this role, they act as prefixes (e.g., *un-*) or suffixes (e.g., *-ment*). Students benefit from seeing the connections between spelling and meaning. Words may be related in meaning even when the sounds of a word change, such as with *nation* and *national*. Learning

Latin and Greek roots and derivations also helps students understand and remember new words, such as the Latin root common to *cordial, accord,* and *discord.* Morphemic analysis can be used in pre-reading when unfamiliar words provide an opportunity and be integral to vocabulary and spelling development programs.

Students use context clues or surrounding words and illustrations to understand unknown words. When teachers interact with students **during reading**, they help students learn to use the context of the sentence, text, or illustrations to determine what a word means. This instruction helps propel independent reading when no one is available to help them understand unfamiliar words.

Vocabulary instruction that takes place after reading can help students review concepts. Instruction after also can help students understand how concepts relate to each other. Instruction can include the use of semantic maps or diagrams as well as talking about concepts to help students learn. Writing experiences can also be helpful, but students are unlikely to learn by merely copying definitions.

Showing students how to use the dictionary also can help them deal with unknown words. But just asking them to look up words and copy definitions does not by itself promote gains in vocabulary. Teaching them how to use the **dictionary**, however, is practical knowledge to be applied to learning unknown words. Students need to be shown how to locate the word, which, for example, may not be readily apparent if the word has an inflectional ending (e.g., *repairs* or *repairing*). Students should thus be shown that they may need to identify the base word. Then, they must be instructed on how to select the definition that fits with the sentence they are reading, in context.

Teaching Vocabulary for Understanding and Learning in Subject Areas

Teaching all the new words presented in a reading selection typically is not necessary, and may not be effective. Teachers need to decide which words are critical to understanding the meaning of the selection. Teachers also need to decide whether students can gain enough understanding by how the word is used in the selection; this can vary among students, depending upon their language development. For example, a word that could be figured out by a native speaker may not be one that an English learner could understand by using context clues. Teachers should decide how much instruction is needed without disrupting the enjoyment and understanding of the silent reading or reading-aloud experience.

Often vocabulary of informational materials requires direct instruction when the concepts are new. Also, students need to be shown how concepts relate to one another to understand them individually and collectively.

The most basic words in the language are **Tier One words**, high-frequency terms such as *puppy* or *house.* Because students are apt to encounter these words in their daily oral language experiences, explicit instruction is not typically needed for native speakers. Teachers, however, should not assume that English learners will know these words since they may not have encountered them.

Even so, English learners may have a touchstone for the *concept* of words like *family* or *butterfly* in their native language, allowing such words to be more easily taught. Tier One instruction includes expressions and idioms (e.g., "give it a shot" or "piece of cake") that can be especially confusing for English learners.

The next level up contains **Tier Two words**. These words are more apt to require instruction because students are not likely to have encountered them in their daily talking and listening situations. Tier Two, which includes words such as *inhibit*, *adjacent*, and *guarantee*, contains terms likely to be seen in print. Words in this tier also can include those that are commonly confused with each other, such as *fowl* and *foul*. Tier Two words arise in an academic context, cutting across multiple topics and subject areas and allowing more complex topics to be discussed, but students typically understand the concept or a synonym of a Tier Two word, such as *next to* when learning *adjacent*.

Tier Three words are directly associated with a discipline, and these words typically represent new concepts. Examples of terms in this tier include *condensation*, *diameter*, and *senator*. Such words, while occurring with low frequency in everyday communication, are critical to understanding and learning concepts presented in texts in specific disciplines. Instruction may be needed for students to read and understand the text. Often instruction is needed after students read so they can remember or learn concepts and how concepts are connected.

While brief descriptions and examples may be enough to understand some words, the vocabulary associated with new concepts will require more in-depth instruction. As mentioned in connection with dictionary use, research shows that supplying definitions in and of themselves does not help students understand and learn new concepts.

When more in-depth vocabulary instruction is required, teachers must describe or explain the word in a way students can understand. One approach is to ask students to put it in their own words or create a picture or symbolic representation. To help students retain the new vocabulary, they can keep vocabulary notebooks in which they add new vocabulary as it's acquired. The compilation also opens the door to games in which the new words are, for instance, used to pepper conversations with a partner.

Formal Assessment

Formal assessment is a data-driven evaluation method used to assess students' progress in various areas of literacy. Some examples of formal assessment follow:

Criterion-Referenced Tests are developed to assess a specific set of skills or concepts or criteria at a designated level of difficulty. These exams can be used to determine how much a student knows before and after instruction. Each skill or concept is measured by items to obtain an adequate sample of students' knowledge and help control for guessing. Traditionally, the results are presented as percentages. A score of 70% suggests that 70% of the test standards have been mastered.

Norm-Referenced Tests are standardized tests that compare a student's test performance with a sample of similar students (e.g., from the same grade level) who took the test at the same time of the school year. The administration and scoring of the test are standardized by using the same procedures for giving the exam and scoring it. Norms are obtained from the standardization sample. The scores provide information about how the student's achievement compares to that of other students on a national level. A percentile score can range from 1 to 99. A score at the 60th percentile means that 60% of the norm group performed at or below the student's score level.

COMPETENCY 005: READING APPLICATIONS

The teacher understands reading skills and strategies appropriate for various types of texts and contexts and teaches students to apply these skills and strategies to enhance their reading proficiency.

The beginning teacher:

A. Understands skills and strategies for understanding, interpreting, and evaluating different types of written materials, including narratives, expository texts, persuasive texts, technical writing, and content-area textbooks.

B. Understands different purposes for reading and related reading strategies.

C. Knows and teaches strategies to facilitate comprehension of different types of text before, during, and after reading (e.g., previewing, making predictions, questioning, self-monitoring, rereading, mapping, using reading journals, discussing texts).

D. Provides instruction in comprehension skills that support students' transition from "learning to read" to "reading to learn" (e.g., matching comprehension strategies to different types of text and different purposes for reading).

E. Understands the importance of reading as a skill in all content areas.

F. Understands the value of using dictionaries, glossaries, and other sources to determine the meanings, pronunciations, and derivations of unfamiliar words and teaches students to use these sources.

G. Knows how to teach students to interpret information presented in various formats (e.g., maps, tables, graphs) and how to locate, retrieve, and retain information from a range of texts and technologies.

H. Knows how to help students comprehend abstract content and ideas in written materials (e.g., by using manipulatives, examples, diagrams) and formulate, express, and support responses to various types of texts.

I. Knows literary genres (e.g., historical fiction, poetry, myths, fables, drama) and their characteristics.

J. Knows literary nonfiction genres (e.g., biographies, memoirs) and their characteristics.

K. Recognizes a wide range of literature and other texts appropriate for students.

L. Provides multiple opportunities for students to listen and respond to a wide variety of children's and young people's literature, both fiction and nonfiction, and to recognize characteristics of various types of narrative and expository texts.

M. Understands and promotes students' development of literary response and analysis (e.g., formulating, expressing, and supporting responses to various types of literary texts) including teaching students elements of literary analysis (e.g., story elements, literary devices, figurative language, characterization, features of different literary genres, influences of historical and cultural contexts, themes, and settings) and providing students with opportunities to apply comprehension skills to literature.

N. Selects and uses a variety of materials to teach students about authors, including the cultural, historical, and contemporary contexts, and about different purposes for writing.

O. Provides students with opportunities to engage in silent reading and extended reading of a wide range of materials, including expository texts and various literary genres.

P. Engages students in varied reading experiences and encourages students to interact with others about their reading.

Q. Uses strategies to encourage reading for pleasure and lifelong learning.

R. Knows how to teach students strategies for selecting their own books for independent reading.

S. Uses technology to promote students' literacy and teaches students to use technology to access a wide range of appropriate narrative and expository texts.

Reading Comprehension and Applications

Successful reading requires being able to comprehend what is being read. By the time students reach the middle and upper grades, many can correctly pronounce the words they read, but they struggle to understand what they have read. Comprehension hinges on accurate word identification, but simply rendering words accurately does not guarantee that students have understood what they have read.

Learning to Read vs. Reading to Learn

Students in Grades EC–3 are learning how to decode or identify words. In other words, **learning to read is a large part of literacy development in Grades EC–3**. By the time students reach Grade 4, students who are on grade level will know how to recognize words and decode words that are unfamiliar. Word study for students in Grades 4–8 will focus upon morphemic analysis and understanding words, or increasing vocabulary.

Comprehension can start to become difficult for students in Grades 4–6 as the texts they read become longer and more complex. Students must rely more and more upon the print – rather than illustrations – to construct meaning. Along with reading longer stories, students read longer texts in their subject-matter learning. Therefore, a shift takes place where **reading to learn becomes a prime focus in Grades 4–8**. Nevertheless, comprehension development needs to begin, and continue in the upper grades, as students increasingly must understand longer stories as they take in and retain new information.

Levels and Types of Comprehension

To be able to comprehend, students need to be engaged in learning experiences where they need to absorb new information at different levels of comprehension while also understanding various types of texts.

Literal comprehension entails being able to recall what is explicitly stated in a text, which can be the main idea as well as important details. Literal comprehension is the least difficult form of comprehension for children. However, knowing what is explicitly written is important for interpreting and evaluating stories, expository texts in subject-matter learning, and persuasive texts or arguments.

Inferential comprehension requires readers to discern or arrive at understandings for information not explicitly stated. Competent readers are able to use what is in the text to make inferences. Students need to draw inferences as they connect ideas to comprehend what takes place in a story (or understand the plot), to make predictions, and to uncover themes that emerge as the story unfolds. Students also need to know how to make inferences as they comprehend informational text and persuasive texts or arguments by drawing conclusions based on what is presented in the text. Many students assume that comprehension entails only understanding what is explicitly stated, but authors assume readers will make inferences.

Evaluative comprehension also requires readers to think at higher levels as they analyze, evaluate, and take a position or stance. Students need to be able to understand what is presented in the text as they engage in evaluating, and they need to be able to explain and support their claim by marshaling evidence in the text to support or prove it.

Dyslexia and Comprehension Assessment

Students also may be highly proficient in listening comprehension and have a level of intelligence that indicates facility in grasping the texts they read. Yet these students may struggle when processing print, hindering their comprehension.

Students' inability to read words accurately may stem from a lack of effective instruction, but it also may signal the need for assessment to determine whether the student has dyslexia or another specific learning disability. Primary difficulties of students with dyslexia include single-word recognition, reading fluency, and spelling. Difficulties in comprehension and written expression are secondary consequences stemming from the difficulties in reading and spelling words. Teachers are required to seek assessment for students who might have dyslexia or a related disability; this is mandated to prevent delays in receiving the instruction they need.

Metacognition and Comprehension Monitoring

Metacognition pertains to thinking about one's thinking. Proficient readers understand that reading entails awareness and understanding about what we read. Proficient readers do not solely say words, but rather monitor their thinking as they read. This is metacognition in action. Proficient readers know they need to use so-called "fix-up" strategies when their comprehension breaks down: Read a sentence or section again, look up a word in the dictionary, look at other parts of the text, ask someone for help.

Teachers also can foster metacognition before students read the text. When students read stories or informational texts, teachers can (1) activate and/or build background knowledge and (2) introduce new vocabulary which helps students start to think about what they will read.

Pre-reading of stories can include a gist statement where the teacher provides the names of characters and a brief statement of what the story will be about without telling the plot. Pre-reading of informational texts, students can preview text features such as headings, photographs, captions, and maps to help students start to think about ideas they will encounter.

By listening to students read individually, teachers can provide prompts that help students monitor their reading. When a student makes a miscue (or oral reading error) that does not make sense, the miscue indicates that the student is not paying attention to meaning. Rather than telling the student the word, the teacher can say, "Does that make sense?" Using this same wording/ prompt, as needed, helps students monitor their reading and self-correct. Many students in upper grades are able to identify words and not make many errors or miscues. But not all students are on grade level.

When students can decode words of a story but cannot retell it, the teacher can help them monitor their comprehension by highlighting selected sections of text during reading rather than waiting until the end. Over time, students will be able to read the entire story and then discuss it. These discussions in turn can encourage students to pay attention to meaning by "saying" to the students that reading entails understanding. Hearing the comments from the teacher and fellow students, they experience how rewarding it is to connect ideas.

Metacognition of informational texts can be fostered as teachers guide students' reading, showing them strategies for comprehending and learning from informational texts. Effective teaching entails in-depth modeling and guided practice during and after reading. Rather than telling students what to do or just assigning text and testing to assess comprehension and learning, teachers support students as they engage in the process of reading informational/expository texts such as those found in science and social studies.

Strategies to Support Students' Reading Informational/ Expository Texts

Adjusting Reading to Fit the Purpose and Text

Students should be shown that proficient readers change their approach when reading for pleasure as compared to reading to learn. Additionally, different types of texts place different demands on readers. When reading fiction, students often can read a text at their comprehension level straight through and be able to provide a sound retelling. Conversely, when reading informational texts for subject-matter learning, even strong readers cannot remember all of the important details. The teacher's modeling and guidance illuminate approaches to flexibly address (1) the purpose for reading the text at hand, and (2) the type of text being read.

Previewing and Text Features

What happens when readers pause to predict aspects about what they're going to read? Previewing can help students anticipate the process. But there's more at stake. When students read expository text, they can overlook features of text that are important for comprehension and learning. Proficient reading includes recognizing features of text and using them to understand.

The many features of text include illustrations, images, diagrams, labels, captions, graphs, charts, timetable, bold print, italics, headings and subheadings, a glossary, a table of contents, and an index. The best way to familiarize students with text features is to pinpoint the ones relevant to the text they are reading.

Topics in the expository text of social studies, science, and other subjects have their own structure, and this is determined by how a subject is inherently organized. The author of an informational or expository text uses the organization in presenting ideas and in connecting ideas. Successful reading and learning requires an understanding of the major ideas, the important supporting details, and how these ideas relate to one another to create an understanding of the broader topic.

At times, the author may not use any headings, but in such instances, students can be instructed how to infer the major ideas by reading the section.

Question-Answer Relationships (QAR)

Question-Answer Relationships, or QAR, is a strategy used after reading to help students understand that questions presented about a passage can vary in what they require a reader to do to answer the question. Often, students assume that they need to search in a passage to find the answer to a question, not realizing that questions can instead ask readers to connect information in the text and to use their background/prior knowledge to answer a question. In this strategy, types of questions are categorized on the basis of the question-answer relationship. Here are the categories:

- **Right There**—The answer to these questions can be found in the text. These are literal questions that often have the same words as those in the text.

- **Think and Search**—The answer to these questions can be found in the text, too; however, the answer is found by searching parts of the text to put information together.

- **Author and You**—These questions require the student to use information in the text and to relate the information to their prior/background knowledge.

- **On My Own**—The questions require students to use their prior/background knowledge to answer the questions. The answers are found by drawing solely upon past experiences and not the text.

The teacher should explain to students that they can expect to encounter the four different types of questions listed above. Then the teacher should read aloud a short passage as students follow along. The teacher then presents questions about the passage and thinks aloud to model how to answer the question. With practice, students gain in thinking about a text and answering questions they could encounter on exams.

Directed Reading Thinking Activity (DRTA)

Directed Reading Thinking Activity, or DRTA, is a comprehension strategy that encourages students to activate their prior knowledge, make predictions, and monitor their understanding. Teachers need to provide modeling and other support as students engage so that the experiences in applying the strategy are effective. The procedures are as follows:

- **Direct**—Teachers point students' attention to the title, chapter heading(s), illustrations, and captions, and any other related text features. Teachers ask a general question based on the overall title along with the heading of the assigned reading (e.g., "What do you think we will learn, based upon this title?" "Look at this heading. What do you think we will learn?"). As with any strategy, teachers need to think aloud when introducing it. Teachers also need to be prepared to help by providing prompts or adding to what students say to provide differentiated instruction for students who are English learners, less capable readers, or have a learning disability.

- **Read**—The teacher decides in advance what is a good stopping point for students as they read, keeping in mind that students often need to read small chunks rather than an entire section at once. The amount to be read corresponds with the difficulty of the material and the reading ability of the students. After students read, the teacher asks them what they found out and how this relates to their predictions. Then the students continue in this vein until they have read the entire section of the passage or textbook.

- **Think**—When students finish reading a section, the teacher guides them in evaluating their predictions about what they have read. Students think about what they have discovered, and whether as a consequence they need to modify their predictions. Teachers record students' predictions and what they have learned to provide a record of the thought process and the basis of a later review of the passage or chapter. Such modeling teaches note-taking, thus instructing students not only how to read but also how to study to learn information.

Reciprocal Teaching

Reciprocal teaching is instruction that encourages students to be active readers and monitor their reading. Reciprocal teaching incorporates four strategies students use to read and understand text: summarizing, question-generating, clarifying, and predicting. Teachers model and make sure students have had ample practice to learn each strategy of reciprocal teaching. Once teachers are sure students know what to do, students are divided into small groups organized to lead the dialogue about what they have read, teaching each other. The procedures are as follows:

- The teacher demonstrates how to perform the four strategies. This can be done in whole- or small-group work before students use reciprocal teaching. Students must know what to do before they work with each other in a small group. The time teachers devote to making sure students can apply reciprocal teaching strategies is worthwhile because (1) students are learning the content through the guidance, and (2) the payoff is considerable because students can work successfully on their own after learning the strategies:

Summarizing—Students read a chunk of the information to be read in a section of the text. As a summarizer, students tell what the key ideas are so far.

Question-Generating—After the summarizer shares, the questioner asks whether any parts are unclear and/or asks how ideas connect to each other or concepts presented so far.

Clarifying—The clarifier answers the questions presented by the questioner.

Predicting—The predictor anticipates what the author will present next in the text.

Here are the practical steps to put reciprocal teaching to work in the classroom:

- The teacher places students in groups of four, and assigns each student a role written on an index card.

- Students read up to the stopping point determined by the teacher to ensure the class deals with appropriately small chunks of the section. Students assume their roles in leading the dialogue and teaching each other.

- Students change roles, passing the card to the right, and repeat the process.

- The teacher guides and monitors to ensure students are successful. The teacher's participation can diminish as students become more proficient.

Think-Pair-Share (TPS)

The Think-Pair-Share, or TPS, strategy encourages students to think on their own as they respond to a question posed by the teacher and then share their thoughts with a classmate before arriving at a conclusion. TPS's scaffolding helping students learn concepts and develop oral language abilities. The procedures are as follows:

- The teacher determines at what points to ask a question and the question to ask. The question can be general: "What did you learn from what you just read?" or "What does the author tell us?"

- The teacher provides demonstrations on how to use each part of TPS by working with a small or whole group to let students learn what to do. The teacher models and then uses a gradual release of responsibility to let students participate with the teacher's guidance and make sure they know what to do before applying TPS on their own:

Think—After reading or viewing, students individually think about the question the teacher has presented.

Pair—Students pair up with a partner or join a small group to share what they have been thinking.

Share—Students share what they have been thinking. Students then also could share with a whole group, which teachers could use as the basis of a whole-group discussion.

Concept Maps

Concept mapping is a visual organizer that enhances students' understanding and retention by depicting relationships between and among concepts. The concept map may be a web, timeline, or Venn diagram. Concept maps also can be used to show terms associated with a process, such as photosynthesis. Concept maps can include photos or illustrations, such as a plant with its parts explained.

When selecting what type pf map to use, the teacher needs to consider the relationships being featured through the topic. For example, students studying mammals may be learning about features of mammals. To capture the important details and relationships among details, the teacher might present a concept map the students and teacher complete as the students encounter information. Such a concept map follows:

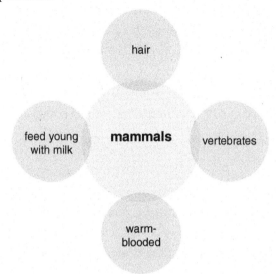

A more extensive concept map could include types of mammals with extending spokes if students were studying these concepts:

- land-dwelling: (extending spokes) skunks, horses, dogs, cats

- flying: (extending spokes) bats, flying squirrels

- marine mammals: (extending spokes) whales, manatees, sea otters

Semantic mapping uses a web of words to highlight meaning-based connections. Typically, a word is placed at the center of the web, and related words and concepts encircle the term at the heart of the lesson.

Examples of a semantic map follow:

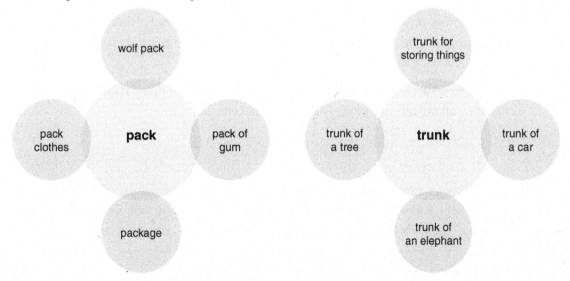

Concept and semantic maps can be used before, during, and after reading or unit of study:

Before—Students can tell what they know or what comes to mind when they think of the topic/ concept/word. The teacher adds students' thoughts to the map. Activating students' prior knowledge can help them have a basis for relating new information.

During—As student read, they can discuss what they are learning to add to the map.

After—The map developed can be reviewed after various points in the unit of study to review and remember.

SQ4R

SQ4R is a comprehension and study strategy that has been used for years to help students navigate expository text. This method adds one step to the original strategy, SQ3R, by including a step for students to create notes. The steps of the strategy are as follows:

- **Survey**—To survey, the students skim the chapter title, headings, illustrations, and bold text to get an overall idea of the topic and the framework for how information is being presented.

- **Question**—When starting to read a section, students turn a heading into the question(s) they anticipate will be answered through the information presented.

- **Read**—Students read to gain answers, and a stopping point can be determined in view of how difficult the materials is.

- **Recite**—After reading a section, students should recite orally what they have found out, putting the information in their own words. In guiding students, teachers can ask them to share, and the teacher writes what they say to create a set of notes students can study later. The students do not copy the notes so that they focus on understanding content they put in their own words.

- **Record**—Once students confirm their understanding of a section of the material and can paraphrase it, they record that understanding by making notes. Teachers can support students by modeling how to proceed from talking about what they have just read (via the "recite" step) to summarizing the ideas in their notes.

- **Review**—The review can take place at the end of reading a section, and it also can take place after reading all the sections by reviewing notes developed.

K-W-L

K-W-L is a strategy where students discuss and complete three columns of a chart as part of reading text: What I **Know**, What I **Want to Learn**, and What I **Learned**. This strategy helps students consciously think about their prior knowledge, set purposes for reading, and monitor their comprehension.

K-W-L Chart

Topic: _____

What I Know	What I Want to Learn	What I Learned

Before reading, students discuss what they know about the topic and the teacher or students list those ideas, which helps them consider their background knowledge. Next, students discuss and list specific questions they think could be answered in the text, which helps them set a purpose for reading and think about what they are reading.

After reading the text or segment of the text, the students discuss and then record what they learned in the corresponding column of the K-W-L chart. Any answers to questions can be written next to the question. Because students put ideas they learned in their own words, the students are better able to process information. Students also can see for themselves which ideas they're familiar with from the reading and which ones merit further study. This strategy is effective when teachers model for students and guide the development of the chart.

Questioning the Author

By **questioning the author**, students read a segment of the text and then collaborate with the teacher to understand the text and learn how to deal with comprehension problems as they read. The students learn how to read actively and see that text is created by someone. Questioning the author takes place as students read a text, not after.

When planning, the teacher first focuses on the major understandings that could create difficulty as they read the text. Next, the teacher determines the best way to segment the text by finding a good stopping point. The teacher develops queries to help promote student understanding. Such questions are designed to be queries rather than comprehension questions. Queries are designed to foster discussion of the information and encourage students to construct meaning by putting what they learn into their own words.

Initial queries about the text help students discuss what the text is saying and prepare them for the next segment as they construct meaning:

- What is the author saying here?

- Am I understanding the author?

Follow-up prompts can help students look at what a text means, not just what is said:

- How does this connect with what the author told before?

- Does the author explain this so that it makes sense?

The teacher and students collaborate. The teacher strives to help students develop and share their thoughts with each other by participating in ways that foster an effective discussion.

Genres of Literature

The form and content of writing determines the **genre** of literature. Literature can be divided into two major types of prose: fiction and nonfiction. Poetry can be designated as a third category of literature. The type of genre is related to the purpose and the audience of the writing. Through reading works of various genres, students learn of various ways people communicate, expand their reading abilities, and become more familiar with techniques writers use, depending upon their audience and purpose.

Nonfiction

Nonfiction is literature that shares factual information. Nonfiction includes biography, autobiography, memoir, essays, technical writing, and informational books. Here are some of the main nonfiction genres.

- **Biography**—factual account of a person's life.

- **Autobiography**—an account of the author's own life.

- **Memoir**—autobiographical but focuses upon selected parts of a person's life.

- **Informational works**—provide factual information about a topic or event.

- **Expository texts**—mainly textbooks, but any text that presents information explicitly to educate its readers.

- **Literary nonfiction**—as with textbooks, presents information, but by using strategies and techniques associated with fiction which help capture the reader's interest.

While expository texts and literary nonfiction are factual, literary nonfiction is meant to compelling even for a person not initially interested in a topic. Though fiction is often assumed to be more interesting to students, many of them, like adults, still enjoy most literary nonfiction or informational literature.

Fiction

Fiction can be realistic and believable, but the story conveyed is not entirely factual. The author may be inspired by an actual event or person in writing, but the author creates characters, episodes, and/or settings.

- **Realistic fiction** offers stories that could have taken place in the real world.

- **Historical fiction** contains stories of history that could have happened and are based upon facts although the actual characters and episodes are fictional.

- **Traditional literature** includes folktales, fairy tales, legends, fables, and myths which are narratives originally told orally that take place in an alternate reality.

- **Fantasy and science fiction** offers stories that are much like traditional literature in exploring an alternate reality, but these stories are written by authors rather than being oral tales that share a culture's beliefs, values, and morals. Science fiction relies upon scientific concepts or technologies.

Poetry

Poetry does not fit neatly or readily under a category of fiction or nonfiction. As a result, it is often recognized by its physical structure—that is, by the way its words are arranged, the length of its lines, and its scheme of rhythm and repetition. Poetry often, but not always, rhymes. Carefully chosen words and arranged words convey a message.

Role of Quality Literature in Meeting Students' Needs

Students who encounter a variety of types of literature are more apt to make more extensive gains. Along with reading aloud fiction and poetry, teachers should add nonfiction, or informational texts, and books. With this should come a concerted effort to ensure that students encounter quality literature that features diverse racial and cultural perspectives. Cultivating this diversity of viewpoints ensures, among other things, that students "see" themselves in books while also expanding their perspectives on the world and particularly with reference to those whose backgrounds differ from their own.

While numerous books have been published expressly for youth, they vary widely in their quality and thus in how well they meet students' needs. However, for the most part, high-quality works for youth are also the ones that students themselves find the most engaging. Rather than search for a book by topic or cultural perspective, teachers should look for *superior* books that feature a given topic or cultural perspective. As is true of the arts generally, mediocre books actually can dampen students' enthusiasm and engagement for reading. By reading aloud to students, teachers help students find authors and types of literature they will want to read on their own. The overarching message: Reading is rewarding.

Literary Elements

Literary elements are inherent components of literary works. Picking out literary elements helps students understand the work. Students need to know literary elements and devices to understand how literature works, which can enhance their study of literature. Knowing literary elements and devices also undergirds development of stories, poetry, and nonfiction. Here's a summary of the main literary elements with which students should be familiar:

- **Plot** is what happens in the story, and the plot should proceed in ways that are logical, even in imaginative works. Even in historical fiction, what takes place needs to be accurate in that it needs to be something that could have taken place. When teachers have discussion about what took place in a story, students are learning about the plot. Through the literary device of **exposition**, the author presents background information, such as about the setting or characters, which introduces the conflict. **Conflict** is the issue that is the basis of the story. The **rising action** is what takes place up to the climax which is the high point or pivotal part of the story. **The falling action or denouement** is what takes place after the climax, which leads to the **resolution**, or conclusion, of the story.

- **Setting** is the time and place of a story. Setting is especially important in historical fiction in determining what can take place. Even in fantasy, the setting should be believable because of the detailed, vivid description.

- **Theme** relates to messages, big ideas, or larger meanings that emerge from a story.

- **Characterization** is how the author reveals characters. Readers learn about characters through what a character says, does, looks like, and and/or thinks. Readers also become familiar with a character through what other characters say about the character. Characters can grow and change, but what characters should seem real and what they do should be plausible even when the reader knows the work is not based upon real events. The **protagonist** is the main character, and the **antagonist** is a character that opposes the protagonist. A **foil** is a character who is presented in contrast to another character, often the protagonist, which highlights certain attributes of the other character. However, the foil is not necessarily an antagonist.

- **Point of View** is who is telling the story, or the narrator, and the way the narrator reveals the story. The **third person, or omniscient, point of view** lets readers know what each character is thinking, saying and doing, and the author can speak to the readers, just as a storyteller would. **Limited third person point of view** takes place when the narrator knows only what one character feels, thinks, says, and understands. In other words, the story is told from that character's viewpoint. First-person narrative is when one or more characters tells the story (e.g., "I …"). In second-person narrative, the author addresses the readers (e.g., "You…").

- **Style** is the way a writer (or speaker) tells a story. The style of the author relates to the types of words used and the way words are arranged. **Diction** refers to the choice of words, which can make an impact on the tone of the writing, how a character is interpreted, and what is revealed. The **voice** of the writing could be the author's voice or that of a character.

- **Dialogue** is the speaking that takes place. **Dialect** is the variety of a language that is spoken by a group of people who belong together socially or geographically, and can serve to reveal a character. Similarly, **colloquialism and slang**, which are everyday, informal uses of language, serve to reveal a character.

Examples of Literary Devices

Literary devices are techniques used by writers to meet aesthetic aims, engage the reader, and provide deeper meanings.

- Through **flashback**, the author relates something that happened previously or before the current place in the story. Through **in media res**, writers begin the narrative at some point in the story other than the beginning of the story, or in the middle of the story. Through **deus ex-machina**, the author uses an unexpected character or divine character to resolve the conflict.

- **Foreshadowing** is a literary device used to give a hint of what will happen. At times, the foreshadowing is subtle, and readers do not discern it until later. In using foreshadowing, writers do not reveal specific details of what will take place, but it is a device used to keep readers interested in how the plot will proceed.

- **Irony** is used when reality differs from what either appears to be or is expected. **Verbal irony** is when the actual meaning of words is not the same as the words presented. **Situational irony** is when situations surprise or do not proceed as expected. **Dramatic irony** is when the audience/reader is aware of something important a character is not aware of yet.

- **Hyperbole** is used for emphasis though consciously exaggerating.

- **Simile and metaphor** are figurative language where two things that are not similar are compared to provide a vivid description. Similes use the words *like* or *as* to compare one thing with another side by side.

- **Personification** provides human characteristics to animals, things, or ideas.

- **Allegory** is a work that conveys a meaning not explicitly set forth in the narrative and that could have meaning on more than two levels to convey a moral/spiritual truth or political/historical situation.

- **Allusion** is a brief reference to a person, place or thing that the author assumes readers will recognize because of the cultural significance.

Characteristics of Poetry

Understanding characteristics of poetry and relationships of characteristics helps students understand how to write and analyze poetry.

Form and Types of Poetry

- The **stanza** is typically a group of lines set off by indentation or spacing from the next stanza. The stanza is the basic recurring metrical unit of a poem.

- The **rhyme scheme** pertains to the pattern of rhyme used. Rhyme scheme is determined by looking at the last word of each line and giving the same letter to designate words that rhyme. For example, ABBA means that the first and fourth lines rhyme, and the second and third lines rhyme.

- The **meter** of a poem is determined by the number of "feet" in a line of the poem, which is determined usually by the number of stressed syllables in a line, such that five stressed syllables would be five "feet" in the line. One foot is a *monometer*, two feet a *dimeter*, three feet a *trimeter*, four feet a *tetrameter*, five feet a *pentameter*, six feet a *hexameter*… An **iamb** exists when the first syllable is unstressed, or the second syllable is stressed. **Iambic pentameter**, then, is when a line has five feet, and each foot is an unstressed syllable followed by a stressed syllable. **Iambic tetrameter** characterizes a line of poetry that has four feet or stressed syllables, and the pattern is unstressed followed by stressed. Meters used include the following:

    - **iambs**—unstressed/stressed

    - **spondees**—stressed/stressed

    - **trochees**—stressed/unstressed

    - **Anapests**—unstressed/unstressed/stressed

    - **dactyls**—stressed/unstressed//unstressed.

- **Blank verse** is when the poet incorporates meter but not rhyme.

- **Free verse** is when the poet does not adhere to a certain pattern in regard to meter nor rhyme.

- A **sonnet** is a form of poetry that traditionally has had 14 lines, and there are two types of sonnets. One type, the **Petrarchan (or Italian) sonnet**, has this rhyme scheme: (1) ABBA ABBA for eight lines which present a problem or solution and (2) CDE CDE or CDE DCE where the problem is addressed or a thought completed. The **Shakespearean** sonnet has (1) three stanzas that are each four lines, or quatrains, and (2) concludes with a couplet, a stanza of two lines. The rhyme scheme for each quatrain is as follows: **ABAB-quatrain one, CDCD-quatrain two, EFEF-quatrain three. The rhyme scheme for the couplet is GG.** The Shakespearean sonnet is written in iambic pentameter.

- **Haiku** is a Japanese form of poetry that traditionally has focused on nature, but also has focused on other topics as poets have used this form. Haiku consists of three lines with a total of seventeen syllables; the first line has five syllables, the second line has seven syllables, and the third line has five syllables.

- **Cinquians** are poems with five lines. Common rhyme schemes are ABABB, ABAAB, and ABCCB.

- A **sestina** is a French form of poetry that has six stanzas with six lines each. This form does not incorporate rhyme, but repeats an ending word according to a pattern.

- A **limerick** is a five-line poem with a particular rhyme scheme: AABBA.

- **Epic** poems are long narratives that portray the story of a hero or adventure.

- **Ballad** poems are narratives that typically share a legend.

Poetic Devices

- **Repetition** of words, phrases, or lines is a way to show emphasis and can be a cue to the themes.

- **Alliteration** is a sound device, the repeated set of a sound in the first syllable of a word or the stressed syllable. Alliteration can entail consonant or vowel sounds. Alliteration adds rhythm to a text.

- **Assonance** is the repetition of a vowel sound.

- **Consonance** is the repetition of a consonant sound within a group of words. In alliteration, the consonant sound must occur at the first syllable, but in consonance, the consonant sound can occur anywhere in the word. The words do not need to be next to each other for consonance to occur as long as the sounds are close together. Like assonance, consonance, adds to the musical aspect of words while also making the words more noticeable to the reader.

- **Metaphor** and **simile** are figures of speech where two things that are not similar are compared to provide a vivid description. Metaphor directly compares things that are unrelated to provide imagery that leads a reader to think about something differently or to stress the impact of something. Simile uses the words *like* or *as* to compare one thing with another side by side.

- **Hyperbole** is used for emphasis though consciously exaggerating.

- **Personification** provides human characteristics to animals, things, or ideas.

- **Onomatopoeia** is when the sounds of a word or group of words describe sounds or imitate the sounds being featured.

Fostering Students' Comprehension of Literary Texts

- Through hearing literature read aloud as well on their own, students gain understandings of how literature works, to the point where they will both consciously and unconsciously incorporate literary elements and devices when they write.

- Instruction that helps students focus on the literary elements and devices can help students gain deeper understandings. However, to be most successful in analyzing literature, students first need to see that they can make connections to literature and that their thoughts are legitimate.

- Traditional literature instruction has assumed that meaning is in the text. However, noted theorist Louise Rosenblatt's **transactional theory** pinpoints meaning as being derived where readers and the text intersect, in a transaction in which both participate. Thus, meaning is neither solely in the text nor in the reader. Through transacting with the text, the reader creates meaning, drawing upon the reader's background of experiences as well as knowledge about language.

- The reader's stance toward the text matters. Reading experience can vary, depending on whether readers are reading to get information or complete a task, rather than having what Rosenblatt termed an "aesthetic" experience, which involves reading simply for enjoyment.

- Although readers often do read informational text to gain information, such reading can also be an aesthetic experience, involving emotions, especially with respect to literary nonfiction.

- Readers need to be able to know how to adjust their reading according to purposes, but schooling has ignored reading as an aesthetic experience, even when students read literature by requiring analysis and tests and not providing opportunities for reading and an aesthetic experience, akin to what readers do in the real world.

Developing Comprehension and Personal Responses to Literature

Teachers who go into the field of reading and the language arts often found reading and writing rewarding during their own schooling. So, when asked to analyze literature during their schooling, they already saw that they could make connections to literature by trusting their own insights. Many students in Grades 4–8, however, have not succeeded in reading and writing, so they need learning experiences where they can become part of the "reading club" and find ways to connect to literature they read. In the real world, reading is a social experience. Even though readers read on their own, they often will want to talk about what they have read with others. Including **grand conversations** makes it possible for students to discuss what they have read. As teacher and students share their personal responses, important ideas or rigorous questions are highlighted, a phenomenon consistent with the tenets of Rosenblatt's transactional theory. Ways to promote comprehension and personal responses to literature include the following:

- Grand conversations provide authentic reading experiences in which students share their personal responses, akin to the way readers do in the real world via individual conversations, email exchanges and texts, and book clubs. Through such conversations, students hear the views of others, including the teacher, which expands their experiences with a literary work.

- Students need to learn how to analyze literature. However, Rosenblatt points out, before students can analyze literature, they need to be confident that their thoughts about it are legitimate. In addition, students are likely to miss the aesthetic reading experience when reading just to complete a task or for the sake of analysis.

- Teachers support students' comprehension by providing instruction that recognizes the role of personal responses in reading. Students read a work and share their personal responses orally to a work before they analyze a work.

- By sharing their responses through grand conversations, students read and reflect upon a work. As they formulate their thoughts in the course of discussion, they consider what they like or do not like, evaluate big ideas that emerge from the work, and draw connections between concepts in the work and with their own life experiences.

- Students' interpretations need not be consistent with what happens in the text, but when two diverge, an opportunity for teaching arises. The teacher and fellow students can then share alternative understandings based on what is in the text.

- Rather than assessing comprehension by asking questions, teachers model by sharing their responses to what took place in the work and by reflecting on big ideas that emerge. This sharing by the teacher teaches comprehension by modeling how a competent reader thinks about a work. The sharing by the teacher also "invites" students to share, just as conversations do in other settings.

- The teacher expands students' understanding of a work, including by highlighting critical points they want students to focus on. This fosters critical thinking. However, instead of asking questions that point directly to something in the work, the teacher shares reaction to the work.

- Modeling by the teacher shows how a competent reader thinks. In so doing, the teacher sets the tone and invites students to share by joining a conversation rather than taking part in a question-and-answer recitation. The replies of the teacher to students' comments also can show and encourage evaluative/critical thinking, thereby expanding students' reading experiences.

- Although all students may not feel confident in sharing, all will gain as they hear the thoughts of their peers, and more will feel confident over time as they feel safe in sharing.

- Competent readers' responses are consistent with what the text presents, so students also can be encouraged to look more closely at the text if the text has been overlooked as they formed a response (rather than being told the response is wrong).

- The oral language experiences provide scaffolding for students as they subsequently analyze a literary work and learn to commit that analysis to writing.

Instruction Featuring Literary Elements & Devices

- As students see that their thoughts are accepted as legitimate, they engage in closer reading to analyze literature and are freed to engage with big ideas elicited in the text.

- By reflecting on a work through subsequent close reading, teachers and students can focus on literary elements or literary devices writers use to understand the work and the craft of writing.

- While it is important to help students understand literary elements, instruction should not sap the joy of literature in the name of teaching. Don't let memorization overtake engagement.

    o   As with informational/expository texts, literature, too, warrants a **gradual release of responsibility**, teachers provide scaffolding as students learn to analyze or interpret literature. The time necessary for the release of responsibility varies with the **difficulty of the task** and **students' abilities** to accomplish the task. However, bear in mind that students are indeed learning, and gaining the necessary tools at each phase, to move toward independent work.

    o   The teacher provides demonstrations or thinks aloud to show how to engage in a task.

    o   The teacher and students work together.

    o   The teacher provides guided practice for students, offering feedback as needed.

    o   Students work independently once the teacher knows they can.

Levels of Comprehension and Abilities of Successful Readers

Comprehension is the central goal of reading. Readers' levels of comprehension should be taken into account in teaching and assessment. A look at those varying levels follows:

- **Literal**—Literal comprehension is "reading the lines," or understanding what is stated in the text. This level of comprehension is the least demanding of readers; still, being able to understand what is directly stated is the basis for higher levels of comprehension. Questions that assess literal comprehension require an answer that is explicitly stated or can be quoted.

- **Inferential**—Inferential comprehension, or "reading between the lines," requires the reader to arrive at understanding by connecting ideas between the literal sentences or connecting what is said in the text to what the reader knows. Questions that assess inferential comprehension do not have an answer explicitly stated and require the reader to conjecture by using evidence from the text and reasoning. When reading literature, drawing inferences can entail thinking about what is known in the text about the characters, the plot, and the setting along with what the reader knows. Students can find making inferences challenging because they assume that all questions have an answer explicitly stated in the text.

- **Evaluative**—Evaluative comprehension or "reading beyond the lines" requires the reader to arrive at understanding by contemplating what they believe, think, and have experienced in relation to what is stated in the text. Evaluative questions can require the reader to refer to the text as they share personal feelings, explain whether they agree or disagree with decisions, and examine positive or negative factors about a situation.

Strategies and Techniques for Fostering Comprehension of Literary Texts

Research has provided insights that teachers can draw upon to foster students' comprehension. Comprehension strategies are approaches that students can use to control their comprehension. While strategies can be helpful, teaching the strategy should be a means to helping students be and feel successful as readers. Knowing a strategy is not the overall purpose of reading, and learning the strategy should not be frustrating for students.

In deciding whether to teach or incorporate a strategy, teachers should assess and then decide. Rather than require all students to engage in a strategy, teachers should incorporate a strategy based upon the reading needs of the students, the difficulty of the text, and the purposes of the reading.

Visualization

Rather than solely reading words, competent readers create a mental picture as they read. If students are unable to retell or recall what they have read, visual imagery can help students become active readers as they interact with the text. The teacher reads and then pauses after reading—leaving enough time to provide a good description. The teacher then tells the students the picture created, including what the teacher sees and feels and how words that helped create the picture that helps understand what is happening in the story. Depending upon what the teacher has just read, the picture could include the setting or what characters said/did. Next, the teacher continues to read and shares the mental picture again. The teacher then asks the student(s) to share. The mental images may be different—owing to differing prior knowledge—even though both are accurate. The teacher may point out, crucially, that two people can have accurate pictures in mind even when those pictures don't match. Then the teacher reads a longer segment, and the teacher and students share again. Once this strategy is familiar to students, they will use visualization when reading.

Self-Monitoring

As we mentioned earlier, comprehension requires forming connections between and among ideas during reading. Proficient readers monitor their understanding of texts as they read. This close attention to the text lets them adjust their rate of reading to fit the purpose and difficulty of the text. A proficient reader, for example, re-reads a section or pauses to contemplate more difficult ideas.

How do teachers encourage self-monitoring? When encountering miscues, step in and ask students whether what they're saying makes sense when a written or oral miscue shows they're missing the meaning of the text. Teachers also can create opportunities for students to engage in self-monitoring by engaging them in discussion of short segments of text rather than waiting until the end. Such discussions help students stay attentive to, and draw out, meaning, and serve to encourage a generally more thoughtful way to read.

Think-Alouds

Through a think-aloud, the teacher helps students monitor their thinking. The teacher reads a section orally and verbalizes while reading. Through a think-aloud, the teacher shows students the type of thinking a competent reader uses or how to create meaning. The verbalizing is what the teacher is doing to monitor comprehension. The section read orally is selected with a view toward the students and the text. Thus, the teacher could pick a section with vocabulary or sentence structure (syntax) that could be challenging. This gives the teacher the opportunity to show students how to reread a sentence they do not initially understand; how to use context clues to figure out unknown words; and how to continue reading to see whether the text bears out their predictions.

Gist Statements and Setting Purposes for Reading

Before students read, teachers should provide gist statements—that is, brief statements (20 words or less) that list the names of characters and hint at the plot, in a bare-bones way, without revealing all that takes place. Similarly, students also can be given a purpose for reading that encourage students to read actively, such as reading to talk about what happened in the story and what you feel about what happened.

Retelling

As discussed earlier under Competency 001 (Oral Language), after reading a story or segment of a story, students retell what they have read. Students in the group relate what has taken place. Retelling helps students recall what they just read as they tell what happened in their own words. Before students are asked to retell, the teacher should model and should join in students' retellings if students leave out important information. A basic retelling would include the setting, characters, and what took place. In retelling what took place, the retelling includes the major events of the story as well as the problem and resolution of the problem. Retelling can help ensure students have understood the plot or what has taken place. As students' retellings become more advanced, they could include inferences about what took place and evaluations.

Teaching Students Strategies for Comprehending Literary Works

In guiding students how to analyze literature featuring literary elements or devices, teachers should use a **gradual release of responsibility** when introducing a strategy. Students should not be asked to use a strategy on their own until the students are familiar with the strategy and can benefit from it. The time needed for gradual release of responsibility to take place depends upon the **difficulty of the task** and **students' abilities** in performing the task. However, students are learning at each phase to move towards independent work.

Using a **gradual release of responsibility**, teachers provide scaffolding:

1) The teacher provides demonstrations or thinks aloud to show how to engage in a task. ("I do.")

2) The teacher and students work together. ("We do.")

3) The teacher provides guided practice for students, offering with feedback as needed. ("You do, and I help if needed.")

4) Students work independently once the teacher knows they can. ('You do.")

Guided Reading Groups and Small-Group Instruction

Guided reading is small-group instruction where the teacher works with students who are reading at approximately the same reading level. Although students can profit from heterogeneous groups for the independent work, guided reading groups works best with homogenous grouping where students are reading a text at the instructional level for all. Students can be overwhelmed and unable to make gains when they are reading texts that are not too hard because too many words are unknown. The texts for guided reading are ones the student can read with some support from the teacher, so the students can make gains. Through this small-group instruction, the teacher also can provide more individualized attention.

Guided reading/small-group reading can take place during language arts blocks, but it also can take place during science and social studies when students learn from textbooks that are more difficult to read. If students cannot read the textbook, teachers can use shared reading, where students follow along as the teacher reads. In time, students will gain in sight vocabulary so that they can read a text.

The three parts of a guided reading lesson work together to help the students learn how to be more proficient readers: before reading, during reading, and after reading. A story the students read with a teacher during one week could be one the students are able to read independently subsequently. Through support in learning how to read textbooks or other types of informational texts, students will be better able to read them as they advance in their schooling.

Before Reading

Before reading, the teacher builds or activates background knowledge helpful for understanding the text. As discussed earlier, the teacher also helps students equip themselves to handle aspects of the text which are unfamiliar, including unknown words. These unknown words can be terms the students cannot identify or that they need to understand. The teacher also can help students preview the text to examine speech bubbles, charts, bold print, and headings to point out how these features of the text play a role in reading the text successfully.

During Reading

During reading, the students read silently (or in a soft voice if the students are young children/beginning readers) the story or designated segment. If some students finish and others have not, those that have done so know to read the text again, which helps with fluency. The teacher listens to individual students read aloud to assess their ability to recognize words and to provide prompts to help decode unknown words. The teacher usually cannot listen to all read in one day, but the teacher can listen to some read one day and the rest the next day.

During reading is a critical time because the teacher can determine what needs to be addressed during word study, such as which words students do not know, whether students read fluently, and whether students know how to use multiple cues for word analysis. Lower ability readers often will over-rely upon context clues such as illustrations or what makes sense because they do not have strong word identification abilities. Teachers create brief anecdotal notes so they can address the needs of students during word-study instruction.

Teachers also teach during reading as they respond to a student's miscues because students are shown how to use all sources of information or cueing systems: to look at the print (visual cues), to think about what sounds right (language structure cues), and what makes sense (meaning cues).

During reading also can encompass time devoted to developing comprehension. If texts are not complex for students, they can read the text without support from the teacher during reading. However, if students have difficulty with comprehension of stories, during reading can be a time to guide the students by reading with them short segments and showing students how to visualize what they have read.

Informational texts present demands that stories do not, so even capable readers can profit from the teacher showing them strategies for comprehending the text. The amount of support from the teacher would depend upon the students' ability, the purpose for reading, and how complex the informational text is for students. When students are reading expository texts as part of subject-matter learning, all can profit from the teacher showing a strategy for not only comprehending but also learning information. Students may be able to understand what they read as they encounter ideas, but that does not ensure they are able to connect ideas as they read and know the relationships among ideas.

After Reading

After reading, the teacher and students discuss the story. Teachers can begin by asking students to recall what happened to ensure students understand while also helping them to remember and write about what happened. After retelling, students can discuss the story to engage in higher levels of comprehension by making inferences, forming connections among texts (text-to-text connections), or connections to their lives (text-to-self connections). Students also can discuss themes or lessons that emerge from the text. Through authentic discussions, students can learn through the contributions or modeling of the teacher where important ideas can be brought up without a question-and-answer recitation. Students also learn from each other.

Reading informational texts requires reading and discussing short segments to check for understanding and recall. Working with students can take place during reading or afterward as they apply a strategy to read a text more carefully and process the information. Students can discuss ideas and how to take notes by using headings to help remember details about a topic.

After reading also is devoted to word study, during which the teacher can teach students, when needed, how to spell and determine meanings of words. Teachers also can share reading strategies with which students are less well acquainted, such as how to use context, how to read with expression, or how to read charts.

Providing Scaffolding for Students' Silent Reading

Silent reading is critical for students' reading development because it provides the opportunity for students to orchestrate skills, which is when students grow as readers. In other words, students learn to read by reading. Students do need direct, systematic instruction. However, engaging in sustained, silent reading is necessary. Reading short passages and answering comprehension questions may help students learn strategies for taking exams and becoming test sophisticated. However, the strongest readers actually read, and they read literature.

Teachers often are not sure students will read or can read the text on their own, so they resort to asking students to read a text aloud, taking turns. Instead of using round-robin reading, which is detrimental to reading development, teachers can show students how to read in soft voices or silently thorough guided reading/small-group instruction. Students can be assigned to small groups while the rest of the class engages in independent reading activities. For students struggling to identify words in a text, the teacher can use shared reading where the teacher reads and students follow along. For students who can read words but are unable to stay engaged, the teacher can ask them to read and discuss short segments; this will help students monitor their reading while also building stamina. Audio-recordings of books provide another way for students to engage in reading silently as they follow along with the book being read aloud.

A most important way to provide scaffolding for students' silent reading is to read aloud each day to show students that reading can be rewarding. When teachers read aloud from books students enjoy, students want to read those books once more. By carefully selecting books to read aloud, teachers can ensure students become aware of a range of types of quality literature students enjoy. In addition to fiction, daily reading aloud can include literary nonfiction and poetry. Teachers often assume that older students enjoy solely chapter books, but current picture books also provide works older students find engaging. Some of the finest illustrators create picture books based upon short stories or traditional literature where illustration becomes a prime vehicle for storytelling. For young children, picture books bring to life folktales that often were originally created orally by adults for adults, but are accessible to, and enjoyed by, all ages.

Teachers can feature books to read aloud by setting them in a special place in the classroom library. Teachers also can set aside a time regularly to showcase books the teacher is adding to the classroom library, which can be ones borrowed from the school library. These books can include special requests from students, such as a book by a particular author.

Another important dimension of daily silent reading is to include letting students select what they read rather than limiting silent reading to assigned reading. When students self-select, they have "ownership" of their reading, the way readers do in the world beyond the classroom.

COMPETENCY 006: WRITTEN LANGUAGE—WRITING CONVENTIONS

The teacher understands the conventions of writing in English and provides instruction that helps students develop proficiency in applying writing conventions.

The beginning teacher:

A. Knows predictable stages in the development of writing conventions (including the physical and cognitive processes involved in letter formation, word writing, sentence construction, spelling, punctuation and grammatical expression) and recognizes that individual variations occur.

B. Knows and applies appropriate instructional strategies and sequences to teach writing conventions and their applications to all students, including English learners (in accordance with the ELPS).

C. Knows informal and formal procedures for assessing students' use of writing conventions and uses multiple ongoing assessments to monitor and evaluate students' development in this area.

D. Uses ongoing assessment of writing conventions to determine when a student needs additional help or intervention to bring the student's performance to grade level, based on state content and performance standards for writing in the Texas Essential Knowledge and Skills (TEKS).

E. Analyzes students' errors in applying writing conventions and uses the results of this analysis to develop and adjust future instruction.

F. Knows writing conventions and appropriate grammar and usage and provides students with direct instruction and guided practice in these areas.

G. Understands the use of conventional spelling and its importance for success in reading and writing.

H. Understands stages of spelling development (prephonetic, phonetic, transitional and conventional) and how and when to support students' development from one stage to the next.

I. Provides systematic spelling instruction and gives students opportunities to use and develop spelling skills in the context of meaningful written expression.

Role and Importance of Writing Conventions

Think of writing conventions as a way to be "polite" to the reader. Establishing content can be the most challenging part of writing, but teachers also need to devote time to writing conventions such as handwriting, capitalization, punctuation, usage, and spelling. Instruction needs to regularly include time for skill development and for students to apply writing conventions as they write.

Handwriting instruction needs to help students know how to use manuscript as well as cursive writing. Because of the large amounts of time students spend using keyboards, some may question the usefulness of handwriting instruction. However, many legal documents require a signature, and some documents require printing as well as providing a signature. Additionally, some people prefer to hand-write a manuscript and then type the final draft, and people also use writing in their lives in other ways, such as signing a card. Handwriting instruction should help students write in legible, efficient ways. Letter-formation guides have been developed for teachers to show students how to properly form letters; if these are used, students can write more efficiently since English is written left to right.

Systematic spelling instruction should be a part of schooling. Once students know some consonants and at least one short vowel sound, they can start to build words by changing the initial consonant, such as *sat* to *cat*, and then changing the final consonant such as *cat* to *can*. Once another vowel sound is known, students can see how to change the medial vowel of CVC words, such as *cat* to *cut*. Other phonics generalizations and high-frequency words also need to be taught early on because these appear not only when students read but also when they write. Spelling instruction should include aspects of morphemic/structural analysis, including multisyllabic words. Knowing the spelling patterns featured in phonics generalizations provides a basis for knowing the major types of syllables, such as closed syllables, open syllables, *r*-controlled syllables, and vowel team syllables (as discussed under Competency 003: Word Identification Skills and Reading Fluency). Students also can learn commonly confused and misspelled words.

Students also need regular skill lessons on capitalization, punctuation, and usage. The TEKS curriculum delineates the aspects of capitalization, punctuation, and usage students need to know according to grade level. English handbooks provide guidance that teachers can use as they help ensure their students receive instruction. By developing checklists and using anecdotal records, teachers can make sure students master skills. Skill instruction of any type is best provided for no more than 10 to 20 minutes at a time, focusing upon one type of skill or a few words to learn how to spell. Spending more time can lead to diminishing returns and take time away from other important facets of instruction. However, reinforcement and review over time will allow students to build upon what they have learned.

Role of Proofreading in Publishing Conferences

Along with systematic skills instruction, students need to be able to apply skills for real reasons. During the **publishing conference**, the teacher meets with a small group of students to guide students as they proofread their draft to create a final draft or "publish" their work. Students understand that just as professional writers rely upon proofreading, they also can develop a polished product. Students may write final drafts to be displayed on the bulletin board, or they could develop a book to be added to the class library or a classroom document, or given as a gift. Because students are writing for a broader audience beyond solely the teacher, students are more apt to want to invest time in proofreading.

To prepare for the conference, the teacher reads each student's draft and decides upon two skills to teach to each student. During the conference, the teacher shows students how to use an editing checklist to check for spelling, capitalization, and punctuation. The children use one color of ink pen to mark these. The editing checklists become more sophisticated as students learn more about writing conventions (i.e., spelling, capitalization, and punctuation, and usage.) The teacher has short lessons on one or two aspects of writing conventions with each student, while the others listen. The teacher always should start off by telling the student what he or she did well, and then show what needs to be changed. The focus of the revision should be on just a couple of factors to avoid overwhelming the student and blocking the very learning that should take place. After the student makes the edits, the teacher reviews the document again, using different color of pencil, to identify any other possible errors, and to guide the students to produce the final product.

Stages of Spelling Development

Researchers have studied the writing of children and described stages of spelling development. The movement to different stages is gradual; in fact, a speller can have facets of more than one stage at a time. Age levels are approximate, as children vary according to their experiences with print and the extent of spelling instruction they receive. In fact, some experts recommend not thinking of development in terms of grade levels at all, but instead view each student as a unique individual and provide instruction based upon ability.

Precommunicative stage (typically 4 to 6 years old)

The child uses letters, but there is no correspondence between letters and words when the child reads the writing. The child shows knowledge that letters are used in writing. The writing looks like a random array of letters. The child has a message in mind, but a reader would not be able to read the message. The child may not know that writing moves left to right on the page.

M E M M S (I am with my dog.)

Semiphonetic stage (typically 4 to 6 years old)

The child knows that sounds in words are represented by letters. The child uses the name of a letter to represent sounds, words, and syllables. Spelling is abbreviated. This stage is the beginning of "invented spelling" where the child starts to account for the sounds heard in words.

R (are) U (you) B (be)

The child begins to establish letter-sound correspondence—which defines how sounds are assigned to specific letters and letter combinations. At this stage, the child often uses rudimentary logic, using single letters, for example, to represent words, sounds, and syllables (e.g., *U* for *you*).

Phonetic stage (typically 5 to 7 years old)

The child represents all the major speech sounds he/she can hear in a word. Although the words may not be spelled in a conventional manner, the spellings are systematic and can be understood.

TAK (take)   CHRAN (train)   CHRUK (truck)

Transitional stage (typically 6 to 11 years old)

The child starts to not rely solely upon representing sounds to spell. The child also starts to use visual and morphological information. Many common words are known, and the child may use common letter strings, such as *igh*. Using visual information may result in reversing letters in words: *siad* (said).

Correct/Conventional stage (typically 10 to 11+ years old)

The speller knows nearly all the sound-symbol principles. The speller has learned generalizations as well as irregular spellings of words. The speller can use prefixes, suffixes, and silent consonants. Commonly misspelled words and instances of individual words could create difficulty.

COMPETENCY 007: WRITTEN LANGUAGE—COMPOSITION

The teacher understands that writing to communicate is a developmental process and provides instruction that promotes students' competence in written communication.

The beginning teacher:

A. Knows predictable stages in the development of written language and recognizes that individual variations occur.

B. Promotes student recognition of the practical uses of writing, creates an environment in which students are motivated to express ideas in writing and models writing as an enjoyable activity and a tool for lifelong learning.

C. Knows and applies appropriate instructional strategies and sequences to develop students' writing skills (e.g., effective introduction, clearly stated purpose, controlling ideas).

D. Knows characteristics and uses of informal and formal written language assessments and uses multiple, ongoing assessments to monitor and evaluate students' writing development.

E. Uses assessment results to plan focused instruction to address the writing strengths, needs, and interests of all individuals and groups, including English learners (in accordance with the ELPS).

F. Uses ongoing assessment of written language to determine when a student needs additional help or intervention to bring the student's performance to grade level, based on state content and performance standards for writing in the Texas Essential Knowledge and Skills (TEKS).

G. Understands the use of self-assessment in writing and provides opportunities for students to self-assess their writings (e.g., for clarity, interest to audience, comprehensiveness) and their development as writers.

H. Understands differences between first-draft writing and writing for publication, and provides instruction in various stages of writing, including prewriting, drafting, editing, and revising.

I. Understands and teaches writing as a tool for inquiry, research, and learning.

J. Provides instruction about plagiarism, academic honesty and integrity as applied to students' written work and their presentation of information from different sources, including electronic sources.

K. Teaches students to critically evaluate the sources they use for their writing.

L. Understands the development of writing in relation to the other language arts and uses instructional strategies that connect these various aspects of language.

M. Understands similarities and differences between the language (e.g., syntax, vocabulary) used in spoken and written English and helps students use knowledge of these similarities and differences to enhance their own writing.

N. Understands writing for a variety of audiences, purposes, and settings and provides students with opportunities to write for various audiences, purposes, and settings.

O. Knows how to write using voices and styles appropriate for different audiences and purposes, and provides students with opportunities to write using various voices and styles.

P. Understands the benefits of technology for teaching writing and writing for publication and provides instruction in the use of technology to facilitate written communication.

Process and Product in Writing

Writing instruction should help students learn the strategies and techniques successful writers use, and the conditions for writing should be those that foster growth in writing proficiency. Much of traditional writing instruction focuses solely or mostly on the end product. Typically, students get a writing assignment and work on their own to complete it. The teacher then grades the finished assignment. The grade may depend on how well the writing establishes content or presents ideas. The grade also may be based on how well the student applies the conventions of spelling, punctuation, capitalization, and usage. This focus on the final product fails to keep in mind the process of writing—what happens when people write. Focusing on the finished product provides feedback only at the end of the process without providing support for the process itself.

Current theory and research emphasize that effective writing instruction should support students *during* the process to help them develop a better product and become proficient writers. During the process, attention first focuses on establishing content, but instruction should not dismiss the application of writing conventions when writing is going to be "published" or shared with others. Students thus should be shown how to proofread their writing for others to read.

By writing rough drafts, students learn to establish content and share their writing so that others can understand it. By paying attention to the final product, students then further learn to apply conventions of spelling, punctuation, capitalization, and usage.

Writing instruction should recognize that students can vary where they are in the process even when they all are writing daily. Some students may finish a piece on the second day, while others may be working on a piece for several days. Students just need to know that when they finish a piece, they should begin another. Over a few weeks, teachers can ask students to select one piece for "publishing" and thus sharing its final draft. They then learn further proofreading so that what they share adheres to conventions of spelling, punctuation, capitalization, and usage.

Daily Writing Instruction and Structure of Writing Workshop

By using a **writing workshop** approach, teachers can provide conditions for learning akin to how writers write in the real world. In a writing workshop, students write daily to gain fluency through practice, as they do when engaging in reading and other learning. Progress does not come with occasional writing or doing it only for periodic assessments.

A writing workshop is a structured way to help students gain proficiency. Each part plays a role, and, when combined, support students' development by helping them learn strategies and techniques as well as providing authentic writing experiences and conditions for learning. The simple, predictable structure of a workshop helps students by letting them know what to expect each day. Students who know they will write each day also think about topics even when they are outside of school. A predictable structure also helps teachers because they know what they will do rather than having to choreograph something each day or week. Structure is not regimentation; it avoids chaos.

Through **mini-lessons**, teachers help students learn what they need to learn. At the start of the writing workshop each day, students meet as a group. Mini-lessons are brief but maintain the same focus over more than one day, depending on students' needs. The teacher first must devote attention to procedures of the writing workshop. These include how to get such materials as each student's writing folder as well as paper and pencils. Procedures also include writing names and dates on drafts and starting another writing task once a draft is finished. Rather than sharpening pencils, students can get another pencil from the materials shelf if a pencil breaks and place the broken pencil in a container.

Mini-lessons focus mostly on the craft of writing, reflecting strategies and techniques that writers use. Instead of lecturing, teachers should think aloud and show students the writing process. For example, the teacher can model how to select a topic by brainstorming and listing what the teacher knows and cares about. The teacher also might show the nature of revision by sharing a draft the teacher is working on and then adding needed details to it. Because teachers also write, teachers can use their drafts to demonstrate what they see students need to learn. Literature previously read aloud also can be reviewed as a **mentor text** to show students how a professional writer uses a strategy or technique.

Mini-lessons could be longer when teaching students about conducting research and writing a report. The teacher does plan mini-lessons based upon the strategies and techniques needed for writing a report. However, the students and teacher should work together in learning how to locate information from sources and take notes, depending upon whether the resources call for reading a book, viewing a video, interviewing a person, and/or observing a plant or animal. Along with needing to know how to gather information, students need to know how to organize notes to write a rough draft. The teacher models the process, but also works with the students as part of a gradual release of responsibility. The scaffolding provided can include selecting the resources for students and developing the headings for the parts of the report, used to organize notes and the drafts, such as where wolves live, the wolf pack, wolf pups, and survival of the wolf. Providing the scaffolding students need helps ensure students can make progress.

Small-group work can build upon mini-lessons. For additional scaffolding, teachers can provide small-group instruction while other students write. Each student should meet the teacher during the week according to a daily schedule created for each group.

During **writing, conferences or small-group work**, the teacher and students write. After about 10 minutes, the teacher should move about the room for **rough-draft conferences** with students. These conferences should go about one to three minutes and focus solely on establishing content, with later proofreading reserved for addressing conventions. As is true of most writers, the student or the teacher reads the piece aloud. The teacher then "receives" the work by telling the student what the teacher heard or learned, using the student's exact words. For example, the teacher might say, "I like the way you told me you wanted to get the red sparkly shoes. That helped me understand exactly the shoes you wanted your grandma to buy for you." Next, the teacher asks questions about anything that needs to be clarified. For example, the teacher might say, "You said you loved the gift your sister gave you. What was the gift she gave you at your birthday party?" This structure lets students know what is working and what needs to be clearer. The conference also can let the teacher help a student with a specific problem, such as selecting a topic. Teachers should not assign a topic— let the students pick it and maintain ownership. Nonetheless, teachers should talk to students and *help* them pick a topic they know and care about. By talking with the teacher, students can discover a topic of interest. This way, students are more apt to express their own ideas.

Whole-class sharing can occur daily to let students share their writing beyond the teacher. A few students can sign up to share each day. All who want to share should have the opportunity, but it should not be required of students who do not wish to do so. Students learn from each other in whole-group conferences, which should be structured like the rough-draft conferences with the teacher. The student reads the piece aloud. The students then "receive" the work by telling the student what they heard or learned. Next, the students ask genuine questions that can show where the piece needs clarification.

The structure of a writing workshop can remain the same with any writing. The content to be learned changes according to what students need and what needs to be taught. The structure provides opportunities for growth while managing the class. The structure also provides differentiated instruction because students participate according to their abilities while getting support from the teacher as well as their classmates.

Publishing Conferences

Publishing conferences can occur while students write. Kindergartners and early first-grade students do not proofread, and their invented spelling should be recognized as positive, not as an error. Invented spelling contributes to phonemic awareness, which is central to learning to read and write, and should not be discouraged. Once students master conventional spelling, however, teachers should have publishing conferences. After two or three weeks, students should select one piece to be published from their folders. While students should move at their own pace in writing, they should write daily. During those two or three weeks, students should put a piece for "publishing" in an editing tray. When enough students do this, the teacher conducts a publishing conference at the table. For rough-draft conferences, the teacher moves among students, but publishing conferences take place in small groups gathered at a table.

The teacher prepares for publishing conferences by reading each draft to determine what the student can do and where the student needs help. The teacher records this on an anecdotal record sheet kept for each student to document skill development. When focusing on writing to capture their thoughts, students devote attention to establish content. First drafts thus may have errors in such writing conventions as spelling, punctuation, capitalization and usage even when they can otherwise spell a word or use another convention correctly. As students gain proficiency, they will apply the skill more often when writing drafts.

During the publishing conference with a small group, the teacher shows how to use an editing checklist for spelling, capitalization, punctuation, and usage. Students use one ink color for marking. Students' checklists become more sophisticated as they learn more about the conventions of writing.

The teacher conducts short lessons on one or two writing conventions with each student while classmates listen. The teacher starts by telling the student what works and then suggests what should be revised according to the one or two conventions. By limiting the focus of the revision, the teacher avoids overwhelming the student, but the goal is still a final draft without errors.

The teacher corrects errors in a different ink color to distinguish them from the student's. This is done before a final draft is typed or written and not during the conference. The teacher or the student then types or hand-writes the piece without errors. If the student types well, the teacher lets them produce the final draft on the computer. However, reluctant and less capable writers may rely on the teacher to type a final draft without errors.

Strategies and Techniques of Effective Writing

The most difficult part of writing is establishing content that will be understood by the reader in the way the author intends. The writer expresses a message or purpose. But the writer must also write to be read, and so must work to hold the reader's attention. To develop the best possible piece, writers must develop multiple drafts. Students must follow suit to establish content.

In trying to help students meet the demands of writing a draft, teachers can show students strategies and techniques used by professional writers, much as a coach does. Rather than just "telling" someone what to do, a coach also "shows" and provides support while the student works to mimic the strategy or technique.

Depending on the students' needs and the type of writing being taught, the teacher shows strategies and techniques that writers use, including how to:

- select a topic,

- write rough drafts that focus on establishing content rather than disrupt the process by devoting attention to writing conventions,

- add or delete a word, sentence, or set of sentences,

- spell a word the best you can rather than use a less effective word that is easy to spell,

- elaborate by adding details,

- select a title,

- add dialogue,

- create a picture with words to convey what happened,

- use strong verbs rather than adverbs,

- locate and organize information for writing reports, and

- use resources for reports without plagiarizing.

Voice and Types of Writing

How should the teacher cultivate development of each student's unique **voice** when writing? The teacher first helps students write stories about themselves because personal narratives are meaningful. Students also know what has happened, making it easier to use details and dialogue to create a picture with words. Students also may select topics they know and care about (e.g., soccer, motorcycles, pets) for informal reports that let them share information they have. When students select the topic, they are more likely to be invested in the writing than with a topic chosen by the teacher. Professional writers often write what they know and care about, and it is reasonable to assume that beginning writers will progress more when they share their own experiences and ideas.

State exams and school reports assign topics, but when students get experience at forming their thoughts when writing, they have developed abilities that will help them respond to assigned topics. By writing about what they know and care about, students learn they have something to say when they write. Exams and signed reports also often provide a choice of topics or prompts.

As the school year progresses, students can learn about writing reports, essays, fiction, and poetry. The structure of the writing workshop stays the same, with teachers adapting mini-lessons and group work to the writing to be learned.

Teachers consider the strategies and techniques required to develop the writing and plan mini-lessons that let students implement and practice those strategies. For example, in teaching students how to take notes for a report, the students and the teacher can read the information together. The students then put the ideas on note-taking into their own words.

COMPETENCY 008: VIEWING AND REPRESENTING

The teacher understands skills for interpreting, analyzing, evaluating, and producing visual images and messages in various media and provides students with opportunities to develop skills in this area.

The beginning teacher:

A. Knows grade-level expectations in the Texas Essential Knowledge and Skills (TEKS) and procedures for assessing students' skills in interpreting, analyzing, evaluating, and producing visual images, messages, and meanings.

B. Uses ongoing assessment and knowledge of grade-level expectations in the Texas Essential Knowledge and Skills (TEKS) to identify students' needs regarding the interpretation, analysis, evaluation and production of visual images, messages and meanings and to plan instruction.

C. Understands characteristics and functions of different types of media (e.g., film, print) and knows how different types of media influence and inform.

D. Compares and contrasts print, visual, and electronic media (e.g., films and written stories).

E. Evaluates how visual image makers (e.g., illustrators, documentary filmmakers, political cartoonists, news photographers) represent messages and meanings and provides students with varied opportunities to interpret and evaluate visual images in various media.

F. Knows how to teach students to analyze visual image makers' choices (e.g., style, elements, media) and evaluate how these choices help to represent or extend meaning.

G. Provides students with opportunities to interpret events and ideas based on information from maps, charts, graphics, video segments, and technology presentations and to use media to compare ideas and points of view.

H. Knows steps and procedures for producing visual images, messages, and meanings to communicate with others.

I. Teaches students how to select, organize and produce visuals to complement and extend meanings.

J.   Provides students with opportunities to use technology to produce various types of com-munications (e.g., digital media, class news-papers, multimedia reports, video reports, movies) and helps students analyze how language, medium, and presentation contribute to the message.

Visual Images and Messages of Media

Literacy development is not limited to spoken and written language. Students also must pro-duce and understand visual images as well as learn and solve problems in visual spheres. Just as they engage in authentic use and get scaffolding from the teacher to gain oral and written literacy, students will progress in visual literacy when they get systematic opportunities to engage in it while supported by effective instruction.

Students need to develop the skills needed to create and understand images and messages presented in different media. The skills increase in complexity as students move from lower to upper elementary grades. For example, even younger students can produce visual representations as they they learn as (e.g., create an image of a plant to document the growth of the plant). Students also must know how to discuss the visual representations they have created. As students advance in schooling, they must understand, interpret, analyze, critique, and produce these visual repre-sentations as well as discuss their meaning or significance through the multiple media, including newsletters, charts, and electronic presentations.

Being able to glean insights and respond to multiple media also is important. Additionally, stu-dents need to be able to synthesize as they engage with various sources of media as part of learning in a discipline. Students also should understand an author's purpose and choice of elements used to convey messages via multiple media. The characteristics and functions of the different media are explained next.

Types and Characteristics of Media

A medium is considered to be any means used to convey information to others. At least three main media are available: **print**, **visual**, and **electronic**. **Print media** disseminate information in print form and include newspapers, magazines, and direct mail. Print media are static; that is, once the information is published, it cannot be changed.

Visual media incorporates visual imagery to complement or supplement the message. Visual media includes photographs, illustrations, paintings, graphic art, films, videos, maps, charts, and graphs. Visual media can also stand alone. For example, photographs and paintings can convey meaning without text. Moreover, visual media are also an integral part of print media to illus-trate messages. As such, visual media can take many forms, including photography, film, and even cartoons. Visual media can be static (e.g., still photograph) or dynamic, as seen in movies or videos. Because visual literacy abilities are used in a variety of disciplines, visual literacy can be developed as part of students' learning in reading/language arts as well as other subject areas. At a basic level, students must observe well enough to identify details accurately. Higher-level abilities include understanding what is seen, including comprehending visual relationships. Some contexts require students to create meaning by integrating images they receive or produce with language they read or write. To facilitate progress in comprehending and producing visual images, teachers must help students learn vocabulary and concepts as well as strategies and techniques used in creating images.

Besides incorporating print and visual imagery, **electronic media** require such external devices as a television, computer, or personal assistant device to display the information and images. Electronic media are used in different fields, including journalism, fine arts, commerce, education, and communications. A primary electronic medium that encompasses different electronic tools is the Internet, which contains photographs, videos, blogs, email, and multiple articles. Electronic books also are available on the web.

When using these electronic media, teachers must remember that technology changes quickly. Tools for presenting information are improved and refined. For instance, photography has evolved from being created on photographic plates and then film to now being created digitally. Teachers should realize a vast array of possibilities to create and display information is available via existing media. As the need for using and sharing massive amounts of information with others becomes necessary, some media will take precedence over others. For example, the use of online information has become so pervasive that static media, like print media, are now being channeled electronically (e.g., newspapers and books). The use of online resources and Web sites has become a staple. Students expect those around them to know how to use these tools. Students seek opportunities to use and produce different products through different media.

Representing Messages and Meanings through Media

Charts, tables, graphs, pictures, and print and non-print media are examples of materials used to present or summarize information and/or to complement messages. For instance, a chart can summarize much information without written explanations. Students should understand that visual representations are important and that their purpose is to present information and facilitate communicating the message. Visual images should also be used to make information more understandable.

A graphic can expand or illustrate a concept, support points, summarize data, organize facts, add a dimension to the content (such as a cartoon adding humor), compare information, show change over time, or furnish additional information. Through graphics, the reader can interpret, predict, and apply information with careful observation. Questioning students as they create visual images (e.g., asking what they are trying to convey or how they think someone will interpret their image) as well as providing ongoing feedback may help students to focus and clarify the information they are presenting with graphics.

Understanding How Students May Interpret and Evaluate Visual Images

Teachers should realize that even a graphic that looks uncomplicated may challenge a reader's interpretive skills. Many inferences may be necessary for even the simplest visual aid or graphic. Students may first skip the graphics or skim them without interpreting them. Students also may just focus on the graphics without paying attention to the written explanations. Even students with training in the use of graphic information may fail to transfer that knowledge to other content areas or have trouble going from print to graphic and then back to print. In either case, students may not have been taught how to use multiple representations of information. Teachers can help students use multiple representations of information via open-book and guided reading. A teacher can also show how to use a chart or graph via electronic tools, including computerized overhead projectors and interactive whiteboards. Examples of effective presentations and how to create them can be shared with the students. Resources and software to improve their writing, typically described as mentor texts (Dorfman & Cappelli, 2007), provide examples of how to select images to use with text (e.g., consideration of how the image parallels or complements the text).

Visual design can be viewed as containing its own grammar (Kress & van Leeuwen, 2001). Teachers can help students to understand and apply such visual grammar by teaching its component parts (Wysocki, et al., 2004). Some of these key components are:

- **Visual impact:** how the overall visual design appeals to the reader (e.g., through detail, layout, and color).

- **Visual coherence:** how the design creates unity and wholeness (e.g., via shapes, line, imagery).

- **Visual salience:** using design features to generate a desired effect (e.g., through varying sizes, colors, clip art, etc.)

- **Organization:** how the layout of the page creates a unique pattern understandable to the readers, through consideration of how items in the layout might be arranged on the page).

These features of visual literacy overlap and can guide students toward an awareness of the visual literacy.

Teachers should model how to read, complement, and interpret visual images whenever students are required to create them. Pictures and other graphics can arouse interest and stimulate thinking. Graphics also can add clarity, prevent misunderstanding, show step-by-step development, and exhibit the status of things, events, and processes, as well as demonstrate comparisons and contrasts (Vacca and Vacca 1989).

Integrating Technology in the Classroom

Teachers should provide students with opportunities to use state-of-the-art technology and tools. Doing so will motivate children to read and write as well as monitor their writing and enable them to communicate with different media. For instance, one could assume that the goal of word-processing software is simply to record written information. With technological advances, such software now offers writers help with the editing their documents. Other uses for this software include creating semantic maps, tables, charts, and graphs. Such writing-related elements as spell check, definitions of terms, thesaurus, and even suggestions for sentence constructions are commonly available in programs like Microsoft Word. A spell checker not only helps identify misspelled words but also frees students from the pressure of spelling things right, at least at the drafting stage. Students should be encouraged to put their ideas in writing without stopping to check spelling. When they finish writing, they address other important concerns like spelling. Students also should be reminded that the spell checker won't always work, owing, for instance, to its ignorance of proper nouns (including names) and homophones. Therefore, children should be guided to pay attention to corrections and learn from them.

Teachers should show children how to take advantage of programs available for communicating and creating electronic products. The products they can create include a classroom newsletter, a multimedia presentation, and a video response to a group project. Students should keep their audience and purpose in mind when they create their pieces. Doing so will also help them make sure the language they use is appropriate and understandable for their audience.

Multimodal literacy

Leaders in reading/language arts education provide guidance for fostering **multimodal literacy**, which includes art, text, speech, drama, and physical movement as well as digital literacy. Multimodal literacy takes the following into account:

- Developing students' learning in different modes of expression should be among their curricular goals. In addition, ample time and resources should be allocated.

- Electronic environments should provide students with quick access to a wide range of information platforms to meet the expanded the ways of acquiring information and understanding concepts. However, students also must be shown techniques for locating, selecting, organizing, and evaluating information.

- Multimodal projects are inherently complex, and students will vary in the abilities they bring to the projects, which thus will require substantial collaboration and teamwork. When students work together, the process should foster increased learning as well as better outcomes when they create such products as brochures, magazines, books, videos, or greeting cards.

- An exclusive emphasis on digital literacy can limit (crowd out) students' exposure and access to other modes of communication.

COMPETENCY 009: STUDY AND INQUIRY SKILLS

The teacher understands the importance of study and inquiry skills as tools for learning in the content areas and promotes students' development in applying study and inquiry skills.

The beginning teacher:

A. Understands study and inquiry skills (e.g., using text organizers; taking notes; outlining; drawing conclusions; applying test-taking strategies; previewing; setting purposes for reading; locating, organizing, evaluating, synthesizing and communicating information; summarizing information; using multiple sources of information; correctly recording bibliographic information for notes and sources; interpreting and using graphic sources of information) and knows the significance of these skills for student learning and achievement.

B. Knows grade-level expectations for study and inquiry skills in the Texas Essential Knowledge and Skills (TEKS) and procedures for assessing students' development and use of these skills.

C. Knows and applies instructional practices that promote the acquisition and use of study and inquiry skills across the curriculum by all students, including English learners (in accordance with the ELPS).

D. Knows how to provide students with varied and meaningful opportunities to learn and apply study and inquiry skills to enhance their achievement across the curriculum.

E. Uses ongoing assessment and knowledge of grade-level expectations in the Texas Essential Knowledge and Skills (TEKS) to identify students' needs regarding study and inquiry skills, to determine when a student requires additional help or intervention and to plan instruction.

F. Responds to students' needs by providing direct, explicit instruction to promote the acquisition and use of study and inquiry skills.

Challenges of Reading and Writing to Learn

Students' learning in subject areas entails comprehending what they read. But textbooks and other information documents present varying and specific challenges. For one thing, students may assume that content-area texts can be read the same way they read a story. But even students who can read fiction easily may find content-area texts to be challenging. Students must read these texts to learn, and that means they must also know how to study.

Academic Vocabulary

A major challenge in content-area texts is an **academic vocabulary** that often consists of words students encounter only in that discipline. Acquiring content-specific vocabulary is essential to relating concepts that require in-depth understanding. Such understanding does not come from merely memorizing a glossary definition.

Text Structure

Another challenge of informational texts is using their **text structure** to understand and remember how concepts and ideas relate. Readers have a schema for stories, and they can retell stories and comprehended them as they read. The text structures of informational texts differ from the structure of narratives and are instead based on how information is organized in each field. The text structure in a chapter also can differ depending on how ideas relate. For example, a description of a battle could be presented, and description is a type of text structure. At the same time, however, the description of the battle could be part of the cause and effect type of text structure the author uses to present a major event in history. Expository texts typically demand more than a single straight-through reading to allow for complete understanding and recall of the information.

Comprehension and Learning

Even when students comprehend a content-area text, their education depends on learning new information. They need to retain that information and be able to write about what they have read.

With new information, students typically must study it to learn it. Some information can be grasped readily when students have relevant background information or prior learning. However, *even capable readers* face challenges when reading and writing to learn. Students rely on instruction to help them comprehend the texts, and they also must be shown how to take notes and prepare for tests.

Demands of Reading Informational or Expository Texts

Students have a schema for stories or the narrative structure of fiction, so a story can often be read straight through, and students can recall what took place. However, topics in the expository text of social studies, science, and other subjects have their own inherent structures, and this is determined by how a subject is organized. The author of an informational or expository text uses the organization in presenting ideas and in connecting ideas. Students must discern this text structure when reading the text to create a text model in their minds.

Successful reading and learning requires understanding the major ideas, the important supporting details, and how these ideas relate to one another to create a larger understanding of the broader topic.

Previewing by examining the title, headings, and illustrations can help readers anticipate what they are going to read. Proficient reading also includes recognizing features of text and using them to understand. **Text features** include the following: illustrations, images, diagrams, labels, captions, graphs, charts, timetable, bold print, italics, headings and subheadings, glossary table of contents, index.

When students read expository text, they can overlook features of text that are important for comprehending and learning. Students will best learn about the roles of text features if they are shown how to use text features that are relevant in the text they are reading.

Role of Instruction in Reading to Learn

What is the role of instruction in reading to learn using **informational** or **expository** texts? Consider first that students cannot readily remember the information that is new, but teachers can help put this more readily within students' grasp.

Students need to be shown that proficient readers change their approach when reading to learn. Through modeling and guidance, teachers can help students understand the major ideas (of headings) and supporting details and how these major ideas relate to each other in presenting information about a topic (as indicated in the title). At times, the author does not use headings, but students also can be shown how to infer what the major idea is by reading the section.

Effective strategies can help students not only comprehend text but also learn content. To incorporate the use of a strategy, teachers must focus on helping students learn the content. If students receive demonstrations and guided practice, they also will learn to use the strategy through real reasons to apply it, not just memorizing its steps. In teaching strategies, it is critical that the teacher provide sufficient modeling to demonstrate how to use each strategy. Guided practice is essential as well. In other words, using a gradual release of responsibility helps students use a strategy effectively:

(1) The teacher demonstrates and the students watch.

(2) The teacher and students do the task together.

(3) The students work together, and the teacher provides monitoring to make sure students understand what to do.

(4) The students are able to work on their own.

Students will vary regarding when they are able to apply a strategy on their own. However, guided practice is itself part of instruction, and is valuable because students not only learn in their current subjects but are also primed for future schooling. Teachers who fail to devote enough time to modeling and guidance will have students who are unlikely to gain much from strategy instruction.

Another way to help students learn is to show them how to read short chunks at a time. Students can be asked to read shorter segments before discussion ensues. The length of an appropriate chunk depends upon the difficulty of the materials and the students' abilities.

Finally, students can profit from writing notes to remember key ideas as well as how these ideas relate to each other. Modeling note-taking and working with students by taking notes together can help students learn. Concept mapping and other visual aids can help students remember ideas and see the conceptual relationships they need to see.

Strategies for Reading to Learn

Directed Reading Thinking Activity (DRTA)

> DRTA is a comprehension strategy that helps students activate prior knowledge, make predictions, and monitor their understanding. It also pertains to Competency 005 (Reading Applications), where it is detailed.

Reciprocal Teaching

> Reciprocal teaching is an instructional strategy that entails four strategies students use to read and understand text: summarizing, question generating, clarifying, and predicting. It also pertains to Competency 005 (Reading Applications), where it is detailed.

Concept Mapping

> Concept mapping is a strategy that uses a visual organizer to help students see the relationship between and among ideas and concepts. It also pertains to Competency 005 (Reading Applications).

SQ4R

> SQ4R is a comprehension and study strategy that enables students to deal with expository text. SQ4R stands for **S**urvey, **Q**uestion, **R**ead, **R**ecite, **R**ecord, **R**eview. This strategy also pertains to Competency 005 (Reading Applications).

K-W-L

K-W-L is a strategy where students discuss and complete three columns of a chart as they read informational or expository text: What I **Know**, What I **Want** to Learn, and What I **Learned**. K-W-L also pertains to Competency 005 (Reading Applications).

Note-Taking

Note-taking is a skill that is rarely taught explicitly in school. Teachers assume incorrectly that taking notes is a skill that students will learn naturally. Learning this skill can have multiple cognitive advantages for students. Taking notes help students identify and summarize relevant information. In the process of note-taking, students receive and process information, and write it in their own words. Moreover, taking legible and relevant notes will guide students to develop a better understanding of the content, and thus, be able to ask meaningful questions in class to corroborate information and to expand on it.

A key challenge in note-taking is to decide what information is relevant. One way to help students is to take notes with them to model the process and provide support as they gain proficiency. If note-taking is a regular part of reading in content areas, students will be able to gain expertise. One way to provide note-taking is when reading expository texts. For example, as students are reading to learn about types of rocks, the teacher can ask students to tell what they just learned. The teacher can create a heading, such as SEDIMENTARY ROCKS, then write what the students say. In this way, students are learning together how to read and put what was said in their own words without copying word for word. By not having to actually write the notes, the students focus on the process of reading and extracting. The notes the teacher records can by typed and used for reviewing each day and for studying for a test. On their own, many students would not take notes effectively, but if the teacher models and guides the development of the notes, students gain in expertise over time. Additionally, the note-taking actually enhances learning subject matter.

Similarly, the teacher can help students master note-taking as students conduct research in learning to write reports. Rather than telling students what to do, the teacher and students can take notes together as they read from a book, view a video, or observe something pertinent (e.g., plant growth) to gather information. The notes gathered can be placed on note cards or sticky notes that are placed under headings that are used to organize the information gathered.

Once students have worked with the teacher, they can work in small groups to gather information on a topic, where students can support each other towards learning how to take notes on their own.

Supporting the Complex Process of Writing Reports

Writing a report is a complex process that entails multiple strategies and techniques:

(1) Select a topic and focus in so the topic is not too broad.

(2) Read or observe to gather information.

(3) Document the sources.

(4) Write to take notes, stating ideas so that information is not copied from the source.

(5) Organize notes in categories that will be the headings or sections of the report.

(6) Develop rough draft(s).

(7) Revise/edit wording of draft(s).

(8) Engage in proofreading for spelling, punctuation, and usage.

(9) Write the final draft.

Each step should be demonstrated by teachers and then used by students as they learn and apply it to the subject area.

To provide scaffolding, teachers and students can work first on learning how to read to gather information, and then, without looking back at the material, write notes in their own words. Gathering information also can include observing plants, animals, and people and viewing digital media. Similarly, the teacher and students can first write a report together before students work in small groups as part of learning how to produce a report on their own.

Guidelines for Instruction in Reading and Writing to Learn

Here are guidelines for instruction to support report writing:

- Strategies can help students read and retain information. However, remember that strategies are a means to an end. Rather than focus on teaching an array of strategies, teachers should think of how to help their students before, during, and after reading and be selective in what they incorporate.

- Learning how to read to learn is a complex process. Students need time to master the procedures as they monitor how much time it will take to learn the content they are expected to know.

- Small-group instruction provides differentiated instruction and guided practice. Other students can work independently or with a partner while the teacher meets a group.

- Less capable readers can learn how to read content-area texts. They will need more scaffolding, and this may be needed before, during, and after reading. If students cannot read the text, teachers can try shared reading in which the teacher reads and students follow, joining in when they can.

- Students should read segments rather than an entire section or chapter because of the demands of content-area texts. The length depends on the complexity of the text and the students' background and ability. If students read in small groups, they can reread a section while others finish.

- Instruction must address not only understanding what is read but also connecting ideas. Students may become confused when they try to remember content-area ideas in the same way they would after reading a story. As a result, instruction must include showing how the ideas of a content-area text connect in a section and how ideas of a passage or chapter relate to each other.

- Understanding vocabulary and concept development is integral to learning in subject areas. Dictionary and glossary definitions do not help students grasp and retain concepts. Students need to understand concepts and how they relate in a unit of study.

- Teachers should think aloud and demonstrate as part of instruction. Guided practice also is needed, and students should not work on their own before they are ready. With guided practice, students not only can learn the content but also gain in learning how to learn.

References

Adams, M.J. (1994). *Beginning to read: thinking and learning about print.* Boston: MIT Press.

Anderson, R.C.; Hiebert, E.H, Scott, J.A.; Wilkinson, I.A.G. (1985) *Becoming a Nation of Readers: The Report of the Commission on Reading.* Washington, D.C. National Academy of Education.

Anderson, R.C., & Pearson, P.D. (1984). A schema-theoretic view of basic processes in reading. In P.D. Pearson, R. Barr, M.L. Kamil, & P. Mosenthal (Eds.), *Handbook of reading research.* White Plains, NY: Longman.

Atwell, N, (2015). *In the middle: A lifetime of learning about reading, writing, and adolescents.* Portsmouth, NH: Heinemann Educational Books.

Beck, I., McKeown, M. & Kucan, L (2013). *Bringing words to life: Robust vocabulary instruction.* New York: The Gilford Press.

Bransford, John D., Brown Ann L., and Cocking Rodney R. (2000). *How people learn: Brain, mind, experience, and school.* Washington, DC: National Academy Press.

Baker, Linda, and Brown, Ann L. (1984). Metacognitive skills and reading. In Paul David Pearson, Michael L. Kamil, Rebecca Barr, & Peter Mosenthal (Eds.), *Handbook of research in reading: Volume III* (pp. 353–395). New York: Longman.

Calkins, L. (1994). *The Art of Teaching Writing*, 2nd ed. Portsmouth, NH: Heinemann.

Cambourne, Brian (1995). Toward an educationally relevant theory of literacy learning: Twenty years of inquiry. *The Reading Teacher*, Vol. 49, No. 3.

Cullinan, B. (2000). Independent reading and school achievement. *School Library Media Research*, 3, 1–24.

Chard, D.J., & Osborn, J. (1998). *Suggestions for examining phonics and decoding instruction in supplementary reading programs.* Austin, TX: Texas Education Agency.

Durkin, D. (1978–79). What classroom observations reveal about reading comprehension instruction. Reading Research Quarterly, 14, 481–533.

Ehri, L.C., Dreyer, L.G., Flugman, B., & Gross, A. (2007). Reading Rescue: An effective tutoring intervention model for language minority students who are struggling readers in first grade. *American Educational Research Journal*, 44(2), 414–448.

Fisher, D., & Frey, N. (2013). *Better learning through structured teaching: A framework for the gradual release of responsibility.* ASCD.

Freeman, D. & Freeman, Y. (2008). *Academic language for struggling readers and English language learners.* Portsmouth, NH: Heinemann.

Fountas, I.C., & Pinnell, G.S. (1996). *Guided reading: Good first teaching for all children.* Portsmouth, NH: Heinemann.

Graves, D.H. (1983). *Writing: Teachers and children at work.* Portsmouth, NH: Heinemann Educational Books.

Graves, D. (1994). *A Fresh Look at Writing.* Portsmouth, NH: Heinemann.

Halliday, M.A.K. (1973). Explorations in the Functions of Language. Amersterdam, Netherlands: Elsevier Science Publisher.

Hiebert, E.H. & Reutzel, D.R.(Eds.) (2010). *Revisiting silent reading: New directions for teachers and researchers.* Newark, DE: International Reading Association.

Hasbrouck, J. & Tindal, G. (2017). *An update to compiled ORF norms* (Technical Report No. 1702). Eugene, OR: Behavioral Research and Teaching, University of Oregon.

Kelley, M.J., & Clausen-Grace, N. (2008). From picture walk to text feature walk: Guiding students to strategically preview informational text. *Journal of Content Area Reading*, 7(1), 9–31.

Kibby, M.W. (1995). The organization and teaching of things and the words that signify them. *Journal of Adolescent & Adult Literacy*, 39(3), 208–233.

Krashen, S.D. (1989). We acquire vocabulary and spelling by reading: Additional evidence for the Input Hypothesis. *Modern Language Journal* 73, 440–64.

LaBerge, D., & Samuels, S.J. (1974). Toward a theory of automatic information processing in reading. *Cognitive Psychology*, 6, 293–323.

Lesaux, N.K. & Geva, E. (2006). Synthesis: Development of literacy in language minority learners. In D. L. August & T. Shanahan (Eds.) *Developing Literacy in a second language: Report of the National Literacy Panel.* (pp. 53–74). Mahwah, NJ: Lawrence Erlbaum Associates.

Lindfors, J.W. (1987). *Children's Language and Learning.* Englewood Cliffs, NJ: Prentice-Hall.

Meyer, B.J.F., Middlemiss, W., Theodorou, E.,S., Brezinski, K.L., McDougall, J., & Bartlett, B.J. (2002). Older adults tutoring fifth-grade children in the structure strategy via the Internet. *Journal of Educational Psychology,* 94 (3), 486–519.

Moats, L. (2020). *Teaching Reading is Rocket Science: What Expert Teachers of Reading Should Know.* Washington, DC: American Federation of Teachers.

Moss, B. & Young, T.A. (2010). *Creating lifelong readers through independent reading.* International Reading Association.

National Center for Education Statistics (2019). *The Nation's Report Card: NAEP Reading Assessments.* Institute of Education Sciences, U.S. Department of Education, Washington, DC.

Nagy, W.E., & Scott, J.A. (2004). Vocabulary processes. In R.B. Ruddell & N.J. Unrau (Eds.), *Theoretical models and processes of reading* (5th ed., pp. 574–593). Newark, DE: International Reading Association.

National Reading Panel. (2000, April). *Report of the National Reading Panel: Teaching children to read.* Washington, DC: National Institute of Child Health and Human Development, National Institutes of Health, U.S. Department of Health and Human Services.

Palincsar, A.S., & Brown, A.L. (1984). Reciprocal teaching of comprehension-fostering and monitoring activities. *Cognition and Instruction*, 1, 117–175.

Pearson, P.D., & Dole, J.A. (1987). Explicit comprehension instruction: A review of research and a new conceptualization of instruction. *Elementary School Journal*, 88, 151–165.

Pearson, P.D., & Fielding, L. (1991). Comprehension instruction. In R. Barr, M.L. Kamil, P.B. Mosenthal, & P.D. Pearson (Eds.), *Handbook of reading research: Volume II* (pp. 815–860). White Plains, NY: Longman.

Peregoy, S.F., O.F. Boyle, & Cadiero-Kapplan, K. (2008). *Reading, writing and learning in ESL: A Resource Book for K–12 Teachers* (5th ed.). New York: Pearson.

Pikulski, J.J., & Chard, D.J. (2005). Fluency: Bridge Between Decoding and Reading Comprehension. *The Reading Teacher*, 58, 510–5.

Pressley, M. (2000). What should comprehension instruction be the instruction of? In M.L. Kamil, P.B. Mosenthal, P.D. Pearson, & R. Barr (Eds.), *Handbook of reading research: Volume III* (pp. 545–561). Mahwah NJ: Erlbaum.

Rasinkski, T., & Padak, N. (1996). *Holistic reading strategies: Teaching children who find reading difficult.* Englewood Cliffs, NJ: Merrill/Prentice Hall.

Ruddell, R.B. (2009). *How to teach reading to elementary and middle school students: Practical ideas from highly effective teachers.* Boston: Allyn & Bacon.

Rosenblatt, L.M. (1978). The reader, the text, the poem: The transactional theory of the literary work. Carbondale, IL: Southern Illinois University Press.

Roskos Kathleen, Neuman Susan B. (2014). *Best Practices in Reading: A 21st Century Skill Update.* The Reading Teacher, 67(7), 507–511.

Rupley, W.H., Logan, J.W., & Nichols, W.D. (1998). Vocabulary instruction in a balanced reading program. The Reading Teacher, 52(4), 336–346.

Snow, C.E., Burns, M.S., & Griffin, P. (1998). *Preventing reading difficulties in young children.* Washington, DC: National Academy Press.

Stahl, K.A.D. (2004). Proof, practice, and promise: Comprehension strategy instruction in the primary grades. *The Reading Teacher*, 57(7), 598–609.

Wysocki, A.F., Johnson-Eilola, J., Selfe, L., & Sirc, G. (2004). Writing new media: Theory and applications for expanding the teaching of composition. Logan, UT: Utah State University Press.

CHAPTER 4

Subject Test II: Mathematics (807)

OVERVIEW OF SUBJECT TEST II: MATHEMATICS

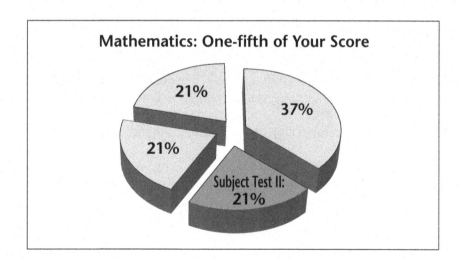

Subject Test II: Mathematics, like the Social Studies and Science subtests, makes up approximately one-fifth of the questions you will see on the TExES Core Subjects 4–8 test. You'll have 1 hour and 5 minutes to answer 42 test items. That gives you about a minute and a half for each question.

The Mathematics subject test assesses eight Texas educator standards, in connection with the statewide curriculum, known as Texas Essential Knowledge and Skills (TEKS). These standards are presented as part of Competency 017, covered later in this chapter.

This subject test embraces 19 competencies, which broadly define "what an entry-level educator in this field in Texas public schools should know and be able to do," according to the Texas Education Agency. These competencies are covered in turn in this chapter. As part of your preparation, we encourage you to drill down in the official test framework to the descriptive statements, which describe the finer points of the knowledge and skills for which you are accountable. With the proviso that the Core Subjects 4–8 test by its nature is notably wide-ranging, this REA guide hits the content you're most likely to see on the exam.

COMPETENCY 001

The teacher understands the structure of number systems, the development of a sense of quantity and the relationship between quantity and symbolic representations.

The beginning teacher:

A. Analyzes the structure of numeration systems and the roles of place value and zero in the base ten system.

B. Understands the relative magnitude of whole numbers, integers, rational numbers, irrational numbers, and real numbers.

C. Demonstrates an understanding of a variety of models for representing numbers (e.g., fraction strips, diagrams, patterns, shaded regions, number lines).

D. Demonstrates an understanding of equivalency among different representations of rational numbers.

E. Selects appropriate representations of real numbers (e.g., fractions, decimals, percents, roots, exponents, scientific notation) for particular situations.

F. Understands the characteristics of the set of whole numbers, integers, rational numbers, real numbers, and complex numbers (e.g., commutativity, order, closure, identity elements, inverse elements, density).

G. Demonstrates an understanding of how some situations that have no solution in one number system (e.g., whole numbers, integers, and rational numbers) have solutions in another number system (e.g., real numbers, complex numbers, and irrational numbers).

H. Approximates (mentally and with calculators) the value of numbers.

I. Represents fractions and decimals to the tenths or hundredths as distances from zero on a number line.

Place Value

Place value is based on powers of 10. It assigns a value to a digit depending on its placement in a numeral.

Millions	Hundred thousands	Ten thousands	Thousands	Hundreds	Tens	Ones		Tenths	Hundredths	Thousandths	Ten thousandths	Hundred thousandths
			7	3	2	5	.	4				

Expanded Form

Any number can be written in expanded form, which shows place value by multiplying each digit in a number by the appropriate power of 10.

Example $7{,}325.4 = 7 \times 10^3 + 3 \times 10^2 + 2 \times 10^1 + 5 \times 10^0 + 4 \times 10^{-1}$

or

$$7{,}325.4 = 7 \times 1{,}000 + 3 \times 100 + 2 \times 10 + 5 \times 1 + 4 \times \frac{1}{10}$$

Natural Numbers

Natural numbers are also called counting numbers and include {1, 2, 3, 4, …}.

Whole Numbers

Whole numbers are the set of natural numbers including zero.

Integers

The set of **integers** includes positive and negative whole numbers. The set of integers includes: {…, −4, −3, −2, −1, 0, 1, 2, 3, 4, …}. Integers are often represented on a number line that extends in both directions from zero.

Rational Numbers

A **rational number** can be expressed as a ratio or quotient of two integers, where the denominator is not zero. Rational numbers are commonly expressed as fractions or decimals, such as $\frac{3}{10} = 0.3$, or $\frac{2}{3} = 0.\overline{666}$. Rational numbers, when represented in decimal form, either terminate or repeat.

Irrational Numbers

Irrational numbers are not rational, meaning they cannot be represented as fractions, and when in decimal form, they do not terminate or repeat. Common examples of irrational numbers are π, e, or $\sqrt{2}$.

Real Numbers

Real numbers are the set of all of the numbers on the number line. The figure below is an illustration of all the subsets of real numbers, which includes irrational and rational numbers, as well as integers, whole numbers, and natural numbers.

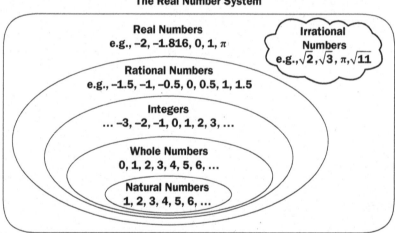

The Real Number System

Scientific Notation

Scientific notation is a form of writing a number in terms of a decimal number between 1 and 10 multiplied by a power of 10.

Example 1 $4,040,700,000 = 4.0407 \times 10^9$

Example 2 $0.005806 = 5.806 \times 10^{-3}$

Absolute Value

The **absolute value** of a number is the distance of that number from zero on a number line.

The absolute value of any number is positive or zero.

> **Example** $|-3| = 3$ since the position of –3 on a number line is 3 units away from zero.

COMPETENCY 002

The teacher understands number operations and computational algorithms.

The beginning teacher:

A. Works proficiently with real and complex numbers and their operations.

B. Analyzes and describes relationships between number properties, operations, and algorithms for the four basic operations involving integers, rational numbers, and real numbers.

C. Uses a variety of concrete and visual representations to demonstrate the connections between operations and algorithms.

D. Justifies procedures used in algorithms for the four basic operations with integers, rational numbers, and real numbers and analyzes error patterns that may occur in their application.

E. Relates operations and algorithms involving numbers to algebraic procedures (e.g., adding fractions to adding rational expressions, division of integers to division of polynomials).

F. Extends and generalizes the operations on rationals and integers to include exponents, their properties, and their applications to the real numbers.

G. Compares and orders real numbers with and without a calculator.

H. Uses models, such as concrete objects, pictorial models, and number lines, to add, subtract, multiply, and divide integers and connect the real-world problems to algorithms, including equivalent ratios and rates.

I. Divides whole numbers by unit fractions and unit fractions by whole numbers.

Operations and Algorithms

Several of the rules of properties of numbers will be helpful as you develop an understanding of this competency.

Properties of Numbers

Closure Property of Addition or Subtraction

If a and b are real numbers, then $a + b$ is a real number.

If a and b are real numbers, then $a - b$ is a real number.

Commutative Property of Addition

The order of the addends does not change the sum.

$$a + b = b + a$$

Associative Property of Addition

Grouping the addends differently does not change the sum.

$$(a + b) + c = a + (b + c)$$

Identity Property of Addition and Subtraction

The sum or difference of a number and zero is the number itself.

$$a + 0 = a \text{ and } a - 0 = a$$

Closure Property of Multiplication

If a and b are real numbers, $a \times b$ is also a real number.

Commutative Property of Multiplication

The order of the factors does not change the product.

$$a \times b = b \times a$$

Associative Property of Multiplication

Grouping the factors differently does not change the product.

$$(a \times b) \times c = a \times (b \times c)$$

Identity Property of Multiplication

The product of a number and 1 is the number itself.

$$a \times 1 = a \text{ and } 1 \times a = a$$

Zero Property of Multiplication

The product of a number and zero is zero.

$$0 \times a = 0 \text{ and } a \times 0 = 0$$

Distributive Property

To multiply a number by a sum or difference, multiply the number by each addend and then add or subtract, respectively.

$$\text{For all numbers } a, b, \text{ and } c, a(b + c) = ab + ac$$

$$\text{and } a(b - c) = ab - ac$$

Order of Operations

Often students learn the distributive property when they investigate problems requiring the order of operations. When presented with the task of evaluating $2(7 + 3)$, two possible approaches will produce the same correct result. One approach is to add first, then multiply: $2(10) = 20$, whereas another approach is to multiply first, then add: $14 + 6 = 20$. Obtaining the same answer using two different strategies may be cumbersome for some students.

Providing more examples of a different nature is needed for students to understand that the order of calculating mathematical problems will impact the outcome. Consider the problems $3 + 4 \times 8$ and $4 \times 8 + 3$. Work both problems from left to right and notice two different results.

Example 1 $3 + 4 \times 8 = 7 \times 8 = 56$ **INCORRECT**

Example 2 $4 \times 8 + 3 = 32 + 3 = 35$ **CORRECT**

Notice that the numbers in both expressions are the same but the order of the mathematical operations is different. In the first example, the addition sign comes before the multiplication, and the second example is the reverse. The second example actually shows the process that should be completed for the first example. Although the addition symbol is the first symbol one encounters in the problem when reading from left to right, addition is one of the last operations when evaluating expressions.

Please Excuse My Dear Aunt Sally or **PEMDAS** is the common phrase and acronym students learn to remember the order of operations. The words in the phrase or the letters of PEMDAS stand for *Parentheses*, *Exponents*, *Multiplication*, *Division*, *Addition*, and *Subtraction*. More important is the understanding of what each word means in regard to evaluating problems. Presenting the order of operations vertically can be helpful to explain the order of the calculations.

Evaluate this equation as you walk through the steps below: $\frac{4}{2} + 2(3 - 1)^2$.

Parentheses: First, compute within any grouping symbols, which may include parentheses ( ), brackets [ ], and absolute value $|\ \ |$. So, in our example, we can replace the set of parentheses with 2, giving $\frac{4}{2} + 2(2)^2$.

Exponents: Next, evaluate exponents or square roots. This gives us $\frac{4}{2} + 2 \times 4$.

Multiplication/Division: Read the problem from left to right and top to bottom. If a division symbol comes before a multiplication symbol, perform the division first. If a multiplication symbol occurs before a division symbol, perform the multiplication first. Performing the multiplication gives us $\frac{4}{2} + 8$. Then, dividing the fraction, we have $2 + 8$.

Addition/Subtraction: The process is similar to the rule for multiplication and division. Subtraction will occur before addition if the subtraction symbol comes before the addition symbol, whereas addition will precede subtraction if an addition symbol occurs before a subtraction symbol. In our example, only addition remains: $8 + 2 = 10$.

Computations with Fractions

A fraction is a number that represents part of a set, part of a whole, or a quotient in the form $\frac{a}{b}$, which can be read as a divided by b. Computations with fractions include finding equivalent fractions and simplifying; converting improper fractions to mixed numbers; and addition, subtraction, multiplication, and division.

Equivalent Fractions and Simplifying

Although the fractions $\frac{1}{4}$ and $\frac{2}{8}$ do not look alike, they represent the same value and are called equivalent or equal fractions; hence $\frac{1}{4} = \frac{2}{8}$.

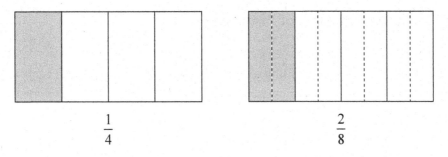

$$\frac{1}{4} \qquad\qquad\qquad \frac{2}{8}$$

Simplifying fractions requires identifying common factors among the numerator and denominator of a fraction. For example, to simplify we may recognize that both 60 and 140 are divisible by 10.

$$\frac{60}{140} = \frac{6 \cdot 10}{14 \cdot 10} = \frac{6}{14}$$

Also, both 6 and 14 are divisible by 2.

$$\frac{6}{14} = \frac{3 \cdot 2}{7 \cdot 2} = \frac{3}{7}$$

It was shown that $\frac{60}{140}$ was simplified to $\frac{6}{14}$ by factoring out a common factor of 10; then $\frac{6}{14}$ was simplified to $\frac{3}{7}$ by factoring out a common factor of 2. This means that $\frac{60}{140} = \frac{3}{7}$. Since there no remaining factors to simplify by, the fraction is now in its simplest form. Since the simplification process identified two common factors of 10 and 2, the **greatest common factor** (GCF) or **greatest common divisor** (GCD) of 60 and 140 is 20. This means the simplification process could have been completed in one step instead of two by factoring out the greatest common factor of both numbers.

$$\frac{60}{140} = \frac{3 \cdot 20}{7 \cdot 20} = \frac{3}{7}$$

The greatest common factor of a and b is the greatest number that divides both a and b evenly.

Converting Improper Fractions to Mixed Numbers

To convert an improper fraction like $\frac{7}{2}$, divide the numerator by the denominator. An improper fraction has a numerator greater than or equal to its denominator, so problems like this can be computed mentally by asking yourself, "How many times does 2 go into 7 evenly?" The answer is 3 times. "How much is left over?" One. The remainder is the numerator of the fractional portion of the mixed number and the denominator stays the same. So, $\frac{7}{2} = 3\frac{1}{2}$.

Addition and Subtraction of Fractions

There are two different cases to consider when adding or subtracting fractions: fractions with like denominators and fractions with unlike denominators. To add or subtract fractions with like, or the same, denominators, combine numerators and the denominator stays the same. For example, $\frac{2}{7} + \frac{4}{7} = \frac{6}{7}$ and $\frac{3}{5} - \frac{1}{5} = \frac{2}{5}$.

When denominators are unlike, first determine a common denominator, create equivalent fractions with that common denominator, and then combine numerators as above. For example, find the sum of $\frac{2}{7} + \frac{1}{3}$. To determine a common denominator, find the **least common multiple** of 7 and 3, which is 21. Next, change both fractions into equivalent fractions with 21 as the denominator. Finally, combine numerators.

$$\frac{2}{7} + \frac{1}{3} = \frac{2 \cdot 3}{7 \cdot 3} + \frac{1 \cdot 7}{3 \cdot 7} = \frac{6}{21} + \frac{7}{21} = \frac{13}{21}$$

Depending on the resulting fraction, you may need to simplify it.

Multiplication of Fractions

If $\frac{a}{b}$ and $\frac{c}{d}$ are any rational numbers, then $\frac{a}{b} \cdot \frac{c}{d} = \frac{a \cdot c}{b \cdot d}$. In short, find the product of the numerators and the product of the denominators, and simplify if possible.

$$\frac{5}{6} \times \frac{3}{4} = \frac{15}{24}$$

$$\frac{15}{24} = \frac{5 \cdot 3}{8 \cdot 3} = \frac{5}{8}$$

Division of Fractions

If $\frac{a}{b}$ and $\frac{c}{d}$ are any rational numbers and $\frac{c}{d} \neq 0$, then $\frac{a}{b} \div \frac{c}{d} = \frac{a}{b} \cdot \frac{d}{c} = \frac{a \cdot d}{b \cdot c}$. To divide fractions, multiply the first fraction by the reciprocal of the second fraction, and simplify if possible. A common phrase to recall is *invert and multiply.*

$$\frac{1}{6} \div \frac{2}{3} = \frac{1}{6} \cdot \frac{3}{2} = \frac{3}{12}$$

$$\frac{3}{12} = \frac{1 \cdot 3}{4 \cdot 3} = \frac{1}{4}$$

Computations with Decimals

Rational numbers can be expressed in the form of **decimals**, which are fractional numbers written using base 10. A mixed decimal number has a whole number part, too. For example, 2.8 is a mixed decimal number, and 0.75 is a mixed decimal number. The whole number part of .75 is zero.

Addition and Subtraction of Decimals

Decimal numbers can be written as fractions whose denominators are powers of 10 (i.e., 10, 100, 1,000, etc.). For example, 0.125 written in word form is one hundred twenty-five thousandths and is equivalent to the fraction $\frac{125}{1000}$. Consider that when adding or subtracting fractions earlier, we created equivalent fractions that had common denominators, then combined numerators. Similarly, with decimal addition or subtraction, we will combine digits of the same place value. Using the standard algorithm to add or subtract two decimal numbers, arrange the decimal numbers vertically, aligning the decimal points, and then combine the digits in the same place values.

Example   Find the sum of 25.07 and 14.326.

$$\begin{array}{r} 25.07 \\ + \ 14.326 \\ \hline 39.396 \end{array}$$

Multiplication of Decimals

Multiplication of decimals does not require aligning decimal points. Like addition/subtraction, the numbers can be arranged vertically but with right justification. The numbers can be multiplied as if they were whole numbers and the number of digits to the right of the decimal point in the product should be equal to the total number of decimal places within the two factors.

Example   Find the product of 3.25 and 0.3.

$$\begin{array}{r} 3.25 \\ \times \ 0.3 \\ \hline 0.975 \end{array}$$

Division of Decimals

Division of decimals can be calculated in the same way as division of traditional whole numbers. When the divisor is a whole number, the division can be handled as with whole numbers and the decimal point placed directly over the decimal point in the dividend. When the divisor is not a whole number, as in 1.44 ÷ 0.2, we can obtain a whole-number divisor by treating the quotient as a fraction and multiplying both numerator and denominator by a power of 10. Thus, 1.44 becomes 14.4, and 0.2 becomes 2.

$$\begin{array}{r} 7.2 \\ 2\overline{\smash{\big)}14.4} \\ \underline{-14} \\ 0\,4 \\ \underline{-4} \\ 0 \end{array}$$

Laws of Exponents

Product of Powers

$$a^n \cdot a^m = a^{n+m} \qquad\qquad 5^2 \cdot 5^1 = 5^{2+1} = 5^3 = 125$$

Power of a Product Rule

$$(ab)^n = a^n \cdot b^n \qquad\qquad (4 \cdot 3)^2 = 4^2 \cdot 3^2 = 16 \cdot 9 = 144$$

Power of a Power

$$\left(a^n\right)^m = a^{nm} \qquad\qquad \left(4^3\right)^2 = 4^{3 \cdot 2} = 4^6 = 4{,}096$$

Power of a Quotient

$$\left(\frac{a}{b}\right)^n = \frac{a^n}{b^n} \qquad\qquad \left(\frac{1}{3}\right)^4 = \frac{1^4}{3^4} = \frac{1}{81}$$

Fractional Exponents

$$a^{1/n} = \sqrt[n]{a} \qquad\qquad 27^{1/3} = \sqrt[3]{27} = 3$$

Negative Exponents

$$a^{-n} = \frac{1}{a^n},\, a \neq 0 \qquad\qquad 6^{-2} = \frac{1}{6^2} = \frac{1}{36}$$

Complex Numbers

Complex numbers, which combine real numbers and imaginary numbers, are not a part of the real number system, but instead exist in their own number system. Similar rules or properties for computation exist in the complex number system. The standard form for complex numbers is $a + bi$, where a and b are real numbers. The imaginary number i is defined as

$$i = \sqrt{-1}$$

Also,

$$i^2 = \left(\sqrt{-1}\right)^2 = -1$$

A pattern can be developed for investigating the powers of i.

$$i = \sqrt{-1} \text{ (this is the definition of } i\text{)}$$
$$i^2 = \left(\sqrt{-1}\right)\left(\sqrt{-1}\right) = \left(\sqrt{-1}\right)^2 = -1$$
$$i^3 = \left(\sqrt{-1}\right)\left(\sqrt{-1}\right)\left(\sqrt{-1}\right) = \left(\sqrt{-1}\right)^2\left(\sqrt{-1}\right) = (-1)\left(\sqrt{-1}\right) = (-1)(i) = -i$$
$$i^4 = \left(\sqrt{-1}\right)\left(\sqrt{-1}\right)\left(\sqrt{-1}\right)\left(\sqrt{-1}\right) = \left(\sqrt{-1}\right)^2\left(\sqrt{-1}\right)^2 = (-1)(-1) = 1$$
$$i^5 = i$$
$$i^6 = -1$$
$$i^7 = -i$$
$$i^8 = 1$$

Computations with Complex Numbers

Computations with complex numbers are similar to those of variable expressions—combining like terms. However, if an i^2 appears in the problem, we can substitute the value -1.

Example 1 Evaluate $5 + 7i - 3i + 9$.

Combine the constants and the imaginary terms.

$$14 + 4i$$

Example 2 Evaluate $3i(-2 + 5i)$.

Begin by distributing the $3i$ through the parentheses.

$$-6i + 15i^2$$

Next, substitute $i^2 = -1$ and multiply 15 by -1.

$$-6i + 15(-1) = -6i - 15$$

Then write the expression in standard form, $a + bi$.

$$-15 - 6i$$

Example 3   Evaluate $(7 + 2i)(3 - 4i)$.

FOIL is a common mathematical process used to multiply two binomials. It is similar to the distributive property. Take the first term in the first set of parentheses and distribute through the second set of parentheses. Continue the process with the second term in the first set of parentheses. FOIL stands for

First: multiply the first terms in the parentheses $7(3) = 21$

Outer: multiply the outside terms of the problem $7(-4i) = -28i$

Inner: multiply the inside two terms of the problem $2i(3) = 6i$

Last: multiply the last two terms in the parentheses $2i(-4i) = -8i^2$

After calculating each product, combine like terms, substitute -1 for i^2, and write the expression in standard form, $a + bi$.

$(7 + 2i)(3 - 4i)$

$21 + (-28i) + 6i + (-8i^2)$

$21 - 22i + (-8)(-1)$

$21 - 22i + 8$

$29 - 22i$

Rationalize the Denominator

To rationalize a quantity literally means to make the quantity rational. Recall that a rational number is one that can be expressed as the ratio or quotient of two non-zero integers. Rational numbers are commonly expressed as fractions or decimals, such as $\frac{3}{10} = 0.3$, or $\frac{2}{3} = 0.\overline{666}$. So, to rationalize the denominator of a fraction, we will create an equivalent fraction with a rational denominator.

Consider the example $\frac{6 + i}{3i}$. The denominator, $3i$, is imaginary and not a rational number. However, we will use the fact that $i^2 = -1$ to rationalize the denominator. Multiply $\frac{6 + i}{3i}$ by a factor of one, which can be written as $\frac{i}{i}$.

$$\frac{6 + i}{3i} \cdot \frac{i}{i} = \frac{6i + i^2}{3i^2}$$

Next, substitute -1 for i^2, and simplify.

$$\frac{6i + (-1)}{3(-1)} = \frac{-1 + 6i}{-3} = \frac{1 - 6i}{3}$$

The new denominator, 3, is a rational number; therefore, the quantity is now rational. In addition, we can say $\frac{6+i}{3i}$ is equivalent to $\frac{1-6i}{3}$, or $\frac{6+i}{3i} = \frac{1-6i}{3}$.

If the denominator to be rationalized is a binomial, multiply by a factor of 1, changing the sign within the binomial. (A binomial is a polynomial with two terms.) For example, consider $\frac{5i}{3 - 2i}$. To rationalize this denominator, we multiply by $\frac{3 + 2i}{3 + 2i}$. This is called a conjugate.

$$\frac{5i}{3 - 2i} \cdot \frac{3 + 2i}{3 + 2i} = \frac{15i + 10i^2}{9 + 6i - 6i - 4i^2}$$

Substitute -1 for i^2, and simplify.

$$\frac{15i + 10(-1)}{9 - 4(-1)} = \frac{-10 + 15i}{9 + 4} = \frac{-10 + 15i}{13}$$

COMPETENCY 003

The teacher understands ideas of number theory and uses numbers to model and solve problems within and outside of mathematics.

The beginning teacher:

A. Demonstrates an understanding of ideas from number theory (e.g., prime factorization, greatest common divisor) as they apply to whole numbers, integers, and rational numbers and uses these ideas in problem situations.

B. Uses integers, rational numbers and real numbers to describe and quantify phenomena such as money, length, area, volume, and density.

C. Applies knowledge of place value and other number properties to develop techniques of mental mathematics and computational estimation.

D. Applies knowledge of counting techniques such as permutations and combinations to quantify situations and solve problems.

E. Applies properties of real numbers to solve a variety of theoretical and applied problems.

F. Makes connections among various representations of a numerical relationship and generates a different representation of data given another representation of data (such as a table, graph, equation, or verbal description).

Composite Number

A **composite number** is a number that is divisible by at least one other number besides 1 and itself. For example: 12 is a composite number because it has more than two factors: 1, 2, 3, 4, 6, 12.

Prime Numbers

A **prime number** is a whole number greater than 1 that is divisible by only 1 and itself, meaning it has only two factors. For example, 11 is a prime number since its only factors are 1 and 11.

Prime Factorization

Exponents can be used to write the **prime factorization** of a number; that is, every whole number except 1 or 0 can be written as a product of prime numbers. When a factor is repeated in a prime factorization, express the repeated factor in exponential form. Most often, students use a factor tree to find the prime factorization of a composite number. To begin factoring, choose two factors of the number and continue factoring each number until you have all prime numbers.

Example   What is the prime factorization of 36?

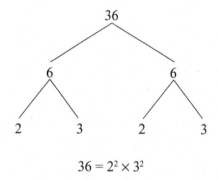

$$36 = 2^2 \times 3^2$$

Divisibility Rules

Sometimes it is handy to know if one number is divisible by another just by looking at a number or by performing a simple test.

Divisibility Rule of . . .	Rule
2	Any integer is divisible by 2 if it is an even number.
3	Any integer is divisible by 3 if the sum of its digits is divisible by 3.
4	Any integer is divisible by 4 if the last two digits of the integer represent a number divisible by 4.
5	Any integer is divisible by 5 if it ends in 0 or 5.
6	Any integer is divisible by 6 if it is divisible by both 2 and 3.
8	Any integer is divisible by 8 if the last three digits of the integer represent a number divisible by 8.
9	Any integer is divisible by 9 if the sum of the digits is divisible by 9.
10	Any integer is divisible by 10 if it ends in 0.

Common Multiple

A **common multiple** is a whole number that is a multiple of two or more given numbers. For example, the common multiples of 2, 3, and 4 are 12, 24, 36, 48, ...

Some students might claim 6 and/or 8 are common multiples of 2, 3, and 4, but this is incorrect. Six is a common multiple only among the numbers 2 and 3, but not 4. Likewise, 8 is a common multiple among the numbers 2 and 4, but not 3.

Greatest Common Divisor

The **greatest common divisor** (GCD) of two or more non-zero integers is the largest positive integer that divides into the numbers without producing a remainder. The GCD is useful for simplifying fractions into lowest terms, which was explored earlier in this chapter. The term *greatest common factor* (GCF) is often used when simplifying fractions.

Example: Find the greatest common divisor of 40 and 56. To identify the GCD, make a list of all the factors of each number. Then, identify the largest common factor between the two sets of numbers.

$$\begin{cases} 40 : 1, 2, 4, 5, 8, 10, 20, 40 \\ 56 : 1, 2, 4, 7, 8, 14, 28, 56 \end{cases}$$

The largest or greatest common factor of each list is 8. Therefore, the GCD of 40 and 56 is 8.

Decimal Representations with Base-10 Blocks

Base-10 blocks are handy manipulatives for fractional and decimal representations and computations. Graph paper or 10-by-10 grids can be used to transform the concrete use of base-10 blocks into pictorial form. The number 1.45 is represented in the figure below.

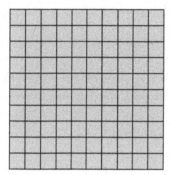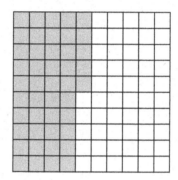

The first shaded 10-by-10 grid shows $\frac{100}{100} = 1$, and the second grid has 45 of the 100 cells shaded; therefore, it models $\frac{45}{100} = 0.45$. The pictorial representation is also an area model, meaning the visual representation shows the amount of space taken up by the shaded region. By modeling multiple decimal numbers in this form, students can more easily order a set of numbers from least to greatest.

Mental Mathematics and Estimation

The ability to make accurate estimates is important in today's society. Always look for **combinations** (like halves and doubles) or **compatible numbers** when doing mental calculations. Consider the two examples below:

Example 1   Evaluate 25×8.

Compute $25 \times 4 = 100$ and then $100 \times 2 = 200$. Ultimately, the number 8 was broken down to its factors of 4×2 to rearrange the problem to be $25 \times 4 \times 2$.

Example 2   Evaluate $25 + 17 + 15$.

First combine $25 + 15 = 40$, and then find $40 + 17 = 57$. The numbers 25 and 15 are good compatible numbers since they both have 5 in the ones place-value; 40 is a nice round even number to add any other value to, hence we add 17 last.

Rounding is common practice in mathematics. The **5-up rule** is the standard method used when rounding numbers to a certain place value. First, determine which position you are rounding. If the digit to the right of this position is 5 or more, add 1 to the digit in the position to which you are rounding and replace zeros for all of the digits to the right of the position to which you are rounding. If the digit to the right of the position to be rounded is less than 5, leave the digit unchanged and drop all of the digits to the right of the position.

For example, round 37,250 to the nearest (a) hundred and (b) thousand.

(a) The digit 2 is in the hundreds position with the digit 5 to its right. Since the digit to the right is 5, round 2 to 3. Rounding the given number to the nearest hundred produces 37,300.

(b) The digit 7 is in the thousands place, and 2 is the digit to the right. Since 2 is less than 5, we will leave the 7 as is and replace all numbers to its right with zeros. Rounding the given number to the nearest thousand produces 37,000.

Permutations

The **counting principle** allows you to determine the number of possibilities of a real-life event or activity.

When dealing with the occurrence of more than one event or activity, it is important to be able to quickly determine how many outcomes exist, rather than actually listing them. If there are "m ways" for one activity to occur and "n ways" for a second activity to occur, the counting principle states that there are "$m \times n$ ways" for both to occur.

Example: A vending machine sells snacks and soft drinks. If there are 8 different snacks and 5 different soft drinks, there are 8 • 5 = 40 different ways to choose a snack and a soft drink.

Example: A popular car comes in 10 different colors, 4 different interiors, 3 engine sizes, and with or without a navigation system. There are 10 • 4 • 3 • 2 = 240 configurations of the car that are possible.

A permutation is a set of objects in which position (or order) is important. An example is a password to a bank account. If the password is HJ2M6, the order is important. MH62J will not gain access to the account.

Permutations with replacement: An object can be repeated. In the example, it is possible for a password to be HJ22M or HH22H. If we have n things to choose from each time we choose, the counting principle says that there will be $n • n • n • ...$ permutations.

Example: In the password example containing 5 characters, there are 36 possibilities for each character: a through z is 26 letters and 0 through 9 is 10 digits. Therefore, there are $36 \times 36 \times 36 \times 36 \times 36 = 36^5 = 60,466,176$ permutations. Note that this assumes that it is possible for a number to repeat.

Permutations without replacement: An object *cannot* be repeated. Once we choose it, it can no longer be chosen.

Example: In the password example, suppose that you cannot use a character over again. Once you use it, you cannot reuse it. The first character has a choice of 36. Once you use it, you now have only 35 choices for the second character. Once you use it, you only have 34 choices for the third character. So, there are $36 \times 35 \times 34 \times 33 \times 32 = 45,239,040$ permutations.

Example: An ice cream shop has 25 flavors. If a person orders a triple-decker cone, how many different cones are possible if (a) it is allowed to repeat a flavor and (b) no replacement of flavors is allowed? Note that a cone of vanilla on top, chocolate in the middle, and strawberry on the bottom is different than a cone of chocolate on top, strawberry in the middle, and vanilla on the bottom because usually the scoop on the bottom is larger than the scoop on top.

Solution:

a) $25(25)(25) = 15,625$

b) $25(24)(23) = 13,800$

Permutations with Like Objects

In the above examples, each object was distinct. Suppose we wanted to arrange the letters in the words ALMOST and BANANA. ALMOST has 6 distinct letters, so in the first position of the word, you have 6 letters to pick from (A, L, M, O, S, and T). For the next position in the word, you have just 5 letters to pick from (L, M, O, S, and T). This continues for each position, resulting in $6 \times 5 \times 4 \times 3 \times 2 \times 1 = 720$. Another way to write $6 \times 5 \times 4 \times 3 \times 2 \times 1$ is 6!. "!" is the symbol for factorial, which means to multiple a number by every number that precedes it.

BANANA has the letter A appearing 3 times and the letter N appearing twice. So the number of arrangements in the word BANANA is $\dfrac{6!}{(3! \cdot 2!)}$.

Combinations

A set of objects in which position (or order) is *not* important. An example is a dish of ice cream including scoops of vanilla, chocolate, and strawberry. Unlike a cone, we don't care about the order of the flavor scoops. A dish of vanilla, chocolate, and strawberry is the same as a dish of strawberry, vanilla, and chocolate.

The way to determine the number of combinations possible is to use a formula. The number of combinations of n objects taken r at a time has several notations and is computed as follows: $_nC_r = \dfrac{n!}{r!(n-r)!}$. When calculating combinations using this formula, we can usually use cancellation, or simplifying, to make the calculations easier.

Example: A basketball team has 9 members and 5 players are on the floor. The number of combinations of teams on the floor that are possible is given by:

$$_9C_5 = \frac{9!}{5!(9-5)!} = \frac{9!}{5! \cdot 4!} = \frac{9 \cdot 8 \cdot 7 \cdot 6 \cdot 5 \cdot 4 \cdot 3 \cdot 2 \cdot 1}{5 \cdot 4 \cdot 3 \cdot 2 \cdot 1 \cdot 4 \cdot 3 \cdot 2 \cdot 1}$$

$$= \frac{9 \cdot 8 \cdot 7 \cdot 6 \cdot 5 \cdot 4 \cdot 3 \cdot 2 \cdot 1}{5 \cdot 4 \cdot 3 \cdot 2 \cdot 1 \cdot 4 \cdot 3 \cdot 2 \cdot 1} = 126$$

It is important to be able to determine whether a problem defines a permutation or a combination.

Permutation	Combination
Picking a player to pitch, catch, and play shortstop from a group of players.	Picking three team members from a group of players.
In a dog show, choosing 1st place, 2nd place, and 3rd place from a group of dogs.	In a dog show, choosing 3 dogs that will go to the finals from a group of dogs.
From a color paint brochure, choosing a color for the walls and a color for the trim.	From a color paint brochure, choosing two colors to paint the room.

An alternate notation for combinations is sometimes used: $\binom{n}{r} = {}_nC_r$. So ${}_9C_5$ can be written as $\binom{9}{5}$.

Example: An essay exam has 10 questions and students are instructed to answer exactly 4 of them. How many ways can this be done?

Solution: ${}_{10}C_4$ or $\binom{10}{4} = \dfrac{10!}{4! \cdot 6!} = \dfrac{10 \cdot 9 \cdot 8 \cdot 7 \cdot 6 \cdot 5 \cdot 4 \cdot 3 \cdot 2 \cdot 1}{4 \cdot 3 \cdot 2 \cdot 1 \cdot 6 \cdot 5 \cdot 4 \cdot 3 \cdot 2 \cdot 1} = 210$

COMPETENCY 004

The teacher understands and uses mathematical reasoning to identify, extend, and analyze patterns and understands the relationships among variables, expressions, equations, inequalities, relations, and functions.

The beginning teacher:

A. Uses inductive reasoning to identify, extend and create patterns using concrete models, figures, numbers, and algebraic expressions.

B. Formulates implicit and explicit rules to describe and construct sequences verbally, numerically, graphically, and symbolically.

C. Makes, tests, validates, and uses conjectures about patterns and relationships in data presented in tables, sequences, or graphs.

D. Gives appropriate justification of the manipulation of algebraic expressions.

E. Illustrates the concept of a function using concrete models, tables, graphs, and symbolic and verbal representations.

F. Uses transformations to illustrate properties of functions and relations and to solve problems.

G. Uses graphs, tables, and algebraic representations to make predictions and solve problems.

H. Uses letters to represent an unknown in an equation.

I. Formulates problem situations when given a simple equation and formulates an equation when given a problem situation.

Patterns

There are two types of patterns explored in Grades 4 through 8: repeating patterns and growing patterns. An important concept in working with repeating patterns is identifying the core of the pattern, or the string of elements that repeats. Consider the musical pattern created by clapping and stomping: *stomp, stomp, clap, stomp, stomp, clap, stomp, stomp, clap, ...* The core of the unit is *stomp, stomp, clap* and can be written in the form of *AAB*. Number patterns can be used to predict numbers down the line. For example, consider 3, 5, 7, ... The number pattern is odd numbers beginning with 3. Add 2 each time. The next three numbers in the pattern would be 9, 11, and 13.

Growing patterns involve a progression from step to step. Students should not only extend these patterns but also look for a generalization or an algebraic relationship to create a function that represents the pattern. Investigate the three steps below and generalize the growing pattern.

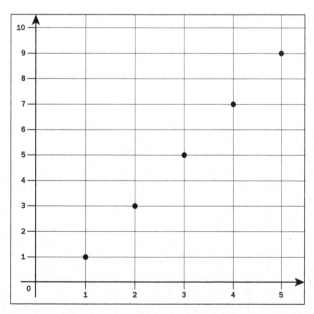

A table can be constructed to record the number of objects per step and identify the pattern.

Step	1	2	3	4	. . .	n
Number of Objects	1	3	5		. . .	

The pattern is increasing by 2 on each step, so on the fourth step there will be 7 objects, and on the nth step there will be $2n - 1$ objects. Moreover, we can graph this relationship or function:

$$f(n) = 2n - 1$$

The function $f(n) = 2n - 1$ represents the number of objects is one less than twice the step. This problem illustrates the concept of a function using models, tables, graphs, and symbolic and verbal representations, which are important concepts within mathematics.

Variables

Variables can express relationships. Consider the following statement and question: Jose was born on his three-year-old sister Kendra's birthday. How are their ages related? Three different relationships can be represented:

- Jose is three years younger than Kendra. $J = K - 3$

- Kendra is three years older than Jose. $K = J + 3$

- The difference in age between Kendra and her younger brother Jose is three years. $K - J = 3$

COMPETENCY 005

The teacher understands and uses linear functions to model and solve problems.

The beginning teacher:

A. Demonstrates an understanding of the concept of linear function using concrete models, tables, graphs, and symbolic and verbal representations.

B. Demonstrates an understanding of the connections among linear functions, proportions, and direct variation.

C. Determines the linear function that best models a set of data.

D. Analyzes the relationship between a linear equation and its graph.

E. Uses linear functions, inequalities, and systems to model problems.

F. Uses a variety of representations and methods (e.g., numerical methods, tables, graphs, algebraic techniques) to solve systems of linear equations and inequalities.

G. Demonstrates an understanding of the characteristics of linear models and the advantages and disadvantages of using a linear model in a given situation.

H. Uses multiplication by a given constant factor (including unit rate) to represent and solve problems involving proportional relationships, including conversions between measurement systems (e.g., ratio, speed, density, price, recipes, student teacher ratio).

I.   Identifies proportional or nonproportional linear relationships in problem situations and solves problems.

Linear Functions and Slope

Linear functions are commonly written in the form of $y = mx + b$, where m is the slope of the function and b is the y-intercept, $(0, b)$, or the point at which the line crosses the y-axis. When the slope of a line is positive, $m > 0$, the line goes up from left to right (increases); if the slope is negative, $m < 0$, the line goes down from left to right (decreases).

Example 1   The function $y = x$ has a positive slope of $m = 1$ and a y-intercept of $(0, 0)$.

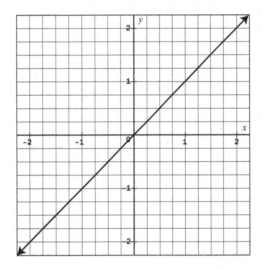

This particular function is called the linear parent function.

Example 2   The function $y = -x$ has a negative slope of $m = -1$ and a y-intercept of $(0, 0)$.

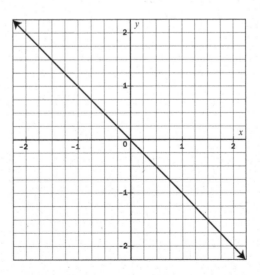

A line segment is a section of a line that is bounded by two points. Two points can also be used to graph a line—which extends in opposite directions forever. To find the equation of a line passing through two points, (x_1, y_1) and (x_2, y_2), we will calculate the **slope** and use the **point-slope formula**.

$$\text{slope} = m = \frac{y_2 - y_1}{x_2 - x_1} \qquad \text{point-slope formula: } y - y_1 = m(x - x_1)$$

Example 3 Find the equation of a line passing through the points $(-1, -3)$ and $(2, 2)$.

Begin by calculating the slope between the two points.

$$m = \frac{2 - (-3)}{2 - (-1)} = \frac{2 + 3}{2 + 1} = \frac{5}{3}$$

Next, choose one point and the slope to evaluate the point-slope formula.

$$y - (-3) = \frac{5}{3}[x - (-1)]$$

$$y + 3 = \frac{5}{3}(x + 1)$$

$$y + 3 = \frac{5}{3}x + \frac{5}{3}$$

$$y + 3 - 3 = \frac{5}{3}x + \frac{5}{3} - 3$$

$$y = \frac{5}{3}x - \frac{4}{3}$$

The equation of the line passing through points $(-1, -3)$ and $(2, 2)$ is $y = \frac{5}{3}x - \frac{4}{3}$, where $m = \frac{5}{3}$ and the y-intercept is $(0, -\frac{4}{3})$. The graph of the line is shown below.

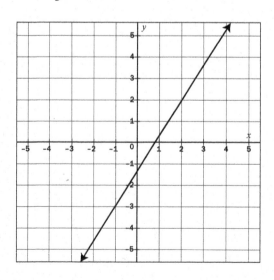

Linear equations can also be written in **standard form**, $Ax + By = C$, where A, B, and C are integers and $A \neq 0$ and $B \neq 0$. Let's take the equation from above, $y = \frac{5}{3}x - \frac{4}{3}$, and write it in standard form. First, all coefficients need to be integers. Since the slope is in fractional form, we can multiply both sides of the equation by 3 (the denominator) to clear the fractional portion of the equation, making all coefficients integers:

$$3(y) = 3\left(\frac{5}{3}x - \frac{4}{3}\right)$$
$$3y = 5x - 4$$

Then, subtract $5x$ from both sides to isolate the constant from the variable terms.

$$-5x + 3y = -4$$

By multiplying both sides of the equation by -1, it can also be written as $5x - 3y = 4$.

Modeling Linear Functions to Solve Problems

Applications, or word problems, are frequently used to help students understand linear functions and modeling problems. They can prepare students for situations they might encounter later in life. The following scenario requires students to perform multiple mathematical tasks such as creating a table, drawing a graph, and evaluating problems within the posed scenario.

Scenario:

A survey of car owners shows that the monthly cost (in dollars) to own and drive a car is given by the function $f(x) = 0.41x + 225$. Here, x represents the number of miles driven throughout the month and 225 represents the monthly expenses that come with ownership of a vehicle, such as insurance, vehicle license fees, and so on, which are independent of the miles driven.

(a) Make a table that shows the cost of having a car that is driven 0, 100, 200, . . . , 500 miles per month.

(b) Use the table to draw a graph that shows the cost of driving a car for up to 500 miles in a month.

(c) Use your graph to estimate the corresponding limit on the number of miles driven in a month if your monthly budget is limited to $400.

(d) What is the approximate number of miles driven throughout the month if the expenditures are $350?

Solution:

(a) To create a table we must first identify the variables: x is the miles driven, and y is the cost (in dollars) of owning and driving the car. We will evaluate the function $f(x) = 0.41x + 225$ when x is 0, 100, 200, 300, 400, and 500. The outputs represent the cost of owning and driving the car based on those numbers of miles driven in the month.

Miles, x	0	100	200	300	400	500
Cost, y	225	266	307	348	389	430

(b) To use the table to create a graph, plot the coordinates from the table. For example, (0, 225) is the y-intercept of the graph.

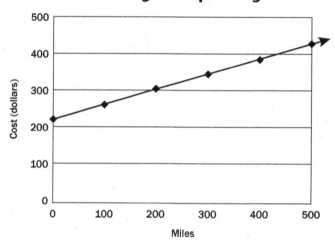

Cost of Owning and Operating a Car

(c) To use the graph to determine how many miles can be driven if there is a budget of $400, place your finger where 400 is on the y-axis and then slide your finger to the right until it meets the function. The x-value below this intersection tells how many miles can be driven if the budget is $400. Based on the graph above, one could drive about 425 miles for the cost of $400.

(d)   To determine the approximate amount of miles driven if the expenditures are $350, we will evaluate the function when $f(x) = 350$. Therefore, our equation to solve is

$$
\begin{array}{r}
350 = 0.41x + 225 \\
-225 \qquad\quad -225 \\
\hline
\dfrac{125}{0.41} = x
\end{array}
$$

$$x \approx 304.88 \text{ miles driven}$$

COMPETENCY 006

The teacher understands and uses nonlinear functions and relations to model and solve problems.

The beginning teacher:

A.   Uses a variety of methods to investigate the roots (real and complex), vertex, and symmetry of a quadratic function or relation.

B.   Demonstrates an understanding of the connections among geometric, graphic, numeric, and symbolic representations of quadratic functions.

C.   Demonstrates an understanding of the connections among proportions, inverse variation, and rational functions.

D.   Understands the effects of transformations such as on the graph of a nonlinear function $f(x)$.

E.   Applies properties, graphs, and applications of nonlinear functions to analyze, model, and solve problems.

F.   Uses a variety of representations and methods (e.g., numerical methods, tables, graphs, algebraic techniques) to solve systems of quadratic equations and inequalities.

G.   Understands how to use properties, graphs, and applications of nonlinear relations including polynomial, rational, radical, absolute value, exponential, logarithmic, trigonometric, and piecewise functions and relations to analyze, model, and solve problems.

Quadratic Functions

A function defined by $f(x) = ax^2 + bx + c$, where a, b, and c are constants with $a \neq 0$, is called a quadratic function. The most elementary **quadratic function** is $f(x) = x^2$, often referred to as the quadratic parent function. The graph of a quadratic function is called a **parabola** (see figure below).

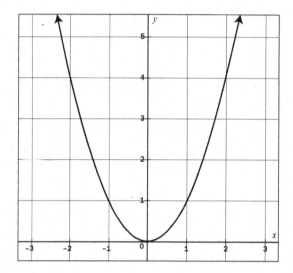

The parabola is a symmetrical function, meaning it has a **line of symmetry** through the **vertex**. In the figure above, the vertex is at (0, 0), or the bottom point on the graph, also called the **minimum**. This graph of $f(x) = x^2$ opens upward, but a similar quadratic function of $f(x) = -x^2$ opens downward (see graph below). The vertex on a parabola that opens downward is the topmost point of the function, called the **maximum**.

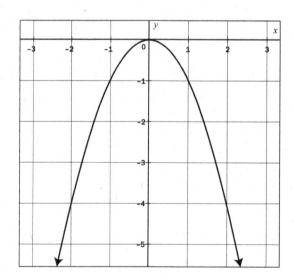

The value of the leading coefficient a determines if the graph of a quadratic function will open up or down. If $a > 0$, the parabola opens up, as in the function $f(x) = x^2$, where $a = 1$. If $a < 0$, the parabola opens down, as in the similar function $f(x) = -x^2$, where $a = -1$.

Transformations

We often call the function $f(x) = x^2$ the parent function for quadratics, and any manipulation to this function performs a transformation of the graph. As shown above, the graph of $f(x) = -x^2$ opens downward, whereas the parent function opens upward. The graph of the function when $a = -1$ was reflected across the x-axis. To reflect the graph across the x-axis, examine the function $g(x) = -f(x)$ or in our case $g(x) = -x^2$. Below is a table of transformations that may occur on any type of function.

Transformations of Functions

Examining the function $g(x)$	Result	Example $\left[f(x) = x^2 \right]$
$g(x) = -f(x)$	Reflects $f(x)$ across the x-axis.	$g(x) = -x^2$
$g(x) = f(-x)$	Reflects $f(x)$ across the y-axis.	$g(x) = (-x)^2$
$g(x) = f(x) + c$	Translates $f(x)$ c units up.	$g(x) = x^2 + 2$
$g(x) = f(x) - c$	Translates $f(x)$ c units down.	$g(x) = x^2 - 2$
$g(x) = f(x + c)$	Translates $f(x)$ c units left.	$g(x) = (x + 2)^2$
$g(x) = f(x - c)$	Translates $f(x)$ c units right.	$g(x) = (x - 2)^2$
$g(x) = af(x)$	Dilates the graph vertically. If $a > 1$, graph is stretched. If $0 < a < 1$, graph is compressed.	$g(x) = 2x^2$ $g(x) = \frac{1}{2}x^2$
$f(ax)$	Dilates the graph horizontally. If $a > 1$, graph is stretched. If $0 < a < 1$, graph is compressed.	$g(x) = (2x)^2$ $g(x) = \left(\frac{1}{2}x\right)^2$

Vertex and Line of Symmetry

The **vertex** of a parabola occurs at the point $\left(\frac{-b}{2a}, f\left(\frac{-b}{2a}\right) \right)$, where the values for a and b are found in the function $f(x) = ax^2 + bx + c$. As mentioned before, parabolas are symmetrical about a line of symmetry. Such a line is $x = \frac{-b}{2a}$, a vertical line through the vertex. This may also be called the axis of symmetry.

Identify the vertex and line of symmetry in the function $f(x) = -16x^2 + 32x - 10$. To find the x-coordinate of the vertex, we compute $\frac{-b}{2a} = \frac{-32}{2(-16)} = \frac{-32}{-32} = 1$. Next find the y-coordinate by computing $f(1) = -16(1)^2 + 32(1) - 10 = 6$. Therefore, the vertex or maximum is located at $(1, 6)$ and the line of symmetry is at $x = 1$. Below is the graph of $f(x) = -16x^2 + 32x - 10$.

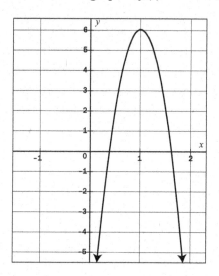

Solving Quadratic Equations

The solutions to a quadratic equation are called **zeros** or **roots**. Graphically, the solutions are x-intercepts, or where the graph crosses or touches the x-axis. We determine the value(s) when $y = 0$, which are the x-intercepts.

If the graph crosses the x-axis in two places, there are two solutions to the equation when $f(x) = 0$. The function above, $f(x) = -16x^2 + 32x - 10$, crosses the x-axis at two places that are both positive. Therefore, the two answers for x are both positive.

The function $f(x) = x^2$ does not cross the x-axis, but it touches it at the point $(0, 0)$. Quadratic functions that touch but do not cross the x-axis have only one solution when $f(x) = 0$: the x-value of the coordinate at which it touches the axis. The one solution to $f(x) = 0 = x^2$ is $x = 0$.

Some quadratic equations do not touch or cross the x-axis. Instead, they are suspended above or below the x-axis, and their solutions are complex or imaginary. The function $f(x) = x^2 + 2$ lies above the x-axis and has two complex solutions when $f(x) = 0$ (see graph that follows).

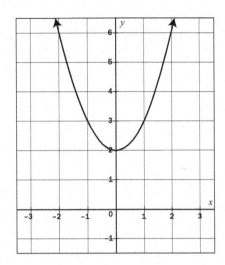

The solutions for $f(x) = 0$ can be found by evaluating the **quadratic formula**: $x = \dfrac{-b \pm \sqrt{b^2 - 4ac}}{2a}$, where a, b, and c are the coefficients in the function $ax^2 + bx + c = 0$. Determine the values for a, b, and c, and then substitute them into the quadratic formula. For the function $f(x) = x^2 + 2$, the x-intercepts can be calculated as:

$$a = 1, b = 0, c = 2$$

$$x = \frac{0 \pm \sqrt{0^2 - 4(1)(2)}}{2(1)} = \frac{\pm\sqrt{-8}}{2} = \frac{\pm\sqrt{-4(2)}}{2} = \frac{\pm 2i\sqrt{2}}{2} = \pm\sqrt{2}\,i$$

The $\pm$ symbol means there are two answers for x: $\sqrt{2}\,i$ and $-\sqrt{2}\,i$. The fact that the two solutions are imaginary is an indication that the graph does not cross the x-axis and thus has no x-intercepts.

To determine the type (real or complex) and number of solutions (one or two), calculate the **discriminant**, $b^2 - 4ac$, and follow these rules:

If $b^2 - 4ac > 0$, there are two real solutions.

If $b^2 - 4ac = 0$, there is one real solution.

If $b^2 - 4ac < 0$, there are two complex solutions.

Example   Determine the type and number of solutions to the function $f(x) = 0 = x^2 - 7x + 12$, then find the solutions. First, determine the values for a, b, and c and use them to find the discriminant.

$$a = 1, b = -7, c = 12$$

$$(-7)^2 - 4(1)(12) = 49 - 48 = 1$$

Since $1 > 0$, there are two real solutions. Next, compute the quadratic formula to find these two real solutions.

$$x = \frac{-(-7) \pm \sqrt{(-7)^2 - 4(1)(12)}}{2(1)} = \frac{7 \pm \sqrt{49 - 48}}{2} = \frac{7 \pm 1}{2}$$

$$x = \frac{7 + 1}{2} = \frac{8}{2} = 4 \text{ and } x = \frac{7 - 1}{2} = \frac{6}{2} = 3$$

Therefore, $x = 3$ and 4, or the x-intercepts are $(3, 0)$ and $(4, 0)$.

Factoring can be a helpful method for solving some quadratic equations. Consider the example we just solved using the quadratic formula: $x^2 - 7x + 12 = 0$. When the leading coefficient, a, equals 1, as is the case here, the first step is to determine the factors of c that when added together equal b. In this example, the factors of 12 whose sum is -7 are -3 and -4. Next, use these factors to factor the quadratic into $(x - 3)(x - 4) = 0$. To solve the factored quadratic, set each binomial equal to zero and solve for x.

$$x - 3 = 0 \quad \text{and} \quad x - 4 = 0$$
$$x = 3 \qquad\qquad x = 4$$

As seen on the graph below, the x-intercepts are $(3, 0)$ and $(4, 0)$.

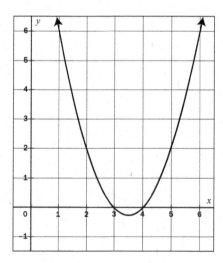

Additional Nonlinear Functions

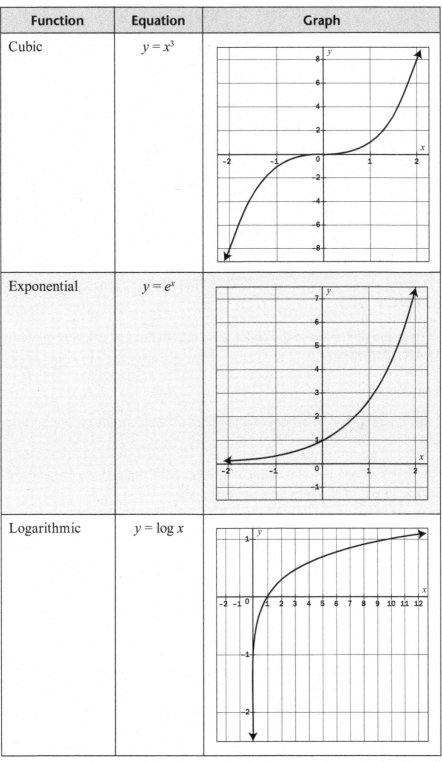

Function	Equation	Graph
Cubic	$y = x^3$	
Exponential	$y = e^x$	
Logarithmic	$y = \log x$	

(continued)

Function	Equation	Graph
Absolute value	$y = \lvert x \rvert$	

COMPETENCY 007

The teacher uses and understands the conceptual foundations of calculus related to topics in middle school mathematics.

The beginning teacher:

A. Relates topics in middle school mathematics to the concept of limit in sequences and series.

B. Relates the concept of average rate of change to the slope of the line and the concept of instantaneous rate of change as a slope of the line.

C. Demonstrates an understanding of the use of calculus concepts to answer questions about rates of change, areas, volumes, and properties of functions and their graphs.

In terms of the Core Subjects 4–8 Mathematics subject test, you are required to understand only the most rudimentary aspects of calculus. Calculus is the study of how things change. Since change is all around us, it is obviously applicable to the real world. Many real-life examples of calculus occur in the world of physics, economics, engineering, and medicine.

Calculus studies three basic problems, all concerning themselves with the concept of infinity.

Slopes of Secant Lines and Tangent Lines

Given a curve $y = f(x)$, we define the secant line between two points P and Q as the line connecting the two points (diagram 1).

We define the tangent line at point P as the line that touches $y = f(x)$ only at point P (diagram 2).

We draw the secant line through PQ. Point Q moves along $y = f(x)$ towards point P. The closer that Q gets to P, the more the secant line resembles the tangent line at P (diagram 3). So, the closer that Q gets to P, the closer the slope of the secant line gets to the slope of the tangent line at P.

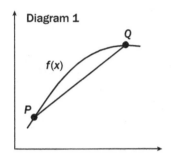
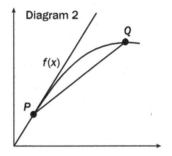
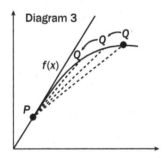

The formula for the slope of the secant line between the points $(a, f(a))$ and $(b, f(b)) = \dfrac{f(b) - f(a)}{b - a}$. It looks confusing but is merely the formula for the slope of a line. The slope of the tangent line at $(a, f(a))$ is beyond what is asked on the TExES Core Subjects exam, but if you choose another point close to $x = a$, you can approximate the slope of the tangent line at $x = a$ with great accuracy.

Example: If $f(x) = x^2 + x - 2$, find a) the slope of the secant line between $x = -1$ and $x = 2$. Then b) approximate the slope of the tangent line at $x = 1$.

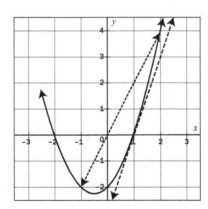

Solution: a) $f(2) = 4 + 2 - 2 = 4$

$f(-1) = 1 - 1 - 2 = -2$

slope of secant line $= \dfrac{f(2) - f(-1)}{2 - (-1)} = \dfrac{4 - (-2)}{2 + 1} = \dfrac{6}{3} = 2$

b) To approximate the slope of the tangent line at $x = 1$, we will use $x = 1$ and $x = 1.1$

$f(1) = 1 + 1 - 2 = 0$

$f(1.1) = 1.21 + 1.1 - 2 = 0.31$

slope of tangent line is approximately $\dfrac{f(1.1) - f(1)}{1.1 - 1} = \dfrac{0.31 - 0}{0.1} = 3.1$

The closer you choose your second point to $x = 1$, the more accurate the slope of the tangent line. If you get infinitely close, it turns out that the slope of the tangent line is exactly 3.

The reason that the slopes of secant lines and tangent lines are so important is that we can use them to make an analogy to the concept of motion. When we have motion in a straight line, we can find the average velocity between two times as well as the instantaneous velocity at a certain time.

If $s(t)$ describes the position of a particle moving along a straight line, the average velocity between t_1 and t_2 is given by $\dfrac{s(t_2) - s(t_1)}{t_2 - t_1}$. This formula is similar to the one used for the slope of a secant line.

If a train is traveling along a straight track and is 50 miles from a station at $t = 2$ hours and 70 miles from the station at $t = 2.5$ hours, its average velocity is $\dfrac{s(2.5) - s(2)}{2.5 - 2} = \dfrac{70 - 50}{0.5} = \dfrac{20}{0.5} = 40 \text{ mph}$. However, just because the train averages 40 mph between $t = 2.5$ hours and $t = 2$ hours doesn't mean we know how fast the train is traveling at $t = 2.25$ hours. It could be traveling at 60 mph. It could even be stopped. This is called the instantaneous velocity, and the way it is found is similar to the way we found the slope of the tangent line.

Area Under a Curve

The second problem that calculus studies is finding the area between a curve and the x-axis. For instance, given the function $y = 1 - x^2$, we wish to find the area under the curve between $x = -1$ and $x = 1$ as shown in the following graph. The problem is that the parabola is curved and that means that it is difficult to find the exact area. Similar to finding the slope of the tangent line, we approximate the area using rectangles. Since the curve is symmetric to the y-axis, we will start building rectangles at $x = 0$.

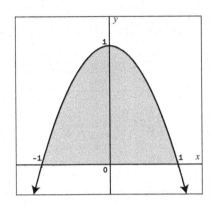

We choose to have the width of each rectangle equal to $\frac{1}{4}$. We start at $x = 0$ and draw a rectangle whose height is the value of the function at $x = 0$ and whose width is $\frac{1}{4}$. We build a second rectangle whose height is the value of the function at $x = \frac{1}{4}$ and whose width is $\frac{1}{4}$. We build a third rectangle whose height is the value of the function at $x = \frac{1}{2}$ and whose width is $\frac{1}{4}$. We continue the pattern until we get to the x-intercept. The following graph illustrates what we are describing.

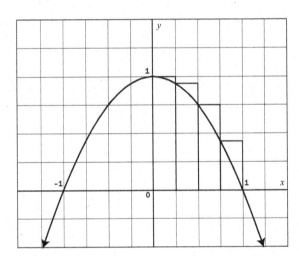

Since all the bases of the rectangles are $\frac{1}{4}$, we need to find the height of each rectangle. This involves finding the value of the function at $x = 0$, $x = \frac{1}{4}$, $x = \frac{1}{2}$, and $x = \frac{3}{4}$.

Rectangle	x	Height = $f(x)$	Base	Area = Base • Height
1	0	$1 - 0 = 1$	$\frac{1}{4}$	$\frac{1}{4}(1) = \frac{1}{4}$
2	$\frac{1}{4}$	$1 - \frac{1}{16} = \frac{15}{16}$	$\frac{1}{4}$	$\frac{1}{4}\left(\frac{15}{16}\right) = \frac{15}{64}$
3	$\frac{1}{2}$	$1 - \frac{1}{4} = \frac{3}{4}$	$\frac{1}{4}$	$\frac{1}{4}\left(\frac{3}{4}\right) = \frac{3}{16}$
4	$\frac{3}{4}$	$1 - \frac{9}{16} = \frac{7}{16}$	$\frac{1}{4}$	$\frac{1}{4}\left(\frac{7}{16}\right) = \frac{7}{64}$

Adding these areas $\frac{1}{4} + \frac{15}{64} + \frac{3}{16} + \frac{7}{64}$ and changing to a decimal, we get 0.78125. Since this is half of the area under the curve, we double it to find the total area under the curve is approximately 1.5625.

Between $x = 0$ and $x = 1$, we used "outer rectangles" and the sum of the areas of these rectangles will be greater than the actual area. It is possible to use "lower estimate rectangles" as well and the sum of the areas of these rectangles will be less than the actual area. The picture looks like this:

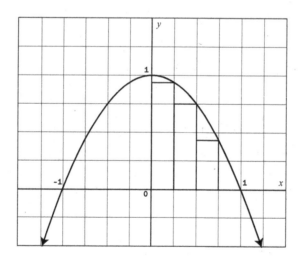

Note that there are only 3 rectangles as the height of the 4th rectangle has height zero.

Another way to solve this is to use "upper estimate rectangles." These rectangles both over-estimate and underestimate the true area at the same time making it a very accurate technique. However, the calculations are more cumbersome.

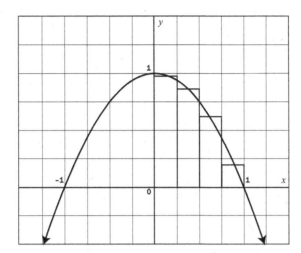

The more rectangles that are chosen, the more work is necessary but the more precise the answer. As the number of rectangles gets infinitely large, the area under the curve becomes infinitely close to $1.\overline{33}$.

Infinite Series

The third problem calculus studies is more theoretical and has to do with whether a sequence of numbers gets infinitely large or small or approaches a specific number.

We define a **sequence** $\{a_n\}$ as a set of numbers following some algebraic rule for $n = 1, 2, 3, 4,$ ... going to infinity. For instance, if $\{a_n\} = n^2 + n + 1$, the terms of the sequence are 3, 7, 13, 21, ...

We say a sequence **diverges** or is **divergent** if the terms of the sequence get infinitely large or small. $\{a_n\} = n^2 + n + 1$ is divergent because as n gets larger and larger, the terms get larger and larger without bound. No matter how large the number you can think of, $\{a_n\} = n^2 + n + 1$ will eventually become larger than it.

But if the terms of the sequence never get larger than a number L, then we say that the sequence is **convergent** or **converges to L**.

For instance, if the sequence is given by $\{a_n\} = \dfrac{1}{n}$, its terms are $1, \dfrac{1}{2}, \dfrac{1}{3}, \dfrac{1}{4}, ...$ These terms get smaller and smaller and get infinitely closer to zero. We say that the sequence converges to zero. It doesn't actually reach zero, but then again, the terms are generated infinitely.

If the sequence is given by $\{a_n\} = \dfrac{n}{n+1}$, its terms are $\dfrac{1}{2}, \dfrac{2}{3}, \dfrac{3}{4}, \dfrac{4}{5}, ... \dfrac{99}{100}, ... \dfrac{99999}{100000}, ...$ These terms get larger and larger and because the numerator is one smaller than the denominator, the sequence gets closer and closer to 1. We say that the sequence converges to 1.

A **series** is the sum of the terms of a sequence. For instance, if we add the terms of the sequence $\{a_n\} = n^2 + n + 1$, we get $3 + 7 + 13 + 21 + \ldots$, it is clear that the sum of these terms gets infinitely large, and we say that the series is divergent as well as the sequence being divergent.

If we add the terms of the convergent sequence $\{a_n\} = \dfrac{n}{n+1}$, we get $\dfrac{1}{2} + \dfrac{2}{3} + \dfrac{3}{4} + \dfrac{4}{5} + \ldots + \dfrac{99}{100} + \ldots + \dfrac{99999}{100000} + \ldots$, our terms are getting closer to one so eventually we will be adding numbers similar to $1 + 1 + 1 + \ldots$ This gets infinitely large and the series is divergent although the sequence is convergent.

If we add the terms of the convergent sequence $\{a_n\} = \dfrac{1}{2^n}$, we get $1 + \dfrac{1}{2} + \dfrac{1}{4} + \dfrac{1}{8} + \dfrac{1}{16} + \ldots$. This sum will never get larger than 2, and we say that the series converges to 2.

On the other hand, if we add the terms of the convergent sequence $\{a_n\} = \dfrac{1}{n}$, we get $1 + \dfrac{1}{2} + \dfrac{1}{3} + \dfrac{1}{4} + \ldots$, and even though the terms are getting smaller and smaller, it turns out that contrary to logic, the series is divergent, meaning its sum will eventually get larger than any number you can think of.

On the TExES Core Subjects 4–8 exam, any questions about the convergence and divergence of a sequence or series will be easily answerable if you generate just a few terms of the sequence.

COMPETENCY 008

The teacher understands measurement as a process.

The beginning teacher:

A. Selects and uses appropriate units of measurement (e.g., temperature, money, mass, weight, area, capacity, density, percents, speed, acceleration) to quantify, compare, and communicate information.

B. Develops, justifies, and uses conversions within measurement systems.

C. Applies dimensional analysis to derive units and formulas in a variety of situations (e.g., rates of change of one variable with respect to another) and to find and evaluate solutions to problems.

D. Describes the precision of measurement and the effects of error on measurement.

E. Applies the Pythagorean Theorem, proportional reasoning, and right triangle trigonometry to solve measurement problems.

Measurement is an area of mathematics used by many on a daily basis, whether it be calculating the area of a garden, estimating time to complete a project, or calculating distance of travel from point A to B. Often we are asked to convert units of measure. Below are charts of the U.S. and metric units of measure. Note that U.S. units are sometimes called U.S. customary units, standard units, or English units.

Units of Measure

U.S.	
12 inches	1 foot
3 feet	1 yard
5,280 feet	1 mile
Metric	
10 millimeters	1 centimeter
1,000 millimeters	1 meter
100 centimeters	1 meter
10 centimeters	1 decimeter
10 decimeters	1 meter
10 meters	1 decameter
1,000 meters	1 kilometer

Example   Sasha walked $\frac{1}{4}$ mile from home to her friend Nick's house. Together they walked 30 yards to the public pool. How many feet did Sasha walk altogether?

We use the fact that 1 mile = 5,280 feet and 1 yard = 3 feet to answer this question. First, we need to convert $\frac{1}{4}$ of a mile into feet: $\frac{1}{4}$ (1 mile) = $\frac{1}{4}$ (5,280 feet) = 1,320 feet. Next, we convert 30 yards into feet: 30(3 feet) = 90 feet. Finally, find the sum of the two distances: 1,320 + 90 = 1,410 feet. Sasha walked a total of 1,410 feet.

Units of Mass

U.S.	
16 ounces	1 pound
2,000 pounds	1 ton
Metric	
1,000 grams	1 kilogram
1,000 kilograms	1 metric ton

Example   Jesse sells heavy furniture. For shipping purposes, he must inform the movers of the weight of each shipment in metric tons. Jesse will be shipping an order of furniture that weighs 750 kilograms. How many metric tons will he be shipping?

Creating a proportion can be handy when converting units.

$$\frac{1 \text{ metric ton}}{1,000 \text{ kilograms}} = \frac{x \text{ metric tons}}{750 \text{ kilograms}}$$

$$750 = 1,000x$$

$$x = \frac{750}{1,000} = 0.75 \text{ metric tons}$$

Jesse will be shipping 0.75 metric tons of furniture.

Units of Capacity

U.S.	
3 teaspoons	1 tablespoon
2 tablespoons	1 fluid ounce
8 fluid ounces	1 cup
16 fluid ounces	1 pint
2 cups	1 pint
2 pints	1 quart
4 quarts	1 gallon
Metric	
10 milliliters	1 centiliter
10 centiliters	1 deciliter
1,000 milliliters	1 liter
10 deciliters	1 liter
1,000 liters	1 kiloliter

Example   A recipe for lemonade spritzer requires 1 pint of fresh lemon juice, 1 cup of sugar, 2 quarts of club soda, and 2 limes sliced very thin for garnishing. How much liquid, in cups, is needed for this recipe?

First, we need to know which ingredients are liquid: 1 pint of lemon juice and 2 quarts of club soda. Next, we need to convert pints and quarts into cups. We know 1 pint = 2 cups. We know 1 quart = 2 pints, so 2 quarts = 4 pints. Since 1 pint = 2 cups, then 4 pints = 8 cups. Altogether, we need 2 cups of lemon juice and 8 cups of club soda for a total of 10 cups of liquid for the recipe.

Units of Time

60 seconds	1 minute
60 minutes	1 hour
24 hours	1 day
7 days	1 week
52 weeks	1 year
12 months	1 year

Example   Mercedes determined she worked on her science project for a total of 1 day, 7 hours, and 24 minutes. How many total hours did she spend on her project?

First, let's start by converting the 24 minutes into a portion of an hour. We know 60 minutes = 1 hour, so 24 minutes = $\dfrac{24}{60}$ = 0.4 hours. Also, 1 day = 24 hours. Mercedes spent 24 + 7 + 0.4 = 31.4 hours working on her science project.

Temperature

A thermometer measures temperature in **Fahrenheit** and/or **Celsius**. Conversion formulas can be used to convert temperatures from Fahrenheit to Celsius and vice versa.

$$F = C \cdot \dfrac{9}{5} + 32$$

$$C = \dfrac{5}{9}(F - 32)$$

Error of Measurement

Often, measuring physical objects with tools such as rulers and protractors can result in a slight error of measurement. For example, most textbooks are rectangular in shape and have four right angles. If using a protractor to measure the angle of a book corner results in finding the angle to be 88.5 degrees instead of 90 degrees, there is a 1.5 degree error of measure. To determine the percent of error, divide the amount of error by the original amount that should be present. For example, $\frac{1.5}{90} = 0.01\overline{66}$ or $1.\overline{66}\%$ error.

Right Triangle Trigonometry

The study of right triangles and their measures of sides and angles is right triangle trigonometry.

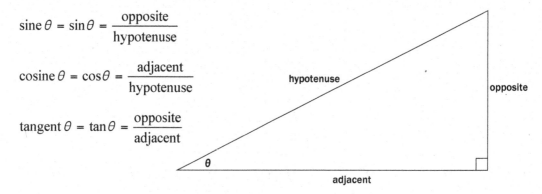

$$\text{sine } \theta = \sin\theta = \frac{\text{opposite}}{\text{hypotenuse}}$$

$$\text{cosine } \theta = \cos\theta = \frac{\text{adjacent}}{\text{hypotenuse}}$$

$$\text{tangent } \theta = \tan\theta = \frac{\text{opposite}}{\text{adjacent}}$$

A good way to remember this is the mnemonic **SOH CAH TOA** (Sine Opposite Hypotenuse, Cosine Adjacent Hypotenuse, Tangent Opposite Adjacent). Notice that the first letter in each triplet refers to the trig function, the second letter refers to the numerator of the quotient, and the third refers to the denominator of the quotient.

SOH   CAH   TOA

↓   ↓   ↓

$$\sin\theta = \frac{O}{H} \qquad \cos\theta = \frac{A}{H} \qquad \tan\theta = \frac{O}{A}$$

Example   Using the figure below, find the sine, cosine, and tangent of θ.

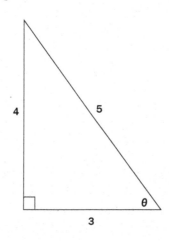

$$\sin\theta = \frac{\text{opposite}}{\text{hypotenuse}} = \frac{4}{5}$$

$$\cos\theta = \frac{\text{adjacent}}{\text{hypotenuse}} = \frac{3}{5}$$

$$\tan\theta = \frac{\text{opposite}}{\text{adjacent}} = \frac{4}{3}$$

Similar Triangles

Triangles are said to be similar if they have congruent corresponding angles (equal measure) and their corresponding sides are proportional. Consider the figure below of similar triangles $\triangle ABC$ and $\triangle ADE$. Find the measure of x using proportional reasoning.

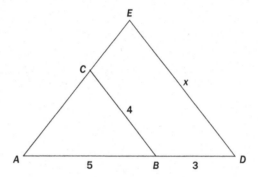

In the figure, we can see $\overline{AB} = 5$, $\overline{AD} = 8$, and $\overline{CB} = 4$. Using this information, we can create a proportion to solve for $\overline{ED} = x$.

$$\frac{AB}{CB} = \frac{AD}{ED}$$

$$\frac{5}{4} = \frac{8}{x}$$

Using cross products or cross multiplication, we find

$$5x = 32$$

$$x = \frac{32}{5} = 6.4$$

Pythagorean Theorem

The Pythagorean Theorem is a relation among the three sides of a right triangle, $a^2 + b^2 = c^2$, where a and b are the **legs** of the right triangle and c is the **hypotenuse**, or side opposite the right angle. We use the equation $a^2 + b^2 = c^2$ when given two of the side lengths of a right triangle and we need to find the third.

Example   Diane is going to mount a new 40-inch LED TV on the wall. The base of the TV is 35 inches. What is the height? Round your answer to the nearest inch.

Before beginning this problem, some background knowledge on televisions is needed. When buying a 40-inch television, the 40 inches refers to the diagonal (see the figure that follows). A television is also a rectangle, not a triangle. However, the diagonal of the rectangle creates two right triangles, allowing the Pythagorean Theorem to be a solution strategy.

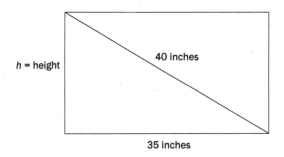

Next, substitute the values into the Pythagorean Theorem and solve for h.

$$35^2 + h^2 = 40^2$$

$$1,225 + h^2 = 1,600$$

$$h^2 = 375$$

$$\sqrt{h^2} = \sqrt{375} \approx 19.36 \approx 19 \text{ inches}$$

The LED TV is about 19 inches high and 35 inches wide, with a 40-inch diagonal.

COMPETENCY 009

The teacher understands the geometric relationships and axiomatic structure of Euclidian geometry.

The beginning teacher:

A. Understands concepts and properties of points, lines, planes, angles, lengths, and distances.

B. Analyzes and applies the properties of parallel and perpendicular lines.

C. Uses the properties of congruent triangles to explore geometric relationships and prove theorems.

D. Describes and justifies geometric constructions.

E. Applies knowledge of right angles to identify acute, right, and obtuse triangles.

F. Measures angles correctly using a protractor.

The fundamental building blocks of geometry are **points**, **lines**, and **planes**. These terms are called undefined terms, but an intuitive notion of these terms is illustrated in the table that follows.

Term and Symbol	Description	Figure
Point A	Point A is a vertex of the triangle.	
	Point A is located at $(-3, 0)$.	
Line ℓ	Line ℓ is similar to the center line of a road. The outer lines and the center line are *parallel* lines.	
Perpendicular lines	$\overleftrightarrow{PQ}$ and $\overleftrightarrow{RS}$ are *perpendicular* lines.	
Ray	A portion of a line that starts at a point and extends infinitely in a particular direction to infinity	
Line segment	A portion of a line which links two points without extending beyond them	

Term and Symbol	Description	Figure
Plane γ	Plane γ is like a tabletop or a flat surface; however, a plane would extend infinitely and have zero thickness.	
Plane *ABC* or plane γ		

Angles and Their Measures

When two rays or lines meet at a point, they form an **angle**, measured in **degrees**. Congruent angles are two or more angles that have the same size or measure, regardless of their orientation or how they are drawn. If angles *A* and *B* are congruent, we write $\angle A \cong \angle B$. Descriptions of types of angles are given below.

- **Right angles** measure exactly 90 degrees.

- **Acute angles** measure between 0 and 90 degrees.

- **Obtuse angles** measure greater than 90 degrees but less than 180 degrees.

- **Straight angles** measure 180 degrees and are also called lines.

- **Reflex angles** measure greater than 180 and less than 360 degrees.

- **Supplementary angles** are any two angles whose sum is 180 degrees.

- **Complementary angles** are any two angles whose sum is 90 degrees.

- **Vertical angles** are opposite angles formed by two intersecting lines, where vertical angles are congruent.

Angles Formed by Parallel Lines Cut by a Transversal

Let parallel lines *m* and *n* be cut by another line, called a transversal *t*. The following congruent angles are formed by these lines (see figure below):

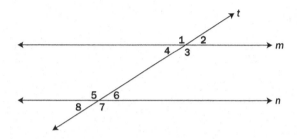

- There are four pairs of congruent **vertical** or **opposite angles:** $\angle 1 \cong \angle 3$, $\angle 2 \cong \angle 4$, $\angle 5 \cong \angle 7$, $\angle 6 \cong \angle 8$.

- There are four pairs of congruent **corresponding angles:** $\angle 1 \cong \angle 5$, $\angle 4 \cong \angle 8$, $\angle 2 \cong \angle 6$, $\angle 3 \cong \angle 7$.

- There are two pairs of congruent **alternate interior angles:** $\angle 4 \cong \angle 6$, $\angle 3 \cong \angle 5$.

- There are two pairs of congruent **alternate exterior angles:** $\angle 1 \cong \angle 7$, $\angle 2 \cong \angle 8$.

- There are two pairs of **same side interior angles** that are supplementary: $\angle 4 + \angle 5 = 180°$, $\angle 3 + \angle 6 = 180°$.

Constructions with a Compass and Straight Edge

Constructing Parallel Lines

Parallel lines never intersect as they have the same slope or incline.

Example   Given line ℓ and point *P*, we will construct a parallel line to line ℓ.

To construct a line parallel to a given line follow these four steps:

Step 1: Choose a point A anywhere on line ℓ, and draw the line passing through it and point P.

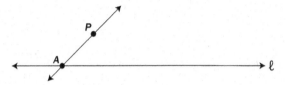

Step 2: Set the compass to the width of $\overline{AP}$, with the point on point A and the pencil on point P. With the pointer still on point A, draw an arc that intersects line ℓ. Where the arc intersects line ℓ, label this point X.

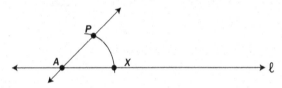

Step 3: With the same opening of the compass, draw intersecting arcs, first with the pointer at P and then with the pointer at X to create a point Y. Point Y is the fourth vertex of the rhombus.

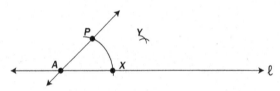

Step 4: Draw $\overleftrightarrow{PY}$. Line $\overleftrightarrow{PY} \parallel$ line ℓ.

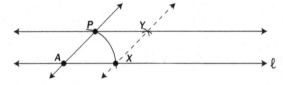

Constructing an Angle Bisector

An angle bisector is a ray that divides an angle into two congruent parts. To construct an angle bisector, follow these three steps:

Step 1: With the compass pointer on *A*, the vertex of the angle to be bisected, draw an arc intersecting the angle at points *B* and *C*.

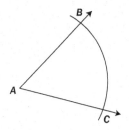

Step 2: Keep the compass set at the same distance as in Step 1. Place the pointer on point *B* and create a small arc near the center of the angle, then place the pointer on point *C* and make an intersecting arc near the center of the angle. Where the two small arcs intersect, label this point *D*.

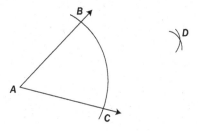

Step 3: Draw $\overline{AD}$, which is the angle bisector of ∠*A*. Therefore, ∠*BAD* ≅ ∠*CAD*.

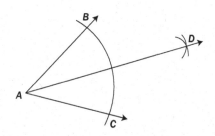

Constructing Perpendicular Lines

Lines that are perpendicular form right angles. To construct a line perpendicular to line ℓ going through point P, follow these three steps:

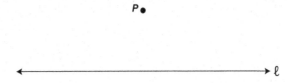

Step 1: Place the compass pointer on P and draw an arc that intersects line ℓ at points A and B.

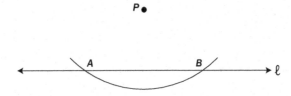

Step 2: With the same compass opening, place the pointer on A and make an arc below line ℓ, and then place the pointer on B and make an intersecting arc. Call the intersection point C.

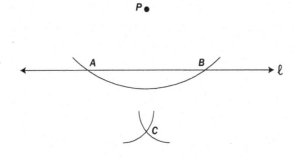

Step 3: Draw a line from point P through C, creating a perpendicular line. Line $\overleftrightarrow{PC} \perp$ line ℓ.

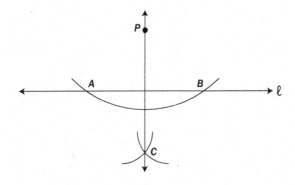

Constructing a Perpendicular Bisector

A perpendicular bisector is a line that is perpendicular to a given line segment and bisects the line segment into two congruent parts. To construct a perpendicular bisector of segment $\overline{AB}$, follow these two steps:

Step 1: Set the compass pointer on A and the pencil between points A and B, but more than halfway between the points. Then, create an arc through the line. Keeping the same compass setting, place the pointer on B and create an arc intersecting the first. Label the points of intersection C and D.

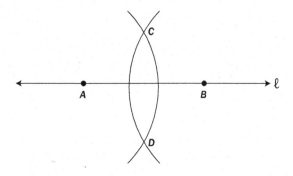

Step 2: Draw a line through points C and D. Label point M the point of intersection of $\overleftrightarrow{CD}$ and $\overleftrightarrow{AB}$. Point M is the midpoint of $\overline{AB}$.

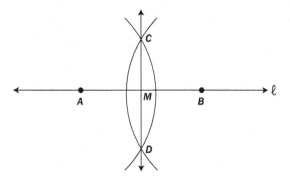

We now know $\overleftrightarrow{CD} \perp \overleftrightarrow{AB}$, $\overleftrightarrow{CD}$ bisects $\overline{AB}$, and $\overline{AM} \cong \overline{MB}$.

COMPETENCY 010

The teacher analyzes the properties of two- and three-dimensional figures.

The beginning teacher:

A. Uses and understands the development of formulas to find lengths, perimeters, areas, and volumes of basic geometric figures.

B. Applies relationships among similar figures, scale, and proportion and analyzes how changes in scale affect area and volume measurements.

C. Uses a variety of representations (e.g., numeric, verbal, graphic, symbolic) to analyze and solve problems involving two- and three-dimensional figures such as circles, triangles, polygons, cylinders, prisms, and spheres.

D. Analyzes the relationship among three-dimensional figures and related two-dimensional representations (e.g., projections, cross-sections, nets) and uses these representations to solve problems.

E. Generates formulas involving perimeter, area, circumference, volume, and scaling.

Area (A) and Perimeter (P) Formulas

		Area	Perimeter
Square		$A = s^2$	$P = 4s$
Rectangle		$A = l \times w$	$P = 2(l + w)$ or $2l + 2w$
Parallelogram		$A = b \times h$	$P = 2(a + b)$ or $2a + 2b$
Trapezoid		$A = \frac{1}{2}(b_1 + b_2)h$	$P = b_1 + b_2 + a + c$

		Area	Perimeter
Triangle		$A = \dfrac{1}{2}(h \times b)$	$P = a + b + c$
Right triangle		$A = \dfrac{1}{2}(a \times b)$	$P = a + b + c$ $P = a + b + \sqrt{a^2 + b^2}$
Equilateral triangle		$A = \dfrac{\sqrt{3}}{4}s^2$	$P = 3s$
Circle		$A = \pi r^2$	$C = 2\pi r = \pi d$ (C = circumference d = diameter = $2r$)

Volume (V) and Surface Area (SA) Formulas

B = area of the base shape

P = perimeter of the base shape

		Volume	Surface Area
Rectangular solid		$V = l \times w \times h$	$SA = 2lw + 2wh + 2lh$
Triangular prism		$V = B \times h$ or (area of triangle) $\times h$	$SA =$ 2 (Area of Base) + (Perimeter of Base) (Height of Solid)

(continued)

		Volume	Surface Area
Pyramid	(Note: The base shape can change.)	$V = \dfrac{1}{3} \times B \times h$	$SA = B +$ (area of each triangle)
Cylinder		$V = \pi r^2 h$	$SA = 2\pi rh + 2\pi r^2$
Cone		$V = \dfrac{1}{3}\pi r^2 h$	$SA = \pi r^2 + \pi rs$
Sphere		$V = \dfrac{4}{3}\pi r^3$	$SA = 4\pi r^2$

Nets

A **net** of a three-dimensional solid is what it would look like if it were opened out flat.

Three-dimensional Solid	Net
Cube	

Three-dimensional Solid	Net
Rectangular prism	
Triangular prism	
Square-based pyramid	
Tetrahedron	

Three-dimensional Solid	Net
Cylinder	
Cone	

Euler's Polyhedra Formula

A **polyhedron** is a solid object whose surface is made up of polygons. The **vertices** are the points at which the polygons meet. Each polygon is called a **face** of the polyhedron, and an **edge** is the side of the polygon. For any convex polyhedron, the sum of the **vertices** and **faces** is two more than the number of **edges**: $V + F = E + 2$.

Solid	Vertices	Faces	Edges
Cube	8	6	12
Rectangular prism	8	6	12
Triangular prism	6	5	9
Square-based pyramid	5	5	8
Tetrahedron	4	4	6

Dimensions and Relationships

Example 1   A certain cylinder has height 5 units and radius 3 units. If the height triples, how is the volume affected?

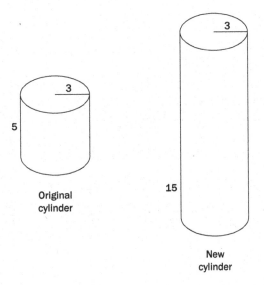

Original
cylinder

New
cylinder

The volume of the original cylinder is $V = \pi r^2 h = \pi(3^2)(5) = 45\pi$.

The volume of the new cylinder with the height tripled is $V = \pi r^2 h = \pi(3^2)(15) = 135\pi$.

The new volume is three times that of the original cylinder.

Example 2   A certain cylinder has height 5 units and radius 3 units. If the radius triples, how is the volume affected?

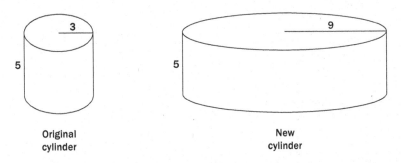

Original
cylinder

New
cylinder

The volume of the original cylinder is $V = \pi r^2 h = \pi(3^2)(5) = 45\pi$.

The volume of the new cylinder with the radius tripled is $V = \pi r^2 h = \pi(9^2)(5) = 405\pi$.

The new volume is nine times that of the original cylinder.

COMPETENCY 011

The teacher understands algebra and geometry through the Cartesian coordinate system and demonstrates knowledge of transformational geometry.

The beginning teacher:

A. Describes and justifies geometric constructions made using a reflection device and other appropriate technologies.

B. Uses translations, reflections, glide-reflections, and rotations to demonstrate congruence and to explore the symmetries of figures.

C. Uses dilations (expansions and contractions) to illustrate similar figures and proportionality.

D. Uses symmetry to describe tessellations and shows how they can be used to illustrate geometric concepts, properties, and relationships.

E. Applies concepts and properties of slope, midpoint, parallelism, and distance in the coordinate plane to explore properties of geometric figures and solve problems.

F. Applies transformations in the coordinate plane.

G. Uses geometry to model and describe the physical world.

H. Identifies, locates and names points on a coordinate plane using ordered pairs of real numbers in all quadrants.

I. Graphs in the first quadrant of the coordinate plane ordered pairs of numbers arising from mathematical and real-world problems, including those generated by number patterns or found in an input-output table.

J. Graphs reflections across the horizontal or vertical axis and graphs translations on a coordinate plane.

Transformations

Transformations for algebraic functions were discussed in Competency 006. The same concepts apply to shapes defined in the Cartesian coordinate system with several more included. Translation, reflection, rotation, glide reflection, and dilation are the five basic types of transformations. Glide reflection is distinct from the other four by being a composite of two transformations: translation and reflection.

Translations

A **translation** is a motion or transformation of a plane that moves every point of the plane a specified distance in a specified direction along a straight line. A **translation in a coordinate plane** is a function that slides a point (x, y) to the corresponding point $(x + a, y + b)$, where a and b are real numbers.

Reflections

A **reflection** about a line ℓ is a transformation of the plane that pairs each point P of the plane with a point P' in such a way that line ℓ is the perpendicular bisector of $\overline{PP'}$, as long as P is not on line ℓ. If P is on line ℓ, then $P = P'$.

The coordinates of a **reflection in a coordinate plane** about the x- or y-axis can be quite easy to find, given the coordinates of the original point. A reflection across the x-axis takes a point (x, y) to the corresponding point $(x, -y)$. A reflection across the y-axis takes a point (x, y) to the corresponding point $(-x, y)$. A reflection about the line $y = x$ interchanges the coordinates of the point. For example, if we reflect the point $(1, 3)$ across the line $y = x$, the new point is $(3, 1)$.

Rotations

A **rotation** is a transformation of the plane determined by holding one point, the center, fixed, and rotating the plane about this point by a certain amount (degrees) in a certain direction (clockwise or counterclockwise).

Glide Reflections

Another basic transformation is called a **glide reflection**. A glide reflection is a transformation consisting of a reflection followed by a translation in a vector parallel to the line of reflection.

Dilation

A dilation is also referred to as a **size transformation** that assigns some point A to a collinear point A'. To dilate a point or figure we use a scale factor r and multiply both the x- and y-coordinates by r. When dilating a figure, if $r > 0$, the figure is enlarged by a factor of r; if $0 < r < 1$, the figure is contracted or made smaller by a factor of r.

For example, suppose we have a triangle with vertices at A $(1, 2)$, B $(3, 5)$, and C $(5, 3)$ and we want to dilate the figure by a scale factor of 3. The transformed points are A' $(3, 6)$, B' $(9, 15)$, and C' $(15, 9)$. The triangles are similar and the side lengths are proportional by a scale factor of 3.

Lines of Symmetry

Figures may have **lines of symmetry**, which can be thought of as imaginary folding lines that produce two congruent mirror-image figures. In the figures below, we can see a square has four lines of symmetry and a circle has an infinite number of lines of symmetry.

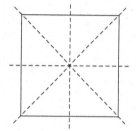 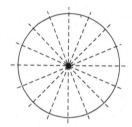

Tessellations

A **tessellation** is a pattern formed by repeating a single unit or shape that when repeated fills the plane with no gaps and no overlaps. Brick patterns or a cross section of a beehive are common tessellations found in the real world.

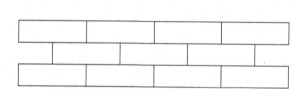 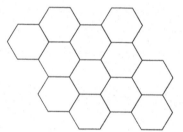

COMPETENCY 012

The teacher understands how to use graphical and numerical techniques to explore data, characterize patterns, and describe departures from patterns.

The beginning teacher:

A. Organizes and displays data in a variety of formats (e.g., tables, frequency distributions, stem-and-leaf plots, box-and-whisker plots, histograms, pie charts).

B. Applies concepts of center, spread, shape, and skewness to describe a data distribution.

C. Supports arguments, makes predictions and draws conclusions using summary statistics and graphs to analyze and interpret one-variable data.

D. Demonstrates an understanding of measures of central tendency (e.g., mean, median, mode) and spread (e.g., range, interquartile range, variance, standard deviation).

E. Analyzes connections among concepts of center and spread, data clusters and gaps, data outliers, and measures of central tendency and dispersion.

F. Calculates and interprets percentiles and quartiles.

We describe data analysis as a process of inspecting, describing, and summarizing data with the goal of discovering useful information, suggesting conclusions, and making decisions. We use statistical methods to analyze what occurred in the past in order to predict what may happen in the future. So while probability concerns itself with the future, statistics and data analysis concerns itself with the past.

A number of graphs can be used to organize and describe data. Categorical data represent characteristics of objects of individuals in groups or categories. Numerical data are collected on numerical variables (distance, time, scores, etc.).

Pictographs

A picture graph, or **pictograph**, represents tallies or frequencies of categories. A picture, or symbol, represents a quantity of items and is denoted in a legend. In the following example, a class of students was surveyed about the types of animals they have at home. The frequencies are displayed in the table below, followed by a pictograph representing the data. For instance, 7 students have a dog, 4 students have a cat, etc.

Type of Animal	Frequency
Dog	7
Cat	4
Snake	2
Fish	10

Type of Animal	☺ = 2 Animals
Dog	☺ ☺ ☺ ☾
Cat	☺ ☺
Snake	☺
Fish	☺ ☺ ☺ ☺ ☺

Bar Graphs

A **bar graph** is used to depict frequencies of categorical data. The following bar graph represents the same data as the pictograph just shown.

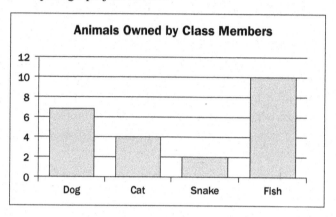

Circle Graphs or Pie Charts

A **circle graph**, also called a **pie chart**, is used to depict frequencies of categorical data. The data from the pictograph and bar graph produces the circle graph below. The reason that the percentages do not add to 100% is because of round-off error.

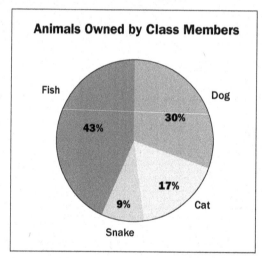

Line or Dot Plots

A **line or dot plot** provides a quick way of organizing numerical data when the number of values is not excessively large. Suppose there is a set of test scores: 70, 72, 83, 75, 88, 81, 94, 94, 80, 85, 93. A line plot for the set of test scores consists of a horizontal number line on which each score is denoted by an X or a dot.

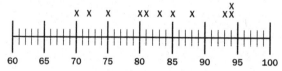

Stem and Leaf Plots

The **stem and leaf plot** is akin to the line plot, but the number line is typically vertical and digits are used to represent data rather than dots or X's. The numbers on the left side of the vertical segment are called the **stem**. The **leaves** are the numbers on the right side.

The high temperatures for Jack's recent trip to Dallas, Texas, were as follows: 65, 72, 69, 81, 74, 78, 73, 78, 70, 82, 71, 77, 80, 67, 78, 73. The stemplot for this data is as follows:

Temperatures in Dallas, Texas, in October

8	0, 1, 2
7	0, 1, 2, 3, 3, 4, 7, 8, 8, 8
6	5, 7, 9

Legend: 6|5 = 65

Histograms

Histograms look similar to bar graphs, but they display grouped numerical data and have adjoining bars. Below is a stem and leaf plot showing ages of presidents at death with its accompanying histogram.

The histogram is similar to the stemplot in that it gives the number of data entries in each bin, but loses the actual data.

4	6, 9
5	3, 6, 7, 7, 8
6	0, 0, 3, 3, 4, 5, 6, 7, 7, 7, 8
7	0, 1, 1, 2, 3, 4, 7, 8, 8, 9
8	0, 1, 1, 2, 3, 5, 8
9	0, 0, 3, 3

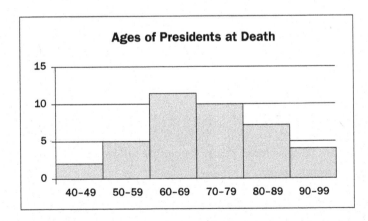

Bivariate Data

Bivariate data examines the relationship between two variables. The two variables are called the response variable and the explanatory variable. The data is given as points (explanatory, response).

The response variable measures the outcome of a study. The explanatory variable attempts to explain the response variable.

Example: How does studying affect the score in a final exam? The explanatory variable is hours of study which explains the response variable, the score. Someone who studies 8 hours and received a score of 75 would have the point (8, 75).

A **scatter plot** shows the relationship between two quantitative variables measured on the same individuals.

The values of one variable appear on the horizontal (*x*) axis and the values of the other variable appear on the vertical (*y*) axis. Each piece of bivariate data appears as a point in the plot. The explanatory variable is placed on the *x*-axis and the response variable is placed on the *y*-axis.

Interpreting scatter plots

- Form—does the data appear linear or curved?

- Direction of association

    ○ **Positive association**—data goes up to the right

    ○ **Negative association**—data goes down to the right

- Strength of an association—how closely the points follow a clear form. Both of the associations above are strongly linear.

- Line of best fit (sometimes called the regression line)—The line of best fit is a straight line that describes how a response variable *y* changes as an explanatory variable *x* changes. Lines of best fit are used to predict the value of *y* for a given value of *x*. These lines require an explanatory variable and a response variable.

The closer that the line of best fit comes to the data points, the stronger the association is:

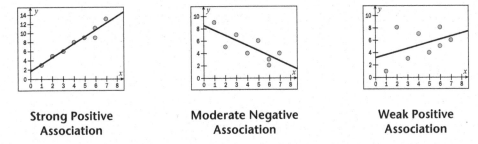

**Strong Positive
Association**

**Moderate Negative
Association**

**Weak Positive
Association**

- Meaning—an association between x and y means that as x changes, y changes. An association between x and y does not mean necessarily that x causes y.

    Example: There is a strong positive association between the number of firefighters sent to a fire and the amount of damage the fire does. However, sending firefighters to a fire surely does not cause damage.

We can measure the strength of the association. The **correlation coefficient**, denoted by r, measures the strength and direction of a linear relationship between variables. The value of r will be between –1 and 1 inclusive. Positive values of r mean a positive association (as x increases, y increases) while negative values of r mean a negative association (as x increases, y decreases). The closer r is to 1 or –1, the stronger the association is.

For the hours-studied-versus-final-exam example, below is a scatter plot of the data and the line of best fit. We would interpret this as a fairly strong positive association between the duration of study and the final grade. Computer analysis confirms what we see by eye: r is equal to 0.9. But we must not assume that studying causes grades to be higher. There are other factors that determine the grade ranging from how smart the student is to how much sleep he or she got the night before.

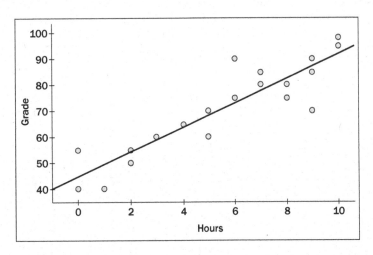

Measures of Central Tendency

When we have a great deal of data in numerical form such as the heights of every student in the school, your grades in all the math tests you took this year, every purchase that was made in a store today, or the yearly salary of every worker in a building, there is usually too much data to grasp at one time. Usually we prefer to have a single number that can represent that data. We call this a measure of central tendency.

- **Mean or average:** The mean of a set of data is the average and is usually denoted $\bar{x}$. To find it, you add up all the data and divide by the number of pieces of data.

  Example: 8 people went out to dinner. Following are the amounts they spent. Find the average cost.

  $18.55, $21.35, $17.45, $20.50, $24.25, $14.75, $19.65 and $22.90.

  $$\bar{x} = \frac{18.55 + 21.35 + 17.45 + 20.50 + 24.25 + 14.75 + 19.65 + 22.90}{8}$$

  $$= \frac{159.40}{8} = \$19.93$$

- **Median:** The median of a set of data is the middle score. To find the median, first put the data in increasing or decreasing order. Let n represent the number of pieces of data. If n is odd, the median is the data value: $\frac{n+1}{2}$. If n is even, take the average of data $\frac{n}{2}$ and the piece of data directly after it. When one of the data is much larger or smaller than the rest of the data, the mean can be strongly affected while the median is not.

  Example: A small class is made up of the students with first names: Susie, Joe, Michael, Shawn, Caroline, Steve, Kurt, Jennifer, Matthew, and Jonathan. Find the median name length.

  The lengths of the names are 5, 3, 7, 5, 8, 5, 4, 8, 7, and 8. When put in order we get: 3, 4, 5, 5, **5, 7**, 7, 8, 8, 8. Since there are 10 pieces of data, the median is the average of the 5th and 6th pieces of data, which are 5 and 7. The median is 6.

- **Mode:** The mode of a set of data is the data that occurs the most often.

  Example: In the class mentioned above, since a name with 8 letters occurs more often than any other number of letters, 8 is the mode.

Example: When leaving a movie, people rated it 1 to 5 with 5 the strongest positive rating and 1 the strongest negative. As the moviegoers voted, their ratings were tallied. At right are the results. Find the average score, the median score, and the mode.

5	⠀⠀⠀⠀ |||
4	⠀⠀⠀⠀ ||||
3	⠀⠀ ||
2	⠀ ||
1				

Solution:

Score	Frequency
5	18
4	19
3	12
2	7
1	3

$$\overline{x} = \frac{18(5) + 19(4) + 12(3) + 7(2) + 3(1)}{59}$$

$$= \frac{219}{59} = 3.71$$

Median is the 30th score, which is 4.

Mode is the most common score, which is 4.

It is sometimes useful to make comparisons about the relative values of the mean and median. We can do that sometimes without knowing the actual data.

The most common shape of a smoothed-out histogram is one of the following three. In a symmetric distribution the mean and median are very close to each other. If the data is right-skewed with the bulge of the data to the left and the tail of the data to the right, the mean will be to the right of the median as some larger values tend to make the mean greater while the median is not affected by size. Similarly, if the data is left-skewed with the bulge of the data to the right and the tail of the data to the left, the mean will be to the left of the median as some smaller values tend to make the mean smaller while the median is not affected by size. Knowing the mode is impossible unless we actually see the data.

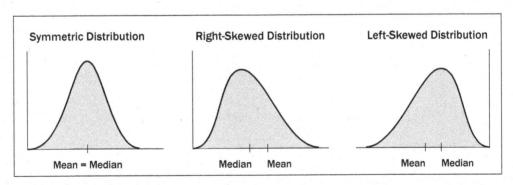

Box-and-Whisker Plots

A **box-and-whisker plot**, or box plot, is a way to represent the **five-number summary** of the data. The five numbers are the minimum, first quartile, median (or second quartile), third quartile, and maximum (or fourth quartile). A box plot can be either horizontal or vertical. We draw lines at the first, second, and third quartiles, which will form the box, and place dots or short lines at the minimum and maximum values; draw segments from each end of the box to these extreme values to create the whiskers.

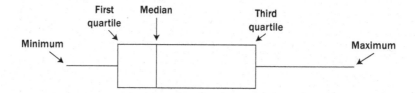

The quartiles of a data set divide the data into four regions with the same number of data values in each. The first quartile has 25% of the data values below it, the second quartile has 50% of the data values below it, the third quartile has 75% of the data values below it, and the fourth quartile has 100% of the data values below it. If there are 12 data points in the set, the third quartile includes the first 9 data values when in order from least to greatest.

Notice, the lengths of the whiskers and portions within the box are not the same. Many students confuse this to mean there are more data values represented between the median to the third quartile, but this is untrue. Box-and-whisker plots divide the data set into four regions with the same amount of data values in each region. The lengths differ based on the ranges of each area. The data described by the box plot above is skewed to the right as 50% of the data lies below the median while there is a much greater spread of data above the median. The **interquartile range** is the range between the values at the third and first quartiles.

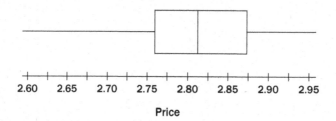

Price

The box-and-whisker plot above describes the price of a gallon of gas at filling stations along the main street of a town. Although the actual data is not given, we see that the median price is about $2.81, with 50% of the prices within the interquartile range of 12 cents (approximately $2.88 – $2.76). Since the data tails off to the left, the prices are skewed left and the mean price will be less than the median of $2.81.

Measures of Variability

While mean, median, and mode measure the center of a data set, they say nothing about how spread out the data is. We call this spread a measure of **variability**. A manufacturer of light bulbs would like small variability in the number of hours the bulbs will likely burn. A track coach who needs to decide which athletes go on to the finals may want larger variability in heat times because it will be easier to decide who are truly the fastest runners. There are two measures of variability that you are responsible for: range and standard deviation.

- **Range:** The range is the difference between the highest and lowest data values. If we are given all of the data, the range is easy to find. The larger the range, the greater the spread of the data.

    Example: If the heaviest person in a room is 205 pounds and the lightest person is 130 pounds, the range is 205 – 130 = 75 pounds.

- **Standard Deviation:** The standard deviation is a measure of how spread out the data is from the mean and is quite useful for data that is fairly symmetric. The greater the standard deviation, the greater the spread of the data from the mean. On the exam, you are not responsible for the actual calculations of standard deviation and variance, which is the square of the standard deviation.

    Example: 6 people are standing on a subway platform. If the average position on the platform is measured, arrange the following choices in order from smallest to largest standard deviation.

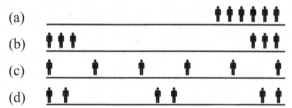

    Solution: In (a) all the people are standing at the end of the platform so the standard deviation should be close to zero. In (b), (c), and (d), the mean position is in the center of the platform. Choice (b) has the people furthest from the center so it will have the largest standard deviation.

- **Outliers:** An outlier is a score that is dramatically different from the other scores in a group of data. Outliers can have a huge effect on the mean and standard deviation and it is important to know whether the outlier is a true score and not a typographical error, or occurring because of special circumstances.

At this stage of statistics, the standard deviation by itself tells us little about how the data is distributed. However, when two or more data sets are compared, the standard deviations of each allow us to compare the data sets.

Example: The chart shows exam scores of 4 classes of 5 students each. Each class has a mean of 80 but the data is quite different. Students should be able to compute the mean, median, and range of each. The standard deviation was also calculated. Interpret the variability of the classes.

Solution: Class 1 has a standard deviation of 0 because there is no spread about the mean of 80. Classes 2, 3, and 4 have larger standard deviations, meaning that there is a bigger spread about the mean. 0 is an outlier in class 4, which dramatically changes the mean and standard deviation.

Class 1	Class 2	Class 3	Class 4
80	90	100	100
80	85	90	100
80	80	80	100
80	75	70	100
80	70	60	0
$\bar{x} = 80$	$\bar{x} = 80$	$\bar{x} = 80$	$\bar{x} = 80$
Median = 80	Median = 80	Median = 80	Median = 100
Range = 0	Range = 20	Range = 40	Range = 100
St. Dev = 0	St. Dev = 7.07	St. Dev = 14.14	St. Dev = 40

Normal Distributions

One of the most important distributions in statistics is called the **normal distribution.** If a histogram is "smoothed out," many times its curve will appear symmetric, single-peaked, and bell-shaped. Such a distribution is depicted by a **normal curve,** sometimes called a **bell curve** because of its flared shape. At right is a picture of a normal curve. Note how the data is more concentrated in the center than in the tails.

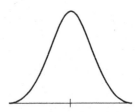

The reason these curves are so important in statistics is that so much of real-life statistics appears "normal." Here are some common examples:

- **Most data about the human body:** Examples include height, weight, fingernail length, hair length, how long people live, and so on.

- **Consumer prices:** Go to many markets and price a 2-liter bottle of soda. The data will appear normal with most prices about average, and fewer much cheaper and fewer much more expensive.

- **Wages:** Most people make an average amount of money while fewer make little money and fewer make a lot of money.

- **Time it takes to get to work:** Most days it might take 30 minutes to drive to work while fewer days it might take 20 minutes and fewer days it might take 40.

- **Grades:** Collect GPAs for a class of students and many students will have an average GPA, with fewer with low GPAs or with high GPAs.

The normal distribution follows an important rule called the **68-95-99.7% rule**. It states that in any normal distribution,

- 68% of the data lies within one standard deviation of the mean. In the figure provided, we have a normal distribution with the mean $\bar{x}$ in the center. Going out one standard deviation to the left and right of $\bar{x}$ will encompass 68% of the data.

- 95% of the data lies within two standard deviations of the mean. In the figure at right, we have a normal distribution with the mean $\bar{x}$ in the center. Going out two standard deviations to the left and right of $\bar{x}$ will encompass 95% of the data.

- 99.7% (or just about all) of the data lies within three standard deviations of the mean.

The more "normal" a distribution is, these relationships become closer to being perfectly true. No distribution is perfectly normal and therefore, these relationships are approximations in most real-life settings.

Example: The distribution of heights of adult American men is approximately normal with mean 69 inches and standard deviation 2.5 inches. On the normal curve at right, we mark the values for the mean and 1, 2, and 3 standard deviations above and below the mean.

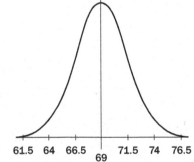

Although many distributions are normal, there are some that are not. For instance, although the time relative to the start of a class in which students arrive might be normal, the time that students leave relative to the end of class is not normal as everyone usually leaves at the same time.

We can make the following observations:

- 68% of adult American men are between 66.5 and 71.5 inches (5'6.5" and 5'11.5") tall.

- 95% of adult American men are between 64 and 74 inches (5'4" and 6'2") tall.

- 99.7% of adult American men are between 61.5 and 76.5 inches (5'1.5" and 6'4.5") tall.

COMPETENCY 013

The teacher understands the theory of probability.

The beginning teacher:

A. Explores concepts of experimental and theoretical probability through data collection, experiments and simulations.

B. Uses the concepts and principles of probability to describe the outcome of simple and compound events, including independent and dependent events.

C. Generates, simulates, and uses probability models to represent a situation.

D. Determines probabilities by constructing sample spaces to model situations.

E. Solves a variety of probability problems using combinations, permutations, and geometric probability (i.e., probability as the ratio of two areas).

F. Uses the binomial, geometric, and normal distributions to solve problems.

Sample Spaces and Counting

In an event or activity that has a few or many possible outcomes, a sample space lists all of those possible outcomes.

Example: A piggy bank contains a good number of nickels, dimes, and quarters. Two coins are chosen at random. Write the sample space of possible sums.

Solution: $\{.10, .15, .20, .30, .35, .50\}$

In probability, we are usually concerned with how many ways an event can occur. You should review the section on permutations and combinations under Competency 003 — Number Theory.

Probability

Probability refers to how likely an event is to occur. The probability of an event is a number between 0 and 1 inclusive. A probability of 0 means the event cannot occur, a probability of 1 means the event must occur, and a probability of 0.5 means that the event is as likely to occur than not. Probability can be expressed as a fraction, decimal, or percent. If a fair coin is tossed, the probability of heads is 0.5, and the probability of tails is 0.5.

In general: the probability of an event happening $= \dfrac{\text{number of ways the event can happen}}{\text{total number of outcomes}}$.

Example: A class has 20 students with 14 boys and 6 girls. The teacher calls on a student at random. The probability that she chooses a boy is $\dfrac{14}{20} = \dfrac{7}{10} = 0.7 = 70\%$.

Example: 5 people line up at random. If Jack and Jill are boyfriend and girlfriend, what is the probability that they will be next to each other?

Probability that Jack and Jill are together =

$\dfrac{\text{Number of ways Jack and Jill can be together}}{\text{Number of ways 5 people can line up}}$

Number of ways 5 people can line up $= 5! = 5 \bullet 4 \bullet 3 \bullet 2 \bullet 1 = 120$.

It is easy to simply generate the sample space of the possibilities with Jack and Jill together:

1	2	3	4	5
Jack	Jill			
	Jack	Jill		
		Jack	Jill	
			Jack	Jill

1	2	3	4	5
Jill	Jack			
	Jill	Jack		
		Jill	Jack	
			Jill	Jack

For each row where Jack and Jill are together there are $3! = 3 \bullet 2 \bullet 1 = 6$ different ways of lining up the three other people. So, there are 6 ways Jack can be in the 1st position and Jill in the 2nd position. There are 6 ways that Jack can be in the 2nd position and Jill in the 3rd position, and so forth. So

Probability that Jack and Jill are together $= \dfrac{8(6)}{120} = \dfrac{48}{120} = 40\%$

Example: There are 5 ice cream flavors and Consuela chooses a dish at random with 3 different flavors. What is the probability that she has both chocolate and vanilla?

Probability of having chocolate & vanilla =

$$\frac{\text{Number of dishes with chocolate, vanilla, and 1 other flavor}}{\text{Number of dishes with 3 flavors}}$$

Number of dishes with 3 flavors $= {_5}C_3 = \dfrac{5!}{3!\,2!} = \dfrac{5 \bullet 4 \bullet 3 \bullet 2 \bullet 1}{3 \bullet 2 \bullet 1 \bullet 2 \bullet 1} = 10$

Number of dishes with chocolate, vanilla, and 1 other flavor $= 3$

Probability of having chocolate and vanilla $= \dfrac{3}{10} = 0.3 = 30\%$.

Mutually Exclusive and Complementary Events

Events that are **mutually exclusive** (also called disjoint) are events that cannot happen at the same time. Examples of choosing mutually exclusive events are:

- Choose a whole number. It is either even or odd.

- When you get to a traffic light, you can go either straight, turn left, or turn right.

Two events are described as **complementary** if they are the only two possible outcomes. The two examples above are complementary events. For any event A, the probability of A complement is given by $P(A)^C = 1 - P(A)$.

Examples:
- If the probability of choosing a boy is 62%, the probability of choosing a girl is $1 - 0.62 = 0.38$, which is 38%.

- If the probability that a lamp turns on is 98%, the probability that it does not turn on is $1 - 0.98 = 0.02$, which is 2%.

- If two events A and B are mutually exclusive, the probability of A or $B =$ Prob(A) + Prob(B).

Example: If a cooler contains 5 Cokes, 8 Pepsis, 10 Sprites, and 7 Waters, the probability of choosing a Coke or a Pepsi $= \dfrac{5}{30} + \dfrac{8}{30} = \dfrac{13}{30}$. The probability of not choosing a Water is $1 - \dfrac{7}{30} = \dfrac{23}{30}$. That is because choosing a Water and not choosing a water are complementary events.

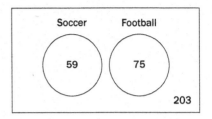

Probability questions can be answered by examining a Venn diagram. In a school, students can only be in one fall sport. This Venn diagram shows how many students participate in soccer or football or neither. The probability that a student is chosen who plays soccer or football $= \dfrac{59}{337} + \dfrac{75}{337} = \dfrac{134}{337}$. The probability of choosing a student who does not play soccer is $\dfrac{337 - 59}{337} = \dfrac{278}{337}$.

Non-Mutually Exclusive Events

If two events A and B are *not* mutually exclusive (meaning that they *can* occur at the same time), we cannot add the respective probabilities, as we have to concern ourselves with the overlap.

- A poll was taken in an office building as to how people got to work. The result is shown in the Venn diagram. There are 120 people taking the car exclusively, 55 people taking the train exclusively, 15 people taking both, and 10 people taking neither. To find the probability that someone takes a car *or* a train (which are *not* mutually exclusive events), compute $\dfrac{120 + 15 + 55}{120 + 15 + 55 + 10} = \dfrac{190}{200} = 95\%$.

Note: In probability theory, computing the probability that A or B occurs is interpreted as A occurring, B occurring, or both.

- In a class of 30 students, their status is shown by this table. The probability of choosing a student who is a boy *and* passing is $\dfrac{15}{30} = \dfrac{1}{2} = 50\%$. The probability of choosing a student who is a boy *or* passing is found by either $\dfrac{15 + 7 + 3}{30} = \dfrac{25}{30} = \dfrac{5}{6} = 83.3\%$.

	Passing	Failing	Total
Boy	15	3	18
Girl	7	5	12
Total	22	8	30

Conditional Probability

In Florida, it is more likely to rain if it is summer, rather than winter. So, the probability of rain in Florida is dependent on the month of the year. This is called conditional probability. Conditional probability is the probability event A occurs, given that event B occurs. For instance, the probability of a rainy day in South Florida is only 2% but, given that the month is June, the probability is over 50%.

Example: Suppose we have a class with this makeup: A student is chosen at random.

	Senior	Junior	Total
Boy	8	4	12
Girl	3	5	8
Total	11	9	20

The probability of choosing a boy is $\frac{12}{20} = \frac{3}{5} = 60\%$.

The probability of choosing a senior is $\frac{11}{20} = 55\%$.

The probability of choosing a senior boy is $\frac{8}{20} = \frac{2}{5} = 40\%$.

Suppose we wish the probability of choosing a senior *given* that we have chosen a boy. This is an example of conditional probability. The condition is choosing a boy. Since there are 12 boys and 8 of them are seniors, the denominator is no longer 20 but 12. So, the probability of choosing a senior given that we have chosen a boy is $\frac{8}{12} = \frac{2}{3} = 66.\overline{6}\%$. Since, as we saw, the probability of choosing a senior is 55%, it is more likely to choose a senior, given that we chose a boy.

If we want the probability of choosing a boy *given* that we have chosen a senior, we see that there are 11 seniors and 8 of them are boys, so $\frac{8}{11} = 72.7\%$.

One special type of probability question that occurs quite regularly in the real world has to do with binomial experiments.

Binomial experiments have all four of the following conditions:

1. Each observation falls into one of two categories—we call them "success" or "failure."

2. There is a fixed number of *n* observations.

3. The *n* observations are independent. Knowing the result of one observation tells you nothing about the other observations.

4. The probability of success *p* is the same for each observation.

Example: We pick 5 cards from a standard deck and count the number of hearts. We replace the card each time and reshuffle. This is a binomial experiment as success is a heart and failure is a non-heart. There are 5 observations and since we replace the card each time, the chances of drawing a heart on any pick has nothing to do with previous draws. The probability of choosing a heart is always 25%.

If we pick 5 cards from a standard deck and count the number of hearts but do not replace the cards, we do not have a binomial experiment as the chance of drawing a heart on any pick is dependent on whether we chose a heart on the previous pick. If we did, then there are fewer hearts in the deck and thus the probabilities are not the same.

Example: Suppose a teacher gives a short quiz with 3 multiple-choice questions with choices A, B, C, and D. A student didn't study and randomly guesses. What is the probability that he gets at least 2 of the 3 questions correct?

First, we determine that this is a binomial experiment. Success means getting a problem right and failure means getting it wrong. There are 3 observations and getting a problem correct has nothing to do with getting another problem correct. The chance of getting a problem correct by guessing is 25% and the chance of getting a problem wrong is 75%.

There are two ways to solve this. First, we can create the sample space for getting 3 questions either right (R) or wrong (W). We then multiply the probabilities.

Sample Space	Probability
RRR	$(0.25)\,(0.25)\,(0.25) = 0.1015625$
RRW	$(0.25)\,(0.25)\,(0.75) = 0.046875$
RWR	$(0.25)\,(0.75)\,(0.25) = 0.046875$
RWW	$(0.25)\,(0.75)\,(0.75) = 0.140625$
WRR	$(0.75)\,(0.25)\,(0.25) = 0.046875$
WRW	$(0.75)\,(0.25)\,(0.75) = 0.140625$
WWR	$(0.75)\,(0.75)\,(0.25) = 0.140625$
WWW	$(0.75)\,(0.75)\,(0.75) = 0.42187$

Getting at least 2 questions right means getting either 2 questions right or all 3 questions right. So, we add the probabilities of the boxed items: $0.15625 + 3(0.46875) = 0.15625$. So, there is less than a 16% chance of getting 2 or more questions correct by mere guessing.

We can also do this by using the binomial formula. This formula uses combinations as reviewed in Competency 002. Recall that $_nC_r = \dfrac{n!}{r! \cdot (n-r)!}$ with 0! defined as 1.

In a binomial experiment, the chances of r successes from n trials with the probability of success equal to p is given by the formula: $_nC_r \cdot p^r \cdot (1-p)^{r-n}$.

The probability of all 3 questions correct is:

$$_3C_3 \cdot (0.25)^3 \cdot (1 - 0.25)^{3-3} = \frac{3!}{3! \cdot 0!}(0.25)^3 \cdot (0.75)^0 = 0.015625.$$

The probability of 2 questions correct is:

$$_3C_2 \cdot (0.25)^2 \cdot (1 - 0.25)^{3-2} = \frac{3!}{2! \cdot 1!}(0.25)^2 \cdot (0.75)^1 = 0.140625.$$

The probability of 1 question correct is:

$$_3C_1 \cdot (0.25)^1 \cdot (1 - 0.25)^{3-1} = \frac{3!}{1! \cdot 2!}(0.25)^1 \cdot (0.75)^2 = 0.421875.$$

The probability of no questions correct is:

$$_3C_0 \cdot (0.25)^0 \cdot (1 - 0.25)^{3-0} = \frac{3!}{0! \cdot 3!}(0.25)^0 \cdot (0.75)^3 = 0.421875.$$

So, the probability of at least 2 questions correct is:
$0.015625 + 0.140625 = 0.15625$.

Geometric Probability

Geometric probability typically refers to finding a ratio of two areas. For example, if a blindfolded player throws a dart that lands in the square with side length s, find the probability that it lands in the shaded region. For example, find the probability of throwing a dart at the shaded region in a square with side length s.

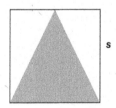

The probability of throwing a dart at the shaded region is the area of the shaded region divided by the area of the total region or square. We know the area of a square with side length s is s^2. The shaded region is exactly half of the square. One might draw a line through the middle of the triangle to see that there are four congruent triangles that make up the whole square (see the following figure). Of course, this makes the assumption that the vertex of the triangle is at the midpoint of the top side of the square. But it doesn't matter. No matter where the vertex hits the top side of the square, its base is s and its height is s and the area is $\frac{1}{2}s^2$.

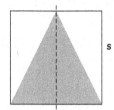

The area of half of the square is $\frac{1}{2}s^2$. Therefore, the probability of throwing a dart in the shaded region is $\dfrac{\frac{1}{2}s^2}{s^2} = \dfrac{1}{2}$.

COMPETENCY 014

The teacher understands the relationship among probability theory, sampling, and statistical inference and how statistical inference is used in making and evaluating predictions.

The beginning teacher:

   A. Applies knowledge of designing, conducting, analyzing, and interpreting statistical experiments to investigate real-world problems.

   B. Demonstrates an understanding of random samples, sample statistics and the relationship between sample size and confidence intervals.

   C. Applies knowledge of the use of probability to make observations and draw conclusions from single variable data and to describe the level of confidence in the conclusion.

   D. Makes inferences about a population using binomial, normal, and geometric distributions.

   E. Demonstrates an understanding of the use of techniques such as scatter plots, regression lines, correlation coefficients and residual analysis to explore bivariate data and to make and evaluate predictions.

We saw that Competency 012 for the most part deals with descriptive statistics. **Descriptive statistics** uses the data to provide descriptions of the population, either through numerical calculations or graphs or tables. In contrast, **inferential statistics**, the focus of Competency 014, which we'll look at now, makes inferences and predictions about a population based on a sample of data taken from the population in question.

For example, suppose we were interested in the average monthly price of renting an apartment in Killeen, Texas. We will call all apartments that are currently rented in Killeen as the **population**. One way we could accomplish our goal is by taking a **census**: finding the cost of every apartment that is currently being rented in Killeen and averaging them. By doing so, there would be no question of accuracy. But although theoretically possible, in practice it is not doable. There are too many apartments. Unless you had a large number of people to help, a census makes absolutely no sense.

Another strategy is to **sample**. We examine the rental cost of a smaller number of apartments, perhaps 100 of them. Because we expect the distribution of their cost to be normal (following the bell-shaped curve), with a few of them very expensive and a few of them very cheap, we then believe that the average of this sample to be very close to the average of our population: all apartments currently rented in Killeen.

The key to this process is how the sample is taken. The best way to accomplish this is by taking a **simple random sample (SRS)**. Although there are technical ways to do this, an SRS is taken by essentially placing the name of every apartment in the city in a hat and choosing 100. From there, necessary work is done to find the rental price to the point of knocking on doors. A SRS makes every apartment and every combination of apartments equally likely to be chosen.

If the sample is not done correctly, **bias** can enter the process and any conclusion of the study may be flawed. Here are some types of sampling involving bias.

- A **convenience sample** might be taken by just sampling the rental prices on a major tourist street. It is less work for the sampler. But, by doing that, the average rental cost of the sample may be higher than that of the population.

- We could use the internet to help choose the apartments, but our sample would possibly suffer from **undercoverage** as it wouldn't include some of the lower-rent apartments that may not be advertised on the internet.

- Sometimes **systematic sampling** is used where all the apartments are placed in some kind of order, maybe alphabetical. Then maybe the first apartment on the list is taken, the 100th, the 200th, and so on. This may appear to be fair, but if the first apartment is the Acme and the second is the Adelphia, once Acme is chosen, then Adelphia cannot be taken and that introduces bias.

- **Stratified sampling** could involve taking exactly one apartment from every street in Killeen. Again, this appears fair but if a street only has one apartment, then that apartment must be taken as opposed to streets that have multiple apartments.

Bias can be quite subtle and when it is introduced, it is called **hidden bias**. For instance, in a taste test between two brands of soda, if one is served at 35° and the other served at 40°, then people's judgment might be clouded by the temperature and not the taste.

Once the sample has been chosen and the data averaged, we are ready to create a **confidence interval**. This is in the form of:

sample average ± margin of error for n% confidence.

For example, we might find that the average cost of an apartment in Killeen is $1,700 ± $150 for 95% confidence. The interpretation for this statement is:

We are 95% sure that the average cost of renting
an apartment in Killeen is between $1,550 and $1,850.

Using a confidence interval, we hedge our bets in two ways:

- We say that we believe the average rental cost is $1,700. But the margin of error says that our average could be off as much as $150 in either direction.

- We say that we are 95% sure of our estimate, acknowledging that perhaps we could be wrong. This means that if we were to repeat this process doing it a total of 100 times, in 5 out of 100 times, our confidence interval wouldn't contain the true average rental price.

If the true average price of an apartment in Killeen is $1,825, our 95% confidence interval is correct as $1,825 lies between $1,550 and $1,850.

If the true average price of an apartment in Killeen is $1,600, our 95% confidence interval is correct as $1,600 lies between $1,550 and $1,850.

But if the true average price of an apartment in Killeen is $1,930, our 95% confidence interval is incorrect as $1,930 does not lie between $1,550 and $1,850.

But whether our calculated confidence interval is right or wrong, we never know it. The only true way to know the average cost of a Killeen apartment is to do a census, and again that is impractical.

Think of it as a court trial. A jury makes a judgment on whether a defendant has committed a crime. Their conclusion is based on a degree of confidence. If it is a murder trial, the degree of confidence must be 99.9% (it is never 100%). If the jury votes guilty, the defendant goes to jail. If the jury votes not guilty, the defendant goes free. But ultimately only the defendant truly knows whether he or she committed the crime. So, in our case, we estimate the average rental cost to the best of our ability and make decisions based on that. But we never really truly know if our estimate is correct.

This type of estimation is done all the time during elections. A poll might proclaim that a candidate is expected to win 52% of the vote in an election with a margin of error of 3% for 95% confidence. That is saying that the pollsters are 95% certain that the candidate will win between 49% and 55% of the vote. This means that it is possible that he could lose because 49% is within the confidence interval. And they are only 95% sure of this. Is it any wonder that we are told not to believe polls! Still, typically when polls are proved wrong by the actual election (which is a census), it was because there was bias in the selection of the data.

Confidence intervals can have smaller margins of error or have greater confidence (like 99%) by increasing the sample size. The greater the sample size, the smaller the margin of error. But increasing the sample size creates more work and if the sample size gets too large, it becomes similar to actually taking a census which gives the exact information rather than an estimation. The goal of statistical inference is to estimate an unknown average using a relatively small sample compared to the size of the population.

On the TExES exam, you are not responsible for calculating a confidence interval. Rather, you simply need to be able to interpret what a given confidence interval means as well as to examine a sampling technique to see if there is any bias.

Example: A farmer has just cleared a cornfield that can be divided into 64 smaller plots. The farmer isn't sure whether harvesting the entire field is worth the expense. So, he decides to harvest 8 plots and use this information to estimate the total yield for the entire field. Based on this information, he will decide whether to harvest the remaining plots.

Match the samples with the most likely sampling technique.

A.

C.

B.

D.

I. Stratified

II. Simple Random

III. Systematic

IV. Convenience

Solution:

    I. B. It appears stratified sampling was used—one plot of land was taken from each column.

    II. C. There appears to be no pattern to the plots taken, which is a clear sign that simple random selection was used.

    III. D. There appears to be a specific pattern to the plots taken that is, a systematic sampling.

    IV. A. All the plots taken are in one corner, making it convenient to obtain the data.

Example: The farmer finds that after sampling his chosen plots, the average yield from each plot was 10.2 bushels of corn with a margin of error of 1.8 plots for 95% confidence. Interpret this.

Solution: The farmer is 95% confident that the average yield of his field will be between 8.4 and 12.0 bushels of corn per plot. Since he has 64 plots, this also means that he is 95% confident that his total field will yield between 537.6 and 768 bushels of corn.

COMPETENCY 015

The teacher understands mathematical reasoning and problem solving.

The beginning teacher:

A. Demonstrates an understanding of proof, including indirect proof, in mathematics.

B. Applies correct mathematical reasoning to derive valid conclusions from a set of premises.

C. Demonstrates an understanding of the use of inductive reasoning to make conjectures and deductive methods to evaluate the validity of conjectures.

D. Applies knowledge of the use of formal and informal reasoning to explore, investigate, and justify mathematical ideas.

E. Recognizes that a mathematical problem can be solved in a variety of ways and selects an appropriate strategy for a given problem.

F. Evaluates the reasonableness of a solution to a given problem.

G. Applies content knowledge to develop a mathematical model of a real-world situation and analyzes and evaluates how well the model represents the situation.

H. Demonstrates an understanding of estimation and evaluates its appropriate uses.

Teachers need to create opportunities to motivate children to develop logical thinking skills through exploratory mathematics and problem solving. Such exploration can be done with partners or in learning centers designed to expose students to manipulatives and teach mathematical concepts in an indirect fashion through student-selected activities.

Problem solving requires frequent opportunities to formulate, grapple with, and solve complex problems. Students are able to acquire ways of thinking, habits of persistence, and curiosity in unfamiliar situations (NCTM, 2000). Solving problems requires more than numerical computations. There are a number of problem-solving strategies. These can include drawing a picture, making a list, acting out a problem, creating a graph, using logical reasoning, looking for a pattern, developing a systematic list, working backward, writing an equation, and using guess-and-check methods.

George Polya wrote a classic book, *How to Solve It* (1945), which outlined four steps for doing mathematics. These steps are widely adopted in textbooks and resource books to help students develop problem-solving skills. The four steps are described briefly in the following list:

1. *Understanding the problem.* In this phase students determine what the problem is about and identify what question or problem is being posed.

2. *Devising a plan.* Students think about how they intend to solve the problem and select a problem-solving strategy.

3. *Carrying out the plan.* Students implement the plan they just devised. If they get stumped, students can reevaluate their plan and try a different approach if needed.

4. *Looking back.* This phase can be the most important as well as the most skipped by students. Once they've arrived at an answer after the first three steps, students should determine whether their answers make sense and check their work if possible.

Logical reasoning is thinking about something in a way that makes sense to the student. Thinking about mathematics problems involves logical reasoning. Logical reasoning can be used to find patterns in a set of data, then those patterns can be used to draw conclusions about the data, which can then be used to solve problems. Finding patterns involves identifying characteristics that numbers or objects have in common. A sequence of geometric objects may have some property in common. For example, they may all be quadrilaterals or all have right angles.

Through mathematical reasoning skills, students should investigate mathematical conjectures and develop, as well as evaluate, mathematical arguments and proofs (NCTM, 2000). Strong reasoning skills are needed for building skill sets in all five content strands: Number and Operations, Algebra, Geometry, Measurement, and Data Analysis and Probability.

Deductive reasoning requires moving from the assumptions to the conclusion, or from the general to the specific. Deductive reasoning is often used in students' daily lives. For example, if a student sees it is raining outside before leaving home to head to school, she might conclude she needs an umbrella. The student's conclusion is reached through deductive reasoning.

Inductive reasoning involves examining particular instances to come to some general assumptions, and should be intuitive. When thinking inductively, students will make hypotheses, extend patterns of thought, use analogies, and make reasonable conclusions by examining what appears to be a body of evidence.

COMPETENCY 016

The teacher understands mathematical connections within and outside of mathematics and how to communicate mathematical ideas and concepts.

The beginning teacher:

A. Recognizes and uses multiple representations of a mathematical concept (e.g., a point and its coordinates, the area of circle as a quadratic function in r, probability as the ratio of two areas).

B. Uses mathematics to model and solve problems in other disciplines, such as art, music, science, social science, and business.

C. Expresses mathematical statements using developmentally appropriate language, Standard English, mathematical language and symbolic mathematics.

D. Communicates mathematical ideas using a variety of representations (e.g., numeric, verbal, graphic, pictorial, symbolic, concrete).

E. Demonstrates an understanding of the use of visual media such as graphs, tables, diagrams, and animations to communicate mathematical information.

F. Uses the language of mathematics as a precise means of expressing mathematical ideas.

G. Understands the structural properties common to the mathematical disciplines.

H. Explores and applies concepts of financial literacy as it relates to teaching students (e.g., describes the basic purpose of financial institutions, distinguishes the difference between gross income and net income, identifies various savings options, defines different types of taxes, identifies the advantages and disadvantages of different methods of payments).

I. Applies mathematics to model and solve problems to manage financial resources effectively for lifetime financial security as it relates to teaching students (e.g., distinguish between fixed and variable expenses, calculate profit in a given situation, develop a system for keeping and using financial records, describe actions that might be taken to balance a budget when expenses exceed income and balance a simple budget).

Mathematics is an integrated field of study. When students connect mathematical ideas, their understanding is deeper and more lasting. Students can come to view mathematics as a coherent whole (NCTM, 2000). One of the challenges teachers face in promoting interest in mathematics is to convince students that mathematics plays an important role in their lives. Based on this assumption, teachers may wish to introduce mathematics concepts in a problem-solving format using situations that are real to the students' lives. Some examples to connect mathematics to students' lives are explained below.

Planning Projects

- Have students plan a field trip for the class. As a class or in small groups, students might have to decide where the field trip will take place and estimate the cost of the trip. They will need to determine a means of transportation, number of adult volunteer chaperones, the duration of the field trip including travel time, cost per student, and total cost of the trip. Students can also develop a plan to pay for the field trip, including fund-raising opportunities, and create a field trip permission slip form for parents/guardians to sign. Once all information is collected, they can write a proposal for the field trip and present it to the principal and potentially get approval to take the trip.

- Have students plan a road trip to a vacation spot they would like to visit one day. Using an on-line mapping website, students can obtain the appropriate information to determine distance from one place to the other, and use this distance to calculate travel time and gas expenses based on mileage of driving their family car. Students can also investigate traveling by bus, train, or plane, and then they can compare costs to determine the most cost-effective trip.

- Organize cooking activities using recipes requiring specific units of measurement. These activities should include some that can be completed in school and at home. The recipes should require students to convert units and use proportional reasoning to double recipes or make portions of a recipe.

- Develop a "class store" to help students with concepts of fractions, decimals, and percents, as well as basic computational skills. Using a token or sticker system, students can earn forms of money as tokens or stickers, and use them to purchase items in the class store. Often teachers reward students for good behavior for following directions or having good listening skills. However, students could earn their tokens/stickers by helping students in class mathematically, presenting a problem to the class, posing questions, leading class discussions, or explaining where they used mathematics outside of school and/or bringing proof of such experience.

- To lend added real-world dimension to geometry class, plan a scavenger hunt outside of the classroom by having students snap pictures of various shapes that they see throughout the day and give their own definitions. Another activity could have students plan like an architect—design a floor plan and then calculate the materials needed for floors and walls. Plans can be compared by square footage or, say, number of basketballs that could fit inside—and other ways that would create opportunities to talk about the concepts of area and volume.

COMPETENCY 017

The teacher understands how children learn and develop mathematical skills, procedures, and concepts.

The beginning teacher:

A. Applies theories and principles of learning mathematics to plan appropriate instructional activities for all students.

B. Understands how students differ in their approaches to learning mathematics with regards to diversity.

C. Uses students' prior mathematical knowledge to build conceptual links to new knowledge and plans instruction that builds on students' strengths and addresses students' needs.

D. Understands how learning may be assisted through the use of mathematics manipulatives and technological tools.

E. Understands how to motivate students and actively engage them in the learning process by using a variety of interesting, challenging and worthwhile mathematical tasks in individual, small-group, and large-group settings.

F. Understands how to provide instruction along a continuum from concrete to abstract.

G. Recognizes the implications of current trends and research in mathematics and mathematics education.

Contextual factors are important elements that help teachers plan and meet the needs of all students. Understanding students' backgrounds, prior knowledge, and personal experiences can influence what content is taught and how to teach it. Understanding how students differ in their problem-solving approaches can create an effective learning environment.

Students should experience mathematics through the use of manipulatives and technological tools that allow learning to occur at a concrete level. Manipulatives and tools allow students to touch, move, rearrange, and explore mathematics. From these experiences, students can then transfer their knowledge to the pictorial level, where they use pictures to problem solve. They can create and design their own pictorial representations for the given task. Once students master the concrete and pictorial phases, they can then apply the mathematical content in a more abstract form.

The teacher is responsible for motivating and engaging students in challenging and worthwhile mathematics, through individual, small-group, and large-group settings. The five Process Standards defined by the National Council of Teachers of Mathematics (NCTM) are essential for students to successfully learn mathematics. They are problem solving, reasoning and proof, representations, communication, and connections (NCTM, 2000). Rarely are these standards experienced in isolation. Rather, students oscillate among and within the standards regularly during their mathematical learning experiences.

The NCTM, established in 1920, is one of the most well-known organizations in mathematics education. NCTM's goals include the development and improvement of mathematics education through six principles and ten standards that children in kindergarten through grade 12 should master. In 2000, NCTM published the *Principles and Standards for School Mathematics*, a resource intended for all who make decisions that affect mathematics education for K–12 students. This document has influenced state and district curricula development, and specifies the mathematics content students should learn.

Principles of Mathematics

The NCTM (2000) identified six principles that should guide mathematics instruction. These include equity, curriculum, teaching, learning, assessment, and technology.

- **Equity:** Excellence in mathematics education requires equity: high expectations and strong support for all students.

- **Curriculum:** A curriculum must be coherent, focusing on important mathematics and clearly articulating concepts across grades. Curriculum is more than a collection of activities.

- **Teaching:** Effective mathematics teaching requires understanding what students know and need to learn and then challenging and supporting students to learn it well.

- **Learning:** Students must learn mathematics with understanding, actively building new knowledge from experience and former knowledge.

- **Assessment:** Assessment should support the learning of important mathematics, and furnish useful information to both teachers and students.

- **Technology:** Technology is essential in teaching and learning mathematics; it influences the teaching of mathematics and enhances students' learning.

Standards of Mathematics

NCTM (2000) has identified five Content Standards and five Process Standards. The Content Standards explicitly describe the mathematical content students should learn, whereas the Process Standards highlight ways of attaining and using content knowledge.

Texas Mathematics Standards

The Texas State Board of Educator Certification (SBEC) and the State Board of Education (SBOE) approved Texas educator standards that outline what the beginning educator should know and be able to do. These standards are based on the required state curriculum for students, the Texas Essential Knowledge and Skills (TEKS). The Texas Education Agency (TEA, 2009) has defined eight mathematical standards as follows:

Standard I—Number Concepts

The mathematics teacher understands and uses numbers, number systems and their structure, operations and algorithms, quantitative reasoning, and technology appropriate to teach the state-wide curriculum in order to prepare students to use mathematics.

Standard II—Patterns and Algebra

The mathematics teacher understands and uses patterns, relations, functions, algebraic reasoning, analysis, and technology appropriate to teach the statewide curriculum in order to prepare students to use mathematics.

Standard III—Geometry and Measurement

The mathematics teacher understands and uses geometry, spatial reasoning, measurement concepts and principles, and technology appropriate to teach the statewide curriculum in order to prepare students to use mathematics.

Standard IV—Probability and Statistics

The mathematics teacher understands and uses probability and statistics, their applications, and technology appropriate to teach the statewide curriculum in order to prepare students to use mathematics.

Standard V—Mathematical Processes

The mathematics teacher understands and uses mathematical processes to reason mathematically, to solve mathematical problems, to make mathematical connections within and outside of mathematics, and to communicate mathematically.

Standard VI—Mathematical Perspectives

The mathematics teacher understands the historical development of mathematical ideas, the interrelationship between society and mathematics, the structure of mathematics, and the evolving nature of mathematics and mathematical knowledge.

Standard VII—Mathematical Learning and Instruction

The mathematics teacher understands how children learn and develop mathematical skills, procedures, and concepts; knows typical errors students make; and uses this knowledge to plan, organize, and implement instruction; to meet curriculum goals; and to teach all students to understand and use mathematics.

Standard VIII—Mathematical Assessment

The mathematics teacher understands assessment and uses a variety of formal and informal assessment techniques appropriate to the learner on an ongoing basis to monitor and guide instruction and to evaluate and report student progress.

Standard IX—Professional Development

The mathematics teacher understands mathematics teaching as a profession, knows the value and rewards of being a reflective practitioner, and realizes the importance of making a lifelong commitment to professional growth and development.

Mathematics and Cognitive Development

Learning mathematics requires students to create mathematical relationships and develop meanings for abstract ideas. Students need concrete interactions with mathematical ideas that may not be accessible from abstractions and symbols. Jean Piaget, a developmental psychologist, observed and recorded the intellectual abilities of infants, children, and adolescents. Piaget developed stages of intellectual development related to brain growth that led him to conclude that thinking and reasoning skills of children were dominated by preoperational thought, a pattern of thinking that is egocentric, centered, irreversible, and nontransformational (Piaget and Inhelder, 1969). His theory included the growth of intelligence and emergence and acquisition of schemata—schemes of a child using "developmental stages" to explain how children acquire new information. The four main stages are the Sensorimotor stage (Birth– Age 2), Preoperational stage (Age 2–7), Concrete Operational stage (Age 7–11), and the Formal Operational stage (Age 11–Adult).

Piaget describes the Preoperational stage of development to include the processes of symbolic functioning, centration, intuitive thought, egocentrism, and inability to conserve. Students in the Concrete Operational stage exhibit the developmental processes of decentering, reversibility, conservation, serialization, classification, and elimination of egocentrism. The Formal Operational stage of Piaget's cognitive development focuses on the ability to use symbols and to think abstractly (Piaget and Inhelder, 1969).

Students in the Preoperational stage experience problems with at least two perceptual concepts: conservation and centration, according to Susan Sperry Smith (2008). Conservation is the understanding that the quantity, length, or number of items is unrelated to the arrangement or appearance of the object or items. Students encountering problems with conservation may have difficulty measuring volume or understanding the value of money. For example, students may think a dime is worth less than a nickel since it is thinner and smaller in diameter. Centration is characterized by a child's focus on one aspect of a situation or problem. For example, take two 8.5-inch-by-11-inch sheets of paper and roll each into a tube, one a long skinny tube, and the other a short wider tube. A young student might judge the capacity of the shorter tube to be less than that of the taller tube based on his perception of short and tall.

Children ages 7 to 11 years old (roughly second through seventh grades) experience rapid growth during the Concrete Operational stage of cognitive development. At this time students are developing the ability to think logically about concrete objects or relationships. Some of the characteristics of students at this stage are:

- **Classification:** The student can identify and name sets of objects according to appearance, size, color, or other characteristics. The student can arrange objects based on characteristics.

- **Conservation:** The student understands that the quantity, length, or number of items is unrelated to the arrangement or appearance of the object. The student can discern that if water is transferred from a glass to a pitcher, the quantity of water will be conserved; that is, the quantity of water in the pitcher will be equal to the quantity that had been in the glass.

- **Decentering:** The student can take into account multiple aspects of a problem to solve it. The student can form conclusions based on reason rather than perception.

- **Elimination of egocentrism:** The student is able to view things from another student's perspective. The student can retell or summarize a story from another child's perspective.

- **Reversibility:** The student understands that objects can be changed and then returned to their original state. The student can determine that four rows of two crayons is the same original quantity as two rows of four crayons.

Piaget's stages of cognitive development were foundational during his time. Contemporary researchers have found Piaget underestimated the abilities of children in preschool and early elementary years. Some students can develop more sophisticated thinking and reasoning skills by as early as second or third grade, especially if they have adequate instruction and support from teachers and peers (Vygotsky, 1986). Students' cognitive development is influenced by their culture and instruction and is related to cognitively guided instruction (CGI) (Carpenter et al., 1999; Kamii, 2000; Santrock, 2003).

Mathematical Literacy

Literacy skills are essential for students to be successful learners. More than reading and writing, literacy includes purposeful social and cognitive processes that help students discover ideas and create meaning; it requires analysis, synthesis, organization, and evaluation of reading tasks (Jacobs, 2008; Moss, 2005; Tovani, 2000). Mathematical literacy involves the capacity to identify, understand, and engage in mathematics; it includes the ability to make sound judgments about the role mathematics plays in one's present and future life as a constructive, concerned, and reflective citizen (Kramarski and Mizrachi, 2006). NCTM (1989) describes mathematically literate students as having an appreciation of the value and beauty of mathematics and being able, as well as being inclined, to value and use quantitative information.

Successful readers determine what is important. They synthesize information to create new thinking, construct sensory images, and self-monitor their own comprehension. Students struggle when reading if they lack the comprehension strategies needed to unlock meaning, sufficient background knowledge, and the ability to recognize organizational patterns (Tovani, 2000). Gardner (1983, 1993) would describe students with mathematical literacy to have logical-mathematical intelligence, which is the ability to understand and use logical structures including patterns, relationships, statements, and propositions through experimentation, quantification, conceptualization, and classification.

Students may face a number of challenges with the technical vocabulary and literacy skills of mathematics. The mathematics classroom tends to abound in assumptions concerning students' prior knowledge of specialized academic terms such as *numerator, denominator, product, quotient, minuend, divisor, subtrahend,* and other technical concepts and vocabulary. The terms that have one meaning in one subject domain can have an entirely different meaning in the vocabulary of mathematics. These terms include *quarter, column, product, rational, even,* and *table.* Also, mathematics vocabulary tends to encompass a variety of homophones (words pronounced in the same way but having different meanings). Table 4-1 depicts various mathematics terms and their structures that may be confusing for all students. Table 4-2 lists homophones that may pose challenges for students.

Table 4-1 Mathematical Terminology and Meanings

Terminology	Common Meaning	Mathematical Meaning
Even	Equal amount, same level	Numbers divisible by 2
Face	Front of a human head	Surface of a geometric solid
Plane	Aircraft	A two-dimensional surface
Mean	Not nice, or to express a particular message	Arithmetic average of a set of data values
Right	Correct, proper; or a direction	A 90-degree angle
Volume	Loudness of sounds	Capacity or quantity of liquid

Table 4-2 Homophones

Mathematical Term	Everyday Term
Sum	Some
One	Won
Two	To, too
Whole	Hole
Plane	Plain
Hour	Our
Chord	Cord
Eight	Ate
Weigh	Way
Real	Reel

Contextual Mathematics

Mathematical concepts are integral aspects of daily life. Students should encounter mathematics in real-world contexts that are associated with activities found in their daily lives. For instance, children may often be involved in recreational activities such as baseball or softball. Common mathematics associated with these sports includes players' batting averages, calculated by the number of hits divided by the number of times at bat. Providing students with a mathematical context allows students to develop a deeper meaning to the mathematics, assisting in conceptual versus procedural understanding.

Consider the following examples:

Example 1   During the second week of July 2011, the temperatures for Monday through Friday were 98, 102, 99, 99, and 105 degrees. What was the average temperature during this week?

Example 2   Find the average of 98, 102, 99, 99, and 105.

Both examples ask for the same mathematical task: compute the average of the data set by calculating the sum of the numbers and dividing by the number of data values—five. However, Example 1 poses the mathematical problem in a context or real-world scenario that students can relate to: temperature. Knowledge of the daily temperature is helpful to determine what a student might wear to school one day. In warm temperatures, as depicted in the problem, students might wear shorts to school, but if the temperatures were in the 30s and 40s, they'd probably choose to wear jeans and a jacket. Example 2 has less connotation or meaning to students, as the problem is not posed in a specific context. Although having the ability to calculate the mean or average of a set of values is important, students should have a balance of problems presented and not presented in real-world contexts.

Manipulatives in the Mathematics Classroom

Manipulatives are powerful tools to help students explore mathematics in a concrete and hands-on approach. Manipulatives provide a visual representation of a concept that assists in developing deeper understanding, which will help explain and improve the abstract meaning of mathematics. Students need opportunities to work collaboratively, applying numeric and algebraic reasoning; generating and analyzing data; and developing an understanding of ratios, proportions, and rate, as well as of critical thinking and making sound predictions and estimates. The importance of using manipulatives to teach these skills and mathematical concepts is reinforced by Piaget's theories on the cognitive development in children (Dienes and Sriraman, 2008).

Two-Color Counters

Two-color counters are circles, often with one side red and the other white. Sometimes the product is sold in sets of yellow and red. In primary grades, two-color counters are used for building number concepts from 0 to 20 using five-frames and ten-frames. In grades 4 through 8, two-color counters can depict multiplication problems in the form of rectangular arrays. They are great tools for teaching operations with integers, specifically zero pairs and why the product of two negative numbers is positive.

Fraction Bars

Fraction bars can be constructed from paper using paper-folding techniques, or the product can be purchased. As their name implies, fraction bars are length models of fractions. They model relationships and equivalencies. For example, by the diagram below, we can see two $\frac{1}{4}$ bars is equivalent to one bar the length of $\frac{1}{2}$. So, $\frac{2}{4} = \frac{1}{2}$. Although students learn how to simplify fractions by finding a GCF and removing a factor of 1, the fraction bars approach equivalent fractions by using length to model the equivalencies. In addition to exploring fraction equivalencies, students can use fraction bars to display mixed numbers and to solve addition and subtraction problems.

1															
$\frac{1}{2}$								$\frac{1}{2}$							
$\frac{1}{4}$				$\frac{1}{4}$				$\frac{1}{4}$				$\frac{1}{4}$			
$\frac{1}{8}$		$\frac{1}{8}$		$\frac{1}{8}$		$\frac{1}{8}$		$\frac{1}{8}$		$\frac{1}{8}$		$\frac{1}{8}$		$\frac{1}{8}$	
$\frac{1}{16}$	$\frac{1}{16}$	$\frac{1}{16}$	$\frac{1}{16}$	$\frac{1}{16}$	$\frac{1}{16}$	$\frac{1}{16}$	$\frac{1}{16}$	$\frac{1}{16}$	$\frac{1}{16}$	$\frac{1}{16}$	$\frac{1}{16}$	$\frac{1}{16}$	$\frac{1}{16}$	$\frac{1}{16}$	$\frac{1}{16}$

Fraction Circles

Fraction circles are similar to fraction bars. However, this manipulative models fractions in an *area* model. Students can explore equivalent fractions, mixed numbers, and computations with fraction circles.

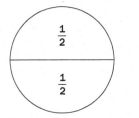

Pattern Blocks

Pattern blocks consist of six different polygons that are identified by color and shape: orange square, green equilateral triangle, yellow regular hexagon, red isosceles trapezoid, blue rhombus, and brown parallelogram. Pattern blocks can be used to teach number and operation skills of basic fractional concepts and relationships, as well as addition, subtraction, multiplication, and division of fractions. In geometry, they are used for modeling transformations, tessellations, and geometric probability.

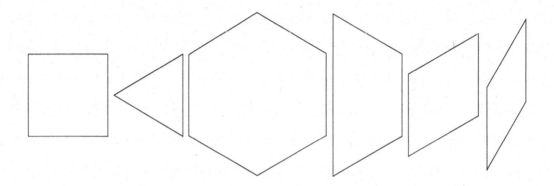

Cuisenaire Rods

Cuisenaire rods are similar to fraction bars as they depict length models. There are 10 different rods denoted by color and length. The rods are used in primary grades to discuss whole number addition and subtraction. In grades 4 through 8, they are frequently used to explore fractional concepts, equivalencies, and computations.

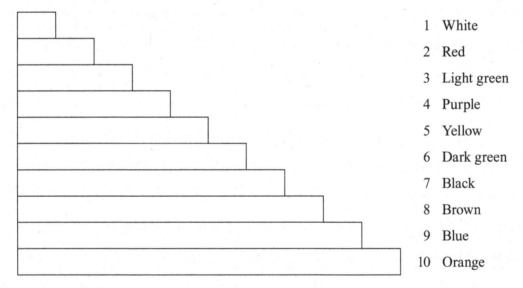

1 White

2 Red

3 Light green

4 Purple

5 Yellow

6 Dark green

7 Black

8 Brown

9 Blue

10 Orange

Algebra Tiles

Algebra tiles comprise three different shapes, each with two different-colored sides. They represent variables and constants and are used to solve equations, factor polynomials, expand or multiply polynomials, and investigate zero pairs. A strong foundation of integer operations should be formed prior to using algebra tiles. Specifically, students should understand why the product of two negative numbers is a positive number, most often taught using two-color counters. Then, when students apply their knowledge of integer operations to algebra tiles, the approach is less procedural and more conceptual.

Often, the constant has one side red and the other beige or yellow. The x bar has one side red and the other green. The square has one side red and the other blue. The red side is to represent negative values. The beige, green, and blue sides are to represent positive values.

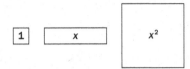

Double-Sided Geoboard

Double-sided geoboards include a five-by-five pin array on one side and a circular array on the other side. They come with rubber bands to create various shapes used to explore properties, area, and perimeter. The side with the circular array can be used to investigate chords, angle measures and their relationships, sectors, and so on. The circle can represent a clock, too, so students can represent a time and then discuss angle measures and fractions or portions of a circle. Of course, with more and more students only being exposed to digital clocks, the use of analog clocks in math problems is on the wane.

COMPETENCY 018

The teacher understands how to plan, organize and implement instruction using knowledge of students, subject matter, and statewide curriculum to teach all students to use mathematics.

The beginning teacher:

A. Demonstrates an understanding of a variety of instructional methods, tools, and tasks that promote students' ability to do mathematics described in the TEKS.

B. Understands planning strategies for developing mathematical instruction as a discipline of interconnected concepts and procedures.

C. Develops clear learning goals to plan, deliver, assess, and reevaluate instruction based on the TEKS.

D. Understands procedures for developing instruction that establishes transitions between concrete, symbolic, and abstract representations of mathematical knowledge.

E. Applies knowledge of a variety of instructional delivery methods, such as individual, structured small-group and large-group formats.

F. Understands how to create a learning environment that provides all students, including English learners, with opportunities to develop and improve mathematical skills and procedures.

G. Demonstrates an understanding of a variety of questioning strategies to encourage mathematical discourse and to help students analyze and evaluate their mathematical thinking.

H. Understands how technological tools and manipulatives can be used appropriately to assist students in developing, comprehending and applying mathematical concepts.

Substantial thought to lesson planning is crucial for all teachers regardless of experience. Every class of students is different, so choices of which tasks to use and how they are presented to students must be made daily. Addressing all students' needs for a diverse classroom and including the state and local curriculum objectives are essential components of the lesson-plan process. The following are key components to consider when planning a lesson:

- Determine the mathematics and learning objectives.

- Consider the students' needs.

- Select, design, or adapt a task or activity.

- Identify essential questions.

- Design lesson assessments.

Differentiated instruction is a teaching method in which the teacher's plan includes strategies to support the range of different academic backgrounds. Students' interests and their prior knowledge impact instruction. Three elements to consider when differentiating instruction are content (what you want each student to be able to do), process (how you will engage students in that learning), and product (what students will show for what they have learned at the end of the lesson) (Tomlinson, 2001).

The Texas state curriculum should guide the mathematical content taught in the classroom. How the specific content is taught is up to the classroom teacher but can often be guided by curriculum specialists within school districts.

COMPETENCY 019

The teacher understands assessment and uses a variety of formal and informal assessment techniques to monitor and guide mathematics instruction and to evaluate student progress.

The beginning teacher:

A. Demonstrates an understanding of the purpose, characteristics, and uses of various assessments in mathematics, including formative and summative assessments.

B. Understands how to select and develop assessments that are consistent with what is taught and how it is taught.

C. Demonstrates an understanding of how to develop a variety of assessments and scoring procedures consisting of worthwhile tasks that assess mathematical understanding, common misconceptions, and error patterns.

D. Understands how to evaluate a variety of assessment methods and materials for reliability, validity, absence of bias, clarity of language, and appropriateness of mathematical level.

E. Understands the relationship between assessment and instruction and knows how to evaluate assessment results to design, monitor, and modify instruction to improve mathematical learning for all students, including English learners.

One of NCTM's (2000) six principles for school mathematics is assessment, which should support the learning of important mathematics and furnish useful information to both teachers and students. In traditional testing, the focus is on what students do not know, but a shift toward assessing students has led to an emphasis on determining what students do know. This shift resulted in the *Assessment Standards for School Mathematics* published by NCTM in 1995. This document outlines four specific purposes of assessment: (1) monitoring student progress, (2) making instructional design, (3) evaluating student achievement, and (4) evaluating programs. Additional considerations about what should be assessed were identified as concepts and procedures, mathematical processes, and productive dispositions (NCTM, 1995).

Assessments can be formative or summative. **Formative assessments** are regularly planned checkups of students' progress. When implemented well, formative assessments can increase the speed of learning by providing feedback that promotes learning. Formative assessments should also guide instruction, impacting decision making for future steps in the learning progression (NCTM, 1995; Van de Walle et al., 2010). Some formative approaches include performance-based tasks, journals, observations of problem solving, and diagnostic interviews.

Summative assessments are cumulative evaluations that often generate a single score, such as a unit exam or standardized test. This type of assessment shows what students know at that particular point in time, whereas formative assessments depict active student thinking and reasoning over time.

REFERENCES

Carpenter, T.M., E. Fennema, M.L. Franke, L. Levi, and S.B. Empson. 1999. *Children's Mathematics: Cognitively Guided Instruction*. Portsmouth, NH: Heinemann.

Dienes, Z.P., and B. Sriraman, eds. 2008. *Mathematics Education and the Legacy of Zoltan Paul Dienes*. Charlotte, NC: Information Age Publishing.

Gardner, Howard. 1983. *Frames of Mind*. New York: HarperCollins Publishers, Inc.

Gardner, Howard. 1993. *Multiple Intelligences: The Theory in Practice*. New York: HarperCollins Publishers, Inc.

Jacobs, V. A. 2008. "Adolescent Literacy: Putting the Crisis in Context." *Harvard Educational Review* 78: 7–39.

Kamii, C. 2000. *Young Children Reinvent Arithmetic: Implications of Piaget's Theory*. New York: Teachers College Press.

Kramarski B., and N. Mizrachi. 2006. "Online Discussion and Self-regulated Learning: Effects of Instructional Methods on Mathematical Literacy." *Journal of Educational Research* 99: 218–230.

Moss, B. 2005. "Making a Case and a Place for Effective Content Area Literacy Instruction in Elementary Grades. *The Reading Teacher* 59: 46–55.

National Council of Teachers of Mathematics (NCTM). 1989. *Curriculum and Evaluation Standards for School Mathematics*. Reston, VA: NCTM.

National Council of Teachers of Mathematics (NCTM). 1995. Assessment Standards for School Mathematics. Reston, VA: NCTM.

National Council of Teachers of Mathematics (NCTM). 2000. *Principles and Standards for School Mathematics*. Reston, VA: NCTM.

Piaget, J., and B. Inhelder. 1969. *The Psychology of the Child*. New York: Basic Books.

Polya, G. 1945. *How to Solve It*. Princeton, NJ: Princeton University Books.

Santrock, J.W. 2003. *Children*, 7th ed. Boston: McGraw-Hill.

Sperry Smith, S. 2008. *Early Childhood Mathematics*, 4th ed. Boston: Allyn and Bacon.

Texas Education Agency (TEA). 2009. Texas Essential Knowledge and Skills. Texas Administrative Code (TAC), Title 19, Part II, Chapter 111. Texas Essential Knowledge and Skills for Mathematics. Austin: Texas Education Agency.

Tomlinson, C. 2001. *How to Differentiate Instruction in Mixed-Ability Differentiated Classrooms*, 2nd ed. Alexandria, VA: Association for Supervision and Curriculum Development.

Tovani, C. 2000. *I Read It, but I Don't Get It: Comprehension Strategies for Adolescent Readers*. Portland, ME: Stenhouse Publishers.

Van de Wall, J.A., K.S. Karp, and J.M. Bay-Williams. 2010. *Elementary and Middle School Mathematics: Teaching Developmentally*, 7th ed. Boston: Allyn and Bacon.

Vygotsky, L.S. 1986. *Thought and Language*, new rev. ed. Cambridge, MA: MIT Press.

Subject Test III: Social Studies (808)

OVERVIEW OF SUBJECT TEST III: SOCIAL STUDIES

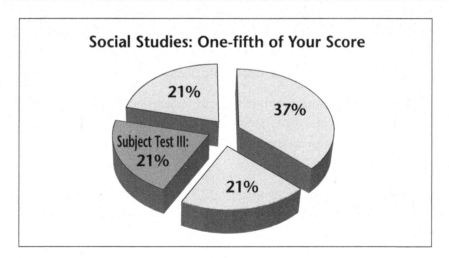

Subject Test III: Social Studies, like the Mathematics and Science subject tests, makes up approximately one-fifth of the questions you will see on the TExES Core Subjects 4–8 test. You'll have 50 minutes to get through 42 test items. That gives you just over one minute for each question. Each of the four subject tests that make up the Core Subjects 4–8 test is individually timed.

The Social Studies subject test assesses 10 Texas educator standards for teaching middle school social studies, including that the teacher:

I. Has a comprehensive foundational knowledge of social sciences, understands and applies the many social studies skills, and recognizes the value of the social sciences.

II. Effectively integrates the social science disciplines into the curriculum;

III. Commands the social studies subject matter, as framed by the Texas Essential Knowledge and Skills (TEKS), to plan and carry out effective curriculum, instruction, assessment, and evaluation;

IV. History: Applies knowledge of significant historical events and developments, as well as of multiple historical interpretations and ideas, in order to foster student understanding of relationships across historical periods and eras as well as implications for the future;

V. Geography: Applies knowledge of people, places, and environments to foster students' understanding of geographic relationships in Texas, the United States, and the world.

VI. Economics: Demonstrates ability to apply knowledge of how economic systems are organized to produce, distribute and consume goods and services, and deploys this knowledge to enable students to understand economic systems and make informed economic decisions;

VII. Government: Demonstrates ability to apply knowledge of how governments and structures of power function, provide order, and allocate resources, as well as using this knowledge to foster student understanding of how individuals and groups achieve their goals through political systems, particularly in the United States and Texas;

VIII. Citizenship: Demonstrates ability to apply knowledge of the United States, Texas, and other societies and deploys this knowledge to prepare students to participate in our society through an understanding and application of citizenship and democratic principles;

IX. Culture: Demonstrates ability to apply knowledge of cultures and how they develop and adapt and deploys this knowledge to foster students' appreciation for and respect of cultural diversity in Texas, the United States and the world; and

X. Science, Technology, and Society: Demonstrates the ability to apply knowledge of the dynamic relationship of science, technology, and society as well as the diversity, adaptation, and cultural development in modern and historical societies in the United States, Texas, and the world.

The Social Studies subject test embraces seven competencies, which broadly define, as the Texas Education Agency puts it, "what an entry-level educator in this field in Texas public schools should know and be able to do." This chapter synthesizes the material under each competency most likely to benefit you when you sit for the test.

COMPETENCY 001: HISTORY

The teacher understands and applies knowledge of significant historical events and developments, multiple historical interpretations and ideas and relationships between the past, the present, and the future as defined by the Texas Essential Knowledge and Skills (TEKS).

The beginning teacher:

A. Understands traditional historical points of reference in the history of Texas, the United States, and the world.

B. Analyzes how individuals, events, and issues shaped the history of Texas, the United States, and the world.

C. Analyzes the influence of various factors (e.g., geographic contexts, processes of spatial exchange, science, and technology) on the development of societies.

D. Demonstrates knowledge of common characteristics of communities, past and present.

E. Applies knowledge of the concept of chronology and its use in understanding history and historical events.

F. Applies different methods of interpreting the past to understand, evaluate, and support multiple points of view, frames of reference, and the historical context of events and issues.

G. Understands similarities and differences among Native-American groups in Texas, the United States, and the Western Hemisphere before European colonization.

H. Understands the causes and effects of European exploration and colonization of the United States, and the Western Hemisphere.

I. Understands the impact of individuals, events, and issues, on the exploration of Texas (e.g., Cabeza de Vaca, Alonso Álvarez de Pineda, Francisco Coronado, La Salle, the search for gold, conflicting territorial claims between France and Spain).

J. Can identify important events, issues, and individuals related to European colonization of Texas; Mexico becoming an independent nation, including the establishment of Catholic missions, towns, and ranches (e.g., Fray Damián Massanet, José de Escandón, Antonio Margil de Jesús, Francisco Hidalgo, the Mexican Federal Constitution of 1824, and the State Colonization Law of 1825).

K. Understands the foundations of representative government in the United States; significant individuals, events, and issues of the revolutionary era; and challenges confronting the U.S. government in the early years of the republic (e.g., Mayflower Compact, Virginia Houses of Burgesses, John Adams, Abigail Adams, George Washington, Crispus Attucks, Battle of Saratoga, winter at Valley Forge, Battle of Yorktown, the arguments of the Federalists and Anti-Federalists, Articles of Confederation, United States Constitution, War of 1812).

L. Demonstrates knowledge of the individuals, events, and issues related to the independence of Texas, the founding of the Republic of Texas, and Texas statehood (e.g., Moses Austin, Samuel Houston, Erasmo Seguín, Antonio López de Santa Anna, the Fredonian Rebellion, the Battle of the Alamo, the Battle of San Jacinto, the annexation of Texas, the U.S.-Mexican War).

M. Understands westward expansion and analyzes its effects on the political, economic and social development of the United States and Texas — including its effects on American Indian life (e.g., Louisiana Purchase, Monroe Doctrine, building of U.S. forts, the destruction of the buffalo, Indian Removal Act, Trail of Tears, Red River Indian War).

N. Analyzes ways in which political, economic, and social factors led to the growth of sectionalism and the Civil War (e.g., nullification crisis, Compromise of 1850, the roles of John Quincy Adams, John C. Calhoun, Henry Clay, and Daniel Webster).

O. Demonstrates knowledge of individuals, issues, and events of the Civil War and analyzes the effects of Reconstruction on the political, economic, and social life of the nation and Texas (e.g., Abraham Lincoln, Jefferson Davis, John Bell Hood, Vicksburg Campaign, Battle of Gettysburg, Emancipation Proclamation, Battle of Galveston, Battle of Palmito Ranch).

P. Demonstrates knowledge of major U.S. and Texas reform movements of the nineteenth and twentieth centuries (e.g., abolition movement, women suffrage movement, temperance movement, Civil Rights movement, agrarian groups, labor unions, James L. Farmer Jr., Jane Addams, Hector Pérez García, Oveta Culp Hobby, the League of United Latin American Citizens (LULAC), the evangelical movement).

Q. Understands important issues, events, and individuals of the twentieth and twenty-first centuries that shaped the role of Texas in the United States and the world (e.g., Great Depression, First and Second World Wars, Civil Rights movement, Lyndon B. Johnson, emergence of a two-party system, political and economic controversies, immigration, migration).

R. Understands and traces the impact of boom-and-bust cycles of leading Texas industries (e.g., railroads, cattle, oil and gas, cotton, real estate, banking, computer technology).

S. Understands the contributions of people of various racial, ethnic, and religious groups in Texas, the United States, and the world.

T. Analyzes ways in which particular contemporary societies reflect historical events (e.g., invasions, conquests, colonizations, immigrations).

World History

The *World History Encyclopedia* divides the history of the world into five periods: the **Ancient World**, the **Middle Ages**, the **Age of Discovery**, **Revolution and Industry**, and the **Modern World** (Ganeri, Martell, and Williams, 1999). A summary and timeline of key events in each period, keyed to the Grades 4–8 TEKS, follow.

The Ancient World (4 Million Years Ago to 500 CE[2])

Though neither the ancient world nor the Middle Ages is a focus of teaching in the middle school years, we nonetheless present a snapshot of these periods here for the sake of historical context. Study of the ancient world focuses on the development of the first humans, the first farmers, and the first civilizations. It documents the critical change in human behavior from hunter-gatherer to agrarian societies, which occurred after man learned to domesticate plants and animals. This time period emphasizes the history of the ancient civilizations of Mesopotamia, Sumer, Assyria, Babylon, Egypt, the Indus Valley, megalith Europe, ancient China, Phoenicia, ancient America, ancient Greece, the Celts, the Romans, and empires in Africa and India.

Timeline of the Ancient World

4000 BCE	Homo sapiens appear in various regions in the world
3500 BCE	The Sumerians of Mesopotamia invent writing and the wheel
3100 BCE	Egypt becomes unified
2800 BCE	Building begins in Stonehenge, England
2500 BCE	Indus civilization flourishes in India
1600–1100 BCE	Mycenaean control of Greece
1200–400 BCE	Olmecs civilization flourishes in western Mexico
1000–612 BCE	New Assyrian Empire flourishes
753 BCE	Foundation of Rome
605–562 BCE	King Nebuchadnezzar rebuilds the city Babylon
476–431 BCE	Golden age of Athens
336–323 BCE	Alexander the Great rules the world
27 BCE to 14 CE	Augustus rules as the first Roman emperor
1 CE	Birth of Christ (Est.)
476 CE	Western Roman Empire falls

---

[2] The terms "Before the Common Era (BCE)" and "Common Era (CE)" are used here in place of the traditional "Before Christ (BC)" and "Anno Domini (AD)." These designations cover the same historical periods.

The Middle Ages (500–1400 CE)

This period includes the Byzantine civilization, the rise of Islam, civilizations of the Americas, the Vikings, the feudal system, the Crusades, Genghis Khan and China, the African kingdoms, and the Hundred Years' War.

Timeline for the Middle Ages (CE)

500	Eastern Roman (Byzantine) Empire at its peak
600	Teotihuacán civilization flourishes in Mexico
600	Rise of Islam
700	Mayan civilization at its height in Central America
700	Feudal system begins in Europe; peasants serve a lord in exchange for protection
711	Moors invade Spain
750	Abbasid dynasty is founded; Arab Empire at its peak
800	Charlemagne crowned emperor of the Holy Roman Empire
900	Rise of Toltec civilization in Mexico
1000	Vikings land in North America
1095	Muslim Turks take Jerusalem and ban Christian pilgrims from the city
1096–1270	Crusades try to rescue Jerusalem from the Muslims
1215	Genghis Khan and the Mongols invade China
1271	Marco Polo travels to China from Italy
1300	Renaissance begins in Europe
1325	Aztecs established Tenochtitlán near modern day Mexico City
1368	Foundation of the Ming dynasty in China
1453	Fall of the eastern Roman Empire (Constantinople)
1454	Gutenberg invents the printing press
1500	Inca Empire at its peak in Peru

Age of Discovery (1400–1700)

The Age of Discovery was a period in history starting in the early 15th century and continuing into the early 17th century during which Europeans engaged in intensive exploration and mapping of the world, and establishing contact with Africa, the Americas, and Asia. This period in history bridges the distance between the Middle Ages, which was characterized by a rise in Islam, the feudal system, the Crusades, the Hundred Years' war, and the Modern Era. Accounts from exploring distant lands and maps spread with the help of the new printing press, which increased curiosity about the world and ushered in a new age of scientific and intellectual inquiry. European colonization led to the rise of colonial empires; increased and diversified trade routes; a wide transfer of plants, animals, foods, and human populations (including slaves); the spread of communicable diseases; and the sharing of culture between the Eastern and Western hemispheres. The Age of Discovery includes the Renaissance, the development of the Aztec and Inca civilizations, voyages of discovery from Spain and Portugal, African empires, the Reformation, and the Ottoman Empire. This period also marks when European citizenry became more educated and questioned the power of the church and the monarchy. The Age of Discovery resulted in a new world-view as distant civilizations came into contact with one another.

Timeline for the Age of Discovery

1441	Portuguese begin slave trade from Africa to Europe
1448	Portuguese explorers reach the southern part of Africa
1453	Fall of the eastern Roman Empire (Constantinople)
1454	Gutenberg invents the printing press
1492	Columbus sails from Spain to America
1492	Spain becomes unified and expels the Moors
	Colonization of the Americas begins with Christopher Columbus in the Dominican Republic
1497	Portuguese reach India
1500	Inca Empire at its peak in Peru
1508	Begin the colonization of Puerto Rico
1511	Begin the colonization of Cuba
1517	Martin Luther begins the religious Reformation in Europe
1520	Suleiman rules the Ottoman Empire
1522	Magellan travels around the world
1535	Spain completes the conquest of the Aztecs in Mexico and the Incas in Peru
1543	Copernicus suggests that the sun is the center of the universe, not the Earth
1571	Europeans defeat the Muslim Ottomans in the battle of Lepanto
1588	England defeats the Spanish Armada and becomes the greatest naval power in the world
1607	England begins the colonization of North America
1609	Galileo uses a new invention, the telescope, to study the universe
1618	Thirty Years' War begins (The key participants in the war included: The Holy Roman Empire, Great Britain, the Dutch Republic, Denmark, Germany, Sweden, France, Spain, and Austria)

Revolution and Industry (1700–1900)

This period includes the Russian Empire, the Manchu dynasty in China, the period of Enlightenment in Europe, the growth of Austria and Prussia, the birth of the United States, the French Revolution, the Napoleonic Era, the Industrial Revolution, the British Empire, the American Civil War, and the unification of both Italy and Germany.

Timeline for the Age of Revolution and Industry

1644	The Manchu overthrow the Ming dynasty of China
1682–1725	Peter the Great rules Russia; expanded territory, strong military
1740	Frederick the Great becomes king of Prussia—Domination of Europe
1756–1763	Seven Years' War ensues, with France, Austria, and Russia clashing against Prussia and England
1768	James Cook visits regions in the Pacific
1775–1783	American War for Independence ends with Treaty of Paris
1776	America declares independence from England
1789	French Revolution begins with the fall of the Bastille in Paris
1791	As part of the Enlightenment period, Thomas Paine publishes *The Rights of Man*, his best-seller
1804	Napoleon declares himself emperor of France, beginning the Napoleonic Era
1808	Wars for independence begin in Spanish America
1812–1815	War of 1812, considered a second war for American independence, waged by U.S. and its Indigenous allies against the UK over British violations of U.S. maritime rights
1835–1836	Texas War for Independence ends with the Battle of San Jacinto
1836	Texas declares independence from Mexico
1837–1901	British Empire at its peak under Queen Victoria
1846–1848	Mexican-American War
1848	Year of revolution in all of Europe
1861–1865	American Civil War
1869	Union Pacific Railroad links the East and West coasts of the United States
1898	Spanish-American War

The Modern World (1900–Present)

This period includes the struggle for equal rights for women, World War I, the Russian Revolution, the Great Depression, the rise of fascism, revolution in China, World War II, Israel versus Palestine, the Cold War, the space race, the Korean and Vietnam wars, and globalization. The early 1900s also saw some revolutions, the seeds for which were sown in the previous period.

Timeline for the Modern World

1910	Mexican revolution begins. Large numbers of Mexicans immigrate to the United States
1914	World War I begins when Austria declares war on Serbia and Germany on Russia
1917	Woodrow Wilson signs Jones-Shafroth Act into law, granting American citizenship to Puerto Ricans
	The United States declares war against Germany and the Central Powers
	Russian Revolution starts when the Bolsheviks, led by Lenin, seize power from Czar Nicholas II and kill his family; this is also called the Bolshevik Revolution
1918	World War I ends; Europe is in ruins, and Germany is heavily punished
1929	Great Depression begins in the United States
1933	Adolf Hitler achieves power in Germany
1936–1939	Spanish Civil War brings Francisco Franco to power
1939	World War II begins when Germany invades Poland and Czechoslovakia
1941	The United States enters World War II following the Japanese bombing of the American Fleet at Pearl Harbor
1945	Germany surrenders to the Allied Forces, and Japan surrenders after the United States detonates two atomic bombs over Hiroshima and Nagasaki
1947	Pakistan and India obtain independence from Great Britain
1948–1949	The State of Israel is founded in Palestine, and the Arabs declare war
1949	Communist Mao Zedong (Tse-tung) gains control of China
1959	Cuban Revolution
1960	Many countries in Africa gain independence
1965–1972	America participates in the Vietnam War
1969	Neil Armstrong becomes the first person to set foot on the moon
1986	U.S. Space Shuttle *Challenger* breaks apart 73 seconds after launch
1990	Germany is reunited
1991	Soviet Union collapses, and the Cold War ends

1994	Free elections in South Africa and the end of apartheid
2001	9/11 terrorist attacks in New York City and near Washington, D.C.
2001–2021	War in Afghanistan against the Taliban
2003	U.S. Space Shuttle *Columbia* disintegrates over Texas during re-entry on Feb. 1
	Iraq War (2003–2011), also called the Second Persian Gulf War, led by combined forces of the U.S. and Great Britain
2004	Boxing Day Earthquake and Tsunami occurs on Dec. 26 in Indian Ocean, killing 230,000 people
2005	The Provisional Irish Republican Army ends its military campaign in Northern Ireland
2006	Ellen Johnson Sirleaf become president of Liberia, and thus Africa's first elected female head of state
2009	Barack Obama inaugurated as the first Black President of the United States
2010	A 7.0 magnitude earthquake in Haiti kills 230,000 people on Jan. 12
	Deepwater Horizon, the largest oil spill in US history occurs in the Gulf of Mexico on April 20
2011	Wedding of Prince William and Catherine Middleton on April 29
	Osama bin Laden is shot dead by U.S. Navy SEALs in Pakistan on May 2
2012	Barack Obama wins second term as President of the United States
2013	Pope Benedict XVI resigns, the first Pope to do so since 1415, and Pope Francis is elected, becoming the first Pope from Latin America
2014	Worst Ebola epidemic in recorded history occurs in West Africa; first case of Ebola contracted in the United States
2015	Greece announces bankruptcy, becoming the first developed country to default the International Monetary Fund
	Heads of China and Taiwan meet for the first time; the U.S. and Cuba resume diplomatic relations
2016	United Kingdom votes to leave the European Union (Brexit)
	Donald Trump wins the presidential election on Nov. 8
2017	Three massive hurricanes hit the United States, Hurricanes Harvey, Irma, and Maria
2018	Wildfires in northern California are the deadliest in that state's history
2019	President Donald Trump is impeached by the U.S. House of Representatives

2020	Death of George Floyd sparks #BlackLivesMatter protests across the U.S. and world
	Covid-19 pandemic spreads from China to the rest of the world, killing at least 1.8 million people in the first year
	China National People's Congress grants itself sweeping powers to control civil liberties in Hong Kong
	Joe Biden is elected president; the incumbent president, Donald Trump, leads an unprecedented effort to prevent official recognition of the newly elected president
2021	Covid-19 pandemic continues, infecting more than 220 million and killing at least 3.6 million people in its second year
	United States ends military support in Afghanistan; the Taliban takes control of the country
2022	Russia invades Ukraine

For details about these historical periods, go to these websites: History Channel (*https://www.history.com/*) and Encyclopedia Britannica *(https://www.britannica.com)*, as well as *http://www.bbc.com/news/world-europe-34814203; http://www.bbc.com/news/world-europe-36800730; http://www.bbc.com/news/uk-40258989.* For more information regarding the Space Shuttle tragedies, visit *https://www.history.com* and *http://www.space.com.*

The Enlightenment—The Age of Reason

The Enlightenment refers to a period during the 17th and 18th centuries when people questioned religious dogmas and emphasized scientific reasoning and knowledge. This quest for knowledge resulted in the development of modern chemistry and biology. People questioned governments and demanded more individual freedoms. The search for freedom led countries to seek independence and fight tyranny. For example, the quest for freedom led to the American War of Independence and the French Revolution. The American Revolution motivated the Spanish colonies to seek independence. Some of the leading thinkers of this period were Jean-Jacques Rousseau, John Locke, Charles Montesquieu, Voltaire, and Francis Bacon. Enlightenment ideas quickly reached the British colonies. Many leaders responsible for the writing of the Constitution were familiar with the leading Enlightenment thinkers, and framed the Constitution to protect the natural rights of the individual and limit the power of the government.

The Industrial Revolution and Modern Technology

The Industrial Revolution began in England in the mid-18th century. Inventions that made mining of fossil fuel (coal) easier provided the energy needed to expand and promote industrial development. Improvement on the steam engine and industrial machines led to the mass production of goods and a better distribution system. The economic growth motivated people to leave the rural areas and move to the cities. The following timeline highlights inventions that supported the industrial revolution and modern life:

Timeline for Industrial and Technological Development

1769	Richard Arkwright patents the spinning machine powered by a waterwheel, which marks the beginning of industrial mass production of textiles
1814	German Printer Friedrich Koenig's improved printing press is used by *The Times* of London
1831	An American, Cyrus H. McCormick, invents the mechanical reaper, which revolutionizes farming so that more crops can be harvested by machines. This allowed for greater food production, marking a move toward commercial farming. Mass food production supported urbanization by providing a food source for cities.
1836	Samuel Colt invents the first revolver in the U.S. to be used as a practical weapon. Colt's manufacturing firm would later produce the pistols most widely used in the U.S. Civil War.
1832–1838	Samuel Morse develops the telegraph and Morse Code
1846	Ascanio Sobrero, an Italian chemist, invents nitroglycerin
1856	French chemist and microbiologist Louis Pasteur invents the process of pasteurization
1858	Belgian Étienne Lenoir invents the first commercially successful internal-combustion engine
1867	Alfred Nobel invents dynamite
1876	Alexander Graham Bell patents the telephone
1885	Gottlieb Daimler invents the first gas engine motorcycle
1900	Ferdinand von Zeppelin invents a rigid dirigible airship
1903	The Wright brothers invent the first gas-powered airplane (but their historic first flight on Dec. 17 is mentioned in only three newspapers)
1905	Albert Einstein publishes the theory of relativity: $E = mc^2$
1914	Henry Ford introduces the assembly line to mass-produce automobiles
1928	Biologist Alexander Fleming discovers penicillin
1930	Vannevar Bush at the Massachusetts Institute of Technology invents the first modern analog computer
1940	Peter Goldmark invents the first commercial color-television system (eight years later, in 1948, he would unveil the long-playing phonograph record)
1945	The atomic bomb is tested in Alamogordo, New Mexico
1955	The antibiotic tetracycline is invented
1959	Jack Kilby and Robert Noyce invent the microchip
1969	The predecessor of the internet, called the ARPAnet, is invented
1971	Ray Tomlinson invents internet-based email

	Engineer Ted Hoff develops the first microprocessor
1973	First mobile cellular phone call placed
1974	Micro Instrumentation and Telemetry Systems (MITS) makes the Altair available, a mail-order personal computer building kit
1975	Paul G. Allen and Bill Gates form Microsoft
1985	Microsoft invents the Windows program
1988	Digital cell phones are invented
1990	Tim Berners-Lee creates the internet protocol HTTP and the World Wide Web language HTML
	Hubble space telescope is launched
1992	The first form of email becomes available to the public
1993	The European Organization for Nuclear Research (CERN) opens the World Wide Web to the public, a decision that profoundly alters how information is stored and shared, not to mention the very fabric of society
	Global Positioning System (GPS) becomes commercially available
1994	The Channel Tunnel connecting England and France opens
1996	The first animal is successfully cloned (Dolly the sheep)
1997	Mars Pathfinder lands on the Martian surface
	A NASA Shuttle mission is commanded by a woman for the first time
	Toyota releases the the Prius, the first mass-produced hybrid car
1998	Construction begins on the International Space Station
	DVDs are introduced, revolutionizing data storage
2000	The first cellphone with a camera is introduced
	Bluetooth-enabled cellphones debut
	USB flash drive is made available in the U.S. by IBM
2003	Space Shuttle *Columbia* is lost on Feb. 1
2004	Facebook is founded
2006	The International Astronomical Union creates the first formal definition of a planet, making Pluto a dwarf planet
2007	iPhone comes to market on June 29
2011	The U.S. Space Shuttle program is officially ended
2019	Astronomers capture first photo of a black hole
2020	Crewed spaceflight resumes in the U.S.
	The U.S. Food and Drug Administration issues Emergency Use Authorizaton on Dec. 11 for the first Covid-19 vaccine, from Pfizer-BioNTech

Settlements, Building Communities, and Understanding Culture

Historically, communities have formed to fulfill a number of needs. They include security, religious freedom, and material well-being, as well as the protection provided by laws. For example, farmers and townspeople under feudalism during the Middle Ages would offer their allegiance to a noble who promised to protect them. As another example, immigrants throughout history have come to the United States to practice the religion of their choice as well as to have their rights and freedom protected under the law. As communities develop, they seek to meet their needs by educating their members, creating a system to govern and to protect the people, establishing communication and transportation systems, and providing recreation. Throughout history, certain members rise to meet or advocate for the needs and well-being of others within a community or for the community as a whole. These leaders are often recognized as patriots and become historical figures. They help shape societies and can even impact the development of a state or nation. Good members of the community include such people as political and military leaders (e.g., mayors, governors, presidents, generals), police officers, firefighters, educators (e.g., principals, teachers), doctors, inventors, scientists, athletes, doctors, artists, writers, activists, etc.). In the United States many individuals have shaped communities as well as the nation. They include George Washington, Benjamin Franklin, Harriet Tubman, Abraham Lincoln, Upton Sinclair, Susan B. Anthony, Ida Tarbell, Henry Ford, Steve Jobs, Franklin D. Roosevelt, Dwight Eisenhower, Harry Truman, Jonas Salk, Thomas Dewey, Mark Twain, Edward Hopper, Georgia O'Keeffe, Charlie Chaplin, Louis Armstrong, Billie Holiday, Booker T. Washington, W.E.B. Du Bois, Martin Luther King, Jr., Daniel K. Inouye, Cesar Chavez, Jackie Robinson, and Lyndon Johnson (from Gillespie County, Texas) to name but a few. In Texas, many patriots and historical figures shaped our communities such as Sam Houston, Davy Crockett, Stephen F. Austin, Sarah Driscoll, José de Escandón, Capt. Anthony F. Lucas, James Stephen Hogg, Molly Ivins, and Ann Richards.

Culture is "the sum total of knowledge, attitudes, and habitual behavior patterns shared and transmitted by the members of a society" (De Blij & Murphy, 1999). Cultures change and adapt for a number of reasons. For example, cultural attire can be a simple adaptation to account for cold or hot weather, mild or harsh climates. For example, during the winter, a parka may be worn in Alaska while light jackets are worn in Texas. Native Americans exemplified adaptation when some groups used grease from animal fat to ward off mosquitoes. Cultures may also change through modifications. For example, the extreme heat and humidity in the South are better withstood through the invention of air conditioning. Modifications, such as roads and railroads, as well as steel frames for buildings, allowed cultures to develop and expand their population and their geographic area over time. Moving to a new location and interacting with communities can also impact groups of people. For example, in Texas, many cultural groups (e.g., Hispanic, Germans, Polish, Czech, African-American, etc.) have learned from each other through cultural diffusion. **Cultural diffusion** is "the process of dissemination, the spread of an idea or innovation from its source area to other cultures" (De Blij, Murphy, Alexander, 1999). This can be seen in Texas through many foods (e.g., tacos, burritos, pork rinds, cornbread, sauerkraut, and sausage) and cultural traditions (e.g., Oktoberfest, Cinco de Mayo, festivals and state fairs, Kwanzaa, Christmas, Hanukkah, etc.). These are also examples of a **cultural exchange**, whereby groups of people take on some of the traits of other cultural groups.

Ancient Civilizations of the Americas

Native Americans lived throughout what we now call the Americas for centuries prior to European colonization. These ancient civilizations each had a unique and rich cultural heritage. They made major contributions to the development of the Americas in all aspects of social, political, and cultural life. Their legacies continue to influence modern day history. Unfortunately, many of the ancient civilizations were destroyed as a result of European colonization. Among the most developed ancient civilizations in the Americas were the Olmecs, Mayas, Toltecs, Aztecs, and Incas.

Mayans (1800 BCE to 900 CE)

One of the earliest civilizations of Mesoamerica was the Mayan, from regions of Mexico's Yucatán Peninsula, Guatemala, and Honduras. The Mayas developed a highly integrated society with elaborate religious observances for which they built stone and mortar pyramids. The center of the Maya civilization was the city of Chichén Itzá and its religious centers, where human victims were sacrificed. The Mayas developed an elaborate calendar, a system of writing, and the mathematical concept of zero. They also had highly advanced knowledge of astronomy, engineering, and art. By the time the Spanish conquerors arrived, most of the Mayan religious centers had been abandoned and the civilization was in decline.

Zapotecs, Olmecs, and Toltecs

Further north in Mexico, three highly sophisticated civilizations emerged: the Olmecs, Zapotecs, and Toltecs. Beginning with the Olmecs, who flourished around 1200 BCE and followed by the Toltecs and Zapotecs, these groups developed highly sophisticated civilizations. They had already begun to use a ceremonial calendar and had built stone pyramids on which they performed religious observances. Teotihuacán is the best-known example of religious ceremonial sites built by these civilizations. They developed a partly alphabetic writing system and left codices describing their history, religion, and daily events. They also built pyramids starting in about 1000 BCE, which predates the pyramids in Egypt. Two of the most famous are the Pyramid of the Sun and the Pyramid of the Moon in Teotihuacán, Mexico, built between 1 and 250 CE.

Aztecs (6th century to 1525 CE)

The Aztec civilization achieved the highest degree of development in Mexico. They had a centralized government headed by a king and supported by a large army. The Aztecs were also skilled builders and engineers, and accomplished astronomers and mathematicians. They built the famous city of Tenochtitlán, with many pyramids, palaces, plazas, and canals. At the zenith of their civilization, the Aztecs had a population of about five million. According to the Native Languages of America, Classical Nahuatl, the administrative language of the Aztec empire, is practically extinct. However, modern Nahuatl varieties are still being used in Mexico, and used in their bilingual education programs (Rosado, Hellawell & Zamora, 2011). For more information on native languages go to *http://www.native-languages.org.*

Incas—Children of the Sun

The Inca civilization ultimately encompassed a large swath of western South America which incorporated the modern countries of Ecuador, Peru, and central Chile. Although they were not as advanced in mathematics and the sciences as the Mayans and Aztecs, the Incas had a well-developed political system. They also built a monumental road system to unify the empire. Their civilization was at its peak when the Spanish conquerors arrived in Cuzco, the capital of the empire. The Quechua are descendants of the Incas and still live in large numbers in South America, mainly in the Andes Mountains.

Native Americans

Native Americans are aboriginal peoples of the Western Hemisphere who are also revered as American Indian, Indian, and First Nation persons, to list a few. Many American Indian groups were either hunter-gatherer cultures or agrarian peoples. They are known for domesticating such plants as corn (maize), beans, and potatoes and such animals as turkeys, llamas, and alpacas. These plants and animals in turn were used to support communities. Culturally, these indigenous people are grouped as Arctic peoples and American Indians, which are culturally grouped by location (e.g., North America, Mesoamerica, South America, and so on).

Native Americans of North America

In North America, American Indians are identified by cultural area. For example, some areas are referred to by cardinal directions (i.e., Northeast and Southeast), whereas others combine such groups based on physical geography. Thus, the Northeast and Southeast areas may be referred to as the Eastern Woodland cultural areas. The Mound Builders are an example of peoples known by the physical geography of their location. Known as the Woodland and Mississippian peoples, they lived in the Great Lakes and Mississippi area. These people built burial mounds dated as early as 500 CE. The Mississippian peoples built flat-topped mounds as foundations for wooden temples. The chiefs and the priests of these groups lived in residences built atop the mounds, while the rest of the population lived in houses below. These mound-building civilizations declined gradually, disappearing altogether by the 14th century.

On the other hand, other groups were identified by their cardinal location. For example, two ancient cultures who are recognized as indigenous groups from the southwestern United States and northern Mexico are the Anasazi and the Hohokam. The Anasazi developed adobe architecture consisting of individual apartments, storage areas, and a central plaza. They worked the land, developed a system of irrigation, and made clothes and baskets. The Hohokam built separate stone and timber houses surrounding a central plaza. Neither group developed a written language. Drought and attacks from rival tribes contributed to the decline of these civilizations. Historians believe that the Anasazi built the cliff dwellings at Mesa Verde, Colorado, during the 14th and 15th centuries to protect against these attacks. Additionally, Native Peoples of the Northwest Coast consisted of cultural groups known for fishing, woodworking, large communities (e.g., villages), and a more complex, hierarchical society. This area is home to a number of groups such as the Chinook, Kwakiutl, Haida, among others.

For more about these indigenous groups see *https://www.britannica.com/topic/Native-American/The-Arctic* and *https://www.history.com/topics/native-american-history/native-american-cultures*.

Algonquians

The **Algonquians** were the first Native Americans to interact with the English settlers at Plymouth. Algonquians were skilled hunters, gathers, and trappers who were adept at farming. They wore clothing made from animal skins and lived in wigwams. The Algonquians shared their extensive knowledge of agriculture with the English settlers, a practice that likely saved the colonists' lives.

Iroquois

The **Iroquois** inhabited the area of modern-day Ontario, Canada, and upstate New York for at least 4,500 years before the arrival of Europeans. They hunted and fished, but farming became the main economic activity for the group. The Iroquois had a matrilineal line of descent, with women doing most of the farming to support the community. They developed the Iroquois Confederation to discourage war among the groups and to provide for a common defense.

Seminoles and Muscogee Creeks

The **Seminoles** and **Muscogee Creeks** lived in the Southeastern United States in open bark-covered houses called *chickees*. They were excellent hunters and planters. They are best known for their struggle against Spanish and English settlers in the mid-1800s.

Cherokee

The **Cherokee** also lived in the Southeast, and were one of the most advanced tribes, with their domed houses and deerskin and rabbit-fur clothing. Accomplished hunters, farmers, and fishers, they were known on the continent for their basketry and pottery. Covered in the Grade 7 TEKS is Cherokee leader Chief Bowl, also called "Bowles" and "Duwali." Born in North Carolina circa 1756 to a Scottish father and a Cherokee mother, in the early 19th century, Bowl led the first large Cherokee emigration that crossed the Mississippi River, with stops in Missouri, then Arkansas, and finally to Nacogdoches in the Mexican province of Texas.

Though Bowl helped Mexico defeat Anglo settlers in the Fredonian Rebellion of 1827, the Mexican government would not recognize Cherokee claims to land in East Texas.

Pueblo

Evidence suggests that the Anasazi settled along the Rio Grande and intermarried with the local population, leading to the emergence of the **Pueblo** people. The Pueblo culture improved on the architectural tradition and farming techniques of their predecessors. The Pueblo people lived in dwellings called pueblos and wore clothes made of wool and woven cotton. They were able to produce drought-resistant corn and squash, which became the foundation of their diet. The Pueblo Indians managed to survive the Spanish conquest and colonization period.

Apache

The **Apache** and their famous leader Geronimo lived in wickiups, simple dome-shaped shelters made of bark, grass, and branches. They wore cotton clothing and were skilled hunters and gatherers. The Apache lived in the Southwestern portion of the United States. The Grade 4 TEKS curriculum embraces the Lipan Apache, who were one of six sub-tribes of the Apache. The Lipans' traditional territory extended across the Southern Plains from southern Kansas to northwest Texas. They were mainly bison hunters, had limited involvement in agriculture, and were some of the earliest Plains Indians to get horses, which they used for trade and to raid their neighbors for supplies.

Navajo

The **Navajo** people lived in the Southwest as well, and were excellent weapon makers, weavers, and silversmiths. They lived in Hogans, round homes built of forked sticks, and wore rabbit-skin clothes.

Jumano

The **Jumano** territorial base was in central Texas between the lower Pecos and the Colorado rivers. They were bison hunters and traders and played an active role as middlemen between the Spanish colonies and various Indian tribes. *https://www.tshaonline.org/handbook/entries/jumano-indians*

Karankawa

The **Karankawa** Indians are an American Indian cultural group whose traditional homelands are located along the Texas Gulf Coast. They were a nomadic people who migrated seasonally to obtain food. With their traditional territory located at the flashpoint of the French and Spanish rivalry and later at an immigration pathway for Anglo Americans, the Karankawas struggled to survive as a group.

Caddo

The term **Caddo** once denoted only one of at least 25 distinct but closely affiliated groups centered around the Red River who lived in Texas, Arkansas, Louisiana, and Oklahoma. They settled along stream valleys in densely populated settlements, manufactured ceramics, domesticated plants to raise such crops as corn (maize), squash, and beans, and carried on extensive trade in fur, guns, and horses. Their societies had a well established social and political hierarchy that was intertwined with other Caddo societies. In the late 1600s to the 1800s, Spanish and French explorers sustained contact with Caddo groups along the Red River and in East Texas in the vicinity of Nacogdoches, Caddo Lake, and the Sabine and Brazos Rivers (Perttula, 2020).

For more information about American Indians in Texas see also *https://www.tshaonline.org*.

American History

Colonization

In the early 15th century, Portugal, under the leadership of Prince Henry the Navigator, began sea exploration. Over the next few decades, the Portuguese explored further south along the African coast. In 1498, Vasco da Gama successfully navigated the Cape of Good Hope at the southern tip of Africa, opening a new route to India.

Columbus's voyage to the New World in 1492 had tremendous impact on both Europe and the New World. By opening the Western Hemisphere to political and economic development by Europeans, Columbus changed the face of the world. Native populations that had existed prior to Columbus were decimated by disease and warfare. As Spanish, French, and English settlers began claiming territories in the Americas as their own, they displaced and killed millions of Native Americans.

In 1565, the Spaniards established the first successful European settlement in North America in St. Augustine, Florida, near what is now Jacksonville, Florida. Following the Spaniards, the English attempted to establish a permanent colony on Roanoke, an island off the coast of North Carolina. This colony eventually disappeared. Nearly 20 years later, the first permanent English settlement in North America was established on May 14, 1607, near present-day Williamsburg, Virginia. Further north, the Dutch settled colonies in the region of present-day New York and New Jersey. Following the Dutch, numerous private companies received royal charters, or patents, permitting them to begin the colonization process in North America. Three of the first and most successful companies were the Plymouth Company, the Massachusetts Bay Company, and the London Company. The London Company was the first to exercise this patent.

The English Colonies

Thirteen colonies were established on the Atlantic coastline. Three types of colonies developed and were based on three different charters: corporate colonies, royal colonies, and proprietary colonies. These were divided in three geographical regions: the New England Colonies, the Middle Colonies, and the Southern Colonies. The New England Colonies consisted of Massachusetts, Connecticut, Rhode Island, and New Hampshire. Their economy was based on farming and such small industries as fishing, lumber, and crafts. The Middle Colonies consisted of New York, New Jersey, Delaware, and Pennsylvania. Their economy was based on farming, shipping, fishing, and trading.

The Southern Colonies were: Maryland, Virginia, North Carolina, South Carolina, and Georgia. Their economy, which was centered around agriculture, was based on tobacco, rice, and indigo. Plantations produced agricultural crops in large scale and exploited workers as well as the environment. Each colonial region had unique cultures, communities, and geographical settings that affected their political and economic development.

Virginia (1607)

The Virginia Company established the first English colony in Jamestown, Virginia. The governor of the colony was Sir Edwin Sandys. During the difficult early years of the colony, a power struggle ensued between Sandys and Capt. John Smith, with Smith becoming the de facto leader. Natives of the area captured Smith and sentenced him to death. Pocahontas, daughter of the tribe's chief, intervened and saved his life. Contrary to popular belief, John Smith did not marry Pocahontas. She married John Rolfe, a tobacco farmer from the same colony. In 1619, the colony of Virginia established the first European-style form of government in North America, the **House of Burgesses**.

Massachusetts (Plymouth Colony, 1620), (Massachusetts Bay, 1630)

The Puritans, who fled England to avoid religious persecution, founded Plymouth in 1620. Plymouth was the first permanent colony in New England. The group obtained a patent from the Virginia Company. Among the Puritans were both separatists and non-separatists. The Pilgrims were separatists, a radical faction of Puritans who wanted to separate from the Church of England rather than merely purify it. The group obtained a patent from the Virginia Company of London to finance their pilgrimage to America; hence the name *Pilgrim*. The ship used for the journey was called the *Mayflower*. Approximately two-thirds on board were non-separatist Pilgrims. Before arriving, they wrote the **Mayflower Compact**, a document containing rules to guide life in the community. This compact, signed November 11, 1620, established one of the first types of government in North America.

New Hampshire (1623)

Two groups founded the New Hampshire colony. The first group was led by London merchant Capt. John Mason, who established a fishing village in 1623. Mason was one of several proprietors, but never lived in the colony. He acquired a charter for the colony of New Hampshire in 1622 and named the territory after his home county of Hampshire. But the first settlers were fishermen led by a David Thompson who settled near Portsmouth in 1623. Later villages were founded by other arrivals. In 1638, a group led by John Wheelwright founded a second settlement called Exeter. That colony began as a proprietorship but became a royal colony.

Maryland (1634)

In 1632, King Charles I granted to Lord Baltimore (Cecil Calvert) a charter establishing the colony of Maryland under Lord Baltimore's proprietorship. The colony was established as a refuge for Roman Catholics.

Rhode Island (1635)

Roger Williams founded the Rhode Island colony in 1636, and in 1637 Anne Hutchinson settled an additional part of the colony after being expelled from Massachusetts. Both Williams and Hutchinson had been banned from Massachusetts for their religious and political views and were looking for sanctuary. The colony was granted a corporate charter (or legally founded) in 1640.

Connecticut (1635)

Dutch fur traders explored the region that would become Connecticut as early as 1614 and settled in the Hartford area around 1623. The earliest English settlers were Puritans from Massachusetts who began to settle in the region as early as 1635. The largest contingent of English early settlers were led by Thomas Hooker and arrived in 1636 after falling out with the Puritans in Massachusetts. In 1662, Connecticut obtained a royal charter under the leadership of John Winthrop Jr.

South Carolina (1663)

In 1663, King Charles II created the colony of Carolina by granting the territory, of what is now North Carolina, South Carolina, and Georgia, to loyal supporters. It began as a proprietary colony and became a royal colony in 1719. Sir John Yeamans was one of a number of a plantation owners from Barbados involved in the founding of the city of Charleston in 1670.

New York (1664)

The British colony of New York began as the Dutch colony called New Netherlands. The town today known as New York City was originally called New Amsterdam, after the Dutch city of the same name. In 1664, the English took control of New Netherlands, renaming it New York in honor of its new proprietor, the brother of King Charles II, the Duke of York. The colony remained a proprietary colony until 1685 when it became a royal colony.

New Jersey (1664)

The Dutch founded the New Jersey colony in 1623, though the Swedes also claimed part of southwestern New Jersey. After taking over the Dutch territory between Virginia and New England in 1664, King Charles II of England gave it to his brother, the Duke of York. The duke then gave the territory as a proprietary grant to Sir George Carteret and Lord Berkeley. In 1702, New Jersey became a royal colony.

Pennsylvania (1681)

As early as 1638, Swedish, Dutch, and English settlers tried to establish permanent settlements in Delaware, part of which would be incorporated into Pennsylvania. In 1681, William Penn was granted the larger territory now known as Pennsylvania. He was a Quaker, a religion persecuted in England. He made Pennsylvania a safe haven for Quakers. In 1682, Penn established the city of Philadelphia. Though Quakers were the most prominent group to settle in Pennsylvania, large numbers of German Mennonites also came to Pennsylvania. These "Pennsylvania Dutch," from the word *Deutsche* (or "German"), established the city of Germantown near Philadelphia in 1683.

Delaware (1701)

Dutch, Swedish, and Finnish settlers first settled the colony between 1631 and 1638. The region was claimed by both Cecil Calvert, Lord Baltimore, and by the Duke of York, but was granted to William Penn in 1681. The colony became self-governing in 1701.

North Carolina (1712)

By 1653, Virginia colonists had begun moving south and settling in the North Carolina region. In 1663, King Charles II rewarded key allies with proprietorship of the colony of Carolina, which included North Carolina, South Carolina, and Georgia. Disputes over how the colony was to be governed resulted in the division of North and South Carolina in 1712. In 1729, most of the proprietors of North Carolina ceded their ownership to the crown and the colony became a royal colony.

Georgia (1732)

Georgia was founded as both a haven for the English poor and as a buffer between England's more profitable colonies and Spain's territories in Florida. English settlement of the region began after James Oglethorpe, a social reforming member of parliament, proposed that a colony be founded to house England's poor and those jailed for their inability to pay their debts. He and other reformers acquired a charter for their colony in 1732. In 1752, Georgia became a royal colony and soon was increasingly settled by plantation owners and their slaves.

Table 5-1 summarizes the key historical figures involved in the founding of the colonies.

Table 5-1: The Thirteen American Colonies

Colony	Year Founded	Founded By
Virginia	1607	Virginia Company of London. Chartered in 1606, becomes a royal colony in 1624.
Massachusetts	1620 - Plymouth Colony	Puritans, with a patent from the Virginia Company of London, later incorporated into Massachusetts Bay Colony.
	1630 - Massachusetts Bay Colony	Puritans. Chartered in 1629, becomes a royal colony in 1679.
New Hampshire	1623	Settled in early 1620s as small villages but was placed under government of Massachusetts Bay Colony until chartered in 1641; becomes a royal colony in 1679.
Maryland	1634	Granted to Lord Baltimore as proprietor in 1632. Haven for Roman Catholics.

(continued)

Colony	Year Founded	Founded By
Rhode Island	1635	Roger Williams, exiled by Massachusetts Bay Colony, established Providence.
Connecticut	1635	Thomas Hooker. Government organized in 1636.
South Carolina	1663	Eight nobles with a royal charter from Charles II granted in 1663; unauthorized settlement had begun earlier in what is now North Carolina.
New York	1664	Originally settled by the Dutch, granted to the Duke of York in 1664.
New Jersey	1664	Originally settled by the Dutch, granted as part of New York to Duke of York. Ceded in 1664 to Sir George Carteret.
Pennsylvania	1681	Granted to William Penn as proprietor in 1681. Haven for Quakers.
Delaware	1701	Settled by Dutch (1631), Swedes (1638) and part of New Netherlands; was acquired in 1664 by England and granted to Duke of York as part of New York. Ceded to William Penn in 1681; became self-governing in 1701.
North Carolina	1712	Settled by Virginians; governed as part of the Carolina colony that combined both North and South Carolina.
Georgia	1732	James Oglethorpe. Became a royal colony in 1752.

Representative Government in Colonial America

The United States was settled by pioneers who wanted to experience freedom and have a voice in how they were governed. These settlers were influenced by such enlightened individuals as John Locke, Montesquieu, Thomas Hobbes, and Thomas Paine, as well as by their experiences in establishing and governing their settlements. Colonists thus developed greater expectations for representation in their government. Actions and documents such as the Magna Carta (English Bill of Rights), the Mayflower Compact, the Virginia House of Burgesses, and the Fundamental Orders of Connecticut exemplify this belief.

The colonies were founded with the idea that people would have a substantial autonomy and liberty in regards to political and religious life. The colonists were unique because they were English citizens who chose to move to the New World. They were not natives who were conquered and forced to become a colony. They brought with them their tradition of hard work, individual freedom, and representative government that reflected English values and the influence of Locke and the Age of Reason. When the colonists first arrived in America they were still under British rule. Believing in the right to elect the people who would represent them on issues such as taxation, the colonists felt that they should have representation in the British Parliament. Unfortunately, the colonists (those in America and in other British colonies) were not given a seat in parliament or given the right to vote for any member of parliament. As such the colonists did not have any form of representation in the British political system. This reality would later be a major cause of the American Revolution and formation of a new nation.

The idea of representative government, or the idea that people can vote for their own lawmakers, would become fundamental to the formation of the United States. Along with the ability to elect lawmakers, representative government also includes the notion that concepts and ideas can be deliberated and discussed by both legislators and the people who elected them. This principle would later be reflected in the design of the United States Congress.

The Virginia House of Burgesses was the first colonial assembly of elected representatives from the Virginia settlement. It was established in Jamestown to represent the colonists in the state of Virginia in the lawmaking process and met for the first time in July 1619.

The Mayflower Compact was drawn and signed in 1620 by the Pilgrims aboard the Mayflower. They pledged to consult one another to make decisions and to act by the will of the majority. It is one of the earliest agreements to establish a political body and to give that political body the power to act for the good of the colony. Eventually, the lack of representation for colonists led to rebellions, like the Boston Tea Party, and to such meetings as the Continental Congress and the Second Continental Congress, which led to the Declaration of Independence July 4, 1776. After the colonists won the War for Independence, also called the Revolutionary War, their desire for representational government led to the development of the Articles of Confederation and then to the Constitution of the United States.

Indentured Servants

The indentured servant system was used to bring workers to the New World. In practice, the indentured servant would sell him or herself to an agent or ship captain before leaving England. In turn, the contract would be sold to a buyer in the colonies to recover the cost of passage. Criminals and people in debt could also be sold for life or until they paid their debts. In some cases, at the end of the service, servants remained as salaried workers, or in the best situations, the servants were given a piece of land for their services. This system of provisional servitude was not applied to Africans; instead, permanent slavery was instituted.

The Enlightenment—The Age of Reason

The Enlightenment refers to a period during the 17th and 18th centuries when people began questioning religious dogmas and emphasizing scientific reasoning and knowledge. As a result of this quest for knowledge, modern chemistry and biology were developed. Additionally, people also began to think critically about the rights, freedoms, and powers of man in relation to political systems. The Enlightenment stirred people to action in fighting the tyranny of religious and political oppression. For example, the quest for freedom led to the American and the French Revolutions. Some of the leading thinkers of this period were Jean-Jacques Rousseau, John Locke, Montesquieu, Voltaire, and Francis Bacon. The ideas of the Enlightenment quickly reached the British colonies. Many of the leaders responsible for the writing of the Constitution were familiar with and influenced by the leading thinkers of the movement. They framed the Constitution around the powerful ideas of these thinkers, including the protection of the natural rights of the individual and limiting the power of the government.

The French and Indian War

The French and Indian War, the North American part of the Seven Years' War, began in 1754 as part of a larger imperial war in Europe between France and Britain. Both countries sought to expand their control in the Americas. Their poorly defined borders and attempts to militarily strengthen their claims caused increased tensions that led to war. The war officially ended with the Treaty of Paris in 1763 and a solid British victory. However, the conflict was expensive. Therefore, the British government levied heavy taxes on the American colonists to help pay for the war, adding to the rising tensions in the colonies. Coupled with limitations on colonists' westward expansion and increased war with the Indians, the colonists would soon rebel and fight for their independence.

American Revolution

The main reasons why the British colonists revolted against British control were economic. England, as well as other European nations, had established **mercantilism** to exploit the colonies. This system had three main principles:

1. The wealth of the nation is measured in terms of commodities accrued, especially gold and silver.

2. Economic activities can increase the power and control of the national government.

3. The colonies existed for the benefit of the mother country.

England used the system of mercantilism quite effectively in the 13 colonies, but after more than a century of British rule, the colonists resented England's economic and political control. Outraged and spurred on by Enlightenment ideas, the colonists were primed for independence, and war with England became inevitable.

Another reason for the rebellion was the cost of the French and Indian War. This war emptied the British coffers and the British Crown needed a quick way to recover financially. The taxation system that followed the French and Indian War was unbearable for the colonies. The colonies responded with civil disobedience and by boycotting the government of King George. In response to civil disobedience, the British sent troops to Boston, where the groups clashed and several colonists were killed. The event was called the **Boston Massacre**. One of the best-known boycotts was the **Boston Tea Party**, in which the colonists dumped tea in the Boston Harbor to protest against taxation. "No taxation without representation" became a rallying cry for the colonists. All these events and the repression that followed led to the **American Revolution**, which is also known as the **American War of Independence** or **American Revolutionary War**.

Continental Congress

Following the events in Boston, representatives of the colonies met in Philadelphia to discuss the political and economic situation in the colonies. No clear solutions were reached at this congress. Once the hostilities started, the Second Continental Congress met to discuss preparations for war. George Washington was elected commander of the American forces, and war was declared against the British. The congress named a committee, led by Thomas Jefferson, to prepare the Declaration of Independence, which was officially signed (primarily) on August 2, 1776.

The Declaration of Independence

The **Declaration of Independence** pronounced the colonies free and independent states (hence the celebration of "Independence Day"). It consists of a preamble, or introduction, followed by three main parts. The first part stresses natural unalienable rights and liberties that belong to all people from birth. The second part consists of a list of specific grievances and injustices committed by Britain. The third part announces the colonies as the United States of America. This document provided the foundation to establish equal rights for all people. By signing this document, the colonists formally declared they were independent from English rule, thus officially beginning the American Revolution. Because it was signed on July 4, 1776, we celebrate "Independence Day," also known as "The 4th of July." **Note:** Students will remember "The 4th of July," but do not always understand that it is America's Independence Day and the reason for this celebration.

American Revolution (April 19, 1775–September 3, 1783)

The **American Revolution** began in Massachusetts on the outskirts of the towns of Concord and Lexington. In 1775, while the colonists were preparing for war, hundreds of British soldiers marched against them. Paul Revere warned the colonists of British troop movements, and minutemen took up arms to face the enemy. At Concord, the British were repelled and forced back to Boston. On their way back, American sharpshooters ambushed and killed hundreds of British soldiers. Following this initial victory for the colonists, the battle of Bunker Hill was fought near Boston. In this battle, the British lost large numbers of soldiers but managed to defeat the colonial troops. Later, in Long Island, the British won another decisive victory over the Americans. The French joined the war in support of the Americans, in retaliation for the French defeat at the hands of the British in the Seven Years' War. Eventually, with the support of the French, the American troops defeated the British forces in Yorktown, Virginia, in 1781. The **Treaty of Paris**, officially signed in 1783, ended the war and gave independence to the new nation. For additional details about the American Revolution, go to *http://www.historycentral.com*.

Articles of Confederation

During the Revolutionary War, the Second Continental Congress ran the government. After independence, the Articles of Confederation defined a new form of government. The **Articles of Confederation** was an agreement among the 13 founding states that legally established the United States of America as a confederation of sovereign states and served as its first constitution. It was drafted by the Continental Congress in 1776–77, went into use in 1777, and was formally ratified by all 13 states in 1781. The Articles gave legitimacy to the Continental Congress to direct the American Revolutionary War, conduct diplomacy with Europe, and deal with territorial issues and Indian relations. The Articles of Confederation established a new government, with limited power, that was comprised of representatives from 13 independent states. The Congress could not declare war or raise an army. It could, however, ask the states for money or for soldiers, but it was up to the states to agree to provide them. Under this type of government, each state printed its own money and imposed taxes on imports from the other states.

On the positive side, the new government provided for a common citizenship—citizens of the United States. It organized a uniform system of weights and measurements and a postal service. It also became responsible for issues related to Native Americans living within the borders of the new nation. The confederation served as the official government of the young republic until 1789, when the states ratified the **Constitution of the United States**.

United States Constitution

After six years under the Articles of Confederation, the leaders of the nation realized that the American government needed revision to bolster its strength. To accomplish this goal, a constitutional convention was held in Philadelphia in 1787. The leaders of this initiative were George Washington, James Madison, Benjamin Franklin, and Alexander Hamilton. From this convention, a new form of government emerged. The Constitution was officially ratified in 1788, and in 1789 George Washington was selected to be the first president of the United States. The U.S. Constitution allowed for a much stronger national government, with a president, courts, and taxing powers. The republic defined by the Constitution was composed of three branches—the executive, judicial, and legislative—with a system of checks and balances to regulate each branch. To learn more about historical American documents, go to "A Chronology of U.S. Historical Documents," a website created and maintained by the University of Oklahoma Law Center, at *www.law.ou.edu/hist*.

War of 1812

Twenty-nine years after the end of the American Revolution, conflict between Great Britain and the young United States flared up again. The **War of 1812** broke out for a variety of reasons, including Britain's seizure of American ships, impressment of American sailors into the British navy, and restriction of trade between the United States and France. In June 1812, James Madison became the first U.S. president to ask Congress to declare war. In 1814, Francis Scott Key had boarded a British ship in hopes of persuading officials to release a prisoner. Due to an impeding battle, he was forced to remain on the ship during a relentless effort by the British to take Fort McHenry in Baltimore Harbor. While watching the bombardment of the fort, he wrote a poem describing what he saw and felt. It was originally published by the name "Defence of Fort M'Henry." It is now called **"The Star-Spangled Banner."** In 1916, President Woodrow Wilson announced that it should be played at all official events and was designated as the National Anthem of the United States with the stroke of President Herbert Hoover's pen on March 3, 1931. Fought in three theaters, the War of 1812 ended with the Treaty of Ghent in 1815. Learn more about the War of 1812 visit *http://www.history.com* and *http://www. smithsonianmag.com/history/the-story-behind-the-star-spangled-banner-149220970/*

Monroe Doctrine

In 1823, President James Monroe made clear to European countries that the United States was not going to permit the establishment of colonies in the Western Hemisphere. Monroe also banned European countries from attacking the new American republics that were just becoming established in the early 19th century. The U.S. was not to become involved in European affairs. This concept of "America for Americans" is known as the **Monroe Doctrine**.

Westward Expansion (1807–1912)

After the War of 1812, much of America's attention turned to exploration and settlement of its territory to the West, which had been greatly enlarged by the Louisiana Purchase. Pioneer families moved westward and founded new communities throughout what is now the Midwest. Between 1816 and 1821, six new states were admitted to the Union. This westward expansion occurred for a number of reasons, primarily economic.

First, cotton had become an important resource in the southern states. As the effects of the industrial revolution—which began in England—reached the United States, new inventions, for example Eli Whitney's cotton gin, encouraged faster and more efficient production of goods. With the invention of the cotton gin, the demand for cotton grew, and more and more farmers became involved in the production of cotton. Innovations in long-distance transportation, most notably the railroad, allowed cotton and other goods to be shipped cross-country with more ease. As demand for cotton and prices increased, southern farmers began expanding their farms toward the West where there was fertile soil. As farm sizes increased, so did the demand for a large supply of cheap labor. As a result, the system of slavery expanded both in numbers and in regional movement to the West.

Secondly, expansion westward continued as people moved west to seek their economic fortunes. Miners, trappers, ranchers, merchants, and others went west to find new resources and economic riches. The Lewis and Clark Expedition played a prominent role in promoting westward expansion and in mapping the West. Fur companies recruited "mountain men" to search for fur-bearing animals that would increase the supply of such goods and meet the needs of the East and of Europe. Finally, the California Gold Rush attracted easterners to push westward in hopes of finding riches.

Thirdly, increased settlement in the West encouraged missionaries to travel west with the fur traders to seek converts among the native peoples. Missionaries sent word back to the East encouraging more settlers to come to the West. This encouragement by missionaries helped produce a tremendous influx of westward settlers.

Finally, **Manifest Destiny**, or the belief that the United States was foreordained to expand across the continent, encouraged westward expansion. In 1844, President James K. Polk declared to the world that the United States would eventually become a world power and expand to its natural borders. Some of the borders mentioned were the Pacific to the west and Mexico to the south. Manifest Destiny would ultimately cause huge issues between the U.S. Government and Native Americans, England, Spain, and Mexico. Eventually, Polk's expectations became a reality as a result of the war between Mexico and the United States that lasted from 1846 to 1848.

Many Americans believed it was the country's destiny to stretch from the Atlantic Ocean to the Pacific Ocean. This belief helped propel and justify westward expansion, wars, land purchases, treatment of the Native Americans, and economic development. Still, it was not a conviction supported by everyone. Some Americans, most notably members of the Whig party, did not believe that it was America's divine right to expand; rather, the United States should be a virtuous example of democracy for others to follow. However, Jefferson's purchase of the Louisiana territory in 1803, netting 827,000 square miles of land west of the Mississippi River for $15 million, created conditions to support America's westward growth and development.

Results of Westward Expansion

As America grew in the 19th century, so did its need for resources, land, and expansion. European settlers had originally claimed much of the terrain, although Native Americans had long-established territories of their own. Therefore, when land was garnered through agreements (e.g., the Louisiana Purchase from the French), annexation (e.g., Texas), and war (e.g., with Mexico), the American people expected that they had a right to the land. Acquiring more land made the country stronger economically. For example, more crops could be grown to provide a food source for American cities or to be exported to other countries. The natural resources fueled the country's industrial power. The **Transcontinental Railroad** was built to move resources and people across the nation and thus tied the nation together from the East Coast to the West Coast. The railroad was pivotal to the economic growth and development of the United States and to the rapid settling of the West.

Expansion came at great cost to the Native Americans. Some Native Americans may have coexisted peacefully with settlers when peace agreements were made and kept. Others groups, such as the Comanche and Apache, were more aggressive and given to war. The expansion of American settlements in the 1800s caused tensions to increase between Native Americans and settlers. In the end, Native Americans were forced to give up their lands and eventually their way of life. The American government set aside reservations, land specifically designated for these groups. However, this land was typically poor quality and unwanted by both Americans and Native Americans. This forced Native Americans into a state of dependency and poverty. If life on the reservation was refused, war ensued to compel Native Americans to comply. In many cases, Native Americans were killed in raids or in war. Native Americans also attacked settlers, which added to the distrust and increased military action.

One of the most controversial actions taken by the federal government occurred in 1830 when Andrew Jackson signed the Indian Removal Act. The law, covered in the Grade 8 TEKS, forced Native Americans out of the cotton-producing lands in the South, east of the Mississippi River. Although this action did not follow the legal negotiation of a fair removal of the treaty with the Indians, Jackson's administration wanted all Native Americans out of the economically productive Eastern part of the country. The Indian removal process, also known as the Trail of Tears, forced Native Americans to vacate their homes in the southeastern part of the United States to lands in the West, mainly in what is now Oklahoma. The U.S. Army crushed any resistance to removal.

With the West cleared, Westerners focused on developing new methods of transporting their goods to market. The canal and railroad systems, which were developed in the North, facilitated a much larger volume of trade and manufacturing while greatly reducing costs. Great cities sprang up throughout the North and Northwest, bolstered by the improvement in transportation.

After the Midwest had been substantially developed, the national focus turned toward the far West. The territory of Texas, controlled by the Spanish, was settled by Americans, who eventually undertook the Texas Rebellion in efforts to win independence. When the United States admitted Texas to the Union in 1845, the Mexican government was outraged, and from 1846 to 1848, the two nations squared off in the Mexican War. As a result of this war, the United States gained control of Texas, New Mexico, and California. When the Oregon Territory was annexed in 1846, the U.S. stretched all the way to the Pacific Ocean.

As the population of the West soared and the prospects of statehood for western territories appeared clearer and clearer, the nation battled over the future of slavery in the West. This battle was one reason for the Civil War, which slowed the acceleration of expansion. However, the last three decades of the 19th century saw the return of accelerated expansion due to the successful struggle to contain the Plains Indians in reservations, and the completion of the **Transcontinental Railroad** in 1869. By the early 20th century, the organization of the West was complete, and the United States consisted of 48 contiguous states.

Slavery in the United States

As the nation grew, so did local, state, and national politics. The issue of slavery was a constant concern. Agreements were made to limit the number of states that did or did not allow slavery. Expanded territories became states as the population increased, thereby adding to the number of members of Congress in the Senate and House of Representatives. The influx of legislators affected laws and policies. These legislative decisions included laws about Native Americans, slavery, and big businesses (e.g., railroads, steel, meatpacking industries, etc.).

The Dutch brought the first African slaves to Virginia in 1619 to work on plantations. From 1640 to 1680, large numbers of slaves were brought to the Americas. With the invention of Eli Whitney's cotton gin, cotton became the economic mainstay of the South, and the demand for labor increased the slave trade. From 1798 to 1808, more than 200,000 African slaves were brought to America, mostly to the southern region.

Beginning in 1774, the North began regulating and eventually prohibiting slavery. By 1804, New York and New Jersey had passed gradual emancipation laws. Meanwhile, the slave trade in the South grew to meet the economic needs of the area. Eventually, the issue of slavery, along with other economic and ideological differences between the regions, resulted in the American Civil War. In 1862, Abraham Lincoln issued the Emancipation Proclamation, granting freedom to slaves in the rebellious states. After the war, the 13th Amendment to the Constitution officially abolished slavery. Additionally, in 1866 the 14th Amendment gave African Americans full citizenship, and in 1870 the 15th Amendment granted voting rights to Black men.

Compromises

The late 17th and early 18th centuries were marked by a number of compromises between the various regions. Most of the time these compromises were short-lived and broke down quickly. One of the compromises was the **three-fifths compromise** proposed at the Constitutional Convention of 1787. This compromise centered on how to count slaves in deciding the number of representatives for the House of Representatives and the amount of taxes to be paid. Residents of the South wanted to count the slaves for the purposes of representation, but not for taxation. Northerners, on the other hand, wanted the opposite. As a compromise, the two sides agreed to count three-fifths of the slave population for both taxation and representation purposes.

The **Missouri Compromise** was an agreement passed in 1820 between the pro-slavery and anti-slavery factions in the United States Congress, involving primarily the regulation of slavery in the western territories. In 1819, the United States had 21 states: 10 slave states and 11 free states. The Territory of Missouri allowed slavery; its admittance as a state into the Union would cause an imbalance in the number of U.S. senators. Alabama had recently been added to the Union, thus equalizing the representation of free and slave states at 22 senators each. To resolve the conflict, the first Missouri Compromise allowed Maine to be admitted as a free state to the Union along with Missouri as a slave state.

Additionally, the Missouri Compromise prohibited slavery in the former Louisiana Territory north of the parallel 36°30' except within the boundaries of the proposed state of Missouri. Prior to the agreement, the House of Representatives had refused to accept this compromise and a conference committee was appointed. Southern congressmen accepted this proposal since growing cotton on land north of this line was not profitable. One year after the first compromise was passed, tensions heated up again as Missouri's state constitution discriminated against free Blacks. Antislavery advocates demanded that Missouri not be admitted to the Union. Under the leadership of Henry Clay, known as the great compromiser, it was proposed that the Constitution of the United States guaranteed the protection and privileges of citizens in states and thus Missouri's state constitution could not deny any person these rights. This proposal was accepted in 1820 and Missouri was admitted to the Union.

The **Compromise of 1850** was another agreement crafted by Henry Clay and Stephen Douglas aimed at ending the continuing struggle between slave and non-slave states. This compromise included a series of five bills intended to stave off sectional strife over slavery. Its goal was to deal with the spread of slavery to territories in order to keep northern and southern interests in balance. The five bills are summarized below:

1. California was entered as a free state.

2. New Mexico and Utah were each allowed using **popular sovereignty,** or the idea that people living in territories or states should decide for themselves if slavery should be permitted.

3. The Republic of Texas gave up lands that it claimed in present-day New Mexico and received $10 million to pay its debt to Mexico.

4. The slave trade was abolished in the District of Columbia.

5. The **Fugitive Slave Act** made any federal official who did not arrest a runaway slave liable to pay a fine. This was the most controversial part of the Compromise of 1850 and caused many abolitionists to increase their efforts against slavery.

The **Kansas–Nebraska Act** of 1854 created the territories of Kansas and Nebraska, opened new lands that would help settlement in them, repealed the Missouri Compromise of 1820, and allowed settlers in those territories to determine via popular sovereignty if they would allow slavery within their boundaries. Designed by Democratic Senator Stephen Douglas, the Kansas-Nebraska Act created a huge controversy because of the popular sovereignty provision. Both pro- and anti-slavery supporters flooded into Kansas with the goal of voting slavery up or down. One group of northern abolitionists, led by **John Brown**, also flocked to the territory and set up their own government in Lawrence. A band of pro-slavery men, however, burned Lawrence to the ground in 1856. In revenge, an abolitionist gang killed five men in the **Pottawatomie Massacre**. In 1859, Brown and his followers seized the federal arsenal at Harper's Ferry in what is now West Virginia. Their purpose was to steal the guns in the arsenal, give them to slaves nearby, and begin a widespread rebellion. Brown and his men were captured by Colonel Robert E. Lee and found guilty. Brown was later hanged. These two events sparked an internal war so savage that many referred to the territory as **"Bleeding Kansas."**

The decision rendered in the ***Dred Scott v. Sandford*** Supreme Court case served to intensify the debate regarding the issue of slavery in the United States. Dred Scott was a slave whose owner had taken him from Missouri, a slave state, to Illinois and Minnesota, both free states, and back to Missouri. Scott petitioned the Supreme Court (after petitioning two lower courts) for his freedom based on his having resided in two free states, each with state laws that declared that slaves brought into the state were set free. The Supreme Court ruled that Scott and all other slaves were not citizens of any state or the United States and thus had no rights. A slave was deemed property, neither a person nor a citizen. Thus, Scott or other slaves had no right to sue in either state or federal court. Further, the court held that the federal government had no legal right to interfere with the institution of slavery. Slavery advocates were encouraged and began to make plans to expand slavery into all of the western territories and states, thus creating much of the tension that led to the Civil War.

Civil War (April 12, 1861–May 9, 1865)

Political, Economic, Social Differences

As the nation expanded and territories became states, each new state developed its own unique political, social, economic, and cultural identity. Over time, regional identities evolved, leading to regionalism or the political division of and loyalty to the interests of particular regions. Each region came to be defined by the economic and social institutions most prevalent in the area. In the North, the industrialized factory system created a division between factory owners who reaped huge profits and factory workers who were subjected to poor working conditions. The industrialized North had a boom in the number of factories and towns, while the South remained primarily agricultural where slaves and indentured servants worked on large plantations owned by wealthy whites. The South defended their economy on the basis that states had the right to self-determination with regard to their economic and social institutions. The West was a vast expanse of newly explored and settled land in which ranching became a mainstay. Settlers who traveled to the West were looking for land, wealth, and opportunity. Many settlers were from the South and brought slaves with them. As such, the identity of each of these regions was distinctly different, especially in the role of children, women, trade, religion, and labor systems. As might be expected, these differences led to conflicts among the inhabitants of each region.

Slavery and Sectionalism

The issue of slavery became a major issue between the North and South and created deep divisions for the young nation. By the 1800s, slavery had been virtually abolished in the North. The northern states' reasons for turning against slavery were primarily economic: the North had become more urban and industrialized than the South, and northern states received large numbers of immigrants who provided the necessary labor. Southern states remained mostly rural and received few immigrants, making slavery the foundation of their economy. This economic disparity coupled with the publication of Harriet Beecher Stowe's book *Uncle Tom's Cabin* as well as efforts by the national government to control trade between the regions created a huge rift between the North and the South. The disagreement over slavery, specifically over the issue of who was guaranteed the inalienable right to be free, led to sectionalism, or the excessive devotion to local interests and customs. This growing sectionalism would be a primary cause of the Civil War.

The issue of slavery became the main topic of the presidential election of 1860. The candidates were clearly aligned either in favor of or against slavery. The southern Democrats backed a strong proslavery candidate, John C. Breckinridge of Kentucky, while the new Republican Party selected a strong antislavery candidate in the figure of Abraham Lincoln. The election of Abraham Lincoln resulted in the secession of the southern states from the Union (January 1861), the creation of the Confederacy, known as the Confederate States of America, and the start of the American Civil War (1861-1865). The southern states created the **Confederate States of America** in February 1861 and selected Jefferson Davis as president. For more information about events of the Civil War, see *https://www.britannica.com/summary/American-Civil-War-Timeline* and *https://www.nps.gov/gett/ learn/historyculture/civil-war-timeline.htm.*

Secession

In response to the election of Abraham Lincoln, 11 southern slave states, led by South Carolina, seceded from the Union and formed the Confederate States of America, or the Confederacy. Twenty-five states supported the federal government and remained part of the Union. Both sides began preparations for war. The North had a greater advantage over the South because of a larger population, financial security, industrial resources, increased means of transportation, and natural resources. The South, largely agricultural in nature, did not have the same caliber of resources or infrastructure as the North. The South, however, had some advantage in the sheer vastness of their territory and the know-how of their army leaders, many of whom were educated at West Point and had extensive experience in previous wars.

The major aim of the Confederacy's war efforts was to win independence, protect the institution of slavery, and earn the right to govern themselves. The war efforts of the North coalesced around protecting the sanctity of the Union under the leadership of Lincoln. However, the abolition of slavery became an increasingly more important issue as the war continued.

Battle of Gettysburg

Hundreds of battles were fought in this war, but none was as devastating as the **Battle of Gettysburg**. Fought in 1863, this battle was the most disastrous event of the war and marked a major turning point; more than 50,000 soldiers from the North and the South lost their lives. In a speech delivered on the battlefield in November 1863, President Lincoln eulogized the fallen Union soldiers in what became the famous **Gettysburg Address**.

The End of the American Civil War

In 1865, after five years of fighting, the loss of thousands of lives and millions of dollars in property, the commander of the Confederate army, General Robert E. Lee, surrendered to General Ulysses S. Grant, commander of the Union forces. The Civil War took more American lives than any other war in U.S. history. The South lost nearly one-third of its soldiers, while the North lost about one-sixth. More than 50% of the deaths were attributed to the terrible conditions of field hospitals and to disease.

The loss of human life was not the only devastation; the economic losses were significant for both sides. The physical destruction, almost all of it in the South, was enormous: burned or plundered homes, pillaged countryside, untold losses in crops and farm animals, ruined buildings and bridges, devastated college campuses, and neglected roads all left the South in ruins.

Reconstruction Era (1865–1877)

Post–Civil War physical reconstruction focused on the South because the war was primarily fought in this region. However, the emotional reconstruction and the reconstruction of American unity had to be done nationwide, and admission of rebel states back into the Union was not automatically granted. The Reconstruction period was characterized by hatred and violence. Because Lincoln was assassinated shortly after the end of the war, leadership of southern reconstruction fell to Lincoln's vice president, Andrew Johnson, a southerner who was disliked by both northerners as well as southerners. Eventually, Johnson was impeached and almost removed from power, surviving the removal vote in the U.S. Senate by one vote. One of the immediate changes to take place was to officially abolish slavery. Passed by Congress on January 21, 1865, and ratified by the states on December 6, 1865, the 13th Amendment to the Constitution formally ended slavery. Next, former slaves had to be granted due process, which came with the recognition of citizenship. On July 9, 1868, the 14th Amendment of the Constitution granted citizenship to "all persons born or naturalized in the United States."

A major obstacle to reunification were the restrictive laws enacted immediately after the Civil War by every southern legislature. These **Black Codes** barred the newly freed slaves from free assembly, regulated Black labor, and, among other restrictions, denied **Freedmen** the right to vote, serve on juries, and testify against whites. After major electoral victories in the election of 1866, Republicans placed the South under military rule, and held new elections in which the Freedmen could vote.

By 1867, the U.S. Congress, still composed entirely of northerners, passed legislation to eliminate the Black Codes. On February 26, 1869, Congress passed the **15th Amendment** of the Constitution that provided universal male suffrage (right to vote), made the Bill of Rights applicable to the states recognizing all substantive and procedural rights under the law, and providing equal protection under the law to all people in their jurisdiction. The 15th Amendment was ratified on February 3, 1870. Furthermore, the U.S. Congress required that each state ratify the 13th, 14th and

15th amendments as a prerequisite for reentry into the Union. Finally, in 1870, the last two states (Texas and Florida), having satisfied all requirements, were allowed back into the Union. For more information on the 13th, 14th, and 15th amendments go to *https://www.loc.gov/.*

Ku Klux Klan

After first emerging as a secret society during Reconstruction, the **Ku Klux Klan** flourished in the 1860s and died out in the 1870s, only to reemerge in the 1920s and again in the 1950s and 1960s. During Reconstruction, Klan members enforced the Black Codes through violence and terror. Subsequent Klan activities, both overt and covert, upheld **Jim Crow laws** reinforcing segregation and spreading intimidation. Racial separation continued to characterize life in the South and other parts of the nation throughout most of the 20th century.

Economic Development

After the reunification of the country, energy was redirected to the economic development and growth of the nation. New inventions, together with the development of the railroad, paved the way to economic recovery. The reconstruction that followed the war also played a vital role in the development of the United States as a solid economic and industrial nation.

In the late 19th and early 20th centuries, Americans recognized opportunities in cities. Migration to urban areas caused the cities to grow exponentially in size, population, and population density. This is called **urbanization**. The fast growth caused issues with housing, transportation, sanitation, and employment (De Blij & Murphy, 2005). People from diverse backgrounds were forced to live and work in proximity. The surrounding countryside was absorbed as an area grew. Poor areas, called shantytowns, sometimes developed on the periphery of the cities. The rapid increase in population provided more workers than needed for manufacturing, resulting in a surplus of labor. In Texas, the greatest examples of urbanization occurred in cities that served as major transportation and economic centers. They include Galveston, Houston, Corpus Christi, El Paso, San Antonio, Austin, Dallas, Fort Worth, and Amarillo. Urbanization also led to urban sprawl, the multidimensional expansion of a city. Urban sprawl may not always coincide with proper coding and planning.

In the 19th and 20th centuries, American farmers used exploitive agricultural methods that rarely conserved the soil. Overgrazing, expanding farmland, and new mechanized practices increased production, but also created a problem: The land could not replenish the nutrients at the same rate they were being used. In the 1930s, the area encompassing the Texas and Oklahoma panhandles, as well as parts of Kansas, Colorado, and New Mexico, suffered from a severe drought. The thin, dry soil did not have enough plants to anchor the topsoil. Strong winds blew the topsoil into dust storms. The affected region was called the Dust Bowl.

Temperance Movement—Prohibition

Early Americans drank alcohol in enormous quantities. Their yearly consumption at the time of the American Revolution has been estimated at the equivalent of three-and-a-half gallons of pure, 200-proof alcohol for each person. After 1790, American men began to drink even more. By the late 1820s, imbibing had risen to an all-time high of almost four gallons per capita. This pattern went unchallenged until early in the 19th century, when local efforts to curb drinking by individual clergymen were amplified by the founding of the American Temperance Society in 1826, sponsored by a wide range of groups and individuals. Temperance reformers acted for a variety of reasons, but we can describe four powerful perspectives on temperance that motivated most advocates and shaped their arguments and campaigns. For many of them, of course, all four viewpoints were linked together.

1. *Social order.* Many reformers feared that drunkenness—particularly the increasing prevalence of binge drinking—was a threat to law-abiding society and economic prosperity. How could men act as responsible workers and vote as responsible citizens if they were insensible with drink?

2. *Evangelical religion.* Religiously motivated temperance advocates came to see drinking as a sin—a way of giving in to the animal or depraved self that was incompatible with Christian morals, self-control, and spiritual awakening.

3. *Damage to the family.* Looking at family destitution and violence, reformers reckoned the cost to American wives, mothers, and children of heavy drinking by their husbands and fathers. The Woman's Christian Temperance Union, founded in 1874, brought the concerns of religion and family together in the battle to outlaw alcohol.

4. *Medical.* Health-minded reformers popularized a radically new way of looking at alcohol. Americans had traditionally considered strong drink to be healthy and fortifying; but after 1810, many physicians and writers on health were telling their patients and readers that alcohol was actually a poison.

By the end of the 19th century and the beginning of the 20th century, alcohol abuse had reached such heights that the movement focused on an outright prohibition of its consumption. In 1919, the U.S. Constitution was amended to prohibit alcohol consumption at the national level; this marked the adoption of the **18th Amendment** (Cardinale, 2007). However, the prohibition was never fully enforced. Battles between law enforcements agents, like Eliot Ness, and organized crime characterized the prohibition era. Leaders of organized crime, like Al Capone, made millions bootlegging alcohol. After 14 years of prohibition and unsuccessful attempts to enforce the law, the 18th Amendment was finally repealed in 1933 with the **21st Amendment**.

Civil Rights Movement

In the United States, the Constitution and the Bill of Rights guarantee civil rights to American citizens and residents. The first 10 amendments to the U.S. Constitution are known as the **Bill of Rights**. Following these initial amendments and as a result of the American Civil War, three additional amendments were ratified.

1. The 13th Amendment freed all the slaves without compensation to slave owners.

2. The 14th Amendment declared that all persons born in the United States were citizens (excluding Native Americans, due to their legal sovereignty) and, that all citizens were entitled to equal rights, and that their rights were protected by due process.

3. The 15th Amendment granted universal male suffrage, thereby granting Black men the right to vote.

Even after the 13th, 14th, and 15th Amendments extended constitutional protections, Blacks continued to be denied full civil rights through discriminatory state and local laws and practices. These laws, known as Jim Crow laws, reinforced a strict racial separation in the South. African Americans were kept from voting by poll taxes and literacy tests. Segregation rules restricted Blacks to separate facilities in public places such as theaters, restaurants, buses, restrooms, and schools. In 1896, *Plessy v. Ferguson* legalized segregation, allowing "separate but equal facilities" for Black and white students.

In response to the horrific practice of lynching that undergirded the program of terror to enforce Jim Crow laws, and specifically in reaction to the 1908 race riots in Springfield, Illinois, a group of white liberals issued a call for a meeting to discuss racial justice. Sixty people, seven of whom were African American (including W.E.B. Du Bois, Ida B. Wells-Barnett and Mary Church Terrell), signed the call, which was released on the centennial of Lincoln's birth. This heralded the birth, on February 12, 1909, of the **National Association for the Advancement of Colored People (NAACP)**. Throughout the early 20th century, the NAACP saw enormous growth in membership, recording roughly 600,000 members by 1946. It continued to act as a legislative and legal advocate, pushing for a federal anti-lynching law and for an end to state-mandated segregation.

Several historic events marked the beginning of what is today known as the **Civil Rights Movement**. In 1947, Jackie Robinson became the first African American to play baseball on a Major League team. In 1948, President Truman ordered the desegregation of the armed forces and introduced civil rights legislation in Congress. In 1954, the NAACP Legal Defense and Educational Fund, headed by Thurgood Marshall, secured an important milestone through the landmark Supreme Court ruling in *Brown v. Board of Education of Topeka* (1954), which outlawed segregation in public schools.

The **Montgomery bus boycott** began in December 1955 when **Rosa Parks**, a well-known NAACP activist and respected citizen of Montgomery, Alabama, refused to give up her seat on a bus to a white man as Alabama's Jim Crow laws required. She was arrested and consequently sent to jail. Her actions prompted local community leaders of the NAACP to form a new organization called the Montgomery Improvement Association.

The association chose a young Baptist minister, **Dr. Martin Luther King Jr.**, to lead the organization and to direct a boycott of the Montgomery bus company. The boycott began in December 1956 and ended about a year later when the Supreme Court ruled segregation on buses unconstitutional. This victory gained national attention and Dr. King became one of the most prominent figures of the civil rights movement. He founded the Southern Christian Leadership Conference (SCLC) with other African American leaders. The SCLC favored nonviolent forms of protest such as sit-ins, boycotts, freedom rides, and protest marches. On August 28, 1963, a march in Washington in support of the Civil Rights Act culminated in Dr. King's influential and memorable "I Have a Dream" speech. The eloquent speech and orderly, large-scale demonstration gained more supporters for the cause.

President **John F. Kennedy** proposed new civil rights laws as well as programs to help the millions of Americans living in poverty. After his assassination in Dallas in 1963, President **Lyndon B. Johnson** urged Congress to pass the laws in honor of Kennedy, persuading the majority of Democrats and some Republicans. The **Civil Rights Act**, passed in 1964, prohibited segregation in all public facilities and outlawed discrimination in education and employment. On April 4, 1968, Martin Luther King was assassinated in Memphis, Tennessee, taking his place alongside the other martyrs who lost their lives in the struggle for freedom during the modern Civil Rights Movement, which extended from 1954 to 1968.

The Mexican American Civil Rights Movement

During the 1960s, Mexican Americans were engaged in the struggle for human rights. As part of the process, the Mexican-American leaders initiated a movement called the **Chicano Movement**. This movement was cultural as well as political (Rosales Castañeda, n.d.). It embraced four main goals: the restoration of land grants, farm workers' rights, and education and political rights (Mendoza, 2001). The movement also sought to rescue the cultural and linguistic identity of Mexican Americans.

Activist **Reies López Tijerina** initiated the Chicano Movement in New Mexico with the land grant movement, which sought to recover the land taken from the Mexican Americans as a result of the Guadalupe Hidalgo Treaty of 1848 and the eventual annexation of the American Southwest. In Colorado, Rodolfo "Corky" Gonzales founded the Crusade for Justice as a platform for the political movement (Mendoza, 2001). He also defined the movement through his epic poem "Yo Soy Joaquín/I Am Joaquin." In this poem he provided a historical development of Mexican-American identity and described their struggles in the United States.

As part of the effort to support the rights of farm workers, human rights leaders **César Chávez** and **Dolores Huerta** founded the **United Farm Workers (UFW)** union. Through the UFW they fought for better working conditions and fair compensation for agricultural workers.

In Texas, the movement focused its attention on the educational and political rights of Mexican Americans. In Crystal City, students took a leadership role by organizing Mexican-American voters and joining the political process. As part of this process, **Mexican American Youth Organization (MAYO)**, under the leadership of **José Ángel Gutiérrez** and **Mario Compean**, founded the **Raza Unida Party (RUP)** in 1970. Through the RUP, they sought to bring greater economic, social, and political autonomy to Mexican Americans (Acosta, n.d.). As a result of this movement, the RUP nominated candidates for mayor, city councils, and school boards in three South Texas cities—Crystal City, Cotulla, and Carrizo. In these communities, the RUP won 15 seats. This political awakening of the Mexican-American voters in Texas paved the way for better schools and programs for Mexican-American and minority children in general.

Women's Rights

While the **19th Amendment** to the Constitution guaranteed women the right to vote in 1920, women remained the subject of discrimination. The civil rights movement provided a backdrop for the women's movements of the 1960s as women of varying classes and races, working in the civil rights movement and in the anti-war movement, began to recognize their own second-class status. The liberal women's movement attained better employment and professional opportunities for women through legislation such as the Equal Pay Act of 1963, the Civil Rights Act of 1964, the Equal Credit Opportunity Act (1974), and the Pregnancy Discrimination Act of 1978. All this legislation prohibited discrimination based on gender. In 1966, **Betty Friedan**, author of *The Feminine Mystique*, and other women leaders founded the **National Organization for Women (NOW)**, and the 1970s saw an exponential growth of organizations and associations formed to promote women's equality.

Conflicts and Wars

Spanish-American War of 1898

The war between Spain and the United States in 1898 made the United States a world power. Setting the tone for the **Spanish-American War** were blaring headlines accompanied by sensationalized reporting of the sinking of the *U.S.S. Maine*. Though it's too much to claim that the newspapers started the war, what came to be known as "yellow journalism" certainly helped sound the drumbeat for it. As a result of this war, the United States established its power and influence in the Caribbean Sea and Pacific Ocean. Cuba became an independent nation, and the United States gained control of the Philippines, Guam, and Puerto Rico. Eventually, the Philippines became an independent nation, while Puerto Rico and Guam remained U.S. territories. Eventually, the people from Guam and Puerto Rico became American citizens.

World War I

The first global war, **World War I**, began in Europe and involved two alliances: the Allies and the Central Powers. The **Allies** were England, France, Russia, and Italy. The **Central Powers** were Germany, the Austria-Hungary Empire, Turkey, and Bulgaria. Initially, the Americans remained neutral and benefited extensively from trading with the Allies. America's neutrality was challenged, however, when the Germans developed a new weapon, the submarine, and used it successfully to destroy Allied ships. In 1915, the Germans sank a British liner, the *Lusitania*, killing more than 1,100 passengers, including 128 Americans. Additionally, American cargo ships were sunk, which forced President Wilson to ask Congress to declare war against Germany and the Central Powers. The influx of fresh American forces fostered the Allies' victory in 1918.

With the **Treaty of Versailles**, the war officially ended. In this treaty, the Central Powers were severely punished and forced to pay for the war. Additionally, the Austria-Hungary Empire was dismembered and new countries created. The punitive conditions of the Treaty of Versailles created the resentment among the Germans that eventually led to the second global confrontation, World War II.

The Great Depression

After World War I, the United States enjoyed a period of prosperity, the golden 1920s. However, it all came to an abrupt end on October 29, 1929, when the stock market crashed, initiating a ten-year period that we now call the **Great Depression**. During the Depression, millions of people lost their capital and jobs. Between 1933 and 1937, **President Franklin D. Roosevelt** implemented a series of government-sponsored programs called the **New Deal**, designed to revitalize the economy and alleviate poverty and despair caused by the Depression.

World War II

The emergence of totalitarian countries like the USSR, Germany, and Italy created instability in Europe and led to war. The Communist Soviet Union under **Joseph Stalin** became a threat to European countries. Italy, ruled by **Benito Mussolini** was a fascist, belligerent state where individual liberties were ignored. Germany under **Adolf Hitler** was ready to avenge the humiliating treatment it suffered as a result of World War I. In the Pacific, meanwhile, Japan was building an empire that had already conquered parts of China. These conditions promoted the creation of military alliances that led to **World War II**. Germany, Italy, and Japan created the **Axis Powers**, and the USSR, France, and England became the Allies. The war started with the German invasion of Poland in 1939. Two days later, France and England declared war against Germany. Hitler conquered most of Europe in a short time. France was occupied, and England was brought close to submission. The United States supported the Allies with supplies and weapons, but did not send troops. Although it remained neutral for the first few years of the war, the United States joined the Allies when Japan attacked its naval base in Pearl Harbor, Hawaii, in 1941. Three days later, Hitler declared war on the United States. Believing Germany to be the greater threat, the United States concentrated on the war in Europe before turning its attention to Japan.

D-Day

With Hitler in full control of Europe, the United States joined England and representatives of the French government to plan and execute the invasion of Europe in 1944. On June 6, **General Dwight D. Eisenhower**, together with a quarter of a million Allied soldiers, crossed the English Channel into France and launched one of the largest offensives ever seen against the German occupying forces. This massive attack was known as **D-Day**. As a result of the collective effort of the Allies, France was freed from German occupation. With the combined forces of England, Russia, Canada, and the United States, Hitler and the Axis forces were finally defeated. **Victory in Europe** day, or **VE Day**, occurred on May 8, 1945. **Victory over Japan** day, or **VJ Day**, occurred on August 15, 1945.

Yalta Conference

The Allies met in Yalta, Russia, to discuss the terms of the treaty to end the war in Europe. In this meeting, the leaders of the Allied forces—Winston Churchill, Joseph Stalin, and Franklin D. Roosevelt—met to discuss peace. Under the terms of peace agreed to at Yalta, Germany was to be divided into four sections, each controlled by an Allied country—Britain, France, Russia, and the United States. The Germans were to pay the Russians for war reparations in money and labor. Poland was divided, and the Russians received control of one section (later they took full control of the nation). Finally, plans were set to organize the United Nations to prevent future conflicts in the world.

Hiroshima and Nagasaki

The United States was fighting the war on two fronts, and the Japanese appeared to be invincible. The best available option seemed to be the atomic bomb. An island nation, Japan had gained control of much territory in the Pacific, most of it islands. Securing each island would take much time and cost many American soldiers' lives. After asking for the Japanese to surrender, by the order of **President Harry Truman**, the United States dropped two atomic bombs, one each on the cities of Hiroshima and Nagasaki. The death and destruction caused by these two bombs forced the Japanese government to surrender in 1945, which officially ended World War II.

Marshall Plan

The **Marshall Plan** was a U.S.-supported program to rebuild the economic infrastructure in Europe. The United States provided money and machinery for the reconstruction of the continent.

The Holocaust and Creation of Israel

During World War II, Hitler devised a "master plan" to exterminate the Jewish population. Germany placed European Jews in concentration camps and systematically killed millions. This act of genocide is known today as the **Holocaust**. At the end of the war, under the leadership of Great Britain, the United States, and the United Nations, the state of Israel was created in Palestine.

On that same day, the Arab Liberation Army (ALA) was created to fight the Jewish state. This liberation movement has resulted in several wars between Israel and the Arabs.

Truman Doctrine

In response to the threat of the Soviets, Harry Truman issued a proclamation warning communist countries that the United States would help any nation in danger of falling under communist control. This declaration was called the **Truman Doctrine**. As a result of this doctrine, the United States became involved in two major military conflicts: the **Korean War** and the **Vietnam War**.

Cold War

As a result of the Yalta agreement, Russia became the most powerful country in the region. After taking over Poland and East Berlin, and building the Berlin Wall, a new war emerged between the Soviet Union and the United States—the **Cold War**. Although war was never formally declared between the two nations, confrontations occurred from 1945 to 1991. In 1963, the two nations were on the verge of nuclear war after **Premier Nikita Khrushchev** ordered the deployment of nuclear missiles to Cuba. An intense negotiation between Premier Khrushchev and President Kennedy avoided war between the two countries. This most intense confrontation of the Cold War was called the **Cuban Missile Crisis**.

The Cold War finally ended with the fall of the Soviet Union under the leadership of **Mikhail Gorbachev**. The fall of the Soviet empire resulted in the reunification of Germany and the creation of multiple smaller countries in Russia that gained independence.

War on Terrorism

On September 11, 2001, terrorists from abroad attacked Americans on American soil. The assailants hijacked four domestic aircraft and used two of them as missiles to crash into the twin towers of the World Trade Center in New York and a third to strike the Pentagon just outside Washington D.C. A fourth plane crashed in Shanksville, Pennsylvania, as passengers tried to wrest control of the plane from the hijackers. The attacks killed nearly 3,000 people. As a result of the attacks, the United States declared war on terrorism and attacked and ultimately toppled the ultra-conservative Taliban regime early in the course of the Afghanistan War (2001–2014). The Taliban had harbored al-Qaeda, the terrorist group that planned the 9/11 attacks. Al-Qaeda's leader, Osama bin Laden, the mastermind of the 9/11 attacks, was hunted for nearly a decade and was killed by U.S. special forces on May 2, 2011. The search for alleged weapons of mass destruction (WMD), as well as Iraq's support of terrorist organizations, led the United States into the Iraq War (2003–2011). Weapons of mass destruction were never found, and this topic continues to stir debate. In hindsight, the American government came to recognize that faulty intelligence paved the way for the rationale for the Iraq invasion. Once elected, President Obama worked to reduce the number of troops in this region. He formally declared the war in Iraq over in October 2011.

War in Syria

The recent war in Syria has given rise to the Islamic State, also known as the Islamic State of Iraq and Syria (ISIS), an extreme al-Qaeda faction from Iraq. The Syrian conflict began in March 2011 with pro-democracy protests that ended when demonstrators were shot by Syrian security forces. This action triggered protests across the nation. The violence and fighting and the conflicts grew to be more than issues with President Assad. The Sunni majority was against the Shia Alawite sect supporting the president. Neighboring countries and key world powers were drawn in as well. The United Nations Commission of Inquiry on the Syrian Arab Republic found human rights violations on both sides. According to the BBC, the Islamic State capitalized on the turmoil to seize large amounts of territory in Iraq and Syria. "In September 2014, a United States-led coalition launched air strikes inside Iraq and Syria in an effort to 'degrade and ultimately destroy' ISIS." (BBC, 2016). The conflict continues, with Iran and Russia supporting the Alawite-led government. Turkey, various Arab states, the United States, the United Kingdom, and France have been supporting the Sunni-led opposition. For more information, see *http://www.bbc.com/news/world-middle-east-39500947* and *http://www.bbc.com/news/world-middle-east-39037609*.

Brexit

"Brexit" is the portmanteau for when the people of the United Kingdom voted to leave the **European Union** (EU). The European Union is the partnership among 28 European countries connected economically and politically. The decision to leave the EU, which took effect in January 2020, was made by a referendum, a poll in which every person of legal voting age within the United Kingdom was able to vote. For more information, see *http://www.bbc.com/news/uk-politics-32810887* and *http://www.bbc.com/news/uk-politics-eu-referendum-36574526*.

Weather, Climate, and Natural Disasters

The first two decades of the new millennium have been marked by a number of severe weather and natural disaster events around the globe. When storms are particularly damaging or have a high death toll, the name of the storm is retired, thus providing a way to judge event severity in a particular time span. The hurricane seasons from 1980 to 1999 had 22 such storms. However, 44 names were retired from 2000 to 2020. Catastrophic natural disasters also occurred during this time. In 2004, a tsunami in the Indian Ocean led to over 230,000 deaths. The 2010 magnitude 7.2 Haiti earthquake was the deadliest natural disaster of the decade, killing over 200,000 people.

The following year, a record-breaking 9.0 earthquake hit Japan, triggering a tsunami and the meltdown of the Fukushima Daiichi Nuclear Power Plant. Wildfires in the United States from 2012 to 2021 burned 635,264 acres. As a result, concerns about the environment and climate change grew. Issues highlighted poor stewardship of the land and its resources. For instance, environmental and human factors caused the Yangzi River dolphin to be declared functionally extinct (2007), as was the northern white rhinoceros (2018). Oil spills heightened awareness of environmental challenges; these included the 2006 Guimaras oil spill in the Philippines and the 2010 Deepwater Horizon oil spill in the Gulf of Mexico (largest such spill on record worldwide). Citizens increasingly demanded reform (e.g., 2014 People's Climate March and 2016 Dakota Access Pipeline). This coincided with the United States hitting record-breaking energy consumption rates in 2017 and 2018. The year 2019 marked the first time that renewable power capacity surpassed coal energy. Growing concerns led to the landmark 2016 Paris Agreement where key world leaders were among 196 parties to sign an international treaty to address climate change and set goals to limit global warming. However, protests calling for change continued. Among those voices was 17-year-old activist Greta Thunberg, who led the 2019 Climate Strike to call attention to such issues as environmental justice and sustainability as well as respect for native land and protection of biodiversity.

Firsts for American Presidents (2008–2022)

Recent U.S. presidents reflect a changing America. In 2008, Barack Obama was the first African American to be elected president and went on for reelection in 2012. In 2016, Hillary Clinton became the first woman nominated as a presidential candidate of a major party. Donald Trump won the 2016 presidential election, becoming the first president to have neither held public office nor any military position. He later became the first president to actively protest the election of his successor in 2020, which led to an insurrection and attack by his supporters on the United States Capitol on January 6, 2021. He is also the third president to have been impeached by the House of Representatives, and the only president to have been impeached twice (2019, 2021). Former U.S. Senator Joseph Biden became the oldest elected president of the United States in 2020.

Revolutions, Conflicts, and Movements for Change

The decades since the turn of the 21st century have marked a time of tension, protests, and calls for change. Globally, people have sought protections of human rights; political recognition; widespread policy changes; and that climate change be addressed and environmental awareness be heightened. Revolutions and uprisings were seen in Georgia, Kyrgyzstan, Lebanon, Ukraine, and Myanmar (2003–2007). Arab conflicts that came to be known as the Arab Spring, Arab Winter, and Second Arab Spring (2010–2021) consisted of a number of protests, uprisings, and riots in Southwest Asia (also known as the Middle East) and North Africa. In addition, civil unrest sparked a wave of protests in Latin America (2018–2021) and in the United States (2020–2022). Moreover, the 2010–2020 decade saw several movements for independence or autonomy (e.g., Catalonia, Ukraine, Crimea, Hong Kong, Kurdistan, and Kashmir, to list a few). Several countries—including Armenia, Mexico, Serbia, Honduras, and the United States—also witnessed protests of the conduct of elections.

Across the world, protests and marches were organized to bring about change for a myriad of reasons, with issues at the forefront including women's rights, abortion, same-sex marriage, and civil rights. In 2015, 10 countries, including the United States, legalized same-sex marriages.

Change for rights remains a constant theme, as exemplified by women's strikes in Switzerland (2019) and Poland (2020–2021), and anti-abortion protests in Europe, the United States, and Latin America. In the U.S., the new millennium began with protests for gun control (the Million Mom March in 2000), the Iraqi war protests (2003), and the immigrants' boycott (2006) in the U.S. which sought to show what one day without immigrants would cost the nation. Economic inequality was protested in the 2011 Occupy Wall Street demonstrations, which sparked other similarly themed actions. Calls for racial equality came alive with the #BlackLivesMatter movement, which began in 2013 and gained strength in 2014 and 2015 with protests initially inspired by the not guilty verdict for George Zimmerman, who shot a black teenager, Trayvon Martin, in South Florida. Issues of women's rights and sexual harassment galvanized millions to march in the Women's March 2017, the largest march ever for women's rights, which took place on the heels of Donald Trump's inauguration as the new American president. The march inspired over 600 similar marches worldwide, which coincided with the evolution of the #MeToo movement, whose ranks swelled in 2017 as women spoke out publicly against sexual harassment, naming key figures in American society. Another issue facing society was the call for making rational policy decisions using science (March for Science 2017), which reflected the tensions regarding climate change and demands for environmental accountability. For more, see *https://en.wikipedia.org/wiki/List_of_protests_in_the_21st_century*, *https://www.usatoday.com/story/money/2020/09/06/the-worlds-most-important-event-every-year-since-1920/113604790/*, and *https://www.history.com/news/2010s-decade-major-events*.

Texas History

Timeline

1519	Álonso Alvarez de Pineda explores and maps the Texas coastline
1528	Spanish explorer Álvar Núñez Cabeza de Vaca explores the Texas interior on his way to Mexico
1685	French explorer, René-Robert Cavelier, Sieur de La Salle establishes Fort St. Louis at Matagorda Bay, establishing French claim to Texas territory
1688	French colony is massacred
1689	The French continue to claim Texas but no longer physically occupy any of the territory
1690	First mission in East Texas established by Alonso de Leon
1700s	Spain establishes Catholic missions throughout Texas
1718	Mission San Antonio de Valero (the Alamo) founded
1762	As a result of the The Seven Years War (French and Indian War) the French give up their claims to Texas and cede Louisiana to Spain until 1800
1800	North Texas territory is returned to French and later sold to the U.S. in the Louisiana purchase (1803)

1821	Texas becomes a Mexican state as Mexico becomes free from Spain
1823	Stephen Austin establishes the Old Three Hundred colony along the Brazos River
1830	Mexico bans emigration into Texas by settlers from the United States
1832	Battle of Velasco—first casualties of the Texas Revolution
1835	The Texas Revolution officially begins at the Battle of Gonzales
1835	Texans lead by Jim Bowie win the Battle of Concepcion, near San Antonio
1836	The Convention of 1836 signs the Texas Declaration of Independence on March 2 at Washington on the Brazos
	The Alamo—Texans under Colonel William B. Travis were defeated on March 6 by the Mexican army after a two-week siege at the Battle of the Alamo in San Antonio
	The Battle of San Jacinto—Texans under Sam Houston defeat Santa Anna and win independence on April 21
1837	Sam Houston, the first President of the Texas Republic, begins operating the seat of government from Houston
1839	Austin becomes the capital of the Republic of Texas
1845	Texas admitted as the 28th state in the Union
1846	The Mexican-American War due to disputes over claims to Texas boundaries. The outcome fixed the southern boundary at the Rio Grande River.
1850	The compromise of 1850 adjusts the state boundary and assumes Texas's debts
1861	Texas secedes from the Union and becomes part of the Confederacy
1865	Texas slaves freed on June 19 (Juneteenth) after Union soldiers land in Galveston and put the Emancipation Proclamation into effect
1865–1890	Era of the great Texas cattle drives
1870	Texas is readmitted into the United States
1876	Adoption of current Texas State Constitution
1876	Texas A&M University opens its doors as the first public institution of higher learning in Texas
1883	The University of Texas at Austin is founded
1887–1891	Lawrence Sullivan "Sul" Ross serves as Governor of Texas. Ross was a Texas Ranger and the principal author of the Texas Constitution of 1876, oversaw the completion of the state capitol building, and was president of Texas A&M; Sul Ross State University in Alpine is named after him
1900	Hurricane destroys Galveston and kills over 6,000 people
1901	Oil discovered at Spindletop

1914–1918	Texas becomes a primary staging area for military training during World War I
1919	Texas ratifies the 19th Amendment giving women the right to vote
1924	Miriam "Ma" Ferguson is elected Texas's first woman governor after her husband, James, is impeached for misapplication of public funds and barred from holding office. Her campaign slogan: "Two governors for the price of one."
1929	League of United Latin American Citizens (LULAC) founded in Corpus Christi
1929–1933	Great Depression envelops the nation, hitting Texas when such factors as overproduction of oil tip the economy
1931–1933	John Nance Garner ("Cactus Jack") of Uvalde, serves as Speaker of the U.S. House of Representatives
1933–1941	John Nance Garner serves as Vice President of the United States under Franklin D. Roosevelt; Garner would split with FDR on major New Deal policies including the Wagner Labor Relations Act, the Social Security Act, and the Revenue Act
1935	Dust Bowl (actually four distinct events in the 1930s that failed to let Texans recover from one before the next came) causes severe economic and social damage, especially in the Texas Panhandle
1940–1961	Sam Rayburn of Bonham is the longest serving Speaker of the U.S. House of Representative (1940–1947, 1949–1953, and 1955–1961)
1941–1945	Audie Murphy, from Kingston, becomes the most decorated soldier of World War II
1950	"Babe" Didrikson Zaharias of Beaumont named "Woman Athlete of the Half-Century"
1957–1961	Raymond L. Telles serves as the first Mexican-American mayor of a major American city, El Paso. He later becomes the first Hispanic appointed as a U.S. ambassador
1961	Henry B. Gonzalez beceoms the first Hispanic from Texas to serve in the U.S. Congress; his term spanned 1961–1998
1962–1963	Humble Oil and Refining Co. (now ExxonMobil) and Rice University donate land to base NASA in Houston
1963	President John F. Kennedy is assassinated in Dallas on Nov. 22; Texas Governor John Connally wounded. Vice President Lyndon Johnson sworn in as President
1964	Lyndon Johnson defeats Barry Goldwater and is elected President
1967	Barbara Jordan elected to Texas Senate, the first African American to serve in the Texas Senate since 1883
1973	Barbara Jordan elected to the U.S. Congress, the first African American woman from a Southern state to serve in Congress

1981	Sandra Day O'Connor becomes the first woman appointed to serve on the U.S. Supreme Court
1984–1998	Raul A. Gonzalez becomes the first Hispanic to serve on the Texas Supreme Court
1987–1989	Jim Wright of Nuecestown serves as Speaker of the U.S. House of Representatives
1988	Houston's George H.W. Bush elected President of the United States
1989–1992	James Baker III of Houston serves as United States Secretary of State
1991–1995	Ann Richards elected 45th Governor of Texas, becoming the first female governor to hold office in her own right ("Ma" Ferguson was elected in 1924 after impeachment barred her husband from holding elective office.)
1993	Kay Bailey Hutchison becomes first woman from Texas elected to the U.S. Senate
2000	Texas Governor George W. Bush elected President of the United States
2003	Space shuttle *Columbia* disintegrates upon re-entry over East Texas on Feb. 1
2005	Hurricane Rita forces over 1 million residents to evacuate the Texas coast
2006	Two Enron executives convicted of conspiracy to commit fraud after the company, which had become one of the largest firms in the U.S., was found to have a long list of fake holdings and to have conducted off-the-books accounting that hid billions in debt
2007	Category 3 Hurricane Ike strikes Texas Gulf Coast
2011	Texas wildfires destroy over 1 million acres, burn over 1,000 homes
2013	Massive explosion at a fertilizer plan in the town of West
2014	First known case of the Ebola virus documented in Dallas, resulting ultimately in 11 patients being treated
2017	Category 4 Hurricane Harvey makes landfall at San Jose Island and then near Rockport, in south-central Texas, causing massive flooding
2020	The Texas Department of State Health Services reports first case of Covid-19 on March 4
	Governor Greg Abbott declares a state of disaster on March 13 due to the Covid-19 pandemic
2021	Winter storms combine with record low temperatures to stress the state's power grid, causing extensive, lengthy blackouts

Before European Colonization

Several Native American groups inhabited the territory known today as Texas. They adopted different customs, different farming, hunting, and gathering methods, and made slightly different weapons. At times they fought against one another, and at other times they lived in cooperation. It is important to recognize that Native American tribes had established important cultural, social, and economic systems in the United States long before European colonizers arrived on the continent.

Archeologists have found evidence of Native American civilization in Texas dating back to at least 9,200 BCE. The three groups living in the coastal plains—the Coahuiltecans, Karankawas, and Caddos—were food gatherers, fishermen, and farmers. When the Spanish arrived in Texas, they made initial contact with these groups. The name *Texas* came as a result of contact with the Caddos. Attempting to communicate to the Spaniards that they were not hostile, some Caddos identified themselves with the word *taysha*, which in their language meant "friend" or "ally." When the Spaniards heard the word *taysha*, they thought the Caddos were identifying the name of the region. From that exchange, the name Texas and the state motto, "Friendship," emerged.

A fourth group, the Jumanos, lived in the mountains and basins of West Texas. The information about this group is limited because they virtually disappeared before the Spaniards arrived in the area. The last two groups are the Comanches and the Apaches. These two groups coexisted with Europeans and resisted colonization efforts. After they domesticated horses, previously introduced by the Spanish, the Comanches and Apaches became fearless warriors and successful buffalo hunters. The domestication of the horse allowed the development of the culture of the buffalo. When buffalo were later annihilated in the area, these two groups became practically extinct. Table 5-2 presents a summary of Native American groups in Texas.

Table 5-2
Native American Groups in Texas[3]

Regions	Native Group
Coastal plains, flatland	**Coahuiltecan** (Rio Grande Valley) **Economic Activity:** Food gatherers and hunters—roots, beans of the mesquite tree, rabbit, birds, and deer **Features:** Lived in family groups
	Karankawa (Southeastern Texas) **Economic Activity:** Fishing and food gathering **Features:** Lived as nomads and used canoes for fishing
	Caddo (East Texas, Piney Woods) **Economic Activity:** Farming—squash, pumpkins, tobacco, and corn (good food supply) **Features:** Built villages and lived in groups

(continued)

[3] The Native American groups listed in the table were important to the regional and historical development of Texas. In addition, other Native American groups that still reside in Texas are there because of American Indian relocation efforts. These groups are Ysleta Del Sur Pueblo (West Texas, El Paso County), Alabama-Coushatta (East Texas, Travis County), and the Kickappo (South Texas, Maverick County). For more information about American Indians in Texas, visit the Texas State Historical Association at *https://www.tshaonline.org*.

Regions	Native Group
Central plains, flatland, and hills	**Apache** (Central and western Texas); Lipan Apache **Economic Activity:** Farming and hunting **Features:** Lived as nomads, built portable housing called tepees, domesticated horses, and hunted bison
Great Plains, flatland, and hills	**Comanche**; Quanah Parker was the last chief of the Kwahadis, a band of Comanches. He was the main spokesman and peacetime leader of Native Americans in Texas. **Economic Activity:** Hunters **Features:** Lived as nomads and built portable housing; also domesticated the horse and hunted the buffalo
Mountains and basins	**Jumano** (West Texas) **Economic Activity:** Farming and hunting **Features:** Mostly sedentary and built homes of adobe

European Colonization

Cabeza de Vaca

The Spanish exploration of the territory known today as Texas began in 1528, when **Álvar Núñez Cabeza de Vaca** and three companions landed in the territory. The four Spaniards made contact with the Caddo in the southeastern part of the state, near modern-day Houston. In his account of the meeting, de Vaca described the Caddo as a very sophisticated Native American group. From there, de Vaca continued exploring the region of modern-day New Mexico and Arizona. No other significant events happened in the region until 1541, when **Francisco Vázquez de Coronado** explored Texas.

Francisco Vázquez de Coronado

In response to reports of the mythical Seven Cities of Cibola, Coronado led an expedition of almost a thousand men in search of the golden cities. The expedition left Mexico City and explored the southwestern United States and northern Texas. In 1542, Coronado returned to Mexico empty-handed. For the next 140 years, the Texas region remained isolated, and no other attempts were made to colonize it.

Alonso Álvarez de Pineda

Alonso Álvarez de Pineda was a Spanish conquistador and cartographer who was the first to map the Gulf of Mexico. His map established the boundaries while disproving the idea of a sea passage to Asia.

Robert de La Salle and French Influence over Texas

In 1685, **Robert de La Salle**, a French explorer, established a French settlement at Matagorda Bay called Fort St. Louis in East Texas. This settlement established France's claim on this region of Texas. A few years later, the French colony was massacred by Native Americans. Spain then established a series of missions in East Texas to control the French threat in the region. The French continued to claim Texas for decades following the massacre, even though they had no physical presence in the region. In 1762, France relinquished its claim on Texas, turning it over to Spain.

Spanish Missions in Texas

In 1632, the Spanish began establishing Catholic missions throughout Texas, beginning with San Clemente near San Angelo, which was abandoned on account of its remoteness. The revival of Spanish missions began again in the 1680s, starting in the El Paso area. In 1690, **Alonso de León** along with **Fray Damián Massanet** established the San Francisco de los Tejas Mission in East Texas. Spain continued to establish missions across Texas throughout the 18th century. A persistent advocate for Indians in East Texas through the Mission system was **Father Francisco Hidalgo**. (*https://www.tshaonline.org/handbook/entries/margil-de-jesus-antonio*) In 1718, the Spanish established a mission and a fort—San Antonio de Valero and Fort San Antonio de Bexar, respectively—near what is now the city of San Antonio. There, in 1720, **Antonio Margil de Jesús** founded the most successful of all Texas missions, San Jose y San Miquel de Aguayo. (*https://www.tshaonline.org/handbook/entries/margil-de-jesus-antonio*) The Spanish missions were designed not only to promote religious conversion, but also to provide territorial claim and protection over Texas. The Catholic missions established throughout Texas helped the Spanish maintain control over the region from 1682 to 1821. *https://www.tshaonline.org/handbook/entries/spanish-missions*

Mexican War of Independence

During the first part of the 19th century, the Spanish empire began crumbling. Mexico obtained its independence in 1821 and took control of the colony of Texas. Up until this point, Texas had been a sparsely populated area that served as a buffer between the territories claimed by France and Spain. To encourage settlement in this area, Mexico invited European and American settlers to move to the region.

Stephen F. Austin and Anglo Presence in Texas

In 1821, Moses Austin received permission from the Spanish government to bring Anglo-American families to settle in Texas. This agreement was voided when Mexico took control of the territory. Later, Austin's son, Stephen, negotiated with the Mexican government and obtained a similar agreement to allow Anglo-Americans to settle in Texas. Stephen F. Austin established a colony called the *Old Three Hundred* on the Brazos River, which opened the way for further settlement in this area. By 1835, the settlers were the majority in the region, which antagonized the Mexican government and eventually resulted in war. The best known and most successful of the land agents, or contractors, known as *empresarios*, Austin earned the moniker "Father of Texas." Other prominent empresarios included Green DeWitt and Martin De León.

The Texas War for Independence

Conflicts between Texans and the Mexican government started as early as 1830. The colonists felt that the government was not providing adequate support and protection to Texas. Initially, they wanted to negotiate with the new president, **Santa Anna**, and sent Stephen Austin to Mexico City to represent the colony. The Mexican government was not willing to negotiate and jailed Austin for a year. By the fall of 1835, it had become clear to many Texans that the democratic principles in the Mexican Federal Constitution of 1824 were being undermined by Santa Anna and the rich landowners who supported him.

Battle of Gonzales

The power struggle between the Mexican government and Texas settlers continued to escalate. The town of Gonzales had a cannon to protect the colonists from Native Americans. By order of the government, Mexican soldiers came to take the cannon from the colonists in October 1835. The Texans refused to relinquish their weapon and fired the cannon against the Mexican soldiers. The soldiers were told to "come and take it!" Although the battle was lost, the motto "Come and take it" became a symbol of Texas independence and a rallying cry for the soldiers. With this incident in Gonzales, the war for Texas independence began.

Sam Houston and William Goyens

On March 1, 1836, delegates representing the 17 municipalities in Texas met at Washington-on-the-Brazos. The elected delegates voted to send a delegation of Texans to the United States to solicit men, money, supplies, and sympathy for the Texas cause. On March 2, the assembly adopted the Texas Declaration of Independence. Two days later, on March 4, 1836, they selected **Sam Houston**, a former governor of Tennessee, as the Major General of the Texas army. During the Texas Revolution, Houston appointed **William Goyens**, a Black man, as his agent to deal with the Native Americans to ensure peace, a concern especially during the time of the Texas Revolution. Goyens was a highly trusted businessman and effective negotiator with strong ties to Native Americans, Mexicans, and Anglo-Americans throughout East Texas. After Texas won her independence from Mexico in 1836, Sam Houston served as the first and third president of the Republic of Texas. Once Texas joined the United States in 1845, Sam Houston became one of the state's United States senators.

Battles of the Alamo and Goliad

The next major battle of the Texas War for Independence took place near the present-day city of San Antonio in a small mission and fort known as the Alamo, originally called Misión San Antonio de Valero. When the battle began, fewer than 200 men, led by **Colonel William Travis**, protected the Alamo. Eventually, **James Bowie** and **Davy Crockett**, along with 30 Tennesseans, joined Travis, **Juan Seguín**, and their men in defending the fort. But in the midst of the siege, Seguín was pressed into service as a courier to warn the settlers in the area of Santa Anna's coming attack. The letter he carried, written by Travis on Feb. 24, 1836, was famously addressed "To the People of Texas and All Americans in the World," and was a passionate plea for help. After 13 days of fighting, on March 6, 1836, Santa Anna's Mexican army took the fort and killed all its defenders, including Texans of Mexican ancestry. Among the few survivors were Susanna Dickinson (sometimes spelled Dickerson) and her infant daughter. General Santa Anna had Dickinson carry a letter meant as a warning for General Houston and the Texas army. Santa Anna wrote, "The obstinancy of Travis and his soldiers was the cause of the death of the whole of them, for not one would surrender." Following the victory at the Alamo, Santa Anna continued marching against the rebels and took the city of Goliad, where more than 300 rebels were killed. These two battles provided the battle cry that resulted in the creation of the Texas army led by Houston.

As for Seguín, the Alamo fell before he was able to return with reinforcements. But between its fall and the Battle of San Jacinto, Captain Seguín led a company that provided a rear guard for General Houston; he thus protected the civilians fleeing ahead of Santa Anna's advancing army.

Runaway Scrape

The Runaway Scrape events took place mainly between September 1835 and April 1836. They involved the evacuations by Texas civilians fleeing the Mexican Army of Operations during the Texas Revolution, from the Battle of the Alamo through the decisive Battle of San Jacinto. Houston had told the people to leave nothing behind for the Mexicans. People across Texas were dropping everything in their effort to escape the carnage they expected after Santa Anna took his revenge for the rebellious Texans, which he did by killing everyone in the town of Goliad. The exodus continued until word came by horseback that the Mexican Army had fallen at San Jacinto.

Texas Declaration of Independence

As fighting grew worse, another Convention of Texas delegates discussed earlier was called in 1836 at Washington-on-the-Brazos. This convention led to the creation of the Texas Declaration of

Independence, which established the Republic of Texas and the *ad interim* government with **David G. Burnet** as president and **Lorenzo de Zavala** as vice president. The principal author of the Texas Declaration of Independence was **George Childress**. This document was signed on March 2, 1836, four days before the Battle of the Alamo ended.

Battle of San Jacinto

While the colonists were fighting the Mexican army at the Alamo and in Goliad, General Sam Houston was strengthening the army of the new republic. The Texan army continued retreating ahead of the Mexican forces until they reached the San Jacinto River, near the city of Houston. In a battle that lasted less than 20 minutes, Houston's troops defeated the Mexican army and captured General Santa Anna. Texas President Burnet and Mexican President Santa Anna signed the Treaty of Velasco, with Santa Anna agreeing to withdraw his troops from Texas in exchange for safe conduct back to Mexico, where he would lobby for recognition of Texas independence. But Santa Anna's commitment never materialized, and the Mexican government refused to recognize Texas as an independent republic. Nevertheless, Sam Houston became the president of the new republic, and from 1836 to 1845, Texas functioned as an independent nation. However, the Mexican government still considered it one of its rebellious provinces that it could one day reclaim (Barker & Pohl, 2009).

The Republic Period (1836–1845)

Despite the economic hardship typical of new nations, Texas managed to remain independent for 10 years and was recognized by several nations in the world, including the United States. This period was marked by tensions between those who wished to remain independent and those who wished to become part of the United States. Sam Houston was one who advocated for Texas to join the Union. Unable to secure its borders and reverse its financial situation, Sam Houston's vision would gain traction as the Republic of Texas sought the support of the United States. The first president of the Republic of Texas was **Sam Houston** whose vice president, **Lorenzo de Zavala**, an empresario, was a former Mexican elected official, author of Mexican history, a signer of the Texas Declaration of Independence, and a contributor to the Texas constitution. Poor health led him to step down, with his place taken by **Mirabeau B. Lamar**, who later became the second president of Texas. Lamar was known for his harsh treatment of Indians; opposition to annexation to the United States; moving the capital to Austin; establishing a system of education by endowing public lands for what would ultimately become a school and university system (causing him to be dubbed today as the "Father of Texas Education." Owing to financial failures during Lamar's tenure, Sam Houston was again elected, serving now as the republic's third president. The last president of Texas, who paved the way to annexation to the United States, was **Anson Jones**.

Texas Rangers

Starting in 1823, Stephen F. Austin unofficially created the Texas Rangers by hiring a small group of experienced frontiersmen to protect settlers. In 1835, the Rangers were formally constituted and continued to grow throughout the years of the Republic of Texas and continue today in service to the state of Texas. **John "Jack" Coffee Hays** became the most famous Texas Ranger during the early era when the Rangers would patrol the frontier to protect immigrants. He helped make the Texas Rangers into a tough and effective military force by creating a disciplined, cohesive group with the latest in firearms technology. The Colt revolver, the Rangers' handgun of choice, became the preferred weapon of the West. For more information: *https://texasrangers.org/history/ more-about-texas-rangers/.*

Texas Joins the United States

In 1845, Texas became the 28th state of the American Union. Texas was admitted as a slave state. Immediately, the U.S. government sent troops to the Rio Grande (which Mexicans considered their territory) to secure the Texas border. The ensuing clashes between Mexican and U.S. forces resulted in Congress declaring war in May 1846.

Mexican-American War

Between 1846 and 1848, Mexico and the United States waged a war that ended with a decisive victory and tremendous land acquisitions for the United States. As a result of the Treaty of Guadalupe Hidalgo, Mexico withdrew its claim over Texas and established the Rio Grande, or *Rio Bravo*, as it is known in Mexico, as the official border between the two countries. Mexico also ceded California and the territory known today as the American Southwest to the United States. Figure 5-1 presents a timeline of important events in Texas history from 1528–1861.

Figure 5-1
Texas Timeline from 1528 to 1861

1528	1541	1682	1682	1690	1718	1820
Cabeza de Vaca lands in Texas	Coronado explores Texas	Mission founded in El Paso	La Salle (French) lands in Texas	First mission in East Texas San Francisco de los Tejas	Mission and fort founded in San Antonio	Austin arrives in San Antonio

1861	1848	1846	1845	1836	1835	1833
Texas secedes from the Union	Treaty of Guadalupe Hidalgo	Mexican-American War begins	Texas becomes the 28th state in the Union	Battle of San Jacinto; Texas declares independence	Battle of Gonzales marks beginning of Texas revolution	Santa Anna becomes president of Mexico

Confederacy Period (1861–1865)

The American Civil War in Texas

Initially, Texas was divided about entering the Civil War. The state had fought hard to be admitted into the Union, but many Texans did not like the northern legislators' control of the government. Sam Houston, the governor of the State of Texas, refused to declare allegiance to the Confederacy and was thus replaced. Texans also did not like the antislavery sentiment, though only about one-fourth of its people owned slaves. Once in the war, the state provided many troops and was essential to westward expansion, protecting the Gulf Coast and supporting major battles in the Deep South. Three Civil War battles were fought in Texas: the Battle of Galveston, the Battle of Sabine Pass, and the last battle fought in the Civil War – the Battle of Palmito Ranch.

After five years of war, the Confederate army, led by General Robert E. Lee, surrendered to General Ulysses S. Grant, the leader of the Union forces. With the Union victory came freedom for slaves. In June 1865, news of the Emancipation Proclamation, which abolished slavery, reached Galveston. "**Juneteenth**" is a holiday that celebrates this event.

For more information visit the Texas State Historical Association, *http://www.tshaonline.org/handbook/online http://www.tshaonline.org/handbook/online/articles/qdc02.*

Reconstruction Period (1865–1877)

After the war, the Union forces occupied the South for a period of 12 years (1865–1877). This era was called the Reconstruction Period. During Reconstruction, Texas was briefly under occupation by U.S. troops. Texas was allowed to rejoin the Union in 1870. The Ku Klux Klan became very active at this time, terrorizing African Americans in Texas and across the South.

Economic Development after Reconstruction

After Reconstruction, the Texas economy flourished, largely based on the growth of the cattle industry. Barbed wire was introduced in 1880, and ranchers began using scientific cattle breeding to increase production and improve the quality of meat.

Woman Suffrage Movement in Texas

The Woman Suffrage Movement in Texas was a long fight of determination that began in the 1860s. Although women worked and paid taxes like men, they lacked the right to vote and rarely participated in government and politics. Opponents of woman suffrage feared that allowing a change in women's status would undermine cultural customs and traditions. In fact, recent male immigrants could vote before women could. Women not only had to convince political leaders to stop the disenfranchisement of women, they also had to persuade average citizens, including other women, that women's roles at home, in the community, and at work would not change simply because they could vote. The Texas legislature considered and/or voted on women's suffrage multiple times from the 1860s to the early 1900s. In June 1919, the **19th Amendment** to the U.S. Constitution, giving women the right to vote nationally, was submitted to the states for ratification. On June 28, 1919, Texas became the ninth state to ratify it. To learn more, see *https://www.tshaonline. org/handbook/online/articles/viw0.*

Civil Rights in Texas

Texas civil rights issues center mainly on African Americans and Mexican Americans, the state's largest ethnic minority groups. Although both groups have fought for equal treatment since the mid-1800s, true change did not come until the 20th century. This change was fraught with violence and intimidation from such factions as the Ku Klux Klan, the White Caps, as well as community leaders, law officials, and the Texas Rangers. Such factors as the poll-tax and Jim Crow laws limited African American and Mexican American involvement in politics and society. The **League of United Latin America Citizens** (LULAC) was founded on February 17, 1929, in Corpus Christi, Texas. Its establishment stemmed from the rise of the Texas-Mexican middle class and resistance to racial discrimination. The strength of the organization has historically been in Texas. Schools and communities were segregated by ethnicities until the Supreme Court's landmark *Brown v. Board of Education* (1954) decision started a move toward integrated schools. Civil rights transformation was a long, arduous process. It required laws to change, and communities had to modify their cultural customs, traditions, and mindsets. Much support for civil rights came from the middle class. After World War II, many Mexican-American and African-American men pushed for equal treatment, which influenced the tumultuous 1960s when many men and women spoke out against inequality. These ethnic groups have made gains in their struggle for civil rights and continue to work to ensure that they are treated equally by the law and within their Texas communities. A key civil rights landmark case in 1950 was *Sweatt v. Painter*, in which the U.S. Supreme Court held that the Fourteenth Amendment prohibited the University of Texas from rejecting applicants solely on the basis of race. To learn more, follow this link: *http://www.tshaonline.org/handbook/ online/articles/pkcfl"www.tshaonline.org/handbook/online/articles/pkcfl.*

Great Depression and the Dust Bowl

Most Texans lived on farms, ranches, or small towns prior to the Great Depression. During the 1920s, oil was showing signs of success, but the Texas economy was still primarily cotton in the north, citrus farming in the south, and livestock ranching in the West. While most Texans were optimistic that they would make it through the economic downturn because of the state's largely rural nature, the Texas economy nonetheless collapsed. A major drought devastated the Southern Plains, setting the stage for the crippling effects of the Dust Bowl in the Texas Panhandle. New Deal programs offered relief, hope, and improvements to everyday living. And the 1936 Texas Centennial—with the main event hosted at the Texas State Fair Grounds in Dallas—proved especially timely to help boost the state's economy as well as its psyche. The event helped bring the world to Texas's doorstep.

The depression, while amplifying issues of segregation across the state, also helped create a fresh slate for change. Change came slowly but laid the foundation for bigger gains after World War II. *https://texasourtexas.texaspbs.org/the-eras-of-texas/great-depression-ww2/*

Boom or Bust Economic Cycles in Texas

As Texas developed in the latter part of the 19th and into the 20th and 21st centuries, it experienced a number of "boom-or-bust" economic cycles. These cycles affected railroads, the cattle industry, oil and gas production, cotton, real estate, banking, and computer technology. A "boom-or-bust" economy undergoes sharp fluctuations from boom, a period of strength and wealth, to bust, a period of weakness and poverty. These variations affect the stability of the economy and the ability for the state to plan its future.

Cattle

Cattle that were left untended during the Civil War greatly multiplied. After the war, they were rounded up and driven to major rail lines to be shipped to the east where the demand for beef was the greatest and where they were willing to pay about 10 times more than the prices in Texas. Many of these cattle trails followed old Indian paths and some formed the route for major roads today. The four major cattle trails in Texas were the Shawnee Trail, the Chisolm Trail, the Western Trail, and the Goodnight-Loving Trail. With the arrival of the railroad and the invention of barbed wire in 1873, the long cattle drives came to an end around 1880. The best known rancher in the American West was **Charles Goodnight**, who is sometimes called the "Father of the Texas Panhandle." Another well known rancher was **Richard King**, founder of the King Ranch in South Texas with over 825,000 acres. **Lizzie Johnson**, the "Cattle Queen of Texas," was the first woman to drive cattle up the Chisholm Trail. See also *https://tpwd.texas.gov/education/resources/* (search "vaqueros and cowboys"), *http://www.historynet.com/* (search "Texas Longhorns: A Short History"), and *https://texasourtexas.texaspbs.org/* (search "The Eras of Texas: Cotton, Cattle, Railroads").

Railroads

Railroads changed the way Texas farms. With increased access to railroads, farmers could ship their surplus goods to market and ranchers could ship cattle to other states. As such, the building of rail lines in Texas led to an increase in both commercial agriculture and cattle ranching. Governor **James Hogg**, the first native governor of Texas, established the Railroad Commission of Texas in 1894, which compelled railroads to respect Texas laws and protected the public interest against the powerful corporate railways.

Oil

In 1901, oil was discovered in the Spindletop Oil Field near Beaumont. **Patitillo Higgins** was an American businessman and self-taught geologist who showed people where to drill for Spindletop as well as many other oil fields throughout Texas. The ensuing development of the oil industry catapulted Texas to its position as the leading producer of oil in the United States. As a result of this boom, cities like Houston and Dallas became large urban and industrial centers.

Military and Wartime Industry

As a result of World War I, Texas emerged as a leading military training center. Several military bases were established in the state, bringing economic growth. The rapid development of the aircraft industry and highly technological businesses led to rapid industrialization in the state. By World War II, Texas was a leading state in the defense industry. The modern economy of Texas still relies on agriculture, ranching, and oil production, but new high-tech industries are rapidly becoming the top economic forces in the state. More factories are moving to Texas and other places in the South because land is abundant and cheap, and the labor costs and regulations are fewer than the Northeast.

Six Flags over Texas

The phrase "Six flags over Texas" describes the different countries that have exerted control in Texas from 1519, when the first European exploration of the region by Cortés took place, to the present:

- Spain (1519–1821)
- France (1685–1690)
- Mexico (1821–1836)
- Republic of Texas (1836–1845)
- United States (1845–1861)
- Texas in the Confederacy (1861–1865)
- Back to the American Union (1870–present)

State Facts and Symbols

Texas has adopted the following symbols to represent the state:

- State flower   Bluebonnet
- State bird   Mockingbird

- State tree   Pecan

- State motto   Friendship

- Border states   Oklahoma, Louisiana, Arkansas, and New Mexico

- State song   "Texas, Our Texas," by William J. Marsh and Gladys Yoakum Wright

  Here are the lyrics to "Texas, Our Texas":

  Texas, our Texas!
  All hail the
  mighty State!
  Texas, our Texas!
  So wonderful so great!

  Boldest and grandest, withstanding ev'ry test;
  O Empire wide and glorious, you stand supremely blest.

  [Refrain]
  God bless you Texas! And
  keep you brave and strong,
  That you may grow in
  power and worth, thro'out
  the ages long.

- United States Pledge of Allegiance

  I pledge allegiance to the Flag of the United States of America, and to the Republic for which it stands, one Nation under God, indivisible, with liberty and justice for all.

- Texas Pledge of Allegiance

  Honor the Texas flag; I pledge allegiance to thee, Texas, one state under God, one and indivisible.

COMPETENCY 002: GEOGRAPHY

The teacher understands and applies knowledge of geographic relationships involving people, places, and environments in Texas, the United States, and the world, as defined by the Texas Essential Knowledge and Skills (TEKS).

The beginning teacher:

  A. Understands and applies the geographic concept of region.

B. Knows how to create and use geographic tools and translate geographic data into a variety of formats (e.g., grid systems, legends, scales, databases, construction of maps, graphs, charts, models).

C. Knows the location and the human and physical characteristics of places and regions in Texas, the United States, and the world.

D. Analyzes ways in which humans adapt to, use, and modify the physical environment.

E. Knows how regional physical characteristics and human modifications to the environment affect people's activities, settlement, immigration, and migration patterns.

F. Analyzes ways in which location (absolute and relative) affects people, places, and environments.

G. Demonstrates knowledge of physical processes (e.g., erosion, deposition, and weathering; plate tectonics; sediment transfer; the flows and exchanges of energy and matter in the atmosphere that produce weather and climate) and their effects on environmental patterns.

H. Understands the characteristics, distribution and migration of populations in Texas, the United States, and the world.

I. Understands the physical and environmental characteristics of Texas, the United States and the world, past and present, and how humans have adapted to and positively and negatively modified the environment (e.g., air and water quality, building of dams, use of natural resources, the impact on habitats and wildlife).

J. Analyzes how geographic factors have influenced settlement patterns, economic and social development, political relationships and policies of societies and regions in Texas, the United States, and the world (e.g., the Galveston hurricane of 1900, the Dust Bowl, limited water resources, alternative energy sources).

K. Analyzes interactions between people and the physical environment and the effects of these interactions on the development of places and regions.

L. Understands comparisons among various world regions and countries (e.g., aspects of population, disease and economic activities) by analyzing maps, charts, databases, and models.

Geographic Concepts

Geography

Geography studies the Earth's surface, the organisms that populate it, and their interaction within the ecosystem by examining spatial patterns, processes, and relationships from a local to global scale. Geography can be divided into two main areas: physical and cultural. **Physical geography** refers to the physical characteristics of the surface of the Earth and how those features affect life (e.g., plate tectonics, landforms, bodies of water, climate, biomes, weathering, erosion, etc.). **Cultural**, or **human geography** deals with the interaction of humans with their environment and how that interaction produces changes. Humans can alter the physical environment of the Earth, but the physical environment can also shape humans and their culture. For example, the Incas built the capital of their empire, Cuzco, in the Andes Mountains in what is now Peru. This city has an altitude of 11,152 feet above sea level, where oxygen is scarce and agriculture is a challenge. However, the Incas managed to live and flourish. They carved the land for agriculture and built roads and cities. In turn, the environment changed the Incas, who had to evolve to tolerate the low levels of oxygen. Studies conducted on the Indians from Peru suggest that people of the Andes developed genetic adaptations for high-altitude living (Discovery Channel, March 10, 2004). By adapting to environmental conditions, the inhabitants not only survived but also flourished in less-than-ideal conditions.

Physical Geography Influences Settlement Locations

People typically settle where there is good land, good climate, and good, clean water. The location of such renewable and nonrenewable natural resources as fresh water, fossil fuels, fertile soils, and timber affect decisions about where to build a community. For example, the settlement patterns in Texas and in the United States show that people did not simply settle where the climate was good for crops, or along the coast where land was easily accessed. People also settled away from the coast along waterways. This provided a fresh source of water as well as a resource for food and transportation. However, settlement decisions can also cause stress on the natural resources. For example, in San Antonio the Edward's Aquifer is one of the most prolific underground sources of water in the world. The demand for the water may become greater than the capacity of the aquifer, which will affect the livelihood of the people as well as the potential development of urban areas in the region.

Locating Places and Regions on a Map

Maps have two categories: reference and thematic. **Reference maps** show the locations of places, boundaries of countries, states, counties, towns, landforms, and bodies of water. They are sometimes referred to as political and physical maps. A **physical map** shows the topography of the Earth, including land features and elevations. A **political map** shows how a country is organized. Atlases are examples of reference maps. **Thematic maps**, or **special purpose maps**, show such specific topics as population density or distribution of world religions as well as physical, social, economic, political, agricultural, or economic features. An *economic map* shows the important resources of a country or region. A **historical map** shows the location of historical events. **Population maps** show where people live.

A globe is a scale **model** of the Earth shaped like a sphere. Because a globe models the shape of the Earth, it shows sizes and shapes accurately. The Mercator projection map is a flat representation of the Earth, and it thus distorts the shape, size, and/or distance in some way. This projection, used initially for shipping, is most accurate nearest the equator. The portability of maps makes them more useful than globes. The position of people, places, and things can be identified using relative or absolute location. **Relative location** uses references to help describe where something is. For example, a house may be located next to a big soccer field. **Absolute location** provides the exact position of the destination. This could be as simple as an address for a house or the coordinates of the location using latitude and longitude. It is important to say "latitude and longitude" in that order because the coordinate system identifies latitude first. For example, Dallas is located at 33°N, 97°W.

The Grid System

A **grid system** is a network of horizontal and vertical lines used to locate points on a map or a chart by means of coordinates. This grid shows the location of places. Latitude and longitude lines form divisions in this grid system that consist of geometrical coordinates used in designating the location of places on the surface of the Earth on a globe or map. The lines measure distances in degrees.

Latitude lines are horizontal lines that run parallel around the Earth measuring the distance north and south of the equator. The **equator** is identified as the 0 degree line of latitude, and it divides the Earth into the Northern and the Southern hemispheres. The United States is located in the Northern Hemisphere, while Brazil, for example, is located in the Southern Hemisphere. **Longitude lines** are vertical lines that run north and south going east and west. The 0 degree line of longitude is known as the prime meridian. It goes through Greenwich, England, and it divides the Earth into the Eastern and Western hemispheres. The United States is in the Western Hemisphere and Japan in the Eastern Hemisphere.

Geographic Symbols

A **compass rose** is a design printed on a chart or map for reference. It shows the orientation of a map on Earth and shows the four cardinal directions (north, south, east, and west). A compass rose may also show in-between directions such as northeast or northwest. Symbols are used for a map to contain a large amount of information that can be easily understood. Common symbols used on a map include dots, stars, and small pictures to represent cities or places. Some maps use different colors to represent features such as elevations and divisions. These symbols and colors are defined in the map's key, or **legend**. A map **scale** shows the distance between two places in the world. The scale to which a map is drawn represents the ratio of the distance between two points on the Earth and the distance between the two corresponding points on the map. When teaching cardinal and intermediate directions, teachers sometimes label walls with N, S, E, W to aid students when giving directions. Teachers need to take precautions to assure that each wall is labeled accurately. This means that the wall that faces north is labeled "North." If North is in a corner, label the corner North. The wall can then have a sign for the correct intermediate direction.

Time Zones

Time zones are established based on the lines of longitude, or meridians. These lines run from north to south. The prime meridian, or the meridian at 0 degrees, has been set in Greenwich, England. On the other side of the globe is the 180th meridian along which the International Date Line (IDL) generally follows. The prime meridian divides the Earth into the Western and Eastern hemispheres. Following the sunlight as it travels along the rotating Earth, the time decreases moving from east to west. Crossing the IDL eastward, you subtract a day, whereas moving westward means you add a day. So in the first example, Monday would become Sunday; in the second case, it would be Tuesday.

The United States is divided into six time zones, all one hour apart—Eastern, Central, Mountain, Pacific, Alaska, and Hawaii. Figure 5-2 represents the six time zones in the United States with a key city for each zone. Technically, the United States has four time zones in the contiguous 48 states, five in the continental U.S. with the addition of Alaska, and when we add Hawaii, we add the sixth time zone. For more information about time zones, go to the website provided by the National Institute of Standards and Technology (an agency of the U.S. Department of Commerce) and the U.S. Naval Observatory at *https://time.gov*.

Figure 5-2
Time Zones in the United States

West ←					→ East
Hawaii	Alaska	Pacific	Mountain	Central	Eastern
1:00 PM	2:00 PM	3:00 PM	4:00 PM	5:00 PM	6:00 PM
Honolulu	Anchorage	Los Angeles	Phoenix	Dallas	New York City

Locations and Human and Physical Characteristics of Places and Regions

Texas

As measured by area, Texas is the second-largest state in the United States. Only Alaska is larger. Covering 268,601 square miles, the state contains five geographic regions within its boundaries. Table 5-3 lists the regions and the key cities and main economic activities of each.

Table 5-3
Regions and Economic Activity in Texas

Region	Key Cities	Main Economic Activities	Key Statistics
Coastal Plains, flatland	Dallas, Houston, San Antonio, Austin, Corpus Christi, Laredo	**Lumber:** East Texas (Piney Woods) **Oil:** Refineries in Houston **Farming:** Rice, oranges, cotton, wheat, milo **Ranching:** Cattle in Kingsville **Shipping:** Houston	**Population:** High: 1 of 3 Texans **Rainfall:** High **Distinguishing Mark:** Hurricanes
North Central Plains, flatland and hills	Fort Worth, Arlington, San Angelo, Abilene	**Ranching:** Cattle, wool (mohair), sheep **Farming:** Grains	**Population:** High **Rainfall:** Medium **Distinguishing Marks:** Tornadoes, northerlies (cold winds), hailstorms; large ranches
Great Plains, flatland and hill country	Midland, Odessa, Lubbock, Amarillo, Texas Panhandle	**Ranching:** Cattle, sheep **Minerals:** Graphite **Oil:** Odessa and Midland **Farming:** Wheat	**Population:** Average **Rainfall:** Medium **Distinguishing Marks:** Snowstorms, dust storms, windmills, use of aquifers
Mountains and Basins, Rocky Mountains, Davis, Chisos, and Guadalupe	El Paso	**Ranching:** Limited large ranches	**Population:** Low **Rainfall:** Low; hard rain wears out the rocks and land **Distinguishing Mark:** Big Bend National Park

The United States

The concept of regions facilitates the examination of geography by providing a convenient and manageable unit for studying the Earth's human and natural environment.

Regions in the United States

The United States can be divided into various regions based on different criteria. For example, according to the U.S. Census Bureau, there are four main regions: the Northeast, Midwest, South, and West.

The National Geographic Society delineates five region-defining geographic positions in the continental United States: the Northeast, Southwest, West, Southeast, and Midwest. For more information, visit National Geographic at *https://www.nationalgeographic.org/maps/united-states-regions/.* Sometimes regions are based on physical geography. For example, the contiguous United States may be divided into seven broad physiographic divisions, which, from east to west, are as follows: the Atlantic–Gulf Coastal Plain; the Appalachian Highlands; the Interior Plains; the Interior Highlands; the Rocky Mountain System; the Intermontane Region; and the Pacific Mountain System. An eighth division, the Laurentian Uplands, a part of the Canadian Shield, dips into the United States from Canada in the Great Lakes region. *https://www.infoplease.com/encyclopedia/places/north-america/us/united-states/physical-geography*

Rivers in the United States

These are the largest and most important rivers in the United States:

- The **Mississippi** is the longest river in the United States and the 14th longest in the world. It begins in Minnesota and ends in the Gulf of Mexico.

- The **Ohio River** begins near Pittsburgh and runs southwest, ending in the Mississippi River on the Illinois and Missouri borders.

- The **Rio Grande** begins in the San Juan Mountains of southern Colorado and ends in the Gulf of Mexico. The river is the official border between the United States and Mexico, where it is known as the **Rio Bravo**.

- The **Colorado River** begins in the Rocky Mountains and flows to the wetlands of northwestern Mexico and the Gulf of California.

- The **Missouri River** begins in the Rocky Mountains, flowing north first and then generally southeast across the central United States, ending at the Mississippi River, just to the north of St. Louis, Missouri.

For information about significant rivers in the continental United States, visit *http://www.worldatlas.com.*

Regions of the World

A world region is an area of the world that shares similar, unifying cultural or physical characteristics that are different from those of surrounding areas. The physical features refer to topographic characteristics like elevation, rivers, and mountains. The cultural features include all the features that distinguish different groups of people, for example: language, religion, government, economics, food, architecture, shared values, and family life.

Geographers divide the world into ten regions: North America, Central and South America, Europe, Central Eurasia, the Middle East, North Africa, Sub-Saharan Africa, South Asia, East Asia, and Australasia. These divisions are based on physical and cultural similarities. North America consists of Canada, the United States, and Mexico. It is the third-largest continent, and it is located between the Arctic Circle and the Tropic of Cancer. The Europeans colonized the North American region. Table 5-4 presents an overview of the world regions by physical and cultural features. World region names and scope can vary depending on the purpose of those defining the area. For example, when discussing North America and Latin America, North America in this instance only refers to Canada and the United States, while Latin America consists of everything south of the United States (Mexico, Central America, the Caribbean, and South America).

Table 5-4
World Regions

World Region	Physical Features	Cultural Features
North America	• Consists of Canada, the United States, and Mexico. • The United States is the fourth-largest country in the world. • Oil is an important resource in the U.S. • Most of the U.S. has a humid-continental or humid-subtropical climate. • Most of Canada has a subarctic or tundra climate. • Over 75% of Canadians live along the southern border. • The areas of greatest concentration of population in the U.S. are along the East Coast and California. • The climate of Mexico ranges from humid tropical and subtropical to desert and highland. • Mexico has rich mineral resources including oil.	• Europeans colonized this region. • Languages spoken are predominantly English, Spanish, and French. • Most people hold Christian beliefs.

World Region	Physical Features	Cultural Features
Central and South America	• Includes the countries of Central America, the Caribbean islands, and South America. • The majority of this continuous mass of land is south of the Equator. • South America extends from Point Gallinas in Colombia to Cape Horn. • Part of South America lies closer to the South Pole than any other land mass of this size. • Venezuela is one of the world's leading exporters of oil. • Most of Eastern Central America and equatorial South America have a humid tropical climate.	• Most people speak Spanish, but many other languages are spoken: Portuguese, French, Dutch, English, and several Native American languages and dialects. • Christian beliefs, the Roman Catholic religion is predominant. • Architecture, law, religion, traditions, and language are strongly influenced by Europe's colonial rule of this region. • The many ethnic groups in this region are separated by geographical barriers such as the Andes and the Amazon.
Europe	• Western section of the Eurasian continent • Shares a mountain chain, the Alps. • Most of Europe has a temperate climate. • Europe's irregular coastline has many harbors that are important manufacturing and trade centers. • The rivers of Europe are important resources for trade, water, and hydroelectricity. • European population growth rates are the smallest in the world.	• Shares a common history in the Roman Empire and later the Catholic Church and Latin language. • English is the most spoken language in Europe, German and French are also widespread. • Cultural diffusion or shared cultural traits spread throughout Europe. • Ninety percent of all adults ages 15–24 speak a second language and some countries are considered multilingual. • Europeans practice many different religions. • Roman Catholicism is the predominant religion of many European countries. • Most of Northern and Central Europe is Protestant. • Jews live in many parts of Western Europe.

(continued)

World Region	Physical Features	Cultural Features
Russia and the Eurasian republics	• Central Asia and Eastern Europe • United around one continuous mass of land located in the middle of the continent. • Little access to the sea • The borders of Eastern European countries have changed many times. • From WWII to the late 1980s, the Soviet Union controlled Eastern Europe and introduced communism to the region.	• Conquered at different times by the Persians, Mongolians, Tartars, the French, the Germans, and the Russians. • Slavic languages are predominant. • Most people in the Eastern part of the region follow the Eastern Orthodox church; people in the Northern area are mostly Roman Catholic.
Southwest Asia (sometimes referred to as the Middle East)	• Consists of the area of southwest Asia and North Africa. • Access to sea water • The majority of the land is desert. • Rich in oil	• While the majority of people follow the religion of Islam there are also groups that follow Christianity and Judaism. • The religion defines the law in many places. • The most ancient of human civilizations. Egyptians, Assyrians, Babylonians, Persians, Greeks, and Romans have left their mark in this region. • This region has been the fighting ground for many religious battles.
North Africa	• Part of the African continent • Includes Egypt, Libya, Tunisia, Algeria, and Morocco • Extensive coastline • The Sahara desert and the Nile river are two important physical features of this area. • Rich in oil • Egypt is undergoing rapid growth, urbanization, and industrialization.	• The majority of people follow the religion of Islam. • People speak Arabic predominantly. • Religious issues influence the politics of this area.

World Region	Physical Features	Cultural Features
Sub-Saharan Africa	• Consists of Africa south of the Sahara • Most of the area is a savanna. • Has abundant rain • Extensive coastline • Fertile land • Most people live in the forest zone and the dry savannas. • Agriculture is the predominant activity in West Africa. • Livestock is the predominant economic activity in the northern area.	• Cultural diversity reflects indigenous, Arab, and European influences. • Majority follows tribal beliefs, Christianity, or a combination of both. • Most people speak native African or European languages. • Over 500 ethnic groups live in this region.
South Asia	• Consists of a large Indian peninsula that extends into the Indian Ocean. • Abundant rainfall • Strong seasonal winds called monsoons • Rice is an important crop. • One of the most populated regions in the world. • The world's highest mountains are located in the northern area of this region. • Many major manufacturing and trade centers are located along the coast.	• People in South Asia speak many languages. • Predominant beliefs are of Eastern origins such as Buddhism and Hinduism. • Many South Asians are farmers who live in small villages. • Many cultural influences • Through the efforts of Mohandas Gandhi the region gained its independence from Britain in 1947.
East Asia	• Consists of China, Korea, Taiwan, and Japan. • It is the most densely populated region in the world. • Large expanse of coastline.	• Buddhism and Taoism are predominant religions. • Confucian philosophy • People speak Chinese, Japanese, Korean, Mongolian, and many other languages. • Chinese Script or characters influence many of the writing systems of these languages. • Culturally, China has had a major influence in this region.
Australia and the Pacific Realm	• It is composed of the Australian continent and surrounding islands. • South of the equator	• English is the predominant language of most nations in this region • Population contains a large Christian majority.

World Mountains

With the notable exception of the peak known as K2, which is part of the Karakoram Range, the tallest mountains in the world are located in the Himalayas, ranging across the countries of China, Pakistan, Nepal, and Tibet. Table 5-5 lists the top ten tallest mountains in the world. For additional information about the world's mountains, see *http://www.infoplease.com/ipa/A0001771.html*.

Table 5-5
Tallest Mountains in the World

Mountain	Location	Height (in feet)
Everest	Nepal/Tibet	29,035
K2	Pakistan/China	28,250
Kanchenjunga	India/Nepal	28,169
Lhotse I	Nepal/Tibet	27,940
Makalu I	Nepal/Tibet	27,766
Cho Oyu	Nepal/Tibet	26,906
Dhaulagiri	Nepal	26,795
Manaslu I	Nepal	26,781
Nanga Parbat	Pakistan	26,660
Annapurna	Nepal	26,545

Compared to the world's tallest peaks, mountains in the United States are smaller, with the highest mountain being Mt. McKinley in Alaska, which is 20,310 feet high. The state of Alaska has the 16 highest peaks in the United States. A list of U.S. mountains with elevations of 16,000 feet or above is presented in Table 5-6.

Table 5-6
Tallest Mountains in the United States

Mountain	Location	Height (in feet)
Denali[4]	Alaska	20,310
Mt. St. Elias	Alaska	18,008
Mt. Foraker	Alaska	17,400
Mt. Bona	Alaska	16,500
Mt. Blackburn	Alaska	16,390
Mt. Sanford	Alaska	16,237

[4] Also called Mt. McKinley. Denali's official elevation was established by the U.S. Geological Survey in 2015.

Physical Processes

The Earth's surface is shaped by powerful physical processes held in dynamic balance that both demolish and restore the continental and oceanic crust.

Weathering

Weathering describes the breaking down or dissolving of rocks and minerals on the surface of the Earth. Water, ice, acids, salts, plants, animals, and changes in temperature are all agents of weathering. *https://www.nationalgeographic.org/encyclopedia/weathering.*

Erosion

Erosion is the geological process by which earthen materials are worn away and transported by natural forces such as wind or water. For more information, visit the National Geographic Society at *https://www.nationalgeographic.org/encyclopedia/erosion.*

Deposition

Deposition is the process of carrying soil from one place to another, usually by means of water or wind. This process is responsible for the creation of beaches, sand dunes found in desert areas, and landforms created by glaciers.

Plate Tectonics

The theory of plate tectonics revolutionized the earth sciences by explaining how the movement of geologic plates causes mountain building, volcanoes, earthquakes, rift valleys, etc. For more information, visit the National Geographic Society at *https://www.nationalgeographic.org/ encyclopedia/plate-tectonics.*

Human Adaptation, Modification, and Use of the Physical Environment

Humans can alter the physical environment of the Earth, but the physical environment can also shape humans and their culture. For example, the Incas built the capital of their empire, Cuzco, in the Andes Mountains in what is now Peru. This city has an altitude of 11,152 feet above sea level, where oxygen is scarce and agriculture is a challenge. However, the Incas managed to live and flourish under these conditions. They carved the land for agriculture and built roads and cities. In turn, the environment changed the Incas, who had to evolve to tolerate the low levels of oxygen. Studies conducted on the Indians from Peru suggest that people of the Andes developed genetic adaptations for high-altitude living (Discovery Channel, 2004 March 10). By adapting to the conditions of their environment, inhabitants of the area not only survived but also flourished in less-than-ideal conditions.

How Regional Physical Characteristics and Human Modifications to the Environment Affect People's Activities and Settlement Patterns

The intended and unintended consequences of how humans modify the physical environment result in constant change to the human and physical world.

Advances in technology can bring a continuum of positive to negative consequences for people and for the environment. For example, humans often supply their energy needs from the Earth. The United States has long relied on coal as an energy source. Much of U.S. coal comes from Pennsylvania and West Virginia. Humans cannot have the energy benefits of coal without altering the physical landscape from which the coal is taken. This physical reshaping of mining the Earth changes how rainfall runs, where people can build homes, and how they maintain safe drinking water.

Humans often redefine environmental systems and reshape the Earth in order to plant and harvest food. Some farming methods, such as intercropping, feature greater measures for sustainability, while other methods maintain focus on maximizing yield and are more detrimental to the environment.

How Location (Absolute and Relative) Affects People, Places and Environments

Both relative and absolute location tell us about where we are in the world. We use latitude and longitude to determine a global location. We use a street address to determine local location. Both of these are examples of absolute location. Often we describe a location by what is around a location. This is relative location. Referencing a landmark or the distance a location is from another well-known location would be examples of giving a relative location.

Most of us interact daily with our environment. Dolphin-safe tuna, bottled water, and sunscreen, are all real-life examples of products people create to interact safely and sustainably with their environment. Geography, in part, contributes to the pattern of how people organize space on the Earth. People use location, place, territory, geopolitics, migration, gender, race, language, economic change, and power to manage their relationship to the space around them. All of these have both local and worldwide effects.

Characteristics, Distribution, and Migration of Populations

The global population is more than seven-and-a-half billion people, with much of the growth occurring in the last two centuries. Population density of hyper-urban areas is also growing. For example, Tokyo, Japan, has over 36 million people. The New York and Sao Paulo, Brazil, metropolitan areas both have over 20 million people. Mumbai and Delhi, both urban areas in India, have over 21 million people each! Increases in population places strains on cities, regions, countries, and the Earth to keep up with the daily needs and wants of people, from access to clean water and medical care, to maintaining and growing schools and industry to support basic needs to extended quality of life. Population growth sometimes causes migration. Some migration is voluntary, as when humans search for a better quality of life. Other migration is involuntary, as when humans must move to maintain their culture or life, as in the face of famine, war, or ecological devastation. World events, as varied as war or the use of vaccines, can also affect population. Shifts in population density affect supply and demand of goods and services for people.

Culture

The culture of a group is reflected in what its people write, create, and wear as well as their government, decisions, customs and ceremonies, way of life, and dwellings. Humans share their culture through oral traditions, stories, real and mythical heroes, music, paintings, and sculptures. Significant historical periods represent cultural ideals at a given time and may continue to influence following generations as well as other regions of the world. For example, the Renaissance, Baroque, Classicism, Neoclassicism, and Romanticism are key historical periods that gave birth to influential literature, art, and music. The **Renaissance**, or "rebirth," was a time of great creativity. **William Shakespeare**'s plays explored humanity in plays that are still read and performed. **Leonardo da Vinci** created inspiring paintings and sculptures. He also was known as the "Renaissance Man" who learned about and pursued different disciplines that enabled him to follow his interest in science and inventions as well. Literature and art often also reflect their time as well as the societies in which they are produced. The Renaissance also reflected reformation of attitudes toward political authority, which was mainly embodied in the church and monarchs. Society questioned and challenged decisions made by the church—as well as the monarch's rule. (For more information go to *http://www.britannica.com/EBchecked/topic/497731/Renaissance*.)

In the United States, the American Renaissance occurred in literature from the 1830s through the Civil War and into the 1880s. As with the European renaissance, literature and the arts explored humanity and challenged beliefs in the church, politics, and society. It was a period of time that was greatly governed by Transcendentalism. **American Transcendentalism**, a term derived from the philosopher Kant, was heavily influenced by the great minds of England and Germany. In America, this philosophy, or belief, was idealistic in nature, rooted in faith, and had a visionary bent. As stated by Thomas Hampson and Carla Maria Verdino-Süllwold in the PBS "Song of America" program, it was a collection of complex beliefs "that the spark of divinity lies within man; that everything in the world is a microcosm of existence; that the individual soul is identical to the world soul, or Over-Soul, as Emerson called it. . . . By meditation, by communing with nature, through work and art, man could transcend his senses and attain an understanding of beauty and goodness and truth." (see *http://www.songofamerica.net/library/ami/the-american-renaissance-and-transcendentalism*) This philosophy permeated American life through literature, poetry, artwork (e.g., painting, sculpture), architecture, and music. Well-known authors in American Transcendentalism include Emerson, Thoreau, Hawthorne, Whitman, and Dickinson. The renaissance is just one example of how creative expression is influenced by societal issues, and how it can transcend the societal boundaries with art, music, and literature and explore such universal ideas as religion, justice, and the passage of time.

Culture can be also analyzed by the effects of race, gender, socioeconomic class, and status and stratification on the ways of life. Historically, individuals differentiate themselves, and this affects their societies. For example, race has been used as a way to segment society and to allow certain groups to achieve status or some reward over another group. Race groups people according to such common features as hair, eye, or skin color. Ethnicity identifies a group of people by cultural traits. During World War II, Adolf Hitler, the leader of Germany, identified Jews as the reason for the economic and social crisis Germany was facing. He gradually stratified society by Jew and non-Jew. Although he referred to the Jewish ethnic group, Jews were recognized by characteristics that Hitler identified as the Jewish race. In the United States, people have recognized race as both unifying and divisive. For example, enclaves developed in cities where people with similar ethnic backgrounds lived. In this way, the immigrants felt at home and could ease into American culture. However, cultural differences sometimes have divided people. After a series of potato famines in Ireland, Irish immigrants moved to America to find a new life—and were met with such signs as "Don't hire Irish" and such comments as "dirty Irish." Texas was settled by cultural groups who created towns to reflect their German, Polish, Mexican, and other heritages. At the same time, societies were often stratified by race, gender, and socioeconomic class.

Cultural Diffusion

The term **cultural diffusion** describes the exchange or transmission of cultural information and lifestyles from people around the world. For example, most people in the world use cotton, a fabric developed in India; and silk, developed in China. Chickens and pigs were originally domesticated in Asia, but by the process of cultural diffusion, these animals are common today in most countries in the world. Many countries are predominantly Christian today, but Christianity was born in the Middle East, a place where most people are Muslim. The Romans facilitated the cultural diffusion of Christianity around the ancient world. Travelers visiting Morocco, a Muslim country in North Africa, may be surprised to hear Puerto Rican salsa and Jamaican reggae music being played in local nightclubs. The popularity of Latin and Caribbean rhythms in a predominantly Muslim country is an example of the powerful effect of cultural diffusion.

Cultural diffusion influences the development of multicultural societies, which may have unifying and divisive qualities. The influx of people can aid the social and economic development of a nation. All cultures have unique characteristics and knowledge that can add to a society. These include inventions, art, music, and technology as well as production techniques. However, tensions can rise when people compete for housing, jobs, and land. Large cultural groups also may seek to dominate and exploit smaller, weaker cultural groups. Conflict also may occur if cultural groups try to force their way of life on others.

Relationships among cultural groups are dynamic. The relationships are influenced by conflict, cooperation, and change and are based on such factors as race, ethnicity, and religion. For example, in the 1960s tensions between the Caucasian and African-American races in the United States brought about much change. Although in the South some conflicts occurred in the form of riots, protests, and attacks, both races also cooperated through marches, speeches, peaceful demonstrations, and, eventually, new laws. Religion can also cause tensions. For example, in Northern Ireland, Catholics and Protestants have fought for many years. Although both groups are Christian, their religion has come to symbolize geopolitical issues.

Improved communication, transportation and economic development can also impact cultural change. For example, the country of Malawi, on the continent of Africa, has a poor infrastructure resulting in a few people owning a telephone in their house or village. Telephones with landlines require electricity, wiring under or above ground, and other infrastructure. However, satellites allow farmers in this country to operate satellite mobile telephones that need little infrastructure. The people in Malawi, like many African cultures, have a strong oral tradition, meaning they learn by listening as experienced elders pass knowledge and traditions. Many cannot read and write. Satellite phones let members of this society gain new knowledge to improve their agriculture by using their oral traditions rather than written language.

Geographical Tools

Social scientists (e.g., geographers, historians, political scientists, and economists) use an assortment of geographical tools to help examine physical and cultural geographic data. First, the globe is recognized as a mathematical model of the world and is important to students' development of spatial thinking. It shows accurate distance, shape, and size of continents and bodies of water. As will be discussed, colors are used to symbolize elevation or other concepts. The complexity of the globe increases with the grade level. Maps are a flat representation of the world or a region of the world. As with globes, the complexity of maps increases developmentally with the grade level. Charts, graphs, and diagrams are also used to analyze data. Some mathematical representations, such as Dot Plots, offer an opportunity to reinforce mathematical concepts while examining cultural and historical data sets. Digital geospatial tools can offer teachers an alternative to paper maps and allow for more depth and rigor when used appropriately. These tools can provide an easy way to explore data spatially, such as in the Annie E. Case Foundation "Kids Count" website (*http://datacenter.kidscount.org/*) and the Census Bureau webpage for kids (*https://www.census.gov/schools/facts/*). Others provide interactive online maps such as *http://mrnussbaum.com/united-states/amwest/* or *https://mrnussbaum.com/western-states-interactive-map*. A popular digital globe is Google Earth (*https://https://www.google.com/earth/*), which allows users to add data layers and to spatially analyze data from a local to global scale. The National Geographic Society also has an interactive map (*https://mapmaker.nationalgeographic.org*). Finally, ArcGIS Online (*http://www.arcgis.com/features/*) offers an online tool that facilitates inquiry-based discussions and lets students and teachers explore data and create maps.

Map Skills by Grade—Scope and Sequence

Students should create and interpret maps of places and regions of the world that contain developmentally appropriate map elements and symbols. A compass rose and grid system should be used to locate places on maps and globes as well. Place location, or memorizing countries, cities, bodies of water, and landforms on a map, is critical to learning geography and other social studies. It provides a foundation on which content about Texas, the United States, and the world can be built. Its importance is akin to the multiplication tables in mathematics. Maps may be provided through an online or desktop digital source or on paper. Paper maps may already have an outline of a region or require students to sketch the area. Sketch maps are important because they require students to create a mental image, or map, of the area. Doing so will help them visualize the region when learning about social studies, and it will also help them to make connections to other content, including literature and science.

In addition to knowing the specific knowledge and skills required at each grade level in the Texas Essential Knowledge and Skills (TEKS), it is important to be aware of areas in the curriculum for vertical alignment. For example, in each grade level in elementary school, the following skills are reinforced. Savvy elementary teachers would work together to ensure that these skills are supported and extended to appropriately challenge students. As you read the geography knowledge and skills for each grade level, consider ways you can continue to build and develop curriculum to make it rigorous and relevant while preparing students for their next grade level.

Prior Grades Knowledge and Skills for Social Studies (TEKS)

- Understands and uses terms related to location, direction, and distance (e.g., *up*, *down*, *left*, *right*, *here*, *near*, *far*).

- Recognizes a globe as a model of the Earth.

- Recognizes and uses terms that express relative size and shape (e.g., *big*, *little*, *large*, *small*, *round*, *square*).

- Identifies school and local community by name.

- Recognizes and uses models and symbols to represent real things.

- Uses a compass rose to find true directions.

- Identifies bodies of water—oceans, seas, lakes, rivers, ponds, and bayous.

- Identifies landforms—plains, mountains, deserts, hills, and canyons.

- Identifies natural resources—water, soil, trees, metals, and fish.

Grade 4 Knowledge and Skills for Social Studies

- Interprets pictures, graphs, charts, and tables.

- Works with distance, directions, scale, and map symbols.

- Relates similarities and differences between maps and globes.

- Uses maps of different scales and themes.

- Recognizes the common characteristics of the map grid system.

- Compares and contrasts regions on a state, national, or world basis.

- Understands such concepts of adaptation and modification as changing the landscape to meet survival needs and building to adjust to a new environment.

- Identifies elements that affect the climate.

- Identifies key explorers and their achievements.

- Identifies how geography affects the settlement and development of places.

- Understands the connection between climate and vegetation.

- Identifies global divisions, like the prime meridian, the equator, and the four hemispheres.

Grade 5 Knowledge and Skills for Social Studies

- Uses geographic tools to collect, analyze, and interpret data.

- Applies such geographic tools as grid systems, legends, symbols, scales, and compass roses to make and interpret maps.

- Translates geographic data into such formats as graphs and maps.

- Understands the concept of regions and can describe regions in the U.S. that result from patterns of human activity, including political, population, and economic regions as well as from physical characteristics, including landform, climate, and vegetation regions.

- Locates the 50 states on a map and can identify regions made by features such as the Appalachian Mountains, Great Lakes, Mississippi River, Great Plains, and the Rocky Mountains.

- Understands and describes location and patterns of settlement as well as their distribution.

- Analyzes the location of U. S. cities, including the five largest cities by population in the U.S.

- Understands how people adapt and modify their environment to meet human needs.

- Analyzes the consequences of human modification of the environment in the United States.

Grade 6 Knowledge and Skills for Social Studies

- Uses maps, globes, graphs, charts, models, and databases to answer geographic questions.

- Creates maps, graphs, models, and databases.

- Poses and answers questions about geographic distributions and patterns from selected world regions and countries.

- Compares selected world regions and countries by using data from maps, graphs, charts, databases, and models.

- Understands the characteristics and relative locations of major historical and contemporary societies.

- Locates major historical and contemporary societies on maps and globes.

- Identifies and explains how geography affects patterns of population in places and regions.

- Understands how geography influences the economic development, political relationships, and policies of societies.

- Understands the impact of physical processes on patterns in the environment.

- Understands the impact of interactions between people and the physical environment on the development of places and regions.

Grade 7 Knowledge and Skills for Social Studies

- Uses geographic tools to collect, analyze, and interpret data.

- Creates and interprets thematic maps, graphs, charts, models, and databases.

- Analyzes and interprets geographic distributions and patterns.

- Locates the mountains and basins, Great Plains, North Central Plains, and Coastal Plains regions and places of importance.

- Compares places and regions in terms of physical and human characteristics.

- Analyzes the effects of physical and human factors.

- Identifies ways people have modified and adapted to the environment.

- Analyzes positive and negative consequences of modifications.

- Explains ways in which geographic factors have affected political, economic, and social development.

• Analyzes why immigrants moved and where they settled.

• Analyzes how immigrants and migrants influenced Texas.

• Analyzes the effects of changing population distribution and growth.

• Describes the structure of the population.

Grade 8 Knowledge and Skills for Social Studies

• Understands United States history from early colonial period in the 16th and 17th century through Reconstruction in the 19th century.

• Understands the location and characteristics of places and regions of the U.S., past and present.

• Locates places and regions of importance.

• Compares places and regions in terms of physical and human characteristics.

• Understands the physical characteristics of the U.S. and how humans adapted and modified the environment.

• Analyzes how physical characteristics influenced population distribution, settlement patterns and economic activities.

• Analyzes positive and negative consequences of modifications.

• Analyzes how different immigrant groups interacted with the environment.

COMPETENCY 003: ECONOMICS

The teacher understands and applies knowledge of economic systems and how people organize economic systems to produce, distribute, and consume goods and services, as defined by the Texas Essential Knowledge and Skills (TEKS).

The beginning teacher:

A. Understands that basic human needs are met in many ways.

B. Understands and applies knowledge of basic economic concepts (e.g., goods and services, free enterprise, interdependence, needs and wants, scarcity, economic system, factors of production).

C. Demonstrates knowledge of the ways in which people organize economic systems and the similarities and differences among various economic systems around the world.

D. Understands the value and importance of work and purposes for spending and saving money.

E. Demonstrates knowledge of occupational patterns and economic activities in Texas, the United States and the world, past and present (e.g., the plantation system, the spread of slavery, industrialization and urbanization, transportation, the American ideals of progress, equality of opportunity).

F. Understands the characteristics, benefits and development of the free enterprise system in Texas and the United States.

G. Analyzes the roles of producers and consumers in the production of goods and services.

H. Understands the effects of government regulation and taxation on economic development.

I. Demonstrates knowledge of how businesses operate in the U.S. free enterprise system and international markets (e.g., government regulation, world competition, the importance of morality and ethics in maintaining a functional enterprise system).

J. Applies knowledge of the effects of supply and demand on consumers and producers in a free-enterprise system.

K. Demonstrates knowledge of categories of economic activities and methods used to measure a society's economic level.

L. Uses economic indicators to describe and measure levels of economic activity.

M. Understands the causes of major events and trends in economic history (e.g., factors leading societies to change from agrarian to urban, economic reasons for exploration and colonization, economic forces leading to the Industrial Revolution, processes of economic development in world areas, factors leading to the emergence of different patterns in jobs, economic activity in regions of the United States).

N. Analyzes the interdependence of Texas, the United States, and world economies.

O. Understands how geographic factors such as immigration, migration, location, climate and limited resources have influenced the development of economic activities in Texas, the United States, and the world.

P. Applies knowledge of significant economic events and issues and their effects in Texas, in the United States, and the world.

Basic Principles of Economy

Economics, the subject covered by Competency 003, is a social science that analyzes the principles that regulate the production, distribution, and consumption of resources in society. It emphasizes how these principles operate within the economic choices of individuals, households, businesses, and governments. Economics can be divided into two main areas: macroeconomics and microeconomics. Macroeconomics is the study of the economy at the world, regional, state, and local levels. Some of the topics include reasons and ways to control inflation, causes of unemployment, and economic growth in general. Microeconomics deals with specific issues related to the decision-making process at the household, firm, or industry levels.

Four key economic concepts help explain the many individual decisions people make: scarcity, opportunity cost, and supply and demand incentives.

The study of economics can also be summarized under six key principles.

1. People choose.

2. People's choices have costs.

3. People respond to incentives in predictable ways.

4. People create economic systems that influence individual choices and incentives.

5. People gain when they trade voluntarily.

6. People's choices have consequences that lie in the future.

Scarcity

Economics centers on the notion of scarcity. **Scarcity** refers to the reality that there are limited resources despite consumer's unlimited wants. The result is that people must choose among competing alternatives. The choices people make about which alternative to choose are generally purposeful and based on their desire to obtain the most utility or satisfaction from their choices. Time, money, and natural resources are all examples of scarce resources.

Needs and Wants

Needs and wants drive the economy. As Britannica Kids puts it, "Needs are things that people require to survive. Food, water, clothing, and shelter are all needs. If a human body does not have those things, the body cannot function and will die. Wants are things that a person would like to have but are not needed for survival. A want may include a toy, expensive shoes, or the most recent electronics." See *https://kids.britannica.com/kids/article/needs-and-wants/630969* for more information on this topic.

Opportunity Costs

All choices have benefits and costs. Every time an investor, saver, consumer, or producer makes a decision, there is an alternative course of action that could be taken. Economists refer to the best alternative forgone as the **opportunity cost** of a decision. Opportunity costs are both monetary and nonmonetary in nature, and are an important consideration in the choices people make. Let's consider your decision to read this book and study for the TExES exam. There are probably several other things you could be doing rather than reading this book and studying for the TExES exam, such as watching television, spending time with family or friends, or exercising. If you were to rank your alternatives in order, the alternative ranking right behind your decision to read this book is the opportunity cost of your choice.

For instance, if you were to rank your choices in the following order, the opportunity cost of your decision to read this book would have been exercising.

1. Read this book (choice)

2. Exercise (opportunity cost: best alternative forgone)

3. Watch television

4. Spend time with family and friends

Theory of Supply and Demand

The theory of supply and demand states that prices vary based on the balance between the availability of a product or service at a certain price (supply) and the desire of potential purchasers to pay that price (demand). This balance of supply and demand can occur naturally or be created artificially. An example of an artificially created balance is the intentional destruction of a surplus of a given product on the world market to maintain the price level. Another way is to control the production and availability of the product to create a scarcity of a product. For instance, the OPEC oil cartel often reduces its production of oil to cause an increase in price.

Goods and Services

The use of machines increases the availability of goods and services to the population. This kind of production can decrease the cost of producing the goods and consequently their price. For example, as a result of the division of labor and the use of assembly lines developed by Eli Whitney in 1799, production costs of manufactured goods decreased and productivity increased. Mass production that came as a result of the Industrial Revolution made contemporary families and children more likely to become consumers rather than producers. However, before the Industrial Revolution, especially in colonial America, children were used to produce goods and contribute to the group.

Economic activities are categorized into five major categories: primary, secondary, tertiary, quaternary, and quinary. *Primary* economic activities directly use natural resources by such activities as farming, mining, logging, etc. *Secondary* economic activities take the primary goods and change, or manufacture, them in some way. For example, fresh vegetables are canned or put into a frozen dinner. *Tertiary* activities typically refer to the service industry. To carry the previous examples further, the grocery store where canned and frozen foods are bought is considered part of the tertiary sector. *Quaternary* activities typically require specialized knowledge or technical skills and refer to the "collection, processing, and manipulation of information and capital (finance, administration, insurance, legal services, computer services, etc.)" (de Blij & Murphy 1999, 320). Finally, the *quinary* sector "denotes activities that facilitate complex decision making and the advancement of human capacities (scientific research, high-level management, etc.)" required for jobs like "research professors, the heads of corporations, and top government officials." (de Blij & Murphy 1999, 320).

Factors of Production

The resources required for the production of goods and services are generally classified into four categories: natural resources, labor, capital, and entrepreneurship.

Natural resources include timber, land, fisheries, farms, oil, and other similar natural resources. Natural resources are generally a limited resource for many economies. Although some natural resources, such as timber, food, and animals, are renewable, the physical land is usually a fixed resource. Nations must carefully use their natural resources by creating a mix of natural and industrial uses.

Labor represents the human capital available to transform raw or national resources into consumer goods. Human capital includes all able-bodied individuals capable of working in the economic system and providing various services to other individuals or businesses. This factor of production is a flexible resource as workers can be allocated to different areas of the economy for producing consumer goods or services. Human capital can also be improved through training or educating workers to complete technical functions or business tasks when working with other economic resources.

Capital has two economic definitions as a factor of production. Capital can represent the monetary resources companies use to purchase natural resources, land, and other capital goods. Monetary resources flow through an economic system as individuals buy and sell resources to individuals and businesses. Capital also represents the major physical assets individuals and companies use when producing goods or services. These assets include buildings, production facilities, equipment, motor vehicles, and other similar items.

Entrepreneurship is considered a factor of production because economic resources can exist in an economy and not be transformed into consumer goods. Entrepreneurs usually have an idea for creating a valuable good or service and assume the risk involved with transforming economic resources into consumer products. Entrepreneurship is also considered a factor of production since someone must complete the managerial functions of gathering, allocating, and distributing economic resources or consumer products to individuals and other businesses in the economy.

Economic Indicators

The strength of an economy is determined by assessing indicators. An indicator is a statistic used to evaluate and to make economic and geopolitical predictions about a country or its subdivisions. Such measures are used to identify and analyze patterns and trends on a local to global scale. There are a number of indicators that provide insight into the economic development of a country. They include but are not limited to manufactured goods, construction spending, housing purchases and rentals, retail sales, international trade, inventories, investments, credit, unemployment and employment, wages, inflation, deflation, number of doctors, life expectancy, etc. (For more information, visit Investopedia at *https://www.investopedia.com/articles/personal-finance/020215/top-ten-us-economic-indicators.asp* or the U.S. Census Bureau at *https://www. census.gov/economic-indicators.*)

Some economic indicators provide more comprehensive, aggregate data about a country's economy; among them are gross domestic product (GDP), gross national product (GNP), and the purchase power of parity (PPP). Four broad sectors are used to calculate economic output (spending and production): consumers, businesses (investments), government, and foreign sectors. The *gross domestic product (GDP)* is the total market value of a country's goods and services produced within the country's borders (domestically) over a specific amount of time. On the other hand, the *gross national product (GNP)* is the total market value of goods and services produced both domestically and abroad. For example, GNP includes data from McDonald's restaurant chain revenue in countries outside the United States, while GDP does not include such statistics.

The *purchase power of parity (PPP)* is yet another indicator used to compare countries' economic strength. PPP basically recalculates a country's goods and services to that of another country as if they were using the same currency. For example, McDonald's standard for their products is consistent regardless of location. But there are economic variables across jurisdictions. For example, in December 2020, the Big Mac in the U.S. was $5.66 USD compared to 22.4 yuan in China, which calculates to $3.47 USD. Governments use PPP to compare and contrast the output (goods and services) of countries with different exchange rates. However, PPP has limitations, as a number of factors must be considered, such as varying costs, tariffs, taxes, fluctuating exchange rates, access to international trade, services, etc.). On the other hand, awareness of these indicators provides unique insight that furthers understanding of people and their systems of government around the world. Overall, GDP is most commonly used to compare global economies. (For more information see *https://www.thebalance.com/purchasing-power-parity-3305953, https://www.britannica. com/topic/gross-domestic-product, https://www.britannica.com/topic/gross-national-product*, and *https://www.investopedia.com/ask/answers/030415/what-functional-difference-between-gdp-and-gnp.asp.*)

Economic Interdependence

Interdependence is the idea that you as an individual depend on other people for certain things. Within economies, there is a natural web of interdependence on others for some needs because no one country can produce everything they need. There is also a web of interdependence among economies. Visit Social Studies for Kids for more: *http://www.socialstudiesforkids.com/articles/economics/interdependence.htm.*

Economic Systems

Because resources are scarce and wants are unlimited, societies often devise economic systems to help regulate this divide between demand and supply. Economic systems are generally created based on three important questions:

1. What goods and services to produce?

2. How to produce these goods and services?

3. How are these goods and services allocated?

The way a society answers these questions determines the type of economic system they will create. The three main economic systems are:

1. Free enterprise or market economy (also referred to as capitalism)

2. Communism (or centrally planned economies)[5]

3. Socialism (or mixed economies)

Market Economy, or Free Enterprise

Free enterprise is an economic and political doctrine of the capitalist system. The concept is based on the premise that the economy can regulate itself in a freely competitive market through the relationship of supply and demand, and with minimum governmental intervention. This economic system allows entrepreneurship, or individually owned and operated businesses. One of the main benefits of free enterprise is the competition among businesses. This results in a greater choice and better prices for consumers as well as in increased specialization and trade. Americans believe strongly in equal opportunities for all. All citizens expect to be given an equal chance to succeed. Individual ownership and engagement in the free-market system comes with the responsibility and importance of employing moral and ethical business practices. The federal government

---

[5] **Note:** Although *communism* is sometimes used to describe both an economic and political system in the context of strong government control, meaning that the government gives little power to the citizens of the country, it is more appropriately used to describe a system of government, i.e., an example of a totalitarian regime. This can be confusing for students. Be sure to be clear how you phrase your discussion with students. For more information, see *https://www.britannica.com/topic/command-economy.*

sometimes needs to step in to protect workers, small businesses, and the consumer. For example, business cannot discriminate, or treat someone differently, based on such things as skin color, ethnicity, or gender. The United States government is also supposed to safeguard small business by preventing monopolies, which occur when one business controls part of the market. The U.S. government tries to encourage small businesses to flourish. Additionally, regulations are laws that require businesses to use safe practices. For example, in the early 20th century, President Theodore Roosevelt pushed through a meat inspection act to make sure that meat is packaged properly to prevent people from getting sick. The Food and Drug Administration now requires additional information, such as the expiration date, to inform consumers about a product.

The three questions of economic systems are answered in the marketplace by the interaction of buyers and sellers. One of the main benefits of the system of free enterprise is the competition among businesses that results in a greater choice and better prices for consumers. The system of free enterprise has led to **globalization**. Globalization can be defined as a continuous increase of cross-border financial, economic, and social activities. It implies some level of economic interdependence among individuals, financial entities, and nations. As a result of globalization, trade barriers have been eliminated and tariffs imposed on imported products have been largely discontinued. In a global market, it is difficult to determine the origins of products. For example, Japan-based Toyota, and U.S.-based Ford joined forces to build cars using parts and labor from Mexico. The concept of **economic interdependence** describes a positive, close connection between producers and consumers of goods and services within a nation or across nations. This economic interdependence has guided nations to establish large markets of free trade zones like the European Union (EU) trade agreement and the North American Free Trade Agreement (NAFTA) for Canada, Mexico, and the United States. The European Union went a step further; in 2002 they adopted a common currency for the Union—the *euro*. This alliance has resulted in the euro's ranking as one of the strongest currencies in the world.

Centrally Planned or Command Economy

The opposite of a market or free enterprise economy is called a **centrally planned economy**, also referred to as a command economy or centralized economy. In a planned economy, supply and price are regulated by the government rather than market forces (i.e., the interaction between consumers and businesses). Government planners answer the three questions of economic systems and decide which goods and services are produced and how they are distributed. Most planned economies direct resources into the production of capital and military goods leaving little resources for consumer goods. A planned economy discourages individualistic profit motives and consumeristic needs.

A **command economy** is the extreme form of a planned economy that discourages individualistic profit motives and consumeristic needs. Under such a planned system, rewards, wages, and perks are distributed based on the social value of the service performed. Certain sectors get preferential allocation at the expense of others, which may lead to shortages in some essential goods. Absence of profit motives precludes any need for competitiveness. This acts as a disincentive in individual contribution to collective efforts. The former Soviet Union was an example of a command economy. China also has a command economy, but, in recent years, it has brought changes allowing for some form of more open economies in certain regions. Today, countries using a command economy are rare. Remaining examples of countries with a command economy include Cuba and North Korea.

Mixed Economies

In between market and planned economies are mixed economies. A mixed economy, also referred to as a **socialist economy** or **socialism**, is an economic system that answers the three questions both in the marketplace and in the government. It is a system in which the central government controls the production and distribution of goods, services, and labor to some degree. Economic systems can be viewed as part of a continuum moving from strict government control (a command or communist economy) to one with little or no government control (free enterprise or market economy). Mixed, or socialist, economies can be anywhere along the continuum, in between command and market economies. Planning is usually used to direct resources at the upper levels of the economy, with markets being used to determine prices of consumer goods and wages. The former Yugoslavia was a mixed economy. Although the United States government plays a role in our economy, a mixed economy usually involves producers working closer with the government than they do in the United States, so the U.S. economic system is still a market economy.

Money and Banking

Under the presidency of Woodrow Wilson, the **Federal Reserve System** was established in 1913. The main purpose of this institution is to keep the banking industry strong to ensure a supply of currency. The Federal Reserve is run by the Federal Reserve Board of Governors, a seven-member body appointed to a four-year term, with the option of being reappointed to a maximum of 14-year terms. The main function of the Fed, as it is commonly called, is to promote monetary stability and economic growth in the nation and to regulate inflation and deflation. The Board of Governors controls the flow of money and sets the interest rate that banks use to lend money. They increase the interest rate to control inflation and lower the interest rate when business slows down. To learn more about the Federal Reserve System go to *http://www.federalreserve.gov*.

Inflation and Deflation

Inflation reduces the purchasing power of money, which technically affects the value of the currency. Countries generally devalue their currency to keep up with inflation. Deflation is the opposite of inflation: the purchasing power of money increases, thereby lowering the prices of goods and services. In a period of deflation, consumers benefit but industry suffers. The Federal Reserve controls the flow of money and seeks to keep a healthy balance between inflation and deflation.

Government Regulations and Taxation

City, state, and national governments regulate businesses to ensure safe, fair, and consistent practices as well as to create a framework for standardizing production of certain products. Taxes support regulations by providing the money to pay people to inspect products and practices as well as to enforce sanctions. Regulations are important to build consumer trust. For example, children's toys are not allowed to use lead-based paint because a child may put a toy in his or her mouth and become sick. Taxes pay for inspectors to monitor toy manufacturers as well as the people who take these cases to court. Buildings are also examined during construction to check that the frame and materials are up to code. When businesses fail to comply with regulations, the owners are fined or in some cases put in jail. However, if the regulations are viewed as burdensome to businesses, it can be said that the regulations will negatively affect business development or be too great of a tax burden for the community. A careful balance must be struck between providing a safe, consistent product and being too restrictive and thereby hindering businesses.

American Federal Income Tax System

In 1913, the 16th Amendment to the U.S. Constitution allowed the imposition of direct taxation of citizens. This direct taxation is known as the **federal income tax**. Federal income tax dollars are used to fund various government agencies and projects.

Major Historical Events and Trends of State, National, and World Economies

It is important to understand the major events and trends that have shaped economic history. These events and trends helped create and shape the economic system of Texas, the United States, and the world.

Agricultural Revolution

The invention of the plow around 3500 BCE set in motion a significant transformation in the way people lived, and led to the agricultural revolution. The plow made mass agriculture possible and facilitated the development of agrarian societies. In addition to the plow, the invention of the wheel and formalized writing structures helped shift hunter/gatherer societies toward more agricultural societies that were self-sustaining.

The continued advances in agricultural technology led to the ability of societies to produce surplus goods. The surplus of goods created a trade market in which people trading their surpluses for other desired goods. As such, traders and trade routes developed between different communities and villages. Protecting these surplus goods became a prime concern of societies and led to the construction of fortified communities.

United States

Post-Civil War America witnessed a surge in farming as the West opened up and scientific discoveries and innovations improved crops and harvest yields. The number of farms tripled—from 2 million to 6 million—during the 50 years after the Civil War. The farms also grew in size, heralding an increase in commercial farming. Production of grain, cotton, beef, pork, and wool rapidly surpassed American needs, creating great surpluses to sell abroad. The number of land grant colleges expanded and focused on scientific farming. The growth of colleges and universities had a significant impact on the development of an educated populace. In addition, farm machinery was rapidly developing (e.g., automatic wire binder, threshing machine, planters, cutters, huskers, manure spreaders, poultry incubators and more). One of the earliest inventions, the reaper he first demonstrated in 1831 by **Cyrus McCormick** revolutionized harvesting crops. Global travel increased causing the diffusion of technology such as rust and drought-resistant winter wheat (Russia) and kaffir corn from North Africa. New scientific discoveries conquered illnesses such as hog cholera and hoof-and-mouth disease, while others developed new fruits and vegetables. The agriculture revolution in the United States paved the way for cities to grow (urbanization) and the U.S. to develop as an economic and geopolitical powerhouse. For more information, visit the U.S. Department of Agriculture at *https://www.usda.gov/sites/default/files/documents/history-american-agriculture.pdf.*

Texas

Texas identity is tied to the land. The Texas Agriculture Revolution reflects changes in America as well as a rich history of European and Native American influence. When Europeans first arrived in Texas, most Native Americans were nomadic, with a few advanced agriculture communities in the East (Caddo Indians) and the Far West (Pueblo cultures) that had permanent crops and some farming tools. The Spanish developed livestock industries focused on cattle, sheep, goats, and hogs. Active settlement campaigns of Mexico through empresario, or colonial, grants, that led to Moses Austin and Stephen Austin leading 300 families to central Texas. The American settlers introduced new crops and expanded commercial and small, subsistence farming. Small farming communities continued to flourish. From 1830–1860, plantations growing cotton expanded, as did the cattle industry. Cotton production soon led the Texas economy and Texas beef production fed people across the country. After the Civil War, the number of farms surged from 61,000 in 1870 to 350,000 by 1900, and land grant colleges and universities were established to research agriculture and natural resource production (e.g., oil). Inventions and scientific discoveries improved harvest yields and durability of crops. Texas production rivaled that of national output of global markets. Economic strength led the impressive development of the state as influential in the nation while enabling the state to be an independent political power. The focus on diversification, education, innovation, and science coupled with its strong connection with the land honed the independent, proud, and strong identity of Texas people. Today, farms continue to evolve with Global Positioning Systems (GPS) and satellite imagery. Technological innovations and scientific discoveries increase farm surplus and capability to sustain large urban populations, thus allowing the urban economic sectors to flourish. Today, land ownership is becoming increasingly centered on recreation, which is sustained by the robust agriculture and other economic markets. See also *https://texasheritageforliving.com/texas-living/a-history-of-texas-agriculture/* and *https://www.texasalmanac.com/articles/the-state-of-texas-agriculture*.

Industrial Revolution

The industrial revolution of the 18th and 19th centuries led to even greater changes in human societies and increased opportunities for trade, production, and the exchange of goods and ideas. The first phase of the industrial revolution (1750–1830) included improvements in mining, the invention of the steam engine, improvements in transportation including canals and railroads, and the mechanization of the textile industry. The second phase of the industrial revolution (1830–1910) resulted in improvement in the mechanization of a variety of industries. Important innovations of this time period included the Bessemer steel process, the steamship, electricity, photography, hydroelectric power, and petroleum engineering. It was during this phase of the industrial revolution that these ideas and inventions spread to the United States.

The industrial revolution led to some major economic shifts including: an increase in productivity, specialization and division of labor, increase in global trade, mass production, growth in large corporations and monopolies. During this time, ideas and knowledge spread rapidly with the increase in mobility. Additionally, immigration to industrialized countries also increased. As immigration increased, so did the clashing and blending of cultures. In the United States, as the economy grew and developed, people began spreading north, south, and westward. Each of these regions developed unique economic systems. The southern states had economies based primarily on agriculture, plantations, and slave labor. The North developed into a primarily industrial economy.

The Roaring Twenties Give Way to the Great Depression

Prior to World War I, the United States remained fairly isolationist with few trade partners. Following the war, international trade became an increasingly common reality for the United States. After the war, the U.S. economy of the "Roaring Twenties" saw huge increases in mass production. Manufacturing output doubled during this period from 1918–1929. The building and loan sector also saw a huge boom. The stock market was booming, with investors buying and selling with borrowed money, or, on margin. Unfortunately, when stock prices fell in 1929, many speculators could not meet their margin demands and this shortfall eventually led to the Great Depression.

The Great Depression (1929 to about 1939) had devastating effects in virtually every country. Personal income, tax revenue, profits and prices dropped, while international trade plunged by more than 50 percent. Unemployment in the United States rose to 25 percent, and in some countries went as high as 33 percent. Cities around the world were hit hard, especially those dependent on industry. Construction was virtually halted in many countries. Farming and rural areas suffered as crop prices fell by approximately 60 percent.

World War II (1939–1945)

As America prepared to enter World War II, the nation's wartime efforts demanded the production of various wartime goods and services. This demand for increased production also led to increased employment opportunities. World War II drove a dramatic increase in GDP, the export of vast quantities of supplies to the Allies and to American forces overseas, the end of unemployment, and a rise in civilian consumption even as 40 percent of the GDP went to the war effort. This was achieved by workers moving from low-productivity occupations to high-efficiency jobs, improvements in productivity through better technology and management, by students, retired people, housewives, and the unemployed moving into the active labor force, and an increase in hours worked. FDR's New Deal relief programs helped stabilize the economy. Most durable goods became unavailable, and meat, clothing, and gasoline were tightly rationed. In addition, prices and wages were controlled, and individual savings eventually increased as the war effort kicked manufacturing into high gear.

The Texas Economy

Texas continues to play a unique role in the U.S. economy and in the world. Texas interacts with other states and the national government through trade and commerce. Cattle, livestock, and agriculture were important factors in the development of the Texas economy. As railroads and cities developed, the Texas economy continued to expand. Dallas became a trading post for grain and cotton. Houston's port location was at the heart of the sugar trade and later the oil industry. In 1901, the discovery of oil at Spindletop also led to increased economic production in Texas as it became the leading producer of oil in the U.S. In the 1940s, the Texas economy continued to grow as major corporations relocated to Texas providing more jobs.

Today, the Texas economy is still highly bound up in agricultural and serves as the leading exporter of cattle and cotton in the U.S. High-tech industries, defense contracting, telecommunications, biotechnology, oil, and tourism are also important economic activities in Texas. A large percentage of these products are exported to NAFTA members—Mexico and Canada—and to world markets. The Texas economy relies heavily on exports of goods and services. Texas ranks as the No. 1 state in terms of export revenues. In 2022, Texas accounted for 20% of all U.S. exports. Without its exports, the Texas economy could not sustain its growth. Because of the interdependence of state and global economies, political turmoil and economic problems in the world can have a direct impact on the Texas economy. For example, because part of the economy of Texas is based on petroleum, the decisions of OPEC have a direct impact on the state's economy. The Texas economy weathered the Great Recession of 2008–2009 better than most states, but the unemployment rate in the state continued to climb even after the recession ended. In 2011, the jobless rate stood at almost 8.5 percent. Later, nonfarm employment found its footing again. With more factories and other businesses moving to the state, the housing market improved, especially in urban markets like the Dallas-Fort Worth area. In 2017, the unemployment rate stood at 4.8 percent, about half a percentage point higher than the national average. The largest employment sectors of Texas are retail trade, professional services, leisure and hospitality, and health care. Like the rest of the nation, Texas's economy was dealt a major blow by the rapid spread of Covid-19 in early 2020. The pandemic begat a widespread economic shutdown that gripped the state, and the nation, for months afterward. Nevertheless, in 2021, the Texas economy was listed as the ninth largest in the world by GDP, meaning that it was larger than that of many countries. The largest employment sectors of Texas are retail trade, professional services, leisure and hospitality and health care, all of which were hit hard by the pandemic. Though Texans mounted a post-pandemic recovery whose pace was stronger than the U.S. as a whole, signs of a possible slowdown hung over the state (as did the possibility of a nationwide recession) in late 2022, even as the state continued to see employment expansion well above historical averages. For more information on the Texas economy, visit *http://www.dallasfed.org*.

COMPETENCY 004: GOVERNMENT AND CITIZENSHIP

The teacher understands and applies knowledge of government, democracy, and citizenship, including ways in which individuals and groups achieve their goals through political systems, as defined by the Texas Essential Knowledge and Skills (TEKS).

The beginning teacher:

A. Demonstrates knowledge of the historical origins of democratic forms of government, such as ancient Greece.

B. Understands the purpose of rules and laws; the relationship between rules, rights, and responsibilities; and the individual's role in making and enforcing rules and ensuring the welfare of society.

C. Knows the basic structure and functions of the U.S. government, the Texas government and local governments (including the roles of public officials) and relationships among national, state, and local governments.

D. Demonstrates knowledge of key principles and ideas in major political documents of Texas and the United States (e.g., Articles of Confederation, Declaration of Independence, U.S. Constitution, Bill of Rights, Texas Constitution) and relationships among political documents.

E. Understands early United States political issues, including those surrounding Alexander Hamilton, Patrick Henry, James Madison, George Mason; the arguments of the Federalists and Anti-Federalists; states' rights issues; and the nullification crisis.

F. Knows how American Indian groups and settlers organized governments in precolonial America, and during the early development of Texas and North America.

G. Demonstrates knowledge of how state and local governments use sources of revenue such as property tax and sales tax, and the funding of Texas public education.

H. Demonstrates knowledge of types of government (e.g., constitutional, totalitarian), their effectiveness in meeting citizens' needs, and the reasons for limiting the power of government.

I. Knows the formal and informal process of changing the U.S. and Texas constitutions and the impact of constitutional changes on society.

J. Understands the impact of landmark Supreme Court cases (e.g., *Marbury v. Madison*, *Dred Scott v. Sandford*, *McCulloch v. Maryland*, *Gibbons v. Ogden*).

K. Understands components of the democratic process (e.g., voting, contacting local and state representatives, voluntary individual participation, effective leadership, expression of different points of view) and their significance in a democratic society.

L. Demonstrates knowledge of important customs, symbols, landmarks, and celebrations that represent American and Texan beliefs and principles and that contribute to national unity (e.g., Uncle Sam, "The Star-Spangled Banner," the San Jacinto Monument, "Texas, our Texas").

M. Demonstrates knowledge of the importance, accomplishments, and leadership qualities of United States and Texas leaders (e.g., presidents Washington, Adams, Jefferson, Madison, Monroe, Lincoln; U.S. senators Calhoun, Webster, Clay; Texas governors and local Texas representatives).

N. Analyzes the relationship among individual rights, responsibilities, and freedoms in democratic societies.

O. Applies knowledge of the nature, rights, and responsibilities of citizens in Texas, the United States, and various societies, past and present.

P. Understands the contributions and importance of political figures, members of Congress, military leaders, and social reformers who modeled active participation in the democratic process in Texas and in the United States (e.g., Frederick Douglass, Susan B. Anthony, Sam Houston, Barbara Jordan, Henry B. González, Kay Bailey Hutchinson, Audie Murphy, William Carney, Philip Bazaar).

Forms of Government

Forms of government or political systems can be defined by the way nations govern themselves. The U.S. Department of State identifies 26 forms of governments in the world (CIA, n.d.). Three of the most common forms of government are democracy, monarchy, and totalitarian. A description of these types of government follows:

- **Democracy** is a form of government in which the majority rules. The government's power is limited, meaning that a constitution, or agreement with the people, delineates the authority that the government is allowed. Citizens in this government enjoy an abundance of civil liberties. In the United States, these civil liberties are unique because they are called "inalienable rights," meaning that they cannot be ever taken away from the citizens by the government or any other entity. Though rare, pure democracies, a form of government in which each individual votes on all decisions, exist in some places. In the United States, pure democracies are still used in some town hall meetings, where people meet to make decisions for their municipality. In practice, it becomes a representative democracy, in which the people elect candidates to represent them in the government. Democratic governments typically have either free enterprise or socialist economies.

- **Monarchy** is a system in which a king or queen leads the nation. The monarch gains power by inheriting it from his or her parents. The monarch can have supreme powers and control the entire government, or he or she can have limited or ceremonial powers circumscribed by a parliament or a constitution, as in a constitutional monarchy.

- **Totalitarian** is a form of government in which one person or a few people have all of the governing power and authority. The central government controls nearly all aspects of its citizens' political, social, cultural, and economic lives, including education, employment, housing, reproduction, and movement. This form of government typically has either a communist or socialist economic system. Additionally, citizens have few individual rights, while the government has unlimited rights. It can also be in the form of an oligarchy. Incidences of human rights violations, or abuses, are typically more frequent under this government. **Note:** Sometimes a totalitarian government is referred to as a communist government or a communist state. This means it is a country in which the state (government) controls the economic activity in the nation. The state rejects free enterprise; consequently, private ownership is discouraged and often prohibited. (See Economics section for more about communism.)

There are three broad classifications or forms of government based on the number of people in power—government by one person, a group, or by many people, and vary regarding the degree of limitations and freedom citizens experience.

Rule by One

In this form of government, one person becomes the supreme leader of the nation. Some of the terminology and concepts linked to this type of government are:

- **Autocracy:** Ruler has unlimited power, uses power in an arbitrary manner.

- **Monarchy:** A system in which a king or queen leads the nation. The monarch can have supreme powers and hold complete control over the subjects. Typically, the ruler is determined by birth or divine rights. Titles of monarchs may be King/Queen, Emperor/Empress, Tsar/Tsarina, etc. (For monarchs who have limited or ceremonial powers determined by a parliament or a constitution, see the section below titled "Ruled by Many, Parliamentarian Monarchy.")

- **Dictatorship:** The ruler holds absolute power to make laws and to command the army.

Ruled by a Few

In this system, a group of influential people takes control of the government. Traditionally, they appoint one of their own to function as the supreme leader of the government. Some examples of this type of government are:

- **Theocracy:** Ruled by a group of religious leaders, e.g., the Islamic Republic in Iran, or, the Taliban in Afghanistan.

- **Aristocracy:** A group of nobles controls the economy and the government.

- **Oligarchy:** A small group of people controls the government. Generally, power rests with an elite class distinguished by royalty, wealth, family ties, commercial, and/or military legitimacy.

- **Military:** A committee of military officers or a junta becomes the rulers of the nation.

Rule by Many

In this government, the citizens technically are the government because they make the decisions for the community being governed (e.g., cultural group, town, state, or nation). This is called a democracy. In its purest form, each person participates in voting on each decision made for the community. In practice, the citizens elect members to represent them and elected officials become the government. This is called a representative democracy. Today, most democracies are also a constitutional democracy, meaning that they are regulated by a constitution. Examples of representative governments include constitutional democracy and parliamentarian (or constitutional) monarchy.

The historical origins of democratic governance can be found in Ancient Greece where the cultures participated in pure and representational democracy and developed a court system with a jury. More information about Ancient Greece and the roots of democracy can be found online at *http://www.history.com/topics/ancient-history/ancient-greece-democracy*.

Some examples of this type of government are:

- **Democracy:** A form of government in which the majority rules. The citizens of the nation directly or through elected members make important decisions, and become part of the government. In practice, it becomes a representative democracy, in which the people elect candidates to represent them in the government.

- **Republic:** A representative democracy is led by someone who is not a monarch, such as a president. Example: the United States of America.

- **Constitutional Democracy:** It is a democratic form of government regulated by a constitution.

- **Parliamentarian Monarchy:** The monarch shares the power with the parliament. Often, the powers of the monarch are ceremonial in nature, like in the United Kingdom. This government is also referred to as a "constitutional monarchy" because the monarch's power is limited by the constitution for the given country.

- **Federal Republic:** A constitutional government in which the powers of the central government are restricted to create semi-autonomous bodies (states or provinces) with certain degrees of self-governing powers, e.g., the United States.

Government Power Structure

The structure of the governmental power can be designed so that either almost all of the decision-making capabilities are held within the centralized government (unitary government), such as the United Kingdom, or the power is shared between the central and local governing bodies (federal government), such as the United States.

The American Government

The governmental system of the United States has been identified as a federal republic and a constitutional representative democracy. It is a federal republic because the U.S. government is limited by law; in this case, the government is limited by the Constitution. It is a constitutional representative democracy because the citizens elect members of Congress to represent them in the bicameral (two house) system. (Senators are elected to the Senate. Representatives are elected to the House of Representatives. Both houses, together, are referred to as Congress.) This combination is referred to as a Constitutional Republic in the revised social studies TEKS.

The American democratic system is based on popular sovereignty. **Popular sovereignty** grants citizens the ability to participate directly in their own government by voting and running for public office. This ideal is based on the notion that all citizens have equal rights to engage in their own governance. Certainly, over time, this notion of equal rights has expanded to include a respect for minority rights, including women and ethnic minority citizens.

The American government is also based on majority rule. In public elections, the candidate who receives the most votes wins; in Congress, legislation is decided based on how the majority of the body votes. Majority rule ensures that authority cannot be concentrated in a small group of people. This majority rule system also shapes the two-party system of the U.S. government. There are two major political parties in the U.S.: the Republican and Democratic parties.

The Constitution is the supreme law of the nation. It contains a description of the government and the rights and responsibilities of its citizens. The document can be amended with the approval of two-thirds of the House and the Senate and the ratification of individual state legislatures. Amendments to the U.S. Constitution have made it more democratic than the original document.

Effective leadership in a constitutional republic is critical for the success of the country. The leader must collaborate with opposing parties to make the best possible decisions for the nation. The following links list U.S. presidents and Texas governors and describes their term in office *http://www.whitehouse.gov/about/presidents* and *https://www.tsl.texas.gov/ref/abouttx/governors.* Students can look up their members of Congress at *https://www.govtrack.us/congress/members.* To develop a better understanding of effective leadership, teachers can ask students to compare and contrast leaders, the decisions they made, and the long-term impact of those decisions.

The U.S. Constitution

The Constitution is the supreme law of the nation. It contains a description of the government and the rights and responsibilities of its citizens. The document can be amended with the approval of two-thirds of the House and the Senate and the ratification of three-fourths of the individual state legislatures. Amendments to the U.S. Constitution have made it more democratic than the original document. The first ten amendments to the Constitution are known as the Bill of Rights. For more on the Constitution go to *https://www.archives.gov/founding-docs/constitution.*

The U.S. Constitution was based on four fundamental principles, which are listed below.

1. *Federalism:* This is a system in which government powers are divided between the national and state governments. This established four types of governmental powers: (1) delegated or expressed—those directly listed; (2) implied powers—those not stated directly but suggested; (3) reserved powers—those not given to the national government but reserved for the people or for the states; and (4) concurrent powers—given to both national and state governments at the same time.

2. *Separation of Powers:* This constitutional principle is based on a system of checks and balances. The constitutional writers wanted to protect their new nation from tyranny or the possibility of one branch of government becoming more powerful and influential than another. Thus, they created a three-branch system of separation of powers and checks and balances.

3. *Protection of individual rights and liberties:* These provisions of the Constitution include: the prohibition of "ex post facto laws," or laws passed after the crime was committed, providing the penalty for an act that was not illegal at the time it was committed, and "bills of attainder," or laws that mete out punishment to someone without a court trial first. Individual rights are protected through the "writ of habeas corpus" that required persons be released from jail if they had not been formally charged or convicted of a

crime. The Bill of Rights also guarantees protection of individuals against federal action that would threaten their life, liberty, or property without proper legal proceedings.

4. *Adaptation to changing times and circumstances:* This allows governing bodies to meet the needs of changing times through the process of amendments. The necessary and proper or elastic clause also provides Congress the power to make additional laws needed to implement other powers.

In the United States, the national government makes decisions for the benefit of the country as a whole (e.g., laws, coin money, regulate trade and commerce, protection of rights, foreign affairs, declaration of war, banking regulations, education, taxation, postal services, etc.). Each state government makes decisions pertaining to the people and businesses within its borders. These include elections, business regulations, education, taxation, transportation and communication, and so on. The national, or federal, government's powers are delineated in the U.S. Constitution. All powers not mentioned belong to the states. Local governments provide direct governance of the people in an immediate area. Many duties of local government mirror those of the state (taxation, communication, transportation, business regulation, etc.) on a smaller scale. State legislatures determine local governments' power. The official White House website (*http://www.whitehouse.gov/our-government/executive-branch*) provides more details about the federal government. Government responsibilities and programs are largely funded by taxes. All Americans contribute a portion of their paycheck to the federal income tax. Each state decides whether to allow state and local taxes. Texas has no state and local taxes. Governments can also issue bonds, which are a mechanism to allow the government to borrow money from its citizens or from other countries. According to the U.S. Department of the Treasury, the U.S. outstanding debt was $23,861,554,218,139.08 (approximately $23.86 trillion) as of May 17, 2022. For updated information, consult the U.S. Treasury website at *https://fiscaldata.treasury.gov/datasets/debt-to-the-penny/debt-to-the-penny*.

Federalism: Power Sharing Between State and Federal Governments

One of the most significant principles of the U.S. Constitution is the concept of power sharing between the federal and state governments. Some of the powers reserved to the federal and state governments follow.

Powers Reserved for the Federal Government

- Regulate interstate and foreign commerce

- Print money and regulate its value

- Establish laws for regulation of immigration and naturalization

- Regulate admission of new states

- Declare war and ratify peace treaties

- Establish a system of weights and measures

- Raise and maintain armed forces

- Conduct relations with foreign nations

Powers Reserved for State Governments

- Conduct and monitor local, state, and federal elections

- Provide for local government

- Ratify proposed amendments to the Constitution

- Regulate intrastate commerce

- Provide education for its citizens

- Establish direct taxes like sales and state taxes

- Regulate and maintain police power over public health and safety

- Maintain control of state borders

Concurrent Powers of Federal and State Governments

- Both may tax

- Both may borrow money

- Both may charter banks and corporations

- Both may establish courts

- Both may make and enforce laws

- Both may take property for public purposes

- Both may spend money to provide for public welfare

In addition to the powers reserved to the states, the Tenth Amendment to the U.S. Constitution provides additional powers to the state. In this amendment, the powers not specifically delegated to the federal government are reserved for the states.

Separation of Powers: Branches of Government

The U.S. Constitution set up a federal system of government, dividing up power between the state and national governments. The national government is further balanced through the three branches of government that provide checks and balances on each other's power. The three branches of government are the executive, legislative, and judicial branches. To learn more, go to *https://www.usa.gov/branches-of-government*. Each of the branches is described in more detail below.

Executive Branch

The executive branch of the U.S. government is composed of a president and a vice president elected every four years by electoral votes. The president can be elected for a maximum of two terms. The president is the commander-in-chief of the armed forces. He or she appoints cabinet members, nominates judges to the federal court system, grants pardons, recommends legislation, and has the power to veto legislation. The president also appoints American representatives to carry out diplomatic relations in foreign lands and to serve in international organizations. The president also performs a variety of ceremonial duties.

Legislative Branch

The legislative branch is composed of the Congress, which is bicameral, or divided into two parts—the Senate and the House of Representatives. The Senate is composed of two senators from each state, for a total of a 100 members. Senators are elected for six-year terms. The composition of the House is based on the population of people in each state, for a total of 435 members, who each serve two-year terms. The Congress makes the laws of the nation, collects taxes, coins money and regulates its value, can declare war, controls appropriations, can impeach public officials, regulates the jurisdictions of federal courts, and can override presidential vetoes. The vice president presides over the Senate as its leader, while the Speaker of the House serves as the leader of the House of Representatives.

Judicial Branch

The judicial branch is composed of a federal court system that includes the Supreme Court and a system of lower courts—district courts, appeals courts, bankruptcy courts, and special federal courts. Federal judges are nominated by the president of the United States and confirmed by the Senate. All federal judges are appointed for life. The Supreme Court is composed of nine judges, and their ruling is considered final. Under a process called "judicial review" (set forth in *Marbury v. Madison*, 1803), the Supreme Court has the power to declare unconstitutional any executive orders or legislative acts of both the federal and state governments. Some of the major responsibilities of this body are to interpret the Constitution, resolve conflicts among states, and interpret laws and treaties.

System of Checks and Balances

The U.S. Constitution provides for a system of checks and balances among the three branches of the government. In this type of system, individual branches check the others to be sure that no one branch assumes full control of the central government. The legislative branch can check the executive branch by passing laws over presidential veto (by a two-thirds majority in both houses). This branch exerts control over the judicial branch by having to confirm the president's judicial appointments. The executive can check the legislative branch by the use of the veto and the judicial branch by appointing federal judges. The judicial branch can check the other two branches through the process of judicial review, which can declare legislation unconstitutional or illegal.

Protection of Individual Rights and Liberties: The Bill of Rights

After the U.S. Constitution was enacted in 1783, the founders felt that additional measures were necessary to preserve basic human rights. The first 10 amendments to the U.S. Constitution are called the **Bill of Rights**. A summary of those 10 amendments follows:

- *First Amendment*—separation of church and state; freedom of religion, speech and press; and the right to peaceful assembly

- *Second Amendment*—right to keep and bear arms

- *Third Amendment*—makes it illegal to force people to offer quarters to soldiers in time of peace

- *Fourth Amendment*—rights to privacy and unreasonable searches or seizures

- *Fifth Amendment*—rights of due process, protection against self-incrimination, and protection from being indicted for the same crime twice (double jeopardy)

- *Sixth Amendment*—rights to speedy public trial by an impartial jury and to counsel for one's defense

- *Seventh Amendment*—right to sue people

- *Eighth Amendment*—protection against cruel and unusual punishment

- *Ninth Amendment*—enumeration of specific rights in the Constitution cannot be taken as a way to deny other rights retained by the people

- *Tenth Amendment*—rights not delegated to the federal government by the Constitution are reserved to the states or to the people

Adapting to Change: The Amendment Process

When the Constitution was written, the writers knew their creation was not perfect. They knew that new ideas and changes would need to be considered. They wanted to make it possible to change the Constitution through a thoughtful and democratic process. Thus, the Constitution provides for an amendment process. An amendment to the Constitution is a change that can add to the Constitution or change a part of it. An amendment can even overturn a previous amendment, as the 21st Amendment overturned the 18th Amendment. There are several methods to amend the Constitution, but the most common is to pass an amendment through the Congress, on a two-thirds vote. After that, the amendment goes to the states; if three-quarters of the state legislatures pass the amendment, it has been ratified and is considered a part of the Constitution. To date, there are 27 amendments to the Constitution; the first 10 comprise the Bill of Rights.

Additional Key Amendments to the U.S. Constitution

- **13th Amendment**—Slavery abolished

- **14th Amendment**—Citizenship and rights: Citizenship to African-Americans including former slaves; reaffirmed privileges and rights for all citizens

- **15th Amendment**—Race, color, or previous servitude/No bar to vote: Right to vote for African American males

- **16th Amendment**—Ratified in 1913, it gives the federal government power to levy taxes

- **19th Amendment**—Women's suffrage (right to vote)

- **25th Amendment**—Presidential disability and succession

- **26th Amendment**—Voting age set to 18 years

For a detailed analysis of the U.S. Constitution and the 27 amendments, see the U.S. Constitution online at *http://www.usconstitution.net/const.html*.

Landmark Supreme Court Cases

Judicial Review Process—*Marbury v. Madison* (1803)

A dispute that occurred as the Thomas Jefferson administration came into power fundamentally altered the system of checks and balances of the American government. In this case, the judicial branch confirmed its power to review and assess the constitutionality of the legislation passed by Congress and signed by the president. This process is now called *judicial review*.

National Supremacy—*McCulloch v. Maryland* (1819)

A dispute occurred between the Bank of the United States and the State of Maryland in 1819. At that time, the United States still had a federal bank, the Bank of the United States (which has since died out). The State of Maryland voted to tax all bank business not done with state banks. This was meant to be a tax on people who lived in Maryland but did business with banks in other states, and with the federal bank. Andrew McCulloch, who worked in the Baltimore branch of the Bank of the United States, refused to pay the tax. The State of Maryland sued, and the Supreme Court accepted the case. Chief Justice Marshall wrote in his opinion that the federal government did indeed have the right and power to set up the federal bank. He wrote that the state did not have the power to tax the federal government.

Federal Regulation of Commerce—*Gibbons v. Ogden* (1824)

The New York Legislature in 1808 granted Robert Livingston and Robert Fulton a 20-year monopoly to operate steamboats in New York waters. In 1811, Fulton in turn granted Aaron Ogden a license to operate steamboats between New York and New Jersey. In 1818, the U.S. Congress, using the power given it by the commerce clause of Article I, Section 8 of the Constitution, granted Thomas Gibbons a license to engage in the coastal trade and operate steamboats between New York and New Jersey. Claiming that his monopoly rights were being violated, Ogden obtained an injunction from a New York court forbidding Gibbons from continuing to operate his steamboats in these U.S. Supreme Court. The majority opinion, written by Chief Justice Marshall, said that the U.S. Constitution had a commerce clause that allowed the federal government to regulate commerce, in this case trade, wherever it might be, including within the borders of a state. Previously, it was thought that the federal government had power over only *interstate commerce*. However, Marshall's opinion said that the commerce clause applied here, too. Thus, the Supreme Court extended the definition of interstate commerce and cemented the power of the federal government over the states when laws conflicted.

Federal vs. States Rights in Indian Affairs—*Worcester v. Georgia* (1832)

In December 1829, President Andrew Jackson announced his Indian removal proposal in an address to the U.S. Congress. In 1830, the Congress passed the Indian Removal Act, which authorized the president to grant the Indians unsettled lands west of the Mississippi River in exchange for Indian lands within existing state borders. The Georgia legislature had passed a law requiring anyone other than Cherokees who lived on Indian territory to obtain a license from the state. Samuel Worcester and several other non-Cherokee Congregational missionaries settled and established a mission on Cherokee land at the request of the Cherokees, and with permission of the United States government. The state of Georgia charged them with residing within the limits of the Cherokee nation without a license. They were tried, convicted, and sentenced to four years of hard labor. Worcester and the other missionaries appealed their convictions to the U.S. Supreme Court. The Supreme Court ruled in favor of Worcester and the Cherokees arguing that the Cherokee nation was a "distinct community" with self-government "in which the laws of Georgia can have no force." It established the doctrine that the national government of the United States, and not individual states, had authority in American Indian affairs.

Slavery/Due Process—*Dred Scott v. Sandford* (1857)

Dred Scott, a slave in Virginia, was moved by his owner to Illinois, a non-slave (free) state. In 1836, they moved to Minnesota, which was part of the non-slave Wisconsin territory, before being moved to Missouri. Then, Dred Scott sued his owners, claiming that he was no longer a slave because he had become free when he lived in a free state. The jury decided that Scott and his family should be free. His owners did not like the decision and appealed to the Missouri Supreme Court in 1852. That court said that Missouri does not have to follow the laws of another state. As a slave state, Missouri's laws meant that Scott and his family were not free. Scott finally took his case to the U.S. Supreme Court, which ruled that Scott and all other slaves were not state or U.S. citizens, and thus had no rights. A slave was considered property, not a person or a citizen. Thus, Scott or any other slave, had no right to sue in state or federal court. Further, the court ruled that the federal government had no legal right to interfere with the institution of slavery.

Separate but Equal—*Plessy v. Ferguson* (1896)

In 1890, Louisiana passed a law called the Separate Car Act. This law said that railroad companies must provide separate but equal train cars for whites and Blacks. Two parties wanted to challenge the constitutionality of the Separate Car Act. A group of Black citizens who raised money to overturn the law worked together with the East Louisiana Railroad Company, which sought to terminate the law largely for monetary reasons. They chose a 30-year-old shoemaker named Homer Plessy, a citizen of the United States who was one-eighth Black and a resident of the state of Louisiana. On June 7, 1892, Plessy purchased a first-class passage from New Orleans to Covington, Louisiana, and sat in the railroad car for white passengers. The railroad officials knew Plessy was coming and arrested him for violating the Separate Car Act. Plessy argued in court that the Separate Car Act violated the 13th and 14th Amendments to the Constitution. The 13th Amendment banned slavery and the 14th Amendment requires that the government treat people equally. After both a lower court and the Supreme Court of Louisiana found Plessy guilty, he took his case to the Supreme Court of the United States. The high court upheld the decisions of the two lower courts, arguing that separate but equal practices were constitutional. This decision legitimized the move toward segregation practices begun earlier in the South and provided an impetus for further segregation laws.

Desegregation—*Brown v. Board of Education of Topeka* (1954)

In the early 1950s, many students went to different schools based on their race. Many other public facilities were also segregated. Segregation was legal because of the *Plessy v. Ferguson* case. Under segregation, all-white and all-Black schools sometimes had similar buildings, buses, and teachers. Sometimes, the buildings, busses, and teachers for the all-Black schools were lower in quality. Often, Black children had to travel far to get to their school. In Topeka, Kansas, a Black student named Linda Brown had to walk through a dangerous railroad switching station to get to her all-Black school. Her family believed that segregated schools should be illegal. The Brown family sued the school system (Board of Education of Topeka). After losing their cases in two lower courts, the Browns took their case to the U.S. Supreme Court, which unanimously ruled that "separate educational facilities are inherently unequal." This case paved the way for integration and the civil rights movement.

Local and State Governments

Most states in the United States follow the type of government established for the federal government in the U.S. Constitution. State governments generally have three branches—executive, legislative, and judicial. The main difference is that the executive branch is led by a governor and the judicial branch is composed of a state court system subordinate to the federal court system. The city government is generally headed by a mayor or city manager with the support of a city council.

Citizenship in the U.S.

Citizenship is membership in a political state such as a country or state. Citizenship confers the right to participate politically in a society. Anyone born in the United States is a U.S. citizen, regardless of the nationality or citizenship of his or her parents. Additionally, children who are born on foreign soil, but whose parents are U.S. citizens, are also citizens of the United States.

Citizenship in the United States provides individuals with certain rights, including the right to life, liberty, and the pursuit of property. Along with rights, however, come specific responsibilities. In the United States, citizens have the right to vote at the age of 18. With this right comes the responsibility to be an informed voter who makes wise decisions. Citizens of the U.S. are also eligible to run for public office. With this right comes the responsibility of representing one's constituents as well as possible. The right to free speech is also given to citizens of the United States. This means that citizens also have the responsibility to allow others to speak freely. Additionally, the U.S. Constitution guarantees freedom of religion. This means that citizens have both the right to choose their religious affiliation and the responsibility to allow others to practice their religion. Being a good citizen means exercising one's own rights, meeting one's responsibilities, and allowing others to do the same.

Citizenship rights and responsibilities in Texas and the United States include obeying local, state, and national laws; paying taxes; and voting in elections. Good citizens should also develop a respect that recognizes and values the feelings, interests, beliefs, and values of others. While citizenship involves being respectful of one another and obeying the laws of the land, it does not mean that we need to teach students to simply comply and conform. Dissent is an important part in any governmental system and provides necessary checks and balances on governmental authority. Dissent may be expressed in a number of ways, including voting, protesting, writing to one's legislator, etc. Certainly, there are some forms of dissent that are more socially and politically acceptable.

The development of civic ideas and practices is a lifelong process that begins in school by observing patriotic holidays, learning about the contribution of historical characters, and pledging allegiance to the American and Texas flags each day, unless excused. Students should develop foundational knowledge about what each pledge means, as well as the history of their development and why the pledges are important to American citizens. In this way, saying the pledge will be meaningful rather than rote memorization and recitation of words that students do not understand. In lower elementary, encouraging good citizenship continues with the introduction of the American anthem and the mottoes of Texas and the United States, which should be reinforced in later grades as well. Civic education and the principles of democracy are infused through active participation in community activities. To promote civic responsibility, students can get involved in discussions about issues that affect the community. Teachers guide students to suggest possible solutions to community problems, while students are guided to listen and analyze contributions. Through this exchange, students are guided to practice principles of democracy and to value individual contributions to solve community problems.

Children in these grade levels should be developing **civic responsibility**. Teachers can promote this sense of responsibility by involving students in real-life situations in which they take civic responsibility. For example, teachers can make children aware of how producing trash can affect the environment. As part of this process, students can be guided to examine the amount of trash that they produce daily and explore ways to reduce it. Promoting a sense of responsibility for the well-being of everyone constitutes the main principle for developing responsible citizenship.

Additionally, students should define "civic responsibility" (referred to in early grades as a "good citizen") and connect their definition with historical and contemporary examples from the community, state, and nation. Americans value such things as recognizing social responsibilities; helping each other; making sure everyone has food, shelter, and clothing; caring for the elderly; keeping the land clean; using things wisely; caring for others; being patriotic; respecting our men and women in uniform (e.g., military, police, firefighters); respecting our state and country flags and what they symbolize; and so on. Teachers can invite speakers from such organizations as food pantries, the Red Cross, the League of Women Voters, Boy Scouts, Girl Scouts, and Meals on Wheels to show examples of good citizenship. Interdisciplinary service learning can be developed to help students explore this topic in-depth. Students can investigate ways that good citizens keep the land clean via recycling as well as with larger projects. For example, Chad Pregracke as a teenager was concerned about the trash in the Mississippi River. Realizing no one else was going to clean up the river, he began to fill his little boat with trash and haul it away. He developed an organization that now has over 70,000 volunteers who work to clean the rivers. (For more information, see *http://livinglandsandwaters.org/*.) Inspiring stories help students realize they can be good citizens as well. Clara Harlowe Barton was a teacher who risked her life to help soldiers during the Civil War. She later founded the American Red Cross. Teachers should help students recognize the values that made these people good citizens and show students how they can also be good citizens. (For more information go to *http://www.redcross.org/about-us/ history/clara-barton.*)

In Grades K–6, students should learn the meaning and importance of national holidays. Holidays with historic significance include Memorial Day, Labor Day, Columbus Day, Independence Day, Veterans Day, and Martin Luther King Jr. Day. Memorial Day honors members of the military who died in war. Labor Day recognizes the importance of workers and labor unions. Columbus Day commemorates the arrival of Christopher Columbus to the Americas. Independence Day commemorates the adoption of the Declaration of Independence. Often it is referred to as the "Fourth of July"; however, sometimes its purpose can be lost. By referring to it as "Independence Day," teachers can remind students of its meaning and historic importance. Martin Luther King Jr. Day honors the leader of the civil rights movement. Veterans Day celebrates those who have served in the country's armed forces.

Texas is among a handful of U.S. states that have set aside a week each year to appreciate America's founding documents, known collectively as the Charters of Freedom. In Texas, schools mark Celebrate Freedom Week (TEC § 29.907) during the week in which September 17 falls. The holiday, according to the Texas Education Agency, highlights the founding principles and ideals of the United States, "as well as the sacrifices that were made for freedom in the founding of the country. Students learn about the intent, meaning, and importance of the Declaration of Independence and the U.S. Constitution, including the Bill of Rights. Students also examine the relationship between the ideas in these documents and subsequent American history."

Celebrate Freedom Week coincides with Constitution Week, established by Congress to commemorate the signing of the Constitution at the Constitutional Convention on September 17, 1787.

American Symbols

American Patriotic Symbols

Patriotic symbols are visible signs of national pride. The U.S. National Flag, the Pledge of Allegiance, the Statue of Liberty, the Liberty Bell, and the White House are important examples of patriotic symbols for Americans.

The United States of America National Flag has 50 stars representing the 50 states of the Union. The color red represents hardiness and valor; the white symbolizes purity and innocence; and the blue symbolizes vigilance, perseverance, and justice. Congress approved a new flag with 13 red and white alternating horizontal stripes and 13 stars representing the original colonies in 1777. A star and stripe were added to the flag each time a state entered the Union. Congress set the number of stripes at 13 in 1818 and decided to add one star for each new state. In Texas, the state flag is a symbol of state pride. It can fly equal to or below the United States flag because it was a sovereign nation when it entered the United States of America. Many Texans fly both flags as a symbol of their American patriotism.

The U.S. Pledge of Allegiance is a declaration of patriotism. First published in 1892 in *The Youth's Companion*, it was believed to have been written by the magazine's editor, Francis Bellamy. The original purpose for the pledge was as an activity by schoolchildren to celebrate the 400th anniversary of the discovery of America. The Pledge was widely used in morning school routines for many years and received official recognition by Congress on 1942. The phrase "under God" was added in 1954, along with a law indicating the proper behavior to adopt when reciting the pledge, which includes standing straight, removing hats or any other headgear, and placing the right hand over the heart.

The Star-Spangled Banner is the national anthem of the United States. It was originally a poem written by Francis Scott Key during the Battle of Baltimore in the War of 1812 against the British. In 1931, it was made the official national anthem of the United States.

The Statue of Liberty was a gift of friendship from the people of France to the people of the United States commemorating the 100th anniversary of the United States. It is a universal symbol of freedom, democracy, and international friendship.

The Liberty Bell is a symbol of freedom and liberty. The Pennsylvania Assembly ordered the Liberty Bell to commemorate the 50th anniversary of Pennsylvania's original constitution, William Penn's Charter of Privileges. It is traditionally believed that it was rung to summon the people of Philadelphia to hear the Declaration of Independence. It became an icon when the abolitionists adopted it as a symbol of freedom. The abolitionists changed its name from The State House Bell to the Liberty Bell.

The White House was originally planned by President George Washington in 1791 and was completed in 1800 when its first resident, President John Adams, moved in with his wife, Abigail. It was originally called the President's House. President Theodore Roosevelt christened it The White House in 1901. For more than 200 years, it has been the home of U.S. presidents and their families. It is recognized as a symbol of the Presidency of the United States throughout the world.

The Great Seal of the United States consists of a bald eagle holding an olive branch and a bundle of arrows. The olive branch represents peace and the arrows represent military strength. The eagle holds a scroll in its beak with the nation's original motto, "E Pluribus Unum," which means "from many, one."

For additional information about symbols of the United States, see *http://www.ushistory.org.*, a website created and hosted by the Independence Hall Association in Philadelphia.

Texan Symbols

Texas Patriotic Symbols

Patriotic symbols are also signs of state pride. The Texas Flag, the Texas Pledge of Allegiance, bluebonnets, longhorns, oil rigs, and the state capitol are important symbols of Texas state pride. Places such as King's Ranch, the Alamo, cattle trails, the Capitol, Gruene Hall, and the San Jacinto battlegrounds are examples of landmarks that are meaningful symbols. For additional information about symbols of Texas, go to *http://www.statesymbolsusa.org/Texas/state_symbols.html*. For additional information about national monuments and landmarks in Texas, go to *http://texastimetravel.com/node/28774*. *(See also the additional symbols covered under Social Studies Competency 001: History.)*

COMPETENCY 005: CULTURE; SCIENCE, TECHNOLOGY, AND SOCIETY

The teacher understands and applies knowledge of cultural development, adaptation, and diversity and understands and applies knowledge of interactions among science, technology, and society, as defined by the Texas Essential Knowledge and Skills (TEKS).

The beginning teacher:

A. Understands basic concepts of culture and the processes of cultural adaptation, diffusion, and exchange.

B. Analyzes similarities and differences in the ways various peoples at different times in history have lived and met basic human needs.

C. Applies knowledge of the role of families in meeting basic human needs and how families and cultures develop and use customs, traditions, and beliefs to define themselves.

D. Demonstrates knowledge of institutions that exist in all societies and how characteristics of these institutions may vary among societies.

E. Understands how people use oral tradition, stories, real and mythical heroes, music, paintings, and sculpture to create and represent culture in communities in Texas, the United States, and the world.

F. Demonstrates knowledge of significant examples of art, music, and literature from various periods in U.S. and Texas history (e.g., John James Audubon, Henry David Thoreau, transcendentalism, the painting American Progress, "Yankee Doodle," "Battle Hymn of the Republic," Amado Peña, Diane Gonzales Bertrand, Scott Joplin).

G. Understands the universal themes found in the arts and their relationship with the times and societies in which they are produced, including how contemporary issues influence creative expressions and how the arts can transcend the boundaries of societies (e.g., religion, justice, the passage of time).

H. Understands the contributions of people of various racial, ethnic, and religious groups in Texas, the United States, and the world.

I.   Demonstrates knowledge of relationships among world cultures and relationships between and among people from various groups, including racial, ethnic, and religious groups, in the United States, and throughout the world.

J.   Analyzes relationships among religion, philosophy, and culture, and the impact of religion on ways of life in the United States and throughout the world.

K. Understands the concept of diversity within unity.

L.   Analyzes the effects of race, gender, socioeconomic class, status, and stratification on ways of life in the United States and throughout the world.

M. Understands the various roles of men, women, children, and families in cultures past and present.

N. Understands how the self develops and the dynamic relationship between self and social context.

O. Demonstrates knowledge of the discoveries, technological innovations and accomplishments of notable inventors and individuals in the field of science from the United States, Texas and the world (e.g., Benjamin Franklin, Eli Whitney, Cyrus McCormick, Thomas Alva Edison, Alexander Graham Bell, Michael DeBakey, Millie Hughes-Fulford, Walter Cunningham, Denton Cooley, Michael Dell).

P. Applies knowledge of the effects of scientific discoveries and technological innovations on political, economic, social, and environmental developments and on everyday life in Texas, the United States, and the world in the past, present, and future.

Q. Analyzes how science and technology relate to political, economic, social, and cultural issues and events.

R. Demonstrates knowledge of the origins, diffusions, and effects of major scientific, mathematical, and technological discoveries throughout history.

S. Knows how developments in science and technology have affected the physical environment; the growth of economies and societies; and definitions of, access to, and use of physical and human resources.

T. Knows how changes in science and technology affect moral and ethical issues.

The Role of Families in Meeting Basic Human Needs

While all young people need food, clothing, and shelter, families may have different ways of meeting these needs. Cultural, religious, and familiar traditions may influence families' preferences and choices in meeting basic needs.

How Families and Cultures Develop and Use Customs, Traditions, and Beliefs to Define Themselves

Educators should give students and families opportunities to share and express their culture throughout the social studies curriculum. Parents are children's first and constant teachers. Educators must realize that a student's cultural or religious beliefs could at times be incompatible with school activities and thus, students may opt not to participate in certain school events. Teachers should help students feel positively about their cultural differences. Family values and culture fuel children's self-esteem, identity, and pride surrounding who they are and who they aspire to become as educated adults. Schools should make space for students' cultural heritages to be respected, valued, and incorporated into their education.

Knowledge of Institutions that Exist in All Societies and How Characteristics of These Institutions May Vary among Societies

Geneva Gay, a professor of education at the University of Washington, defines culturally responsive teaching as using the cultural knowledge, prior experiences, and performance styles of diverse students to make learning more appropriate and effective for them; it teaches to and through the strengths of these students (Gay, 2000). All societies have norms, rules, and laws; however, these may differ from one society to the next.

Use of Oral Tradition, Stories, Real and Mythical Heroes, Music, Paintings, and Sculpture to Create and Represent Culture in Communities

Stories, art, and music help people express and share culture. While some mythic archetypes exist across cultures, such as the hero's journey, the trickster, the quest, and creation stories, cultural aspects of stories vary from one culture to the next.

In Texas

Texas has unique cultural traditions and celebrations, such as Juneteenth. Juneteenth is uniquely Texan, representing the oldest celebration commemorating the end of U.S. slavery. On June 19, 1865, two-and-a-half years after Lincoln's *Emancipation Proclamation*, Major General Gordon Granger landed in Galveston, Texas, and announced, "The people of Texas are informed that in accordance with a proclamation from the executive of the United States, all slaves are free."

In the United States

Thanksgiving, Memorial Day, and Independence Day on the Fourth of July are holidays unique to the United States. We have localized myths and folktales from various American Indian tales to frontier folklore such as Paul Bunyan and Babe the Blue Ox. In addition to mythical heroes, all cultures, including the United States, have real heroes of cultural expression. The Harlem Renaissance in the 1920s and 1930s represents a uniquely U.S. convergence of cultural expression with many real-life cultural leaders and heroes.

In the World

Cultural stories exist in any culture. Humans tell stories as part of cultural expression. *Beowulf, The Odyssey, The Aeneid, El Cid, Paradise Lost, Mahabharata, Metamorphoses,* and *Epic of Gilgamesh* all represent cultural stories from differing languages and origins that are still valued today.

Relationships among World Cultures, and Relationships between and among People from Various Groups, Including Racial, Ethnic, and Religious Groups

According to the *Curriculum Guidelines for Multicultural Education* by the National Council for the Social Studies, "A democratic society protects and provides opportunities for ethnic and cultural diversity at the same time having overarching values—such as equality, justice, and human dignity—that all groups accept and respect." (Fullinwider, 2001)

Relationships among Religion, Philosophy, and Culture, and the Impact of Religion on Ways of Life in the United States and World Areas

Though the Harlem Renaissance is perhaps best known for its artistic and religious movements, Harlem also had significant political movements at this same time period. Marcus Garvey, who ascribed to a Black Nationalist philosophy, founded the Universal Negro Improvement Association, and was a proponent of a Black migration back to Africa. He also founded African Orthodox Church. While Garvey advocated for separation, W.E.B. Du Bois favored integration. Du Bois was the leading African American politician and philosopher during the Harlem Renaissance. James Weldon Johnson was the first appointed African American officer in the NAACP. Louis Armstrong and Duke Ellington were noted musicians during this period.

Concept of Diversity within Unity

As we said earlier, "E Pluribus Unum" means "from many, one." In 1776, John Adams, Benjamin Franklin, and Thomas Jefferson proposed this Latin saying as the motto to be printed on the first Great Seal of the United States. While the original intent involved a single unified nation from many states, the motto stands the test of time and still affirms U.S. identity even though the U.S. national motto since 1956 has been "In God We Trust." James Banks (2001) and several co-authors, published a document entitled *Diversity within Unity Essential Principles for Teaching and Learning in a Multicultural Society*. It centered on 12 principles aligned to five key areas:

1. teacher learning

2. student learning

3. intergroup relations

4. school governance, organization, and equity

5. assessment

The concept of diversity within unity underscores that our cultural differences make society stronger. We achieve unity through civic ideals and practices and an acknowledged commitment to the greater good. As citizens of the United States, we share in common challenges and collective joys of our nation, bound by both geographic union and shared American identity, not by any law that would impose a forced unity. Americans uphold and affirm citizens' rights to decent lives and publicly speak against policy via peaceful protest. In part, it is our affirmation and respect of differences that hold us in our unity.

Effects of Scientific Discoveries and Technological Innovations

In Texas

Some Texas leaders in science and technology include:

- *Walter Cunningham*—NASA's second civilian astronaut, fighter pilot, retired military physicist

- *Michael DeBakey*—Surgeon who helped develop innovative treatments in heart and vascular surgery

- *Denton Cooley*—Native Houstonian known for heart surgery and transplants, as well as adept surgical work with children

- *Benjy Brooks*—Native Texan and the first female pediatric surgeon in Texas. She conducted research on congenital defects, burn treatment, spleen reparation, and the prevention of hepatitis. A foundation set up in her name has advanced the surgical care of young children in Texas.

- *Michael Dell*—Founder of Dell Computer Corporation. He is a native Houstonian known for technology, business, and philanthropy.

- *Howard Hughes Sr.*—Designer of a drill bit that could drill through hard rock. Previously, oil drillers could not reach large pockets of oil lying beneath hard rock. He co-founded the Sharp-Hughes Tool Company, which held the patent for the new drill bit, manufactured the bit, and leased the bit to oil companies.

Major Scientific, Mathematical, and Technological Discoveries throughout History

- *Archimedes*—One of the greatest mathematicians and scientists; worked in hydrostatics, static mechanics, the measurement of the volume or density; made key contributions to calculus

- *Copernicus*—Mathematician and astronomer; discovered that the Earth revolved around the sun, which was stationary in the center of the universe; created a conceptualization of our universe as a place where the distances of the planets from the sun had a direct relationship to the size of their orbits; often considered to be the initiator of the Scientific Revolution.

- *Eratosthenes*—A mathematician who worked on prime numbers and measuring the diameter of the Earth

- *Galileo*—Scientist who formulated basic laws of falling bodies; constructed a telescope to study lunar craters; discovered four of Jupiter's moons

- *Pythagoras*—Philosopher and mathematician; contributed to math systems; however, none of his writings are known, so his contributions are not distinctly defined

- *Robert Boyle*—Chemist and philosopher; worked toward establishing chemistry as based on a mechanistic theory of matter

- *Marie Curie*—Scientist who discovered the radioactive elements polonium and radium; first person awarded two Nobel prizes. Her work influenced the development of medical research and treatment.

- *Thomas Edison*—Scientist and inventor, most famous for developing the incandescent light bulb

- *Albert Einstein*—Physicist who heavily contributed to the modern vision of physics including his general theories of relativity.

- *Robert Fulton*—Artist, engineer, and inventor who made the steamboat designs viable and put this mode of transportation into actual practice.

- *Sir Isaac Newton*—Philosopher, scientific theorist, and inventor of the infinitesimal calculus and a new theory of light and color. He transformed physical science through conceiving the three laws of motion and the law of universal gravitation.

- *Louis Pasteur*—Biologist, chemist, and humanitarian, known for germ and immunization theories; he uncovered origins of rabies, anthrax, chicken cholera, and silkworm diseases; contributed to the development of the first vaccines; he described the scientific basis for fermentation.

- *James Watt*—Engineer and inventor known for improvements made to Newcomen's atmospheric engine, which turned steam into the major power source of the Industrial Revolution.

COMPETENCY 006: SOCIAL STUDIES FOUNDATIONS AND SKILLS

The teacher understands the foundations of social studies education and applies knowledge of skills used in the social sciences.[6]

The beginning teacher:

A. Understands the philosophical foundations of the social science disciplines and knows how knowledge generated by the social sciences affects society and people's lives.

B. Understands how social science disciplines relate to each other.

C. Understands practical applications of social studies education.

D. Relates philosophical assumptions and ideas to issues and trends in the social sciences.

E. Knows characteristics and uses of various primary and secondary sources (e.g., databases, maps, photographs, media services, the internet, biographies, interviews, questionnaires, artifacts) and uses information from a variety of sources to acquire social science information and answer social science questions.

F. Knows how to formulate research questions and use appropriate procedures to reach supportable judgments and conclusions in the social sciences.

G. Understands social science research and knows how social scientists locate, gather, organize, analyze and report information using standard research methodologies.

H. Evaluates the validity of social science information from primary and secondary sources regarding bias issues, propaganda, point of view, and frame of reference.

I. Understands and evaluates multiple points of view and frames of reference relating to issues in the social sciences.

---

[6] Social Studies Texas Essential Knowledge and Skills include eight strands of essential knowledge and skills that are intended to be integrated for instructional purposes. Typically, the last 3 to 5 Social Studies TEKS identify the Social Studies Skills students are to know. Constructing lessons based on one TEKS is a common error. Every Social Studies lesson should include a minimum of one Social Studies Skills and at least one other TEKS from another strand.

J. Knows how to analyze social science information (e.g., by categorizing, comparing and contrasting, making generalizations and predictions, drawing inferences and conclusions).

K. Communicates and interprets social science information in written, oral, and visual forms and translates information from one medium to another (e.g., written to visual, statistical to written or visual).

L. Uses standard grammar, spelling, sentence structure, punctuation, and proper citation of sources.

M. Knows how to use problem-solving processes to identify problems, gather information, list and consider options, consider advantages and disadvantages, choose and implement solutions, and evaluate the effectiveness of solutions.

N. Knows how to use decision-making processes to identify situations that require decisions, gather information, identify options, predict consequences and take action to implement decisions.

O. Knows how to create maps and other graphics to present geographic, political, historical, economic, and cultural features, distributions, and relationships.

P. Analyzes social science data by using basic mathematical and statistical concepts and analytical methods.

Q. Knows how to apply skills for resolving conflict, including persuasion, compromise, debate, and negotiation.

R. Understands and uses social studies terminology correctly.

Social Studies Inquiry

Research in social studies involves the use of systematic inquiry. Engaging students in inquiry involves the ability to acquire information from various resources. Inquiry involves the ability to design and conduct investigations, which requires students to develop an understanding of key information in social studies content. To gather content information, students should become familiar with the various resources used in social sciences research. Those resources include primary and secondary sources, encyclopedias, almanacs, atlases, government documents, artifacts, and oral histories. Students need to apply critical-thinking skills to organize and use information acquired from a variety of sources including electronic technology.

Information about social studies is available from the internet; however, students need to evaluate the scholarship of the many sources available and use only those known to be reliable. Teachers should equip middle-grade social studies students to think, research, and communicate like historians, sociologists, geographers, economists, political scientists, and other social studies processionals. Asking and answering appropriate levels of higher-order questions is imperative to teaching students to think like a social scientist. For more information, see *https://www.socialstudies.org/professional-learning/questioning-key-unlocking-power-inquiry-social-studies* and *https://c3teachers.org/what-are-compelling-questions/* and *http://www.esc4.net/users/0001/docs/107-DWilliamsTCSS2005.ppt.* Inquiry is the mechanism to achieve professional-level social studies skills.

The Problem-Solving Process

Just like scientists, social scientists utilize the basics of the scientific method. Educators should guide students to:

1. Identify a social science problem.

2. Formulate research questions and hypotheses.

3. Gather and analyze information, look for patterns.

4. Raise discipline-appropriate questions, identify possible positive and negative consequences, and use data to support ideas.

5. Test and report findings.

Data (facts) must be used to support one's conclusions. In a democracy, an informed citizenry must be able to make statements and support (or defend) them with evidence (data) from multiple perspectives. Social studies education seeks to develop content knowledge and skills communities expect their citizens to have. In America, we strongly value being able to articulate well-reasoned conclusions, thoughts, and beliefs that consider different points of view. Social studies classrooms in the United States prepare youth to be able to function in an active participatory democracy.

Professionally Modeled Thinking

When studying history, an educator should guide students to think like historians. Likewise, when studying geography or culture, the teacher will prompt students to work like geographers and anthropologists. This approach builds core social studies skills while simultaneously preparing students with college and career readiness skills. Professionals who work in the field of social studies do not rely on memory skills alone, nor should students in the middle grades. Professionally modeled thinking involves leading students through the interrogation of primary and supporting secondary sources to test hypotheses. Often, students may come away with more questions than they started with in their initial hypothesis, which is natural for this type of educational experience. Professionally modeled thinking prompts students to be critical consumers of information and it empowers them to think critically about the social worlds around them. Students acquire life-long learning skills through classroom activities that foreground professionally modeled thinking. Social studies teachers do not always recognize how to or what to model. Modeling how to think and reason in various situations or about different issues is critical. Social studies teachers can do this using think-aloud strategies. Teachers need to be cautious when thinking through events and issues to use the different social studies "hats"—history, geography, political science, and economics to develop a complete understanding of the topic at hand.

How Social Science Disciplines Relate to Each Other

Social studies is an umbrella term used to encompass the disciplines of history, geography, civics and government, economics, and psychology. All five components are intertwined with the standards or strands developed by the National Council for the Social Studies in 1997 (NCSS, 2018). The Texas Education Agency (TEA) used these strands and curriculum standards as a foundation to develop the state social studies curriculum for kindergarten through grade 12. In many ways, social studies is a hub at the center of all other disciplines. Social studies brings together reading, writing, and other linguistic processing skills with mathematical reading and thinking skills as students read and interpret maps, charts, and other social science data immersed in both linguistic and numerical data. Social studies subjects also relate to students' everyday life interactions with all subject areas. For example, when students encounter chemistry and health in the real world, it often takes laboratory science to the everyday social setting of the breakfast table where nutritional charts inform them about their own eating choices and where digestion becomes an internal body chemistry validation of what they read. When teachers overtly connect all the other disciplines linked to students' everyday worlds through their study of the social studies, then students begin to understand the applicability of the entire curriculum through the study of their own and others' social lives. Social studies can become the real-world connection hub for all other disciplines.

Relating Philosophical Assumptions and Ideas to Issues and Trends in the Social Sciences

Core philosophical assumptions align with various historical and social traditions. For example, the Enlightenment pulls ideas from Jefferson, Locke, and Rousseau. The scientific revolution relies on ideas from Copernicus (Ptolemaic Astronomy; Earth's revolution around the sun), Galileo (refracting telescope, objects of various weights descend at the same rate), and Newton (universal gravitation, calculus, laws of motion). Political science origins rely on Aristotle, Plato, and Aquinas. Machiavelli and Hobbes contribute to ideas of power. Historical and philosophical trends go hand-and-hand. Students begin to understand the works of philosophers like Heidegger and Arendt more fully when they can process the information within the historical backdrop of that period in time.

In part, people think about philosophy as they do because of what is going on in the world around them. In powerful and transformative social studies classrooms, educators help students to explore and make sense of how social theory, philosophical development, and history intermingle and influence one another. Students can then apply the continuity of historical and philosophical ideas to the worlds of today and tomorrow.

Sources of Information

Teachers should use various primary and secondary sources (e.g., databases, maps, photographs, media services, the internet, biographies, interviews, questionnaires, artifacts, works of historical fiction, interviews, etc.) and information from a variety of sources to acquire social science information and answer social science questions. Students and teachers must evaluate the validity of social science information from primary and secondary sources regarding bias issues, propaganda, point-of-view, and frame of reference.

Educators should help students to formulate social studies research questions and use appropriate procedures to reach supportable judgments and conclusions in the social sciences, as well as analyze social science information (e.g., by categorizing, comparing and contrasting, making generalizations and predictions, drawing inferences and conclusions). Students should be able to pull together, synthesize, apply, and evaluate contemporary internet resources alongside historical sources. Teachers should always consider students' everyday worlds as sources or comparative sources to help make the study of social studies meaningful to students' lives. Likewise, educators should include familial and local oral histories and other historical and cultural documents and artifacts that make students' immediate geographies and histories relevant to the majority of the social studies curriculum.

See the National Archives (*www.archives.gov*) for more information on locating primary sources and lesson ideas related to social studies.

Spatial Thinking

Social scientists continually use space and place as vehicles for analyzing patterns, relationships, and processes within and between places from multiple perspectives (i.e., historical, geographical, political, economical, etc.). These professionals seek to organize and understand the world around them. Using a spatial perspective is a vital part of what they do. Educators must model for students how to think spatially and show them how this analysis differs on a local, state, national, and global scale. Recently, methods of spatial analysis have been enhanced through geospatial tools such as digital globes (i.e., Google Earth) and geographic information systems (GIS). Due to the participation of Esri, a mapping and spatial data analytics supplier, in President Obama's 2013 ConnectED initiative, the online, cloud-based ArcGIS software is available to all educators in the U.S. Educators can create an account for their school from which each teacher can have a space for students to interact with, create, and upload maps using GIS. For more, go to *http://www.esri.com/connected* and *http://geospatialrevolution.psu.edu/*. By visualizing data, educators can teach students how to better understand the patterns, relationships, and connections throughout time and place.

COMPETENCY 007: SOCIAL STUDIES INSTRUCTION AND ASSESSMENT

The teacher plans and implements effective instruction and assessment in social studies.

The beginning teacher:

A. Knows state content and performance standards for social studies that are used in the Texas Essential Knowledge and Skills (TEKS).

B. Understands the vertical alignment of the social sciences in the Texas Essential Knowledge and Skills (TEKS) from grade level to grade level, including prerequisite knowledge and skills.

C. Understands the implications of stages of child growth and development for designing and implementing effective learning experiences in the social sciences.

D. Understands the appropriate use of technology as a tool for learning and communicating social studies concepts.

E. Selects and uses effective instructional practices, activities, technologies and materials to promote students' knowledge and skills in the social sciences.

F. Knows how to promote students' use of social science skills, vocabulary, and research tools, including technological tools.

G. Knows how to communicate the value of social studies education to students, parents/caregivers, colleagues, and the community.

H. Knows how to provide instruction that relates skills, concepts, and ideas in different social science disciplines.

I. Provides instruction that makes connections between knowledge and methods in the social sciences and in other content areas.

J. Demonstrates knowledge of forms of assessment appropriate for evaluating students' progress and needs in the social sciences.

K. Uses multiple forms of assessment and knowledge of the Texas Essential Knowledge and Skills (TEKS) to determine students' progress and needs and to help plan instruction that addresses the strengths, needs, and interests of all students, including English learners.

Educators have a crucial responsibility because they lay the foundation of American core values, citizenship, democracy, and patriotism. Social studies often gets less attention in the classroom than the intended state curriculum calls for. Teachers must learn to find ways to infuse their curricula with social studies lessons and recognize that social studies strongly supports literacy and other content areas. Understanding maps, diagrams, charts, and graphs as well as analysis of spatial patterns and relationships support students' spatial and mathematical reasoning capabilities.

The middle-grades teacher should plan and implement effective instruction and assessment in social studies, aligned to state content and performance standards for social studies that comprise the TEKS. Additionally, educators must understand the vertical alignment of the social sciences in the TEKS from one grade level to the next, including prerequisite knowledge and skills. Educators should account for the implications of stages of child growth and development for designing and implementing effective learning experiences in the social sciences and understand the appropriate use of technology as a tool for learning and communicating social studies concepts.

Educators should select and use effective instructional practices, activities, technologies, and materials to promote students' knowledge and skills in the social sciences in order to promote students' use of social science skills, vocabulary, and research tools, including technological tools. Prepared educators know how to communicate the value of social studies education to students, parents/caregivers, colleagues, and the community and how to provide instruction that relates skills, concepts, and ideas in different social science disciplines.

Optimally, educators should provide instruction that makes connections between knowledge and methods in the social sciences and in other content areas. Teachers must demonstrate knowledge of forms of assessment appropriate for evaluating students' progress and needs in the social science and use multiple forms of assessment and knowledge of the TEKS to determine students' progress and needs and to help plan instruction that addresses the strengths, needs, and interests of all students, including English learners.

Texas Essential Knowledge and Skills (TEKS) in Social Studies

As the state curriculum for kindergarten to Grade 12, the TEKS organizes the social studies content inductively, from the known to the unknown. In this vertical alignment, children begin learning about the self in kindergarten and expand their knowledge with each successive grade, eventually encompassing the community, the state, the nation, and the world. This is sometimes referred to as thinking on a local to global scale. Secondary grade-level social studies courses build and rely on the foundation laid by 4–8 teachers. Social Studies nationally is divided into 10 strands that are infused throughout each of the social studies disciplines (See Table 5-7 below). This is reflected in the Social Studies Texas Essential Knowledge and Skills (TEKS), where eight strands are present in the social studies course for each grade level. In Texas, social studies is built on the foundation of the following strands: history, geography, economics, government, citizenship, culture, science, technology, and society, and social studies skills.

Table 5-7
NCSS vs. TEKS Social Studies Strands

National Social Studies Strands (NCSS)	Texas Social Studies Strands (TEKS)
Time, Continuity, and Change	History
People, Places, and Environment	Geography
Global Connections	Culture
Culture and Cultural Diversity	Government
Individual Development and Identity	Economics
Individual Groups and Institutions	Citizenship
Power, Authority, and Governance	Science, Technology, and Society
Production, Distribution, and Consumption	Social Studies Skills
Civic Ideals and Practices	
Science, Technology, and Society	

A summary of the key components of the social studies curriculum covered in Grades 4–8 follows.

Grades 4 & 7 Focus—History of Texas

- History of Texas from its beginning to the present. Several Native American groups inhabited the territory that became Texas.

- Geographic regions of Texas (i.e., location, biomes, resources, economic products, settlements, groups of people)

- Events and individuals of the 19th and 20th centuries

- Human activity and physical features of regions in Texas and the Western Hemisphere

- Native Americans in Texas and the Western Hemisphere (i.e., tribes, customs, location, time period, movement, interaction with other people)

- European exploration and colonization

- Types of Native American governments

- Characteristics of Spanish and Mexican colonial governments

- Anthems, mottoes, and pledges of Texas and the United States

Grades 5 & 8 Focus—United States History

- Anthem, motto, and pledge of the United States of America

- History of the United States from its early beginnings to the present

- Major events and significant individuals of the late 19th and 20th centuries including contributions of famous inventors and scientists

- Regions of the United States that result from physical features and human activity

- Characteristics and benefits of the free enterprise system

- Roots of representative government

- Important ideas in the Declaration of Independence

- Meaning of the Pledge of Allegiance

- Fundamental rights guaranteed in the Bill of Rights

- Customs and celebrations of various racial, ethnic, and religious groups in the nation

Grade 6—People and Places of the Contemporary World

- This part of the curriculum is designed to introduce students to the concepts of cultural geography. The discipline of geography explores patterns, relationships, and processes at local to global scale.

- People and places of the contemporary world

- Societies from the following regions in the world: Europe, Russia and the Eurasian republics, North America, Middle America, South America, Southwest Asia-North Africa, Sub-Saharan Africa, South Asia, East Asia, Southeast Asia, Australia, and the Pacific Realm

- Influence of individuals and groups from various cultures on selected historical and contemporary events

- Different ways of organizing economic and governmental systems

Different Ways of Organizing Economic and Governmental Systems

Using Maps and Globes

Symbolic representation can pose challenges for students. Maps and globes are tools for representing space symbolically. Globes are a mathematical model of the Earth and show correct, unaltered (not distorted) distance, size, and shape of continents and bodies of water. Maps are a flat representation of the world and distort the distance, size, or shape of continents and bodies of water. This distortion can confuse the young learner. In the early grades, the main purpose for using globes is to familiarize children with the basic roundness of the Earth and to begin developing a global perspective. It can also be used to study the proportion of land and water. In grades 4 through 6, students can use a 16-inch globe containing additional details. Generally, seven colors are used to represent land elevation and three colors to represent water depth. For ideas for lessons, and for personal practice, go to *http://www.nea.org/tools/lessons/teaching-with-maps.html*. For creating online maps go to *http://www.arcgis.com/features/index.html* or *https://www.google.com/help/maps/education/*.

Activities for Students in Grades 4–8

Teaching map concepts in Grade 4 should include the following activities:

- Stress that the globe is a very small representation that is a model of the Earth.

- Stress that the map is a flat representation of the Earth and why maps are used more often than globes.

- Show children different kinds of maps of Texas (i.e., climate, precipitation, resources, vegetation, physical, population, etc.) as well as from different time periods throughout the year (i.e., Indian tribe locations, exploration paths, settlement patterns, battles, land acquisition, etc.) to better understand place and change over time.

- Show children how land areas and water bodies are represented on the globe.

- Identify major landforms and water bodies.

- Show and explain the location of the North Pole and the concept of the Northern Hemisphere, where most of the world's land is located.

- Show and explain the location of the South Pole and the concept of the Southern Hemisphere, where most of the world's water is located.

- Show the relationship and location of the Earth in the solar system.

- Use the globe to find the continent, the country, the state, and the city where the children live.

- Encourage children to explore the globe and maps to find places by themselves as well as the connections between places.

- Compare the size of the continents represented on a globe with their representation on a Mercator projection—the flat representation.

Teaching map concepts in Grades 5 and 6 should include the following activities:

- Identify countries, capitals, and other major cities in the United States and the world.

- Identify major landforms and bodies of water.

- Create and interpret maps.

- Use maps and globes to pose and answer questions.

- Locate major historical and contemporary societies on maps and globes.

- Use maps to solve real-life problems, i.e., using road maps to plan a route to a specific destination.

Latitude and Longitude—Developmental Considerations

Latitude and longitude are imaginary lines used to create a coordinate system to determine the absolute location of any place on Earth. **Absolute location** is the exact place on Earth where something is located. Often it is given in terms of latitude and longitude, but could also be a postal address. Location can also be expressed as **relative location**, meaning it is described in relationship to another known location or place. For example, Austin is south of Dallas, or the shopping mall is located just past the Texaco gas station. (For more on this topic, visit the National Geographic Society at *https://www.nationalgeographic.org/encyclopedia/location*.)

Lines of latitude, also called parallels, are measured in an angle north or south from the Equator and are measured in degrees like all mathematical angles. The Equator is the first line of latitude, measured at 0°. All lines of latitude are measured between 0 and 90 degrees. It is also a latitude line that divides the Earth into two halves, also called **hemispheres**. One half is north of the Equator, referred to as the **Northern Hemisphere**, and the other half is south of the Equator and thus called the **Southern Hemisphere**.

Lines of longitude, also referred to as meridians, are imaginary lines that run from the north to the south pole and are measured east or west of the **Prime Meridian**. While latitude has a natural middle line formed by the Equator, lines of longitude do not. Therefore, a starting point identifying the first (prime) line of longitude (meridian) was identified to create a line from which all other meridians are measured. The meridian that goes through Greenwich, England, was officially recognized as the Prime Meridian in 1884 at the International Meridian Conference. This was essential to standardize mapping and shipping. Like the Equator, the Prime Meridian is the first line of longitude measured at 0°; the last line of longitude is 180°. (See *https://www.rmg.co.uk/stories/topics/what-prime-meridian-why-it-greenwich*.) These lines form the boundaries for two hemispheres. To the east of the Prime Meridian is the *Eastern Hemisphere*, and to the west of the Prime Meridian is the *Western Hemisphere*.

Establishing a geographic coordinate system to identify absolute location of places became increasingly important as trade across the seas evolved. Coordinates are written using parentheses, degrees from the line of origin, degree symbols, and cardinal directions (*N, S, E, W*). For example, the absolute location of the Empire State Building in New York City is at 40 degrees north (latitude) and 74 degrees west (longitude). It is correctly written as (40° N, 73° W).

For more information, see also *https://www.britannica.com/science/latitude* and *https://gsp. humboldt.edu/olm/Lessons/GIS/01%20SphericalCoordinates/Latitude_and_Longitude.html.*

**Figure 5-3
Latitude and Longitude**

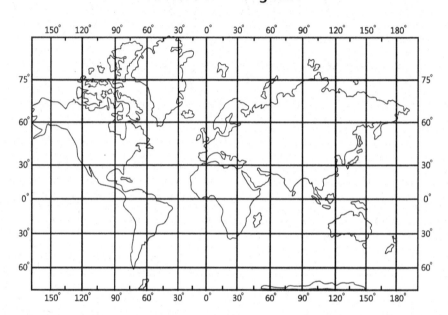

Using Technology Information in Social Studies

Research in social studies involves the use of systematic inquiry. Engaging children in inquiry involves the ability to acquire information from various resources. Inquiry involves the ability to design and conduct investigations, which requires students to develop an understanding of key information in social studies content.

To gather information, students should learn about the sources used in social sciences research. They should learn to distinguish between primary and secondary sources as they become familiar with encyclopedias, almanacs, atlases, government documents, artifacts, and oral histories. Students should apply critical-thinking skills to organize and use information acquired from sources including electronic technology. Information about social studies is available from the internet; however, students need to evaluate the scholarship of the many sources available and use only those known to be reliable. Students can use commercially developed programs like *Oregon Trails* and *Where in the World is Carmen San Diego?* Digital globes, such as Google Earth (*https://*

www.google.com/earth/), National Geographic's Map Machine (*maps.nationalgeographic.com/map-machine*), and ArcGIS Online (*http://www.arcgis.com/features/index.html*) are **geospatial technologies** that provide a forum to analyze relationships and patterns at a local to global scale. Another excellent recourse is MapStats for Kids that allows students to experience the dynamic relationships of charts, diagrams, and maps as they work to achieve a goal (*https://www.geovista.psu.edu/grants/MapStatsKids/MSK_portal/*). These interactive programs expose students to problem-solving skills and social studies content in a fun and supportive environment. These kinds of interactive programs can expose students to problem-solving skills and social studies content in a fun and supportive environment.

Integration of Social Studies

As mentioned earlier, the teaching of social studies by definition implies integration of content from five disciplines: history, geography, civics and government, economics, and psychology. However, teachers can go beyond this integration and add components from other content areas. The use of a literature-based approach is an ideal way to integrate social studies with language arts. Using authentic multicultural literature, teachers can expose children to quality reading and the cultures of the many ethnic and linguistic groups living in the United States. Social studies is strongly linked with English Language Arts and Reading. It not only requires strong reading and writing skills but also supports reading by providing an understanding of the history as well as the physical and cultural characteristics of a place.

The use of thematic units can also help teachers to integrate the content areas. In this approach, a teacher or teachers select a theme and organize content area instruction around it. Thematic instruction can be done in a self-contained classroom or in a departmental format in which several teachers teach the content. However, units may be organized by key time periods in history or regions of the world with key themes serving as "big ideas" or "guiding questions" to drive instruction. This method allows learners to "chunk" the material historically or geographically while simultaneously analyzing major themes or "big ideas" that connect to other units of instruction. Some educators may prefer this method because it divides content into units familiar to both the educator and students.

Thematic instruction is ideal for English learners because the use of a common theme in multiple content areas makes content more cognitively accessible for them. For example, in a unit on the **solar system**, the names of the planets and the terminology used to describe the system can be introduced and repeated in several subjects through the duration of the unit. The presentation and repetition of content in different subjects and conditions allow students the opportunity to develop English vocabulary while learning content.

Graphic Representations of Historical Information

Information in social studies can be presented in a visual form with graphs and charts to make content accessible to all children, including ELs.

Graphs

The most commonly used graphs are the pictorial graph, the bar graph, the pie or circle graph, and the line graph. The **pictorial graph** is the most concrete type of graph because it uses a picture of the object being represented. **Bar graphs** are more concrete than pie graphs (also known as pie charts or circle graphs). In elementary school, social studies teachers can use a **Dot Plot** from mathematics, which is a simple histogram-like chart that is similar to a bar graph. A common bar graph in social studies is the population pyramid, which shows the number of males and females for each age group in a community. The population pyramid is appropriate for upper elementary because it uses percentages as well as whole numbers. Visit the U.S. Census Bureau's website for more information at *https://www.census.gov/library/visualizations/2005/demo/2005-us-region-poppyramid.html*. When possible, teachers should also incorporate such charts and graphs common to other disciplines as the dot plots in mathematics, to reinforce concepts and show that learning is continuous and can be applied in different ways.

Although the **pie graph** appears to be simple, students need to understand the concept of percentages to interpret correctly the meaning of this type of graph, and the concept of percentages is not acquired until late in the elementary grades. Teachers can use more sophisticated graphs like the pie graph to represent research information. For example, children can take 5 to 10 minutes a day to observe the types of transportation used by people in the neighborhood. Teachers can use this information to guide children to make inferences about the information contained in the graph. Why are so many people using pickup trucks as a mode of transportation? Why are only a small number of people walking? Graphs provide a great opportunity to integrate social studies into mathematics and vice versa.

Charts

Charts can be used to record information and present ideas in a concise way. Charts are ideal for promoting concept formation in a concrete fashion. **Data retrieval charts** are used to gather and keep track of data gathered from research, observation, or experimentation. This type of chart is constructed to allow the easy comparison of two or more sets of data. An example of a data retrieval chart appears below in Table 5-8.

Table 5-8
Data Retrieval Chart—Country Leaders

Country	Head of the Government	Type of Government
United States	President	Constitutional Federal Republic
United Kingdom	Prime Minister	Parliamentary Constitutional Monarchy
Saudi Arabia	King and Prime Minister	Absolute Monarch

Source: The CIA World Factbook (*https://www.cia.gov*)

Narrative charts are used to show events in a sequence. For example, students can develop charts showing the steps in making their favorite dishes. A narrative chart can also be used to present a timeline of historical events. An example of a simple timeline is Figure 5-4 below, which shows a child's personal history.

Figure 5-4
Timeline—My History

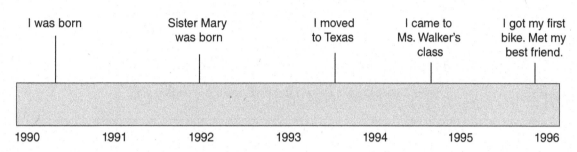

A **tabulation** or **classification** chart provides an orderly columnar display of information for comparison. For example, Table 5-9 compares data based on the 2010 United States census.

Table 5-9
Tabulation or Classification Chart—U.S. and Texas Populations by Group

Race/Ethnic Group Population	Percentage of U.S. Population	Percentage of Texas Population
Caucasian/not Hispanic	76.3%	78.70%
Hispanic or Latino	18.5%	39.7%
African American	13.4%	12.9%
Asian	5.9%	5.2%
American Indian/Alaskan Native	1.3%	1.0%
Native Hawaiian/Pacific Is.	0.2%	0.1%

Source: U.S. Census Bureau (2022): online *https://www.census.gov/quickfacts/fact/table/US/PST045221*
Texas Quick Facts online: *https://www.census.gov/quickfacts/TX*

Using developmentally appropriate vocabulary, teachers can guide students to recall and infer data from the chart. It is important to move between various social studies tools (i.e., maps, graphs, charts, diagrams, and pictures) to help build learners cognitive ability and skills that increase in complexity with age and grade level.

A **flowchart** shows a process involving changes at certain points.

Figure 5-5
Flowchart for Program Completion

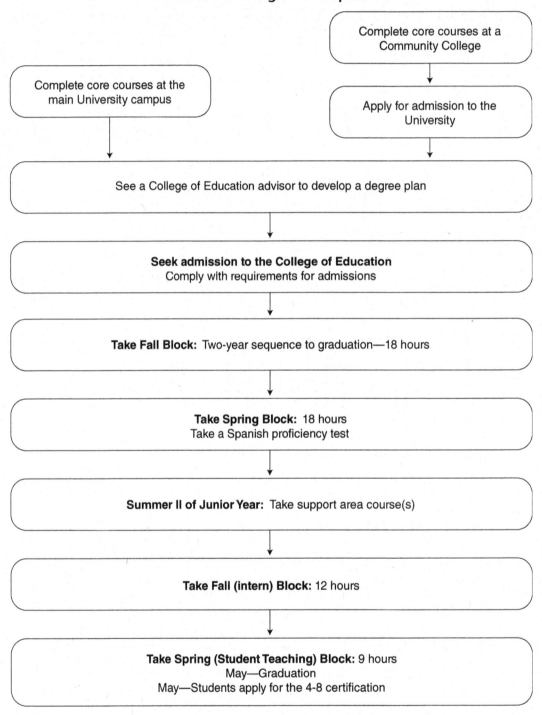

Addressing the Needs of English Learners

English learners can find social studies instruction quite challenging; thus, teachers need to modify instruction to make the content comprehensible for this group. Some textbooks have been written with ELs in mind. These books use numerous visual and graphic representations to make the content cognitively accessible to children learning English. For example, *Adventure Tales of America*, written by Jody Potts (1994), is an American history book that uses cartoons and illustrations to explain complex concepts like the processes of electing the president and making a bill into law. It also uses concrete timelines to represent the historical development of the nation. The illustrations give ELs the fundamental meanings of important concepts from which teachers can develop lessons. Other books integrate language instruction with content to deliver both components in a contextualized format. One example is the English as a Second Language (ESL) series titled *Avenues*, published by Hampton Brown (Schifini et al., 2004). This set of books presents ESL lessons in conjunction with content from other disciplines. The integration of content and language is one of the most effective strategies to promote content area mastery and language development.

Cognates and Suffixes

English and most Western languages have been heavily influenced by the Greek and Roman civilizations. The association has resulted in the creation of multiple cognates—words that are similar in two languages. Most of the sophisticated English words in the content areas and especially in social studies are cognates of Spanish and other Western languages. Teachers can use these similarities to expand the vocabulary of students and enhance content area comprehension. Table 5-10 below presents examples of the connection between English and Spanish words (Rosado & Salazar, 2002–2003).

Table 5-10
Common Greek and Latin Roots and Affixes

Roots/Affixes	Meaning	English/Spanish Cognates
Phobia Xeno	Fear of Foreigners or strangers	Xenophobia/Xenofobia
Phono Logy(ia)	Sound Study of	Phonology/Fonología
Photo Graphy	Light Graph, form	Photography/Fotografía
Homo Sapiens	Same, Man Able to think	Homo sapiens/homo sapiens

Roots/Affixes	Meaning	English/Spanish Cognates
Demo	People	Democracy/Democracia
Cracy	Government	

Instructional Techniques to Support English Learners

Teachers need to implement a variety of activities to teach the state curriculum to English learners (ELs) at the grade level and complexity required of native English speakers. Scaffolding was originally used to describe the way in which adults support children in their efforts to communicate in the native language (L1). The same concept can be used to facilitate language and content development for ELs. The term *scaffolding* alludes to the provisional structure used to provide support during the construction of a building. This support is eliminated when the structure is complete. Following this analogy, ELs receive language support to make content cognitively accessible to them until they achieve mastery in the second language (L2); once that mastery is accomplished, the language support is eliminated. In education, the term "scaffold" is based on research by Jerome Bruner and influenced by Lev Vygotsky. According to Bruner, scaffolding is the helpful interaction between teachers (or other adult) and the learner so that the learners can move from one idea to a more complex one or to achieve a goal. (For more, see *http://www.teacthough.com/learning/learning-theories-jerome-bruner-scaffolding-learning/* or *https://www.simplypsychology.org/bruner.html*) When giving a lecture, remember to keep it to 4- to 10-minute segments. Younger children have shorter attention spans; lectures should be kept to a minimum. Preview vocabulary and key concepts prior to lecture. Use plenty of visuals. Refrain from creating busy or text-heavy presentation slides. After the lecture, provide a minimum of two minutes for students to discuss or otherwise interact with the lecture content.

Graphic organizers are visuals used to show relationships and are important to use with all learners. However, they are particularly helpful with ELs as they learn to break down the language when learning new concepts. These are the most common graphic organizers:

- A **semantic web** or **tree diagram** shows the relationship between main ideas and subordinated components.

- A **timeline** presents a visual summary of chronological events and is ideal for showing historical events or events in a sequence.

- A **flowchart** shows cause-and-effect relationships and can be used to show steps in a process, like the process for admission to a school or program.

- A **Venn diagram** (Figure 5-6) uses circles to compare common and unique elements of two or three distinct components, such as properties of numbers, elements of stories, or events, or civilizations.

Figure 5-6
Venn diagram—Three Civilizations

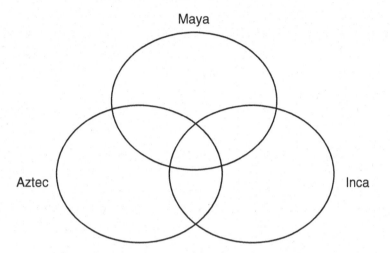

The **SQ4R** is a study strategy in which the learner is engaged in the entire reading process. The acronym stands for **survey**, **question**, **read**, **reflect**, **recite**, and **review**. During the **survey** part, readers examine the headings and major components of the text to develop predictions and generate questions. Through these **questions**, students establish the purpose for reading. As they **read**, students look for answers to the questions they generated. They monitor their comprehension as they **reflect**, write a summary, and **recite** the content they learned. Finally, they **review** to evaluate how much they learned about the content.

Academic Vocabulary in Social Studies

Academic vocabulary is the vocabulary needed to understand the concepts of school. In other words, it is the vocabulary of teaching and learning. Marzano and Pickering (2005) emphasize the importance of teaching academic vocabulary to English language learners and recommend a six-step systematic approach that includes direct instruction as well as practice and reinforcement. The steps to teach academic vocabulary are presented next.

- The teacher provides a description, explanation, or example of the new term.

- Students restate the description, example, or explanation in their own words.

- Students create a representation of the word by drawing a picture, symbol, or graphic of the word.

- Students periodically participate in activities that help to add to their knowledge of terms.

- Students discuss terms with one another.

- Students participate in games and activities that reinforce the new term.

Cooperative learning is a teaching strategy designed to create a low-anxiety learning environment in which students work together in small groups to achieve instructional goals. As a result of this instructional arrangement, students with different levels of ability or language development work collaboratively to support each other to ensure that each member masters the objectives of the lesson. This approach can easily be used to deliver content and language instruction. Traditionally, the strategy is delivered in specific steps (Arends, 1998):

1. **Present Goals**—The teacher goes over the objectives of the lesson and provides the motivation.

2. **Present Information**—The teacher presents information to students either verbally or with text.

3. **Organize Students into Learning Teams**—The teacher explains to students how to form learning teams and helps groups make an efficient transition.

4. **Assist Teamwork and Study**—The teacher assists learning teams as they do their work.

5. **Test Students on the Content**—The teacher tests students' knowledge of learning materials as each group presents the results of its work.

6. **Provide Recognition**—The teacher finds ways to recognize both individual and group efforts and achievements.

To emphasize the cooperative nature of the strategy, specific methods were developed to enrich the lessons such as Student Teams Achievement Division (STAD), Group Investigations, Think-Pair-Share, and Numbered Heads Together. These specialized methods are described in the sections that follow.

Student Teams Achievement Division (STAD)

1. The teacher presents new academic information to students.

2. Students are divided into four- or five-member learning teams.

3. Team members master the content and then help each other learn the material through tutoring, quizzing one another, or carrying on team discussions.

4. Each student receives an improvement score that helps show the growth he or she has made.

5. Daily or weekly quizzes are given to assess mastery.

6. Each week, through newsletters or a short ceremony, groups and individual students are recognized for showing the most improvement (Slavin, 1986).

Think-Pair-Share

This activity was developed as a result of the wait-time research. Wait-time research suggests that pausing for a few seconds to allow children to reflect on the question can improve the quality of the response and the overall performance of children (Rowe, 1986).

1. **Think**—The teacher poses a question and asks students to spend a minute thinking alone about the answer. No talking or walking is allowed.

2. **Pair**—Students pair off and discuss what they have been thinking about, sharing possible answers or information.

3. **Share**—Students share their answers with the whole class. The teacher goes around the classroom from pair to pair until a fourth to a half of the class has a chance to report (Lyman, 1981).

213 Cooperative Learning Strategy

This activity was designed to involve more students in the review of materials covered in class.

1. **Number**—The teacher divides the students into teams with three to five members each and assigns a number to each member.

2. **Question**—The teacher asks a question.

3. **Heads Together**—Students put their heads together to figure out the answer and to be sure everyone knows the answer.

4. **Answer**—The teacher calls a number, and students who have that number from each group raise their hands and provide the answer (Kagan, 1985).

Inquiry

Inquiry as an instructional technique has gained popularity as a relevant way to connect students to authentic careers within given disciplines. Social studies is no different. Inquiry is fundamental to social studies. According to the 2013 National Council for the Social Studies College, Career, and Civic Life (C3) Framework for Social Studies State Standards, inquiry lies at the heart of social studies. According to the C3 Framework, "Now more than ever, students need the intellectual power to recognize societal problems; ask good questions and develop robust investigations into them, consider possible solutions and consequences; separate evidence-based claims from parochial opinions; and communicate and act upon what they know" (p. 6). This document goes on to introduce the Inquiry Arc, which centers the framework and emphasizes disciplinary practices to develop "the capacity to know, analyze, explain, and argue about interdisciplinary challenges in our social world" (p. 6). Focusing on key elements of the C3 Framework, the Inquiry Design Model was designed to help teachers create inquiry-based instruction in social studies. (See *https://c3teachers.org/inquiry-design-model/* for lesson ideas.)

Inquiry is built on the premise that all children and adolescents are inherently curious. Inquiry helps students understand the world, what people do, and why they take the action that they do. The Minnesota Center for Social Studies Education explains inquiry as "an intellectual process used by social scientists to address authentic issues. Inquiry-based instruction gives students practice being political scientists, economists, geographers, and historians" (*http://www.mncsse.org/instruction/inquiry*). According to Edutopia, inquiry-based learning "uses student inquiries, questions, interests and curiosities to drive learning," which makes learning more relevant (*https://www.edutopia.org*). The teacher must carefully select resources and plan for the development of critical thinkers. Evidence is critical when studying the social studies disciplines. Students must be trained to support their statements and conclusions with evidence (data, facts, information). Further refined questions may be warranted to truly understand an issue, a group of people, or phenomenon. Throughout this process, be aware of myths and/or misconceptions so that they can be avoided and explained.

Since 2013, there has been a growth in inquiry-focused tools, blogs, research, and discussions for social studies education. GeoInquiries is one tool that introduces the use of geographic information systems (GIS) by providing short, interactive inquiry-based activities that targets the curricula being taught while modeling for teachers how to have inquiry-focused instruction. (See *https://www.esri.com/en-us/industries/k-12-education/geoinquiries*). The National Geographic Society also promotes inquiry through their Geo-inquiry support for educators. (See h*ttps://www.nationalgeographic.org/education/programs/geo-inquiry.*)

References

Acosta, T.P. (2009). Raza Unida Party. *The Handbook of Texas Online. Texas State Historical Association.*

Adams, C. (2021, March). *Timeline: How coronavirus in Texas unfolded since first case one year ago.* KXAN. *https://www.kxan.com/news/coronavirus/365-days-of-covid-how-the-coronavirus-in-texas-unfolded-one-year-after-the-first-case/.*

Arends, R. (1998). *Learning to Teach.* (4th ed.). Boston: McGraw-Hill.

Banks, J.A., P. Cookson, G. Gay, W.D. Hawley, J.J. Irvine, S. Nieto, J.W. Schofield, and W.G. Stephan. 2001. Diversity within unity essential principles for teaching and learning in a multicultural society. Phi Delta Kappan. Retrieved from *https://www.uwyo.edu/education/_files/documents/diversity-articles/banks_2001.pdf.*

Barker, E.C., & Pohl, J.W. (2009). Texas Revolution. *The Handbook of Texas Online. Texas State Historical Association. Retrieved from https://www.tshaonline.org/handbook.*

Castaneda, O.R. 2006. The Chicano Movement in Washington State 1967-2006. Seattle Civil Rights and Labor History Project. Retrieved from *https://depts.washington.edu/civilr/Chicano-movement_part1.htm.*

Centers for Disease Control and Prevention. (2014, November). *Ebola virus disease cluster in the United States–Dallas County, Texas, 2014.* Morbidity and Mortality Weekly Report (MMWR). *https://www.cdc.gov/mmwr/preview/mmwrhtml/mm63e1114a5.htm.*

Central Intelligence Agency. Central Asia: Russia. *World Factbook.* Retrieved from *https://www.cia.gov/library/publications/the-world-factbook/geos/rs.html.*

CEO Magazine. (2019, December). *28 unforgettable history-defining moments of the past decade.* CEO Magazine. *https://www.theceomagazine.com/business/world-news/historical-moments-decade.*

CUNY: The City University of New York. (2022). *Hurricanes Harvey, Irma, & Maria.* CUNY: The City University of New York *https://www.cuny.edu/about/administration/offices/ovsa/disaster-relief/hurricanes-harvey-irma.*

De Blij, Harm & Murphy, A. B. 1999. Human Geography: Culture, Society, and Space. (7th Ed.) Wiley: New York.

Earth.org. (2021, August) *15 worst wildfires in U.S. History.* Earth.org Ltd *https://earth.org/worst-wildfires-in-us-history.*

Echevarria, J., Vogt, M., and Short, D. (2000). *Making content comprehensible for English language learners: The SIOP model.* Needham Heights, MA: Allyn and Bacon.

Ferguson, J.L. (2021). *Texas History Timeline.* eReferenceDesk.com. *https://www.ereferencedesk.com/resources/state-history-timeline/texas.html.*

Fry, P. L., *Texas State Historical Association.* (n.d.). Origin of Name. *The Handbook of Texas Online. Retrieved from https://tshaonline.org/handbook/online/articles/pft04.*

Fullinwider, Robert K., International Journal of Educational Research, vol. 35, issue 3, 2001, pp. 331–343, Multicultural Education and Cosmopolitan Citizenship.

Ganeri, A., Martell, H. M., Williams, B. (1999). *The World History Encyclopedia.* Bath, UK: Parragon.

García, E. & García, E.E. Villamil, J. (2003). *Avenues: Success in language, literacy and content.* Carmel, CA: Hampton-Brown.

Gay, G. (2000). *Culturally Responsive Teaching: Theory, Research & Practice.* New York: Teachers College Press.

History.com Editors. (2022, January). *Presidential elections.* History. *https://www.history.com/topics/us-presidents/presidential-elections-1.*

Kagan, S. (1985). *Cooperative learning resources for teachers.* Riverside, CA: Spencer Kagan.

Kerr, A., History Department, Ohio State University. (n.d.). Temperance and prohibition. Retrieved from https://prohibition.osu.edu.

Lister, T.R. Sanchez, M. Bixler, S. O'ley, M. Hogenmiller, & M. Tawfeeq (2018). ISIS goes global: 143 attacks in 29 countries have killed 2,043. CNN. Retrieved from *https://www.cnn.com/2015/12/17/world/mapping-isis-attacks-around-the-world/index.html.*

Lyman, F.T. (1981). The responsive classroom discussion: The inclusion of all students. In A.S. Anderson (Ed.), *Mainstreaming Digest (*e109–113). College Park, MD: University of Maryland Press.

Marzano, R., & Pickering, D. (2005). *Building academic vocabulary: Teacher's manual.* Alexandria, VA: Association for Supervision and Curriculum Development (ASCD).

McFarland, A. (2019, December). *In 2018, the United States consumed more energy than ever before.* Independent Statistics & Analysis: U.S. Energy Information Administration. *https://www.eia.gov/todayinenergy/detail.php?id=42335.*

National Council for the Social Studies (NCSS). (2006). National Curriculum Standards for Social Studies—Executive Summary. Retrieved from *https://www.socialstudies.org/standards/national-curriculum-standards-social-studies-executive-summary.*

National Council for the Social Studies (2010). National Curriculum Standards for Social Studies: A Framework for Teaching, Learning, and Assessment. Retrieved from *https://www.socialstudies.org/standards/curriculum.*

National Council for the Social Studies (NCSS), The College, Career, and Civic Life (C3) Framework for Social Studies State Standards: Guidance for Enhancing the Rigor of K–12 Civics, Economics, Geography, and History (Silver Spring, MD: NCSS, 2013).

National Interagency Fire Center. (2022, April). *National Fire News.* National Interagency Fire Center. *https://www.nifc.gov/fire-information/nfn.*

Nieto, S. (1996). *Affirming diversity: The sociopolitical context of multicultural education* (2nd ed.). White Plains, NY: Longman.

Parker, W.C. (2001). *Social Studies in Elementary Education* (11th ed.). Columbus, OH: Merrill Prentice-Hall.

Pauls, E.P. (2021, August). *Native American. Encyclopedia Britannica.* Retrieved from *https://www.britannica.com/topic/Native-American.*

Perttula, T.K. (2020, October). *Caddo Indians.* Texas State Historical Association. *https://www.tshaonline.org/handbook/entries/caddo-indians.*

Potts, J. (1994). *Adventure Tales of America.* Dallas, TX: Signal Media.

Pruitt, S. (2019, December). *14 major events of the 2010s.* History. *https://www.history.com/news/2010s-decade-major-events.*

Rapier, R. (2019, January). *U.S. renewable power capacity surpasses coal for the first time.* Forbes.

Rodgers, L., D. Gritten, J. Offer, and P. Asare. (March 11, 2016). "Syria: The story of the conflict." BBC News. Retrieved from *http://www.bbc.com/news/world-middle-east-26116868.*

Roos, D. (2021, February). *How many U.S. presidents have faced impeachment?* History. *https://www.history.com/news/how-many-presidents-impeached.*

Rosado, L., & Salazar, D. (2002–2003). La Conexión: The English/Spanish connection. *National Forum of Applied Educational Research Journal 15*(4): 51–66.

Rosado, L., Hellawell, M. & Zamora, B.E. (June 6, 2011). An Analysis of the Education System in Mexico and the United States from Pre-Kindergarten to 12th Grade. Education Resources Information Center (ERIC #520900). Available: *https://files.eric.ed.gov/fulltext/ED520900.pdf.*

Rosales Castañeda, O. (2006). *The Chicano Movement in Washington State: Political activism in the Puget Sound and Yakima Valley regions, 1960s-1980s.* Retrieved from *http://historylink.org/File/7922.*

Rowe, M.B. (1986). *Wait Times: Slowing down may be a way of speeding up. Journal of Teacher Education, 37,* 43–50.

Schifini, A. (1985). *Sheltered English: Content area instruction for limited English proficiency students.* Los Angeles, CA: Los Angeles County Office of Education.

Seattle Civil Rights and Labor History Project. 2006.

Sheppard, D.E. (n.d.) *Cabeza de Vaca in North America.* Spanish exploration and conquest of Native America. Retrieved from *http://floridahistory.com.*

Slavin, R. (1986). *Student Learning: An overview and practical guide.* Washington, DC: Professional Library, National Education Association.

Strayhorn, C.K. (2004), Fall. "The Rebound is Here." Texas Economic Update. Window on State Government. Retrieved from *http://www.window.state.tx.us/ecodata/teufall04/.*

Sweet, J. (2022, January). *Famous protests in the U.S. history and their impacts.* Stacker. *https://stacker.com/stories/4302/famous-protests-us-history-and-their-impact.*

Texas Health and Human Services. (2019). *Coronavirus Disease 2019 (COVID-19).* Texas Department of State Health Services. *https://www.dshs.state.tx.us/coronavirus.*

The Weather Company. (2022). *Hurricane and Tropical Cyclones.* Weather Underground. *https://www.wunderground.com/hurricane/archive.*

U.S. Food and Drug Administration. (2021, August). *FDA Approves First COVID-19 Vaccine.* U.S. Food and Drug Administration. *https://www.fda.gov/news-events/press-announcements/fda-approves-first-covid-19-vaccine.*

United Nationals Framework Convention on Climate Change (UNFCC). (2022). *The Paris Agreement.* United Nations Climate Change. *https://unfccc.int/process-and-meetings/the-paris-agreement/the-paris-agreement.*

CHAPTER 6

Subject Test IV: Science (809)

OVERVIEW OF SUBJECT TEST IV: SCIENCE

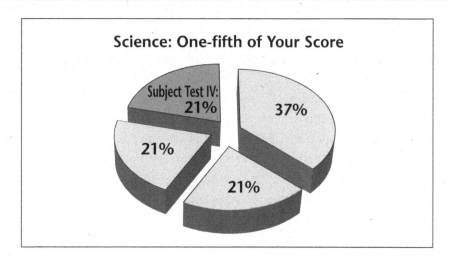

Subject Test IV: Science, as is the case with the Mathematics and Social Studies subject tests, represents approximately one-fifth of the Core Subjects 4–8 test. You'll have 50 minutes to answer 42 test items. As with Social Studies, this gives you slightly more than one minute for each question. Each of the four subject tests that make up the Core Subjects 4–8 test is individually timed.

The Science subject test assesses 11 Texas educator standards for teaching middle school science, including that the teacher:

I.   Manages classroom, field, and laboratory activities to ensure the safety of all students and the ethical care and treatment of organisms and specimens;

II. Understands the correct use of tools, materials, equipment, and technologies;

III. Understands the process of scientific inquiry and its role in science instruction;

IV. Has theoretical and practical knowledge about teaching science and about how students learn science;

V.   Knows the varied and appropriate assessments and assessment practices to monitor science learning;

VI. Understands the history and nature of science;

VII. Understands how science affects the daily lives of students and how it interacts with and influences personal and societal decisions;

VIII. Knows and understands the science content appropriate to teach the statewide curriculum (Texas Essential Knowledge and Skills) in physical science;

IX. Knows and understands the science content appropriate to teach the statewide curriculum (Texas Essential Knowledge and Skills) in life science;

X.   Knows and understands the science content appropriate to teach the statewide curriculum (Texas Essential Knowledge and Skills) in Earth and space science; and

XI. Knows unifying concepts and processes that are common to all sciences.

The Science subject test embraces 23 competencies, which broadly define "what an entry-level educator in this field in Texas public schools should know and be able to do," according to the Texas Education Agency. These competencies are covered in sequence in this chapter. As part of your preparation, we encourage you to drill down in the official test framework to the descriptive statements, which describe the finer points of the knowledge and skills for which you are accountable. We list the descriptive statements under each competency.

The National Science Teachers Association (NSTA) (2012) lists the following standards for effective science teaching (from: *http://www.nsta.org/preservice/docs/2012NSTAPreserviceScienc eStandards.pdf*):

1. Effective teachers of science understand and articulate the knowledge and practices of contemporary science. They interrelate and interpret important concepts, ideas, and applications in their fields of licensure.

2. Effective teachers of science understand how students learn and develop scientific knowledge. Preservice teachers use scientific inquiry to develop this knowledge for all students.

3. Effective teachers of science are able to plan for engaging all students in science learning by setting appropriate goals that are consistent with knowledge of how students learn science and are aligned with state and national standards. The plans reflect the nature and social context of science, inquiry, and appropriate safety considerations. Candidates design and select learning activities, instructional settings, and resources—including science-specific technology, to achieve those goals; and they plan fair and equitable assessment strategies to evaluate if the learning goals are met.

4. Effective teachers of science can, in a P–12 classroom setting, demonstrate and maintain chemical safety, safety procedures, and the ethical treatment of living organisms needed in the P–12 science classroom appropriate to their area of licensure.

5. Effective teachers of science provide evidence to show that P–12 students' understanding of major science concepts, principles, theories, and laws have changed as a result of instruction by the candidate and that student knowledge is at a level of understanding beyond memorization. Candidates provide evidence for the diversity of students they teach.

6. Effective teachers of science strive continuously to improve their knowledge and understanding of the ever-changing knowledge base of both content, and science pedagogy, including approaches for addressing inequities and inclusion for all students in science. They identify with, and conduct themselves as part of, the science education community.

These standards are the hallmark of good science teaching agreed upon by science teachers and experienced professionals in the field. Essentially, for students to learn science, they must be consistently engaged in hands-on, manipulative activities. Teaching practices focusing on experience and direct investigation will best promote students' science learning. It is the teacher's responsibility to plan active learning experiences that engage students in constructing new understandings of scientific phenomena, effectively measure learning, and provide a safe and interactive learning environment for all students.

NSTA strongly supports the idea that scientific inquiry should be a basic component of the curriculum in every grade in American schools (NSTA 2002). The 2016 NSTA position paper *Science Education for Middle Level Students* acknowledges the uniqueness of students in the middle grades with the statement, "The middle school years, Grades 5 through 9, are a time of tremendous physical, emotional, and cognitive changes for students. It also is a pivotal time in their understanding of and enthusiasm for science." (p. 1). It is important, therefore, that teachers gain sound knowledge of the content; however, it is equally important that they teach this content in ways that are motivating, interesting, and meaningful to students—focusing primarily on students having direct, hands-on inquiry-based learning experiences and connecting what they learn to everyday life.

Accordingly, teachers must consistently do the following in teaching science to middle-level students (2016 *Science Education for Middle Level Students*, NSTA Position Paper, p. 1):

- Nurture curiosity about the natural world.

- Provide opportunities for students to engage in science and engineering experiences.

- Engage students in multiple laboratory investigations every week.

- Help students understand the nature of science by experiencing inquiry-based science in the classroom.

- Provide opportunities for students to work both independently and in collaborative groups.

- Integrate science learning with other subjects across the curriculum.

- Provide opportunities for and encourage critical thinking, reasoning, and analyses of evidence-based results.

- Give students experience in communicating and sharing ideas with others.

It is also important that science teaching utilizes scientific findings as well as the advancements of people from a variety of cultures, and ensures equitable learning among all students.

Further, the National Academies report titled *A Framework for K–12 Science Education: Practices, Crosscutting Concepts, and Core Ideas* (National Research Council [NRC], 2012) emphasizes that "one of the principal goals of science education has been to cultivate students' scientific habits of mind, develop their capability to engage in scientific inquiry and teach them how to reason in a scientific context" (p. 3-1). It is essential that teachers provide direct experiences so students may develop the knowledge they need through these experiences. Accordingly, "a narrow focus on content alone has the unfortunate consequence of leaving the students with naïve conceptions of the nature of scientific inquiry and the impression that science is simply a body of isolated facts" (NRC 2011, p. 3-4). To be most effective in helping students learn science, teachers need to understand both the content and process of science. Importantly, teachers must understand and develop skill in implementing experiential, inquiry-based science as the primary teaching practice in all K–12 classrooms.

COMPETENCY 001

The teacher understands how to manage learning activities to ensure the safety of all students.

The beginning teacher:

A. Understands safety regulations and guidelines for science facilities and science instruction.

B. Knows procedures for and sources of information regarding the appropriate handling, use, disposal, care, and maintenance of chemicals, materials, specimens, and equipment.

C. Knows procedures for the safe handling and ethical care and treatment of organisms and specimens.

Teachers need to develop and communicate **safety guidelines** to students, model and implement safe practices in the classroom, and ensure all students follow the safety guidelines at all times. Teachers should prepare a safety contract for students listing all guidelines and behavioral expectations to be read aloud in class. The contract must be signed by both the student and a parent or guardian. Safety rules should be clearly posted in the classroom and periodically reviewed, particularly before engaging in laboratory activities. Safe practices to consistently implement and enforce in the classroom include the following:

- Require students to use appropriate personal protective gear like goggles, laboratory coats, and gloves.

- Use appropriate procedures for cleaning and disposing of materials.

- Adhere to appropriate disciplinary procedures to avoid accidents; for example, do not allow children to play with water or other lab materials.

- Substitute less hazardous equivalent materials when possible; for example, use cleaning products instead of chemicals in their pure form; use mild acids such as vinegar instead of more dangerous acids if appropriate.

- Use polyethylene or metal containers in place of glass.

- Advise children to avoid tasting or ingesting substances or materials.

- Label containers appropriately to avoid confusion.

- Control the distribution of materials to students and provide appropriate containers to safely transport materials.

- Control the use of sharp objects that can puncture the skin, providing strict rules and monitoring behavior at all times.

- Supervise the use of living organisms and ensure humane treatment of organisms is practiced.

- Monitor the cleaning of instruments used to ensure proper sanitation and avoid breakage.

- Avoid experimenting with human cells and bodily fluids.

- Share the responsibility for the safety of the students with the whole group; that is, students should motivate each other to follow safety procedures.

- Make provisions for the movement and handling of equipment and materials for students with special needs.

- Prepare, review, and send home an age-appropriate safety contract requiring parent/guardian signature.

- Organize all materials to be used in class by placing them in separate bins for a member of each student group to pick up for use for the lab activity and for returning materials after the lab activity.

- Clearly label and demonstrate the use of safety equipment with students, such as the eyewash station and fire blanket.

- Prepare and practice an emergency plan with students should an accident occur.

- Document all accidents, regardless of how minor they may be, and have another teacher sign as a witness if possible.

- Clearly write and read to students the safety precautions for the laboratory before beginning the activity. Ensure all students understand by responding to their questions before beginning.

- Place posters around the room emphasizing the safety rules of the classroom and laboratory.

- Keep all chemicals, glassware, and other laboratory materials in locked cabinets with no unsupervised student access.

- Maintain regular inventory of all laboratory materials and chemicals.

- Store acids and other caustic chemicals in cabinets close to the floor in case they fall when retrieving for use.

- When using an open flame, such as lit candles, students must tie long hair back and tape or roll up loose sleeves to avoid contact with the fire.

- Caution students on the use of hot plates and placing materials on the hot plates reminding students that it remains warm long after it has been turned off.

The use of dangerous chemical substances in the middle-level classroom may be generally limited in scope. Many laboratory chemicals can be substituted with household products. However, care needs to be taken even when handling household chemicals. It is important to demonstrate **safe laboratory procedures** for the classroom because household products are still chemicals and pose some level of risk to students. **Safety management** of chemicals in the classroom requires teachers to have knowledge of those chemicals and their properties. For example, teachers need to be aware that a simple tool like a mercury thermometer can break and thus pose a danger to students.

The National Science Teachers Association has an official position and guidelines on animals in the classroom. This information can be found at the NSTA website: *www.nsta.org/about/positions/animals.aspx*. NSTA contends that using animals in the classroom sparks interest and curiosity among students, and is therefore important to their science education experience. However, animals must be cared for and treated in a **humane and ethical manner**. This includes animals that may not be recognized as falling within these guidelines, from ants in ant farms, to mealworms, to guinea pigs and rabbits. Following are a few key guidelines in the treatment of animals in the classroom.

- Send permission slips home to be signed by parents or guardians if you anticipate the children will be handling the animals. This permission can go along with the safety contract previously described.

- Research and learn as much as possible about the animals, their typical behaviors, diet, sleep patterns, and habitats in advance of housing the animals in the classroom.

- Instruct students on how to handle animals and monitor their handling of animals at all times.

- Ensure the animals' habitats, including cages or other living quarters, are clean and regularly maintained. With instruction, cleaning animal housing can be done on a rotating basis by the students, teaching them important lessons on responsibility and fulfilling necessary chores.

- Feed and water the animals on a regular schedule according to the dietary needs of the animal.

- Demonstrate safe and humane treatment, and strictly enforce this standard among all who have access to the animals.

When animals are used in dissection, it is critical that students learn to respect that this animal was a once a living organism, and that the dissection is for their learning. Monitor the dissection to ensure students treat the specimen with respect (e.g., do not "play" with internal organs). Have a backup plan for students who may object to participating in animal dissection, or have low tolerance for the activity.

In addition to NSTA, the American Psychological Association provides guidelines for the ethical treatment of animals. These guidelines can be found at: *www.apa.org/science/leadership/care/guidelines.aspx*. Most of the information presented deals with using animals in scientific research; however, the guidelines also present useful information on caring for animals.

COMPETENCY 002

The teacher understands the correct use of tools, materials, equipment, and technologies.

The beginning teacher:

A. Selects and safely uses appropriate tools, technologies, materials, and equipment needed for instructional activities.

B. Understands concepts of precision, accuracy, and error with regard to reading and recording numerical data from a scientific instrument.

C. Understands how to gather, organize, display, and communicate data in a variety of ways (e.g., charts, tables, graphs, diagrams, written reports, oral presentations, maps, satellite views).

D. Understands various units of measure such as the International System of Units (SI or metric system), light years, and degrees Celsius, and performs unit conversions within measurement systems (e.g., grams to kilograms, meters to millimeters).

Scientific experimentation requires **careful observation and precise measures** beyond what we can determine through our senses alone. To extend what can be observed with our senses scientific instruments are used such as balances, microscopes, beakers, electronic probes, and graduated cylinders to allow precise observations and measurements are made. Science requires the use of standard measuring devices to be sure that the information is clear, accurate, and able to be replicated in experimental settings.

In selecting the appropriate tools to use for a given observation and measurement consider the task that is needed and match that with the instrument as follows.

- To take an object's **mass** (amount of matter in an object), use triple beam or electronic balance and obtain the measurement in grams or kilograms. If taking the mass of a liquid or object that will not stay on the balance or scale, use a container such as a beaker or plastic cup in which to place the liquid or object. First measure and record the mass of the container minus the liquid or object. Then place the liquid or object in the container and measure the mass of both objects together. Subtract the mass of the container from the mass of both the container and liquid or object together to obtain the measure of only liquid or object. Regardless of the device used to measure mass, whether triple beam or electronic balance, the device must be zeroed out before placing the object on the device. This will ensure the mass measured is accurate.

- To measure the **volume** (amount of space something occupies) of a liquid, use a graduated cylinder for a precise measure in milliliters. Liquids that are polar molecules such as water cling to the walls of the container forming a downward arc shape or meniscus. The lowest point in the arc or meniscus is the accurate reading of liquid volume. It is best to have students view the meniscus at eye level to obtain an accurate reading.

- To measure the volume of an irregular object such as a rock, place water in a graduated cylinder to allow room for the object when dropped into the liquid, typically up to about half-way to three-quarters of the way to the top. Measure the water level as described above, reading and recording the water level at the meniscus. Then place the object into the graduated cylinder, being careful not to allow water to splash. The water will rise to a new level according to the volume of water displaced by the object. Measure the new volume of water with the object in the graduated cylinder. Then subtract the beginning volume of water to obtain the volume of the irregular object. One milliliter (ml) is a liquid volume measure that is equal to one cubic centimeter (cc or cm^3) that is a solid volume measure.

- Measuring the volume of a cube is accomplished by taking the length × width × height of the object using a metric tape measure or meter stick. The volume is typically recorded in cubic centimeters (cc or cm^3).

- Beakers are usually used to hold liquids, with a less precise measure of volume. Beakers are useful in making solutions.

- **Compound light microscopes** are used to observe very small specimens, and provide fairly high magnification. Specimens must be very thin when placed on a slide on the stage of the microscope in order that light may pass through.

- **Dissecting microscopes** have lower magnification than compound microscopes and are used for observing larger specimens such as whole insects, leaves, and rock minerals.

The United States uses a combination of the **English system of measurement** (standard) and the **International System of Units** (SI), also known as the metric system. The United States is the only technologically developed country in the world that uses the English system for business transactions and for day-to-day activities. However, for international business, engineering, and natural sciences, all countries use the more standardized, precise system of weights and measurement, the metric system. The English system uses pounds, gallons, and inches for measurement, while the metric system uses degrees Celsius, grams or kilograms, liters, and meters. The metric system uses a system of fractions and multiples of units that are related to each other by powers of 10, allowing conversion and comparison of measures simply by shifting a decimal point, and avoiding the lengthy arithmetical operations required by the English system. Examples of metric conversions include: 1.0 kilograms is equivalent to 1,000 grams and 1.0 meter is equivalent to 1,000 millimeters. The TEKS requires the teaching of both the metric and the English systems; however, all scientific data are reported using the metric system. In addition to the English and metric systems, students should be familiar with the **light-year** as a unit of measurement. It is important to understand that light-years are used to measure astronomical distances for objects in outer space and *not* a measure of time (as the term "years" may imply).

Students should become comfortable with using metric measurements. To help them learn to think metric, it is important to show them exactly what a gram or kilogram, for example, looks and "feels" like, along with meters, centimeters, liters, and milliliters. Have students measure and make items according to these standards as a reference for all to use in the classroom.

In addition to gathering data, such as measurements, students should be able to display their data appropriately. Teachers should be familiar with the varied ways to display data, which include: charts, tables, graphs, diagrams, written reports, oral presentations, maps, and satellite views.

COMPETENCY 003

The teacher understands the process of scientific inquiry and the history and nature of science.

The beginning teacher:

A. Understands the characteristics of various types of scientific investigations (e.g., descriptive studies, comparative data analysis, experiments).

B. Understands how to design, conduct, and communicate the results of a variety of scientific investigations.

C. Understands the historical development of science (e.g., cell theory, plate tectonics, laws of motion, universal gravity, atomic theory) and the contributions that diverse cultures and individuals of both genders have made to scientific knowledge.

D. Understands the roles that logical reasoning, verifiable evidence, prediction, and peer review play in the process of generating and evaluating scientific knowledge.

E. Understands principles of scientific ethics (e.g., honest and complete reporting of data, informed consent, legal constraints).

F. Develops, analyzes, and evaluates different explanations for a given scientific result.

G. Demonstrates an understanding of potential sources of error in an investigation.

H. Demonstrates an understanding of how to communicate and defend the results of an investigation.

I. Demonstrates an ability to identify, review, and evaluate legitimate sources of scientific information.

One common misunderstanding about **scientific inquiry** is that scientific investigations are limited to one method, the **scientific method**. Many science classrooms support this idea with a poster that describes this single method, the experimental method. These posters often describe a number of "steps" including a hypothesis, control, and variable to be manipulated. However, science has more than one way to carry out investigations, with experimental science as *just one* of several recognized forms of scientific inquiry accepted by the scientific community. Some of these forms of scientific inquiry include: descriptive studies, comparative data analysis, and as mentioned, experiments. **Descriptive studies** are those where the purpose of the inquiry is to explain or describe observations. For example, in an animal dissection, the students would describe observations of the internal systems and organs of the animal. The students would observe, illustrate, and label organs and make inferences on their functions or study them more in-depth. The students would record observations through illustrations, labels, and anatomical (appearances) as well as physiological (functions) descriptions. An astronomer, geologist, and ecologist may also use descriptive studies in their work, while still engaging in scientific inquiry. For example, an astronomer would describe planetary motions, a geologist may describe rocks and rock layers, and an ecologist would describe interrelationships between and among living organisms in the natural environment. Descriptive studies simply explain "what is." For more information, see: *http://www.visionlearning.com/en/library/Process-of-Science/49/Description-in-Scientific-Research/151.*

Comparative investigations are more open than descriptive studies; observations and data collected are compared among different existing situations, such as comparing and contrasting data collected on two different populations. Comparative investigations may have students compare the functions of, for example, the gills in fish with the lungs of a fetal pig, viewing cross sections of each under the microscope. Comparative studies share some features with descriptive studies as well as experimental studies. As with experimental studies, the researcher attempts to find the relationships between variables by observing and recording differences and similarities; for example, between different organisms, rock types, stars, and/or populations. However, unlike experimental studies, comparative studies do not involve setting up "treatments" or "controls." Like descriptive studies, comparative investigations describe what exists, making inferences about similarities and differences based on observations and data. Note, however, that simple comparative studies are not simple notations of similarities and differences—there must be "systematic cataloguing of the nature and/or behavior of two or more variables, and the quantification of the relationships between them." For more information, see *www.visionlearning.com/en/library/Process-of-Science/49/ Comparison-in-Scientific-Research/152.*

Experiments attempt to find relationships among variables within a particular phenomenon. Scientists using the experimental method, for example, a chemist experimenting on the effects of a certain chemical on bacterial growth may start with a hypothesis and experimental controls in a more structured manner. Experimental controls mean that all variables are constant between two different situations or groups except the variable being tested. For instance, to determine whether or not "plants need light to survive and grow," the experiment would involve starting with two sets of plants of the same kind (e.g., bean plants) in the same types of pots, with the same amount and type of soil, under the same temperature conditions, receiving the same amount of water, and the same amount of light. These are the **independent variables** because they are the same for all plants. Consistency among the independent variables can also be determined by measuring and recording beginning experiment plant heights, number of leaves, and quality of color, for example. Photos or drawings would also add data to the experiment. Before beginning the experiment, often but not always, the researcher prepares a hypothesis to logically state what he or she predicts will be the result. Then the experiment begins: the researcher keeps one set of plants in the light, and takes one set of equivalent plants and places them in the dark. The set of plants in the light are the experimental "control" group because conditions are not changed. The second set of plants placed in the dark are the "treatment" group—these plants are subjected to only *one* different variable, also called the *dependent* variable—and that is they are no longer exposed to light. The **dependent variable** is the one aspect that is changed or different between one group and another. The plants would be observed and measured over time, still receiving the same amount of water, air, and heat (placed within the same temperature range), and data would be recorded on observed differences between the plants in the light and in the dark. The observed differences would be used to accept or fail to accept the hypothesis. For more information on experimental research in science, see: *http://www. visionlearning.com/en/library/Process-of-Science/49/Experimentation-in-Scientific-Research/150.*

It should be noted that experiments do not always precisely follow the linear set of steps of the scientific method from hypothesis to the reporting of results. Instead, the process is often a cyclical and nonlinear endeavor to establish relationships between variables, and sometimes to attempt to determine cause and effect. Regardless of the type of inquiry investigation being conducted (descriptive, comparative, experimental), all scientific investigations share at least one aspect: a question. The type of scientific inquiry to engage always hinges on the nature of the question(s) and the best way to respond.

In the classroom there are multiple ways to implement inquiry science, often referred to as structured, guided, or open. These instructional methods vary primarily in the amount of control the teacher has in the inquiry process, along with the nature of the scientific research question. Teachers often begin the school year with more structured investigations; then, as students learn the routines and rules of the classroom and laboratory, teachers turn more control over to students to engage in more open inquiry. Allowing more student-directed open inquiry should be a goal of every science teacher so that students experience the true nature of the scientific discipline and understand what scientists do! In helping students understand and become immersed in what scientists do in the profession, teachers must also incorporate practice in developing students' communication skills. In the global scientific community, scientific research and information is always shared with and disseminated to other scientists and the general public using strong communication skills. Therefore, it is critical that students learn to effectively convey what they're doing to others, learning to effectively argue their reasoning and defend the results and explanations derived from their investigations. Students must use logical scientific reasoning and present sound arguments for their findings, not based on opinion but on **experimental evidence**. These communication skills can best be developed and promoted by engaging students in collaborative, inquiry-based science in the classroom, and providing them with regular opportunities to present findings in written and oral forms using a variety of delivery mechanisms (posters, technical papers, technology). Students should also be familiar with peer review—meaning that their investigations and findings are always subject to the critical review of others. In the scientific community, results of investigations are never published before they are carefully and critically reviewed and scrutinized by peers in the same field of study. Communicating results and allowing peer review in a scientific (not personal) manner should be practiced in the science classroom. The National Research Council promotes the need for strong communication among students as stated in the publication *Inquiry and the National Science Education Standards* (NRC, 2000). In this document, the NRC (2000) specifically states that students' scientific explanations "must adhere to criteria such as: a proposed explanation must be logically consistent; it must abide by the rules of evidence; it must be open to questions and possible modification; and it must be based on historical and current scientific knowledge" (p. 20). The book addresses several of the ideas and responsibilities encountered by students while conducting scientific inquiry. Further, according to the Next Generation Science Standards[7] (NGSS), the practices of science involve the following activities. For more information see: *https://www.nextgenscience.org/*.

1. Asking questions (for science) and defining problems (for engineering)

2. Developing and using models

3. Planning and carrying out investigations

4. Analyzing and interpreting data

---

[7] The NGSS are K–12 science content standards that set expectations for what students should know and be able to do. The standards were developed by states to improve science education for all students.

5. Using mathematics and computational thinking

6. Constructing explanations (for science) and designing solutions (for engineering)

7. Engaging in argument from evidence

8. Obtaining, evaluating, and communicating information

Teachers should understand the historical development of science (e.g., the development of cell theory or plate tectonics) and the contributions that diverse cultures and individuals of both genders have made to scientific knowledge. Although the "modern science" we practice today finds its origins in the European Renaissance, it was the "reawakening" to the work of many non-Western cultures (e.g., Arab philosophers and scholars) that led to the knowledge and technological advances seen today in medicine and nearly all other fields of science. These contributions and contributions from the diverse populations and regions of the world need to be regularly introduced and discussed in the classroom. Teaching the history of science will help students better understand how learning leads to discoveries and help them realize that they are the scientists of the present and future.

Important history of science topics for teachers to understand and to incorporate into their teaching are shown in Table 6.1.

It is important to demonstrate to students that women have made tremendous contributions to the body of scientific knowledge. For example, it was astronomer Cecilia Payne (1900–1979) who challenged the assumptions of the prevailing opinion that the sun was composed primarily of iron. It was her spectroscopic work that suggested the sun was actually composed primarily of hydrogen and helium. As it was during her lifetime, her work is often ignored in the classroom today. Yet she is credited with providing a basis for the discovery of how the sun produces its energy (i.e., through fusion).

Teachers should know and use the history of science in their teaching, integrating the diverse number of scientists who made scientific contributions throughout history and in present-day science. The incorporation in classroom discussion of scientists who have made important contributions to present-day scientific understandings and advances must be done with attention to equity. At the core of this competency is the premise that teachers must provide equitable science learning opportunities for their students. That is, science and science education is for *all students* regardless of gender, culture, ethnicity, physical ability, or learning exceptionality. Teachers must ensure that the examples they provide, the students called upon to respond, the opportunity to experience inquiry, and treatment of all students is equitable and fair at all times. It is crucial that students see *themselves* as scientists and as fully capable of solving problems and engaging in the inquiry process.

Table 6.1
History of Important Scientific Concepts to Use in Classroom Teaching

Concept	Description	Who	Timeframe	Resource
Cell theory	All living things are made up of cells and all cells have arisen from other existing cells.	Robert Hooke Henri Dutrochet	1635–1703 1776–1847	*http://www. biologyreference. com/Gr-Hi/ History-of-Biology-Cell-Theory-and-Cell-Structure.html*
Plate Tectonics	Continents on Earth today were long ago formed together in a single landmass.	Alfred Wegener	1880–1930	*http://www.scec. org/education/k12/ learn/plate2.htm*
Laws of Motion	1. An object at rest will remain at rest unless acted on by an unbalanced force. An object in motion continues in motion with the same speed and in the same direction unless acted upon by an unbalanced force. This is known as the law of inertia. 2. Acceleration is produced when a force acts on a mass. The greater the mass, the greater the amount of force needed (to accelerate the object). 3. For every action there is an equal and opposite reaction.	Sir Isaac Newton	1643–1727	*http://teachertech. rice.edu/ Participants/ louviere/Newton/ index.html*
Universal Gravity	Every object in the universe attracts every other object with a force directed along the line of centers for the two objects that is proportional to the product of their masses and inversely proportional to the square of the separation between the two objects.	Sir Isaac Newton	1643–1727	*http://csep10.phys. utk.edu/astr161/ lect/history/ newtongrav.html*
Technology	The invention and development of systematic techniques and/or tools for making and doing things.	Various Scientists and Inventors	2.5 Million Years Ago to the Present	*http://www. historyworld. net/wrldhis/ PlainTextHistories. asp?historyid=ab11*

Ethical standards are an essential aspect of science to preserve the scholarship and rigor of the discipline. Consequently, scientists' research and reporting of research is guided by a strict code of ethics; this practice should also be followed in the classroom. The following list is a summary of ethics that apply to the middle school classroom (Resnik, 1993; Resnik, 2015):

1. **Scientific Honesty:** Do not commit scientific fraud, i.e., do not fabricate, fudge, trim, cook, destroy, or misrepresent data.

2. **Carefulness:** Strive to avoid careless errors or sloppiness in all aspects of scientific work.

3. **Intellectual Freedom:** Scientists should be allowed to pursue new ideas and criticize old ones. They should be free to conduct research they find interesting.

4. **Openness:** i.e., share data, results, methods, theories, equipment, and so on.

5. **Acceptance of Criticism:** Allow people to see your work; be open to criticism.

6. **Assignment of Credit:** Do not plagiarize the work of other scientists; give credit where credit is due (but not where it is not due).

In addition to these six principles, scientists must also:

- Report findings in a complete and thorough manner.

- Consider the principles of informed consent and legal constraints when conducting experiments.

Informed consent pertains to experiments, including surveys conducted with human beings. Informed consent means individuals participating in the experiment or research study have full knowledge of what they will be required to do as part of the study/experiment, including any harmful side effects, and that they understand they may withdraw their participation at any time.

Legal constraints for scientists include the ethical treatment of both humans and animals that participate in the experiment or study. There are multiple laws in place to ensure the safety of humans and animals involved in experimentations.

Teachers should understand the potential sources of error or uncertainty in inquiry-based investigations. Two common sources of error that students might encounter are systematic and random error. Systematic errors are due to faulty instruments. Random errors are not predictable and may stem from a variety of causes, including human error in interpreting data, recording data incorrectly, or inaccurate readings of measurements.

In addition, teachers should be knowledgeable when it comes to establishing reliable sources of scientific information. Teachers should be able to recognize sources that adhere to the above principles and those that do not. Websites and journal articles published by professional associations are generally reliable, **peer-reviewed sources** of information; for example, the journal titled *Science* is published by the American Association for the Advancement of Science. Websites that are sponsored by legitimate agencies such as NASA, the National Science Foundation (NSF), and the National Institutes of Health (NIH) are also reliable. Reliably sourced research and information is screened and reported with great attention to accuracy and quality prior to publishing through a rigorous, peer-reviewed process. It is always good practice to review several sources of information before arriving at conclusions as to the saliency of the information presented. A single source is unacceptable as it may provide a narrow view, may have promotional or self-interest at stake, and/or may provide one-sided or biased information. For example, when conducting research on causes and treatments of cancer, it is best to seek several legitimate sources for information and consistency in findings presented by these sources. The World Health Organization (WHO), NIH, and sources such as a renowned medical facility like the Mayo Clinic are more reliable than unknown sources. Think of it this way: You would not want to depend on citing research funded by the pharmaceutical company whose drugs are sold to treat the disease.

COMPETENCY 004

The teacher understands how science impacts the daily lives of students and interacts with and influences personal and societal decisions.

The beginning teacher:

A. Understands that decisions about the use of science are based on factors such as ethical standards, economics, and personal and societal needs.

B. Applies scientific principles and the theory of probability to analyze the advantages of, disadvantages of, or alternatives to a given decision or course of action.

C. Applies scientific principles and processes to analyze factors that influence personal choices concerning fitness and health, including physiological and psychological effects and risks associated with the use of substances and substance abuse.

D. Understands concepts, characteristics, and issues related to changes in populations and human population growth.

E. Understands the types and uses of natural resources and the effects of human consumption on the renewal and depletion of global resources (e.g., energy, sustainability).

F. Understands the role science can play in helping resolve personal, societal, and global challenges (e.g., water quality, public health, climate change).

Teachers need to remain knowledgeable of the influences of science and technology on the lives of students and the extent to which these fields permeate students' lives. The functioning of their bodies, the potential threat of diseases, issues of sustainability and the natural environment around them, and their everyday use of electrical appliances, computers, and cell phones are examples of biological and physical science in their lives. Many of these topics and technologies can be used productively in classroom science instruction, as they are intertwined in the lives of students. However, teachers need to be aware that students tend to keep the science they learn in school separate from the science they experience in everyday life. Instead of teaching science and technology in isolation and maintaining this pervasive separation, teachers must help students connect the science they are learning in school to the world around them. Integrating everyday life experiences and personal and societal topics into the classroom through science teaching broadens students' conceptual understandings and promotes the usefulness, value, and applicability of science. In inquiry science, the optimal time to make connections with everyday life phenomena is either after or while students experience a hands-on lab activity and construct an understanding of the concept. To make sense of science, the student must have the background needed to relate the newly learned concept to their everyday lives and see how the concept works in differing contexts. Connecting newly learned concepts to the student's life experiences makes learning more meaningful and helps students retain understanding of the concept for later use. Relating science to what students already know and experience in life helps bridge the gap between "school science" and science they observe and experience in everyday life.

Another approach is to place the societal and everyday life connections in the context of science through Project Based Learning or PBL (Krajcik et al., 1994). In PBL, a societal topic is selected as the overarching theme, and the teacher leads the students in, or the students initiate their own, inquiry-based science experiences connected to the overarching theme, or project. Project Based Learning engages students in authentic learning activities that are motivating and designed to answer a question or solve a problem. PBL provides students with experiences that are consistent with learning and workplace activities that are present in the everyday world. More specifically, PBL is defined as "a systematic teaching method that engages students in learning essential knowledge and life-enhancing skills through an extended, student-influenced inquiry process structured around complex, authentic questions and carefully designed products and tasks" (The Buck Institute for Education and Boise State University, 2012).

Science has brought society many advantages that have served to improve health and increase the longevity of human lives, and to improve the quality of life for all. However, there are sometimes unforeseen consequences of scientific discovery and invention that affect society and the natural environment, as well as the habitats and survival of the living organisms that share this planet. To better understand such issues, students must gain scientific knowledge and study evidence of what is known. Armed with appropriate background knowledge, students are put in the position to weigh the pros and cons of various scientific discoveries and debate issues that prevail in our global community. Students should be apprised of such issues as global warming, but before taking a position on the topic, they must be equipped with accurate scientific information. When students are given opportunities to use scientific concepts as support for sound logic and reasoning to debate or evaluate a scientific issue, they operate at high cognitive levels critical to their intellectual development. Equally important is student awareness of the ethical, personal, societal, and economic implications of science, from both positive and negative perspectives. Students must learn to appreciate the trade-offs often inherent in scientific discovery and experimentation. Consider laboratory testing on animals. Many new and important discoveries have improved the quality of human life at the cost of animals' lives. It is important for students to understand and weigh the costs versus benefits of research from not only financial, but also social and ethical, standpoints.

In order to best understand the complexity of how science interfaces with personal and societal issues, students need to be engaged in electronic and library research on impactful science topics and take part in discussion with peers and experts in the science fields. Topics such as cloning, global warming, alternative versus fossil fuels, and space exploration are just a few additional topics tied to ethical, personal, societal, and economic concerns. It is essential that students fully understand the scientific knowledge that undergirds all such complex issues. If so equipped, students can then formulate decisions based on this knowledge.

The scientific processes are skills that last a lifetime, applicable to a vast array of everyday life decisions and experiences. Teachers must help students apply the scientific processes to real-world situations. Making careful observations, experimenting, collecting data and information, and drawing conclusions, as examples, are important in everyday life decisions. Determining which presidential candidate to vote for, which doctor to see (and how to know if the diagnoses are correct!) what product to buy, or how to determine the truth from among competing accounts in the media all require proficiency in scientific processes and the associated reasoning skills. Teachers must provide students with opportunities to apply scientific processes in everyday life decisions so they may see the importance and benefits of learning these skills.

Natural resources and the consumption of natural resources have been prime issues in society over the past century. In today's society, the most pressing issue is the economic and environmental impacts of obtaining natural resources for use as fuel and electricity. It is important to know about fossil fuels, their origin, how they are obtained, and how they are used for energy. Since fossil fuels are nonrenewable and will one day be expended, science is continuing to develop and improve upon alternative sources of energy, such as wind, solar, hydroelectric, and geothermal. Teachers must be knowledgeable about these other sources of energy and be able to guide students toward understanding how these renewable energy sources are used, and how they impact our society's energy needs. This understanding must include the concepts of **sustainability** of global resources and energy sustainability. Teachers should allow students to discover and analyze how energy is used in the United States and in other countries; for example, the type of energy sources that each country is most dependent upon (nonrenewable versus renewable). Energy dependency is a worldwide issue since consumption of resources that cannot be renewed will impact many nations across the globe. Non-regulation of pollutants produced in generating energy impacts more than those within the non-regulated nation; it also has vast transborder implications, such as worldwide concerns of global warming due to unchecked carbon dioxide emissions.

A significant impact of science on a student's daily life relates to personal fitness and health. Childhood obesity is a crisis in the United States, and teachers can play an important role in educating children on the negative health issues associated with poor nutrition and a lack of exercise. Teachers need to help students learn about factors that impact physical and psychological health and about how to make good choices regarding nutrition, hygiene, physical exercise, smoking, drugs, and alcohol. Understanding human biology will help students realize how obesity and other factors such as substance use/abuse affect their physical and mental health. The topics of heart disease, diabetes, and cancer should be included in the curriculum as ways to help students understand the detrimental effects of unhealthy life choices.

Science can also impact societal and global challenges, including **water quality** and **climate change**. Scientists regularly share findings from their research on these issues in order to find solutions to solve problems and replicate research to determine consistency in results. For example, science has found innovative solutions to inexpensively produce clean water in places where it is scarce. See solutions for clean water: *https://www.forbes.com/sites/patrickcox/2016/12/06/biotech-has-a-solution-for-the-clean-water-crisis/* and solutions for global warming: *http://www.climate-hotmap.org/global-warming-solutions/* as examples.

COMPETENCY 005

The teacher knows and understands the unifying concepts and processes that are common to all sciences.

The beginning teacher:

A. Understands how the following concepts and processes provide a unifying explanatory framework across the science disciplines: systems, order, and organization; evidence, models, and explanation; change, constancy, and measurements; evolution, and equilibrium; and form and function.

B. Demonstrates an understanding of how patterns in observations and data can be used to make explanations and predictions.

C. Analyzes interactions and interrelationships between systems and subsystems.

D. Applies unifying concepts to explore similarities in a variety of natural phenomena.

E. Understands how properties and patterns of systems can be described in terms of space, time, energy, and matter.

F. Understands how change and constancy occur in systems.

G. Understands the complementary nature of form and function in a given system.

H. Understands how models are used to represent the natural world and how to evaluate the strengths and limitations of a variety of scientific models (e.g., physical, conceptual, mathematical).

Science is a way of knowing, a **process**—it is a systematic way of looking at the world and how it works. This competency focuses on how science uses a regular, consistent method of collecting and reporting data about scientific phenomena. Science is a way of organizing observations and then seeking patterns and regularity in order to make sense of the world. In science we organize evidence, create models, and explain observations logically. We may make predictions and hypotheses and test our predictions and hypotheses through controlled experimentation, meaning all variables of the experiment remain constant except for the variable being tested. We repeat experiments multiple times and seek **constancy** in our findings in form and/or function. We seek patterns and consistency in our observations and data to construct explanations and make new predictions. We employ different forms of scientific inquiry to best respond to our research questions, including experimental, descriptive, and comparative methods, recognizing that experiments do not always progress as planned.

Science embraces a broad spectrum of subject matter, such as life science, physical science, and earth science, all of which is interrelated. For example, in studying the ecosystem, teachers must understand the biological aspects (e.g., the living organism) and how they interact, as in **predator-prey relationships** and **symbiotic relationships** (e.g., parasitism, commensalism), as well as the chemical aspects of the ecosystem (e.g., nitrogen cycle), the geologic or earth science aspects (e.g., the landscape, the water, and the climate) and the physics aspects (e.g., energy transfer, motion). For example, ecosystems, regardless of their location on Earth, share **unifying components** and characteristics, and teachers must understand this unity. In life science, there is unity in terms of what makes organisms "living"—they all must carry on life functions and are composed of one or more cells. These are the criteria that unify life forms and classify something like a virus, for instance, as non-living (it does not carry on the life functions and is not composed of cells).

All scientific observations can be described by their characteristics or "properties." These properties organize the observations according to commonalities, or classification. Observed properties and patterns are centered on space, time, energy, and matter. Unifying concepts in teaching science in Texas at each grade level are articulated in the *Texas Essential Knowledge and Skills for Science* document, found at: *www.tea.state.tx.us*.

COMPETENCY 006

The teacher understands forces and motion and their relationships.

The beginning teacher:

A. Demonstrates an understanding of properties of universal forces (e.g., gravitational, electrical, magnetic).

B. Understands how to measure, graph, and describe changes in motion using concepts of displacement, velocity, and acceleration.

C. Understands the vector nature of force.

D. Identifies the forces acting on an object and applies Newton's laws to describe the motion of an object.

E. Analyzes the relationship between force and motion in a variety of situations (e.g., simple machines, blood flow, geologic processes).

Universal forces include gravity, electricity, and magnetism, which are important to understanding this competency.

Force is defined as the action of moving an object by pulling or pushing it. Force can cause an object to move at a constant speed or to accelerate. When force is applied over a distance, work is done. Work is the product of the force acting in the direction of movement and causing displacement. Energy is defined as the ability to do work; for example, when a tow truck uses force to pull a car and move it to a different location, energy is used and work is accomplished. **Newton's laws of motion** are important to understand in fulfilling this competency. Newton's first law is that an object at rest will remain at rest unless acted upon by an (unbalanced) force, and an object in motion will continue to stay in motion with the same speed and in the same direction unless acted upon by an (unbalanced) outside force. This first law is also called inertia. Newton's second law is that acceleration is produced when a force acts on mass such that the greater the mass of the object being accelerated, the greater the amount of force needed to accelerate that object. Newton's third law of motion is that for every action there is an equal and opposite reaction.

Force and motion, as well as changes in motion, may be measured through hands-on activities in which variables such as time, speed, distance, and direction can be recorded and graphed, and teachers need to know how to do so. For example, teachers can have students experience and record what happens when an object with higher mass (such as a large marble or ball bearing), collides with an object with less mass (e.g., a small marble or ball bearing). Teachers should also know what happens when the rate of speed is high when the objects collide compared to when the rate of speed is low. The game of pool or billiards is a good example. When forces are unbalanced, it may cause the object to change its motion or position.

Magnetism is the force of attraction or repulsion between objects that results from the positive and negative ionic charges of the objects. Usually, the objects are metals, such as iron, nickel, and cobalt. Magnets have two poles that have opposing charges or forces: north (+) and south (−). When the north pole of a magnet is placed close to the north pole of a second magnet, repulsion occurs. When poles of different kinds (north and south) are placed close, they attract one another. The strength of the forces depends on the size and the proximity of the magnets. The charged area around a magnet is called a magnetic field. The Earth is like a large magnet, with opposing forces—the North Pole and South Pole, and the magnetic field of attraction of Earth that we know as **gravity** is also like that of a magnet. Without gravity, all objects on Earth, including the atmosphere, would not be held onto its surface. Planets and other celestial objects that are more massive than Earth, such as Jupiter, have stronger gravitational forces, and those that are less massive and/or dense, such as our moon, have weaker gravitational forces.

A machine is something that makes work easier. Machines can be as simple as a wedge or a screw or as sophisticated as a computer or gas engine. A simple machine has few or no moving parts and can change the size and direction of a force. A screw, hammer, wedge, and incline plane are examples of simple machines. Simple machines are part of our daily activities. For example, children playing on a seesaw are using a simple machine called a lever. In this manner, teachers and their students can appreciate the practical use of simple machines in everyday life. A complex machine is two or more simple machines working together to facilitate work. Some of the complex machines used in daily activities are a wheelbarrow, a can opener, and a bicycle.

Force and motion are what keep the sun, Earth, moon, and planets in their orbits and explains the structure and changes of the universe. On Earth, force and motion are found in all geologic processes, explaining phenomena such as tides and tsunamis.

COMPETENCY 007

The teacher understands physical properties of, and changes in, matter.

The beginning teacher:

A. Describes the physical properties of substances (e.g., density, boiling point, solubility, thermal, and electrical conductivity).

B. Describes the physical properties and molecular structure of solids, liquids, and gases.

C. Describes the relationship between the molecular structure of materials (e.g., metals, crystals, polymers) and their physical properties.

D. Relates the physical properties of an element to its placement in the periodic table.

E. Distinguishes between physical and chemical changes in matter.

F. Applies knowledge of physical properties of and changes in matter to processes and situations that occur in life science and in Earth/space science (e.g., evaporation, changes in air pressure).

Matter has physical, thermal, electrical, and chemical properties. These properties are dependent upon the molecular composition of the matter.

The **physical properties** of matter are the way matter looks and feels. It includes qualities like color, density, hardness, and conductivity. Color represents how matter is reflected or perceived by the human eye. Density is the mass that is contained in a unit of volume of a given substance. Hardness represents the resistance to penetration offered by a given substance. Conductivity is the ability of substances to transmit thermal or electric current.

Matter is sensitive to temperature changes. Heat and cold produce changes in the physical properties of matter; however, the **chemical properties** remain unchanged. For example, when water is exposed to cold temperature (release of heat), it changes from liquid to solid; and when water is exposed to heat, it changes from solid to liquid. With continued heat, the water changes from liquid to gas (water vapor). Water vapor can be cooled again and turned back into liquid. However, through all these states, water retains its chemical properties—two molecules of hydrogen and one molecule of oxygen, or H_2O.

Matter can be classified as a **conductor** or **nonconductor** of electricity. Conductive matter allows the transfer of electric current or heat from one point to another. Metals are usually good conductors, while wood and rocks are examples of nonconductive matter.

Matter can exist in four distinct **states**: solid, liquid, gas, and plasma. Most people are familiar with the basic states of matter, but they might not be familiar with the fourth one, plasma. Plasmas are formed at extremely high temperatures when electrons are stripped from neutral atoms (University of California, 2006). Stars are predominantly composed of plasmas. Solids have mass, occupy a definite amount of space, or *volume,* or have a definite shape, and are denser than liquids. Liquids have mass, occupy a definite volume, do not have a definite shape, but instead take the shape of their container. Gases have mass, do not have a definite volume, have no definite shape but take the shape of their container, and are the least dense of the three states of matter. Plasma has no definite shape or volume, and is a substance that cannot be classified as a solid, liquid, or gas. When substances change from one state of matter to another, such as ice melting, it is a physical change, and not a chemical change.

A physical change is a change in a substance that does not change what that substance is made of. Examples of physical changes are melting ice, boiling water, tearing paper, chopping wood, writing with chalk, and mixing sugar and water together. In the mixing of sugar with water, or salt with water, even though the sugar or salt may not be visible to the naked eye in the water, it is still there and still has the same composition—that is, the molecules that make up the sugar or salt and water are still the same as when you mixed them. Letting the water evaporate allows you to recover your sugar or salt crystals. Students should be aware of the physical changes that occur in the life and Earth/space sciences. An example of a physical change in life science is when food is broken into smaller pieces during the process of chewing, which begins the process of food digestion in the body. An example of a physical change in Earth/space science would be evaporation during the water cycle. During evaporation, liquid water is heated enough that it becomes water vapor.

COMPETENCY 008

The teacher understands chemical properties of, and changes in, matter.

The beginning teacher:

A. Describes the structure and components of the atom.

B. Distinguishes among elements, mixtures, and compounds and describes their properties.

C. Relates the chemical properties of an element to its placement in the periodic table.

D. Describes chemical bonds and chemical formulas.

E. Analyzes chemical reactions and their associated chemical equations.

F. Explains the importance of a variety of chemical reactions that occur in daily life (e.g., rusting, burning of fossil fuels, photosynthesis, cell respiration, chemical batteries, digestion of food).

G. Understands applications of chemical properties of matter in physical, life, and Earth/space science and technology (e.g., materials science, biochemistry, transportation, medicine, telecommunications).

Matter is anything that takes up space and has mass. The mass of a body is the amount of matter in an object or thing, and volume describes the amount of space that matter takes up. Mass is also the property of a body that causes it to have weight. Weight is the amount of gravitational force exerted over an object. Help your students avoid confusing mass with weight. What students measure on their balances in the laboratory is an object's **mass**. Weight changes as an object goes from one level of gravitational force to another—for example, from Earth to the moon—because the amount of "pull" on that object is different. The mass of the object—how much matter or material is in the object—does not change unless we do something to actually take away or add matter to that object.

There are 118 basic kinds of matter, called elements, which are organized into the periodic table. An element is composed of sub-microscopic components called **atoms**. Atoms are made up of particles called electrons, neutrons, and protons. The mass of the atom is located mostly in the nucleus, which is made up of protons, which have a positive charge, and neutrons, which are neutral or have no charge. The atomic mass of the atom is its protons plus neutrons, where each has a mass of 1 atomic mass unit (AMU). The electron contains little mass (which has a negligible contribution to the overall atomic mass), carries a negative charge, and follows an orbit with a specific distance and shape around the nucleus (electron energy level or shell). The atomic number is the number of protons in the nucleus of the atom. The number of protons is the distinction between one type of atom and another, e.g., hydrogen, which has 1 proton, and helium, an entirely different atom with different properties, which has 2 protons. The number of electrons is equal to the number of protons in a stable atom, so the negative and positive charges are balanced. An ion is an atom or molecule that has lost or gained one or more electrons and thus has negative or positive charge (because there are either more or fewer protons, or positive charges, compared to electrons, or negative charges). It is these chemical properties that determine an element's location on the periodic table. Elements with the same number of electrons in their outer shell (or valence electrons) will be in the same vertical column or group. Elements in the same period, or horizontal row, have fewer properties in common. However, as you move from left to right across a period, the atomic numbers always increase.

Molecules are two or more atoms connected by chemical bonds. There are two types of chemical bonds, ionic bonds and covalent bonds. In ionic bonds, electrons are transferred from one atom to the other that it is bonding with, for example Na (sodium) gives its outer shell electron to Cl (chlorine) to make NaCl (sodium chloride) or table salt. In covalent bonding, electrons are shared, equally or unequally, between the different atoms in the molecule. For example, carbon and two oxygen atoms share outer shell electrons to form covalent bonds to the molecule CO_2 (carbon dioxide). In bonding, the atoms are chemically seeking to fill their outer shell of electrons, usually with the full complement of 8 electrons (2 electrons in the case of hydrogen).

The atoms of a molecule can be more than one of the *same kind* of atom, as in the naturally occurring oxygen molecule, O_2, or a molecule can be two or more *different kinds* of atoms as in carbon dioxide (CO_2), ammonia (NH_3), and glucose ($C_6H_{12}O_6$). Compounds are when you have two or more *different* kinds of atoms in the molecule and you have a given amount of that substance. In other words, compounds consist of matter composed of atoms that are chemically combined with one another in molecules in definite weight proportions. An example of a compound is water; water is oxygen and hydrogen combined in the ratio of two hydrogen molecules to one molecule of oxygen (H_2O). So, you can also call *one* H_2O a molecule.

The chemical properties of one type of matter (element) can react with the chemical properties of other types of matter. In general, elements from the same groups will not react with each other, while elements from different groups may. The more separated the groups, the more likely they will cause a chemical reaction when brought together. A type of matter can be chemically altered to become a different type of matter; for example, a metal trash can will rust when left out in the rain.

Mixtures are combinations of two or more substances (where each substance is distinct from the other) that are made up of two or more types of molecules and not chemically combined. The two substances in the mixture may or may not be evenly distributed, so there are no definite amounts or weight proportions. Mixtures may be **heterogeneous**, which means there is an uneven distribution of the substances in the mixture throughout. A mixture may be **homogeneous**, which means the components are evenly distributed throughout. Examples of mixtures include milk, which is a heterogeneous mixture of water and butterfat particles. The components of a mixture can be separated physically. For example, milk producers and manufacturers remove the butterfat from whole milk to make skim milk.

Solutions are *mixtures* that are *homogeneous*, which means that the components are distributed evenly and there is an even concentration throughout. The solute is the substance in the smaller amount that dissolves and that you add into the substance that is in the larger amount—the solvent. Water is a common solvent. Solids, liquids, and gases can be solutes. Examples of solutions are seawater and ammonia. Seawater is made up of water and salt, and ammonia is made up of ammonia gas and water. In these examples, the salt and the ammonia (NH_3) are the solutes; water is the solvent.

A chemical change is when the substances that were combined are no longer the same molecules—they have changed to new substances. For example, burning wood, mixing baking soda and vinegar, or a rusting nail, which is when the iron of the nail (Fe) combines with oxygen (in the presence of water) to form a new substance—that is, a new molecule is formed: iron oxide, or Fe_2O_3.

Physical changes can be reversed, whereas chemical changes generally cannot be reversed. Evidence of a chemical change include that the combination of the substances gives off a gas (bubbles are observed), it changes color (not always a chemical change, but may be if the other evidences are also present), gives off heat and becomes warmer, or absorbs heat and becomes colder (temperature change), and forms a precipitate (a solid substance). When heat is given off in a chemical change, it is an **exothermic** reaction; and when heat is absorbed in a chemical change (the combination becomes colder), it is an **endothermic** reaction. Everyday examples of exothermic reactions are firewood burning or the use of a hand warmer by many mountain climbers and snow skiers. Examples of endothermic reactions are a cold pack used for sports injuries or the combination of baking soda and vinegar (try it with a thermometer in the vinegar during the reaction and see!).

Chemical reactions occur in everyday life and are an essential part of our physical and biological world. The burning of gasoline in automobiles is a chemical change—as is burning of any kind. Burning is a process involving the combination of oxygen from the atmosphere with substances containing the carbon atom. The proper temperature has to be reached in order to begin this exothermic reaction, but once started, the chemical reaction can continue until the oxygen is used up or is prevented from entering into the reaction. So since gasoline is a fossil fuel (a once living organism), it contains carbon. When we provide the energy it needs to begin the reaction, called activation energy, as long as oxygen is present, the carbon substance will burn. Burning is a chemical reaction because the carbon and oxygen combine to form new substances such as carbon monoxide (CO) and carbon dioxide (CO_2). The same reaction occurs in burning wood, candles, and even in cell respiration—the oxygen we breathe and carry through our bloodstream is combined in our cells with carbon-containing glucose molecules in a type of "controlled" burning. Our bodies give off heat from this reaction, which is why we are able to maintain a fairly high temperature of about 98.6 degrees Fahrenheit. Other examples of chemical reactions in everyday life include chemical batteries, the digestion of food, and cooking/baking. Moreover, the process of photosynthesis, where plants use sunlight to convert carbon dioxide gas and water into food for the plant known as glucose (a simple sugar), is also an important chemical reaction responsible for providing food for and sustaining all life on Earth.

COMPETENCY 009

The teacher understands energy and interactions between matter and energy.

The beginning teacher:

A. Describes concepts of work, power, and potential and kinetic energy.

B. Understands the concept of heat energy and the difference between heat and temperature.

C. Understands the principles of electricity and magnetism and their applications (e.g., electric circuits, motors, audio speakers, nerve impulses, lighting).

D. Applies knowledge of types (longitudinal, transverse); properties (e.g., wavelength and frequency); and behaviors (e.g., reflection, refraction, dispersion) to describe a variety of waves (e.g., water, electromagnetic, sound, seismic waves).

E. Applies knowledge of properties and behaviors of light to describe the function of optical systems and phenomena (e.g., camera, microscope, rainbow, eye).

F. Demonstrates an understanding of the properties, production, and transmission of sound.

Energy is available in many forms, including heat, light, solar radiation, chemical, electrical, magnetic, sound, and mechanical energy. It exists in three states: potential, kinetic, and activation energies. An object possessing energy because of its ability to move has kinetic energy. The energy that an object has as the result of its position or condition is called potential energy. The energy necessary to transfer or convert potential energy into kinetic energy is called activation energy. All three states of energy can be transformed from one to another. A parked vehicle has potential energy. When the driver starts the engine using the chemical energy stored in the battery and the fuel, potential energy becomes activation energy. Once the vehicle is moving, the energy changes to kinetic energy.

Heat is a form of energy. Temperature is the measure of heat. The most common device used to measure temperature is the thermometer. Thermometers are made of heat-sensitive substances—mercury and alcohol—that expand when heated.

The most common form of energy comes from the sun. Solar energy provides heat and light for animals and plants. Through photosynthesis, plants capture radiant energy from the sun and transform it into chemical energy in the form of glucose. This chemical energy is stored in the leaves, stems, and fruits of plants. Humans and animals consume the plants or fruits and get the energy they need for survival. This energy source is transformed again to create kinetic energy and body heat. Kinetic energy is used for movement and to do work, while heat is a required element for all warm-blooded animals, like humans. Cold-blooded animals also require heat, but rather than making it themselves through the transformation of plant sugar, they use solar energy to heat their body. Energy transformation constitutes the foundation and the driving force of an ecosystem. In addition to heat and solar radiation, energy is available in the forms of electricity and magnetism.

When you arrange an energy source, such as a battery, a wire, and a light bulb (or motor, or bell, or any electrical device) such that all metal parts are touching (metal is a good "conductor" of energy) in a circle—the bulb will light (the motor will run, the bell will ring, and so on). What has been created by arranging the items in this circle is known as an "electric circuit." The energy from the battery or other energy source is able to "flow" or be transferred through the metal wires and parts of the circuit. A closed circuit is when all metal parts are touching and the electrical charge is able to continue to be transferred through the circuit. A light switch or other "on" button closes the circuit and allows the electricity to flow. An open circuit is when there is a break someplace in the flow of electricity through the circuit. A switch or "off" button" opens the circuit and stops the electricity flow. When you ring a door bell, you are closing the circuit or allowing all metal parts to touch and send electricity through it to make the bell ring; when you release the doorbell button, the circuit is open, and so the flow of electricity stops and so does the bell's ringing.

Lightning is a form of static electricity, which means it is not "flowing" or being transferred in the way it is through a metal wire, but is instead caused by friction, much the same as walking across a carpet in socks and getting a shock when a metal doorknob is touched. In both kinds of electricity, the electrons in the atoms of the substance, which are negatively charged, are pulled away from their atom's nucleus, giving the object, or cloud, a negative charge. The negative charge is quickly attracted to a positive charge—in the case of lightning, that positive charge could be something (or someone!) on the ground. The positive charge quickly jumps toward the negative charge and the negative charge quickly jumps toward the positive charge, and a flash of lighting and clap of thunder is heard; or in the case of the doorknob, a spark and a snap sound. Electric circuits are just a way to channel the electricity and the opposing charges through a conductor such as metal wires to allow us to use the energy to do work and to transform the energy into different forms such as sound (a radio), light (light bulbs), mechanical (machinery), and/or heat energy.

Light energy, and all energy for that matter, travels in waves and in a straight-line path. The electromagnetic spectrum shows the different wavelengths and frequencies of energy, including the small portion that is visible light. The electromagnetic spectrum includes, for example, microwaves, X-rays, radio waves, infrared radiation, visible light waves, and ultraviolet radiation, all of which have different wavelengths and frequencies that distinguish one type of wave from another.

Visible light is the wavelength of light we can see, which our eyes see as white light. However, this white light is composed of a host of other wavelengths of light that our eyes cannot always distinguish. The segment of the electromagnetic spectrum that the human eye can see is called the **visible light spectrum**, or a rainbow. The colors of white light include red, orange, yellow, green, blue, indigo, and violet (although some sources now eliminate indigo as separate from violet), or ROYGBIV. When light traveling in a straight line hits an object or substance and is bent, it is called **refraction**. The bending of light waves may result in the colors of light in the spectrum becoming visible, as when we see a rainbow in the sky (the water molecules in the air bend the light) or when light travels through cut glass such as with a prism. **Reflection** is when light waves bounce back, as when looking in a mirror. The principles of reflection and refraction are used in periscopes and telescopes in order to be able to see objects not otherwise visible. These principles are often incorporated into magic shows when objects are said to "disappear." In actuality, the light of the object has been refracted or reflected to a place away from our eyes so that we can no longer see it.

Refraction is also used to our advantage through concave and convex lenses. Concave or convex lenses work such that when light passes through it changes the focal point. The eye contains a lens, but when light passing through the eye cannot properly focus on the "screen" known as the retina, the object being viewed may be blurred. Concave or convex lenses are used in eyeglasses to adjust and correct the focal point. These lenses are also used in cameras, microscopes, and telescopes. A spoon is an example of both a concave and a convex lens—if you look into the concave side, you will see yourself upside down. If you look into the convex side of the spoon, you will see yourself right side up. This is due to refraction (and reflection) of light.

Sound also travels in waves. Sounds are caused by vibrations, such as a guitar string (or a rubber band), or banging on a drum or cymbal. Sound has a certain wavelength, frequency, pitch, and amplitude (loudness). Sound waves must travel through a medium, which may be solid, liquid, or gas. Sound travels best through solids because there are more molecules (particles) to vibrate, and least well through gases.

The types of sound waves are longitudinal and transverse. **Longitudinal** waves move parallel to the direction the wave moves, and **transverse** waves move perpendicular to the direction of the wave. Seismic waves are both longitudinal and transverse, as they travel in all directions from the source of the earthquake. An electromagnetic wave moves in a direction that is at a right angle to the vibrations of both the magnetic and electric fields, which are perpendicular to each other.

COMPETENCY 010

The teacher understands energy transformations and the conservation of matter and energy.

The beginning teacher:

A. Describes the processes that generate energy in the sun and other stars.

B. Applies the law of conservation of matter to analyze a variety of situations (e.g., the water cycle, food chains, decomposition, balancing chemical equations).

C. Describes sources of electrical energy and processes of energy transformation for human uses (e.g., fossil fuels, solar panels, hydroelectric plants).

D. Understands exothermic and endothermic chemical reactions and their applications (e.g., hot and cold packs, energy content of food).

E. Applies knowledge of energy concepts in a variety of situations (e.g., the production of heat, light, sound, and magnetic effects by electrical energy; the process of photosynthesis; weather processes; food webs; food/energy pyramids).

F. Applies the law of conservation of energy to analyze a variety of physical phenomena (e.g., specific heat, heat transfer, thermal equilibrium, nuclear reactions, efficiency of simple machines, collisions).

G. Understands applications of energy transformations and the conservation of matter and energy in life and Earth/space science.

The sun is the source of energy that sustains life on Earth. It is one of billions of stars in our galaxy, the Milky Way, and is among the countless trillions of stars in the universe. The sun is actually quite an ordinary star, falling somewhere in the middle range in size. The sun is largely composed of the gases hydrogen and helium and generates energy by nuclear fusion, or the combining of atoms in high speed collisions releasing tremendous amounts of energy.

Electricity is the flow of electrons or electric power or charge. The basic unit of charge is based on the positive charge of the **proton** and the negative charge of the **electron**. Energy occurs naturally in the atmosphere through light. However, it is not feasible to capture that type of energy. The electricity that we use comes from secondary sources because it is produced from the conversion of primary (natural) sources of energy like fossil fuels that are nonrenewable (natural gas, coal, and oil) and nuclear, and renewable resources such as wind and solar energy. All sources of energy are used to produce a common result—to turn a turbine that generates electricity. Electricity that is generated can then be sent through wires for human use, and can be transformed into other forms of energy, including sound, light, heat, and force.

The main principle of **energy conservation** states that energy can change form but cannot totally disappear. For example, the chemical energy stored in a car battery is used to start the engine, which in turn is used to recharge the battery. Another example of energy conservation is placing merchandise on shelves. Energy was used to do the work (placing merchandise on a shelf) and it was stored as potential energy. Potential energy in turn can be converted to kinetic energy when the merchandise is pushed back to the floor. In this case, work was recovered completely, but often the recovered energy is less than the energy used to do the work. This loss of energy can be caused by friction or any kind of resistance encountered in the process of doing the work. For example, as a vehicle's tires roll across the pavement, doing the work of moving forward, they encounter friction. This friction causes heat energy, as well as kinetic energy, to be released.

In essence, energy cannot be created or destroyed, only changed in form (law of conservation of energy). Likewise, matter cannot be created or destroyed, only changed in form (law of conservation of matter). Thus, energy from the sun is changed, for example, to chemical energy when plants use the energy to make glucose in photosynthesis. The energy from the sun is stored in the chemical bonds of the glucose molecule and is released for use by the organism—the plant itself, or any organism that eats the plant and its glucose—when the molecule's chemical bonds are "broken" by oxygen in cell respiration and/or stored in another chemical form known as ATP. Likewise, electrical energy comes from burning, or breaking the bond of carbon-based molecules as in fossil fuels. This electricity generated is then transformed to another form by first capturing and sending that electrical energy through metal wires originating at the power generating plant, and sending it in a complete, closed circuit to homes, businesses, and industries. There the electrical energy may be transformed to sound, heat, light, and/or mechanical energy. In all cases the energy is not lost it is changed in form.

Conserving matter and energy generated from fossil fuels is critical, as these are **non-renewable** sources that will one day be expended. It is also thus important, as a corollary, to continue exploring alternative, **renewable** forms of energy and electricity generation to meet our society's energy demands and maintain our Earth's clean air and water supplies.

COMPETENCY 011

The teacher understands the structure and function of living things.

The beginning teacher:

A. Describes characteristics of organisms from the major taxonomic groups.

B. Analyzes how structure complements function in cells.

C. Analyzes how structure complements function in tissues, organs, organ systems, and organisms.

D. Identifies human body systems and describes their functions.

E. Describes how organisms obtain and use energy and matter.

F. Describes the composition, structure, and function of the basic chemical components (e.g., proteins, carbohydrates, lipids, nucleic acids) of living things.

Major Taxonomic Groups

Living things are divided into five groups, or kingdoms: Monera (bacteria), Protista (protozoans), Fungi, Plantae (plants), and Animalia (animals).

Monera consists of unicellular organisms. It is the only group of living organisms made up of prokaryotic cells—the cells with a primitive organization system. Some examples of this organism are bacteria, blue-green algae, and spirochetes.

Protista contains a type of eukaryotic cell with a more complex organization system. This kingdom includes diverse, mostly unicellular organisms that live in aquatic habitats, in both freshwater and saltwater. They are not animals or plants but unique organisms. Some examples of Protista are protozoans and algae of various types. The Amoeba, Paramecium, and Euglena are in the Protista Kingdom.

Fungi are multicellular organisms with a sophisticated organization system that contains eukaryotic cells. Fungi exist in a variety of forms and shapes. Because they lack chlorophyll, they cannot produce food through photosynthesis. Fungi obtain energy, carbon, and water from digesting dead materials. Some examples of these types of organisms are mushrooms, mold, mildews, and yeast.

Plants are multicellular organisms with a sophisticated organization system. In addition to more familiar plants, moss and ferns also fall under this category. Plant cells have chloroplasts, a component that allows them to trap sunlight as energy for the process of photosynthesis. Through photosynthesis, plants use carbon dioxide from the atmospheric environment and as the by-product of this process, supply the oxygen needed for the survival of animals.

Animals are also multicellular, with multiple forms and shapes, and with specialized senses and organs. The Animalia kingdom is composed of organisms like sponges, worms, insects, fish, amphibians, reptiles, birds, and mammals. Animals are the most sophisticated type of living organisms and represent the highest levels of evolution. Animals live in all kinds of habitats, and they are as simple as flies or as sophisticated as humans.

For additional information about living things, go to the website of the Behavioral Sciences Department of Palomar College, San Marcos, California, at *http://anthro.palomar.edu/animal/default.htm*.

There are relationships between the characteristics, structures, and functions of organisms and corresponding taxonomic classifications. **Homologous** structures refer to different living organisms with structural or anatomical features that look or function in a similar way. Because these organisms have a common ancestor, their homologous structures are of the same origin but have different functions. For example, the bone structure of the wing of a bat is very similar to the bone structure of the human arm. **Non-homologous** structures between two organisms are similar in structure and function, but arose independently and not from a common ancestor. **Parallelism** is when there are similar structures between two organisms in different species that arose after diverging from a common ancestor. The common ancestor did not have the structure, but had the beginning features of that structure. **Convergence** is when similar structures developed after diverging from a common ancestor, but the common ancestor did not have the trait or the beginnings of the trait. **Analogous** structures have the same structure or function but arose from different ancestors. That is, analogous structures developed from unrelated evolutionary lines, but the structure was a positive adaptation to the environment, so both survived and were carried on to offspring in their respective species. An example of analogous structures is the wing of a bird and the wing of a butterfly. Both serve as a beneficial adaptation, even though the species are not related.

For more detailed information see: *http://anthro.palomar.edu/animal/animal_2.htm* and *http://www.majordifferences.com/2013/05/difference-between-homologous-and.html - .WW_RQdPys6t*

Life Functions and Cells

All living things carry on life functions—such as respiration, nutrition, response, circulation, growth, excretion, regulation, and reproduction—all of which characterize them as living as opposed to nonliving. In addition, all living things are composed of the basic unit of life known as **cells**. Organisms, as well as individual cells of an organism and single-celled organisms, carry on these life functions using specialized structures. For example, earthworms carry on respiration through their moist skin; plants excrete gases from tiny pores on the underside of leaves called stomata; a single-celled amoeba ingests food by use of a "false foot" or pseudopodia; and insects respond to chemical attractants called pheromones of the opposite-sex insect for mating.

Cells are the basic unit of all living organisms. Within cells there are specialized organelles that carry on all of the life functions at a microscopic/chemical level. For example, the mitochondria carries on cell respiration, and ribosomes assemble proteins for use both inside the cell and out. Teachers should know the parts of the cell, called organelles, and their functions, particularly, the nucleus, mitochondria, chloroplasts (plants only), ribosomes, Golgi, endoplasmic reticulum, vacuoles, and cell membranes.

Animal and plant cells are similar in appearance, but they do have certain distinctions. Animal cells contain mitochondria, small round or rod-shaped bodies found in the cytoplasm of most cells. The main function of mitochondria is to produce the enzymes for the metabolic conversion of food to energy. This process consumes oxygen and is termed **aerobic respiration**.

Plants cells also contain mitochondria, which allow plants to carry on respiration where they use oxygen and excrete carbon dioxide and water just like animals. However, plants also have specialized organelles called chloroplasts that are used for taking in sunlight and using this energy to convert the gas, carbon dioxide, and water taken in from the roots to make glucose—a simple sugar that is the food for the plant. Chloroplasts contain chlorophyll, which is used in this process of converting light into chemical energy. This process is called photosynthesis. **Photosynthesis** is the process by which chlorophyll-containing organisms convert light energy to chemical energy. Through the process of photosynthesis, a plant containing chlorophyll captures energy from the sun and converts it into chemical energy. Part of the chemical energy is used for the plant's own survival, and the rest is stored in the stem and leaves.

The cell is the basic unit of living organisms and the simplest living unit of life. Living organisms are composed of cells that have the following common characteristics:

- Have a membrane that regulates the flow of nutrients and water that enter and exit the cell

- Contain the genetic material (DNA) that allows for reproduction

- Require a supply of energy

- Contain basic chemicals to make metabolic decisions for survival

- Reproduce and are the result of reproduction

There are two kinds of cells—prokaryotic and eukaryotic. Prokaryotic cells are the simplest and most primitive type of cells. They do not contain the structures typical of eukaryotic cells. Prokaryotic cells lack a nucleus and instead have one strand of deoxyribonucleic acid (DNA). Some prokaryotic cells have external whip-like flagella for locomotion or a hair-like system for adhesion. Prokaryotic cells come in three shapes: cocci (round), bacilli (rods), and spirilla or spirochetes (helical cells). Bacteria (of the Kingdom Monera) are prokaryotic cells.

Eukaryotic cells evolved from prokaryotic cells and in the process became structurally and biochemically more complex. The key distinction between the two cell types is that only eukaryotic cells contain many structures, or organelles, separated from other cytoplasm components by a membrane. The organelles within eukaryotic cells are the nucleus, mitochondria, chloroplasts, and Golgi apparatus. The nucleus contains the information for deoxyribonucleic acid (DNA). The mitochondria have their own membrane and contain some DNA information and proteins. They generate the energy for the cell. The chloroplast is a component that exists in plants *only*, allowing them to trap sunlight as energy for the process of photosynthesis. The Golgi apparatus secretes substances needed for the cell's survival.

An organism may consist of only one cell, or it may comprise many billions of cells of various dimensions. Put another way, cells are complete organisms, such as the unicellular bacteria; others, such as muscle cells, are parts of multicellular organisms. All cells have an internal substance called cytoplasm—a clear gelatinous fluid—enclosed within a membrane. Each cell contains the genetic material containing the information for the formation of organisms. Cells are composed primarily of water and the elements oxygen, hydrogen, carbon, and nitrogen.

Structures and Functions

Moving outward from the cell, students should know that cells communicate with one another on a chemical level and work together to perform specific functions. The shape of these groups of cells and activity levels differ according to their particular function in the body; for example, muscle cells are long and narrow so they may better respond to stimuli and contract. Groups of cells with similar functions are called **tissues**. Tissues are organized together to perform a specific life function. A complex system of tissues working together to carry on one of the body's life functions is an **organ**. A group of different organs working together to support and help carry out a life function and keep the organism alive is called an **organ system**. Examples of systems include the digestive system, the respiratory system, the immune system, the muscular system, the skeletal system, the nervous system, and the circulatory system. Organ systems are organized into an *organism*. The order of organization is as follows:

Cells → Tissues → Organs → Systems → Organ Systems → Organism

Musculoskeletal System

The human skeleton consists of more than 200 bones held together by connective tissues called ligaments. Movements are effected by contractions of the *skeletal muscles*, and skeletal muscles are arranged in pairs, such as the biceps and triceps of the upper arm. When one of the pair contracts, it causes a certain movement of the bones; in the meantime, the opposing muscle relaxes. When the opposing pair of muscle contracts, a different movement of the bones occurs, and the original muscle of the pair relaxes. For example, when the biceps (the muscle on top of the upper arm) contracts, the arm bends upwards; when the opposing muscle of the pair, the triceps, contracts, the arm extends. Skeletal muscles are attached to bones with specialized connective tissue called tendons.

The specialized connective tissue that attaches bones to other bones is called ligament. The soft spongy tissue on the ends of bones is called cartilage. Muscular contractions are controlled by the nervous system.

In addition to skeletal muscle, the body also has muscles that are not part of the musculoskeletal system, and thus not attached to bones. One such muscle type is called *smooth muscle*. Smooth muscle forms the inner linings of our digestive system and is controlled involuntarily by our autonomic (automatic) nervous system. A third type of muscle is *cardiac muscle*, which is the muscle of the heart, and is also controlled by our autonomic nervous system.

Nervous System

The **nervous system** has two main divisions: the somatic and automatic. The somatic allows the voluntary control of skeletal muscles, and the automatic, or involuntary, controls cardiac and glandular functions. Voluntary movement is caused by nerve impulses sent from the brain through the spinal cord to nerves to connecting skeletal muscles. Involuntary movement occurs in direct response to outside stimulus. Involuntary responses are called reflexes. For example, when an object presents danger to the eye, the body responds automatically by blinking or retracting away from the object.

Circulatory System

The **circulatory system** follows a cyclical process in which the heart pumps blood through the right chambers of the heart and through the lungs, where it acquires oxygen. From there it is pumped back into the left chambers of the heart, where it is pumped into the main artery (aorta), which then sends the oxygenated blood to the rest of the body using a system of veins and capillaries. Through the capillaries, the blood distributes the oxygen and nutrients to tissues, absorbing from them carbon dioxide, a metabolic waste product. Finally, the blood completes the circuit by passing through small veins, which join to form increasingly larger vessels. Eventually, the blood reaches the largest veins, which return it to the right side of the heart to complete and restart the process.

Immune System

The main function of the body's **immune system** is to defend itself against foreign proteins and infectious organisms. The system recognizes organisms that are not normally in the body and develops the antibodies needed to control and destroy the invaders. When the body is attacked by infectious organisms, it develops what we know as a fever. Fever is the body's way of fighting invading molecules. The raised temperature of a fever will kill some bacteria. The major components of the immune system are the thymus, lymph system, bone marrow, white blood cells, antibodies, and hormones.

Respiratory System

Respiration is carried out by the expansion and contraction of the lungs. In the lungs, oxygen enters tiny capillaries, where it combines with hemoglobin in the red blood cells and is carried to the tissues through the circulatory system. At the same time, carbon dioxide passes through capillaries into the air contained within the lungs.

Animals inhale oxygen from the environment and exhale carbon dioxide. Carbon dioxide is used by plants in the process of photosynthesis, which produces the oxygen that animals use again for survival.

Digestive and Excretory Systems

The energy required for sustenance of the human body is supplied through the chemical energy stored in food. To obtain the energy from food, it has to be fragmented and digested. **Digestion** begins at the moment that food is placed in the mouth and makes contact with saliva. Fragmented and partially digested food passes down the esophagus to the stomach, where the process is continued by the gastric and intestinal juices. Thereafter, the mixture of food and secretions makes its way down the small intestine, where the nutrients are extracted and absorbed into the bloodstream. The unused portion of the food goes to the large intestine and eventually is excreted from the body through defecation.

Reproductive System

Students in the middle grades should know some basic biological facts about **human reproduction**. They should know that the body matures and develops in order for child-bearing to occur. The menstrual cycle should be understood by students. Instruction should cover what occurs in ovulation to prepare the egg cell, namely, the process of meiosis. In males, the process of meiosis occurs to produce the sperm cell. Students should know that these specialized cells, called gametes (egg and sperm), unite to form a fertilized egg, which grows and develops in distinct stages to produce new offspring.

Energy and Matter

Plants make glucose during the process of photosynthesis. Plant cells' chloroplasts capture energy from the sun, take in carbon dioxide (CO_2) from the atmosphere, and absorb water (H_2O) up through its roots and restructuring these molecules into glucose ($C_6H_{12}O_6$). The glucose is used to make its own body structures and stored in chains, which when assembled together make carbohydrates or starch. The starch is stored in roots, stems, and leaves, and may also be transformed into other substances made by the plant such as oils, waxes, and fruits. Photosynthesis is the way plants make food, but it is *not* the way they metabolize food for energy. The sugars that plants make are metabolized by oxygen in respiration to produce the energy needed for plants to carry on their own life functions (excretion, growth). Thus, it is important to know that similar to animals, *plants carry on respiration* (along with photosynthesis) by taking oxygen into their cells and into the mitochondria—the respiratory centers of their cells—where they break the bonds of the glucose molecule ($C_6H_{12}O_6$) to release stored energy in the form of ATP. Note that it is a common misconception for students to think that plants only carry on photosynthesis. In fact, plants also carry on cellular respiration just like animals. Note, however, that the processes of photosynthesis and respiration are the inverse of one another, only with sunlight as the source of energy in photosynthesis, and energy in the form of ATP being produced in respiration.

Animals need the sugars and stored starches made by plants in order for their own cells to carry on life functions and produce the energy needed to sustain the animal's life. Animals, therefore, must ingest food from plants, or from animals that had ingested plants. Once the food is digested into its smallest components in the small intestine, the glucose enters the bloodstream and is carried to the cells. In the cells, and inside the mitochondria of the cells, oxygen that entered the bloodstream and ultimately the cells through respiration combines with the glucose to break the chemical bonds of the molecule and produce energy in the form of ATP. This energy is needed for the animal to sustain its own life functions.

Photosynthesis

(Chloroplasts of plant cells)

Sunlight energy + $6CO_2$ + $6H_2O$ → $C_6H_{12}O_6$ + $6O_2$

Plant *and* Animal Respiration

(Mitochondria of both plant and animal cells)

$C_6H_{12}O_6$ + $6O_2$ → $6CO_2$ + $6H_2O$ + ATP energy

In addition to aerobic cellular respiration, which requires the use of oxygen in the process, organisms or certain cells of organisms may carry on anaerobic respiration, a form of respiration that does not use oxygen. Anaerobic respiration occurs in organisms such as yeast and in the muscle cells of animals when the demands for energy are high, as during strenuous exercise. Anaerobic respiration yields less energy than aerobic respiration; therefore, it occurs in small organisms (yeast, certain bacteria). In animals, it provides a little extra energy to the muscles in the form of ATP during exercise, when extra energy is needed. The by-products in anaerobic respiration for yeast and certain bacteria (e.g., those used in making wine) are different than in muscle cells. In yeast and wine-making bacteria, anaerobic respiration is called fermentation and the by-products are alcohol and carbon dioxide gas. The carbon dioxide gas is what makes bread dough containing yeast to rise (the alcohol burns off during baking). In the muscle cells the anaerobic respiration that takes place during strenuous exercise results in the production of lactic acid.

Anaerobic Respiration in Yeast and Certain Bacteria (as Fermentation)

$C_6H_{12}O_6$ (Glucose) is broken down to → Energy (ATP) + Ethanol + Carbon dioxide (CO_2)

Anaerobic Respiration in Muscle Cells

$C_6H_{12}O_6$ (Glucose) is broken down to → Energy (ATP) + Lactic acid

Chemical Compounds of Life

All living things contain and/or need four main carbon-based compounds for life, also known as organic molecules. These four compounds or organic molecules are carbohydrates, proteins, lipids, and nucleic acids. The composition of these life molecules is always carbon, hydrogen, and oxygen as the backbone, with nitrogen, phosphorous, and sulfur appearing in some of these molecules as well. These molecules can be remembered with the acronym SPONCH (sulfur, phosphorous, oxygen, nitrogen, carbon, and hydrogen).

Carbohydrates are stored as starches, with the simplest form or basic building block a simple sugar or monosaccharide, such as glucose. Carbohydrates are ultimately digested into simple sugars and used in cellular respiration to produce energy for all life functions. The type of carbohydrate or starch is a factor of the number and types of monosaccharides in the chain. Plant substances contain starch in their roots, stems, leaves, and fruit in particular, with an abundance of starch often stored in the roots. Potatoes, carrots, turnips, corn, peas, celery, spinach, and apples are examples of foods that store sugars and starches, or carbohydrates. Carbohydrates are composed of carbon, hydrogen, and oxygen atoms.

Proteins are complex molecules that are made of a repeating, and often turned and twisted, chain of its smallest component, amino acids. Proteins can be immense in size and perform a variety of essential functions and purposes in the body. Proteins are in cell membranes, and make up connective tissue, bones and muscles, and are the enzymes and hormones that control the body's metabolism and internal actions that maintain life. There are 20 different amino acids that exist on Earth which comprise proteins. Proteins are found in meats, eggs, and cheese, as examples. In addition to carbon, oxygen, and hydrogen atoms, proteins contain nitrogen.

Lipids are fats, and the basic building block or smallest component is one to three fatty acid molecules and one glycerol molecule bonded together. Lipids are stored as energy reserves in the fat of animals, or stored in the form of oils in plants. Lipids stored in the body provide insulation for animals in cold climates, and are also believed to be important for brain development. Lipids can be found marbled within meats, and in substances like butter and oils. Lipids contain carbon, hydrogen, and oxygen molecules.

Nucleic acids include deoxyribonucleic acids (DNA) and ribonucleic acids (RNA) found inside of cells. These nucleic acids provide hereditary information and instructions or "blueprints" that direct the cell's life functions. The smallest component of DNA and RNA are nucleotides, which consist of a sugar, a phosphate group, and a nitrogen base. In DNA the sugar is deoxyribose and the nitrogen base in a nucleotide can be adenine (A), thymine (T), cytosine (C), or guanine (G). DNA is shaped as a "double helix," or twisted ladder, with the rungs of the molecular ladder being paired nitrogen bases, and the sides being the sugars and phosphate groups. The nitrogen bases from one side of the ladder are weakly bonded or attracted to the nitrogen bases on the other side of the ladder by hydrogen bonds. The pairing of nitrogen bases is important: DNA nucleotides with the nitrogen base **thymine** only bonds in the center of the ladder with nucleotides carrying the nitrogen base **adenine**, whereas nucleotides with

cytosine only bond with nucleotides that have the nitrogen base **guanine** (A-T or G-C). The differing sizes of the nitrogen bases, A, T, G, and C, cause the ladder to twist, thus forming the twisted double-helix shape. The particular sequence of DNA nucleotides with their nitrogen bases code for traits and characteristics of the organism. The sequence in a section of DNA that codes for a trait is called a **gene**.

Ribonucleic acid (RNA) is similar to DNA, only it is single-stranded rather than double, the sugar in the nucleotide is ribose instead of deoxyribose, and the nitrogen bases are adenine, uracil, cytosine, and guanine (no thymine). In RNA adenine pairs with uracil, and cytosine pairs with guanine. RNA is important in making proteins (e.g., enzymes, hormones) in the cell to be used for a particular life function such as making the enzyme lipase in pancreatic cells to digest the sugar in milk known as lactose.

Nucleic acids are composed of carbon, hydrogen, and oxygen, as well as phosphorus, nitrogen, and sometimes sulfur.

COMPETENCY 012

The teacher understands reproduction and the mechanisms of heredity.

The beginning teacher:

A. Compares and contrasts sexual and asexual reproduction.

B. Understands the organization of hereditary material (e.g., DNA, genes, chromosomes).

C. Describes how an inherited trait can be determined by one or many genes and how more than one trait can be influenced by a single gene.

D. Distinguishes between dominant and recessive alleles and predicts the probable outcomes of genetic combinations (i.e., genotypes and phenotypes).

E. Evaluates the influence of environmental and genetic factors on the traits of an organism.

F. Describes current applications of genetic research (e.g., related to cloning, reproduction, health, industry, agriculture).

Asexual and Sexual Reproduction

There are two forms of reproduction: **asexual** and **sexual** reproduction. Asexual reproduction has one parent cell that divides by a process called mitosis or binary fission into two daughter cells with identical DNA as the parent, and as each other. This type of reproduction occurs in simple, one-celled organisms and in body cells when they undergo growth and repair, and takes place through a series of steps in the cell's life cycle. Growth in most organisms is caused by mitosis. The importance of mitosis is that the offspring cells, or "daughter" cells, are each an exact copy of the original. Through mitosis, new cells are made; for example, to form a scar after an injury, new bone cells, muscle cells, blood cells, and any cell that is needed by the body throughout life and growth. In single-celled organisms, mitosis is the cell's form of reproduction—making exact copies of the DNA in each of the two daughter cells, and is often called binary fission. Only one organism (the single cell) is involved, and there is no exchange of genetic material, or DNA. Thus, the two offspring cells, or daughter cells, are identical to the original, or parent cell.

In mitosis, the entire DNA within each chromosome in the cell makes a copy of itself (replicates). The replicated chromosomes containing DNA line up along the equatorial plane of the cell, and through a series of events, prepare to be separated from each other. When the cell divides, one copy of each strand or chromosome of DNA goes into one of the daughter cells, and one goes into the other daughter cell. This process preserves the DNA of the parent, but does not allow for much variation in the offspring (daughter cells).

Sexual reproduction, which occurs in more complex organisms, requires two parent cells to contribute genetic information to produce a unique new cell, or offspring. The process of producing the cells that ultimately join together to form the new offspring is meiosis. Meiosis occurs only in specialized cells of the parents—namely, within the sex organs, or gonads, known as the ovary in females and testicles in males. Meiosis is somewhat similar to mitosis, but there are important distinctions. Meiosis is how sperm and egg cells are formed in preparation for being combined in the process of fertilization.

Each species of organism has a certain number of chromosomes (containing DNA and thus the genetic code) in each of its cells; for example, humans have 46 chromosomes arranged in 23 pairs. Any new offspring of that species must have the same number of chromosomes as the parent cells. Thus, in the case of humans, the specialized beginning cells (oocytes and spermatocytes) in the gonads have 46 chromosomes, but they must make cells that have half the number of chromosomes (23 in total), which are called **gametes**. This reduction to half the number of chromosomes occurs because when the gamete from one parent (female egg or ovum) combines with the gamete from the other parent (male sperm cell), the full number of 46 chromosomes (arranged in 23 pairs) is restored in the fertilized egg. In sum, meiosis is the process that reduces the number of chromosomes in half to prepare the new daughter cell(s), namely the egg cell in females and sperm cell in males, to join together in the process known as fertilization to produce a new offspring.

In **meiosis**, the chromosomes duplicate as they do in mitosis; however, the cell divides twice, preserving one of each pair of chromosomes in the resulting four daughter cells (in humans, 23 chromosomes). The result of meiosis, therefore, is four cells with half the number of chromosomes as the original parent cell. In the female, only one of the four daughter cells becomes a viable egg cell, whereas in males all four daughter cells are viable sperm cells. After the egg cell has been fertilized by the sperm, it is called a zygote. The zygote immediately begins to divide by **mitosis** to grow and develop into a new offspring, first forming a structure called the morula, then a blastocyst (ball of cells), and then differentiating its cells into what will become the various structures and organs of the new offspring, called the **gastrula**. Soon the gastrula, with its rapidly dividing and differentiating cells, becomes an embryo, and later a fetus that grows and develops (by mitosis) into the new offspring.

Sexual reproduction allows for more variation in offspring because of the combination of genetic material (DNA) coming from each parent. Many animals carry out sexual reproduction and therefore come from eggs. For some animals, the egg is inside the female animal and is fertilized by the male sperm cells within the body. For other animals, such as most fish species, the eggs are fertilized by the male after being expelled from the female's body. When fertilized internally, the fertilized egg may be laid externally from the female, as happens with many insects, reptiles, and birds, or it may remain in the body of the female until birth. The egg has an outer lining to protect the animal growing inside. Bird eggs have hard shells, while the eggs of amphibians, like the turtle, have hard but flexible coverings. With the appropriate care and heat, an egg will hatch. After hatching, in some species, the parents protect and feed the newborn until it can survive on its own; in other species, the eggs must survive on their own. On reaching adulthood, females begin laying eggs, and the cycle of life continues. Mammals are also conceived through egg fertilization, but the resulting embryo is kept inside the mother until it is mature enough for life outside the womb.

The reproduction of plants can also be divided into asexual and sexual mechanisms. Asexual reproduction of plants takes place by cutting portions of the plant and replanting them. Tubers, or the eyes of potatoes, and the bulbs of tulips grow into roots and are also a form of asexual reproduction.

Sexual reproduction in plants involves seeds produced by flowers of female and male plants, which are cross-pollinated with help from insects or other animals. The flower is the reproductive organ of the plant and consists of several parts that are the male and female reproductive organs. Some flowers may have only the male part, and likewise, some flowers contain only the female part of the same species of plant/tree. So, for example, there actually can be a "male" tree and a "female" tree. In the flower, the male reproductive organ is the **stamen**, which is divided into filament and anther. The filament simply holds up the anther, and the anther contains the pollen in which the sperm nuclei are found. Flowers may also contain the female reproductive organ, the **pistil**, which consists of the ovary, style, and stigma. The ovary contains the egg cells, which in the flower are called ovules. The style is the tube above the ovary, and the stigma is the top of the style, which has a sticky substance. The pollen needs to either be manually placed on the stigma, or blown there by the wind. Another mode of transfer, which is what usually happens, is that the pollen sticks to the body of a bee or butterfly (who are actually in search of sugary nectar in the flower, and not the pollen). When the pollen sticks to the body of the insect, it may then be transferred from the anther (male part) to the stigma (female part). In essence, the sperm nuclei then travel down the style to reach the ovules, where fertilization occurs. The fertilized egg then becomes the seed. The ovary of the flower may swell and become the fruit (as in a peach or apple). This process helps protect the seeds, and also helps with seed dispersal. Animals eat the fruit and excrete the seed unharmed in their fecal matter (the seed has a seed coat that protects it, making it indigestible). Seed germination—where the seed sprouts into a plant—requires the appropriate quantity of air, water, and heat.

Heredity

Hereditary information is contained in the specific sequence of DNA in areas called genes, on chromosomes within the cells of organisms. Traits are inherited from the parent cells to the off-spring according to the genes the offspring receive from the parents for particular traits. More than one trait can be determined by a single gene, and one or many genes can determine a particular trait. For example, the gene for human eye color is located on several genes. However, there may be several different physical expressions of genes. Consider eye color, for example. Offspring could have, say, brown, blue, green, or hazel eye colors. Alleles are the different varieties of a gene that exist for a trait. There may be two or more alleles for a given trait. For example, there are three genes, called alleles, for blood type in the human population: A, B, and O. The National Human Genome Institute explains that though an allele is one of two or more versions of a gene, offspring can inherit only two alleles for each gene (one on each paired chromosome). That is, one allele can be inherited from each parent: one allele from the original sperm cell, and one allele from the original egg cell. For a brief video on alleles, see: *https://www.brightstorm.com/science/biology/mendelian-genetics/alleles/*.

Recall that sperm and egg cells each contain one of each pair of chromosomes from the origi-nal parent cell. When the egg is fertilized, the pairs are restored in a random combination from the mother (egg) and father (sperm). The genes inherited from the parent cells may be **dominant** or **recessive** for certain traits in the offspring. In the pair of chromosomes, dominant gene is the trait that is expressed in the offspring when paired with another dominant gene or with a recessive gene. The recessive gene is only expressed when paired with another recessive gene for a trait. Gene pairs are often shown in science as letters; for example, brown fur color = B (dominant is shown as a cap-ital letter), and white fur color = b (recessive is shown as a lower case letter of the dominant gene).

Genetic problems are solved using **Punnett square** diagrams. These Punnett diagrams help predict the gene combinations and expressed traits in the offspring. The genotype is the actual gene combination, and the phenotype is the trait that is expressed or that "shows up" in the offspring. Recall that the egg or sperm cell will have only one of each allele, whereas the fertilized egg (off-spring) will have two, and that number will be maintained in every cell in the offspring throughout its lifetime (except for its own sperm and egg cells when an adult). Two dominant traits may be shown as two capital letters (BB); a dominant and recessive pair may be shown as a capital letter with a lower case (Bb); and two recessive genes are shown as two lower case letters (bb). Two of the same genes, e.g., two dominant genes or two recessive genes, is called homozygous for that trait; and one dominant and one recessive together is termed heterozygous (hybrid).

A Punnett square problem is solved by placing the egg cell genes along one top (or side) of the diagram, and sperm cell genes along the side (or top). Then the genes are combined within the boxes of the diagram, representing fertilization, to predict the probabilities of certain gene combi-nations occurring in the offspring.

B = dominant for brown fur

b = recessive for white fur

A mother guinea pig is homozygous dominant for brown fur. She is mated with a heterozygous male with brown fur color. What are the expected genotypes and phenotypes of the offspring? The solution is shown in the Punnett square diagram that follows.

		mother	
father	B	B
B	BB	BB
b	Bb	Bb

In this problem, the mother's genotype is BB, and she has brown fur. The father's genotype is Bb, and he also has brown fur; however, the father carries the gene for white fur. Fifty percent of the offspring will be homozygous dominant (BB), and fifty percent will be heterozygous (Bb). One hundred percent of the offspring will have the phenotype of brown fur color.

In addition to the genotype and phenotype directly inherited in offspring, environmental factors may contribute to how, or sometimes even whether, the gene is expressed. Some genes may not be expressed until an environmental condition or stressor triggers the gene into action. It is believed that autoimmune diseases, a situation where antibodies are formed to attack otherwise normal body cells, as in certain forms of hypothyroidism, are triggered by environmental stressors. In addition, factors in the environment, such as viruses or carcinogens, may activate susceptible inherited genes in an individual in the development of certain cancers, food intolerances, or allergies.

Genetics has somewhat recently been transformed into an industry, where crops and cattle are genetically engineered to produce, for instance, greater-quality specimens at higher yields. The healthcare industry has been able to use genetics to produce vaccines and medications that have vastly improved the quality of human life; however, sometimes they have impinged on socially controversial areas, such as stem cell research and cloning. By changing the DNA sequence in genes, scientists may, for example, be able to grow limbs and organs to replace those lost; develop humans with pre-specified desired characteristics; or increase the human lifespan. Thus, genetics has been beneficial to the quality of life; however, if unchecked, it can create ethical dilemmas and possibly yield dangerous results.

COMPETENCY 013

The teacher understands adaptations of organisms and the theory of evolution.

The beginning teacher:

A. Describes similarities and differences among various taxonomical groups and methods of classifying organisms.

B. Describes adaptations in a population or species that enhance its survival and reproductive success.

C. Describes how populations and species may evolve through time.

D. Applies knowledge of the mechanisms and processes of biological evolution (e.g., diversity, variation, mutation, environmental factors, natural selection).

E. Describes evidence that supports the theory of evolution of life on Earth.

Survival in the Environment

Genetics plays an important role in the ability of organisms to be able to survive and thrive in their environment, and ultimately produce new offspring such that they pass on similar genetic material, *like* that which allowed them to survive and thrive, and maybe survive and thrive even better. Some inherited traits, called **adaptations**, could allow the organisms to better survive in their environment or could lead to their demise (and thus prevent the prospect of future offspring). Adaptations do not suddenly arise or develop in the lifetime of organisms. Rather, they occur gradually in the species over time. Imagine that a certain deer-like animal thousands of years ago was particularly fast—that is, it was born with stronger muscle tissue than most, and a better bone and muscle physical structure. Perhaps such traits made it better able to run away from predators and survive. This deer-like animal thus was able to survive long enough for it to have offspring with similar genetic material. At the same time, those deer-like animals that were not born with the same muscular and structural soundness as this one would have been killed as prey before they could reproduce. In time, those animals that are best suited in these qualities, as well as others, are the organisms that survive, as do their offspring. Those not so well-adapted, perish.

It is also the case that the organism that survives will breed with another that also has better-adapted characteristics, and was also able to survive in the natural environment. A change or mutation in the genetic material, that is, the genes that direct the development of a trait, may give rise to a new characteristic that either is or is not better suited for the environment. In the event it is better suited, the organism will survive and produce offspring with this same mutation. Over the years, mutations that are better suited to the environment may make the organism appear quite different than it did hundreds, thousands, or millions of years earlier. If the environment itself changes, however, organisms that were able to survive under the previous conditions (climate, water supply, vegetation, landscape) may be rendered unable to survive in the new environmental conditions. Thus, a catastrophic event, such as perhaps a large asteroid striking the Earth, could change the environmental conditions and either lead to the extinction of organisms, or the survival of organisms that would not have survived under the conditions before the strike. Likewise, selective breeding, which has humans choose desirable traits in organisms, and then act to enhance and perpetuate those traits in future generations, also affects the change over time of organisms. The combination of genetics, adaptations, changes over time, mutations, selective breeding, and environmental conditions/changes contribute to the concept known as **evolution**.

Adaptations come about in a random manner. But this of course was not always known. Nothing in Darwin's writings or Gregor Mendel's (the father of heredity) studies pointed to this phenomenon. It was only discovered later that adaptations occurred due to random mutations of gene sequences that code for certain traits. Genetic codes may change for a multitude of reasons, including chance, environmental conditions, and exposure to toxic material. The change in genetic code may give rise to a variation in a trait that turns out to be more favorable than the original trait. If the change prolongs the life of the species with the mutation, then the mutated species is more likely to survive long enough to produce new offspring with the same favorable mutation.

There are several lines of evidence for evolution. Paleontology contributes to our understanding of past organisms, specifically fossils.

- Fossils found in more recent layers of rock are similar or identical to existing organisms.

- In older rock layers, fossils significantly differ from present-day organisms.

- Discoveries are regularly being made that fill gaps in the fossil record.

- Scientists are finding fossils that have the features they predicted based on known, older, and younger fossils.

- Fossils of any species have only been found in rock layers younger than their ancestor species, and not found in rock layers older than their ancestors.

Because the Earth is constantly changing, with plates shifting and colliding, continents being uplifted, and seas being buried, fossils of once-living organisms have been found in all places over the Earth; the study of the geographic distribution of all forms of life is called **biogeography**. Scientists have been able to reveal from fossils that species originate in one place and spread out to other places from that source. Fossils have been found to do exactly that—where a fossil is found can be traced back to its point of origin.

Developmental biology, the study of how vertebrate embryos develop, provides the basis for further evidence of evolution. During their development from embryos, all vertebrates tend to share common features. Some of these features, such as a tail, appear only in the embryo stage of some species and then disappear or are incorporated into the body, whereas the same feature may remain in another species.

Animals can be grouped according to common physical structures or morphology. Organisms are grouped, for example, as vertebrates and invertebrates due to the presence or absence of a backbone, as described earlier in the discussion of taxonomic groups. There is also enormous diversity among living things. For more information, refer to: *http://anthro.palomar.edu/animal/animal_1.htm.*

With more precise and detailed information now available on genomes and particular gene sequences that make up an organism's genetic code, we are better able to show how closely species may be related based on similarities and differences in the sequence. For example, because of similarities in the genetic code, humans have been found to be more closely related to chimpanzees than to gorillas—a finding that was at first surprising.

COMPETENCY 014

The teacher understands regulatory mechanisms and behavior.

The beginning teacher:

A. Describes how organisms respond to internal and external stimuli.

B. Applies knowledge of structures and physiological processes that maintain stable internal conditions (homeostasis).

C. Demonstrates an understanding of feedback mechanisms that allow organisms to maintain stable internal conditions.

D. Understands how evolutionary history of a species affects behavior (e.g., migration, nocturnality, territoriality).

Response to Internal and External Stimuli

All living organisms respond to stimuli from within and outside in the environment. Stimuli within the organism are **internal stimuli**, including feeling hungry or needing food; stimuli outside of the organism are **external stimuli** such as warmth or cold, light, or dark. Even the tiniest organisms such as bacteria have sensory mechanisms called chemoreceptors in their cell membrane that allow them to sense and move toward food in their environment. Plants have chemical hormone substances called auxins, which cause a variety of growth and movement patterns called tropisms. Auxins in plants root tips sense and cause the roots to grow toward water, called hydrotropism, and downward toward gravity (geotropism). Auxins in the stem tips sense light and cause the stems and leaves to grow toward light (phototropism). Other auxins cause plants twining around other plants to seek anchors, some flowers to open during the day and close at night, and growth patterns called circadian rhythms.

Animals respond to external stimuli using their senses, with many responses to stimuli being automatic, such as the pupils of the eyes dilating in the dark and constricting in light (external stimuli). The nervous system in animals controls responses, sending signals to the spinal cord (if present in the organism) and/or to the brain, which then instructs the appropriate muscles or organs to respond. For example, if you accidentally touch a hot stove with your hand, the nervous system immediately sends a signal to the spinal cord, which sends a signal to the correct muscle (biceps) to pull your hand away. It is only after the hand is pulled away from danger that the signal is sent on to the brain that signals the realization that your hand has been burned. Once the individual verbalizes pain (Ouch!), the hand has already been pulled away. The action of the nerves in the hand to the spinal cord to the muscle is called a "reflex" arc. The purpose of the reflex arc is for protection.

Maintaining Stable Internal Conditions

Organisms respond to stimuli to maintain a stable internal condition called **homeostasis**. Homeostasis is the regulation and maintenance of bodily functions, such as temperature, blood sugar levels, water content, and the amount of carbon dioxide. Homeostasis mechanisms also include maintaining proper and stable pH, respiratory rates, and other important factors that protect the balance of life functions in the organism. Maintaining homeostasis is essential for an organism's survival. For more information see: *http://www.bbc.co.uk/education/guides/ z4khvcw/revision*

In addition to the nervous system, hormones within the body also work to regulate life functions and maintain homeostasis. Hormones are produced in glands in the body within the endocrine system. For example, adrenalin is secreted from the adrenal glands (located on top of the kidneys) in high stress or fear situations, such as being chased by a vicious dog, that triggers a series of other responses in the body that allow the organism to experience "fight-or-flight" reactions. For example, respiration and heart rate is increased, and the brain becomes more alert. Some have reported sudden bursts of strength in such situations, allowing them to survive or escape the stressful or fearful situation. Other hormones, such as those secreted by the thyroid and pituitary gland, control growth and metabolism. In females, hormones, including estrogen and progesterone, control menstrual cycles and pregnancy.

Feedback Mechanisms

Regulatory feedback mechanisms can be positive or negative. Positive feedback mechanisms cause reactions to increase, such as eating when hungry, whereas negative feedback causes reactions to slow down, such as stopping eating when full. Some examples described in this section, such as the secretion of adrenalin in the body, describe feedback mechanisms. Adrenalin secretion is an example of a positive feedback mechanism in which a stimulus causes a reaction, rather than slowing or stopping a reaction.

Evolution and Behavior

Organisms have long developed and displayed behaviors that contribute to their survival as a species. In ant colonies, for instance, individual organisms have specific roles that ensure the survival of the entire colony, e.g., workers, soldiers. A variety of behaviors that serve critical roles in survival have evolved over time, such as mating dances of some animals, echolocation in bats, differing bird calls, migratory patterns, territoriality, and nocturnality.

Migration is when organisms move as a group to different places for reasons such as seasonal climate changes, food sources, mating opportunities, or other causes that support their survival. Many species migrate, including birds, whales, butterflies, and others. For more information on migration, go to *https://www.livescience.com/10235-animals-migrate.html.*

Territoriality refers to defending the area where the organism or species live. Living things have many different defenses against intruders into their territory. For example, bees defend their hive by stinging intruders. The more effective they are at defending and protecting their territory, the more likely they are to survive. For more information on territoriality, see: *https://hewittapbiology.wordpress.com/2012/08/06/territorial-behavior/*

Nocturnality is an adaptation of some animals that are awake and active during nighttime, and inactive or asleep during the day. Nocturnal species are either in search of food or seeking the safety of darkness. Raccoons, bats, mice, moths, and other organisms, both predators and prey, are nocturnal. Nocturnal animals have certain adaptations that support their survival, such as enhanced eyesight and/or hearing. For more information on nocturnal organisms, see: *http://www.enchantedlearning.com/coloring/nocturnal.shtml*

COMPETENCY 015

The teacher understands the relationships between organisms and the environment.

The beginning teacher:

A. Identifies the abiotic and biotic components of an ecosystem.

B. Analyzes the interrelationships among producers, consumers, and decomposers in an ecosystem.

C. Identifies factors that influence the size of populations in an ecosystem (e.g., limiting factors, growth rate).

D. Analyzes adaptive characteristics that result in the unique niche of a population or species in an ecosystem.

E. Describes and analyzes energy flow through various types of ecosystems.

F. Knows how populations or species modify and affect ecosystems.

Ecology studies the relationship of organisms with their physical environment. The physical environment includes light, heat, solar radiation, moisture, wind, oxygen, carbon dioxide, nutrients, water, and the atmosphere. These factors of the physical environment are the **abiotic** (nonliving) components of the ecosystem. The **biotic** components are the living or once-living organisms, such as the remains of a dead organism, that shape their ecosystem. There are three main biotic components of an ecosystem:

- **Producers** are green plants that produce oxygen and store chemical energy for consumers.

- **Consumers** are animals, both herbivores and carnivores. The herbivores take the chemical energy from plants, and carnivores take the energy from other animals or directly from plants.

- **Decomposers**, like fungi and bacteria, are in charge of cleaning up the environment by decomposing and freeing dead matter for recycling back into the ecosystem.

A successful ecosystem requires a healthy balance among producers, consumers, and decomposers. This balance relies on natural ways to control populations of living organisms and is maintained mostly through competition and predation. Predation is the consumption of one living organism, plant or animal, by another. It is a direct way to control population and promote natural selection by eliminating weak organisms from the population. As a consequence of predation, predators and prey evolve to survive. If an organism cannot evolve to meet challenges from the environment, it perishes.

Living organisms like plants and animals need to have ideal conditions for their survival. They need nutrients, the appropriate temperature, and a balanced ecosystem to survive and reproduce. A healthy ecosystem must contain an appropriate system for energy exchange or a food chain. The right combination of herbivorous and carnivorous animals is necessary for a healthy ecosystem. The food chain generally begins with the primary source of energy, the sun. The sun provides the energy for plants; plants in turn are consumed by animals; and animals are consumed by other animals. These animals die and serve as food sources for decomposing bacteria, fungi, and plants. In the food chain, or more accurately, food web, energy from the sun is captured by plants in photosynthesis to make sugars stored as starches. Some of this energy is transferred to the consumers when eaten; however, energy is lost to the plant itself when used in its own life processes. Each level along the food chain receives less and less energy because of the use of some of the energy by the organism itself to sustain its life functions. It is estimated that each level of consumer only receives about 10 percent of the energy from the producer or consumer it ingests, whereas 90% was used in that organism's own life functions. A food chain is shown as follows. Decomposers digest dead organisms and return them to soil so that, with proper sunlight and water conditions, new producers may begin the food chain/web again.

Food chain/web:

Sun → producers → 1st order consumers → 2nd order consumers →
3rd order consumers → decomposers

Example:

Sun → wild corn → mouse → snake → hawk → decomposing bacteria

When the balance of the ecosystem's food chain/web is disrupted either by the removal of organisms or the introduction of nonnative species, the ecosystem is affected, forcing animals and plants to adapt or else die. Thus, the common basic needs of all living organisms for survival are: *air, water, food,* and *shelter.* When a shared resource is scarce, organisms must compete to survive. The competition, which occurs between animals as well as between plants, ensures the survival of the fittest as well as the preservation of the system.

Changes in the environment have led to certain adaptations arising in organisms that are favorable to the new environment, yet allowed the organisms without that adaptation to survive. The behaviors or physical features of organisms that developed due to mutations that were more favorable to the changes in the environment allowed greater chances of survival and so were carried on to future generations. Take the anteater species. Over thousands of years, its offspring were able to survive better if they had a long snout to be able to reach for ants. Or consider frogs, which developed a long, sticky tongue to catch flies. Adaptation for animals, plants, and even humans is a matter of life and death. Another angle on this is found in analyzing the skulls of predators versus prey. It turns out that a pattern emerges in the placement of the eye sockets and shapes of the teeth.

Predators such as wolves, foxes, and lions have eye sockets in the front of their skull, which helps them focus on their prey when hunting. Prey, such as rabbits and squirrels, have eyes on the sides of their skull, which helps them see on both sides of their body at once in order to escape predation. Predators have sharp, pointed teeth for tearing the flesh of their prey, whereas prey (those that are primary or first-order consumers) have flat teeth for chewing and grinding plants they consume. It is important to note that plants and other non-animal organisms also adapt to their environment. For example, coniferous trees have thin but strong needles rather than leaves to protect it against the cold, whereas plants in the tropics have broad leaves allowing it to absorb the abundant sunshine for photosynthesis and release excess water through transpiration. In bacteria, a mutation in the genetic code may result in the bacteria being resistant to antibiotics; bacteria without the mutation are killed by the antibiotic, whereas the mutated variety survives. When the bacterium divides in binary fission, its offspring, or replicated bacteria, contains the mutated DNA, and so is also resistant to the antibiotic. This new, mutated variety of bacteria becomes predominant, whereas the former variety dies off. Scientists work to make new and different antibiotics in order to eliminate the new mutated species of bacteria.

Changes in the food chain of animals often lead to modifications in behaviors and the predominance of certain inherited traits that are favorable adaptations to new conditions. For example, because their habitats are destroyed when land is developed by humans, raccoons and opossums have learned to coexist with humans and to get new sources of food. Bears have managed to successfully adapt to colder climates by hibernating during the winter and living on the fat they accumulate during the rest of the year. Other animals, like the chameleon and the fox, have developed camouflage to hide from predators. Humans are not exempt from the need to adapt to new situations. For example, humans have had to adapt by using tools to produce, preserve, and trade the food supplies they needed to sustain them. All these examples represent ways in which organisms adapt to deal with challenges in their ecosystem.

All species of organisms have limiting factors that impact their population growth. These factors may be biotic, such as the availability of food, or abiotic, such as the amount of freshwater available. A drought for example, would impact the growth of plants, which in turn would impact both the food (biotic) and water (abiotic) factors necessary for survival and growth in the population. For more information see: *https://biologydictionary.net/limiting-factor/*.

COMPETENCY 016

The teacher understands the structure and function of Earth systems.

The beginning teacher:

A. Understands the composition and structure of Earth (mantle, crust, and core) and ana- lyzes constructive and destructive processes that produce geologic change (e.g., plate tectonics, weathering, erosion, deposition).

B. Understands the form and function of surface water and ground water.

C. Applies knowledge of the composition and structure of the atmosphere and its properties.

D. Applies knowledge of how human activity and natural processes, both gradual and cata- strophic, can alter Earth systems.

E. Identifies the sources of energy (e.g., solar, geothermal) in Earth systems and describes mechanisms of energy transfer (e.g., convection, radiation).

The formation of deserts, mountains, rivers, oceans, and other landforms can be described in terms of geological processes. Mountains are formed by colliding plates. For example, the Appala- chian Mountains in the United States were formed 250 million years ago when the tectonic plate car- rying the continent of Africa collided with the plate carrying the North American continent (Badder et al., 2000). Rivers and natural lakes form at low elevations where rainfall collects and eventually runs down to the sea. The sediment gathered by the rivers in turn accumulates at river mouths to cre- ate deltas. These are both constructive and destructive processes that form the Earth. **Constructive processes** include those that build mountains, such as the gradual (over millions of years) collision and crushing together of the Earth's tectonic plates. **Destructive processes** include weathering and erosion—the wearing down of mountains and rock by forces such as water, wind, and ice.

Layers of the Earth

The average circumference of the Earth at the equator is 25,902 miles, and its radius is about 3,959 miles. The Earth is divided into three main parts:

• The **crust** is the outer portion of the Earth where we live. The thickness of the crust varies from about 3 miles to 40 miles, depending on the location. It contains various types of soil, metals, and rocks. The crust is broken down into several floating tectonic plates. Movements of these plates cause earthquakes and changes in landforms.

• The **mantle** is the thickest layer of the Earth located right below the crust. It is composed mostly of rocks and metals. The heat in the mantle is so intense that rocks and metals melt, creating magma and the resulting lava that reaches the surface.

- The **core** is the inner part of the Earth. It is composed of a solid inner core and an outer core that is mostly liquid. The inner core is made of solid iron and nickel. Despite temperatures in the inner core that resemble the heat on the surface of the sun, this portion of the Earth remains solid because of the intense pressure there.

Continental Drift

In 1915, the German scientist Alfred Wegener proposed that all the continents were previously one large continent but then broke apart and drifted through the ocean floor to their present locations. This theory was called continental drift, and it was the origin of today's concept of plate tectonics.

Tectonic Plates

Based on the theory of **plate tectonics**, the surface of the Earth is fragmented into large plates. The upper crust, or lithosphere, rides on top of the layer beneath, called the asthenosphere. The lithospheric plates are in continuous motion, floating on more liquid-like asthenosphere and always changing in size and position. The edges of these plates, where they move against each other, are sites of intense geologic activity, which results in earthquakes, volcanoes, and the creation of mountains. The generator for the movement of the continents/Earth's plates is the Mid-Atlantic Ridge—a huge volcanic mountain range on the floor of the Atlantic Ocean that is continuously erupting and pushing the plates apart in opposite directions from each other.

Forces That Change the Surface of the Earth

Three main forces and processes change the surface of the Earth: weathering, geological movements, and the creation of glaciers.

Weathering

Weathering is the process of breaking down rock, soils, and minerals through natural, chemical, and biological processes. Two of the most common examples of physical weathering are exfoliation and freeze thaw.

- Exfoliation occurs in places like the desert when the soil is exposed first to high temperatures, which cause it to expand, and then to cold temperatures, which make the soil contract. The stress of these changes causes the outer layers of rock to peel off.

- Freeze-thaw cycles break down rock when water gets into rock joints or cracks and then freezes and expands, breaking the rock. A similar process occurs when water containing salt crystals gets into the rock. Once the water evaporates, the crystals expand and break the rock. This process is called salt-crystal growth.

Weathering can be caused by chemical reactions. Two of the most common examples of chemical weathering are acid formation and hydration. Acid is formed under various conditions. For example, sulfur and rain are combined to create acid rain, which can weather and change the chemical composition of rock. Hydration occurs when the minerals in rock absorb water and expand sometimes changing the chemical composition of the rock. For example, through the process of hydration, a mineral like anhydrite can be changed into a different mineral, namely gypsum.

Erosion

After weathering, a second process called **erosion** may take place. Erosion is the movement of sediment from one location to the other through the use of water, wind, ice, or gravity. The Grand Canyon was created by the processes of weathering and erosion. The water movement (erosion) is responsible for the canyon being so deep, and the weathering process is responsible for its width (Houghton Mifflin, 2000).

Deposition

When the forces moving the sediment (water, wind, gravity) stop or slow down, the sediment is dropped. For example, when a river flows into a larger body of water, it slows down. The result of this slowdown is the sediment is deposited. When layer upon layer of sediment is deposited, a delta forms.

Earthquakes and Geologic Faults

The movement of the Earth's plates has forced rock layers to fold, creating mountains, hills, and valleys. This movement causes faults in the Earth's crust, breaking rocks and reshaping the environment. When forces within the Earth cause rocks to break and move around geologic faults, earthquakes occur. A fault is a deep crack that marks the boundary between two plates. The San Andreas Fault in central California is a well-known origin of earthquakes in the area. The epicenter of an earthquake is the point on the surface where the quake is strongest. The Richter scale is used to measure the amount of energy released by the earthquake. The severity of an earthquake runs from 0 to 9 on the Richter scale. Earthquake magnitude is determined by the logarithm of the amplitude of waves recorded by seismographs. Because of its logarithmic basis, each one-point increase on the scale represents a 10-fold increase in magnitude. Small earthquakes, many barely felt, are almost always happening somewhere on the planet. On average, a major quake, magnitude 7.0 to 7.9, happens somewhere on Earth more than once a month. A great earthquake, considered to be magnitude 8 or higher, occurs about once a year. Scientists are researching ways to predict earthquakes, but their predictions are not always accurate. There are various types of earthquake fault lines. These fault lines include normal fault, thrust fault, and strike-slip fault and are named according to how the two sides of the fault interface to cause the earthquake.

Volcanoes

Volcanoes are formed by the constant motion of tectonic plates. This movement creates pressure that forces magma from the mantle to escape to the surface, creating an explosion of lava, fire, and ash. The pressure of the magma and gases creates a monticule, or a small cone, that eventually grows to form a mountain-like volcano. Volcanic activity can create earthquakes, and the fiery lava can cause destruction. There are several types of volcanoes with different characteristics, including cinder cones, composite volcanoes, shield volcanoes, and lava domes.

Gravity

Gravity is the force of attraction that exists between objects. Gravity keeps the Earth in its orbit by establishing a balance between the attraction of the sun and the speed at which the Earth travels around it. However, gravity is also responsible for many of the Earth's forces that change the land. For example, when ice melts on the tops of mountains, it is because of gravity that the water will form streams and rivers that flow down the mountain, eventually making its way to the lowest point. Some of the main functions of gravity are listed here:

- Keeping the Earth's atmosphere, oceans, and inhabitants from drifting into space

- Pulling the rain to the rivers and eventually to the sea

- Guiding the development and growth of plants

- Affecting the way that our bones and muscles function

For information about the Earth and space, go to the official website of the U.S. space agency, the National Aeronautics and Space Administration (NASA), at *www.nasa.gov*. The site includes special sections for students from kindergarten through grade 12 and teachers.

Surface Water and Groundwater

Surface water is the water in streams, lakes, rivers, and all water that is on the surface of the land. Groundwater is water that seeps beneath the surface of the land and forms an underground "river" of water. The groundwater seeps into the soil until it reaches an impermeable layer of rock. The water stays on top of this layer and is a source of drinking water. This water may be tapped into via aquifers and wells.

The Earth's Atmosphere

The Earth is surrounded by a large mass of gas called the **atmosphere**. Roughly 348 miles thick, this gas mass supports life on the Earth and separates it from space. Among the many functions of the atmosphere are these:

- Absorbing energy from the sun to sustain life

- Recycling water and other chemicals needed for life

- Maintaining the climate, working with electric and magnetic forces

- Serving as a vacuum that protects life

The atmosphere is composed of 78 percent nitrogen, 21 percent oxygen, and 1 percent argon. In addition to these gases, the atmosphere contains water, greenhouse gases like ozone, and carbon dioxide. The Earth's atmosphere has five layers. The layer closest to the Earth is called the troposphere, which is where the weather we experience occurs.

Natural and Human Influences on Earth Systems

Many natural processes on Earth can change its systems. For example, earthquakes and volcanoes can be destructive and thus change the structure and composition of the landscape. Tsunamis, often caused by earthquakes or volcanic eruptions, can not only reshape shorelines but cause tremendous destruction well beyond the shoreline. Most tsunamis are under 10 feet high, though they can sometimes reach as much as 100 feet at the source. The powerful rushing water from a large tsunami crashing onshore can inundate low-lying coastal areas more than a mile inland. Human influences may also bring large-scale change to Earth systems. The destruction of the rainforests, called deforestation, can change the structure and composition of the land. The risks of deforestation can widen to the point of affecting the balance of atmospheric gases, including carbon dioxide and oxygen levels. Carbon dioxide emissions from factories, automobiles, and airplanes, as examples, may play a role in changing the atmospheric composition as well. Carbon dioxide, called a **greenhouse gas**, tends to trap heat energy and result in an overall warming of the atmosphere, which has an impact on climate and plant growth that in turn affects all living organisms on Earth. Many natural and human influences contribute to the increase of greenhouse gases in the atmosphere, producing what is known as **global warming**. Other greenhouse gases include methane (CH_4) and ozone, (O_3), which is the primary component of smog found at Earth's ground level.

It is important to distinguish global warming and the ozone that is in smog from the destruction of the ozone layer (hole in the ozone layer), which is a different phenomenon. Ozone forms a layer at the top of the atmosphere that blocks harmful ultraviolet rays from the sun from reaching the Earth's surface ("good ozone"). The "hole" in the ozone layer means there is a destruction of this ozone layer, and thus letting harmful ultraviolet radiation reach Earth's surface wherever this hole is present. Chlorofluorocarbons, found in aerosols, contribute to the destruction of the ozone layer.

Energy Transfer

The transfer of heat is accomplished in three ways: conduction, radiation, and convection.

Conduction is the process of transferring heat or electricity through a substance. It occurs when two objects of differing temperatures are placed in contact with each other and heat flows from the hotter object to the cooler object. For example, in the cooling system of a car, heat from the engine is transferred to the liquid coolant. When the coolant passes through the radiator, the heat transfers from the coolant to the radiator, and eventually, out of the car. This heat transfer system preserves the engine and allows it to continue working.

Radiation describes the energy that travels at high speed in space in the form of light or through the decay of radioactive elements. Radiation is part of our modern life. It exists in simple states as the energy emitted by microwaves, cellular phones, and sunshine or as potentially dangerous energy as X-ray machines and nuclear weapons. The radiation used in medicine, nuclear power, and nuclear weapons has enough energy to cause permanent damage and death.

Convection describes the flow of heat through the movement of fluid matter, meaning gases and liquids, from a hot region to a cool region. In its most basic form, the concept of convection is that warmer gases or liquids rise, and colder gases or liquids sink. The colder gases or liquids contract and their greater density makes them sink. The warmer gases or liquids expand, meaning particles become more spread out, and so are less dense, and rise. Consequently, convection occurs when the heating and circulation of a substance changes the density of the substance. A good example is the heating of air over land near coastal areas coupled with the influx of cooler offshore sea breezes. The heated air inland expands and thus decreases in density, causing the cooler, more dense air to rush in to achieve equilibrium. A more common example of convection is the process of heating water on a stove. In this case, heat is transferred from the stove element to the bottom of the pot by conduction, which heats the water. Heat is transferred from the hot water at the bottom of the pot to the cooler water at the top by convection. At the same time, the cooler, denser water at the top sinks to the bottom, where it is subsequently heated. This circulation creates the movement typical of boiling water. Convection currents created by the combining or colliding of cold and warm air masses is one factor responsible for storms and circular rotation of the air in tornados and hurricanes. Ocean currents are also caused by the collision of cold water and warm water masses in the oceans (Cavallo, 2001). Convection currents occur in the molten or partially molten rock of the mantle, causing plates to move and the crust to have seismic and volcanic activity.

COMPETENCY 017

The teacher understands cycles in Earth systems.

The beginning teacher:

A. Understands the rock cycle and how rocks, minerals, and soils are formed.

B. Understands the water cycle and its relationship to weather processes.

C. Understands biogeochemical cycles (e.g., carbon, nitrogen, oxygen) and their relationship to Earth systems.

D. Understands the relationships and interactions that occur among the various cycles in the biosphere, geosphere, hydrosphere, and atmosphere.

Rock Types

The hard, solid part of the Earth's surface is called rock. Rocks are made of one or more minerals. Rocks like granite, marble, and limestone are extensively used in the construction industry. They can be used in floors, buildings, dams, highways, or the making of cement. Rocks are classified by the way they are formed.

On Earth there are three types of rock:

- **Igneous** rocks are crystalline solids that form directly from the cooling of magma or lava. The composition of the magma determines the composition of the rock. Granite is one of the most common types of igneous rocks and is created from magma (inside the Earth). Once magma reaches the Earth's surface, it is called lava. Lava that has cooled forms a rock with a glassy look, called obsidian.

- **Sedimentary** rocks are called secondary rocks because they are often the result of the accumulation of small pieces broken off from preexisting rocks and then pressed into a new form. There are three types of sedimentary rocks:

  ▸ Clastic sedimentary rocks are made when pieces of rock, mineral, and organic material fuse together. These are classified as conglomerates, sandstone, and shale.

  ▸ Chemical sedimentary rocks are formed when water rich in minerals evaporates, leaving the minerals behind. Some common examples are gypsum, rock salt, and some limestone.

  ▸ Organic sedimentary rocks are made from the remains of plants and animals. For example, coal is formed when dead plants are squeezed together. Another example is a form of limestone rock composed of the remains of organisms that lived in the ocean.

- **Metamorphic** rocks are also secondary rocks formed from igneous, sedimentary, or other types of metamorphic rock. When hot magma or lava comes in contact with rocks, or when buried rocks are exposed to pressure and high temperatures, the result is metamorphic rocks. For example, exposing limestone to high temperatures creates marble. The most common metamorphic rocks are slate, gneiss, and marble.

Rock Cycle

The formation of rock follows a cyclical process. For instance, rocks can be formed when magma or lava cools down, creating igneous rocks. Igneous rocks exposed to weathering can break into sediment, which can be compacted and cemented to form sedimentary rocks. Sedimentary rocks are exposed to heat and pressure to create metamorphic rocks. Finally, metamorphic rocks can melt and become magma and lava again (Badder et al., 2000). For more information on the rock cycle, including an explanatory diagram of the process, please refer to the following website: *www. mineralogy4kids.org/rock-cycle*.

Minerals

Minerals are the most common form of solid material found in the Earth's crust. Even soil contains bits of minerals that have broken away from rock. To be considered a mineral, a substance must be found in nature and must never have been a part of any living organism. Minerals can be as soft as talc or as hard as emeralds and diamonds. Dug from the Earth, minerals are used to make various products:

- Jewelry—Gemstones, such as amethysts, opals, diamonds, emeralds, topazes, and garnets, are examples of minerals commonly used to create jewelry. Gold and silver are another type of mineral that can be used to create jewelry.

- Construction—Gypsum boards (drywall) are made of a mineral of the same name—gypsum. The windows in homes are made from the mineral, quartz.

- Personal Use—Talc is the softest mineral and it is commonly applied to the body in powder form.

Water Cycle

The hydrologic cycle describes a series of movements of water above, on, and below the surface of the Earth. This cycle consists of four distinct stages: storage, evaporation, precipitation, and run-off. It is the means by which the sun's energy is used to transport, through the atmosphere, stored water from the rivers and oceans to land masses. The heat of the sun evaporates the water and takes it to the atmosphere from which, through condensation, it falls as precipitation. As precipitation falls, water is filtrated back to underground water deposits called aquifers, or it runs off into storage in lakes, ponds, and oceans.

Tides

The word *tides* is used to describe the alternating rise and fall in sea level with respect to the land, produced by the gravitational attraction of the moon and the sun. Additional factors such as the configuration of the coastline, depth of the water, the topography of the ocean floor, and other hydrographic and meteorological influences may play an important role in altering the range, interval, and times of the arrival of the tides.

Biogeochemical Cycles

Biogeochemical cycles include the carbon, nitrogen, and oxygen cycles. The carbon cycle is the capture of carbon from carbon dioxide in the atmosphere by plants to make glucose. When this glucose is used as food for the plant or other organisms, it is digested, then by respiration, broken apart again into carbon dioxide and returned back to the atmosphere. The process continues in a life sustaining process.

When thinking about the nitrogen cycle, it is important to recognize that most of the air we breathe is nitrogen, but it is not useful to us in that form, so it is exhaled. Lightning causes nitrogen in the air to combine with oxygen. Certain bacteria that live on the roots of certain plants, called nitrogen-fixing bacteria, are able to take nitrogen in this combined form with oxygen and make it available for use by plants. The plants incorporate the nitrogen into their plant structure, and when eaten by animals and other organisms, this nitrogen becomes available for use. The nitrogen returns to the soil when the plant or other living organism dies and decays, releasing nitrogen gas back into the atmosphere. Nitrogen is important to all living things because it is a major component of DNA, RNA, and amino acids, which are the building blocks of proteins.

In the oxygen cycle, plants and animals use oxygen to complete the process of respiration where it is returned to the air in water and carbon dioxide. Carbon dioxide is then taken up by green plants and algae, allowing for photosynthesis, in which oxygen is a by-product. It is important for students to understand how the biogeochemical cycles interact with each other, as well as with the biosphere, geosphere, hydrosphere, and atmosphere.

COMPETENCY 018

The teacher understands the role of energy in weather and climate.

The beginning teacher:

A. Understands the elements of weather (e.g., humidity, wind speed, pressure, temperature) and how they are measured.

B. Compares and contrasts weather and climate.

C. Analyzes weather charts and data to make weather predictions (e.g. fronts, pressure systems).

D. Applies knowledge of how transfers of energy among Earth systems affect weather and climate.

E. Analyzes how Earth's position, orientation, and surface features affect weather and climate (e.g., latitude, altitude, proximity to bodies of water).

Weather

The elements of weather include interactions between and among wind, water (precipitation), wind speed and direction, air pressure, humidity, and temperature. Wind is caused by air masses that have different amounts of heat (temperatures); for example, when a warm air mass moves toward a cold air mass. Air pressure is related to both the amount of water in the air mass and its temperature (heat content). Warm air has higher pressure than cold air; thus, warm, high pressure air masses move toward cold, low pressure air masses. One simple rule to bear in mind is that energy always moves from *warmer to colder*. So, if you open a window on a hot summer day when your air conditioning is on, the cold does not go out—the warm air comes in. The same is true with larger-scale warm and cold air masses.

Humidity is a measure of the percentage of water that is in the air. Dew point is the temperature of the air at which water condenses out of it in liquid form as precipitation and may be observed as "dew." In other words, air has a certain amount of water vapor (water in the gas state) in it (the percent is measured as humidity). That water vapor turns to liquid water (which we observe as dew) as temperatures drop overnight or when a cold front moves in that lowers the temperature, which can result in a rainstorm or snowstorm.

Wind is measured by an instrument called an **anemometer**. Air pressure is measured by a **barometer**; **rain gauges** and other instruments measure precipitation. Temperature is measured by a **thermometer**. Relative humidity is measured by a **psychrometer**.

Climate

Weather describes the conditions of the atmosphere at a given, relatively short period of time. **Climate**, by contrast, is the long-term weather conditions in an area on a continuous, seasonal basis. The climate is more complex and can be measured by the average variety of weather conditions, such as temperature and precipitation, that occur seasonally in that geographic region of the world over a period of time.

Predicting Weather

Weather can be predicted by tracking weather patterns using maps and charts. These maps have special symbols that indicate, for example, warm and cold air masses, air pressure, and relative humidity in a region. Cold air is denser and hence moves down, and warm air rises. Warmer air always moves toward colder air, and high pressure always moves outward toward lower pressure. Knowing how air behaves, we can track the weather and make predictions. Clouds are also an indication of the type of weather occurring in an area.

Interpreting weather maps is an important skill for weather prediction. It is important that teachers know the various symbols, including warm fronts, cold fronts, stationary fronts, wind speed and direction symbols, high and low pressure systems, and others.

The Earth's Surface and Position as a Factor in Weather and Climate

The Earth's surface is primarily water, and bodies of water affect the weather and climate of an area. Water has a high specific heat, which means that it takes longer to take in heat and longer to release the heat it has absorbed than any other material on Earth. Therefore, coastal areas tend to be warmer than areas inland or away from water, because the water moderates the temperature, even if the locations are at the same latitude. In the United States, for example, areas in the middle of the country will have greater extreme differences in the cold temperatures in the winter and warm temperatures in the summer compared to a location at the same latitude near the ocean.

Large lakes, such as the Great Lakes, also create a situation called "lake effect" in the winter—the air over the lake is relatively warm, and so can carry water vapor (evaporation). As soon as the air carrying water moves over land, however, it rapidly cools and releases its water (precipitation) in the form of snow over the land. Mountains and other landforms also have an effect on the weather. When air holding water hits a mountainside, it is forced upward, which makes the air cool and therefore rain (or snow) on that side of the mountain. In the United States, this is typically the western side of the mountain, as we see in the mountain ranges of the Rocky Mountains. Once the precipitation is gone from that air mass, and the air mass crosses the mountain to the other side, it drops back down and warms; but at that point it is dry air and so may result in an arid region or desert. The Gobi Desert of the United States is a result of this phenomenon.

On a much larger scale, the tilt of the Earth itself—as a planet—influences weather and climate. The Earth is on a 23.4-degree tilt on its axis in space. This tilt means the Earth's North Pole is pointed *away* from the sun when it is in one location in its orbit (path around the sun), and *toward* the sun when it is in the opposite orbital location. This tilt of the Earth results in the seasons, with extreme changes being in locations closer to the North and South poles, and in locations with a higher latitude. For example, when the North Pole is pointing toward the sun in its orbit, it is summer in the Northern Hemisphere; when the North Pole is pointing away from the sun in its orbit, it is winter in the Northern Hemisphere. In addition to latitude, altitude has an effect on weather. At higher altitudes, air pressure is lower and thus temperatures are cooler.

COMPETENCY 019

The teacher understands the characteristics of the solar system and the universe.

The beginning teacher:

A. Applies knowledge of the Earth-Moon-Sun system and resulting phenomena (e.g., seasons, tides, lunar phases, eclipses).

B. Identifies properties of the components of the solar system.

C. Recognizes characteristics of stars, nebulas, comets, asteroids, and galaxies, and knows their distribution in the universe.

D. Demonstrates an understanding of evidence for the scientific theories of the origin of the universe.

The sun is the center of our solar system, which is composed of eight planets, many satellites that orbit the planets, several dwarf planets, and a large number of smaller bodies like comets and asteroids. Short definitions of these terms follow.

- **Planets** are large bodies orbiting the sun.

- **Dwarf planets** are small bodies orbiting the sun.

- **Satellites** are moons orbiting the planets. Our planet has one moon whereas other planets may have no moons (Mercury, Venus), or many moons (Jupiter, Saturn).

- **Asteroids** are small dense objects or rocks orbiting our star, the sun. The Asteroid Belt of our own solar system is located between Mars and Jupiter. Some theorize that the asteroids could be the remains of an exploded planet.

- **Meteoroids** are fragments of rock in space, most originating from the debris left behind by comets that burn up/vaporize upon entering Earth's atmosphere due to friction from the air molecules.

- **Comets** are small icy objects traveling through space in an elongated, elliptical orbit around the sun.

The objects in our solar system revolve around our star, which we call the sun. The **inner solar system** contains the planets Mercury, Venus, Earth, and Mars, in this order. The **outer solar system** comprises the planets Jupiter, Saturn, Uranus, and Neptune, and a number of dwarf planets, including Pluto, Ceres, Eris and others, with likely more yet to be found (see Table 6.2).

Table 6.2
Planets and Dwarf Planets of our Solar System

Inner Planets	Mercury, Venus, Earth, Mars
Outer Planets	Jupiter, Saturn, Uranus, Neptune
Dwarf Planets	Pluto, Ceres, Eris, Haumea, Makemake

Galaxies are large collections of stars, hydrogen, dust particles, and other gases. The universe is made up of countless galaxies. The solar system that includes Earth is part of a galaxy called the Milky Way.

Stars like the sun are composed of large masses of hydrogen pulled together by gravity. The hydrogen, with strong gravitational pressure, creates fusion inside the star, turning the hydrogen into helium. The liberation of energy created by this process causes solar radiation, which makes the sun glow with visible light, as well as forms of radiation not visible to the human eye. Nebulas are clouds of gas (mostly hydrogen) and dust in interstellar space. Stars and planetary systems are formed from this gas and dust.

Earth performs two kinds of movement: rotation and revolution. Rotation describes the spinning of Earth on its axis. Earth takes approximately 24 hours to make a complete (360°) rotation, which creates day and night.

While Earth is rotating on its axis, it is also following an orbit around the sun. This movement is called revolution. It takes a year, or 365¼ days, for Earth to complete one revolution. As we said earlier, the tilt of Earth as it moves around the sun and its curvature create climate zones and seasons. The zones immediately north and south of the equator are called the tropics—Cancer (north) and Capricorn (south). The Arctic Circle (North Pole) and Antarctic Circle (South Pole) are the areas surrounding Earth's axis points. Latitude lines are imaginary horizontal lines around the Earth, and longitude lines are likewise vertical lines around the Earth from the North to the South Poles. These lines form a grid that helps us locate positions on Earth according to their specific latitude and longitude.

During each lunar orbit around Earth (about 28 days), the moon appears to go through several stages based on the portion of the moon visible from Earth. The moon does not have its own source of light but reflects the light from the sun. The shape of the moon varies from a full moon, when Earth is between the sun and the moon, to a new moon, when the moon is located between the sun and Earth. When the Earth is between the sun and the moon and blocks light traveling from the sun to the moon, casting a shadow on the moon, we experience a lunar eclipse. When the moon is between the sun and the Earth and the moon blocks light traveling from the sun to the Earth, casting a shadow on the Earth, this is called a solar eclipse. The gravitational attraction between the sun, Earth, and moon result in tides on Earth.

The most prominent scientific theory for the origin of the universe is called the **Big Bang**. This theory is based on the observations of scientists such as Georges Lemaître, who, in 1927, theorized that the universe started as a single point and then, over time, stretched and expanded, and indeed could continue stretching. Another key Big Bang theorist was Edwin Hubble. He provided evidence just two years later buttressing Lemaître's theory. Scientists theorize that a great explosion occurred 13.8 billion years ago as a result of the compression of all the matter and energy in the universe.

COMPETENCY 020

The teacher understands the history of the Earth system.

The beginning teacher:

A. Understands dating methods and the geologic timescale as it relates to geologic processes.

B. Demonstrates an understanding of theories about the Earth's origin and geologic history.

C. Demonstrates an understanding of how tectonic forces have shaped landforms over time.

D. Understands the formation of fossils and the importance of the fossil record in explaining the Earth's history.

Until the 18th century, it was commonly believed that the Earth was only a few thousand years old. However, **radiometric dating** (the comparison of the amount of parent material to daughter material in a substance) has now placed the Earth at approximately 4.5 billion years old. This amount of time is difficult to imagine, especially since the modern form of humans evolved only about 200,000 years ago. Geologic time is divided into **Precambrian** and **Cambrian** expanses of time, and further divided into **Eons**, **Eras**, **Periods**, and **Epochs**. The division of geologic time is based on geologic features of the Earth and events, and may also be characterized by the living organisms that dominated the Earth during that time.

The Earth originated from a cloud of dust that, as with all celestial objects, originated from the Big Bang and, over time, rotated and condensed into its current form. The condensation of dust and rock particles in space that formed the Earth was caused by molecular attractions between the particles, just as dustballs seem to clump together on the floor of a room in your house. More and more particles collided with Earth, also generating much heat. In its early history, the Earth consisted primarily of hot liquid, which cooled over time, as particle collisions subsided. It is believed that the first primitive living organisms, likely single-celled bacteria, originated on Earth 3 billion years ago.

As discussed in Competency 016, in the early 1900s, it was proposed that all the continents were previously one large continent but then broke apart and drifted across the ocean floor to their present locations. This concept is called **continental drift**, and it was the origin of today's concept of plate tectonics, that is, that the surface of the Earth is fragmented into large plates. The collision of plates is the cause of many geologic features on Earth, and the cause of catastrophic events such as volcanoes and earthquakes. The edges or boundaries of the plates are the sites of much seismic activity and the location of most of the "fault lines" on Earth. The boundaries of the Pacific Plate, in particular, are known as the "Ring of Fire" because the seismic activity forms a circle around the edges of the continents adjoining the Pacific Ocean. This is where most volcanic and earthquake activity occurs.

As the plates collide, they produce a variety of geologic results. One possible result that occurs when plates collide is that one plate is forced beneath the other, creating a subduction zone. The plate that rides over the top pushes upwards and forms mountains, whereas the plate that plunges underneath forms a deep sea trench. This type of boundary exists off the west coast of South America and is responsible for forming the Andes Mountains. In subduction zones, plates are destroyed. Another plate boundary is called a convergent zone, which is where island chains may arise.

As mentioned under Competency 016, the movement of the continents/Earth's plates is caused by a huge "generator" known as the Mid-Atlantic Ridge. This ridge is an extensive volcanic mountain range on the floor of the Atlantic Ocean running north and south, extending through the center of Iceland. The mountains in the ridge are continuously erupting and pushing the plates apart in opposite directions from each other, at a rate of about 1 cm per year. Evidence exists that the Mid-Atlantic Ridge is responsible for pushing the continents apart when they were (at several points in geologic history) joined together as one large supercontinent.

The theory of continental drift was supported by the existence of common preserved remains of organisms along the continents, known as fossils. For example, according to the theory, the continents have been joined together at various times throughout history. Fossils of the same time period have been found on the western coast of Africa that are identical to fossils of the same time period found on the east coast of South America, where the two continents would have been joined. The continents when joined together formed a supercontinent, often referred to as Pangaea.

COMPETENCY 021

The teacher has theoretical and practical knowledge about teaching science and about how students learn science.

The beginning teacher:

A. Understands how the developmental characteristics, prior knowledge and experience, and attitudes of students influence science learning.

B. Selects and adapts science curricula, content, instructional materials, vocabulary, and activities to meet the interests, knowledge, understanding, abilities, experiences, and needs of all students, including English learners.

C. Understands how to use situations from students' daily lives to develop instructional materials that investigate how science can be used to make informed decisions.

D. Understands effective ways to address common misconceptions in science.

E. Understands the use of active learning including the appropriate use of inquiry processes for students and other instructional models (e.g., collaborative learning groups).

F. Understands questioning strategies designed to elicit higher-level thinking and how to use them to move students from concrete to more abstract understanding.

G. Understands the importance of planning activities that are inclusive and accommodate the needs of all students.

H. Understands how to sequence learning activities in a way that allows students to build upon their prior knowledge and challenges them to expand their understanding of science.

Developmentally Appropriate Practices

Children's processing of scientific inquiry can begin as early as age 3 or 4. However, teachers must be aware of the stages of cognitive, social, and emotional development of children to appropriately introduce children to science concepts. For example, observing and experimenting with water and colors can easily be done by 3- or 4-year-olds, but using microscopes to observe and analyze animal or vegetable cells might be more appropriate for children in third and fourth grades. Students in Grades 4–8 need direct experiences in order to understand concepts. According to Piaget (1964), children transition through stages of development that require direct involvement to make sense of their experience. The model of teaching known as the learning cycle and 5-E model are based upon promoting the intellectual development of children. Thus, these models of teaching were designed to be consistent with the nature of science—and importantly, to match how children naturally learn (Marek and Cavallo, 1997; Renner and Marek, 1990). It is essential that teachers understand the theory and research that underlie such models, as well as how to use these models in teaching.

Misconceptions or alternative conceptions are a pervasive problem in science teaching and learning. Children tend to view the world from their own perspectives and draw conclusions based on their limited experiences. Once misconceptions are established in learners' minds, they are difficult to dislodge. As such, misconceptions must be identified and addressed directly. Don't assume that students will correct misconceptions on their own. As their teacher, you should allow children the opportunity for **direct experience** and collecting evidence on their own. Your job is to allow them to experiment under your wing. The learning cycle/5-E model is a research-based and supported teaching model that promotes conceptual change, helps students resolve misconceptions, and leads to more scientifically accurate understandings (Sandoval, 1995). The learning cycle consists of three major phases: Exploration, Concept Invention, and Application (Lawson, Abraham, & Renner, 1989; Marek & Cavallo, 1997). It has been expanded into a five-phase sequence: Engage, Explore, Explain, Elaborate, and Evaluate (Bybee et al., 1989; Bybee, 2014).

In the learning cycle/5-E model, teachers begin lessons with direct, concrete activities, giving students experience with objects, observation, and the opportunity to collect data (exploration, or engage/explore phase). Students use these experiences and evidence-based data to construct the main concept of their explorations (concept invention or explain phase). The students' experimentation and construction of the main idea or concept from their experiences becomes the "anchor" for connecting other ideas and information in their minds, making new learning more meaningful. Students' direct experiences and construction of concepts based on their own findings guide them to developmentally progress from concrete to more abstract reasoners. For example, in learning the concept of density, it is important that students have objects to touch, feel, weigh (take the mass of), and measure in the exploration phase of the learning cycle/5-E model. From direct experience with the objects, students should construct the concept that "a certain amount of matter (mass) is packed into a given amount of space (volume)." The term that labels this concept is "density." It is important that the *label* or new scientific *vocabulary* is attached to the concept only after the students have had direct, hands-on experience and have constructed *meanings* from their experiences; that is, after they have stated the scientific concept in their own words. The teacher guides students toward articulating and understanding the concept, but does not tell them. Instead, the teacher uses the students' findings and words, later substituting more scientific terms and definitions as necessary. This process helps students attach new labels to concepts only after they fully understand the meanings, a strategy that also helps English language learners, as well as fluent English-speaking students, learn new vocabulary. Next, the teacher takes this newly constructed concept and the vocabulary that labels the concept and helps students connect it to real-world experiences and to new scientific concepts (application or elaborate phase). Continuing with the density example, in this phase teachers would help students develop their abstract thinking abilities by having them solve problems using the formula for density, $D = M/V$.

Teachers need to select and design learning experiences such that concrete experiences are used first, leading the students to later use abstract reasoning. In doing so, teachers must focus on promoting students' scientific knowledge, skills, and use of inquiry. Further, students must consistently use prior knowledge and understandings they have constructed (in this example, regarding density), to learn more extended, related concepts (e.g., buoyancy). Teaching this way also promotes more meaningful learning versus rote memorization. In addition, it allows teachers to listen to students' thinking and observe their construction of understandings to better address possible misconceptions or misunderstandings. This example demonstrates the instructional knowledge and skills teachers need to have to prepare the best possible science learning experiences for students. The learning cycle/5-E model is consistent with the goals of this competency. (See Marek & Cavallo, 1997.)

Using collaborative groups in teaching also develops students' language, communication, vocabulary, and ability to articulate ideas to others in both written and oral forms. The learning cycle/5E model described here and further discussed in Competency 022 places students in groups throughout their experimentation so they may interact in sharing findings, ideas, and concepts. With teacher guidance, the students also learn skills of argumentation based on evidence. Project Based Learning is an extended, long-term inquiry model in which the instruction is based on a larger theme or problem. Students work in collaborative groups over a period of time to experientially learn concepts within the theme (e.g., through learning cycles/5E modules) and respond and/or present solutions to the problem. The National Education Association (NEA) supports Project Based Learning (PBL) and provides additional resources here: *http://www.nea. org/tools/16963.htm*. For additional information on PBL, also refer to *https://www.bie.org/about/ what_pbl*.

Formulating good questions is critical to promoting logical thinking and scientific reasoning among students. Good questioning causes students to reflect upon the logic of their data and observations with confidence and also helps pinpoint misinformation or misunderstanding of important concepts. Students learn to effectively use scientific argumentation and respond to challenges to their findings in order to support their conclusions. Teachers use questioning to reveal student learning and assess their progress in forming sound scientific frameworks of understanding. Questioning is the hallmark of scientific inquiry and should be used throughout inquiry-based instruction. In the learning cycle/5-E model, questioning must be designed to lead students toward being able to state the concept, so it is especially critical in the concept invention, or "explain" phase.

Teachers can guide students at various levels of development to observe events. Through questioning, teachers can help students develop high-order thinking skills. For example, a teacher can lead children to make predictions while conducting experiments with objects that float or sink in water. By asking students to predict and explain why an object might sink or float, the teacher is leading students to analyze the properties of the object and the water to make an evaluative decision; that is, the children are using analysis and evaluation to complete that simple task. The following guide uses **Bloom's Taxonomy of Educational Objectives** to help teachers best promote and elevate logical thinking abilities among students.

Use key questioning terms aimed at the full range of the cognitive domain. (Bloom & Krathwohl, 1956; Anderson, Krathwohl et al., 2001; Krathwohl, 2002.) A look at Bloom's Taxonomy follows.

Bloom's Taxonomy: Critical Thinking Skills

LEVEL 1: Remember

Recall factual information.

Examples

List the five Kingdoms.

Label the parts of the cell in the diagram provided.

Write the formula for density.

LEVEL 2: Understand

Communicate an idea in a different form.

Examples

Explain heat transfer through conduction.

Restate what an ecosystem is in your own words.

Submit a definition of photosynthesis in your own words.

LEVEL 3: Apply

Use what is known to find new solutions or apply in new situations.

Examples

Relate the concept of convection to plate tectonics.

Utilize your understanding of density to explain why pennies sink in water but battleships float.

Making use of the clothes you are wearing, how can you stay afloat for several hours?

LEVEL 4: Analyze

Break things and ideas down into component parts and find their unique characteristics.

Examples

Examine blueprints of the electrical circuitry of your school building and explain how it works to bring electricity to your laboratory station.

Study the diagram of human digestion and *reason* what the organ marked #7 might be and explain its function.

Using the given laboratory materials, *deduce* the identities of the substances labeled "A," "B," and "C."

LEVEL 5: Evaluate

Use what is known to make judgments and ratings; accept or reject ideas; determine the worthiness of an idea or thing.

Examples

Decide whether or not you agree with the production of more nuclear power plants and provide justification for your decision.

Make a ruling you would give to car manufacturers on global warming and provide support for your ruling.

Rank the top five greatest discoveries in scientific history and *explain* why you have chosen those discoveries and ranked them in that particular order.

LEVEL 6: Create

A. Use what is known to think creatively and divergently; make something new or original; pattern ideas or things in a new way.

Examples

Create a burglar alarm system for the classroom.

Build an interactive display for a hands-on science museum that demonstrates at least one important concept you have learned in science class this year.

Develop a plan for cleaning the pollutants in the Trinity River.

B. Avoid yes/no questions (unless part of a game) and questions with obvious answers.

Examples

Activity	Ineffective prompt - Yes/No	Better prompt - Critical Thinking
Students are shown a picture of a living cell.	Is this a cell?	What is this structure, and how do you know?
Students watch a chemical reaction in which the solution turns blue.	Did it turn blue?	What happened? What did you observe? Why did this happen?

C. Use questions beginning with the words *why, how, what, where,* and *when* that probe students' thinking.

Examples

How do you know?

Why do you think that? Where did you see a change?

What is your explanation for this observation? When did you notice the change occur?

What do you think?

COMPETENCY 022

The teacher understands the process of scientific inquiry and its role in science instruction.

The beginning teacher:

A. Plans and implements instruction that provides opportunities for all students to engage in investigations.

B. Focuses inquiry-based instruction on questions and issues relevant to students and uses strategies to assist students with generating, refining, and focusing scientific questions and hypotheses.

C. Instructs students in the safe and proper use of a variety of grade-appropriate tools, equipment, resources, technology and techniques to access, gather, store, retrieve, organize, and analyze data.

D. Knows how to guide students in making systematic observations and measurements, including repeating investigations to increase reliability.

E. Knows how to promote the use of critical-thinking skills, logical reasoning, and scientific problem solving to reach conclusions based on evidence.

F. Knows how to teach students to develop, analyze, and evaluate different explanations for a given scientific result.

G. Knows how to teach students to demonstrate an understanding of potential sources of error in inquiry-based investigation.

H. Knows how to teach students to demonstrate an understanding of how to communicate and defend the results of an inquiry-based investigation.

Planning and Implementing Scientific Inquiry

Scientific inquiry is promoted through students engaging in hands-on activities and experimentation. From their experiences conducting scientific experiments, students acquire information firsthand and develop problem-solving skills. Children in Grades 4–8 are inquisitive and want to understand the environment around them. Teachers can use this interest to provide students with opportunities to use digital and printed sources to find answers to their questions and to expand their knowledge about the topic. It is important for children to develop inquiry skills. This can only be accomplished by allowing them to experience science for themselves in hands-on investigations. By doing so, students develop important science inquiry and thinking skills (Table 6.3).

Table 6.3
Science Thinking Skills (Full Option Science System, 2000)

Observing: Using the senses to get information
Communicating: Talking, drawing, and acting
Comparing: Pairing and one-to-one correspondence
Organizing: Grouping, seriating, and sequencing
Relating: Cause-and-effect and classification
Inferring: Super-ordinate/subordinate classification, if/then reasoning, and developing scientific laws
Applying: Developing strategic plans and inventing

As introduced in Competency 021, the model of inquiry that best supports science learning is a model known as the *learning cycle*, consisting of three phases: *exploration*, *concept invention*, and *application* (Lawson, Abraham, & Renner, 1989; Marek & Cavallo, 1997). Over time, the learning cycle was extended with the addition of two new phases becoming what is known as the 5-E model

(Engage, Explore, Explain, Elaborate, Evaluate) (Bybee, 1989). What follows is some history on the development of inquiry-based teaching via the learning cycle and 5-E model.

The original three-phase learning cycle model developed by Robert Karplus in the 1960s was based upon the following theoretical foundation (Karplus & Thier, 1967):

1. Science must be taught in a way that is *consistent with the nature of science*. Science is discovery and investigation, and that means science must be taught as an active process—as something we *do*. The children need to have the opportunity to experience the true nature of science by doing science exploration for themselves through direct experiences and hands-on investigations.

2. Science teaching must be focused on promoting the main purpose of education, namely, to foster the development in our students the *ability to think*—to be critical and independent thinkers. Science must be taught in a way that promotes the students use of independent, critical, and higher-level thinking abilities (e.g., logic). Promoting this purpose of education is best accomplished by *not* giving or telling students the "answers" or information (e.g., as in giving a lecture), but instead by first giving students hands-on, direct experiences in which they use logic and reasoning to find "answers" or explanations for themselves; further discussion and teacher guidance can follow the students' direct experiences.

3. Science must be taught in a way that *matches how students learn,* described as the mental functioning model by Piaget (1964). How individuals learn is through mentally experiencing the following three-phase mental process.

   - First, we **assimilate,** or "take in," information with our senses from our environment and what we are experiencing in our environment. During assimilation, we may have a sense of "disequilibrium," which is confusion or "cognitive conflict" as we try to make sense of our experiences. When in disequilibrium, we need to go back and assimilate more information—make more observations and gather more data.

   - Second, once we have assimilated enough information and made sense of the information we have gathered, our minds experience **accommodation**. This is the "Aha!" moment, the point when we ultimately feel "cognitive relief"—we figured it out, or what we have observed/experienced now makes sense!

   - Third, our minds take that newly accommodated information and we **organize** it into our mental structures. That is, we connect the new idea or what we have just figured out/made sense of to what we already know, what we experience in everyday life, and/or to new related concepts.

The three phases of learning described by Piaget, assimilation-accommodation-organization, *match* the original learning cycle's three phases: Exploration-Concept Invention-Application. The logic in developing the learning cycle in these three phases was that, given what we know about how children (people) *learn*, we should be *teaching* in a sequence or way that matches this learning pattern. To do so, teachers should:

1. First, provide students with an *Exploration* phase in which they can assimilate information using their senses. Students may or may not experience disequilibrium, but teachers should guide them (not tell them!) through the sense-making process.

2. Teachers should then carry out a discussion in the *Concept Invention* phase in which students share their observations and findings. With careful questioning, teachers should guide students to review their data/observations toward helping them reach the "Aha!" moment, or accommodation. The summarizing statement the students are to write, post on the board, and/or state aloud to others in this phase represents their accommodation, or understanding, of the concept.

3. The teacher then helps students organize the new concept by guiding them through *Application* of the concept in new contexts, in which students can connect the concept with what they observe in everyday life, or what they already know.

Teaching via the learning cycle, we stay consistent with the nature of science—as an active, hands-on process characterized by investigation and discovery—and we are teaching in a way that supports the purpose of education, that is, we are promoting children's development of higher-level thinking abilities. The learning cycle and its origins and theory base is more fully described in a book by Marek & Cavallo (1997) titled *The Learning Cycle: Elementary School Science and Beyond*.

Over time, science educators added an additional phase to the learning cycle, namely, the *Engage* phase, with the idea that teachers need to do something that will gain the students' attention before beginning the *Exploration* phase. "Engage" can be a demonstration (without explanation) or the simple posing of a question, challenge, or problem. Thus, over time, the original learning cycle model's first phase, *Exploration*, became two phases: *Engage* and *Explore*.

Changing the names of two of the phases also helped refine the learning cycle. The *Concept Invention* phase's name was changed to *Explain*. To sustain the "E" alliteration, the *Application* phase name was changed to *Elaborate*. *Assessment*, or the measurement of learning, in the original three-phase model was to take place throughout the learning cycle. However, science educators at the time preferred to have assessment articulated as an additional phase; thus (again to carry on the "E" alliteration) *Assessment* was termed *Evaluate*. Consequently, the three-phase learning cycle model was expanded into a 5-E Model: *Engage, Explore, Explain, Elaborate, Evaluate*.

The two models (the original three-phase learning cycle model developed by Robert Karplus and the 5-E model that it grew into) are basically the same, and grew out of the same underlying philosophy and theoretical foundation. However, the three phases more closely follow the model of learning—assimilation, accommodation, and organization—as first described by Piaget; whereas the 5-E model incorporates two additional essentials of classroom teaching: (1) gaining students' focus and attention, and (2) measuring student learning.

Most importantly, in both models—the Karplus learning cycle and 5-E model—students are *not told* the science concept or information before beginning the inquiry, but must discover the concept themselves through hands-on investigation, observation, and collection of data. In using the *Engage* phase (from 5-E) the students' learning experience begins with the teacher posing one or more questions, giving an interesting demonstration, or providing a laboratory guide. In all of these approaches, this phase captures students' curiosity and motivates them to learn. Whether or not an *Engage* phase is used, students next (or first) experience an *Exploration* phase—and it must be a student-centered hands-on activity, investigation, or experiment. In the *Exploration* phase, students make observations and gather data on a science idea or topic area. In this phase, students can determine the experimental design, or it can be pre-determined by the teacher. The main aspect, however, is that students are doing the lab activity themselves, and have not been told the expected outcome beforehand. For example, students may grow plants in the light and in the dark, and make observations, draw and/or take photos, and measure the plants grown under the two differing conditions over a period of time. All other variables are controlled (soil, water, air); only the light received by the plants is different, which is the variable.

After the observations have been made and data has been gathered by students, the teacher begins the next instructional phase called *Concept Invention*, or in the 5-E model, the *Explain* phase. In this phase the students present and share data with their classmates in a teacher-guided discussion of findings. The teacher uses questions to guide students' thinking and encourages the use of logic and reasoning as they interpret their data. For example, students may post the photos or drawings of plants grown in the dark and in the light, make line graphs of plant height over time, or share qualitative information about how the plant appeared after grown under the two conditions (e.g., plants in the light were green, whereas plants in the dark were yellow and pale). At the end of this phase, the students construct an overall statement that summarizes their data and observations, which is the central science *concept*. The science vocabulary is then linked to the concept students "invented."

Next, the teacher helps students through the *Application* (from the learning cycle) or *Elaborate* (from the 5-E model phases) in which students use the new concept they learned as it is applied in new contexts. For example, students can create new questions to investigate, or hypotheses to test based on what they just learned (the concept) and develop a way to answer their questions or test their hypotheses (e.g., What color of light is best for plants to grow?). They can also use the internet to learn more about the concept they just invented. In this phase the teacher can engage students in additional hands-on laboratories, readings, discussions, field trips, and/or writing activities that extend and expand upon the concept. These models of inquiry science teaching and learning are endorsed by NSTA (NSTA, 1998, 2003, 2012).

The diagram in Figure 6-2 shows the inquiry-based learning cycle model as it corresponds to the 5-E model of science teaching. The template shown in Table 6.4 explains each phase of the learning cycle as it relates to the 5-E Model for structuring inquiry-based science teaching for all students.

Figure 6.2
The Learning Cycle and 5-E Model

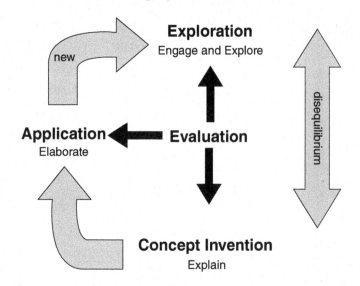

Table 6-4
Description of the Phases of the Learning Cycle and 5-E Model

5-E Definition	Teacher Behavior	Student Behavior
Engage		
• Generate interest • Access prior knowledge • Connect to past knowledge • Set parameters of the focus • Frame the idea	• Motivates • Creates interest • Taps into what students know or think about the topic • Raises questions and encourages responses	• Attentive in listening • Asks questions • Demonstrates interest in the lesson • Responds to questions demonstrating their own entry point of understanding

(continued)

Explore		
• Experience key concepts • Discover new skills • Probe, inquire, and question experiences • Examine their thinking • Establish relationships and understanding	• Acts as a facilitator • Observes and listens to students as they interact • Asks good inquiry-oriented questions • Provides time for students to think and to reflect • Encourages cooperative learning	• Conducts activities, predicts, and forms hypotheses or makes generalizations • Becomes a good listener • Shares ideas and suspends judgment • Records observations and/or generalizations • Discusses tentative alternatives

Explain		
• Connect prior knowledge and background to new discoveries • Communicate new understandings • Connect informal language to formal language	• Encourages students to explain their observations and findings in their own words • Provides definitions, new words, and explanations • Listens and builds upon discussion from students • Asks for clarification and justification • Accepts all reasonable responses	• Explains, listens, defines, and questions • Uses previous observations and findings • Provides reasonable responses to questions • Interacts in a positive, supportive manner

(continued)

Extend/Elaborate		
• Apply new learning to a new or similar situation • Extend and explain concept being explored • Communicate new understanding with formal language	• Uses previously learned information as a vehicle to enhance additional learning • Encourages students to apply or extend the new concepts and skills • Encourages students to use terms and definitions previously acquired	• Applies new terms and definitions • Uses previous information to probe, ask questions, and make reasonable judgments • Provides reasonable conclusions and solutions • Records observations, explanations, and solutions
Evaluate		
• Assess understanding (Self, peer and teacher evaluation) • Demonstrate understanding of new concept by observation or open-ended response • Apply within problem situation • Show evidence of accomplishment	• Observes student behaviors as they explore and apply new concepts and skills • Assesses students' knowledge and skills • Encourages students to assess their own learning • Asks open-ended questions	• Demonstrates an understanding or knowledge of concepts and skills • Evaluates his/her own progress • Answers open-ended questions • Provides reasonable responses and explanations to events or phenomena

Based on the 5-E Instructional Model presented by Dr. Jim Barufaldi at the Eisenhower Science Collaborative Conference in Austin, Texas, July 2002.

Interpreting Findings in Science Inquiry

In planning and conducting experiments, teachers should guide children to develop an appropriate procedure for testing hypotheses, including the use of instruments that can yield measurable data. Even at the early stages of scientific experimentation, the procedure must be clear and tangible enough to allow replication by other students or scientists. Help students understand the concept of controlling variables and testing only one variable at a time. Students need to learn to be precise in the collection of data and measurements. Ensure the use of the metric system in obtaining all measurement data.

Allowing students to gather their own data and observations for interpretation promotes their critical and logical thinking abilities. It also gives them experience with using appropriate tools, resources, and technology of science that will lead to accurate organization and analysis of data. The students will be able to experience and practice science skills by verifying their findings, basing findings on evidence, and analyzing sources of error. Having students collect and report their own data also brings the teacher opportunities to discuss scientific ethics with students. It is important to note that having students repeat investigations will increase the reliability of their results. In the scientific community, scientists repeat experiments possibly hundreds of times, and only report findings if/when they have consistent findings. Other research scientists also replicate experiments to determine whether the same findings are produced independently of the original research. Thus, it is important to allow students opportunity to repeat experiments and share findings with other groups who have conducted the same experiments to more closely model the work of science and scientists.

In explaining data collection procedures and display of findings to English learners, the teacher needs to demonstrate and provide a model of what the end results should look like. In using inquiry, students work in groups, which is particularly helpful for second language learners as they interpret and exchange ideas about data and scientific reasoning.

When students complete their experiments, teachers need to engage them in the process of analyzing their own, and other groups' data for similarities, differences, and variations including error. This occurs in the concept invention or "explain" phase of the learning cycle and 5-E model, and again in any application or "elaborate" activities in which data has been collected. After data has been collected from students' explorations, they display their data in charts and graphs, for example, and communicate their observations and, ultimately, concept statements to the class by posting them on the board and/or through an oral presentation. The data helps them develop conclusions and form new research questions or hypotheses as they evaluate their findings, setting the foundation for new explorations. Students should be able to present pertinent data using graphic representations, and communicate their findings in written and oral forms to others.

In using scientific inquiry as in the learning cycle and 5-E model, scientific vocabulary is introduced *after* students have had hands-on experiences in the (engage and) exploration phase *and* have used their observations and data to construct meaning from their experiences in the *concept invention* or "explain" phase. Once students have had the hands-on direct experience with the concept, and have stated the meaning of their observations, the scientific vocabulary or terms that label the concept can be introduced by the teacher. In the application or elaborate phase, the teacher and students use the new vocabulary in extended experimentation, discussion, readings, writing, and other learning activities. Introducing terms after students have directly experienced the science inquiry and constructed meaning from their experiences by making a concept statement is especially important for second language learners in facilitating the development of understanding of science concepts. For all students, but especially for second language learners, this helps them understand concepts when terms are later *re-introduced*. By giving students the experience—something they *do*—and then allowing them to form meaning from their experience in ways that make sense to them, then when the term that labels what they learned is introduced, they are able to link it to prior knowledge and learning experiences in their minds. The terms are now able to build their background knowledge, which is critical for second language learners to understand the language of science. Making a connection between the hands-on activities and scientific vocabulary is beneficial to all students but especially to English learners who can link the actions with the appropriate concept and vocabulary words without engaging in translations.

Promoting Logical Thinking and Scientific Reasoning

Interpreting results is one of the most challenging phases of scientific inquiry for the middle grades. Students can easily discuss the observable results but might have difficulty discerning their meaning. Teachers have to use developmentally appropriate practices to guide students to make extrapolations and infer information from the data, which involves the teachers' use of questioning, as addressed previously, in Competency 021.

Scientific Tools and Equipment for Gathering and Storing Data

Various tools or instruments are used in scientific experimentation in the middle grades. The classroom should be equipped with measuring devices like graduated cylinders, beakers, scales, dishes, thermometers, meter sticks, and micrometers. They might also have anatomical models showing the body systems. Teachers need to learn to use these tools and equipment properly in order to help their students know how to use them and to collect accurate data in their inquiry investigations.

The TEKS requires students to gather information using specific equipment and tools. Examples of the tools required in Grades 4 through 8 are presented in Table 6.5.

Table 6.5
Sample Tools and Equipment for the Middle-Level Science Classroom

Tools and Equipment	4th	5th	6th	7th	8th
Nonstandard measurements					
Hand lenses	✓	✓	✓	✓	✓
Computers	✓	✓	✓	✓	✓
Balances	✓	✓	✓	✓	✓
Cups and bowls	✓	✓	✓	✓	✓
Thermometers	✓	✓	✓	✓	✓
Clocks	✓	✓	✓	✓	✓
Meter sticks	✓	✓	✓	✓	✓
Light Microscopes	✓	✓	✓	✓	✓
Dissecting Microscopes	✓	✓	✓	✓	✓
Safety goggles	✓	✓	✓	✓	✓
Magnets	✓	✓	✓	✓	✓
Compasses	✓	✓	✓	✓	✓
Timing devices	✓	✓	✓	✓	✓
Calculators	✓	✓	✓	✓	✓
Sound recorders	✓	✓	✓	✓	✓
Hot plates		✓	✓	✓	✓
Burners		✓	✓	✓	✓
Beakers		✓	✓	✓	✓
Graduated cylinders		✓	✓	✓	✓
Flasks (Erlenmeyer and Florence)		✓	✓	✓	✓
Test tubes and holders		✓	✓	✓	✓

COMPETENCY 023

The teacher knows the varied and appropriate assessments and assessment practices to monitor science learning in laboratory, field, and classroom settings.

The beginning teacher:

A. Understands the relationships among science curriculum, assessment, and instruction and bases instruction on information gathered through assessment of students' strengths and needs.

B. Understands the importance of monitoring and assessing students' understanding of science concepts and skills on an ongoing basis.

C. Understands the importance of carefully selecting or designing formative and summative assessments for the specific decisions they are intended to inform.

D. Selects or designs and administers a variety of appropriate assessment methods (e.g., performance assessment, self-assessment, formal/informal, formative/summative) to monitor student understanding and progress.

E. Uses formal and informal assessments of student performance and products (e.g., projects, lab journals, rubrics, portfolios, student profiles, checklists) to evaluate student participation in and understanding of the inquiry process.

F. Understands the importance of sharing evaluation criteria and assessment results with students.

Measuring Student Learning

Teaching cannot occur without student *learning*, and in order to determine that learning is occurring, student progress needs to be assessed on a regular basis. Assessment of learning should occur on some scale, large or small, *every class day*, to monitor students' progress in the learning of concepts, as in the learning cycle and 5-E models. Measuring learning as it is occurring is "authentic assessment" and allows teachers to adjust the instruction according to student learning and immediately and routinely address potential difficulties and/or misconceptions in learning. Alternative, **informal assessment methods**, in addition to the more traditional, **formal testing formats** (e.g., multiple-choice) should be used to obtain a full picture of what students know and do not know, or can and cannot do. Alternative assessments include techniques such as verbal reports, laboratory practical exams, storywriting, developing advertisements or brochures, constructing concept maps, writing essays, creating drawings or models, and developing plays or skits. In each assessment, the concepts to be learned are represented in alternative ways—yet clearly communicate what students have learned and understand.

It is essential that teachers monitor and assess students' understanding of concepts and skills on a regular, consistent basis and use this information to adjust instruction. The results of frequent informal and formal/traditional and alternative assessments should be used as a tool for planning subsequent instruction. Teachers must communicate progress to students so they can learn to self-monitor their own learning and understand what is needed to achieve learning goals.

Formative assessments are assessments that take place during the learning process that allow teachers to regularly monitor learning, and provide measures of student learning at various times and in various manners throughout the process. Summative assessments are tests given at the end of instruction to measure learning, typically by an exam or standardized test. Formative assessments provide teachers with more information and insight into the students' thinking and learning compared to summative assessments, which provide a culminating measure of achievement. It is important that teachers use both forms of assessment, and prepare students on taking a variety of assessments, so the most accurate measure of their learning and accomplishments can be obtained.

Assessing the Science Curriculum

As part of the accountability system, Texas has a very comprehensive assessment system to measure the state uniform curriculum. This system centers on the STAAR exam, short for the State of Texas Assessments of Academic Readiness.

In this system, students take the STAAR test in Grades 3 through 12. However, the science component of STAAR is assessed only in Grades 5, 8, and 10. For further information see: *http://tea.texas.gov/student.assessment/staar/science/*. The fifth-grade and eighth-grade science tests are available in Spanish; thus, Spanish-speaking English learners can take the test in Spanish. In addition to the required science STAAR examinations, students are assessed through teacher- and district-developed tests in kindergarten through Grade 12.

References

Anderson, L.W., Krathwohl, D.R., Airasian, P.W., Cruikshank, K.A., Richard E. Mayer, R.E., Pintrich, P.R., Wittrock, M.C. (2001). *A taxonomy for learning, teaching, and assessing: A revision of bloom's taxonomy of educational objectives.* Boston, MA: Allyn & Bacon (Pearson Education Group).

Houghton Mifflin. (2000). *Discovery works Texas.* Boston: Houghton Mifflin.

Bloom, B.S., & Krathwohl, D.R. (1956). *Taxonomy of educational objectives: The classification of educational goals, by a committee of college and university examiners. Handbook I: Cognitive domain.* New York, NY: Longmans, Green.

Bybee, R. (2014, April/May). The BSCS instructional model: Personal reflections and contemporary implications. Guest editorial. *Science and Children, 51*(8), 10–13.

Bybee, R., Buchwald, C.E., Crissman, S. Heil, D., Kuerbis, P., Matsumoto, C., & McInerney, J.D. (1989). *Science and technology education for elementary years: Frameworks for curriculum and instruction. Opinion paper.* Washington, DC: The National Center for Improving Science Education.

Cavallo, A.M.L. (2001). Convection connections: Integrated learning cycle investigations that explore convection—the science behind wind and waves. *Science and Children, 38,* 20–25.

Full Option Science System (FOSS). (2000). Lawrence Hall of Science, University of California, Berkeley, CA.

Karplus, R. & Thier, H.D. (1967). *A New Look at Elementary School Science.* Chicago: Rand McNally.

Krajcik, J., Blumfield, P., Marx, R., & Soloway, E. (1994). A collaborative model for helping middle grade science teachers learn project-based instruction. *Elementary School Journal, 94,* 483–97.

Lawson, A.E., Abraham, M.R., & Renner, J.W. (1989). *A theory of instruction: Using the learning cycle to teach science concepts and thinking skills.* NARST Monograph No. 1.

Marek, E.A., & Cavallo, A.M.L. (1997). *The learning cycle: Elementary school science and beyond* (rev. ed.). Portsmouth, NH: Heinemann.

National Science Teachers Association (2016). *Science education for middle level students.* Retrieved from *http://static.nsta.org/pdfs/PositionStatement_MiddleLevel.pdf*

National Science Teachers Association (2012). Standards for science teacher preparation. Retrieved from *http://www.nsta.org/preservice/docs/2012NSTAPreserviceScienceStandards.pdf*

National Science Teachers Association. (2003). *Standards for science teacher preparation: Skills of teaching* (revised edition.). Washington, DC: National Science Teachers Association.

National Science Teachers Association. (1998). *Standards for science teacher preparation: Skills of teaching*. Washington, DC: National Science Teachers Association.

National Research Council. (2012). *A framework for K–12 science education*. Washington, DC: National Academy Press.

National Research Council.(2011). *A framework for K–12 science education: Practices, crosscutting concepts, and core ideas*. Washington, DC: National Academy Press.

National Research Council. (2000). *Inquiry and the national science education standards*. Washington, DC: National Academy Press.

National Research Council. (1996). *National science education standards*. Washington, DC: National Academy Press.

Next Generation Science Standards (NGSS) Lead States (2013). Next generation science standards. Washington, DC: The National Academies Press. Retrieved from *https://www.nextgenscience.org/*

Piaget, J. (1964). Cognitive development in children: Piaget, development and learning. *Journal of Research in Science Teaching, 2*, 176–80.

Renner, J. W., and Marek, E.A. (1990). An educational theory base for science teaching. *Journal of Research in Science Teaching*, 27(3), 241–46.

Resnik, D. (1993). "Philosophical Foundations of Scientific Ethics," in *Ethical Issues in Physics: Workshop Proceedings*, Marshall Thomsen (ed.). Workshop: July 17–18, 1993, Eastern Michigan University, Ypsilanti, Michigan.

Sandoval, J.S. (1995). Teaching in subject matter areas: Science. *Annual Review of Psychology, 46*, 355–74.

Resnik, D.B. (2015). What is Ethics in Research & Why is it Important? *National Institute of Environmental Health Sciences*. Retrieved from: *https://www.niehs.nih.gov/research/resources/bioethics/whatis/index.cfm?links=false*.

Texas Education Agency (2010). *Title 19, Part II, Chapter 112: Texas Essential Knowledge and Skills for Science*. Texas Administrative Code (TAC). Retrieved from *www.tea.state.tx.us*

Texas Education Agency. (2012). *STAAR science resources*. Retrieved from *www.tea.state.tx.us*.

University of California Santa Barbara (2017), Regents of the University of California (2017). *http://scienceline.ucsb.edu/getkey.php?key=3144*.

TExES Core Subjects 4–8 Practice Test 1: English Language Arts and Reading (ELAR) (806)

This practice test plus an additional test are available at the online REA Study Center (*www.rea.com/studycenter*).

The TExES Core Subjects ELA and Reading (806) test is computer-based, so we strongly recommend that you take our online practice tests to simulate test-day conditions and to receive these added benefits:

- **Timed testing conditions**—Gauge how much time you can spend on each question.

- **Automatic scoring**—Find out how you did on the test, instantly.

- **On-screen detailed explanations of answers**—Learn not just the correct answer, but also why the other answers are incorrect.

- **Diagnostic score reports**—Pinpoint where you're strongest and where you need to focus your study.

English Language Arts and Reading
Practice Test 1: Answer Sheet

1. Ⓐ Ⓑ Ⓒ Ⓓ	26. Ⓐ Ⓑ Ⓒ Ⓓ	51. Ⓐ Ⓑ Ⓒ Ⓓ
2. Ⓐ Ⓑ Ⓒ Ⓓ	27. Ⓐ Ⓑ Ⓒ Ⓓ	52. Ⓐ Ⓑ Ⓒ Ⓓ
3. Ⓐ Ⓑ Ⓒ Ⓓ	28. Ⓐ Ⓑ Ⓒ Ⓓ	53. Ⓐ Ⓑ Ⓒ Ⓓ
4. Ⓐ Ⓑ Ⓒ Ⓓ	29. Ⓐ Ⓑ Ⓒ Ⓓ	54. Ⓐ Ⓑ Ⓒ Ⓓ
5. Ⓐ Ⓑ Ⓒ Ⓓ	30. Ⓐ Ⓑ Ⓒ Ⓓ	55. Ⓐ Ⓑ Ⓒ Ⓓ
6. Ⓐ Ⓑ Ⓒ Ⓓ	31. Ⓐ Ⓑ Ⓒ Ⓓ	56. Ⓐ Ⓑ Ⓒ Ⓓ
7. Ⓐ Ⓑ Ⓒ Ⓓ	32. Ⓐ Ⓑ Ⓒ Ⓓ	57. Ⓐ Ⓑ Ⓒ Ⓓ
8. Ⓐ Ⓑ Ⓒ Ⓓ	33. Ⓐ Ⓑ Ⓒ Ⓓ	58. Ⓐ Ⓑ Ⓒ Ⓓ
9. Ⓐ Ⓑ Ⓒ Ⓓ	34. Ⓐ Ⓑ Ⓒ Ⓓ	59. Ⓐ Ⓑ Ⓒ Ⓓ
10. Ⓐ Ⓑ Ⓒ Ⓓ	35. Ⓐ Ⓑ Ⓒ Ⓓ	60. Ⓐ Ⓑ Ⓒ Ⓓ
11. Ⓐ Ⓑ Ⓒ Ⓓ	36. Ⓐ Ⓑ Ⓒ Ⓓ	61. Ⓐ Ⓑ Ⓒ Ⓓ
12. Ⓐ Ⓑ Ⓒ Ⓓ	37. Ⓐ Ⓑ Ⓒ Ⓓ	62. Ⓐ Ⓑ Ⓒ Ⓓ
13. Ⓐ Ⓑ Ⓒ Ⓓ	38. Ⓐ Ⓑ Ⓒ Ⓓ	63. Ⓐ Ⓑ Ⓒ Ⓓ
14. Ⓐ Ⓑ Ⓒ Ⓓ	39. Ⓐ Ⓑ Ⓒ Ⓓ	64. Ⓐ Ⓑ Ⓒ Ⓓ
15. Ⓐ Ⓑ Ⓒ Ⓓ	40. Ⓐ Ⓑ Ⓒ Ⓓ	65. Ⓐ Ⓑ Ⓒ Ⓓ
16. Ⓐ Ⓑ Ⓒ Ⓓ	41. Ⓐ Ⓑ Ⓒ Ⓓ	66. Ⓐ Ⓑ Ⓒ Ⓓ
17. Ⓐ Ⓑ Ⓒ Ⓓ	42. Ⓐ Ⓑ Ⓒ Ⓓ	67. Ⓐ Ⓑ Ⓒ Ⓓ
18. Ⓐ Ⓑ Ⓒ Ⓓ	43. Ⓐ Ⓑ Ⓒ Ⓓ	68. Ⓐ Ⓑ Ⓒ Ⓓ
19. Ⓐ Ⓑ Ⓒ Ⓓ	44. Ⓐ Ⓑ Ⓒ Ⓓ	69. Ⓐ Ⓑ Ⓒ Ⓓ
20. Ⓐ Ⓑ Ⓒ Ⓓ	45. Ⓐ Ⓑ Ⓒ Ⓓ	70. Ⓐ Ⓑ Ⓒ Ⓓ
21. Ⓐ Ⓑ Ⓒ Ⓓ	46. Ⓐ Ⓑ Ⓒ Ⓓ	71. Ⓐ Ⓑ Ⓒ Ⓓ
22. Ⓐ Ⓑ Ⓒ Ⓓ	47. Ⓐ Ⓑ Ⓒ Ⓓ	72. Ⓐ Ⓑ Ⓒ Ⓓ
23. Ⓐ Ⓑ Ⓒ Ⓓ	48. Ⓐ Ⓑ Ⓒ Ⓓ	73. Ⓐ Ⓑ Ⓒ Ⓓ
24. Ⓐ Ⓑ Ⓒ Ⓓ	49. Ⓐ Ⓑ Ⓒ Ⓓ	74. Ⓐ Ⓑ Ⓒ Ⓓ
25. Ⓐ Ⓑ Ⓒ Ⓓ	50. Ⓐ Ⓑ Ⓒ Ⓓ	

Practice Test 1: ELAR

TIME: 1 hour and 55 minutes
74 questions

> **Directions:** Read each item and select the best answer. Most items on this test require you to provide the one best answer. However, some questions require you to select all the options that apply.

1. A teacher presents the word *destruction* to the class. The teacher points out that *struct*, a Latin root, means "to build." The teacher adds that *de-* is a common prefix that means "opposite." The teacher also points out how *construct* and *restructure* are related. Which of the following best illustrates how this instruction would help students?

   A. Applying phonics for word identification

   B. Gaining in phonemic awareness

   C. Learning about word structure and meaning

   D. Using knowledge of syntax to identify words

Use the information below to answer questions 2 and 3.

Students in fifth grade start their school year by writing personal narratives and informal reports drawing upon their experiences. The students will learn how to write a report. The teacher knows that even when students are competent writers, they can still find it challenging to orchestrate the skills needed to locate information and write a report.

2. Which of the following is the most effective way to support students' initial learning of how to write a report?

   A. The teacher needs to make sure each student knows how to develop an outline.

   B. The teacher should provide differentiated instruction for English learners to enable them to create an oral version just for them.

   C. The teacher and students could first write a shorter report together to ensure that students know strategies to use.

   D. The teacher needs to instruct students not to copy from a text as they take notes.

3. Which of the following approaches best helps ensure that students use quality sources that meet their needs as they begin to learn how to write a report?

   A. The teacher locates and evaluates websites that students will find helpful.

   B. The teacher provides a checklist for how to evaluate a website.

   C. The teacher shows students how to search for a website.

   D. The teacher lets students work in pairs to support each other.

4. The teacher reads aloud over a period of days from an informational book that provides an overview of a topic of research: wolves. The teacher and students work together to determine questions or aspects of the topic they want to address. The teacher writes each question at the top of a sheet for note-taking. The teacher tells the students that they can add other aspects if they discover other questions as they read to gain information.

How can this demonstration help students gain in inquiry skills?

A. The teacher is providing background knowledge students need for reading.

B. The students are learning how to read for a purpose and organize their note-taking as they gather information from sources.

C. The students are using fiction and nonfiction to learn.

D. The students are learning how to use cohesive ties.

5. The teacher reads aloud an excerpt from an informational book that addresses the topic and that focuses on one category of the topic, baby wolves, also known as wolf pups. The teacher then closes the book and makes a list of what the teacher remembers about pups on the page for note-taking that is devoted to the category of baby wolves.

How can this demonstration help students gain in inquiry skills?

A. The teacher is ensuring students have background knowledge they need.

B. The teacher shows how to preview a text.

C. The teacher next can ask students to copy the notes to use when they write that part of the report.

D. The teacher shows how to take notes without copying the text.

6. A school district wants to monitor students' abilities in learning to understand and spell commonly confused words. Which of the following assessments is best suited to accomplish this?

A. Criterion-referenced

B. Norm-referenced

C. Running records

D. Anecdotal accounts

7. Which of the following statements best describes how to foster fluency?

A. Encourage students to recognize the purpose of headings.

B. Provide students reading materials that have challenging words to foster growth.

C. Make sure students can recognize text structure.

D. Provide opportunities for students to read texts again so that the texts are easy in regard to word identification.

8. Which of the following best pertains to phonology?

A. The study of meaning in a language

B. How words can be combined in language

C. Letter-sound relationships

D. Sounds of a language and how they combine

9. Which of the following represents an accurate analysis of the student's miscue in how the student renders the text extract shown below?

   Student: She needs tap to wrap the gift.

   Text: She needs tape to wrap the gift.

   A. The miscue shows the need for instruction in phonemic awareness.

   B. The student's miscue indicates that the student is not paying attention to meaning and needs phonics instruction.

   C. The student needs instruction in reading multisyllabic words.

   D. The student is not paying attention to meaning and not using any visual cues.

10. Which of the following is a prime advantage of using running records in assessment?

    A. The teacher can keep a record of books the student has read for independent reading.

    B. The teacher can use the running record to help determine the correct text for students' reading instruction and to analyze students' oral reading errors.

    C. The teacher can determine how well the student reads as compared to other students in the state at the end of the school year.

    D. The teacher can keep a record whether the student can spell high-frequency words.

11. A student writes the following:

    I like to play with my cat.

    Which of the following stages of writing development is indicated through this writing sample?

    A. Semiphonetic

    B. Phonetic

    C. Transitional

    D. Conventional

12. A teacher shows students how to identify an unknown word in a sentence by reading the sentence to see what word would make sense. The teacher reveals the first letter of the unknown word. Which of the following describes the ability the teacher is developing?

    A. How to preview the text

    B. How to use visualization when reading

    C. How authors use foreshadowing

    D. Using context clues and phonics for word identification

13. A student writes the following two sentences.

    My best friend lives next to my house, we have fun. Last Friday, we had a sleepover at her house, we stayed up until midnight.

    Which of the following is an accurate assessment of the student's abilities in using writing conventions?

    A. The student does not use correct-subject-verb agreement.

    B. The student knows how to use a period and a comma correctly.

    C. The student needs to learn how to avoid a comma splice.

    D. The student needs to learn about capitalization.

14. Which of the following represents a way a teacher could use a visual organizer to help students think about new terms and see the relationships among terms?

    A. Directed Reading Thinking Activity

    B. Concept maps

    C. Reciprocal Teaching

    D. Question-Answer Relationships

15. During a mini-lesson, the teacher models rough-draft writing by thinking aloud and then saying, "I am not sure about how to spell this word, so I am going to spell it the best I can, so I focus on what I want to say. I can check on the spelling later." Which of the following is the rationale for this mini-lesson?

    A. Teachers need to provide differentiated instruction in teaching writing so that English learners (ELs) are not overwhelmed by learning about writing conventions.

    B. Students are likely to not want to write if they have to care about spelling and punctuation.

    C. Through worksheets, students can obtain ample instruction on writing skills they need to learn.

    D. When writing rough drafts, students should do their best in spelling and using punctuation, but they should not be overly concerned about writing conventions.

16. Which of the following pertains to the semantics of language?

    A. The study of meaning in a language

    B. How words can be combined in language

    C. Letter-sound relationships

    D. Sounds of a language and how they combine

17. Which of the following statements is accurate in describing the demands of reading expository texts?

    A. Expository text is too hard for students to grasp, so it is best to use discussion and visual media.

    B. Students have a schema for the text structure of expository texts, but they can struggle with the narrative structure of fiction because it is unfamiliar.

    C. If students read fiction, they will be prepared for the text structure of expository texts.

    D. Topics in expository text have a structure that is based upon how the subject to topic is organized, so students need to uncover the text structure as they read expository texts.

18. A teacher observes that a student can identify words when reading. However, the student does not read smoothly and does not change intonation when a sentence has a question mark. Which of the following types of instruction does the student most likely need?

    A. Structural analysis

    B. Fluency

    C. Visualization

    D. Phonics

19. Which of the following words has four distinct phonemes?

    A. Stick

    B. Sit

    C. The

    D. Shop

20. After assessing the students, a sixth-grade teacher determines that some students will have difficulty when trying to read a social studies textbook. Which of the following is the most effective way for the teacher to help students gain in reading content-area textbooks?

    A. The teacher could give the students easy questions to answer for each chapter so students can learn information.

    B. The teacher could avoid using the textbook because it is too hard for the students and they will become discouraged.

    C. The teacher could work with students in small groups and use shared reading with students who cannot read at least 90% of the words.

    D. The teacher could give a test each week so that students read and study information in the textbook.

Use the information below to answer questions 21 to 27.

Students in a sixth-grade classroom include some who are English learners as well as native speakers who are reading below grade level. Other students in the class read on or slightly below grade level.

Part 1. During guided reading, the teacher meets with a small group, where students read at the same level. While working independently, the students participate in learning stations where groups are heterogeneous in reading ability level.

Part 2. At the poetry notebook station, the students read the poems the teacher has presented to the class in a previous week for shared reading.

Part 3. When reading the poems at the poetry notebook station, students read with a partner.

Part 4. At another station, students work in a small group and practice a readers' theater script based upon stories or nonfiction that the teacher knows the students can read.

Part 5. At another station, students listen to audio-recordings of books while they follow along and read the book.

Part 6. For the independent reading station, students can select any book for reading, and they record the title on a reading log.

21. Which of the following statements provides the best rationale for the teacher's decisions for grouping in Part 1?

    A. Homogeneous groups are best for instruction so that students receive instruction at a level that meets their needs, and heterogeneous groups work best for productive independent work while the teacher works with a small group.

    B. Older students do not need small groups for instruction because students can identify words and read at the same level.

    C. After forming groups, the teacher will not need to change them.

    D. Heterogeneous groups work best for independent work because worksheets can be adapted, and heterogeneous groups work best for small-group instruction to motivate students.

22. To ensure that students read texts appropriate for their reading ability level, which of the following should teachers do in Part 1?

    A. Give students an interest inventory to find books about topics that interest them.

    B. Examine students' records to determine the correct reading levels for the current year.

    C. Use running records to assess students' use of benchmark books for guided reading instruction.

    D. Select texts that reinforce students' knowledge of sound-letter relationships.

23. In Part 2, the teacher lets the students read poems the class has already read together in a previous week. Which of the following is the best rationale for the teacher's decision?

    A. The activity prepares students to monitor comprehension.

    B. The activity prepares students for making predictions.

    C. Rereading fosters fluency, making it possible for students to focus on understanding what they are reading.

    D. Rereading prepares students for an assignment where the teacher asks the students to memorize the poem.

24. In Part 3, what is the best rationale for the teacher's decision to let students read with a partner?

    A. In reading with a partner, students monitor their comprehension and apply "fix-up" strategies as needed.

    B. Struggling readers can improve their reading proficiency by pairing up with a student who reads more proficiently.

    C. Students are engaging in a text feature walk as they read together.

    D. In reading with a partner, students gain in the regulatory function of language.

25. In Part 4, the students work in a heterogeneous grouping as they read readers' theater scripts together. How can this activity contribute to students' reading development?

    A. The activity prepares students to monitor comprehension.

    B. The activity prepares students for making predictions.

    C. The activity fosters fluency by allowing students to gain in reading smoothly, accurately, and with expression.

    D. The rereading prepares students for memorizing the lines of the script.

26. In Part 5, students listen to audio-recordings of books. How will this activity most likely contribute to students' reading development?

    A. Students can experience gains in listening comprehension and word identification.

    B. Students are apt to stay on task so the teacher can work with others more effectively.

    C. Students can learn more about root words and derivational morphemes.

    D. Students learn to monitor their reading.

27. In Part 6, why does the teacher let students self-select books for independent reading rather than require books of a designated level or length?

    A. When students are allowed to select their own books, they learn to engage in metacognition where they monitor their reading.

    B. When students select books, they experience authentic reading experiences and are more apt to read.

    C. The students read above grade level.

    D. The students read at grade level.

28. A teacher is providing a mini-lesson to help students learn about writing informal reports. The teacher tells the students that she is going to model the writing of informal reports about a specific topic: soccer. The teacher writes "Playing Soccer" in the center of a story web, and then draws lines that extend from the center of the web as she talks briefly about the following: *Starting and Playing; Penalties; Positions*. Why would the teacher provide this mini-lesson?

    A. The teacher is showing students how to take a topic they know about and then create a story web to see possible ways to develop the topic through paragraphs or chapters.

    B. The teacher is encouraging students to write about soccer and demonstrating how to get started.

C. The teacher is showing students how to revise their writing by demonstrating editing strategies.

D. The teacher is teaching a unit of study on information derived about soccer.

29. When teaching phonological and phonemic awareness, which THREE of the following are effective strategies for instruction?

A. Start with easier tasks such as rhyming, then move to blending, and then segmenting.

B. Start with stop sounds because they are easier for students to blend to demonstrate the grapheme-phoneme connection.

C. Use rhyming words and even "invented" spelling to represent the sound-symbol connection.

D. Start with larger units of language such as words and onset-rimes and then move to individual phonemes.

30. A teacher decides that he will devote more attention to the following pairs of words for spelling instruction: *passed—past, stationery—stationary, capital—capitol, aisle—isle*. Which of the following is a rationale for presenting students with these pairings?

A. Each pair represents synonyms that need to be explained.

B. Each pair represents homophones that need to be explained.

C. The teacher can combine spelling and social studies instruction.

D. The teacher can use the words to help students read multisyllabic words.

31. A teacher is focusing on teaching the following two phrases: *for example, for instance*. Which of the following illustrates how this instruction contributes to literacy development?

A. The teacher is showing common affixes used in words.

B. The teacher is teaching antonyms.

C. The teacher is showing how a cohesive tie can be used by writers.

D. The teacher is showing how to use visualization when reading.

32. Which of the following strategies can be used to activate or build background knowledge to prepare students for reading? Select *all* that apply.

A. Teachers can use flashcards with unfamiliar words as a way to have students say the words.

B. Teachers actively engage students in discussion of what they know that relates to new information they will encounter in the text.

C. Students can gain background knowledge needed for understanding content by copying definitions of academic vocabulary.

D. Teachers can explain unfamiliar concepts or aspects of the topic, using student-friendly language.

33. When students are required to read texts independently, the teacher must make sure they can comprehend what they read. Which of the following ranges indicates the correct percentage of words that students should be able to identify to be able to read a text on their own?

A. 95%–100%

B. 90%–94%

C. 85%–89%

D. 80%–84%

34. When evaluating whether to use a website, which of the following are factors that make it a good basis for instruction? Select *all* that apply.

    A. Most of the site's pages present large amounts of information.

    B. The site has accurate, understandable content that relates to the objectives of instruction.

    C. The site has multimedia and visual materials that contribute important information.

    D. The site is easy to navigate.

35. Which of the following represents nonfiction literature?

    A. Fantasy

    B. Mystery

    C. Folktales

    D. Biography

36. After students have read a story or book chapter, the teacher and students have grand conversations in which they share their personal responses. Which of the following support the strategy of "grand conversations"? Select *all* that apply.

    A. The teacher's contributions can show how a competent reader connects events to arrive at big ideas that emerge from a story.

    B. Sharing personal responses to literature helps students make gains in comprehension as important ideas are brought up for discussion.

    C. These learning experiences can help students be able to know how to use text features.

    D. Students are able to see that their thoughts about literature are legitimate, which can foster confidence when students are asked to analyze literature at subsequent points in their schooling.

37. When reading to learn from expository texts, students can benefit from activating their prior knowledge, setting a purpose for reading, and reviewing content. Which of the following strategies helps students engage in these types of thinking?

    A. Reciprocal teaching

    B. Think-Pair-Share

    C. Concept maps

    D. K-W-L

38. Which of the following correctly shows the use of a hyphen?

    A. Twenty five dollars

    B. Ten-year old student

    C. Family-owned restaurant

    D. Very-beautiful sunset

39. Which statement best describes why figurative language can present a challenge for students as they read literature?

    A. Students have trouble understanding the gist of the story.

    B. Students can have difficulty with word identification.

    C. Students achieve literal understanding before mastering the figurative.

    D. Students may not be able to read multisyllabic words.

40. When students learn to write in English, they may use "invented spelling"—accounting for the sounds in a word, but without using conventional spelling. For instance, a student may write *bik* for *bike*. Which of the following best describes the value of invented spelling to the process of developing writing proficiency?

   A.   Students who use invented spelling move toward conventional spelling when exposed to print.

   B.   Students should not write unless they can spell words correctly because the practice of using incorrect spelling interferes with growth in spelling.

   C.   Invented spelling can interfere with the learning of correct spellings because the students have practiced writing using incorrect spelling.

   D.   Invented spelling is an indicator of difficulty in phonological awareness.

41. A student writes the following:

   Since I broke my arm early in the season. I couldn't finish the soccer season.

   Which of the following statements most accurately describes the child's mastery of writing conventions based on the writing sample?

   A.   The student has difficulty with using verb tenses.

   B.   The student does not know that a dependent clause alone does not constitute a complete idea.

   C.   The student does not know about capitalization of seasons.

   D.   The student has difficulty spelling high-frequency words.

42. As part of showing students how to write a report, a teacher reads the opening paragraphs of quality nonfiction books that the class has heard before. Which of the following statements describes a rationale for this type of instruction?

   A.   The teacher can ask students to write a lead-in like one in the books.

   B.   The teacher is showing students how to preview a book.

   C.   Books that students have heard or read can serve as mentor texts.

   D.   Students can find it difficult to comprehend nonfiction as compared to fiction.

43. A story written from the first person point of view does which of the following?

   A.   Presents the events that take place in the story

   B.   Communicates what each character feels, thinks, says, and does

   C.   Describes where and when the story takes place

   D.   Uses a character in the story to tell the story

44. Which of the following is the most effective way to help students navigate expository texts so that they can learn information?

   A.   Provide weekly assessments to make sure students know the content.

   B.   Make sure students write the definitions of words so they will remember the meanings when they read the chapter.

   C.   Guide students to read a small chunk of the text, and let them talk about what they learned before reading the next chunk.

   D.   Tell students to read to the end of a sentence when they encounter a word they do not know so they can use context clues to figure out the unknown word.

45. Where in the writing workshop strategy does the teacher primarily help students address spelling, capitalization, punctuation, and usage?

    A. Mini-lessons and small-group work

    B. Rough-draft stage

    C. Proofreading/publishing conference

    D. Author's chair/whole-class conferences

46. Which of the following is the rationale for asking students to retell what they have read?

    A. The teacher can determine whether the student can make inferences.

    B. The teacher can determine whether the student can evaluate information.

    C. The teacher can determine whether the student is making text-to-self connections.

    D. The teacher can determine whether the student understands what was read at a literal level.

47. A team of teachers has observed that their students have made gains in composing, but the students are not making gains in applying the conventions of writing. Which of the following best describes an effective approach to prepare students to use writing conventions effectively?

    A. Students need to provide systematic instruction in spelling, punctuation, capitalization, and usage to help students be able to apply these when writing.

    B. Students can master writing conventions on their own.

    C. Focusing on spelling, punctuation, capitalization, and usage is not necessary because what matters most is whether students can communicate ideas.

    D. Students need to look up words in a dictionary to correct their spelling for a final draft.

48. Which of the following accurately describes what a score of the 90th percentile on a norm-referenced test means?

    A. The score means that the student answered 90% of the questions correctly.

    B. The score means that 90% of the norm group performed at the same level or above the student's score.

    C. The score means that 90% of the norm group performed at the same level or below the student's score.

    D. The score means the student has earned a 90 for the grading period.

49. What are affixes?

    A. Another name for suffixes

    B. Another name for prefixes

    C. Root or base words

    D. Prefixes and suffixes

50. Which of the following illustrates how viewing a video can be most effectively incorporated as part of a unit of study?

    A. Give students a test to make sure they gained from the video.

    B. Ask students to find a video online to learn about using digital resources.

    C. Have students discuss what they learned and add information to notes based on other sources used during the unit of study.

    D. Have English learners use the video instead of reading the text.

51. When listening to a student read during small-group instruction, a teacher observes that the student stops reading when seeing the word *father*. Which of the following should the teacher do to provide effective support?

    A. The teacher should ask the student to read to the end of the sentence to determine what the word is, based on its initial sound.

    B. The teacher should ask the student to "sound it out" to determine the word.

    C. The teacher should ask the student to "look for the little word" in the word.

    D. The teacher should tell the student the word.

52. Which of the following best defines the term *syntax* in the linguistic context?

    A. The study of meaning in a language

    B. How words can be combined in language

    C. Letter-sound relationships

    D. Sounds of a language and how they combine

53. Which statement describes instructional implications of the alphabetic principle when students learn to read and write in English?

    A. Students need to recognize letters of the alphabet in learning to read.

    B. Students need to know alphabetical order when using the dictionary and other reference materials.

    C. Students need to understand that speech sounds of English are represented through letters or groups of letters when we read and write.

    D. Students need to be able to read and write letters to make progress in literacy.

Use the information below to answer questions 54 to 59.

Part 1. The teacher meets with students in small groups for reading. In preparing English learners to read a story, the teacher presents the word, *exit*. The teacher tells the students that one of the words they will read in the story is *exit*. The students look at the word and say it. The teacher then shows the sentence that appears in the story where the word is used, and the teacher explains what the word means.

Part 2. The teacher shows students a photo of an exit sign above a door in a building, and she discusses that the sign indicates where to leave the building.

Part 3. The teacher then tells students that she is going to exit the classroom and briefly walks out the door and comes back in.

Part 4. After students have read the story silently, they retell the story and share their responses. The teacher brings up the point that the people had difficulty when they tried to exit the building because of the location of the fire.

Part 5. On the next day, the teacher and students talk about the times of the day when they exit the classroom.

Part 6. In a subsequent lesson, the teacher reminds students that they learned the meaning of *exit*. The teacher then shows students the following words: *export* and *expel*. The teacher and students discuss the meaning of the prefix, *ex-* and how this helps understand the meanings of the words.

54. In Part 1, which of the following is a rationale for the teacher's instruction?

    A. The teacher is helping students preview text features.

    B. The teacher is proving direct instruction for a word that English learners may not understand solely by using context clues when reading the story.

    C. The teacher wants to teach phonics so the students can make gains in word identification.

    D. The teacher is helping students be able to make predictions.

55. In Part 2, which of the following is a rationale for the teacher's instruction?

    A.   The teacher is using a visual to help provide a variety of unfamiliar vocabulary that is important know in understanding the story.

    B.   The teacher is helping students preview text features.

    C.   The teacher wants to teach phonics so the students can make gains in word identification.

    D.   The teacher is helping students learn to spell the word by seeing it again.

56. In Part 3, what is a rationale for the teacher's instruction?

    A.   The teacher is helping students be able to develop a concept map.

    B.   The teacher is helping students preview text features.

    C.   The teacher wants students to be able to use pantomime.

    D.   The teacher is using modeling to show the meaning of the intended word.

57. In Part 4, which of the following indicates how the teacher contributes to the English learners' literacy development?

    A.   The students are given opportunities to use language before a whole class.

    B.   The teacher can grade the students' contributions to the discussion to provide feedback.

    C.   The teacher can ask comprehension questions to make sure the English learners understood the story.

    D.   By talking about what took place and sharing personal responses, the students can expand their experiences with the story.

58. Which of the following is a rationale for the teacher's decision to focus again on the word *exit* in Part 5?

    A.   The students will be able to write the word in their personal dictionary.

    B.   Teaching new vocabulary words over several days helps English learners master unknown words.

    C.   The teacher can use the talking experiences as a basis of students' writing.

    D.   Through talking about what took place and sharing personal responses, the students are able to expand their experiences with the story.

59. Why is the teacher's instruction beneficial in Part 6?

    A.   The teacher is helping students be able to apply phonics generalizations.

    B.   The teacher is helping students be prepared for a vocabulary quiz.

    C.   The teacher is preparing students for being able to write sentences using the new words.

    D.   The teacher is using the knowledge and structure of the vocabulary acquired as a foundation for introducing structurally similar new vocabulary.

60. A teacher makes sure students engage in independent reading daily as part of classroom instruction, including time where students select what they want to read?

    Which of the following is a rationale for this instruction?

    A.   Students can make gains in phonics.

    B.   Students need to read connected text and see that they can find books that are rewarding to read.

    C.   The teacher can make sure students read required books.

    D.   The teacher can give tests to make sure students do read.

61. The teacher listens to a student read a text. The student makes a miscue when reading, as shown below. Which of the following describes the type of prompt the teacher should say to help the student become better at identifying words?

   Student: The boat sailed across the over.

   Text: The boat sailed across the ocean.

   A. The teacher should ask the student, "Does that make sense?," to help the student self-correct.

   B. The teacher should tell the child to "sound out" the word the child missed.

   C. The teacher should not say anything because this could discourage the student, especially if she or he is an English learner.

   D. The teacher should tell the child the unknown word so the child knows it.

62. The teacher shows the class the following three sentences:

   Each of the players is able to go to the game.

   Either of us is able to help you.

   Everyone rides on the bus.

   Which of the following is the teacher focusing on for instruction?

   A. The teacher is demonstrating common errors in writing the plural form of a noun.

   B. The teacher is teaching subject-verb agreement.

   C. The teacher is highlighting the use of pronouns in sentences.

   D. The teacher is addressing phonemic awareness.

63. To understand ideas that are implied rather than stated directly in the narrative, students commonly use which of the following strategies?

   A. Summarizing

   B. Recalling

   C. Predicting

   D. Making inferences

64. Which of the following statements describes the cloze procedure?

   A. Encourages students to recognize the purpose of headings.

   B. Guides students to examine the structure of expository texts.

   C. Students examine the structure of a story through a graphic organizer.

   D. Students are given passages with specific words deleted, and they are required to use context to identify the intended meaning.

65. A teacher presents the two pairs of sentences below and reads them aloud to students.

> The **object** of the game is to score more points than your opponent.
>
> The people did not **object** to the change in the delivery date.

> People wondered about the **decrease** in attendance at the games.
>
> She did not **decrease** the amount of time she practiced for the game this week.

Which of the following best represents what the teacher wants students to notice by highlighting the words as shown?

A. The teacher is showing how to use a word in more than one sentence to provide more than one example.

B. The teacher is showing derivatives of words.

C. The teacher is showing examples of words that are spelled the same but pronounced differently, depending upon whether the word is used as a noun or verb.

D. The teacher is providing practice reading a word twice so students are more apt to remember how to recognize a word.

66. Given that the writing process can be recursive, at which of the following stages in the process does the writer devote attention to establishing the intended content?

A. Prewriting

B. Drafting

C. Revising

D. Editing

67. A teacher "publishes" a book with contributions from each student, and these books are added to the classroom library, which students can use for independent reading in class. Which of the following best how this experience supports the students' writing development?

A. The students gain practice in topic selection.

B. The students gain practice in developing a title for their writing.

C. The students learn about elaborating so that important details are included.

D. The students access an authentic audience and are given reasons for writing, including the reasons for proofreading a final draft.

68. When authors use an omniscient point of view in the narrative, they

A. present the events that take place in the story.

B. allow readers to see what each character feels, thinks, says, and does.

C. tell the story, using the names of characters or pronouns

D. present the plot from one character's viewpoint.

69. A teacher has decided that that he will devote additional attention to the following words for his instruction for English learners: *rose, bark, spring, trunk*. What is a rationale for the instruction?

A. Each of these words demonstrates an *r*-controlled vowel for phonics instruction.

B. The words are commonly misspelled words.

C. Each of these words demonstrates the initial consonant sound of *r*.

D. Each word can create confusion as a homonym.

70. Which of the following represents a way to help students understand characterization?

    A. Discussing how, where, and when the story takes place determines events in a work of historical fiction

    B. Discussing the events of the story

    C. Discussing what the author reveals about a person and the techniques used to present the information

    D. Asking students to think about the lesson(s) or big idea(s) that emerge from the story

71. At which of the following steps in the writing workshop can teachers present strategies and techniques writers use in composing drafts?

    A. Writing

    B. Author's chair/whole-class conferences

    C. Mini-lessons and small-group work

    D. Proofreading/publishing conference

72. A teacher works with English learners who are emergent readers in English and have not learned to read in their native language. As part of instruction, the teacher and students read a book together, with the teacher pointing to words as he says a word. The students join in reading with the teacher during additional readings of the book. Which of the following statements provides a rationale for this instruction?

    A. The students can learn about directionality and concepts of print, as well as gain in sight vocabulary.

    B. The students can preview the text through the guidance of the teacher.

    C. The students are being shown how to monitor comprehension.

    D. The students are engaging in reciprocal teaching.

73. Which of the following is not an effective instructional strategy to promote vocabulary development?

    A. Students should be given time to read daily and read various types of texts.

    B. Teachers need to be intentional in selecting words for instruction that meet students' needs.

    C. Teachers can help students by modeling their own strategies for figuring out the meanings of words.

    D. Teachers need to give vocabulary tests on a regular basis and monitor results.

74. Which of the following strategies is least likely to support ELs acquisition of language and content?

    A. Explaining a new concept by building upon background knowledge of the students

    B. Using actions and gestures to explain the definitions of words

    C. Letting students talk to a classmate about what they learned after reading a small chunk of information in a chapter before asking students to share with the whole group

    D. Asking students to look up definitions of unfamiliar words in a dictionary

ELAR Practice Test 1: Answer Key

Test Item	Answer	Competency 806-
1.	C	003
2.	C	009
3.	A	009
4.	B	009
5.	D	009
6.	A	004
7.	D	003
8.	D	001
9.	B	002
10.	B	002
11.	D	006
12.	D	003
13.	C	006
14.	B	004
15.	D	007
16.	A	001
17.	D	009
18.	B	003
19.	A	002
20.	C	005
21.	A	005
22.	C	005
23.	C	003
24.	B	003
25.	C	003

Test Item	Answer	Competency 806-
26.	A	003
27.	B	005
28.	A	008
29.	A, C, D	002
30.	B	006
31.	C	004
32.	B, D	004
33.	A	002
34.	B, C, D	008
35.	D	005
36.	A, B, D	001
37.	D	004
38.	C	006
39.	C	005
40.	A	002
41.	B	006
42.	C	007
43.	D	005
44.	C	009
45.	C	006
46.	D	004
47.	A	006
48.	C	004
49.	D	003
50.	C	008

Test Item	Answer	Competency 806-
51.	A	003
52.	B	001
53.	C	002
54.	B	004
55.	A	004
56.	D	004
57.	D	001
58.	B	001
59.	D	004
60.	B	005
61.	A	002
62.	B	006
63.	D	004
64.	D	003
65.	C	005
66.	B	007
67.	D	007
68.	B	005
69.	D	005
70.	C	005
71.	C	007
72.	A	002
73.	D	004
74.	D	001

ELAR Practice Test 1: Detailed Answers

1. C.

Option (C) is correct because the teacher is using morphemic analysis to show how a Latin root word is featured in English words and how this relates to meaning, which can help students understand other words they encounter. Option (A) is incorrect because phonics involves learning about sound-symbol correspondences to identify words. Option (B) is incorrect because phonemic awareness involves accounting for sounds in words. Option (D) is incorrect because readers use syntax when they use their knowledge of how words can be combined in a language. **(Competency 806-003 Word Identification Skills and Reading Fluency)**

2. C.

Option (C) is correct because students need support as they engage in strategies associated with writing a research report. When the teacher models effective strategies and works with students, they are more apt to be able to write independently. Option (A) is incorrect because even though students are often told to develop an outline, students need to first read to have an overview of a topic and possible areas of the topic that will be addressed. Writers often change outlines between the time they research a topic and when they start writing. Option (B) is incorrect. Making it possible for students to talk about what they want to write is helpful for all students because it provides scaffolding, but English learners also should participate in writing to grow as writers through sheltered instruction. Option (D) is incorrect because students must be shown, not just told, what to do. When students are told not to copy the text, they often just change a few words in a sentence. **(Competency 806-009 Study and Inquiry Skills)**

3. A.

Option (A) is correct. Students eventually do need to learn how to locate and evaluate websites, but as novices they can be overwhelmed and end up using inferior sites that may misguide them and distort their findings. In addition, using quality websites will help students familiarize themselves with the characteristics of a quality site. When teachers narrow the search criteria, students are freed to focus on skills like note-taking, attribution of sources, and producing a draft. Option (B) is incorrect because criteria on a checklist will not be understood if students are unfamiliar with the criteria. Option (C) is incorrect. Even if students know how to search for a site, they may not find a quality site to use on their own. Option (D) is incorrect because students who are novices will not be able to support each other's learning in this situation even though working in pairs is effective for many types of learning situations. **(Competency 806-009 Study and Inquiry Skills)**

4. B.

Option (B) is correct. The designated questions and subject areas provide structure and purpose for students as they read and record information. Option (A) is incorrect. The teacher is not providing information students need to be able to understand a text. Option (C) is incorrect because the teacher has used solely nonfiction in this situation. Option (D) is incorrect because cohesive ties pertain to words that connect, or "glue," ideas together, such as *furthermore*, a word that signals additional ideas. **(Competency 806-009 Study and Inquiry Skills)**

5. D.

Option (D) is correct. Note-taking can be difficult for students to learn, but the teacher shows how to read short segments and then write notes without looking at the text so that students see a way to put ideas into their own words with accuracy. Option (A) is incorrect because the teacher has not focused on building background knowledge in this learning experience. Option (B) is incorrect. Previewing a text entails looking at titles, headings, illustrations, photographs, and captions to prepare for reading. Option (D) is incorrect because when students merely copy the notes, they are directing their attention to copying, not observing the process the teacher is modeling. Instead the teacher should continue to model or work together with students to provide gradual release of responsibility. **(Competency 806-009 Study and Inquiry Skills)**

6.   A.

Option (A) is correct because criterion-referenced test can provide information about what students know in regard to a specific set of predetermined outcomes. Option (B) is incorrect because the scores of a norm-referenced test provide information about a student's ranking in comparison to other students, not specific information about what a student knows and can do. Option (C) is incorrect because running records provide information about a student's oral reading, but not a specific assessment of a set of commonly confused words. Option (D) is incorrect because anecdotal accounts may not include observing students using commonly confused words in their reading and writing, even though anecdotal accounts can be beneficial in other ways. **(Competency 806-004 Reading Comprehension and Assessment)**

7.   D.

Option (D) is correct. Reading fluency is developed when students re-read materials to be able to read smoothly and accurately, as well as with appropriate intonation to better comprehend what they're reading. Option (A) is incorrect because recognizing the purpose of headings pertains to the text structure of expository text. Option (B) is incorrect. Students do need to gain in sight vocabulary words to read fluently, but fluency is developed when students can read the words of the text easily and can devote attention to reading smoothly with expression. Option (C) is incorrect because noting text structure is useful for understanding the way information is presented in expository text, which can foster comprehension and learning. **(Competency 806-003 Word Identification Skills and Reading Fluency)**

8.   D.

Option (D) is correct by definition, as phonemes are the smallest unit of sound in a language. Option (A) is incorrect because semantics pertains to the study of meaning. Option (B) is incorrect because syntax pertains to how words can be combined in a language. Option (C) is incorrect because letter-sound relationships describe only one component of phonology. **(Competency 806-001 Oral Language)**

9.   B.

Option (B) is correct. The student's miscue does not make sense, and the student is not aware of the phonics generalization of how the sound of the vowel differs in a CVC pattern (of short vowels) as compared to the VCe pattern of long vowels. Option (A) is incorrect because phonemic awareness assessment is based on the student hearing and accounting for sounds in words, not reading words. Option (C) is incorrect because the miscue is not based on a word with more than one syllable. Option (D) is incorrect because the student uses the visual cues of the initial and final sounds of the unknown word. **(Competency 806-002 Early Literacy Development)**

10.   B.

Option (B) is correct. Teachers can use running records along with an assessment of the students' comprehension to form reading groups, to monitor students' progress, and teach in view of the miscues. Option (A) is incorrect because a reading log is used by students to record the books they read. Option (C) is incorrect because running records is an informal assessment the teacher uses, not a standardized test (such as might be administered by the state education agency). Option (D) is incorrect because running records are not a record of words the student can spell. **(Competency 806-002 Early Literacy Development)**

11.   D.

Option (D) is correct. At the conventional stage, the student has mostly correct spellings of words. Option (A) is incorrect because in the semiphonetic stage the student uses abbreviated spelling where the word is represented by a letter, such as *u* for *you*. Option (B) is incorrect because in the phonetic stage the students account for every sound in a word, but their spelling may not be conventional, such as *lik* for *like*. Option (C) is incorrect because the student is not relying on visual and morphological information, such as *liek* for *like*. **(Competency 806-006 Written Language—Writing Conventions)**

12. D.

Option (D) is correct because the students can use the surrounding words in using context clues and the initial consonant sound in using phonics to identify the unknown word. Option (A) is incorrect because previewing the text takes place before reading to anticipate what the text will convey. Option (B) is incorrect because the teacher is not asking students to create a picture in their minds to comprehend as they read. Option (C) is incorrect because the teacher is not focusing on words that lead readers to anticipate what is coming later in the narrative. **(Competency 806-003 Word Identification Skills and Reading Fluency)**

13. C.

Option (C) is correct. The student has joined two independent clauses together (between *house* and *we*) with a comma, which is incorrect and is a comma splice. Option (A) is incorrect because the student did use correct subject-verb agreement. Option (B) is incorrect because the student has not used the comma correctly. Option (D) is incorrect because the student has indeed used correct capitalization in the sample (i.e., *Friday*). **(Competency 806-006 Written Language—Writing Conventions)**

14. B.

Option (B) is correct. Concept maps are visual organizers that can help students understand the main ideas and make connections to other ideas in the process of learning content areas. Option (A) is incorrect. The Directed Reading Thinking Activity (DRTA) is a comprehension strategy that guides students to ask questions, make predictions, and then read to confirm or refute their predictions. Option (C) is incorrect. In reciprocal teaching, the teacher models, and then students work in small groups and use four strategies to have a dialogue about what they have learned: summarizing, question generating, clarifying, and predicting. Option (D) is incorrect. Question-Answer Relationships denotes a strategy that helps students think about what can be required to answer questions about material they have read: look in one place in the text; search in more than one place in the text; use what is read in combination with what the reader has experienced; use prior knowledge of the reader. **(Competency 806-004 Reading Comprehension and Assessment)**

15. D.

Option (D) is correct. Students will not be able to devote attention to establishing content if their attention is diverted toward a concern for spelling and punctuation they have not mastered. Option (A) is incorrect because the rationale underlying the instructional scenario does not entail differentiated instruction for ELs. Option (B) is incorrect because students can be supported as they write through proofreading conferences when producing a final draft. Option (C) is incorrect because students need to learn how to apply writing conventions as they write, not just by working on skills in isolation. **(Competency 806-007 Written Language—Composition)**

16. A.

Option (A) is correct because semantics pertains to the study of meaning. Option (B) is incorrect because syntax pertains to how words can be combined in a language. Option (C) is incorrect because letter-sound relationships pertain to phonics. Option (D) is incorrect because phonemes pertain to sounds of a language and how they combine in the pronunciation of words. **(Competency 806-001 Oral Language)**

17. D.

Option (D) is correct. When reading expository, or informational, texts, students must discern the text structure to be able to connect units of information. Option (A) is incorrect because students can learn how to read textbooks and other expository texts if teachers provide support through modeling and guided practice. Option (B) is incorrect because students have a schema for the narrative structure of fiction. Option (C) is incorrect because expository texts make different demands on readers than fiction. Though students do make gains in reading fiction that transfer to reading expository texts, teachers must teach students how to read and learn from expository texts, not assume so. **(Competency 806-009 Study and Inquiry Skills)**

18. B.

Option (B) is correct. Fluency entails being able to read smoothly so what is read can be remembered, and prosody is needed because readers understand better when they read with expression and make changes in intonation in response to indicators in the text. Options (A) and (D) are incorrect because the student does not need word identification instruction. Option (C) is incorrect because the assessment has not focused upon comprehension, and visualization is used to help students create images in their minds to read actively and comprehend. Comprehension can be affected when students do not read fluently, but a comprehension assessment is not described in this situation. **(Competency 806-003 Word Identification Skills and Reading Fluency)**

19. A.

Option (A) is correct because *stick* has five letters but four sounds: /s/ /t/ /i/ /k/. Option (B) is incorrect because *sit* has three sounds: /s/ /i/ /t/. Option (C) is incorrect because *the* has two sounds: /th/ /e/. Option (D) is incorrect because *shop* has four letters but only three phonemes. That is, it contains a consonant digraph—*sh*—and two additional phonemes—/o/ and /p/. **(Competency 806-002 Early Literacy Development)**

20. C.

Option (C) is correct. Through shared reading, the students can participate in reading the textbook because they read with the teacher, which also helps students make gains in word identification. The teacher and students also can use other strategies, such as noticing headings, talking about what they are learning, and recording information by taking notes. Option (A) is incorrect because answering questions does not help students actually read the textbook. Students could search for answers without reading the sections. Option (B) is incorrect because students need to learn how to read expository texts to participate in subsequent reading experiences in their schooling. Teachers need to modify the textbook or provide scaffolding by using shared reading to help students gain in proficiency and not be discouraged. Option (D) is incorrect because fear of a test does not show students how to read a textbook or help them learn its content. **(Competency 806-005 Reading Applications)**

21. A.

Option (A) is correct. When students read a text that is too hard, they can become frustrated and cannot make progress in reading. Heterogeneous grouping for independent work makes it possible for students of diverse ability levels to interact in the same reading group. Option (B) is incorrect because being able to identify words does not ensure that a reader can comprehend, while in small groups it is easier for teachers to meet individual needs. Option (C) is incorrect because grouping for instruction needs to be flexible enough to allow for groups to be rearranged based on progress achieved. Option (D) is incorrect because worksheets are not the focus of the teacher's instruction, and heterogeneous grouping for instruction does not necessarily motivate students to read texts that are too hard or too easy. **(Competency 806-005 Reading Applications)**

22. C.

Option (C) is correct. Through asking students to read an excerpt from a set of benchmark books, teachers can determine the percentage of words a student can read accurately and the types of miscues students make, which reveals the instructional level of each student and type of instruction the student needs. This data can inform the formation of homogeneous reading groups. Option (A) is incorrect because students need to be placed in a guided reading group where they can make progress, and an interest inventory does not reveal reading ability levels. Option (B) is incorrect because students could make progress or decline in progress during the interval between academic years, so current reading levels need to be assessed. Option (D) is incorrect because reading entails decoding and comprehension, and both need to be considered when planning for instruction. The texts cited in this response are better suited for practicing decoding and word recognition. **(Competency 806-005 Reading Applications)**

23. C.

Option (C) is correct. Students gain in fluency by reading a text multiple times so they can learn to say words automatically, use correct intonation, and observe punctuation, which in turn enhances the opportunity to place greater attention on understanding the content. Option (A) is incorrect because the activity does not focus on checking for understanding as students read (even though students might be monitoring comprehension). Option (B) is incorrect because the activity does not focus on making predictions about the content or sequence of events. Option (D) is incorrect because students do not gain in fluency from hearing the story read aloud even though reading aloud is beneficial. **(Competency 806-003 Word Identification Skills and Reading Fluency)**

24. B.

Option (B) is correct because all students (including more advanced classmates) gain in fluency when they read a text again because word identification becomes easier and the content becomes more familiar and easier to understand. Option (A) is incorrect because the focus of this activity is not on checking for understanding and then reading. Option (C) is incorrect because students are not being shown how to examine text features, such as the headings, bold words, illustrations, captions. Option (D) is incorrect because the regulatory function of language pertains to situations where people use language to request or control, which is not an objective of letting students read with a partner. **(Competency 806-003 Word Identification Skills and Reading Fluency)**

25. C.

Option (C) is correct. Students gain in fluency by reading a text multiple times so they can learn to say words automatically, use correct intonation, and observe punctuation, which clarifies the meaning of the text and thus aids the reader in understanding it. Additionally, rereading with others makes it enjoyable, and allows students to learn from others as they practice. Option (A) is incorrect because the activity does not focus on checking for understanding as students read (even though students might be self-monitoring comprehension). Option (B) is incorrect because the activity does not focus on making predictions about what the selection will be about or what will happen next. Option (D) is incorrect because readers' theater is a form of drama where students do not memorize lines or engage in actions because the students read from scripts, with the story shared through the readers' voices. **(Competency 806-003 Word Identification Skills and Reading Fluency)**

26. A.

Option (A) is correct. By listening to the audio-recording of a book, students gain in listening comprehension while following along with the story and making the print-speech connection. Option (B) is incorrect because the purpose of the activity is not to manage the class, but to engage students in a listening comprehension activity. Option (C) is incorrect because listening to audio-recorded stories does not engage students in structural or morphemic analysis. Option (D) is incorrect because the activity does not focus on checking for understanding as students read even though students might be monitoring comprehension. **(Competency 806-003 Word Identification Skills and Reading Fluency)**

27. B.

Option (B) is correct. Outside of school, readers select books they want to read, and have found they types of books they enjoy. If teachers read aloud, students will know of books they want to read for independent reading, and they will feel more ownership of their reading. Option (A) is incorrect because the purpose of the activity is not to help students engage in metacognition, but to become competent readers able to monitor their comprehension even if they are not conscious of doing so. Options (C) and (D) are incorrect because students of all ability levels profit from selecting their own books for independent reading. The teacher can provide instruction needed through guided reading and shared reading. **(Competency 806-005 Reading Applications)**

28. A.

Option (A) is correct because developing a story web can help students organize their writing by breaking down a topic they know and demonstrating its key components. Option (B) is incorrect. While the teacher is encouraging students to write about a topic that they might be familiar with, the activity goes beyond that. It provides the framework for the development of the informal report. Option (C) is incorrect because revising takes place once students start to establish content. Option (D) is incorrect because the scenario does not provide information suggesting that the purpose of the activity is to introduce a unit. **(Competency 806-008 Viewing and Representing)**

29. A., C., D.

Options (A), (C), and (D) are accurate and thus correct. Option (B) is incorrect because teachers actually should start with sounds of longer duration that are easier to blend and can be held continuously, such as /f/, /l/, /m/, /n/, /r/, /s/, /v/, /w/, /z/. Stop sounds are not held continuously (but rather have an "uh" sound): /b/, /d/, /g/, /k/, /p/, /t/. The grapheme *k* often represents the sound /k/]. **(Competency 806-002 Early Literacy Development)**

30. B.

Option (B) is correct. The list of paired homophones can be confusing because they are words that sound the same but have different meanings and spellings. Option (A) is incorrect because the words are not synonyms, words with similar meanings. Option (C) is incorrect because the scenario does not indicate relevance to social studies instruction. Option (D) is incorrect on its face because the first pairing contains only one-syllable words (*passed, past*). Moreover, teaching students how to decode multisyllabic words requires having students, for example, try to identify the vowels in a word in an effort to determine the types of syllables in the word and then read the word to figure out what it is. **(Competency 806-006 Written Language—Writing Conventions)**

31. C.

Option (C) is correct. The words represent ways that writers can use to signal examples in the course of elaboration; knowing this helps students in comprehending and composing text. Option (A) is incorrect because affixes are prefixes and suffixes, which are not present in the question. Option (B) is incorrect because the words are not opposite in meaning, which antonyms would have to be. Option (D) is incorrect because visualization is a comprehension strategy where students are encouraged to think about what they are reading. **(Competency 806-004 Reading Comprehension and Assessment)**

32. B., D.

Options (B) and (D) are correct. Comprehension instruction is enhanced when readers access their background knowledge to what is before them in the text. Additionally, students need a threshold of background knowledge to understand and remember what they read. Option (A) is incorrect because being able to identify a word does not necessarily mean students understand it. Option (C) is incorrect because simply copying definitions does not ensure that students understand the concepts associated with a definition. **(Competency 806-004 Reading Comprehension and Assessment)**

33. A.

Option (A) is correct because students need to read at the independent level (95%–100%) to be able to navigate a text on their own. Option (B) is incorrect. A text is considered to be at the instructional level when students can read at least 90%–94%. At this level, students need additional support to decode and/or comprehend the information read. Options (C) and (D) are incorrect because when a student reads below 90% of words, the text is considered to be too hard, or at the frustration level. **(Competency 806-002 Early Literacy Development)**

34. B., C., D.

Options (B), (C), and (D) are correct because these are all criteria that help ensure students can gain from a site. Option (A) is correct because large amounts of information on a page can be overwhelming. In addition, the focus should be on the information's reliability. **(Competency 806-008 Viewing and Representing)**

35. D.

Option (D) is correct. Biographies, memoirs and other types of nonfiction writings present actual events and facts. Options (A), (B), and (C) represent fictional depictions of the life and aspirations of the characters. **(Competency 806-005 Reading Applications)**

36. A., B., D.

Options (A), (B), and (D) describe ways that authentic discussions, in which the teacher and students share personal responses to literature, can contribute to students' literacy development as well as how oral language experiences can support students' reading development. Option (C) is incorrect because, though the activity would propel gains in listening comprehension, a grand conversation would not focus on study skills. **(Competency 806-001 Oral Language)**

37. D.

Option (D) is correct. K-W-L is a strategy where students complete three columns of a chart to activate prior knowledge by stating what they know (K), what they want to know (W), and what they learned (L). Option (A) is incorrect. Reciprocal teaching is where students engage in small-group discussions about what they have read and use four strategies to talk about what they have learned. Option (B) is incorrect. Think-Pair-Share is a strategy that lets students think about what they have read and learned and talk with a partner as a way of encouraging students to talk as part of their learning. Option (C) is incorrect. Concept maps are visual organizers that can help students understand how ideas relate to other ideas in expository texts. **(Competency 806-004 Reading Comprehension and Assessment)**

38. C.

Option (C) is correct because a hyphen is generally used when two or more words are a single idea that modifies a noun. Option (A) is incorrect because it requires a hyphen. Option (B) is incorrect because the compound noun requires hyphenation in two places; thus, an additional hyphen is needed: *ten-year-old*. Option (D) is incorrect because the intensifier *very*, an adverb, is not hyphenated. **(Competency 806-006 Written Language—Writing Conventions)**

39. C.

Option (C) is correct. Most young readers first attain literal meaning of words before grasping the figurative, or implied, meaning, which requires higher-order thinking. Moreover, students understand cultural or historical references before they can make sense of figurative language. Options (A) and (B) are incorrect because difficulties with figurative language do not stem from difficulty in comprehending stories or recognizing words. Option (D) is incorrect because even when students are able to identify words of figurative language, they can still find figurative language challenging to understand. **(Competency 806-005 Reading Applications)**

40. A.

Option (A) is correct. Students who use invented spelling learn the conventional spellings of words as they progress through exposure to print. In addition, by accounting for the sounds of words, students make gains in phonemic awareness, which is essential in learning to read. Options (B) and (C) are incorrect. When using invented spelling, students do show that they are accounting for the sounds of a word, so errors are not random. Students eventually will learn more about conventional spellings through effective instruction, and invented spelling actually can help literacy development by fostering phonemic awareness. Option (D) is incorrect because invented spelling has students account for phonemes, and phonemic awareness is a dimension of phonological awareness. **(Competency 806-002 Early Literacy Development)**

41. B.

Option (B) is correct. All clauses have a subject and a verb, but a subordinating conjunction such as *since* or *because* or *although* creates a dependent clause, which must be joined to an independent sentence to avoid being left as a fragment. Option (A) is incorrect because this writing sample does not show difficulties with verb tense. Option (C) is incorrect because seasons are not capitalized. Option (D) is incorrect because there are no spelling issues in the sample. **(Competency 806-006 Written Language—Writing Conventions)**

42. C.

Option (C) is correct. Students can learn about how to write effectively through hearing books read aloud and reading books. Teachers can help students notice strategies and techniques writers use by looking back at works. Option (A) is incorrect. Mentor texts help students discern strategies writers use, but they are not used as a model that students must follow. Option (B) is incorrect because the teacher is not focusing on preparation for reading in this situation. Option (D) is incorrect. Students can find it more challenging to read and remember expository text, but in this case the teacher is focusing on showing students how to appreciate and write an effective lead-in. **(Competency 806-007 Written Language—Composition)**

43. D.

Option (D) is correct because in this type of narrative, the author uses a character in the story to tell the story. Option (A) is incorrect because it presents a general description of what the author does, that is, by arranging the events in the plot. Option (B) is incorrect because it simply describes when an author presents the information from an omniscient point of view. Presenting the information as omniscient—with the author knowing everything about the characters—is not uniquely restricted to the first person point of view. Option (C) is incorrect because it just describes the setting of the story—where and when the story takes place. It does not describe the actual role of an author in presenting the information from the first-person perspective. **(Competency 806-005 Reading Applications)**

44. C.

Option (C) is correct because reading small chunks of information helps students to avoid being overwhelmed when encountering new information. Talking about the information helps students review content and monitor their comprehension. Option (A) is incorrect because assessing students is not providing instruction on how to read to learn. Option (B) is incorrect because students are not likely to understand an unfamiliar concept by writing a definition, whereas time could be devoted to effective vocabulary development to help students understand concepts and how concepts relate. Option (D) is incorrect because this strategy is helpful for word identification, but does not help ensure students can comprehend and learn content. **(Competency 806-009 Study and Inquiry Skills)**

45. C.

Option (C) is correct. In proofreading/publishing conferences, students learn to proofread to develop a final draft that would be read by others. Option (A) is incorrect. Mini-lessons take place with the whole class and are brief demonstrations based upon what students need to know. Teachers can meet with students in small groups to provide further support. Option (B) is incorrect. During the daily writing part of the workshop, students and the teacher write, and the teacher also has conferences with students, but these conferences about rough drafts focus upon establishing content, not writing conventions. Option (D) is incorrect. Through author's chair or whole-class sharing, students experience a whole-class conference when they read aloud their writing. **(Competency 806-006 Written Language—Writing Conventions)**

46. D.

Option (D) is correct. When students can retell the events of the story, it shows literal understanding of the information read. Once students demonstrate this literal understanding, the teacher can use it to guide them to go beyond literal comprehension. Options (A), (B), and (C) are incorrect because retelling does not primarily encourage the student to think at higher levels where students infer, evaluate, or relate what they have read to their own experiences. **(Competency 806-004 Reading Comprehension and Assessment)**

47. A.

Option (A) is correct. The students need systematic instruction to learn writing conventions, but they also need opportunities to apply them in their writing. Option (B) is incorrect because students need systematic instruction rather than "discovery" learning to master writing conventions more easily. Option (C) is incorrect because writing conventions are a way of being polite to readers so they can read a text without disruptions. In addition, proficiency in writing conventions is an ingredient for success in the workplace as well as socially. Option (D) is incorrect because this choice is limited to one way of fostering spelling development, and spelling is only one part of writing conventions. Furthermore, students who have to look up a number of words can become overwhelmed and may pull back and start using only words they can spell to avoid using the dictionary. **(Competency 806-006 Written Language—Writing Conventions)**

48. C.

Option (C) is correct because a score of the 90th percentile means that 90% of the norm group performed at the same level or below the student's score. Option (A) is incorrect because the scores of a norm-referenced test provide information about how the student's achievement compares to other students at national levels. Option (B) is incorrect because a score of the 90th percentile means that 90% of the norm group performed at the same level or below the student's score, not above. Option (D) because a norm-referenced score is not based upon a students' performance in the classroom. **(Competency 806-004 Reading Comprehension and Assessment)**

49. D.

Option (D) is correct. Affixes are units of meaning—known as morphemes—added to the word to change or modify it. Some of these affixes have identifiable semantic markings that helps students understand the meaning of the word. Options (A) and (B) are incorrect because affixes include both prefixes and suffixes. Option (C) is incorrect because affixes are combined with root or base words. **(Competency 806-003 Word Identification Skills and Reading Fluency)**

50. C.

Option (C) is correct because this activity helps students learn techniques for selecting, organizing, and evaluating information from the digital environment. Option (A) is incorrect because students need guidance in learning from the video and ample time for learning new information before taking a test. Option (B) is incorrect because the teacher needs to ensure that the students view a quality video, and students need guidance in locating quality digital sources. Option (D) is incorrect because all students need to participate in reading the textbook to gain in proficiency, and teachers can provide scaffolding to support English learners so that they participate in reading a text. **(Competency 806-008 Viewing and Representing)**

51. A.

Option (A) is correct because the teacher is showing how to use context and initial letter sounds to identify an unknown word, which is an effective strategy the student can also use in other situations. Option (B) is incorrect because the word represents an irregular spelling, as do many words in English, so the strategy of "sounding out" will not work for students in many situations. Option (C) is incorrect because using structural analysis or word parts does not work for this word because *fat* is not a root word or part of a compound word in *father*. Option (D) is incorrect because the first response should be to show students how to identify unknown words so that students can be self-reliant in reading. **(Competency 806-003 Word Identification Skills and Reading Fluency)**

52. B.

Option (B) is correct because syntax pertains to how words can be combined in a language. Option (A) is incorrect because semantics pertains to the study of meaning. Option (C) is incorrect because letter-sound relationships pertain to phonics. Option (D) is incorrect because phonemes pertain to sounds of a language and how they combine. **(Competency 806-001 Oral Language)**

53. C.

Option (C) is correct. In learning to read in an alphabetic language, such as English, students learn that sounds of language are represented by letters when they read and write. Option (A) is incorrect. Letter identification is the ability to recognize letters. Option (B) is incorrect because knowing alphabetical order is not needed in learning to read although it is helpful in other ways. Option (D) is incorrect because knowing how to read and write letters is essential to make progress in reading and writing, but the alphabetic principle is understanding that we represent speech sounds through print, not by being able to identify or produce letters. **(Competency 806-002 Early Literacy Development)**

54. B.

Option (B) is correct. If students cannot use context clues to understand new vocabulary, the teacher should ensure students know how to read and understand a word. Option (A) is incorrect. The teacher is not focusing on examining the title, headings, or illustrations of text to be able to comprehend. Option (C) is incorrect because the focus of instruction is on the meaning of a word. Option (D) is incorrect because the focus of this situation is on vocabulary development, not predicting what will take place in the story. **(Competency 806-004 Reading Comprehension and Assessment)**

55. A.

Option (A) is correct. The teacher is strategically using a photo that will help students understand what they will be reading and how they may see the word in other settings. Option (B) is incorrect. The teacher is not focusing examining the title, headings, or illustrations of text to be able to comprehend. Option (C) is incorrect because the focus of instruction is on the meaning of a word, not on using sound phoneme-grapheme relationships to identify the word. Option (D) is incorrect because the focus of this situation is on vocabulary development, not on spelling. **(Competency 806-004 Reading Comprehension and Assessment)**

56. D.

Option (D) is correct. The teacher is using modeling in context to add to the other activities used to foster vocabulary development. Option (A) is incorrect. Concept maps can help students understood words and how concepts are related, but that is not what the teacher is addressing in this situation. Option (B) is incorrect. The teacher is not focusing examining the title, headings, or illustrations of text to be able to comprehend. Option (C) is incorrect because the focus of instruction is on the meaning of a word, not on informal drama. **(Competency 806-004 Reading Comprehension and Assessment)**

57. D.

Option (D) is correct because students gain in oral and written language when given the opportunity to talk about what they have read in authentic ways. Option (B) is incorrect. Teacher should make observations about students' participation to inform their teaching, but grading students is not a way to motivate students. Option (C) is incorrect because the teacher is not asking questions but rather is using retelling and discussion to enhance comprehension. Option (A) is incorrect because the students are talking in a small-group, not whole-class, situation. **(Competency 806-001 Oral Language)**

58. B.

Option (B) is correct because students profit from multiple learning experiences across several days when learning vocabulary. Option (A) is incorrect because the teacher is not helping students write in personal dictionaries in this situation. Option (C) is incorrect. Talking is effective for helping students establish content when they write, but the students are not writing in this situation. Option (D) is incorrect because in this situation, the teacher is focusing upon helping students have in-depth experiences with new vocabulary, not on talking about what took place in the story. **(Competency 806-001 Oral Language)**

59. D.

Option (D) is correct. Teachers should help students relate new concepts to what they know. Understanding the meanings of prefixes, suffixes, and root words can help students understand words independently. Option (A) is incorrect. The focus of instruction is on morphology or word parts, not phonics. Option (B) is incorrect. Research does not show that giving a vocabulary quiz helps students make gains. Option (C) is incorrect because the teacher is not focusing upon writing sentences in this situation. **(Competency 806-004 Reading Comprehension and Assessment)**

60. B.

Option (B) is correct. Students need to experience authentic reading experiences where they select books they want to read daily. Option (A) is incorrect. Students do apply and orchestrate word identification skills when reading independently, but applying phonics abilities is not the main reason for it. Option (C) is incorrect because forcing students to read specific books can be counterproductive—and creates anxiety about reading. Option (D) is incorrect because requiring students to read certain books for independent reading does not let students learn how to select books they like and see how reading can be meaningful for them. **(Competency 806-005 Reading Applications)**

61. A.

Option (A) is correct. The teacher's prompt should help students learn to use language structure (syntax), meaning (semantics), and visual cues (phonics, sight words, morphemic/structural analysis) for word identification. The student's miscue shows that the student is not using meaning cues, and the teacher is reinforcing this by asking if the miscue makes sense. Option (B) is incorrect because sounding out does not work for irregular spellings of English words, so this is not a prompt that helps students for all unknown words. Option (C) is incorrect. Teachers should not disregard a miscue because a prompt is an opportunity to help the child learn more about how to identify words. Option (D) is incorrect because the teacher's prompt should help the child learn how to identify words independently, and the teacher should tell the word only when it is apparent the child cannot figure out the unknown word even

with a prompt. **(Competency 806-002 Early Literacy Development)**

62. B.

Option (B) is correct. The teacher is showing pronouns that are singular and thus require singular verbs. Options (A) and (C) are incorrect because plural forms of nouns are not featured in these options. Option (D) is incorrect because phonemic awareness pertains to hearing words and accounting for their sounds. **(Competency 806-006 Written Language—Writing Conventions)**

63. D.

Option (D) is correct. Readers make inferences when they understand ideas that are not stated explicitly in the text. Option (A) is incorrect. Summarizing is a strategy that helps readers be aware of what is important in a text and bring together ideas, explaining text in their own words. Option (B) is incorrect. Recalling is when students tell what they remember about what they have read, which depends upon their prior knowledge of the topic and the reading level of the text being not too difficult for students to read. Option (C) is incorrect. Predicting is when readers use their prior knowledge along with information they see in the text, such as the title, to predict before reading. They then continue to predict and revise predictions based upon what the text presents. **(Competency 806-004 Reading Comprehension and Assessment)**

64. D.

Option (D) is correct. The cloze procedure can be used to determine if students can decode (identify words) and comprehend as they read. Option (A) is incorrect because helping students recognize the purpose of headings pertains to noting the organization of the information in a text. Option (B) is incorrect because the cloze procedure focuses upon understanding words being read well enough to supply a missing word from a sentence, not the way the information is organized. Option (C) is incorrect because story maps are graphic organizers. **(Competency 806-003 Word Identification Skills and Reading Fluency)**

65. C.

Option (C) is correct. Words with the same spelling—known as homographs—can be pronounced differently depending on how they are used. In the sentences provided, the highlighted words are used either as verbs or nouns. Option (A) is incorrect because the purpose of the activity is not to emphasize the use of the same word, but rather to highlight how context can change the function of words. Option (B) is incorrect because the sentences do not illustrate derivatives, but instead show differences in the pronunciation, which depends on the word's function in the sentence. Option (D) is incorrect because the word featured in each sentence is not pronounced the same way, so the students do not practice reading each word twice. **(Competency 806-005 Reading Applications)**

66. B.

Option (B) is correct because drafting is where the writer first introduces the intended content. Option (A) is incorrect because prewriting is where writers brainstorm and think about what to write before writing. Option (C) is incorrect because revising is where changes are made to refine the content. Option (D) is incorrect because editing is where proofreading takes place and the focus is on writing conventions, or the mechanics of writing, which are spelling punctuation, capitalization, and usage. **(Competency 806-007 Written Language—Composition)**

67. D.

Option (D) is correct. By sharing their writing with others, students earn a broader audience, and they see why using correct spelling, capitalization, and usage matter in developing a final draft. Options (A), (B), and (C) are incorrect. Students can engage in selecting a topic and a title as well as elaborating as part of the writing process, but this activity features publishing and shared writing. **(Competency 806-007 Written Language—Composition)**

68. B.

Option (B) is correct because the omniscient point of view lets the narrator present information otherwise unavailable to readers—about how the characters think and feel. Option (A) is incorrect because it pertains to the plot of the story. Option (C) is incorrect because it pertains to limited third-person point of view, where the author tells the story using the names of characters or third-person pronouns, such as *he*, *she*, or *they*. Option (D) pertains to the first-person point of view that uses first-person pronouns, such as *I* or *we*. **(Competency 806-005 Reading Applications)**

69. D.

Option (D) is correct. Homonyms can be confusing because they are words that are spelled the same and have the same pronunciation but have different meanings. Option (A) is incorrect because only *bark* is a word with an *r*-controlled vowel, *ar*. Option (B) is incorrect because the words adhere to phonics generalizations and common spelling patterns. The difficulty pertains to understanding the correct meanings for the same spelling of each word, so the words are commonly confused. Option (C) is incorrect because only rose is a word with an *r* in the initial position of a word. **(Competency 806-005 Reading Applications)**

70. C.

Option (C) is correct. Authors can reveal how a character looks and what a character does as well as through what other characters say about the character. Option (A) is incorrect because it pertains to the setting of the story. Option (B) is incorrect because it presents the plot of the story. Option (D) is incorrect because it presents information about the theme of the story. **(Competency 806-005 Reading Applications)**

71. C.

Option (C) is correct. Mini-lessons take place using guided instruction with the whole class; the lessons are brief demonstrations based on what students need to know. Teachers can provide further support by meeting with students in small groups. Option (A) is incorrect because during the writing part of the workshop, students and the teacher write, and the teacher also has rough-draft conferences with students. Option (B) is incorrect. Through author's chair or whole-class sharing, students experience a whole-class conference when they read aloud what they've written. Option (D) is incorrect. In proofreading/publishing conferences, students learn to proofread to develop a final draft that will be read by others. **(Competency 806-007 Written Language—Composition)**

72. A.

Option (A) is correct. When emergent readers read with the teacher and track print, they gain in concepts of print, such as knowing that print carries the message and that words are separated by white spaces. Students also learn that print moves left to right and top to bottom in English. Option (B) is incorrect because previewing is a strategy for comprehension that takes place before reading. Option (C) is incorrect because the students are not being shown how to monitor their comprehension or to check that they are comprehending what they are reading. Option (D) is incorrect because reciprocal teaching is a strategy where students work in small groups and assume roles to understand and learn material they read. **(Competency 806-002 Early Literacy Development)**

73. D.

Option (D) is correct because research does not show that tests foster vocabulary development because students often forget the meanings of words and gain a superficial understanding when memorizing definitions. Options (A), (B), and (C) describe instruction that is effective to help students gain in vocabulary development. **(Competency 806-004 Reading Comprehension and Assessment)**

74. D.

Option (D) is correct. ELs (and other students) might not benefit from the definitions provided in dictionaries because of the wording not being clear to them. Options (A), (B), and (C) are ways to develop students' language mastery in effective ways while also making it possible for English learners to participate in subject-matter learning. **(Competency 806-001 Oral Language)**

TExES Core Subjects 4–8 Practice Test 1: Mathematics (807)

This practice test plus an additional test are available at the online REA Study Center (*www.rea.com/studycenter*).

The TExES Core Subjects Mathematics (807) test is computer-based, so we strongly recommend that you take our online practice tests to simulate test-day conditions and to receive these added benefits:

- **Timed testing conditions**—Gauge how much time you can spend on each question.

- **Automatic scoring**—Find out how you did on the test, instantly.

- **On-screen detailed explanations of answers**—Learn not just the correct answer, but also why the other answers are incorrect.

- **Diagnostic score reports**—Pinpoint where you're strongest and where you need to focus your study.

Mathematics Practice Test 1: Answer Sheet

1. Ⓐ Ⓑ Ⓒ Ⓓ
2. Ⓐ Ⓑ Ⓒ Ⓓ
3. Ⓐ Ⓑ Ⓒ Ⓓ
4. Ⓐ Ⓑ Ⓒ Ⓓ
5. Ⓐ Ⓑ Ⓒ Ⓓ
6. Ⓐ Ⓑ Ⓒ Ⓓ
7. Ⓐ Ⓑ Ⓒ Ⓓ
8. Ⓐ Ⓑ Ⓒ Ⓓ
9. Ⓐ Ⓑ Ⓒ Ⓓ
10. Ⓐ Ⓑ Ⓒ Ⓓ
11. Ⓐ Ⓑ Ⓒ Ⓓ
12. Ⓐ Ⓑ Ⓒ Ⓓ
13. Ⓐ Ⓑ Ⓒ Ⓓ
14. Ⓐ Ⓑ Ⓒ Ⓓ

15. Ⓐ Ⓑ Ⓒ Ⓓ
16. Ⓐ Ⓑ Ⓒ Ⓓ
17. Ⓐ Ⓑ Ⓒ Ⓓ
18. Ⓐ Ⓑ Ⓒ Ⓓ
19. Ⓐ Ⓑ Ⓒ Ⓓ
20. Ⓐ Ⓑ Ⓒ Ⓓ
21. Ⓐ Ⓑ Ⓒ Ⓓ
22. Ⓐ Ⓑ Ⓒ Ⓓ
23. Ⓐ Ⓑ Ⓒ Ⓓ
24. Ⓐ Ⓑ Ⓒ Ⓓ
25. Ⓐ Ⓑ Ⓒ Ⓓ
26. Ⓐ Ⓑ Ⓒ Ⓓ
27. Ⓐ Ⓑ Ⓒ Ⓓ
28. Ⓐ Ⓑ Ⓒ Ⓓ

29. Ⓐ Ⓑ Ⓒ Ⓓ
30. Ⓐ Ⓑ Ⓒ Ⓓ
31. Ⓐ Ⓑ Ⓒ Ⓓ
32. Ⓐ Ⓑ Ⓒ Ⓓ
33. Ⓐ Ⓑ Ⓒ Ⓓ
34. Ⓐ Ⓑ Ⓒ Ⓓ
35. Ⓐ Ⓑ Ⓒ Ⓓ
36. Ⓐ Ⓑ Ⓒ Ⓓ
37. Ⓐ Ⓑ Ⓒ Ⓓ Ⓔ Ⓕ
38. Ⓐ Ⓑ Ⓒ Ⓓ
39. Ⓐ Ⓑ Ⓒ Ⓓ
40. Ⓐ Ⓑ Ⓒ Ⓓ
41. Ⓐ Ⓑ Ⓒ Ⓓ
42. Ⓐ Ⓑ Ⓒ Ⓓ

Practice Test 1: Mathematics

TIME: 1 hour and 5 minutes
42 questions

> **Directions:** Read each item and select the best answer. Most items on this test require you to provide the one best answer. However, some questions require you to select all the options that apply.

1. The flu hit Star Elementary School very badly one week. The administration determined that 90 out of 360 students were absent that week. What percentage of students were present?

   A. 25%

   B. 90%

   C. 75%

   D. 40%

2. Nancy is 3 years older than Doug. Kim is 4 years younger than Doug. Nancy is 12 years old. How old are Doug and Kim?

   A. Doug is 8 and Kim is 5

   B. Doug is 9 and Kim is 4

   C. Doug is 9 and Kim is 5

   D. Doug is 8 and Kim is 4

3. Add the following fractions: $\dfrac{2}{3} + \dfrac{3}{5} + \dfrac{5}{6}$.

   A. $\dfrac{5}{7}$

   B. $1\dfrac{9}{10}$

   C. $2\dfrac{1}{30}$

   D. $2\dfrac{1}{10}$

4. The test scores from two different classes are shown below.

   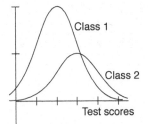

   If the scores for each class are normally distributed, which of the following statements is true?

   A. The mean score for class 1 is greater than the mean score for class 2.

   B. The median score for class 2 is greater than the median score for class 1.

   C. The mode for class 2 is less than the mode for class 1.

   D. The standard deviation for class 1 is much larger than for class 2.

5. Find the equation of the line with x-intercept $\dfrac{1}{2}$ and y-intercept $-\dfrac{1}{2}$.

   A. $y = -x$

   B. $2x + 2y = 0$

   C. $2x + 2y = 1$

   D. $2x - 2y = 1$

6. Jaxson's rectangular sandbox has a perimeter of 34 feet. The length of the sandbox is 9 feet. What is the width of the sandbox?

   A. 16 feet

   B. 9 feet

   C. 8 feet

   D. 72 feet

7. Which of the following statements is true?

   A. All quadrilaterals are squares.

   B. All rectangles are squares.

   C. A square is also a rhombus.

   D. Not all trapezoids are quadrilaterals.

8. Given the following tables of function values, which could NOT be a quadratic function?

   A.

x	$f(x)$
0	1
1	2
2	5
3	10

   B.

x	$f(x)$
0	1
1	4
2	7
3	10

   C.

x	$f(x)$
0	1
1	2
2	4
3	7

   D.

x	$f(x)$
0	–4
1	–1
2	0
3	–1

9. In a triangle PQR the measure of angle PQR is 60°, and the measure of angle QRP is 75°. What is the measure of angle RQP and what type of triangle is it?

   A. 60°, acute triangle

   B. 120°, obtuse triangle

   C. 90°, right triangle

   D. 45°, acute triangle

10. A right circular cone has radius 3 inches and height 6 inches. If the radius doubles and the height is halved, what is the percent change of the cone's new volume compared to its original volume?

   A. 100%

   B. 50%

   C. 200%

   D. 0%

11. Using the following right triangle, find the value of $\dfrac{\sin\theta - \cos\theta}{\tan\theta}$.

   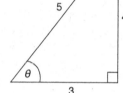

   A. $\dfrac{15}{4}$

   B. $\dfrac{4}{15}$

   C. $\dfrac{3}{20}$

   D. $\dfrac{20}{3}$

12. Which of the following was the advocate of Social Constructivism?

   A. Piaget

   B. Vygotsky

   C. Bruner

   D. Einstein

13. Find the mode for the following stem leaf plot:

   1: 2 2 3
   2: 5 6 6
   4: 7 8
   5: 1 3 5

   A. 26

   B. 12

   C. 12, 26

   D. None

14. Wayne is randomly pulling out golf balls from a bag which contains 3 Nike balls, 5 Srixon balls and 6 Titleist balls. What is the probability that he will pull out a Titleist ball?

   A. $\dfrac{3}{14}$

   B. $\dfrac{3}{7}$

   C. $\dfrac{3}{4}$

   D. $\dfrac{1}{2}$

15. Using the point-slope formula, find the slope of a line passing through the points (5, 4) and (–1, 3).

   A. $\dfrac{1}{6}$

   B. $\dfrac{4}{7}$

   C. $-\dfrac{1}{6}$

   D. $\dfrac{1}{4}$

16. Which of the following is NOT a philosophy of differentiated instruction?

   A. Students work in groups that change membership to discuss problem solving strategies.

   B. Students are given choices in their reading and writing assignments.

   C. The entire class gets the same exam on a subject.

   D. A focus on big ideas when teaching.

17. Triangular flashcards can be used to help with what concept(s)?

   A. Place value

   B. Multiplication and Division

   C. Addition and Subtraction

   D. Both B and C

18. A deck consists of 1 orange, 3 blue, 1 green, 2 yellow, and 3 purple cards. If two cards are chosen randomly from the deck without replacing the first, find the probability P of both of them being purple.

   A. 6.7%

   B. 9.5%

   C. 22.2%

   D. 52.2%

19. What is the prime factorization of 280?

   A. $2^2 \times 5 \times 14$

   B. $2^3 \times 5 \times 10$

   C. $2^3 \times 5 \times 7$

   D. $2^2 \times 5 \times 7$

20. Five runners are competing in a 50-yard dash. If there are not any ties, how many different combinations are possible for a first, second, and third place?

   A. 15

   B. 20

   C. 120

   D. 60

21. In a middle school math class, students have begun activities exploring area relationships among rectangles, triangles, parallelograms, and trapezoids. The classroom teacher wants to identify any aspects of the content that challenges the students in order to adjust future lessons on this topic. Which of the following assessment methods would be most appropriate for achieving this goal?

   A. Regular observation and interviews between teacher and student

   B. Periodic peer review of partner work

   C. Pretest and posttest

   D. Pop quizzes after future lessons

22. The price of a bicycle was reduced from $60 to $45. By what percentage was the price of the bike reduced?

    A. 25%

    B. 15%

    C. 33.3%

    D. 40%

23. Kirk is driving on a highway whose speed limit is 60 mph. He passes a police car traveling at 50 mph. There is a speed trap set up and 2.5 miles down the road, he passes another police car 2 minutes after he passed the first police car. He is traveling at 50 mph when he passes the second police officer as well. The officers radio each other and discuss Kirk. What should they decide?

    A. He gets a ticket because he definitely was speeding.

    B. He gets a warning because he probably was speeding.

    C. He does not get a ticket because he definitely was not speeding.

    D. He is not stopped because there is not enough evidence to determine whether he was speeding.

24. How many ways can all the letters in the word "HAPPINESS" be arranged to form a sequence of 9 letters?

    A. 362,880

    B. 45

    C. 90,720

    D. 181,550

25. A net of a three-dimensional solid appears below. What is the volume of the solid?

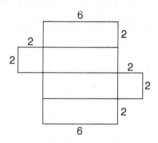

    A. 12

    B. 24

    C. 48

    D. 56

26. Given the graph of the function $f(x)$, what would be the result of graphing $-f(x)$?

    A. Reflects the graph of $f(x)$ across the x-axis

    B. Reflects the graph of $f(x)$ across the y-axis

    C. Shifts $f(x)$ down vertically

    D. Shifts $f(x)$ to the left horizontally

27. A deck of cards has numbers 1 through 10. It is shuffled completely. Which of the following represents a binomial experiment problem?

    A. A card is chosen and not replaced and then another card is chosen. What is the probability of choosing two even numbers?

    B. A card is chosen and replaced and then another card is chosen. What is the probability of choosing two even numbers?

    C. A card is chosen and whether it is even is noted. It is not replaced and another card is chosen. We stop when two even cards have been chosen. We are interested in the average number of cards necessary to get two even cards.

    D. A card is chosen and whether it is even is noted. It is replaced and another card is chosen. We stop when two even cards have been chosen. We are interested in the average number of cards necessary to get two even cards.

28. The graph of $f(x)$ is shown below.

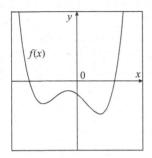

Determine how many of the features the graph has.

	Relative Minimum	Relative Maximum	Absolute Minimum	Absolute Maximum
A.	1	1	Yes	No
B.	1	2	No	No
C.	2	1	Yes	No
D.	2	1	Yes	Yes

29. A teacher asked one set of students to write $y = 3x^2 - 6x + 4$ in standard form while another teacher asked students to graph $y = 3x^2 - 6x + 4$ and report what they see. This is an example of:

A. passive task vs. active task

B. specific task vs. parallel task

C. closed task vs. open task

D. flawed approach vs. effective approach

30. In order to measure the top wind speed of a hurricane, a special plane is needed to fly over the eye of the hurricane. The plane travels over the eye of Hurricane Jay at random times and samples the maximum wind speed. It finds that the maximum wind speed averages 105 mph with a margin of error of 7.5 mph for 95% confidence. Interpret the meaning of this.

A. 95% of the samples had maximum wind speed between 90 mph and 120 mph.

B. We are 95% confident that the maximum wind speed of Jay is between 90 mph and 120 mph.

C. The probability that the maximum wind speed of Jay is between 90 mph and 120 mph is 95%.

D. 95% of hurricanes have a maximum wind speed between 90 mph and 120 mph.

31. Which definition is incorrect?

A. Variable—a letter that represents an unknown number.

B. Exponent—the number of times a number is multiplied by itself

C. Factor of a number—another number that divides into the original number

D. All are correct

32. A number of cruises were sampled with a scatter plot made measuring the length of the cruise in days compared to the cost of the cruise using the same type of accommodations in thousands of dollars. A line of best fit is drawn. A new cruise is added that lasts 7 days and costs $6,000. If the line of best fit is redrawn, how will the relationship between the length of the cruise and the cost change?

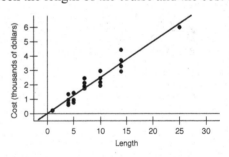

A. It will become less strong.

B. It will become stronger.

C. It will become negative.

D. No real change.

33. If triangle $A'B'C'$ is obtained when triangle ABC shown below is reflected over the line $x = 1$, which of the following would be the location of point B'?

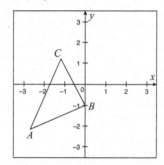

   A. $(0, -1)$

   B. $(1, -1)$

   C. $(2, -1)$

   D. $(1, 0)$

34. The size of a TV is measured by the distance of its diagonal from top left to bottom right. Larry purchased a new television for his family room. The base of the television is 35 inches and its height is 18 inches. What is the size of the television? Round to the nearest inch.

   A.   39 inches

   B.   53 inches

   C.   70 inches

   D.   106 inches

35. During a game of Expanded Form, Parker gave the following clues for his partners to figure out his number:

- The value of the digit 6 is (6×10)
- The value of the digit 5 is (5×100)
- The value of the digit 9 is $\left(9 \times \dfrac{1}{100}\right)$

Which number could fit Parker's description?

   A.   560.9

   B.   568.092

   C.   1,562.009

   D.   65.909

36. A teacher wants to demonstrate to students how to determine the total possible number of sundaes that can be made from 3 flavors of ice cream, 3 sauces, and 2 toppings, where a sundae is comprised of one flavor of ice cream with or without one sauce, and with or without one topping. Select the most effective method(s) to reach all learners.

   A.   Use the Multiplication Principle: Total sundaes = 3(3)(2) = 18

   B.   Use a tree diagram to list all possible combinations

   C.   Both of the above

   D.   Neither of the above

37. $f(x) = \left| 2^x - x^3 \right|$ is evaluated at certain values of x. Which of the following values of $f(x)$ are odd? Select *all* that apply.

   A. $x = 0$

   B. $x = 1$

   C. $x = 2$

   D. $x = 3$

   E. $x = 4$

   F. $x = 5$

38. Which of the following is an example of a formative assessment? Select *all* that apply.

   A.   A math teacher randomly checks several homework problems.

   B.   A math teacher gives a quiz after every topic that was taught.

   C.   A math teacher has students go to the board to show their solution to a problem.

   D.   A math teacher gives a final exam in geometry.

39. A bag of mulch covers 150 feet². Juan has a garden whose shape is a rectangle with a semicircle as shown at right. If he spreads mulch over the entire garden, how many bags must he purchase?

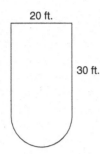

20 ft.

30 ft.

 A. 4

 B. 5

 C. 6

 D. 7

40. In isosceles triangle *PQR*, angle *P* measures 64° which represents the largest angular measurement in the triangle. What is the measure of angle *Q*?

 A. 116°

 B. 52°

 C. 58°

 D. Impossible to say

41. Express the number 0.00000008 • 3,200,000 in scientific notation.

 A. 2.56×10^{-3}

 B. 2.56×10^{-2}

 C. 2.56×10^{-1}

 D. 2.56×10^{0}

42. Which of the following is a list of prime numbers?

 A. 3, 5, 23, 33

 B. 1, 7, 13, 19

 C. 2, 17, 23, 51

 D. 5, 31, 53, 97

Mathematics Practice Test 1: Answer Key

Test Item	Answer	Competency 807-
1.	C	001
2.	C	016
3.	D	002
4.	B	012
5.	D	005
6.	C	009
7.	C	015
8.	B	006
9.	D	009
10.	A	010
11.	C	008
12.	B	017
13.	C	012
14.	B	013
15.	A	005
16.	C	018
17.	D	017
18.	A	013
19.	C	003
20.	D	003
21.	A	019

Test Item	Answer	Competency 807-
22.	A	004
23.	A	007
24.	C	003
25.	B	010
26.	A	011
27.	B	014
28.	C	007
29.	C	018
30.	B	014
31.	B	004
32.	A	012
33.	C	011
34.	A	008
35.	B	001
36.	B	016
37.	A, B, D, F	006
38.	A, B, C	019
39.	C	009
40.	D	015
41.	C	002
42.	D	002

Mathematics Practice Test 1: Detailed Answers

1. C.

$\dfrac{90}{360} = \dfrac{1}{4} = 25\%$. This is the percentage of students absent. Therefore, 75% were present. **(Competency 807-001: Teacher understands the structure of number systems.)**

2. C.

If Nancy is 12, then Doug is 3 years younger than 12, which is 9, and Kim is 4 years younger than Doug (9), which is 5. **(Competency 807-016: Teacher understands mathematical connections within and outside math.)**

3. D.

A lowest common denominator must be found, which is 30. All fractions must be multiplied by the fraction equivalent to 1 which gets the LCD.

$\dfrac{2}{3}\left(\dfrac{10}{10}\right) + \dfrac{3}{5}\left(\dfrac{6}{6}\right) + \dfrac{5}{6}\left(\dfrac{5}{5}\right) = \dfrac{20 + 18 + 25}{30} = \dfrac{63}{30} = \dfrac{21}{10} = 2\dfrac{1}{10}.$

Note that this can also be done using a common denominator of 90. **(Competency 807-002: Teacher understands number systems and computational algorithms.)**

4. B.

For mean and median, we are not concerned with the height of the curve which gives the frequency of each score. We are interested in the test score where the height of the curve is the highest. With normal distributions, the mean and median are the same and it is clear that the median for class 2 is greater than that of class 1. Without seeing the data scores, we have no idea what the mode is. The same is true for standard deviation but the fact that both classes seem to show the entirety of their curves in about 5 units along the axis is an indication that their standard deviations are very similar. **(Competency 807-012:**

Teacher understands exploring data through graphical and numerical processes.)

5. D.

The points are $\left(\dfrac{1}{2}, 0\right)$ and $\left(0, -\dfrac{1}{2}\right)$. The slope m of the line is given by $m = \dfrac{\frac{-1}{2} - 0}{0 - \frac{1}{2}} = 1$. Using the point-slope equation $y - y_1 = m(x - x_1)$, substitute either point: $y + \dfrac{1}{2} = 1(x - 0)$. Multiplying each side by 2, we get $2y + 1 = 2x$ or $2x - 2y = 1$. An easier way is to substitute these points into all choices and see which one is true. **(Competency 807-005: Teacher understands linear functions.)**

6. C.

The perimeter formula for a rectangle is $P = 2L + 2W$. Therefore, $34 = 18 + 2W$ so $2W = 16$ and $W = 8$ feet. **(Competency 807-009: Teacher understands geometric relationships and formulas.)**

7. C.

A rhombus has four sides all the same length and is considered a square when all four angles are 90°. **(Competency 807-015: Teacher understands mathematical reasoning to solve problems.)**

8. B.

Investigate each table. Quadratic equations do not have a linear relationship; therefore, there is not a constant rate of change between the y- and x-values. Option (B) is correct because the table shows a linear relationship. The y-values increase by 3 units for every 1-unit increase in the x-values. Hence the slope of the line is 3. Note that in Option (A), the y-values increase by 1, then 3, then 5. If this pattern is continued, the points form a quadratic function. The same is true in Option (C) as the y-values increase by consecutive integers 1, 2, and 3. Choice (D) is slightly different as the y-values increase by 3 and then 1. At that point, they decrease by 1. This signals a quadratic that reaches its high point at $x = 2$. This analysis is not necessary, though. Once choice (B) is determined as linear, it has to be the correct answer. **(Competency 807-006: Teacher understands non-linear functions.)**

9. D.

The angles in a triangle add to 180°. Therefore, $180 - 75 - 60 = 45°$. Since all of the angles are less than 90°, the triangle is acute. **(Competency 807-009: Teacher uses geometric relationships.)**

10. A.

$$V = \frac{1}{3}\pi r^2 h.$$

$$V_{\text{original}} = \frac{1}{3}\pi\left(3^2\right)\left(6\right) = 18\pi$$

$$V_{\text{new}} = \frac{1}{3}\pi\left(6^2\right)\left(3\right) = 36\pi$$

Change $= 36\pi - 18\pi = 18\pi$.

Percent change $= 100\%\left(\dfrac{V_{\text{change}}}{V_{\text{original}}}\right) = \dfrac{18\pi}{18\pi} = 100\%$.

(Competency 807-010: Teacher understands two- and three-dimensional figures.)

11. C.

$$\sin\theta = \frac{\text{opposite}}{\text{hypotenuse}}$$

$$\cos\theta = \frac{\text{adjacent}}{\text{hypotenuse}}$$

$$\tan\theta = \frac{\text{opposite}}{\text{adjacent}}$$

$$\frac{\sin\theta - \cos\theta}{\tan\theta} = \frac{\frac{4}{5} - \frac{3}{5}}{\frac{4}{3}} = \frac{1}{5} \bullet \frac{3}{4} = \frac{3}{20}$$

(Competency 807-008: Teacher understands the use of measurement.)

12. B.

Vygotsky extended Piaget's theories to include social interactions for increased student understanding. **(Competency 807-017: Teacher understands how children learn.)**

13. C.

12, 26. A stem and leaf plot is read where the first number of the line is the stem (tens or hundreds place) and the following numbers are the ones place. Therefore, Line 5, for example, shows: 51, 53, 55, as the data. There are two 12's and two 26's, so therefore those are the mode. There can be more than one mode. **(Competency 807-12: Teacher understands exploring data through graphical and numerical processes.)**

14. B.

The total number of balls is 14 and the number of Titleist balls is 6. $\dfrac{6}{14}$ reduces to $\dfrac{3}{7}$. **(Competency 807-013: Teacher understands the use of probability.)**

15. A.

The slope of a line is given by $m = \dfrac{y_1 - y_2}{x_1 - x_2} = \dfrac{4 - 3}{5 - (-1)} = \dfrac{1}{6}$. **(Competency 807-005: Teacher understands linear functions.)**

16. C.

Choices (A), (B), and (D) are hallmarks of differentiated instruction. Choice (C) is probably necessary in a math class, but it isn't differentiated instruction. **(Competency 807-018: Teacher understands planning, organizing and implementing instruction.)**

17. D.

Factors and products are given for Multiplication and Division with three numbers, as are the addends and sums for Addition and Subtraction with three numbers. **(Competency 807-017: Teacher understands how children learn.)**

18.　A.

There are 10 cards and 3 are purple. The probability of the first card being purple is $\frac{3}{10}$. For the second card, there are 9 cards remaining and 2 are purple. So, the probability of the second card being purple after you chose a purple card is $\frac{2}{9}$. Both events must happen, so multiply the probabilities. $P = \frac{3}{10}\left(\frac{2}{9}\right) = \frac{6}{90} = \frac{1}{15} = 6.67\%$. This can also be done using combinations: $P = \frac{{}_3C_2}{{}_{10}C_2} = \frac{3}{45} = \frac{1}{15} = 6.67\%$. **(Competency 807-013: Teacher understand the theory of probability.)**

19.　C.

$2^3 \times 5 \times 7 = 8 \times 5 \times 7 = 280$. Choice (A) = 280, but 14 is a composite number. Choice (B) = 400 and 10 is a composite number. Choice (D) = 140, although all factors are prime. **(Competency 807-003: Teacher understands number theory.)**

20.　D.

Any one of the 5 runners has the possibility of finishing first, which leaves 4 possible second-place finishers and 3 possible third-place finishers. Using the multiplication rule, there are 5(4)(3) = 60 possible combinations of how a runner may finish. Note that the word *combination* is used colloquially. Since order counts, we are calculating permutations. **(Competency 807-003: Teacher understands number theory.)**

21.　A.

Frequent observation and interviewing students during observation provide a quick, informal opportunity to judge the progress of student learning, and then allows the teacher to decide whether adjustments to the lesson are necessary. Choice (B) is incorrect because periodic peer reviews of partner work will not allow the teacher to make adjustments to lessons early in a unit. Choice (C) is incorrect because a pretest will provide a teacher with information to plan lessons and a posttest shows what students know at the end of the unit. These types of assessments do not allow for adjustment during the lessons. Choice (D) is incorrect since the quizzes would occur after future lessons, and the adjustments need to happen before future lessons. **(Competency 807-019: Teacher understands assessment techniques.)**

22.　A.

Percentage reduction = $\frac{\text{amount reduction}}{\text{original price}} = \frac{60-45}{60} = \frac{15}{60} = \frac{1}{4} = 25\%$. **(Competency 807-004: Teacher understands mathematical reasoning to identify patterns.)**

23.　A.

This is a calculus problem in disguise. Kirk's average speed is $\frac{\text{total distance}}{\text{total time}} = \frac{2.5 \text{ miles}}{2 \text{ minutes}}$. Multiplying both numerator and denominator by 30 give 75 miles in 60 minutes or 75 mph. If Kirk averaged 75 mph in the 2 minutes, at some point in time he was traveling 75 mph despite his speed when passing the police cars. They are justified in giving him a ticket. **(Competency 807-007: Teacher understands the foundations of calculus.)**

24.　C.

Since "HAPPINESS" has 9 letters and two sets of double letters, the answer may be found by computing $\frac{9!}{2!2!} = \frac{9(8)(7)(6)(5)(4)(3)(2)(1)}{(2)(1)(2)(1)} = \frac{362880}{4} = 90720$. **(Competency 807-003: Teacher understands number theory.)**

25.　B.

The three-dimensional figure would be a rectangular prism that is 6 by 2 by 2. Its volume is 24.

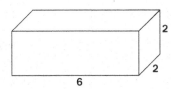

(Competency 807-010: Teacher understands two- and three-dimensional figures.)

26. A.

For instance, if $f(2) = 4, -f(2) = -4$. All points above the x-axis would shift below the x-axis and vice versa. **(Competency 807-011: Teacher understands the coordinate system and transformation.)**

27. B.

In a binomial experiment, every trial must have 2 outcomes: success or failure. For all 4 choices, an even card denotes success. There must be a fixed number of trials. That is not true for Choices (C) and (D) as we only stop choosing cards when 2 even cards have been chosen. The probabilities of success or failure must be the same for each trial. That is not true in choice (A). The probability of choosing an even number is initially $\frac{5}{10} = \frac{1}{2}$. If an even number is chosen, since the card is not replaced, the probability of an even number on the second pick is $\frac{4}{9}$. In choice (B), since the card is replaced, the probability remains at $\frac{1}{2}$. **(Competency 807-014: Teacher understands sampling and statistical inference.)**

28. C.

A relative minimum is the bottom of a hill, and the graph has 2 of them. A relative maximum is the top of a hill and the graph has 1 of them. The curve has an absolute minimum if it has a lowest point, and this curve does. (Note that a relative minimum can also be an absolute minimum). The curve has an absolute maximum if it has a highest point. This curve does not as it goes up to infinity on both sides. **(Competency 807-007: Teacher understands the foundations of calculus.)**

29. C.

Writing the equation in standard form $y - 1 = 3(x - 1)^2$ tells the basic algebra student the vertex and if s/he doesn't know what standard form is, nothing can be done. This is a closed task. Asking them to graph it will tell them the vertex, how it opens, its width, and possibly its roots. This is an example of an open task where many pieces of information can be found. **(Competency 807-018: Teacher understands planning, organizing and implementing instruction.)**

30. B.

In this confidence interval, 95% of the data lies within the margin of error from the mean: $105 \pm 15 = 90$ to 120 mph. We are interested in the maximum wind speed of Jay, which is unknown. Choice (A) is incorrect as it makes no statement about this unknown top wind speed. Choice (C) is incorrect because the maximum wind speed of Jay is either between 90 mph or 120 mph or it isn't. Choice (D) is incorrect because the study is only about Jay. Choice (B) is the correct interpretation because based on the sample, we are willing to say that we are reasonably sure of the range of the maximum winds. **(Competency 807-014: Teacher understands sampling and statistical inference.)**

31. B.

The definition of an exponent is not quite correct. Since $3^2 = 3(3)$, the exponent 2 means 3 is multiplied by itself once and not twice. Since $3^3 = 3(3)(3)$, the exponent 3 means that 3 is multiplied by itself twice. **(Competency 807-004: Teacher understands mathematical reasoning to identify patterns.)**

32. A.

There is already a fairly strong positive relationship between length of cruise and cost (as length goes up, cost goes up) because the line of best fit is close to most of the points and it goes up to the right. This new point will be in the upper left. It acts as a magnet and the line of best fit will still go up to the right, meaning that there still is a positive relationship, but not as strong. **(Competency 807-012: Teacher understands data through graphical and numerical techniques.)**

33. C.

Reflecting triangle ABC across the line $x = 1$ will preserve the y-values but will change the x-values. Point B is at $(0, -1)$ which is a distance of 1 unit left of the point $(1, -1)$ so B' will be one unit to the right of $(1, -1)$ or $(2, -1)$. **(Competency 807-011: Teacher understands the coordinate system and transformation.)**

34. A.

This is solved by the Pythagorean Theorem.

$$c^2 = a^2 + b^2 \Rightarrow c^2 = 18^2 + 35^2 = 1549 \Rightarrow$$

$$c = \sqrt{1549} \approx 39.4 \text{ inches}$$

(Competency 807-008: Teacher understands the use of measurement to solve problems.)

35. B.

This is the only number in which the digits are in the correct place. **(Competency 807-001: Teacher understands the structure of number systems.)**

36. B.

The multiplication principle is true but the number of sundaes = 3(4)(3) = 36 as no sauce is a possibility as well as no topping. With differentiated instruction, a teacher should use a variety of methods to reach all learners. **(Competency 807-016: Teacher understands mathematical connections within and outside math.)**

37. A., B., D., F.

$$f(0) = \left|2^0 - 0^3\right| = \left|1 - 0\right| = \left|1\right| = 1 \text{ (odd)}$$

$$f(1) = \left|2^1 - 1^3\right| = \left|2 - 1\right| = \left|1\right| = 1 \text{ (odd)}$$

$$f(2) = \left|2^2 - 2^3\right| = \left|4 - 8\right| = \left|-4\right| = 4 \text{ (even)}$$

$$f(3) = \left|2^3 - 3^3\right| = \left|8 - 27\right| = \left|-19\right| = 19 \text{ (odd)}$$

$$f(4) = \left|2^4 - 4^3\right| = \left|16 - 64\right| = \left|-48\right| = 48 \text{ (even)}$$

$$f(5) = \left|2^5 - 5^3\right| = \left|32 - 125\right| = \left|-93\right| = 93 \text{ (odd)}$$

(Competency 807-006: Teacher understands non-linear functions.)

38. A., B., C.

A formative assessment is a regularly planned checkup of student progress. Options (A), (B), and (C) fit this description while (D) is a summative assessment that generates a single score and shows what students know and learned over time. **(Competency 807-019: Teacher understands assessment techniques.)**

39. C.

The area of the garden is $20(30) + \frac{1}{2}\pi(10^2) =$ $600 + 157.08 = 757.08 \text{ ft}^2$. $\frac{757.08}{150} = 5.05$ bags, so he must purchase 6 bags. **(Competency 807-009: Teacher understands geometric relationships.)**

40. D.

The sum of the angles of a triangle is 180°. Subtracting 64° from 180° leaves 116° to be split evenly among Angles Q and R. So, each angle equals 58°. But it is possible that angle Q also equals 64° (which doesn't violate the terms of the problem). That would make angle R equal to 52°. So, there are two triangles that fit the criteria. **(Competency 807-015: Teacher understands mathematical reasoning to solve problems.)**

41. C.

$$0.00000008 = 8 \times 10^{-8}$$

$$3,200,000 = 3.2 \times 10^6$$

$$8 \times 10^{-8} \times 3.2 \times 10^6 = 25.6 \times 10^{-2} =$$

$$2.56 \times 10^1 \times 10^{-2} = 2.56 \times 10^{-1}$$

(Competency 807-002: Teacher understands number systems and computational algorithms.)

42. D.

Option (A) is incorrect because 33 is composite, choice (B) is incorrect because 1 is neither prime nor composite, and choice (C) is incorrect because 51 is a composite number. The numbers listed for choice (D) are all prime numbers. **(Competency 807-002: Teacher understands number systems and computational algorithms.)**

TExES Core Subjects 4–8 Practice Test 1: Social Studies (808)

This practice test plus an additional test are also available at the online REA Study Center *(www.rea.com/studycenter)*.

The TExES Core Subjects Social Studies (808) test is computer-based, so we strongly recommend that you take our online practice tests to simulate test-day conditions and to receive these added benefits:

- **Timed testing conditions**—Gauge how much time you can spend on each question.

- **Automatic scoring**—Find out how you did on the test, instantly.

- **On-screen detailed explanations of answers**—Learn not just the correct answer, but also why the other answers are incorrect.

- **Diagnostic score reports**—Pinpoint where you're strongest and where you need to focus your study.

Social Studies Practice Test 1: Answer Sheet

1. Ⓐ Ⓑ Ⓒ Ⓓ
2. Ⓐ Ⓑ Ⓒ Ⓓ
3. Ⓐ Ⓑ Ⓒ Ⓓ
4. Ⓐ Ⓑ Ⓒ Ⓓ
5. Ⓐ Ⓑ Ⓒ Ⓓ
6. Ⓐ Ⓑ Ⓒ Ⓓ
7. Ⓐ Ⓑ Ⓒ Ⓓ
8. Ⓐ Ⓑ Ⓒ Ⓓ
9. Ⓐ Ⓑ Ⓒ Ⓓ
10. Ⓐ Ⓑ Ⓒ Ⓓ
11. Ⓐ Ⓑ Ⓒ Ⓓ
12. Ⓐ Ⓑ Ⓒ Ⓓ
13. Ⓐ Ⓑ Ⓒ Ⓓ Ⓔ
14. Ⓐ Ⓑ Ⓒ Ⓓ

15. Ⓐ Ⓑ Ⓒ Ⓓ
16. Ⓐ Ⓑ Ⓒ Ⓓ
17. Ⓐ Ⓑ Ⓒ Ⓓ
18. Ⓐ Ⓑ Ⓒ Ⓓ
19. Ⓐ Ⓑ Ⓒ Ⓓ
20. Ⓐ Ⓑ Ⓒ Ⓓ
21. Ⓐ Ⓑ Ⓒ Ⓓ
22. Ⓐ Ⓑ Ⓒ Ⓓ
23. Ⓐ Ⓑ Ⓒ Ⓓ
24. Ⓐ Ⓑ Ⓒ Ⓓ
25. Ⓐ Ⓑ Ⓒ Ⓓ
26. Ⓐ Ⓑ Ⓒ Ⓓ
27. Ⓐ Ⓑ Ⓒ Ⓓ
28. Ⓐ Ⓑ Ⓒ Ⓓ

29. Ⓐ Ⓑ Ⓒ Ⓓ
30. Ⓐ Ⓑ Ⓒ Ⓓ
31. Ⓐ Ⓑ Ⓒ Ⓓ
32. Ⓐ Ⓑ Ⓒ Ⓓ
33. Ⓐ Ⓑ Ⓒ Ⓓ
34. Ⓐ Ⓑ Ⓒ Ⓓ
35. Ⓐ Ⓑ Ⓒ Ⓓ
36. Ⓐ Ⓑ Ⓒ Ⓓ
37. Ⓐ Ⓑ Ⓒ Ⓓ
38. Ⓐ Ⓑ Ⓒ Ⓓ
39. Ⓐ Ⓑ Ⓒ Ⓓ
40. Ⓐ Ⓑ Ⓒ Ⓓ
41. Ⓐ Ⓑ Ⓒ Ⓓ
42. Ⓐ Ⓑ Ⓒ Ⓓ

Practice Test 1: Social Studies

TIME: 50 minutes
        42 questions

> **Directions:** Read each item and select the best answer. Most items on this test require you to provide the one best answer. However, some questions require you to select all the options that apply.

1. Which of the following best describes the impact of Spindletop in Texas?

    A. Instrumental in moving Texas from an agrarian-based economy into the industrial age

    B. Major environmental disaster in 1901 that damaged grazing land and the beef industry

    C. Innovative amusement attraction that launched the tourist industry

    D. Caused a mass influx of prospectors that increased the Hispanic population

2. A globe is a scale model of the Earth shaped like a sphere. A globe shows sizes and shapes more accurately than which of the following?

    A. Compass rose

    B. Map

    C. Scale

    D. Grid system

3. A compass rose is printed on a map and used as a tool to

    A. show the orientation of a map of Earth.

    B. show the distance between two places in the world.

    C. represent features such as elevations and divisions.

    D. show the distance between two corresponding points.

4. The New England Colonies consisted of

    A. Virginia, North Carolina, South Carolina, and Georgia.

    B. Massachusetts, Connecticut, Rhode Island, and New Hampshire.

    C. New York, New Jersey, Delaware, Maryland, and Pennsylvania.

    D. North Carolina, Rhode Island, Delaware, and Maryland.

5. To apply the concept of time zones, students need to have a clear understanding of

    A. the International Date Line.

    B. the Earth's yearly revolution.

    C. the concept of the meridians of longitude.

    D. the concept of the parallels of latitude.

Use the photograph below to answer question 6.

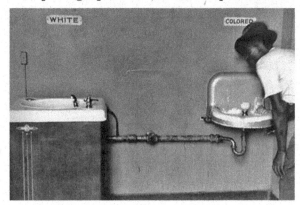

6. In which of the following rulings did the U.S. Supreme Court decide that the conditions of segregation illustrated in the photograph above violated the Fourteenth Amendment?

   A. *Plessy v. Ferguson*

   B. *Marbury v. Madison*

   C. *Brown v. Board of Education of Topeka*

   D. *Dred Scott v. Sandford*

Use the information below to answer question 7 that follows.

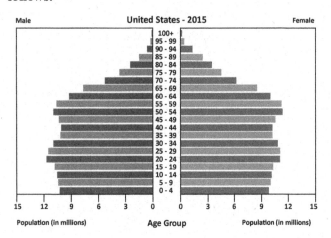

Source: United States Census Bureau

7. A population pyramid as shown in the figure is a complex example of what type of chart, diagram, or graph listed below?

   A. Bar graph

   B. Pie graph

   C. Pedigree chart

   D. Dot plot

8. The first 10 amendments to the U.S. Constitution are known as the

   A. doctrine of the separation of church and state.

   B. Bill of Rights.

   C. Right to Privacy.

   D. Right to Due Process.

9. The United States has 50 states and at least four territories. Based on these figures, what is the maximum number of senators who can serve in the U.S. Senate?

   A. 50

   B. 100

   C. 54

   D. 435

10. In what way did the Gutenberg printing press, invented in 1454, impact the world?

   A. Favorite stories were reprinted on demand.

   B. Affordable books could be illustrated in color.

   C. The spread and democratization of knowledge occurred rapidly throughout society.

   D. Governments embraced the technology to inform the people and to calm rebellions.

Revere, Paul, engraver. "The BLOODY MAS-SACRE perpetrated in King Street BOSTON on March 5th 1770 by a party of the 29th REGT." 1770. Courtesy of Prints and Photographs Division, Library of Congress.

11. The Paul Revere engraving of the Boston Massacre (1770), pictured above, is taught at what grade level?

   A. 6th grade

   B. 5th grade

   C. 4th grade

   D. 3rd grade

12. Cinco de Mayo is a holiday commemorating the victory of the Mexican army over the French forces of Napoleon III on May 5, 1862. This event is important to Mexican Americans because

   A. the Mexicans defeated a ragtag army.

   B. it led to Mexican Independence Day.

   C. the general who led the Mexican forces was born in present-day Texas.

   D. President Benito Juarez joined forces with the United States to defeat France.

13. Determining globes for a first-grade classroom should be based on which of the following characteristics? Select *all* that apply.

   A. Three or fewer colors to represent land

   B. At least seven colors to represent land

   C. Two or fewer colors to represent water

   D. Three or more colors to represent water

   E. A 12-inch globe

14. Probably as a response to the war in Iraq and Afghanistan, the Organization of Petroleum Exporting Countries (OPEC) cut the production of oil. As a result of this action, the cost of gasoline increased to almost $3.00 per gallon in 2005. What is the economic principle or statement that best represents this scenario?

   A. During war, the prices of fossil fuels increase.

   B. The American economy is dependent on foreign oil.

   C. The law of supply and demand determines the prices of goods and services.

   D. OPEC was boycotting the United States.

15. Identify the statement that best describes the country of Iraq.

   A. It is a linguistically and ethnically homogeneous Muslim nation.

   B. It is a Muslim nation with multiple ethnic groups within its borders.

   C. It is located in Southeast Asia.

   D. It is a province of Pakistan.

Use the information below to answer question 16.

Texas GDP Ranking Among Nations
Gross Domestic Product, 2015
(in billions of U.S. dollars)

Rank	Nation	Billion $
1	United States*	$17,418
2	China	$10,380
3	Japan	$4,616
4	Germany	$3,859
5	United Kingdom	$2,945
6	France	$2,846
7	Brazil	$2,353
8	Italy	$2,147
9	India	$2,049
10	Russia	$1,871
11	Canada	$1,788
12	TEXAS†	$1,648
13	Australia	$1,444
14	Korea	$1,416
15	Spain	$1,406
16	Mexico	$1,282
17	Indonesia	$888
18	The Netherlands	$866
19	Turkey	$806
20	Saudi Arabia	$752

* Includes Texas

† If Texas were a nation

Sources: International Monetary Fund and the U.S. Bureau of Economic Analysis. Based on data provided by the Texas Comptroller of Public Accounts staff. Published June 2015.

16. Based on the table given, if Texas were an independent nation, its annual economic output would be which of the following? Select *all* that apply.

    A. Ahead of Canada by approximately US$140 billion

    B. More than double the GDP of Saudi Arabia

    C. More than half the GDP of the United Kingdom

    D. One notch above Australia

17. In Texas, the course that focuses on human or cultural geography is introduced in which of the following grades?

    A. Third

    B. Fourth

    C. Fifth

    D. Sixth

18. The English colonies were established in three regions: the New England Colonies, the Middle Colonies, and the Southern Colonies. The economy of the Southern Colonies was based on

    A. farming, shipping, fishing, and trading.

    B. farming and very small industries such as fishing, lumber, and crafts.

    C. trading and the mining of minerals and other natural resources.

    D. crops of tobacco, rice, indigo, and cotton.

Use the following passage to answer question 19.

We hold these truths to be self-evident. That all men are created equal; that they are endowed by their Creator with certain unalienable rights; that among these are life, liberty and the pursuit of happiness. That, to secure these rights, governments are instituted among men, deriving their just powers from the consent of the governed that, whenever any form of government becomes destructive of these ends, it is the right of the people to alter or to abolish it, and to institute a new government.

19. The excerpt is from which of the following?

    A. Articles of Confederation

    B. U.S. Constitution

    C. Declaration of Independence

    D. Missouri Compromise

20. How do topographic maps differ from other maps?

    A. Topographic maps use census data to show population density.

    B. Topographic maps use contour lines to show elevation change on the surface of Earth.

    C. Topographic maps use latitude and longitude to show relative location.

    D. Topographic maps use latitude and longitude to show absolute location.

21. Assessments that provide the teacher with information about student understanding as they are learning content are called

    A. direct assessments.

    B. informal assessments.

    C. summative assessments.

    D. formative assessments.

22. Which of the following best describes the way in which the Farm Security Administration labor camp in Robstown, Texas, relates to the beginning teacher's knowledge of geography? The beginning teacher

    A. understands the basic concepts of culture and the processes of cultural adaptation, diffusion, and exchange.

    B. understands the characteristics, distribution, and migration of populations in Texas and the United States.

    C. understands how people use oral tradition, stories, real and mythical heroes, music, paintings, and sculpture to create and represent culture in communities in Texas, the United States, and the world.

    D. understands the physical environments of Texas.

23. What is the only branch of government included in the Articles of Confederation?

    A. Judicial

    B. Legislative

    C. Executive

    D. Federal

24. What type of redress did the Civil Liberties Act of 1988, H.R. 442, offer to qualified Japanese Americans who were relocated and interned by the government of the United States?

    A. Payment of $20,000

    B. Guarantees of non-repetition

    C. Restoration of victims to their original situation before the violations occurred

    D. New housing for all detainees

25. On February 1, 1861, the Texas legislature voted to

    A. secede from the Union and join the Confederacy.

    B. relinquish all claims to New Mexico.

    C. annex Texas to the United States.

    D. adopt the Texas Declaration of Independence.

26. Which of the following best describes the way in which the U.S. Constitution assigns governmental power?

    A. It assigns it entirely to the states.

    B. It assigns it entirely to the national government.

    C. It divides it between the states and the national government.

    D. It does not divide power.

27. Which concept is NOT embodied as a right in the First Amendment to the U.S. Constitution?

    A. Peaceable assembly

    B. Freedom of speech

    C. Petition for redress of grievances

    D. Protection against unreasonable search and seizure

28. Which of the following best describes the historical diet of Atakapans and Karankawas American Indians who inhabited the coastal regions of present-day Texas?

    A. Atakapans and Karankawas consumed bear and deer from the land as well as alligators, oysters, clams, ducks, and turtles.

    B. Atakapans and Karankawas grew and consumed beans, squash, and sunflowers, along with eating bear, deer, and occasionally buffalo.

    C. Atakapans and Karankawas ate bison, fish, turtles, crawfish, snails, pecans, acorns, wild fruits, rattlesnakes, and rabbits.

    D. Atakapans and Karankawas gathered wild berries, plants, and other locally grown items.

29. Mr. Whitfield has his seventh-grade students regularly engage in small group discussions following a social studies lesson in which they discuss a shared text. Using small group roles, the students take turns reading the text, pausing to discuss the text according to each student's assigned role. One student is a question generator, one is a summarizer, one is a predictor, and the fourth student is a clarifier of tricky concepts in the text. What is the name of this strategy?

    A. Thinking aloud

    B. Role play

    C. Literature circles

    D. Reciprocal teaching

30. Which of the following played a significant role in the Chicano civil rights movement by fighting for better working conditions and fair compensation for farm workers?

    A. Rosa Parks

    B. Martha Cotera

    C. Dolores Huerta

    D. Ida B. Wells

31. Economics is best described as the study of

    A. how different political systems establish systems for production and consumption.

    B. how individuals and groups with limited resources make decisions to best satisfy their needs and wants.

    C. how currency is used in different societies.

    D. how trade has developed through a historic and systematic process.

32. Which of the following was the original motto of the United States and remains on the Great Seal of the United States?

    A. One nation under God

    B. *Carpe diem*

    C. *E pluribus unum*

    D. Freedom and justice for all

33. One activity used before and after introducing a new time period in history is the K-W-L chart by which students discuss and list what they know, what they want to know, and what they learned about the topic. A rationale for conducting this activity would be to

    A. help students compare and contrast main ideas in a chapter or reading.

    B. provide a structured assessment tool to grade understanding of the new information.

    C. help students better understand the historical time period.

    D. activate background knowledge and generate interest in the historical period.

34. In social studies, students are expected to make evidence-based claims to support larger arguments about a given event, situation, cultural group, and so on. How can primary and secondary sources provide the standards-based content needed for students to support a claim, or statement, made in a social studies class? Select *all* that apply.

    A. Standards-based content comes from textbooks aligned to the Texas Essential Knowledge and Skills with images, diagrams, and text, which should be used to support student claims.

    B. Standards-based content is gathered through a combination of sources, provided by teachers, which deepen and broaden student knowledge, which can be used to support student claims.

    C. Evidence-based reasoning is best if it comes from primary sources that provide firsthand accounts that require students to critically assess situations and events from new perspectives.

    D. Evidence for arguments can be found in related or disparate content-rich information sources of firsthand accounts and high-level synopses of events to support student reasoning.

35. A major conflict between colonial Americans and the British occurred over a series of British Acts of Parliament dealing with

    A. taxes.

    B. slavery.

    C. farming.

    D. Native Americans.

36. Which of the following movements was most influential in the crafting of the U.S. Declaration of Independence and the U.S. Constitution?

    A. Scientific revolution

    B. Industrialism

    C. Enlightenment

    D. Renaissance

Use the image below to answer the question that follows.

Source: National Museum of American History, Smithsonian Institution

37. Which of the following was the purpose of the poster?

    A.   To encourage young women to go back to school

    B.   To encourage women to stand up for themselves

    C.   To encourage women to take factory jobs during World War II

    D.   To encourage men to recognize the rights of women

38. The term *manifest destiny* connotes a culture of

    A.   ancestral harmony.

    B.   territorial expansion.

    C.   geographic isolationism.

    D.   economic capitalism.

39. Which branch of government is responsible for creating the nation's laws?

    A.   Executive

    B.   Legislative

    C.   Judicial

    D.   Fiscal

Use the photograph below to answer the question that follows.

Source: National Archives and Records Administration

40. In reference to the photograph, Eleanor Roosevelt said, "The destiny of human rights is in the hands of all our citizens in all our communities." From a social studies teacher's perspective, this quote applies

    A.   only to U.S. citizens in the 20th century.

    B.   only to U.S. citizens from early civilizations through today.

    C.   only to any human living after the 20th century.

    D.   to any human from early civilizations through today.

41. Which of the following is an example of an activity that students could do to conduct *primary research* for a social studies project?

    A.   Create a poster report using internet resources

    B.   Conduct a survey to gather information

    C.   Synthesize facts from multiple informational texts

    D.   Evaluate websites for accuracy of information

42. Article 55 of which of the following documents calls for "universal respect for, and observance of, human rights and fundamental freedoms"?

    A.   The U.S. Constitution

    B.   The Declaration of Independence

    C.   The United Nations Charter

    D.   The Texas Constitution

Social Studies Practice Test 1: Answer Key

Test Item	Answer	Competency 808-
1.	A	005
2.	B	002
3.	A	002
4.	B	001
5.	C	002
6.	C	001
7.	A	006
8.	B	004
9.	B	004
10.	C	005
11.	B	007
12.	C	001
13.	A, C, E	007
14.	C	003
15.	B	002
16.	B, C, D	002
17	D	007
18.	D	003
19.	C	001
20.	B	002
21.	D	007

Test Item	Answer	Competency 808-
22.	B	001
23.	B	004
24.	A	003
25.	A	001
26.	C	004
27.	D	004
28.	A	001
29.	D	007
30.	C	001
31.	B	003
32.	C	004
33.	D	007
34.	B, D	006
35.	A	001
36.	C	004
37.	C	001
38.	B	001
39.	B	004
40.	D	001
41.	B	006
42.	C	004

Social Studies Practice Test 1: Detailed Answers

1. A.

The correct answer is (A). Spindletop marked the change in the Texas economy from agrarian-based to one that was also based on oil, technology, and innovation. As competition increased, so did innovative uses of technology. Money from the oil business was used to expand the research and development parts of oil companies as well as universities. Companies such as Texas Instruments soon formed and became part of a broad array of innovative, technology-centered firms. Jobs in Texas increased and universities were established and/or supported on account of the oil boom. Option (B) is incorrect. Spindletop was not a natural disaster. Option (C) and (D) are incorrect. Spindletop was the discovery of a large oil formation on a salt dome southeast of Beaumont, Texas. It was not an amusement attraction nor did it impact the Hispanic population. Instead, it marked the birth of the modern petroleum industry. **(Competency 808-005: Culture, Science, Technology and Society)**

2. B.

The correct answer is (B). A globe is a scale model of the Earth shaped like a sphere. Because a globe is the same shape as the Earth, it shows sizes and shapes more accurately than a map (a flat representation of the Earth). Option (A) is incorrect because a compass rose is printed on a map to show the relative position of the cardinal points (north, south, west, and east) and not a representation of the Earth. Some also include the intermediate directions (northeast, southeast, southwest, and northwest). Option (C) is incorrect because a map scale is used to show the distance between two places in the world. Option (D) is incorrect because a grid system provides lines to help determine absolute location. Typically, though not always, these lines are latitude and longitude. **(Competency 808-002 Geography)**

3. A.

The correct answer is (A). A compass rose is a design printed on a chart or map for reference. It shows the orientation of a map on Earth and shows the four cardinal directions (north, south, east, and west). A compass rose may also show intermediate directions (northeast, southeast, southwest, and northwest). Option (B) is incorrect because a map scale shows the distance between two places in the world. Option (C) is incorrect because features such as elevations and divisions are represented by different colors. Option (D) is incorrect because the ratio of the distance between two points on the Earth and the distance between the two corresponding points on the map is represented by a scale and not by a compass rose. **(Competency 808-002 Geography)**

4. B.

The correct answer is (B). The New England Colonies consisted of Massachusetts, Connecticut, Rhode Island, and New Hampshire. Option (A) is incorrect because Virginia, North Carolina, South Carolina, and Georgia formed the Southern Colonies. Option (C) is incorrect because New York, New Jersey, Delaware, Maryland, and Pennsylvania formed the Middle Colonies. Option (D) is incorrect because this answer represents a combination of some of the Southern Colonies and some of the Middle Colonies. **(Competency 808-001 History)**

5. C.

The correct answer is (C). The Earth is divided into 24 zones based on the meridians of longitude, which are determined using the rotation of the Earth and its exposure to sunlight. This rotation creates day and night, and consequently the concept of time. Option (A) is incorrect because the International Date Line is only one of 24 meridians of the Earth. Option (B) is incorrect because the term *revolution* describes the movement of the Earth around the Sun, which affects the seasons but not necessarily the time zones. Option (D) is incorrect because the parallels of latitude do not affect the time zones. **(Competency 808-002 Geography)**

6. C.

The correct answer is (C). The conditions represented in the photograph, which shows separate drinking fountains for whites and for African Americans, were ruled unconstitutional by the U.S. Supreme Court in *Brown v. Board of Education of Topeka* in May 1954. The case struck down *Plessy v. Ferguson* (A), the 1896 case in which the Court had established the "separate but equal" doctrine for determining the constitutionality of racial segregation laws. The Court's ruling in *Marbury v. Madison* (B) in 1803 established the doctrine of judicial review, but did not touch on issues of racial segregation. In contrast, race was central to the thesis put forth in the Supreme Court's *Dred Scott* decision (D) in 1857: that African Americans, regardless of whether they had been slaves or been granted their freedom, were not protected by the U.S. Constitution and could never become U.S. citizens. **(Competency 808-001 History)**

7. A.

Option (A) is correct. A population pyramid uses a series of bar graphs to represent the population of males and females at different ages. A population pyramid is a critical resource in social studies education. Elementary teachers should use them often to help students stay in practice with reading and interpreting the data on these graphs as they apply to different cultures and/or time periods in history. Middle school teachers should use population pyramids to understand current and historical societies and to analyze the graphs for patterns and irregularities to draw conclusions or make predictions. Option (B) refers to a circle divided into parts to represent data. Option (C) is a diagram that looks like a flow chart and is used to show lineage, or a family tree. Option (D) is a type of graph that is often seen in mathematics. It is like a bar graph except that it uses a dot to identify data. For example, if the bar graph extends a bar, or thick line, to the number 9, the dot plot uses a dot at the number 9 to represent the same information. Elementary teachers should use this commonality to help students transfer skills for reading and analyzing data in

multiple forms. **(Competency 808-006 Social Studies Foundations and Skills)**

8. B.

The correct answer is (B). Civil rights are the legal and political rights of the people who live in a particular country. In the United States, the Constitution and the Bill of Rights guarantee civil rights to American citizens and residents. The first 10 amendments to the U.S. Constitution are known as the Bill of Rights. Choices (A), (C), and (D) are incorrect because these name certain rights included in the Bill of Rights, but fail to address the question. **(Competency 808-004 Government and Citizenship)**

9. B.

The correct answer is (B). The U.S. Constitution provides for two senators to represent each of the 50 states, for a total of 100. Territories are not represented in the U.S. Senate. Choice (D) is incorrect because it represents the current number of members of the U.S. House of Representatives. **(Competency 808-004 Government and Citizenship)**

10. C.

Option (C) is correct because for the first time books and other written materials could be produced cheaply and in mass quantities, thus making them available to all classes in society. As the greater masses became more literate, they could read others' ideas and share their own. Ideas for people to have a voice in the government and choice in their daily lives began to spread. Knowledge was spread to all of society, not just the elite few. Option (A) is incorrect. Although it was possible for stories to be reprinted, this was not part of the lasting impact of the Gutenberg printing press. Option (B) is incorrect because the Gutenberg printing press was about the use of movable type, not about providing colored illustrations. Option (D) is incorrect. At the time, many governments did not embrace democracy and, thus, did not set about using the Gutenberg printing press to inform the public. **(Competency 808-005: Culture, Science, Technology and Society)**

11. B.

Option (B) is the correct answer. Students are taught U.S. History in grade 5. The Boston Massacre was an important part of the Revolutionary War. Option (A) refers to World Cultures. Option (C) refers to Texas History. Option (D) refers to the social studies topic, "How Individuals Change their Communities and their World." **(Competency 808-007 Social Studies Instruction and Assessment)**

12. C.

The correct answer is (C). General Ignacio de Zaragoza was one of the leaders of the Mexican Army. He was born south of the city of Goliad when this region was part of Mexico. Because the region is now part of Texas, Mexican Americans celebrate the accomplishment of this "Mexican American" hero. In the Battle of Puebla, the Mexican forces faced anything but a ragtag army (A); Napoleon III's French troops represented one of the world's best fighting forces, so the victory took on symbolic significance. Cinco de Mayo has nothing to do with Mexican Independence Day (B), which was established in 1810, a full half-century before the Battle of Puebla. Option (D) is incorrect because the United States did not participate in this war. The U.S. was fighting its own war—the American Civil War (1860–1865). **(Competency 808-001 History)**

13. A., C., E.

Options (A), (C), and (E) are correct because lower elementary grades (PreK–3) should use a smaller, simpler globe than upper elementary grades (4–6). Options (B) and (D) are characteristics of a globe for older elementary students. **(Competency 808-007 Social Studies Instruction and Assessment)**

14. C.

The correct answer is (C). Reducing the production of oil while keeping the same demand for the product creates an imbalance between supply and demand. This imbalance results in a price increase. Options (A) and (B), while potentially and flatly true, respectively, do not articulate an economic principle, as the question requires. Option (D) presents an opinion that fails to address the true question. **(Competency 808-003 Economics)**

15. B.

The correct answer is (B). Iraq is a Muslim nation with multiple ethnic groups within its borders. The largest groups are the Arabs, consisting of Shiite and Sunni Muslims, who do not always get along. The Kurds are the largest minority group. (A) is incorrect. The multiple groups living in Iraq speak Arabic, Kurdish, Turkish, Assyrian, and other languages. (C) is incorrect because Iraq is located in the Middle Eastern part of Asia. (D) is incorrect because Pakistan is a Muslim country from the region, but there is no political association between the two nations. **(Competency 808-002 Geography)**

16. B., C., D.

Options (B), (C), and (D) are correct. Option (B) is correct because Texas's US$1.65 trillion GDP in 2014 was more than double Saudi Arabia's US$752 billion. Option (C) is correct because the United Kingdom chalked up approximately US$2.95 trillion in GDP in 2014, half of which would be US$1.48 trillion. Option (D) is correct because Texas ranks 12th while Australia ranks 13th, according to the table. Option (A) is incorrect because the statement is actually the inverse of the reality: the figures show Canada in 11th place in terms of GDP, a notch above Texas. **(Competency 808-002 Geography)**

17. D.

The correct answer is (D). The course designed to introduce students to cultural or human geography is introduced in sixth grade. Unfortunately, some teachers teach this from a world history perspective, not from a geographic perspective. A geographic perspective includes history as well as other information such as culture, geopolitics, demographic, and human-environment interaction. Geographic concepts and skills are taught at each grade level. However, the World Cultures course is designed to teach basic understanding of cultural geography in preparation for World Geography at the high school level. **(Competency 808-007 Social Studies Instruction and Assessment)**

18. D.

The correct answer is (D). The economy of the Southern Colonies was based on the crops of tobacco, rice, indigo, and cotton. Plantations produced agricultural crops in large scale and exploited workers as well as the environment. Choice (A) is incorrect because it was the economy of the Middle Colonies that was based on farming, shipping, fishing, and trading. Choice (B) is incorrect because it was the economy of the New England Colonies that was based on farming and very small industries such as fishing, lumber, and crafts. Choice (C) is incorrect because trading and mining for natural resources were not a part of the Southern Colonies' economy. **(Competency 808-003 Economics)**

19. C.

The quotation is from the Declaration of Independence (C), written in 1776 by Thomas Jefferson. The document specifically highlights the reasons the American colonies wanted to seek independence from British rule. The Articles of Confederation (A), adopted in 1781, was an agreement among the 13 founding states that legally established the United States of America as a confederation of sovereign states and served as its first constitution. The U.S. Constitution (B), adopted in 1787, established the governmental structure we still have today. The Missouri Compromise of 1820 (D) dealt primarily with how slave and free states would be admitted to the Union. **(Competency 808-001 History)**

20. B.

Answer (B) is correct, because it reveals the purpose behind why cartographers opt to use topographic maps. Topographic maps use contour lines to show elevation change on the surface of Earth. Even though both relative and absolute location provide information about where we are in the world, they are not what makes a topographic map special. Thus, choices (C) and (D) are incorrect. We use latitude and longitude to determine global location. Population maps show the density of humans in a given location, which means (A) is also incorrect. **(Competency 808-002 Geography)**

21. D.

Formative assessments (D) are ongoing and occur while students are learning information. These types of assessments help teachers make decisions about how the subject is taught, and they can make adjustments as needed. Summative assessments show what students know at a particular time, such as through a unit-based or comprehensive end-of-term exam. **(Competency 808-007 Social Studies Instruction and Assessment)**

22. B.

Response (B), the beginning teacher understands the characteristics, distribution, and migration of populations in Texas and the United States, best describes the way in which the Farm Security Administration labor camp in Robstown, Texas, relates to the beginning teacher's knowledge of geography. There is no explicit detailing of culture exchange or stories. Thus, choices (B) and (C) are incorrect. Choice (D) is an incorrect response because it relates primarily to physical geography and not migration patterns. **(Competency 808-001 History)**

23. B.

The Articles of Confederation mention only the legislative branch (B) in the form of Congress. The judicial (A) and executive branches (C) were later outlined in the U.S. Constitution, but were not mentioned in the Articles of Confederation. The federal branch (D) is not a branch of government, and is thus incorrect. **(Competency 808-004 Government and Citizenship)**

24. A.

Although the *United Nations* draft of Basic Principles and Guidelines on the Right to a Remedy and Reparation for Victims of Gross Violations of International Human Rights Law suggested five forms of redress, including (1) restitution, (2) compensation, (3) rehabilitation, and (4) satisfaction, and (5) guarantees of non-repetition, the United States' Civil Liberties Act of 1988, H.R. 442, offers only an apology and restitution. Thus, responses (B), (C), and (D) are incorrect. Only choice (A), indicating a payment of $20,000, is correct. **(Competency 808-003 Economics)**

25. A.

After the election of Abraham Lincoln, the Texas legislature held a special convention and voted to secede from the Union and join the Confederacy; thus, option (A) is the correct response. Response (B) is incorrect because Texas relinquished all claims to New Mexico in 1850 in line with the terms of the Compromise of 1850. The annexation of Texas by the United States occurred two decades earlier in 1845, making response (C) incorrect. A delegation at Washington-on-the-Brazos adopted the Texas Declaration of Independence on March 2, 1836, creating the Republic of Texas. Thus, response (D) is also incorrect. **(Competency 808-001 History)**

26. C.

The U.S. Constitution divides power between the state and national government (C) in what is referred to as federalism. There are powers that are specifically reserved for the federal government, powers specifically reserved for the state governments, and powers that are shared between the two. Thus, choices (A), (B), and (D) are incorrect. **(Competency 808-004 Government and Citizenship)**

27. D.

The First Amendment to the Constitution reads, "Congress shall make no law respecting an establishment of religion, or prohibiting the free exercise thereof; or abridging the freedom of speech (B), or of the press; or of the right of the people to assemble peaceably (A), and to petition the government for a redress of grievances" (C). Protection against unreasonable search and seizure is a constitutional right found in the Fourth Amendment, and thus option (D) is the only correct choice. **(Competency 808-004 Government and Citizenship)**

28. A.

The Atakapans and Karankawas lived in the coastal areas of present-day Texas. They consumed bear and deer from the land as well as alligators, oysters, clams, ducks, and turtles (A). It was the Caddo, in present-day eastern Texas, who grew and consumed beans, squash, and sunflowers along with eating bear, deer, and occasionally buffalo, so (B) is an incorrect response. Choice (C) is also incorrect. The Tonkawas inhabited the cen-

tral regions of present-day Texas and typically ate bison, fish, turtles, crawfish, snails, pecans, acorns, wild fruits, rattlesnakes, and rabbits, so (D) is also incorrect. **(Competency 808-001 History)**

29. D.

Option (D) is correct because students who practice reciprocal teaching engage in the four "jobs," or roles, described in this question. Option (A) is incorrect because thinking aloud is primarily an individual, cognitive task. Option (B), role play, is incorrect because students are not enacting a scene or scenario from the text; rather, they are discussing the content using the four roles. Option (C) is incorrect because literature circles, while promoting group discussion about a text, are done in a wider variety of ways than described in this scenario. Literature circles also typically focus on the more open-ended responses of the reader. **(Competency 808-007 Social Studies Instruction and Assessment)**

30. C

Dolores Huerta (C) is a noted labor union activist who played a significant role in the Chicano civil rights movement of the 1960s by fighting for better working conditions and fair compensation for farm workers. Rosa Parks (A) was a civil rights activist primarily known for starting the Montgomery bus boycott for refusing to give up her seat to a white man. Martha Cotera (B) is also a Chicana civil rights activist and writer, but her efforts focused primarily around organizing the 1969 Crystal City walkouts that protested the exclusion of Mexican Americans in political representation. Ida B. Wells (D), who was born into slavery, became a fierce antilynching and women's suffrage activist and established several nineteenth century women's organizations. **(Competency 808-001 History)**

31. B.

Economics is *best* described as the study of how individuals and groups with limited resources make decisions to best satisfy their needs and wants. Choice (A) is incorrect because examining how political systems establish systems for production and consumption is only one part of economic study. Choice (C), how currency is used in different societies, might be of interest to anthropologists or sociologists, but is not the primary responsibility of economists. Choice (D), how trade has developed through a historic and systematic process, would be of interest to historians, but not the primary interest of economic study. Thus, option (B) is the best general description of economic study. **(Competency 808-003 Economics)**

32. C.

E pluribus unum is a Latin phrase that means "from many, one." The United States used it as an unofficial motto from 1782 to 1955. This motto appears in the official Great Seal of the United States (adopted in 1782) on the banner in the bald eagle's beak. While both "one nation under God" (A) and "freedom and justice for all" (D) are phrases found in the U.S. Pledge of Allegiance, neither has been a motto of the United States. *Carpe diem* (B), Latin for "seize the day," is incorrect because it has never been recognized as a motto of the United States. "In God We Trust" was adopted as the national motto in 1956 and reaffirmed by Congress in 2011. **(Competency 808-004 Government and Citizenship)**

33. D.

K-W-L stands for "Know," "Want to know," and "Learned," and relates to the types of discussion and questioning that would take place before, during, and after discussing and learning about the topic at hand, which, for this question, is a time period in history. In the "Know" part, the teacher guides students to consider what background knowledge they have that relates to the time period. After these are shared, students pose questions about what they hope to know and learn about the time period. After the lesson or at different points in the lesson, the teacher can discuss with students what they are learning or have learned as a result of the activities, visuals, and readings within the lesson. These activities help students anticipate what they will be learning prior to various activities to engage them by such things as discussing, visualizing, and reading. This will serve to activate their schema or background knowledge. Choice (D) is the correct answer because it best fits this purpose of building and activating background knowledge while helping students to anticipate the key ideas in the text, visuals, or other resources within the lesson. The other choices don't directly relate to this purpose.

(Competency 808-007 Social Studies Instruction and Assessment)

34. B., D.

Options (B) and (D) are the correct responses. Primary and secondary sources are content-rich resources for students, who must be taught how to identify the type of sources as well as the key information provided. Social studies courses should be designed so that students must take a stand on an issue and then support their reasoning. They do this by making a claim stating their position. Teachers should model and expect students to use both primary and secondary resources to construct pieces of the content that will eventually be used to support their reasoning. Therefore, choice (A) is incorrect because it relies solely on a textbook, a secondary resource. The question asks about using both secondary and primary resources together. Choice (C) is also incorrect because it relies solely on primary resources. Choices (B) and (D) illustrate reasons for using both types of resources together, thus answering the question. **(Competency 808-006 Social Studies Instruction and Assessment)**

35. A.

The British imposition of taxes on colonial Americans (A) provoked major conflicts between these two groups. The colonists were upset with the British for implementing taxes when they felt they did not have any direct representation in the British Parliament. For choice (B), even though slavery continued in the colonies after it was abolished in England (1833), it was not a huge source of contention between the colonists and the British because the American Revolution had already occurred and the United States was free from British control. For choice (C), colonial farming was an industry, which received little interference from the British. Choice (D) is incorrect because no British Acts of Parliament were passed that dealt with Native Americans. **(Competency 808-001 History)**

36. C.

Of the four movements listed, the Enlightenment was the greatest influence on the writing of the U.S. Declaration of Independence and the U.S. Constitution, particularly the notion of the social contract. The scientific revolution (A) was an important movement in the sixteenth and seventeenth centuries that had a fundamental impact on Europeans view of the natural world, but did not directly influence the crafting of these documents. Industrialism (B) is incorrect because this revolution occurred in the nineteenth century after the crafting of the Declaration of Independence and U.S. Constitution. The Renaissance (D), which began in Italy and lasted from the fourteenth to seventeenth centuries, was a period of rebirth for literature, language, art, and culture, but had little impact on the crafting of these documents. **(Competency 808-004 Government and Citizenship)**

37. C.

Option (C) is correct. The purpose of the Rosie the Riveter poster produced in the early 1940s was to encourage women to take factory jobs during World War II. As men were deployed to fight in the war abroad, and war efforts demanded the production of more military machinery, women were encouraged to fill the increased demand for factory workers. Using critical and historical thinking skills, we can examine the image by analyzing the clothing and appearance of the woman represented, the choice of words used, and the agency that produced the poster. In examining the image, we can conclude that the poster was not designed to encourage young women to go back to school (A), encourage women to stand up for themselves (B), or encourage men to recognize the rights of women (D). **(Competency 808-001 History)**

38. B.

Manifest destiny is defined as a nineteenth century doctrine that the United States had not only the right, but also the duty, to expand throughout North America. This brought about core American cultural attributes of geographic expansion, so option (B) is the correct response. In many cases, manifest destiny worked against cultural practices of ancestral harmony, as its enactment broke families apart and moved many native peoples away from their cultural connections to ancestral lands; thus, option (A) is incorrect. Option (C) is wrong because manifest destiny resulted in geographic expansion and engagement, which are the antithesis of geographic isolationism. Economic capitalism (D) had a relationship to manifest destiny as an economic influence and often

a result, but it does not connote any cultural aspects of manifest destiny. **(Competency 808-001 History)**

39. B.

Option (B) is correct. The legislative branch of government, comprising the two houses of Congress, is responsible for creating the nation's laws. The executive branch of government (A) is primarily concerned with carrying out the laws of the country. The judicial branch of government (C) is responsible for interpreting and enforcing the nation's laws. The fiscal branch (D) is incorrect because this is not one of the three branches of government. **(Competency 808-004 Government and Citizenship)**

40. D.

Option (D) is correct. When Eleanor Roosevelt said, "The destiny of human rights is in the hands of all our citizens in all our communities," we understand that she was referencing any human from early civilizations through today. The photograph gives us clues to the answer in that we have a United Nations logo and a headline about human rights. Human rights extend beyond the borders of the United States, which eliminates options (A) and (B). This is affirmed in Texas 4–8 social studies teachers' familiarity with the preamble to the declaration of human rights, which begins, "Whereas recognition of the inherent dignity and of the equal and inalienable rights of all members of the human family is the foundation of freedom, justice and peace in the world." Although the United Nations General Assembly adopted the universal declaration of human rights on December 10, 1948, three years after the end of World War II, it pulls from deep and ancient histories of human rights dating before that era, making option (C) incorrect. The Hindu Vedas, the Babylonian Code of Hammurabi, the Bible, the Quran (Koran), and the Analects of Confucius all address people's duties, rights, and responsibilities. Native Americans also addressed human rights via documents, including the Inca Aztec codes of conduct and justice and an Iroquois constitution. **(Competency 808-001 History)**

41. B.

In doing primary research, the student should gather original information from either a primary source document or from a person or group of people. In this case, a survey would be primary research and a way of gathering information that was not collected by someone else. The remaining choices, (A), (C), and (D), are examples of secondary research, or using documents of information that has already been collected. **(Competency 808-006 Social Studies Foundations and Skills)**

42. C.

Article 55 of the United Nations Charter calls for "universal respect for, and observance of, human rights and fundamental freedoms" (C). Responses (A), the U.S. Constitution; (B), the Declaration of Independence; and (D), the Texas Constitution, although seemingly plausible, are incorrect answers to this fact-based question. **(Competency 808-004 Government and Citizenship)**

TExES Core Subjects 4–8 Practice Test 1: Science (809)

This practice test plus an additional test are available at the online REA Study Center (www.rea.com/studycenter).

The TExES Core Subjects Science (809) test is computer-based, so we strongly recommend that you take our online practice tests to simulate test-day conditions and to receive these added benefits:

- **Timed testing conditions**—Gauge how much time you can spend on each question.

- **Automatic scoring**—Find out how you did on the test, instantly.

- **On-screen detailed explanations of answers**—Learn not just the correct answer, but also why the other answers are incorrect.

- **Diagnostic score reports**—Pinpoint where you're strongest and where you need to focus your study.

Science Practice Test 1: Answer Sheet

1. Ⓐ Ⓑ Ⓒ Ⓓ   17. Ⓐ Ⓑ Ⓒ Ⓓ Ⓔ   33. Ⓐ Ⓑ Ⓒ Ⓓ

2. Ⓐ Ⓑ Ⓒ Ⓓ   18. Ⓐ Ⓑ Ⓒ Ⓓ   34. Ⓐ Ⓑ Ⓒ Ⓓ

3. Ⓐ Ⓑ Ⓒ Ⓓ   19. Ⓐ Ⓑ Ⓒ Ⓓ   35. Ⓐ Ⓑ Ⓒ Ⓓ

4. Ⓐ Ⓑ Ⓒ Ⓓ   20. Ⓐ Ⓑ Ⓒ Ⓓ   36. Ⓐ Ⓑ Ⓒ Ⓓ

5. Ⓐ Ⓑ Ⓒ Ⓓ   21. Ⓐ Ⓑ Ⓒ Ⓓ   37. Ⓐ Ⓑ Ⓒ Ⓓ

6. Ⓐ Ⓑ Ⓒ Ⓓ   22. Ⓐ Ⓑ Ⓒ Ⓓ   38. Ⓐ Ⓑ Ⓒ Ⓓ

7. Ⓐ Ⓑ Ⓒ Ⓓ   23. Ⓐ Ⓑ Ⓒ Ⓓ   39. Ⓐ Ⓑ Ⓒ Ⓓ

8. Ⓐ Ⓑ Ⓒ Ⓓ   24. Ⓐ Ⓑ Ⓒ Ⓓ   40. Ⓐ Ⓑ Ⓒ Ⓓ

9. Ⓐ Ⓑ Ⓒ Ⓓ   25. Ⓐ Ⓑ Ⓒ Ⓓ   41. Ⓐ Ⓑ Ⓒ Ⓓ

10. Ⓐ Ⓑ Ⓒ Ⓓ   26. Ⓐ Ⓑ Ⓒ Ⓓ   42. Ⓐ Ⓑ Ⓒ Ⓓ

11. Ⓐ Ⓑ Ⓒ Ⓓ   27. Ⓐ Ⓑ Ⓒ Ⓓ   43. Ⓐ Ⓑ Ⓒ Ⓓ

12. Ⓐ Ⓑ Ⓒ Ⓓ   28. Ⓐ Ⓑ Ⓒ Ⓓ   44. Ⓐ Ⓑ Ⓒ Ⓓ

13. Ⓐ Ⓑ Ⓒ Ⓓ   29. Ⓐ Ⓑ Ⓒ Ⓓ   45. Ⓐ Ⓑ Ⓒ Ⓓ

14. Ⓐ Ⓑ Ⓒ Ⓓ   30. Ⓐ Ⓑ Ⓒ Ⓓ   46. Ⓐ Ⓑ Ⓒ Ⓓ

15. Ⓐ Ⓑ Ⓒ Ⓓ   31. Ⓐ Ⓑ Ⓒ Ⓓ

16. Ⓐ Ⓑ Ⓒ Ⓓ   32. Ⓐ Ⓑ Ⓒ Ⓓ

Practice Test 1: Science[††]

TIME: 55 minutes
       46 questions

> **Directions:** Read each item and select the best answer. Most items on this test require you to provide the one best answer. However, some questions require you to select all the options that apply.

1. The students in Mr. Lawson's class are going to engage in an inquiry-based laboratory investigation during which they will be placing a glass thermometer in a beaker of ice and heating it on a hot plate to graph the heating curve of water. What is the first and most important thing Mr. Lawson should do before students begin this investigation?

   A. Provide students with the materials needed to conduct the investigation and let them begin.

   B. Give students a review sheet that explains and shows a completed graph of the heating curve of water before they begin the investigation.

   C. Read aloud and discuss all safety precautions of the investigation including wearing safety goggles and the use of glassware and heating surfaces.

   D. Instruct students on the clean-up procedures to follow after the investigation including where to store the glassware.

2. A student in Ms. Longfellow's class decided she needed some sodium hydroxide (NaOH) for an experiment she wanted to try at home. She saw a bottle of NaOH behind the glass of the chemical cabinet in the storeroom of her classroom. If Ms. Longfellow were following safety practices in her classroom, what should the student find to be true?

   A. The storeroom and cabinet where the NaOH is located would be open and available for student use because it is not a dangerous chemical.

   B. The storeroom and cabinet where the NaOH is located would be locked and the key not accessible to students, as with all laboratory chemicals.

   C. The NaOH would be stored near the sink and eyewash station in case the chemical spills.

   D. The NaOH would be stored near the fire extinguisher in the classroom in case the chemical catches fire.

3. What is the proper instrument to use in measuring the mass of an object?

   A. Meter stick

   B. Graduated cylinder

   C. Triple beam balance

   D. Sling psychrometer

---

†† This REA Science practice test for the TExES Core Subjects 4–8 exam features slightly more items, and allows proportionately more time, than the actual exam. We do this to more thoroughly expose candidates to the unusually large number of competencies (23) assessed on the Science subject test. Candidates should bear in mind that the actual test is 50 minutes and features 42 questions.

4. The United States is the only industrialized country in the world that uses the English system of measurement in daily life. What is the rationale for using the metric system in scientific research and engineering?

   A. The metric system is widely used in the world.

   B. The English system is an archaic and outdated system used mostly in business.

   C. The metric system is more precise than the English system.

   D. The English system allows for the easy computation of measurements.

5. The parts of any scientific investigation (observations, question, procedure, etc.) are collectively referred to as which of the following?

   A. An experiment

   B. The scientific method

   C. Scientific inquiry

   D. A six-step approach

6. The most meaningful way to teach students about potential sources of error is to

   A. ask the students to conduct an investigation that follows one procedure and leads to only one conclusion.

   B. provide a lecture of sources of error in famous investigations from the history of science.

   C. perform a demonstration and identify sources of error for students.

   D. ask the students to conduct an investigation that is likely to result in findings of instrument error, random results, and/or unsupported personal opinion.

7. In which of the following ways does deforestation (cutting down) of the rainforests in South America impact residents of the United States?

   A. Deforestation does not impact the U.S. population.

   B. Deforestation results in a decrease in the amount of carbon dioxide in the atmosphere, which decreases the threat of global warming.

   C. Deforestation results in contaminated food crops that may be consumed by U.S. residents.

   D. Deforestation results in an increase in the amount of carbon dioxide in the atmosphere, which contributes to the threat of global warming.

8. Which of the following factors could lead to a decrease in the overall size of the human population?

   A. The number of births being higher than the number of deaths.

   B. An outbreak of a fatal virus with no known cure or vaccine.

   C. The number of births being equal to the number of deaths.

   D. The implementation of a new vaccine that will increase the life span of humans.

9. What is true about using models in teaching to represent the natural world in science?

   A. Models are exact in their representation of the actual phenomena.

   B. Models only work as a representation of actual phenomena if computer generated.

   C. Models will always have differences with the actual phenomena.

   D. Models of natural phenomena will always lead students to form misconceptions.

10. _____ and _____ are two related key concepts that are seen across the science disciplines.

    A. Empirical…supernatural

    B. Constancy…change

    C. Form…function

    D. Both (B) and (C)

11. A rocket burns fuel in bursts out of a nozzle allowing it to maneuver and turn in the vacuum of space. Which of Newton's Laws of Motion explains how this maneuvering is able to occur?

    A. An object in motion stays in motion unless an outside force acts on it.

    B. For every action, there is an equal and opposite reaction.

    C. Fast-moving air has low pressure.

    D. An object at rest stays at rest unless an outside force acts on it.

12. What does using two pulleys in a single system (movable pulley) to lift an object do to the force required compared to lifting the object without the movable pulley?

    A. The use of the movable pulley reduces the amount of force required by one-half.

    B. The use of the movable pulley increases the amount of force required by one-half.

    C. The use of the movable pulley changes the amount of force required to 5 Newtons.

    D. The use of the movable pulley does not change the amount of force required.

13. Which of the following is NOT a physical change?

    A. Mixing an acid and base to form a salt and water

    B. Pouring salt (NaCl) in a glass of water to form a mixture

    C. Cars forming rust from salt and ice on roads in winter

    D. Burning sugar in a crucible in the laboratory

14. In an exploration activity, the students measure 50 ml of water and pour it into one cup, and 50 ml of isopropyl alcohol and pour it into a second cup. They then drop one ice cube in the cup of water and one ice cube in the alcohol. The students observe that the ice cube floats in the water, but sinks in the isopropyl alcohol. Why?

    A. The ice cube is less dense than the water and more dense than the alcohol.

    B. The ice cube is more dense than the water and less dense than the alcohol.

    C. The ice cube has equal density as the water and is more dense than the alcohol.

    D. The ice cube has equal density of both the water and the alcohol.

15. Which of the following causes sound waves?

    A. Vibration of air molecules

    B. Vibration of objects such as strings on a piano

    C. Light waves colliding into sound waves

    D. Force equaling mass times acceleration

16. The chemical formula for water is H_2O. Water is which of the following?

    A. Element

    B. Compound

    C. Atom

    D. Ion

17. Which of the following variables need to be known about an object to calculate its density? Select *all* that apply.

    A. Volume

    B. Color

    C. Mass

    D. Texture

    E. Odor

18. What do green plant leaves do with green wavelengths of visible light in the electromagnetic spectrum, and what is the evidence?

    A. Green plants absorb green wavelengths and the evidence is that the leaves are green in color.

    B. Green plants refract green wavelengths and the evidence is that the leaves may be green or yellow in color.

    C. Green plants absorb green wavelengths and the evidence is that the leaves turn red and yellow in the fall.

    D. Green plants reflect green wavelengths and the evidence is that the leaves are green in color.

19. What is the energy source for each of the following nonrenewable and renewable energy types used to generate electricity for human use, listed in the same order as the energy type?

    Nonrenewable and Renewable Energy Types:

    Hydroelectric—Nuclear—Fossil Fuel—Geothermal—Solar

    A. Heat From Beneath Earth's Surface—Coal—Moving Water—Soil—Sun

    B. Soil—Uranium—Wind—Volcanoes—Heat From Beneath Earth's Surface

    C. Moving Water—Uranium—Coal—Heat From Beneath Earth's Surface—Sun

    D. Moving Water—Sun—Heat From Beneath Earth's Surface—Sun—Uranium

20. Which of the following is an example of an exothermic reaction?

    A. Melting ice cubes

    B. Combining baking soda and vinegar

    C. Using a cold pack

    D. Burning firewood

21. Which of the following statements is an accurate description of arteries?

    A. They carry blood away from the heart.

    B. They carry blood toward the heart.

    C. They contain valves to prevent backflow of blood.

    D. They always transport oxygenated blood.

22. Which of the following is the molecular building block of proteins?

    A. Monosaccharide

    B. Glycerol

    C. Fatty acid

    D. Amino acid

23. A scientist crosses a male and female guinea pig, both having a brown coat. Brown coat color is dominant over white coat color. Among the offspring, 75% have brown coats and 25% have white coats. The scientist can conclude that the genotypes of the parent guinea pigs were most likely:

    A. BB × BB

    B. BB × Bb

    C. Bb × Bb

    D. bb × bb

24. Which of the following is true regarding asexual reproduction?

   A. Asexual reproduction is the splitting of one cell, after replicating all of its genetic material, into two daughter cells, with each having genetic material identical to the parent cell.

   B. Asexual reproduction involves the joining of two cells, each consisting of half the number of chromosomes as the parent cells, with their union forming a new cell containing a mixture of genetic materials from each parent cell.

   C. Asexual reproduction involves the exchange of genetic material between two organisms of the same species to produce two identical daughter cells.

   D. Asexual reproduction is a process that occurs only in specialized cells of the organism to produce four daughter cells with half the number of chromosomes as the parent cell.

25. What does the ability of a lizard to lose its tail when pulled represent?

   A. An adaptation for survival when attacked by predators.

   B. A mechanism of reproduction of a new lizard from the tail.

   C. A form of molting as the lizard grows in size.

   D. An indication of environmental stress such as drought.

26. In evolution, the fossil record refers to which of the following?

   A. A large collection of fossils maintained by scientists for use in museums and scientific exhibitions to show the variety of species that lived on Earth long ago.

   B. Evidence that layers of rock are found on Earth in sequence according to age, allowing scientists to trace fossils of organisms buried in these layers during each time period to observe how characteristics of the same species have gradually changed over time.

   C. The finding that appendages of organisms may be homologous, meaning similar in structure, between two different present-day species, such as the bones of the wing of a bat and the arm of a human.

   D. The observation that some species have analogous structures, which are structures with the same function but different evolutionary origin, such as the wing of a bird and wing of a mosquito.

27. Bean seeds are planted in a cup inside a shoebox standing upright on its side with a 3-inch diameter circle cut out of the center of the shoebox close to the bottom of the box, as shown below.

The box is placed in a sunlit room, and the plant is watered regularly without exposing it to sunlight for any length of time. Over time, what will the researcher most likely observe has happened to the bean seeds, and why?

   A. The bean seeds will not have germinated and will die due to lack of sunlight.

   B. The bean seeds will germinate and grow straight up to the top of the box but the plant will be brown, shriveled, and soon die due to lack of sunlight.

   C. The bean seeds will germinate and the plant will be observed to bend and grow out of the cutout circle due to a phototropism reaction.

   D. The bean seeds will germinate and the plant will be observed to bend and grow out of the cutout circle due to a geotropism reaction.

28. When a human is exposed to cold temperatures, the blood vessels constrict, and the person experiences shivering and numbness in extremities. When exposed to warmth, the blood vessels expand or dilate, perspiration occurs, and extremities may swell. Responses to cold and warm temperatures occur

   A. because the body is attempting to cause imbalance in the stable condition, or disrupt homeostasis.

   B. to promote the digestion of proteins for a needed supply of energy or impede the digestion of proteins to slow metabolism.

   C. as feedback mechanisms in response to stimuli in the body's effort to maintain homeostasis, or an internal stable condition.

   D. because changes in temperature and light exposure create a blood cell imbalance in the body that may interfere with feedback mechanisms and homeostatic responses.

29. Which of the following represents a symbiotic relationship known as mutualism?

   A. Mistletoe growing on a tree and using the food and nutrients from the tree for its own growth.

   B. A clown fish living among a type of sea anemone, whereby the fish aggressively protects the anemone from predators and the anemone's poison protects the fish from predators.

   C. Poison ivy producing a toxin that irritates the skin of many animal species, thereby protecting the plant from predation.

   D. Spiders building their web on plants to capture insects for food and to have a protective shelter.

30. In the flow of energy from one organism to the next in a food chain, energy is

   A. gained by each organism in the food chain as one organism gains energy from the organism ingested.

   B. lost by each organism in the food chain as one organism loses energy from the organism ingested.

   C. maintained along the food chain with each organism gaining an equal amount of energy from the organism ingested.

   D. not transferred along the food chain from one organism to the next; only inorganic nutrients are transferred.

31. Which of the following is the order of the layers of the Earth if one were to travel from the surface to its center?

   A. Crust, outer core, mantle, inner core

   B. Mantle, crust, inner core, outer core

   C. Outer core, inner core, crust, mantle

   D. Crust, mantle, outer core, inner core

32. What is the main function of Earth's atmosphere?

   A. To protect and preserve life

   B. To prevent the contamination of Earth

   C. To create a vacuum between Earth's crust and its mantle

   D. To recycle water and gases

33. Which type of rock is formed from the other types of rock after it has been subjected to extreme pressure and temperature over time?

   A. Igneous rock

   B. Metamorphic rock

   C. Sedimentary rock

   D. Conglomerate rock

34. Of the following, which best defines transpiration in the water cycle?

    A. The evaporation of water from the surface of lakes

    B. The condensation of water on the leaves of green plants

    C. The evaporation of water from the leaves of green plants

    D. The precipitation of water on the leaves of green plants

35. Which of the following best describes relative humidity and the instrument used to measure it?

    A. Relative humidity is a measure of the wind speed in a specific region and time, and is measured by an anemometer.

    B. Relative humidity is a measure of the amount of moisture in the air in a specific region and time, and is measured by an anemometer.

    C. Relative humidity is a measure of the moisture in the air in a specific region and time, and is measured by a psychrometer.

    D. Relative humidity is a measure of the air pressure in a specific region and time, and is measured by a barometer.

36. Which of the following regions of the U.S. experiences lake-effect snow in the winter?

    A. The Northeastern states next to the Atlantic Coast

    B. The Northeastern states just east of the Great Lakes

    C. The Midwestern states located in the Great Plains

    D. The Western states just east of the Rocky Mountains

37. What day in the Earth's Northern Hemisphere has the longest daylight hours of the year and why?

    A. The summer solstice because the Northern Hemisphere of the Earth is tilted toward the sun.

    B. The summer solstice because the Earth is closest to the sun at this time of year.

    C. The winter solstice because the Northern Hemisphere of the Earth is tilted toward the sun.

    D. The vernal equinox because the Earth is closest to the sun at this time of year.

38. Which of the following are objects in our solar system?

    A. Asteroids, planets, moons, and comets

    B. Planets, asteroids, moons, and black holes

    C. Planets, meteoroids, asteroids, and black holes

    D. Asteroids, Milky Way, quasars, and comets

39. Fossils of clam-like shells have been found deep in the sedimentary rock in Texas. These fossils indicate

    A. the state of Texas was once covered with small streams.

    B. the state of Texas was once covered by a sea or ocean.

    C. the state of Texas was once seismically active.

    D. there once were mountain ranges across the state of Texas.

40. In radiometric dating, scientists use which of the following information to determine the age of a fossil or rock?

    A. The appearance of the fossil or rock

    B. The location of the fossil or rock

    C. The presence of parent versus daughter isotopes in a fossil or rock

    D. The number of fossils within a rock

41. In Ms. Hernandez's class, the students are studying what plants need to survive. The students generate ideas to share. One need they identify for survival is food. When Ms. Hernandez asks the students where they think plants get their food, she notices that several students respond, "Plants get food from [eating] the soil." Which of the following is the best way to help students change this misconception that plants "eat the soil" to the scientifically accepted conception that plants make their own food from carbon dioxide and water through photosynthesis?

A. Have students conduct an experiment in which they plant seeds in two different containers, one in the dark and one in the light, and make observations over time.

B. Conduct a lecture/discussion session with students, explaining the process of photosynthesis by using pictures and diagrams.

C. Have students conduct an experiment in which they measure the mass of two pots of dry soil before planting seeds in the two pots; Then, after the plants have grown, measure the mass of the pots of dry soil again to see whether there has been a change.

D. Ask students to consult their textbook and search the internet for information on how plants get food.

42. After students concluded their inquiry lab experiments about respiration, Mr. Davis provided real-life examples of anaerobic respiration. He used the example of intensely exercising muscle cells breaking the bonds of sugar molecules to release energy without the use of oxygen (anaerobically). This energy, which is in the form of ATP energy, will be added to the ATP energy made available to the body when sugar is metabolized through aerobic respiration (with the use of oxygen). Mr. Davis described playing football, wrestling, and boxing in his examples. Which of the following is a primary concern with Mr. Davis's approach to teaching?

A. The content of cell respiration is abstract, thus the teacher should not have used inquiry in teaching students this topic.

B. The teacher used only male-dominated sports examples, whereas he should have given a variety of examples that would appeal to a wider range of his students' interests.

C. The content the teacher is presenting to students is not accurate because it is not possible to carry on respiration in the absence of oxygen.

D. The teacher should have described anaerobic respiration and provided real-life examples before the students carried out their inquiry activities.

43. Mr. Freeman conducted an inquiry lesson in which his class of 30 students worked in groups of three and first read and recorded the room temperature with two thermometers. Then, each student group taped one thermometer on a wall of the classroom near the floor, and the second thermometer on a wall of the classroom near the ceiling. After an hour, the students collected their thermometers and again read and recorded the temperature on each. What would be the best strategy to use next to help students reach the desired conclusion that the air near the ceiling is warmer than the air near the floor (demonstrating that warm air rises and cold air sinks, or the concept of convection)?

A. After students have collected their starting and ending temperatures on their thermometers, show a well-designed PowerPoint presentation with diagrams describing and showing convection. Follow the PowerPoint with discussion about other examples of convection, such as hot air balloons and a film about tornadoes.

B. After students have collected their starting and ending temperatures on their thermometers, ask each student group to review their starting and ending temperatures. Then ask each group to make a graph of their findings and develop a conclusion based on their group's measurement and results.

C. After students have collected their starting and ending temperatures on their thermometers, ask one student from each group to enter their starting and ending temperatures for their floor and ceiling thermometers on a class spreadsheet. Using all class data, ask students to make a line graph with one line showing starting and ending floor temperatures and another line showing the same for ceiling temperatures. Ask students to calculate the average starting and ending temperatures for ceiling and floor thermometers using class data.

D. After students have collected their starting and ending temperatures on their thermometers, have students conduct an experiment using a beaker filled with ice. Students measure the temperature of the ice and then place the beaker on a hot plate. After turning on the hot plate, the students measure and record the temperature of the ice every 30 seconds as it changes state from solid to liquid and then reaches the boiling point. The student groups record, share, and analyze findings in class discussion.

44. Which of the following are the best instruments to use in measuring the density of a relatively small, irregularly shaped rock?

A. A beaker of water and a metric tape measure.

B. A graduated cylinder of water and a metric tape measure.

C. A beaker of water and a triple beam or electronic balance.

D. A graduated cylinder of water and a triple beam or electronic balance.

45. Mr. Thomas, a seventh-grade science teacher, wants to use formative assessments to evaluate his students' authentic understanding of the process of scientific inquiry during their lab time. Which of the following would be best suited to this?

A. Do an item analysis of scores on the most recent science standardized test, and chart where students are making progress.

B. Evaluate the content of what students are writing in a scientific notebook by using a teacher-designed rubric.

C. Give a true/false quiz covering content in the most recent science unit, and go over the answers in class.

D. Test students on their knowledge of the vocabulary terms associated with the science unit by using a fill-in-the-blank format.

46. Which of the following best describes the primary role of science notebooks in the science classroom?

A. An opportunity for students to reflect on the day's activities, similar to a diary.

B. An opportunity for students to act like scientists by recording and exploring ideas related to investigative inquiries.

C. An opportunity for the teacher to assess grammar skills.

D. An opportunity for students to act like scientists by writing to inform, explain, persuade, and explore.

Science Practice Test 1: Answer Key

Test Item	Answer	Competency 809-
1.	C	001
2.	B	001
3.	C	002
4.	C	002
5.	C	003
6.	D	003
7.	D	004
8.	B	004
9.	C	005
10.	D	005
11.	B	006
12.	A	006
13.	B	007
14.	A	007
15.	A	009
16.	B	008
17.	A, C	008
18.	D	009
19.	C	010
20.	D	010
21.	A	011
22.	D	011
23.	C	012

Test Item	Answer	Competency 809-
24.	A	012
25.	A	013
26.	B	013
27.	C	014
28.	C	014
29.	B	015
30.	B	015
31.	D	016
32.	A	016
33.	B	017
34.	C	017
35.	C	018
36.	B	018
37.	A	019
38.	A	019
39.	B	020
40.	C	020
41.	C	021
42.	B	021
43.	C	022
44.	D	022
45.	B	023
46.	D	023

Science Practice Test 1: Detailed Answers

1. C.

Option (C) is correct because presenting the safety precautions is the first step in any laboratory investigation. The safety procedures should be printed on the students' laboratory sheets, posted on the walls of the classroom, and read aloud to students before beginning any investigation. Option (A) is incorrect because giving students the materials should not be done prior to a thorough explanation and discussion of both the safety precautions and the laboratory procedures. Failure to do so before allowing students to begin could have disastrous results and cause harm to students. Option (B) is incorrect because providing the "answers" and giving away the concepts to students should not be done before an inquiry investigation—students are to discover the concepts based on their own experiences and data. Option (D) is incorrect because although cleanup instructions are important, these instructions are not to precede a discussion on safety. Safety precautions must be implemented throughout the investigation, including during cleanup activities. **(809-001 Managing Learning Activities)**

2. B.

Option (B) is the correct answer. It is an important safety measure to keep all chemicals in a locked cabinet and ensure the key is not accessible to students. The door to the laboratory storeroom should also be locked. Students should never have access to chemicals without close supervision. The teacher is liable for any accidents due to negligence, such as leaving dangerous chemicals in an unlocked cabinet; therefore, option (A) is incorrect. The eyewash station (C) and fire extinguisher (D) are best placed near areas where chemicals or fire are used, but do not specifically pertain to students' access to chemicals. **(809-001 Managing Learning Activities)**

3. C.

Option (C) is correct because in science the triple beam balance is the instrument or piece of equipment used to measure mass. Option (A), the meter stick, measures length. Option (B), the graduated cylinder, measures liquid amount or volume. Option (D), the sling psychrometer, measures relative humidity. **(809-002 Use of Tools, Materials, Equipment, and Technologies)**

4. C.

Option (C) is the correct answer. The metric system is a very precise system that allows for the measurement of very small amounts of matter. For example, the metric system uses measurements divided into thousands (millimeters or milligrams), while the English system uses larger units of measurement, such as inches and ounces. Options (A) and (B) contain possible true statements and opinions, but they fail to address the question. Option (D) is incorrect; the English system does *not* have a simple way to compute measures. On the other hand, the metric system is a base-10 system, and the computations are typically easier. **(809-002 Use of Tools, Materials, Equipment, and Technologies)**

5. C.

Option (C) is the correct answer. Option (A) is not correct because not all scientific investigations use an experimental method. Option (B) is not correct because there is no single scientific method. Option (D) is not correct because there is no specific number of steps or sequence that makes an approach a scientific investigation. This leaves scientific inquiry, option (C), as the correct answer because it is general enough to describe all scientific investigations. **(809-003 Process of Scientific Inquiry and the History and Nature of Science)**

6.   D.

The best way to teach students about potential sources of error is to have the students experience it themselves. This is what makes Options (B) and (C) incorrect. Option (A) is incorrect because types of error will likely be limited to those associated with the procedure or techniques. Allowing students to do more open inquiry will likely lead to more error personally experienced by nearly every student. **(809-003 Process of Scientific Inquiry and the History and Nature of Science)**

7.   D.

Option (D) is correct because the high quantity of trees and massive foliage in South America carries on photosynthesis, which utilizes carbon dioxide gas to produce glucose, thus decreasing the amount of carbon dioxide in the atmosphere. Carbon dioxide gas in excess has been shown to absorb heat and increase warming of the atmosphere. If the foliage is removed, there will be fewer plants to take carbon dioxide out of the atmosphere, and it will accumulate in ever-increasing amounts. Global warming impacts the growth of food plants elsewhere across the globe, including the U.S., and these food plants have optimal growth within particular temperature and climatic ranges, which could be detrimental to their growth if conditions change. Option (A) is incorrect because there are interactions and interrelationships between what happens in one part of the globe and another. Option (B) is incorrect because the carbon dioxide in the atmosphere will increase rather than decrease. Option (C) is incorrect in that deforestation is not related to crop contamination. **(809-004 Science's Impact on Students' Daily Lives and Its Influence on Personal and Societal Decisions)**

8.   B.

When a population is exposed to a new virus, with no means of fighting it, the virus is able to spread throughout the population. If the virus is deadly, the population is quickly impacted and can decrease in overall number, making Option (B) the correct answer. Answer (A) is incorrect because when the number of births is higher than the number of deaths in a population, the overall population will increase. Option (C) is incorrect because when the number of births is the same as the number of deaths in a population, the population

size is stable, with neither an increase nor a decrease. Option (D) is incorrect because when individuals live longer, the overall population size will increase because more individuals are remaining in the population. **(809-004 Science's Impact on Students' Daily Lives and Its Influence on Personal and Societal Decisions)**

9.   C.

Option (C) is correct because it is not possible to create a model that is exactly the same as the actual scientific phenomena or object being represented. A ball-and-stick model of molecules is only a representation of an atom; the ionic or covalent bonding is due to the charges in the atoms, particularly electrons, which cannot be adequately represented by a stick. Option (A) is incorrect because no model is exact in its representation; it is impossible to represent every detail of a phenomenon with a model—it will simply be the real phenomenon instead. For example, you can make a marsh ecosystem in the classroom in an aquarium to represent an actual marsh, but it could not possibly have all of the elements of the actual marsh ecosystem in nature. Option (B) is incorrect because although computer-generated models are often useful, many physical models are equally or more useful than those that are computer-generated. Making and flying an actual paper airplane to represent real airplane flight gives learners a different experience than making virtual paper airplanes on the computer. Option (D) is incorrect because, although sometimes students may develop misconceptions through the use of models, if implemented correctly, the models will actually help students build sound understandings of natural phenomena. In using models, teachers should ask the students to point out differences between the actual phenomena and the model. Students should understand that the model is simply a tool to help us visualize the natural phenomena but that they have limitations in their applicability. **(809-005 Unifying Concepts and Processes)**

10.   D.

Option (D) is the correct answer because the concepts of constancy, change, form, and function are seen across the science disciplines. Constancy and change are seen in the geologic process, as well as biological processes. Form and function explain the structure of matter, the Earth, and living organisms. Option (A) is incorrect because the science disciplines do not address supernatural concepts. Science only addresses concepts for which observations data can be collected and evaluated. **(809-005 Unifying Concepts and Processes)**

11. **B.**

Option (B) is the correct answer because burning the fuel causes the gases released to be expelled at a very high speed out of a nozzle, which is computer-controlled in the desired direction to push the rocket in the opposite direction. This is Newton's third law, that for every action there is an equal and opposite reaction. Options (A) and (D) are incorrect because the force is not from outside of the rocket in this case. Option (C) is incorrect as it is a simplified version of Bernoulli's principle of lift. **(809-006 Forces and Motion and Their Relationships)**

12. **A.**

Option (A) is correct. A single pulley and movable pulleys are classified as simple machines. The amount of force required to lift an object with 2 pulleys in a single system reduces the force required to lift the object by one-half. Option (B) is incorrect because the movable pulley will not increase, but rather decrease the amount of force required. Option (C) is incorrect because the force will not be changed to a definite value of force; the reduction of force to be applied depends on the weight of the object to be lifted and the number of pulleys in the system. Option (D) is incorrect because the use of a movable pulley does reduce the amount of force required to lift the object. For more information, see: *http://www.ehow.com/how-does_5231254_much-weight-pulley-off.html. (809-006 Forces and Motion and Their Relationships)*

13. **B.**

Option (B) is correct because mixing salt (NaCl) in water does not change the substance in any way and it is reversible. The substance in the water is still salt, and if the water is evaporated, salt crystals will again be restored. Option (A) is incorrect because mixing an acid and base is a neutralization reaction—a chemical reaction that forms new substances, namely a salt and water. For example, mixing hydrochloric acid (HCl) with the base sodium hydroxide (NaOH) produces NaCl and H_2O. Option (C)

is incorrect because rust is the chemical reaction between oxygen in the atmosphere and iron (FeO). The salt and ice on roads in the winter are electrolytes that wear away the protective finish on automobiles and expose the metal to oxygen where rust can form (FeO). Option (D) is incorrect because burning is a chemical reaction in which oxygen combines with the substance to form a new substance. Burning sugar, a hydrocarbon-based substance, will form carbon dioxide and water. **(809-007 Physical Properties of and Changes in Matter)**

14. **A.**

Option (A) is correct because for something to float, it must be less dense than the liquid it is in, and for an object to sink, it must be more dense than the liquid it is in. Density is a measure of how tightly packed the matter is (mass) within a given amount of space (volume) or (D) = M/V. Water is unique with respect to its density because it is the only substance on Earth that is less dense in solid form (ice) than in liquid form (water); therefore the solid form floats in its own liquid. Alcohol is less dense (molecules are less tightly packed) than water, so the ice cube sinks. Option (B) is incorrect because if the ice cube was more dense than liquid water, it would sink in the water, and if less dense than the alcohol, it would float in this liquid. Option (C) is incorrect because if a substance has equal density to the liquid it is in, it would be suspended in the middle of the liquid. This statement is incorrect even though the second part of it—that the ice is more dense than the alcohol—is correct. Option (D) is incorrect because again, equal density means the ice cube would be suspended in the water (neither sink nor float) and in the alcohol. **(809-007 Physical Properties of and Changes in Matter)**

15. **A.**

Option (A) is correct because although sound initiates with vibration of an object, the sound waves are caused by the vibration of the air around the object, not the object itself. The vibrating air reaches the human eardrum, causing it to vibrate, which is sensed by the auditory nerve and carried to the brain for interpretation as sound. Option (B) is incorrect, as previously explained, in that it is not the object itself vibrating that causes sound, it is the movement or vibration of the air molecules in the vicinity of the object. Option (C) is incorrect because light colliding with sound waves is not the cause of sound, and in fact, light waves travel much faster than sound waves. Option (D) is incorrect because this is the formula for Newton's Second Law of Motion. **(809-009 Energy and Interactions between Matter and Energy)**

16. B.

Option (B) is correct because water is made up of two or more different kinds of atoms, hydrogen (H) and oxygen (O), which is a compound. Choice (A) is incorrect because elements are made of only one kind of atom. Option (C) is incorrect because water is made up of more than a single atom. Option (D) is incorrect because ions are positively or negatively charged atoms or molecules and water is a stable molecule. **(809-008 Chemical Properties of and Changes in Matter)**

17. A., C.

This item asks you to select all that apply. Choices (A) and (C) are correct. Mass and volume are the two variables necessary to calculate the density of an object using the formula D = M/V. Color, Texture, and Odor—choices (B), (D), and (E)—are physical characteristics of an object, but are not needed or relevant in calculating its density. **(Competency 809-008 Chemical Properties of and Changes in Matter)**

18. D.

Option (D) is correct because the colors we see around us are the wavelengths of light reflected by that object or substance. Green plants therefore do not absorb green light waves, but this color of visible light of the electromagnetic spectrum reflects off its surface and our eyes see the color green. Option (A) is incorrect because if the plant had absorbed green wavelengths, the color green would not be seen by our eyes because it would be absorbed into the substance of the leaves. Option (B) is incorrect because refraction is the bending of light rather than reflection, so the color would be bent rather than reflected to our eyes. Option (C) is incorrect because green plants in the growing season reflect and do not absorb green wavelengths of light, so the color we see is green. However, in the fall, deciduous trees, which are plants in which the leaves change color and fall off in the

winter, stop producing chlorophyll (the green pigment in plants), and instead produce other pigments, including red and yellow, as they become dormant. The red and yellow colors to which these leaves change indicate a shift in the wavelengths of light reflected. If our eyes see the color red, then the leaves are reflecting light in the red wavelength band of the electromagnetic spectrum. **(809-009 Energy and Interactions between Matter and Energy)**

19. C.

Option (C) is correct in that hydroelectric energy produces electricity through fast-moving water (e.g., the generators that tap the power of Niagara Falls). Nuclear energy utilizes the radioactivity of uranium. Fossil fuel energy produces electricity through the burning of coal, oil, and/or natural gas. Geothermal energy produces electricity by harnessing the energy beneath the Earth's surface to produce electricity. Solar energy captures the energy of the sun to produce electricity. Options (A), (B), and (D) are listed in the incorrect order and/or are incorrect sources of energy. **(809-010 Energy Transformations and the Conservation of Matter and Energy)**

20. D.

Option (D) is the correct answer. Exothermic reactions give off heat during the reaction. Endothermic reactions do the opposite: absorb heat during the reaction. Option (A) is incorrect because melting ice cubes is a physical change and is not a reaction. Options (B) and (C) are incorrect because although these are examples of chemical reactions, heat is not given off during the reaction. **(809-010 Energy Transformations and the Conservation of Matter and Energy)**

21. A.

Arteries always carry blood away from the heart. Veins always carry blood to the heart. There is one artery—the pulmonary artery—that carries blood away from the right side of the heart directly to the lungs and thus does not carry oxygenated blood, making option (D) incorrect. Options (B) and (C) are incorrect because only veins contain valves to prevent backflow of blood as the blood is returning to the heart from all parts of the body. **(809-011 The Structure and Function of Living Things)**

22. D.

Proteins are made up of a chain of amino acid molecules that are arranged in a particular order for that specific protein (for example, hormones, enzymes, hair, fingernails), making option (D) the correct option. There are 20 amino acids, arranged in a vast variety of sequences, with each sequence and shape that results being unique for that particular protein. Option (A) is incorrect because a monosaccharide is the building block of carbohydrates. Options (B) and (C) are incorrect because these molecules are the components of lipids (fats). **(809-011 The Structure and Function of Living Things)**

23. C.

In using the Punnett square diagram, the parental genotypes can be determined as follows:

Parent 1

	B	b
B	BB	Bb
b	Bb	bb

Parent 2

As shown in the Punnett square, the result of the cross of Bb for one parent and Bb for the other parent is 75% with BB and Bb and 25% bb. The "B" allele for *brown* coat is dominant over the "b" allele for *white* coat, so the physical appearance or *phenotype* of 3 out of 4 or 75% of the offspring will be a brown coat. The recessive gene will appear in 1 out of 4, or 25% of the offspring, which is represented in the Punnett square diagram as "bb." Any other cross will not produce these percentages of brown and white coats in the offspring. Options (A) and (B) result in 100% of the offspring with the phenotype of brown coats. Option (D) results in 100% of the offspring with the phenotype of white coats. **(809-012 Reproduction and the Mechanisms of Heredity)**

24. A.

Asexual reproduction is accomplished through a process of binary fission, or mitosis, in which the DNA (genetic material) is first replicated, and, after a series of events, the parent cell divides into two daughter cells with genetic material that is identical to the one parent cell and to each other. Options (B), (C), and (D) all describe sexual reproduction, where parent cells divide into four daughter cells containing half the genetic material (DNA) as the original parent. The daughter cell may be a sperm or egg cell, for example. The daughter cell of one organism joins with the daughter cell of another organism of the same species to form a new cell that has a combination of genetic material from both parent cells. **(809-012 Reproduction and the Mechanisms of Heredity)**

25. A.

Lizards' tails easily drop off when touched or pulled as a form of adaptation that allows the lizard to survive by escaping from predators. The tail will grow back in time. However, a new lizard will not grow from the detached tail, making option (B) the incorrect choice. Lizards do not undergo molting, making option (C) incorrect. Molting is a characteristic of some insects and crustaceans. The lizard also does not lose its tail due to environmental stresses, making option (D) incorrect. **(809-013 Adaptations of Organisms and the Theory of Evolution)**

26. B.

The fossil record is one line of evidence for evolution, which refers to the layers of rocks that indicate periods of time throughout Earth's history, making option (B) the correct answer. These layers contain fossils that show clear patterns of change in species over time. Scientists now know that these changes were due to DNA mutations that provided the organism, and subsequently the offspring, with more favorable traits for survival in that environment. Option (A) is incorrect because it does not refer to the fossil record found in rock layers and sequencing according to geologic age. Options (C) and (D) are incorrect in terms of the fossil record, but do represent other lines of evidence for evolution in the area of morphology, namely homologous and analogous structures, respectively. **(809-013 Adaptations of Organisms and the Theory of Evolution)**

27. C.

The plant will grow and bend toward the light due to chemicals called auxins that create specific responses to stimuli in the plant from the environment. The environmental stimulus that produces a chemical response directing plant stems and leaves to grow toward light is called phototropism, so option (C) is correct. Option (A) is incorrect because seeds do not need sunlight to germinate, only the proper temperature for that particular plant species, as well as water and air (oxygen). Option (B) is incorrect because there will be some light entering the box through the circle cutout opening at the bottom, so although it may not be the healthiest of plants, it will not be entirely shriveled and will likely survive. Option (D) is incorrect because a geotropism is a plant's response to gravity, typically presented by the roots growing downward due to gravity. **(809-014 Regulatory Mechanisms and Behavior)**

28. C.

The body undergoes a series of feedback mechanisms in response to cold and warm temperatures in an effort to maintain a constant internal temperature. This is critical in maintaining an internal stable condition, or homeostasis, making option (C) the correct option. These responses conserve energy when exposed to prolonged cold temperatures and release energy when exposed to prolonged warm temperatures. The mechanisms described in blood vessels constricting or dilating, the body shivering or perspiring, and numbness (indicating lack of blood flow to extremities to maintain warmth and blood flow to critical internal organs) or swelling of extremities (indicating blood going to extremities to cool critical internal organs) are responses to the body's efforts to maintain homeostasis. Option (A) is incorrect because it describes processes that would be in opposition to maintaining homeostasis. Option (B) is incorrect because it describes digestive processes that are not part of the scenario described in this item to maintain homeostasis. Option (D) is incorrect because a blood cell imbalance will not cause the conditions described in the scenario. **(809-014 Regulatory Mechanisms and Behavior)**

29. B.

Mutualism is a form of symbiosis in which both organisms benefit from the relationship, making option (B) the correct option. Option (A) is an example of another form of symbiosis called parasitism, in which one organism benefits from the relationship at the expense of the other. Option (C) is not a form of symbiosis. Option (D) is a form of symbiosis called commensalism, in which one organism benefits and the other organism neither benefits nor is harmed. **(809-015 The Relationships between Organisms and the Environment)**

30. B.

Energy is lost from one organism to the next along the food chain, making option (B) the correct response. The energy originates from the sun and is transferred to green plants in photosynthesis, where it is locked within the chemical bonds of simple sugars (glucose). Thus, green plants contain the most energy from the sun in the chemical bonds of the glucose molecules it forms. As each organism in the chain ingests an organism (sun → grass → rabbit → coyotes → decomposers), some of the original sun energy has already been lost to support the life functions of that organism, so energy content reduces as you progress along the food chain, with the most energy being supplied to the plants, followed by primary consumers, secondary consumers, and so on with the lowest levels of energy being available for decomposers. Option (A) is incorrect because energy is lost and not gained through the food chain. Option (C) is incorrect because energy is not maintained at the same levels since some energy is always used by the organism to carry on its own life functions. Option (D) is incorrect because energy along with inorganic nutrients is transferred from one organism to the next in a food chain. **(809-015 The Relationships between Organisms and the Environment)**

31. D.

Option (D) shows the correct order of the layers of the Earth from surface to center: crust, mantle, outer core, inner core. Options (A), (B), and (C) show an incorrect sequence of the layers of the Earth. For more information see *http://www.factmonster.com* (search "earth structure"). **(809-016 The Structure and Function of Earth Systems)**

32. A.

Option (A) is the correct answer. The main function of the atmosphere is to serve as a buffer between space and the Earth's crust. This buffer provides the ideal conditions to protect and preserve life on Earth. Options (B) and (D) present two functions that can be linked to the atmosphere: recycling water and gases; however, they fail to highlight the real function of the atmosphere.

Option (C) is completely incorrect: the atmosphere is above the crust, not beneath it. **(809-016 The Structure and Function of Earth Systems)**

33. B.

Option (B), metamorphic rock, is correct because this type of rock is formed from igneous or sedimentary rock that is deep in the Earth and has been subjected to extreme pressure and temperature. Metamorphic rock may also exhibit signs of the Earth's folding due to plates colliding, which may also bend and twist the rock. Option (A), igneous rock, is the rock produced from hot lava or magma prior to exposure to pressure and/or folding. Option (C), sedimentary rock, is formed from eroded rock carried in bodies of water as sediments such as clays and sand. The sediments settle out of the water and form rock such as sandstone and shale. Option (D), conglomerate rock, is coarse-grained sedimentary rock. In conglomerates, rocks of different shapes and sizes are cemented together. See *http://flexiblelearning.auckland.ac.nz/rocks_minerals/rocks/index.html*. **(809-017 Cycles in Earth Systems)**

34. C.

Option (C) is correct. Transpiration is the evaporation of water from the stomata located on the underside of leaves on plants. Liquid water is absorbed through the roots and is carried through the plant in small vessels called the xylem. Water that is not needed or excreted evaporates, changing from liquid to gas (water vapor) as it leaves the stomata. This moisture in the air from transpiration contributes to humidity and to cloud formation, along with water evaporated from lakes, rivers, and oceans, which is eventually precipitated to Earth again in the water cycle. Option (A) is incorrect because evaporation from lakes and other bodies of water is simply evaporation—molecules of liquid water on the surface leave the surface in the form of water vapor. Option (B) is incorrect because condensation is water changing from water vapor (gas) to liquid water. Option (D) is incorrect because precipitation is water falling to Earth from clouds in the form of rain, snow, sleet, or hail. **(809-017 Cycles in Earth Systems)**

35. C.

Option (C) is correct because relative humidity is the percentage of water in the air and is measured by a psychrometer. Options (A) and (B) are incorrect because an anemometer measures wind speed. Option (D) is incorrect because humidity is not a measure of air pressure. See *http://www.space.com/17683-earth-atmosphere.html*. **(809-018 The Role of Energy in Weather and Climate)**

36. B.

Option (B) is correct because those states just east of the Great Lakes, such as New York and Pennsylvania, experience the most lake-effect snows. The air contains water evaporated over the Great Lakes (e.g., Lake Erie and Lake Ontario). As the air mass moves east it cools, which causes precipitation in the form of snow if the air is below the freezing temperature of water. Option (A) is incorrect because large bodies of water tend to keep the areas near the coast warmer than land. This is because water has high specific heat, meaning it cools off and warms up more slowly than any other substance on Earth. This is why coastal areas have comparatively warmer winters and cooler summers compared to inland regions at the same latitude. In addition, storms in the U.S. tend to travel from west to east. Options (C) and (D) are incorrect because these regions are not located near significant bodies of water. **(809-018 The Role of Energy in Weather and Climate)**

37. A.

Option (A) is correct because at the location in the Earth's orbit that is the summer solstice, the tilt of the Earth in the Northern Hemisphere is facing toward the sun, making the daylight hours longer than at other times of the year. On the date of the summer solstice, typically June 20 or 21, or the first day of summer, the Northern Hemisphere has approximately 15 hours of sunlight and 9 hours of darkness. Option (B) is incorrect because first, the Earth's distance does not impact daylight hours, and second, the Earth is actually farther away from the sun at the summer solstice than it is at the winter solstice (on or around December 21). Option (C) is incorrect because the Northern Hemisphere is tilted away from the sun at the winter solstice, with 9 hours of daylight, and 15 hours of darkness. So the winter solstice has the shortest number of daylight hours than any other day of the year. The Vernal Equinox occurs in the spring in the Northern Hemisphere, typically around March 20 or the first day of spring, and has an equal number of daylight hours and darkness hours (12 hours each). **(809-019 The Characteristics of the Solar System and the Universe)**

38. A.

Asteroids, planets, moons, and comets are all objects in the solar system. Black holes and quasars are theorized objects in distant galaxies, and the Milky Way is the name of our own cluster of stars or galaxy in which the solar system (sun, planets, dwarf planets, comets, asteroids, and meteoroids) reside. **(809-019 The Characteristics of the Solar System and the Universe)**

39. B.

Option (B) is the correct answer. Modern-day clams are found in both fresh and saltwater habitats, such as seas and oceans. Based on current understandings of clams, it is assumed that clam-like fossils would have inhabited the same environments. When fossils of fresh and/or saltwater organisms are found on currently dry locations, it is assumed that at some point in Earth's history, the location was once covered in water. Option (A) is incorrect because Texas currently has small streams. Option (C) is incorrect because fossils would not be the only indicator of seismic activity. There would also need to be evidence in the rock layers. Option (D) is incorrect because clams are not found on mountain ranges and would not indicate the presence of mountain ranges in Texas's history. **(809-020 The History of the Earth System)**

40. C.

Option (C) is the correct answer. Radioactive parent isotopes decay at particular rates in daughter isotopes. When scientists examine fossils and/or rocks, they can measure the amount of parent and daughter isotopes. With these amounts known, the scientists can then determine the age of the fossil and/or rock. Options (A), (B), and (D) are incorrect because none of these characteristics are used to determine the age of a fossil or rock. **(809-020 The History of the Earth System)**

41. C.

Option (C) is the correct answer. This investigation provides a concrete experience for students to observe that there is no change in the mass of the soil from the beginning to the end of the experiment. They observe that the plant must not be "eating" the soil, but the source of food must be something else. This experiment should be followed by a series of investigations designed to help students discover the source of food as a combination of carbon dioxide and water in the presence of light, thereby constructing the concept of photosynthesis. Option (A) is incorrect because, although student-centered, the concept discovered would be that "plants need light to grow." The seeds planted and placed in the dark will germinate but later die due to lack of sunlight, whereas those placed in the light will germinate, grow, and thrive. This experiment would help students discover the role of light in photosynthesis. Option (B) is incorrect because students do not learn best through lecture/discussion, which is often abstract and meaningless to them. Further, students do not tend to alter their misconceptions when they are simply "told"—they need to discover for themselves. Option (D) is incorrect because students will not know what to focus on in their readings and online searches and will likely be inundated with too much information, making a change from misconception to a more scientifically accepted conception unlikely. **(809-021 Teaching Science and How Students Learn Science)**

42. B.

Option (B) is the correct answer. The examples teachers provide in class should tap into the prior knowledge of students to help promote learning. In the examples given by Mr. Davis, only the prior knowledge of males in his class who have had these types of experiences was activated. Teachers must be careful not to use examples that appeal to only certain groups (e.g., based on gender, ethnicity), which marginalizes the rest of the students. Teachers must develop a wide range of examples that will address the interests of all students in the classroom, making option (B) the best response. Options (A) and (D) address the issue of students needing hands-on, concrete, and inquiry-based experiences (rather than lecture explanations) to best learn science, so Mr. Davis is correct in using inquiry to introduce the topic. Option (C) is incorrect because it is possible for cells to carry on certain types of respiration without the use of oxygen (e.g., anaerobic respiration and fermentation). **(809-021 Teaching Science and How Students Learn Science)**

43. C.

Option (C) is the correct answer. In this scenario, the students use the data collected to make sense of their findings. They are using a larger set of data because they are sharing with all groups. Science requires many trials of the same experiment before conclusions can be drawn. Collecting data in several repeated experiments helps the researcher discover patterns and also errors and outliers. The data in this scenario are represented graphically and mathematically, which also promotes sound interpretations. Option (A) is incorrect because students did not use their own collected data to draw conclusions and gain understanding of the concepts—their work was not *used*, so it became an irrelevant activity. Option (B) is incorrect because sound scientific conclusions cannot be drawn based on one set of data but are accomplished by repeating the experiment several times or days in a row using the whole class's set of data. Option (D) is incorrect because interpretations of the first experiment were not made, and no conclusions were drawn. In addition, the second experiment is not related to the first experiment—the first leads to the concept of convection, whereas the second leads to concept of phase changes in water. **(809-022 The Process of Scientific Inquiry and Its Role in Science Instruction)**

44. D.

Option (D) is the correct answer. Density is the amount of matter (mass) packed into a given amount of space (volume), and is measured by determining the mass of a substance divided by its volume, or density = mass/volume (D = m/v). To measure the density of an irregularly shaped object such as a rock, the proper instruments are a balance, to measure mass, and a graduated cylinder with water, to measure volume. The triple beam or electronic balance will provide the mass of the rock in grams. The volume of the irregularly shaped rock is obtained by filling a graduated cylinder one-half to two-thirds with water. The level of water in the graduated cylinder in milliliters is recorded. The rock is carefully dropped into the graduated cylinder, and

the change in the level of water (or the amount of water that was "displaced" by the rock) in milliliters is measured. One milliliter (liquid volume measure) is equal to one cubic centimeter (solid volume measure); thus, the change in water level after adding the rock is the volume of the rock. These values are then used in the formula (D = m/v) to determine the rock's density. Options (A), (B), and (C) are not the proper instruments to use in determining an irregularly shaped object's density. A beaker does not provide a precise enough measure of the amount of water displaced, or the volume of the rock. A measuring tape is not accurate for determining the volume of an irregularly shaped object. The proper determination of density requires the use of instruments that will measure the volume and the mass of the object. **(809-022 The Process of Scientific Inquiry and Its Role in Science Instruction)**

45. B.

Option (B) is correct because it focuses on the curriculum-based content the students are performing on a regular basis. Because the science notebook contains understandings about related science content, and a rubric is used (informal assessment), it is best suited to assessing students' knowledge about scientific inquiry. For instance, students can describe what the lab process was like and what they did during the process, they can make predictions, and so forth. Options (A), (C), and (D) are less authentic forms of assessment because they are based more on measuring student recall of knowledge rather than deeper understanding. **(809-023 Assessments and Assessment Practices)**

46. D.

The best answer is Option (D) because it describes the major outcomes desired of students in their writing and is also consistent with how scientists use their science notebooks. Option (A) is not correct because scientists do not use science notebooks as a diary but rather as a reflection focused on the ongoing investigation. Option (B) is reasonable, but it leaves students only with the act of recording their observations and "exploring their ideas." Option (D) includes the range of purposes seen in scientists' notebooks. **(Competency 809-023 Assessments and Assessment Practices)**

TExES Core Subjects 4–8
Appendix

Definitions and Formulas for the TExES Math 4–8

Calculus

First Derivative: $f'(x) = \dfrac{dy}{dx}$

Second Derivative: $f''(x) = \dfrac{d^2y}{dx^2}$

Probability

$P(A \text{ or } B) = P(A) + P(B) - P(A \text{ and } B)$

$P(A \text{ and } B) = P(A)P(B|A) = P(B)P(A|B)$

Algebra

i $\qquad\qquad i^2 = -1$

A^{-1} $\qquad\qquad$ inverse of matrix A

$A = P\left(1 = \dfrac{r}{n}\right)^{nt}$ $\quad$ Compound interest, where A is the final value

$\qquad\qquad\qquad\qquad\quad P$ is the principal

$\qquad\qquad\qquad\qquad\quad r$ is the interest rate

$\qquad\qquad\qquad\qquad\quad t$ is the term

$\qquad\qquad\qquad\qquad\quad n$ is the number of divisions within the term

$[x] = n$ $\qquad\qquad$ Greatest integer function, where n is the integer such that $n \le x < n + 1$

Geometry

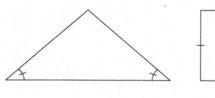

Congruent Angles

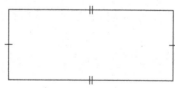

Congruent Sides

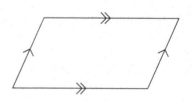

Parallel Sides

Circumference of a Circle: $C = 2\pi r$

Volume

Cylinder: (area of base) $\times$ height

Cone: $\frac{1}{3}$ (area of base) $\times$ height

Sphere: $\frac{4}{3}\pi r^3$

Prism: (area of base) $\times$ height

Area

Triangle: $\frac{1}{2}$ (base $\times$ height)

Rhombus: $\frac{1}{2}$ (diagonal$_1$ $\times$ diagonal$_2$)

Trapezoid: $\frac{1}{2}$ height (base$_1$ $\times$ base$_2$)

Sphere: $4\pi r^2$

Circle: πr^2

Lateral surface area of cylinder: $2\pi rh$

Trigonometry

Law of Sines: $\dfrac{\sin A}{a} = \dfrac{\sin B}{b} = \dfrac{\sin C}{c}$

Law of Cosines: $c^2 = a^2 + b^2 - 2ab\cos C$

$b^2 = a^2 + c^2 - 2ac\cos B$

$a^2 = b^2 + c^2 - 2bc\cos A$

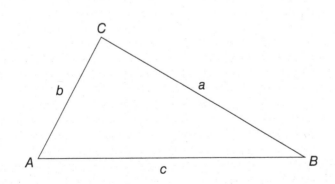

PERIODIC TABLE
Atomic Properties of the Elements

NIST — National Institute of Standards and Technology
U.S. Department of Commerce

Physical Measurement Laboratory www.nist.gov/pml
Standard Reference Data www.nist.gov/srd

§ 1 second = 9 192 631 770 periods of radiation corresponding to the transition between the two hyperfine levels of the ground state of ^{133}Cs

FREQUENTLY USED FUNDAMENTAL PHYSICAL CONSTANTS§

speed of light in vacuum	c	299 792 458 m s^{-1}	(exact)
Planck constant	h	6.626 070 15 × 10^{-34} J Hz^{-1}	(exact)
elementary charge	e	1.602 176 634 × 10^{-19} C	(exact)
Avogadro constant	N_A	6.022 140 76 × 10^{23} mol^{-1}	(exact)
Boltzmann constant	k	1.380 649 × 10^{-23} J K^{-1}	(exact)
electron volt	eV	1.602 176 634 × 10^{-19} J	(exact)
electron mass	m_e	9.109 383 70 × 10^{-31} kg	
energy equivalent	$m_e c^2$	0.510 998 950 MeV	
proton mass	m_p	1.672 621 924 × 10^{-27} kg	
energy equivalent	$m_p c^2$	938.272 088 MeV	
fine-structure constant	α	1/137.035 999	
Rydberg energy	$R_\infty hc$	13.605 693 1230 eV	
Newtonian constant of gravitation	G	6.674 × 10^{-11} m^3 kg^{-1} s^{-2}	

§ For the most accurate values of these and other constants, visit pml.nist.gov/constants.

Solids
Liquids
Gases
Artificially Prepared

Key
Atomic Number — 58
Symbol — Ce
Ground State — $^1G_4^\circ$
Name — Cerium
Standard Atomic Weight (u) — 140.12
Ground-state Configuration — [Xe]4f5d6s^2
Ionization Energy (eV) — 5.5386

† Based upon ^{12}C. ( ) indicates the mass number of the longest-lived isotope.

For the most precise values and uncertainties visit ciaaw.org and pml.nist.gov/data.

NIST SP 966 (July 2019)

Periodic table reproduced courtesy of the U.S. National Institute of Standards and Technology.

Group 1 (IA)
1 H Hydrogen 1.008 1s $^2S_{1/2}$ 13.5984
3 Li Lithium 6.94 1s^{2}2s 5.3917
11 Na Sodium 22.990 [Ne]3s 5.1391
19 K Potassium 39.098 [Ar]4s 4.3407
37 Rb Rubidium 85.468 [Kr]5s 4.1771
55 Cs Cesium 132.91 [Xe]6s 3.8939
87 Fr Francium (223) [Rn]7s 4.0727

Group 2 (IIA)
4 Be Beryllium 9.0122 1s^{2}2s^2 9.3227
12 Mg Magnesium 24.305 [Ne]3s^2 7.6462
20 Ca Calcium 40.078 [Ar]4s^2 6.1132
38 Sr Strontium 87.62 [Kr]5s^2 5.6949
56 Ba Barium 137.33 [Xe]6s^2 5.2117
88 Ra Radium (226) [Rn]7s^2 5.2784

Group 3 (IIIB)
21 Sc Scandium 44.956 [Ar]3d4s^2 6.5615
39 Y Yttrium 88.906 [Kr]4d5s^2 6.2173
57 La Lanthanum 138.91 [Xe]5d6s^2 5.5769
89 Ac Actinium (227) [Rn]6d7s^2 5.3802

Group 4 (IVB)
22 Ti Titanium 47.867 [Ar]3d^{2}4s^2 6.8281
40 Zr Zirconium 91.224 [Kr]4d^{2}5s^2 6.6341
72 Hf Hafnium 178.49 [Xe]4f^{14}5d^{2}6s^2 6.8251
104 Rf Rutherfordium (267) [Rn]5f^{14}6d^{2}7s^2 6.02

Group 5 (VB)
23 V Vanadium 50.942 [Ar]3d^{3}4s^2 6.7462
41 Nb Niobium 92.906 [Kr]4d^{4}5s 6.7589
73 Ta Tantalum 180.95 [Xe]4f^{14}5d^{3}6s^2 7.5496
105 Db Dubnium (268) [Rn]5f^{14}6d^{3}7s^2 6.8

Group 6 (VIB)
24 Cr Chromium 51.996 [Ar]3d^{5}4s 6.7665
42 Mo Molybdenum 95.95 [Kr]4d^{5}5s 7.0924
74 W Tungsten 183.84 [Xe]4f^{14}5d^{4}6s^2 7.8640
106 Sg Seaborgium (269) [Rn]5f^{14}6d^{4}7s^2 7.8

Group 7 (VIIB)
25 Mn Manganese 54.938 [Ar]3d^{5}4s^2 7.4340
43 Tc Technetium (97) [Kr]4d^{5}5s^2 7.1194
75 Re Rhenium 186.21 [Xe]4f^{14}5d^{5}6s^2 7.8335
107 Bh Bohrium (270) [Rn]5f^{14}6d^{5}7s^2 7.7

Group 8 (VIII)
26 Fe Iron 55.845 [Ar]3d^{6}4s^2 7.9025
44 Ru Ruthenium 101.07 [Kr]4d^{7}5s 7.3605
76 Os Osmium 190.23 [Xe]4f^{14}5d^{6}6s^2 8.4382
108 Hs Hassium (269) [Rn]5f^{14}6d^{6}7s^2 7.6

Group 9 (VIII)
27 Co Cobalt 58.933 [Ar]3d^{7}4s^2 7.8810
45 Rh Rhodium 102.91 [Kr]4d^{8}5s 7.4589
77 Ir Iridium 192.22 [Xe]4f^{14}5d^{7}6s^2 8.9670
109 Mt Meitnerium (278) [Rn]5f^{14}6d^{7}7s^2

Group 10 (VIII)
28 Ni Nickel 58.693 [Ar]3d^{8}4s^2 7.6399
46 Pd Palladium 106.42 [Kr]4d^{10} 8.3369
78 Pt Platinum 195.08 [Xe]4f^{14}5d^{9}6s 8.9588
110 Ds Darmstadtium (281) [Rn]5f^{14}6d^{8}7s^2

Group 11 (IB)
29 Cu Copper 63.546 [Ar]3d^{10}4s 7.7264
47 Ag Silver 107.87 [Kr]4d^{10}5s 7.5762
79 Au Gold 196.97 [Xe]4f^{14}5d^{10}6s 9.2256
111 Rg Roentgenium (282) [Rn]5f^{14}6d^{9}7s^2

Group 12 (IIB)
30 Zn Zinc 65.38 [Ar]3d^{10}4s^2 9.3942
48 Cd Cadmium 112.41 [Kr]4d^{10}5s^2 8.9938
80 Hg Mercury 200.59 [Xe]4f^{14}5d^{10}6s^2 10.4375
112 Cn Copernicium (285) [Rn]5f^{14}6d^{10}7s^2

Group 13 (IIIA)
5 B Boron 10.81 1s^{2}2s^{2}2p 8.2980
13 Al Aluminum 26.982 [Ne]3s^{2}3p 5.9858
31 Ga Gallium 69.723 [Ar]3d^{10}4s^{2}4p 5.9993
49 In Indium 114.82 [Kr]4d^{10}5s^{2}5p 5.7864
81 Tl Thallium 204.38 [Xe]4f^{14}5d^{10}6s^{2}6p 6.1083
113 Nh Nihonium (286)

Group 14 (IVA)
6 C Carbon 12.011 1s^{2}2s^{2}2p^2 11.2603
14 Si Silicon 28.085 [Ne]3s^{2}3p^2 8.1517
32 Ge Germanium 72.630 [Ar]3d^{10}4s^{2}4p^2 7.8994
50 Sn Tin 118.71 [Kr]4d^{10}5s^{2}5p^2 7.3439
82 Pb Lead 207.2 [Xe]4f^{14}5d^{10}6s^{2}6p^2 7.4167
114 Fl Flerovium (289)

Group 15 (VA)
7 N Nitrogen 14.007 1s^{2}2s^{2}2p^3 14.5341
15 P Phosphorus 30.974 [Ne]3s^{2}3p^3 10.4867
33 As Arsenic 74.922 [Ar]3d^{10}4s^{2}4p^3 9.7886
51 Sb Antimony 121.76 [Kr]4d^{10}5s^{2}5p^3 8.6084
83 Bi Bismuth 208.98 [Xe]4f^{14}5d^{10}6s^{2}6p^3 7.2855
115 Mc Moscovium (289)

Group 16 (VIA)
8 O Oxygen 15.999 1s^{2}2s^{2}2p^4 13.6181
16 S Sulfur 32.06 [Ne]3s^{2}3p^4 10.3600
34 Se Selenium 78.971 [Ar]3d^{10}4s^{2}4p^4 9.7524
52 Te Tellurium 127.60 [Kr]4d^{10}5s^{2}5p^4 9.0097
84 Po Polonium (209) [Xe]4f^{14}5d^{10}6s^{2}6p^4 8.414
116 Lv Livermorium (293)

Group 17 (VIIA)
9 F Fluorine 18.998 1s^{2}2s^{2}2p^5 17.4228
17 Cl Chlorine 35.45 [Ne]3s^{2}3p^5 12.9676
35 Br Bromine 79.904 [Ar]3d^{10}4s^{2}4p^5 11.8138
53 I Iodine 126.90 [Kr]4d^{10}5s^{2}5p^5 10.4513
85 At Astatine (210) [Xe]4f^{14}5d^{10}6s^{2}6p^5 9.3175
117 Ts Tennessine (294)

Group 18 (VIIIA)
2 He Helium 4.0026 1s^2 24.5874
10 Ne Neon 20.180 1s^{2}2s^{2}2p^6 21.5645
18 Ar Argon 39.948 [Ne]3s^{2}3p^6 15.7596
36 Kr Krypton 83.798 [Ar]3d^{10}4s^{2}4p^6 13.9996
54 Xe Xenon 131.29 [Kr]4d^{10}5s^{2}5p^6 12.1298
86 Rn Radon (222) [Xe]4f^{14}5d^{10}6s^{2}6p^6 10.7485
118 Og Oganesson (294)

Lanthanides
58 Ce Cerium 140.12 [Xe]4f5d6s^2 5.5386
59 Pr Praseodymium 140.91 [Xe]4f^{3}6s^2 5.4702
60 Nd Neodymium 144.24 [Xe]4f^{4}6s^2 5.5250
61 Pm Promethium (145) [Xe]4f^{5}6s^2 5.577
62 Sm Samarium 150.36 [Xe]4f^{6}6s^2 5.6437
63 Eu Europium 151.96 [Xe]4f^{7}6s^2 5.6704
64 Gd Gadolinium 157.25 [Xe]4f^{7}5d6s^2 6.1498
65 Tb Terbium 158.93 [Xe]4f^{9}6s^2 5.8638
66 Dy Dysprosium 162.50 [Xe]4f^{10}6s^2 5.9391
67 Ho Holmium 164.93 [Xe]4f^{11}6s^2 6.0215
68 Er Erbium 167.26 [Xe]4f^{12}6s^2 6.1077
69 Tm Thulium 168.93 [Xe]4f^{13}6s^2 6.1843
70 Yb Ytterbium 173.05 [Xe]4f^{14}6s^2 6.2542
71 Lu Lutetium 174.97 [Xe]4f^{14}5d6s^2 5.4259

Actinides
90 Th Thorium 232.04 [Rn]6d^{2}7s^2 6.3067
91 Pa Protactinium 231.04 [Rn]5f^{2}6d7s^2 5.89
92 U Uranium 238.03 [Rn]5f^{3}6d7s^2 6.1941
93 Np Neptunium (237) [Rn]5f^{4}6d7s^2 6.2655
94 Pu Plutonium (244) [Rn]5f^{6}7s^2 6.0258
95 Am Americium (243) [Rn]5f^{7}7s^2 5.9738
96 Cm Curium (247) [Rn]5f^{7}6d7s^2 5.9914
97 Bk Berkelium (247) [Rn]5f^{9}7s^2 6.1978
98 Cf Californium (251) [Rn]5f^{10}7s^2 6.2817
99 Es Einsteinium (252) [Rn]5f^{11}7s^2 6.3676
100 Fm Fermium (257) [Rn]5f^{12}7s^2 6.50
101 Md Mendelevium (258) [Rn]5f^{13}7s^2 6.58
102 No Nobelium (259) [Rn]5f^{14}7s^2 6.66
103 Lr Lawrencium (266) [Rn]5f^{14}7s^{2}7p 4.96

TExES Core Subjects 4–8
Index

INDEX

Assimilation, 450
Associative property
addition, 136
multiplication, 137
Atlantic–Gulf coastal plains, 303
Atmosphere, 432–433
Atomic bomb, 278
Atoms, 402
Audience, for writing, 120
Austin, Stephen F., 289
Australia and the Pacific Realm, 307
Authentic assessment, 459
Authentic multicultural literature, 365
Autocracy, 332
Automaticity, 65
Average, 200
Axis powers, 277
Aztecs, 251

B

Banking, 325
Bar graph, 196
Base-10 blocks, 148
Bell curve, 204–206
Berkeley, John, 257
Bias, 214
Biden, Joe, 247, 281
Big Bang, 441
Bill of Rights, 274, 339
bin Laden, Osama, 279
Binomial experiments, 210–212
Biogeochemical cycles, 437
Biography, 92
Biotic components, 426–427
Bivariate data, 198–199
Black Codes, 271
Bleeding Kansas, 269
Bloom's Taxonomy, 446–448
Bolshevik revolution, 245
Boston Massacre, 261
Boston Tea Party, 261
Bowie, James, 290
Box-and-whisker plot, 202
Boyle, Robert, 352
Breckinridge, John C., 270
Brexit, 280
Brown, John, 268
Brown v. Board of Education of Topeka, 274, 342–343

Bunker Hill, 262
Burnet, David G., 291

C

Cabeza de Vaca, Álvar Núñez, 287
Caddo, 254–255, 286, 327
Calvert, Cecil, first Lord Baltimore, 256
Cambrian, 442
Capacity, units of, 174
Capital, 321
Capitalism, 323
Capone, Al, 273
Carbohydrates, 414, 416
Carbon cycle, 437
Cardiac muscle, 413
Carteret, George, 257
Cartilage, 413
Catholic missions in Texas, 288
Cattle industry, 295, 329
Celebrate Freedom Week, 345
Cells
animal and plant cells, 410–412
reproduction, 417–419
Cell theory, 392
Celsius, 175
Census, 214
Central America, 305
Central Eurasia, 304
Centrally planned economy, 324–325
Central Powers, 277
Characterization, 94
Charles II, 257
Charts, 366–368
Chávez, César, 276
Checklists, for assessment, 108
Checks and balances, 339
Chemical bonds, 402
Chemical change, 403
Chemical energy, 405
Cherokee, 253
Chicano movement, 275–276
China, command economy of, 325
Chomsky, Noam, 21
Choral reading, 69
Chromosomes, 420
Churchill, Winston, 278
Circle, area and perimeter of, 187
Circle graph, 196
Circulatory system, 412, 413

Citizenship in U.S., 343–345
Civil rights
African American civil rights movement, 274–275
desegregation, 342–343
Dred Scott case, 342
for freed slaves, 274
in Texas, 294
Mexican American movement, 275–276
separate but equal, 342
Civil Rights Act, 275, 276
Civil Rights Movement, 274–276
Civil War, 269–272
end of, 271
Gettysburg, 270
political, economic, and social differences, 269
Reconstruction Era, 271–272
secession and, 270
slavery and sectionalism, 269–270
Classification, 225, 367
Climate, 438
Closed circuit, 405
Closure property
addition, 136
multiplication, 136
Cloze procedure, 63
Coahuiltecan, 286
Cognates, 369–370
Cold War, 279
Colonial America, 255–260
Comanche, 266, 286–287
Combinations
for estimates, 149
numbers of, 151–152
Command economy, 324–325
Commerce, federal regulation of, 341
Common denominator, 140
Common multiple, 147
Communism, 323
Commutative property
addition, 136
multiplication, 136
Comparative investigations, 388–389
Compass rose, 300
Compatible numbers, 149
Compean, Mario, 276
Complementary angle, 180
Complementary event, 208–209

K

K2, 308
Kansas–Nebraska Act, 268
Kant, 311
Karankawa, 254, 286
Kennedy, John F., 275, 279
Khrushchev, Nikita, 279
Kinetic energy, 405
King, Martin Luther Jr., 275
Ku Klux Klan, 272, 293
K-W-L Chart, 91

L

Labor, 321
Land grant movement, 275
Language
    components of, 20
    functions of, 22–23
    language acquisition, 19–20
    oral language, 16–30
    register of, 23
    stages of development, 20–21
Language acquisition, 19–20
Language Acquisition Device (LAD), 21
Language arts. See English language arts
La Salle, Robert de, 288
Latitude, 363
Laurentian highlands, 303
Laws of exponents, 142
Learning cycle, 449–455
Learning to read versus reading to learn, 83
Least common multiple, 140
Lee, Robert E., 271, 293
Legal constraints, 393
Legislative branch, 338
Lexington, 262
Liberty Bell, 346
Life science
    adaptation and evolution, 422–423
    organisms and environment, 426–428
    regulatory mechanisms and behavior, 424–426
    reproduction and heredity, 417–421
    response to stimuli, 424–426

structure and function of living things, 409–417
Ligaments, 413
Light
    heat and, 405
    light energy, 406
Lightning, 406
Lincoln, Abraham, 267
    election of, 270
    Gettysburg Address, 270
Linear functions, 154–159
Line of symmetry, 160
Line plot, 196
Lines
    parallel, 179
    perpendicular, 179
Line segment, 179
Lipids, 416
Literacy assessment
    criterion-referenced tests, 80
    formal assessment, 80–81
    informal assessment, 49–50
    norm-referenced tests, 81
    phonological and phonemic awareness, 32–34
Literacy development, 31–50
    alphabetic principle, 37–38
    foundations for, 31–32
    stages of reading development, 38–40
Literary devices, 95
Logarithmic function, 165
Logical reasoning, 218
Logical thinking, 457
London Company, 255
Longitude, 363
Longitudinal waves, 407
Louisiana Purchase, 265

M

Macroeconomics, 319
Madison, James, 264
Manifest Destiny, 265
Manipulatives, in mathematics, 228
Mantle, of Earth, 429
Maps
    grid system, 300
    locating places and regions on, 299–300

relative and absolute location, 300
skills by grade, scope and sequence, 314–317
teaching map concepts, 362–363
types of, 299
Marbury v. Madison, 338, 340
Margil de Jesús, Antonio, 288
Market economy, 323–324
Marshall Plan, 278
Maryland colony, 256, 258
Mason, John, 256
Mass, 386, 400, 402
    units of, 174
Massachusetts Bay Company, 255
Massachusetts colony, 255, 256, 258
Mass production, 320
Mathematical literacy, 226–228
Mathematics
    assessment, 232–233
    bivariate data, 198–199
    cognitive development and, 224–225
    combinations, 151–152
    communicating mathematical ideas and concepts, 219–220
    complex numbers, 143–145
    curriculum requirements, 223–224, 231–232
    decimal representations with base-10 blocks, 148
    decimals, 141–142
    differentiated instruction, 232
    FOIL, 144
    fractions, 138–140
    geometry, 178–191
    graphs and charts, 195–197
    greatest common factor, 139, 147–148
    infinite series, 171–172
    in real-life situations, 227–228
    laws of exponents, 142
    learning environment for, 221–222
    least common multiple, 140
    linear functions, 154–159
    major discoveries in throughout history, 352–353
    manipulatives in, 228
    mathematical literacy, 226–228
    measurement, 172–176
    mental mathematics and estimation, 149

NOTES

NOTES